The Computer Science Departmental Short Loans Library
Room LF 22

This book must be returned by 11:45am on the date stamped below.

UMCSD UMRCC
COMPUTER LIBRARY
5908   G
12 FEB 2002

# Computer Architecture

Robert J. Baron
*University of Iowa*

Lee Higbie

**ADDISON-WESLEY PUBLISHING COMPANY**
Reading, Massachusetts • Menlo Park, California • New York • Don Mills, Ontario
Wokingham, England • Amsterdam • Bonn • Sydney • Singapore • Tokyo • Madrid • San Juan
Milan • Paris

This book is in the **Addison-Wesley Series in Electrical and Computer Engineering**

*Sponsoring Editor:* Tom Robbins
*Production Supervisor:* Helen Wythe
*Production Coordinator:* Amy Willcutt
*Copy Editor:* Susan Middleton
*Text Designer:* Sally Bindari, Designworks, Inc.
*Compositor:* Beacon Graphics Corporation
*Illustration:* ScotGraphics
*Technical Art Supervisor:* Joseph Vetere
*Manufacturing Manager:* Roy Logan
*Cover Designer:* Peter Blaiwas

Many of the designations used by manufacturers and sellers to distinguish their products are claimed as trademarks. Where those designations appear in this book, and Addison-Wesley was aware of a trademark claim, the designations have been printed in initial caps or all caps.

Library of Congress Cataloging-in-Publication Data

Baron, Robert J.
    Computer architecture/by Robert J. Baron and Lee Higbie.
       p.  cm.
    Includes bibliographical references and index.
    ISBN 0-201-50923-7
    1. Computer architecture.   I. Higbie, Lee  II. Title.
QA76.9.A73H52   1992
004.2'2--dc20                                                                 91-19130
                                                                                               CIP

Copyright © 1992 by Addison-Wesley Publishing Company, Inc.

All rights reserved. No part of this publication may be reproduced, stored in a retrieval system, or transmitted, in any form or by any means, electronic, mechanical, photocopying, recording, or otherwise, without the prior written permission of the publisher. Printed in the United States of America.

1 2 3 4 5 6 7 8 9 10-DO-95949392

# *Foreword*

Computer design is the art of producing a computer to a given specification at a competitive cost and performance. Computer architecture is the art of making a specification that will live through several generations of technologies.

Johann Sebastian Bach, writing for the clavichord, faced the constraints of the instrument and the musical tastes of his times. Within these constraints he produced contrapuntal melodies of complexity and delight that we hear often today, some 250 years later. His genius has survived 10 generations of humanity, outlasting innumerable waves of artistic, political, and social change.

What if Bach were told that every 5 years a new generation of musical instruments would be available, with each new generation capable of producing notes of harmonic richness and depth that far surpassed the qualities of the generation it supplanted? What if Bach's patron had commissioned a series of pieces to be played for the next 20 years on instruments spanning four generations of instruments? Could Bach have conceived of the aural qualities of the future instruments? Could he have produced a sequence of cadences and harmonies to bring out the strengths of each successive generation of instruments?

As a composer of a piece to be played on a specific instrument of the day—the clavichord, the harpsichord, the organ, or the violin—Bach faced a problem analogous to that of the computer designer, namely, how to use talent and cleverness to best exploit existing technology. The computer architect's challenge is much like the hypothetical problem that Bach did not face: how to compose a piece that exploits a sequence of new technologies, especially when you are not sure what those new technologies will be.

The computer architect has to look 20 years ahead and visualize the technology of the future in order to create a family of machines that can use a changing technology to best advantage. Two decades ago most architects did not realize that their decisions for a new machine would have an impact on machines designed 20 or more years into the future. Some design decisions, which seemed optimal for the machine built with then available technology, turned out to have negative and unintended consequences in the future. If each new offering could be designed as if there were no predecessor design and no history, each new design would be free to make optimal use of capabilities provided by newly available technology. But this approach ignores the investment of the customer and the need to remain compatible with the past in order to capture the existing software base.

The 1960s produced the notion of the computer family, in which all family members execute the same programs and maintain compatibility with prior-generation hardware as implementations based on new technology are introduced. What makes a computer family successful? The key is to create an architecture that can be implemented in a variety of ways to span several orders of magnitude of performance and cost. Each distinct implementation has to be competitive, and yet all implementations must be compatible. A program that runs on the bottom-of-the-line family member must run on all higher family members as well. Conversely, a program moved from a high-end machine to a lesser machine must also run compatibly, provided the lesser machine has sufficient memory and disk capacity to support execution.

The lessons of history suggest that when the basic architecture is sound, the architecture will evolve slowly with small, carefully crafted changes introduced several years apart. When a major flaw is embedded in the architecture, the changes are more drastic and more frequent. For the PDP-11, made by Digital Equipment Corporation (DEC), the flaw was too small an address space. Very shortly after its initial introduction, the architecture was expanded to enlarge the physical-address space, but the architecture was hopelessly locked into a 16-bit virtual address. The DEC VAX architecture evolved the good ideas of the PDP-11 into an architecture with a 32-bit virtual address, which at the time of introduction seemed to be essentially infinite. The architecture served DEC and its customers admirably for a decade until ideas embodied in reduced-instruction-set-computer (RISC) architecture produced machines more cost-effective than VAX implementations.

The advent of microprocessors created the roots of new family trees. Microprocessors were necessarily limited because the full implementation had to fit on a single integrated-circuit chip. With integrated-circuit technology in its infancy, early microprocessors had small address spaces and relatively simple instruction sets. Their designers had not foreseen how architectural families would grow from such inauspicious beginnings. Yet architectural evolution is a common theme in the history of computers.

A landmark processor was the Intel 8080. It was in head-to-head competition with other popular microprocessors such as the MOS Technology 6502 (used in the Apple II computer) and the Motorola 6800. Intel used an architecture similar to the 8080 for its successor, the 8086. Although the two chips were not directly compatible, 8080 software could be mapped onto the 8086 fairly easily through reassembly or recompilation.

In the race between Intel and other chip manufacturers to establish a strong market position in microprocessors, the 8086 architecture reached a major turning point when it became the choice of IBM for use in the IBM PC (Personal Computer) in 1981. From this point the 8086 architecture took a major share of the microprocessor market, with the Motorola 68000 architecture taking a strong secondary role through its adoption by Apple for the Macintosh.

The history of the IBM PC is an interesting story in itself, and has many lessons for the computer architect. Baron and Higbie relate many of the technical highlights of this family. The architecture of the IBM PC computer is a superset of the architecture of the 8086 family architecture. The PC architecture includes not only the instruction set of the 8086 but the electrical interfaces of the adapter cards and the operating system interface of DOS (Disk Operating System). The PC appeared about 5 years after the first 8-bit microcomputers were offered, at a time when microcomputers were reaching office, laboratory, and home in large numbers.

We learn that IBM's entry to the microcomputer market was a computer based on the Intel 8088, a chip compatible with the Intel 8086 but with an 8-bit data-bus interface rather than a 16-bit interface. What was unusual about this release was that IBM published the full information for interfacing to this computer. Overnight a large industry developed to supply expansion cards and peripherals for the PC. Eventually manufacturers were able to produce fully compatible computers without violating IBM copyrights and patents. At this point the IBM PC became a de facto standard computer architecture and was offered in full-system configurations and with plug-in components by hundreds of manufacturers.

In 1985 IBM released a new generation of machines, the IBM PC AT (for Advanced Technology), based on the Intel 80286 processor. This computer became the basis of a second de facto standard, and the industry responded quickly by producing peripherals and compatible computers. As the industry grew around these two related architectures, the consumer benefited through lower prices, availability from nearby merchants or through mail order, and easy access to service.

IBM established a new family of computers, the PS/2, in 1987. The PS/2 family is software-compatible with the IBM PC and PC AT lines, but has a different physical and electrical interface for plug-in components. Within a short time after announcement of the PS/2, IBM stopped production of its PCs and PC ATs. The business in IBM PCs and PC ATs continued to grow, however, leaving IBM in the position of being one of the computer manufacturers not making IBM PC or PC AT–compatible machines. Eventually IBM released some PS/2 models that were fully compatible with the IBM PC AT, and offically reentered that market.

In this case the consumer base had a significant investment in the de facto standard, and IBM could not abandon that base overnight. The IBM PS/2 captured only the existing software base but was not immediately able to compete on price and availability of plug-in cards. Also, a number of semiconductor companies had developed very-large-scale-integraton (VLSI) peripheral and control chips to perform the complex functions of the de facto standards. These chips led to further price decreases. These several factors have helped the IBM PC clone manufacturers to offer decreasing prices and higher performance on a continuing basis, thereby keeping the industry alive and healthy well after IBM abandoned compatiblity. Hence the advanced capabilities of the PS/2, which were supposed to woo former PC users to the new line of machines, were not sufficiently attractive to entice the majority of those users to make the change. Eventually IBM chose to return to the market that it had intended to leave behind.

In retrospect, one can see that IBM's decision to make details of the PC and PC AT public information created a market by enabling competitive manufacturers to produce compatible components in high volumes, thereby giving good value to the PC customers. As the market developed and grew to a volume of millions of machines per year, the market dictated what kind of evolution could succeed as new technology replaced old technology.

The 1980s introduced new architectures for parallel processing and vector processing; these machines are described in the text. Pipelining, a technique once relegated to supercomputers, became architecture-independent and now is used in low-end microprocessors and RISC processors, as well as scientific supercomputers that originally hosted the technique. Baron and Higbie touch on pipelining in several of its incarnations, most notably in recent Cray supercomputers and in RISC architectures. Other examples of supercomputers such as the Connection Machine CM-2 and Intel's parallel microprocessors illustrate such concepts as massively parallel machines, vector processing, distributed processing, and hypercube interconnections.

What are the challenges for the future? Baron and Higbie explore a number of advanced notions that have not yet been identified as family architectures. RISC is the most notable of these. Its architecture exposes the interior of the hardware implementation to software in order to give the optimizing compiler an opportunity to improve performance. How will this evolve in time? Perhaps such architectures will be insensitive to new changes in technology. Or perhaps the implementations will change drastically, and the interface that remains the same from generation to generation will be the interface to the optimizing compiler.

The problem we posed earlier for Bach was to compose for a changing family of musical instruments. What a marvelous *tour de force* it would be to compose a masterwork for piccolo and tuba alike. If the composition were for a radically different instrument, say a Moog synthesizer, the composition itself could depart from normal tonal scales and cadences. Imagine, then, composing for an instrument yet to be invented! And yet, that has been the history of computer-family architectures. Thus, as we see the introduction of RISCs, massively parallel machines, and other new roots of future architectures, we wonder what will be the notes and cadences of the new families of machines.

Harold S. Stone<br>
Chappaqua, New York

# *Preface*

This book is about computer architecture, the design of computers, and it is intended as an undergraduate textbook for a one-semester core course in computer science, electrical engineering, or computer engineering. We assume the reader has had the equivalent study of a course in digital logic and is familiar with basic circuit components, such as switches, encoders and decoders, multiplexors and demultiplexors, registers, arithmetic and logic circuits, and control units. Appendix B presents a brief review of these fundamental digital components. We also assume the reader has had some experience with programming.

In developing this book, our goal was to introduce a wide range of fundamental concepts relating to computer architecture. Chapter 1 introduces the major categories of computers and discusses various measures of computer performance. The next three chapters focus on the building blocks of computers, which include the instruction set (Chapter 2); the hardware system, the central processing unit and its control, and the input-output system (Chapter 3); and the memory system (Chapter 4). Chapter 5 integrates these subjects by discussing the architecture of a current computer family, the International Business Machines (IBM) PC. The final two chapters focus on techniques for introducing parallelism into computers and increasing their operating speeds up: Chapter 6 focuses on pipelining, with emphasis on reduced-instruction-set computers (RISCs). Chapter 7 focuses on parallel processors including both massively parallel computers and multiprocessor computers; Chapter 7 also introduces dataflow processors and neural networks, two recent developments in computer architecture. (We will expand this chapter-by-chapter synopsis later in the Preface.)

Students should expect to satisfy two goals from a course on computer architecture. One goal is to become conversant with a large body of concepts and accompanying terminology. With this knowledge students will be able to read and understand technical articles or promotional brochures that describe new computer architectures and appreciate the design issues and tradeoffs of that architecture. They will also understand current trends in computer architecture and thus have some sense of the future directions of computational machines.

A second goal is for students to gain specific knowledge and understanding of the history of computer architectures. A relatively small number of companies and machines have dominated the industry since its inception, and students should know about these machines, their structure, and the contributions their designers have made to the field of computer architecture. It is important to understand why some architectures have survived for 30 years while others have long since become obsolete.

A student can satisfy the first goal by studying the material in this textbook. We have designed the material to satisfy a one-semester course in computer architecture, assuming the instructor progresses through the material at the rate of about one chapter every 2 weeks. A student can satisfy the second goal by reading about specific computers and computer families. We have put descriptions of the following selected machines into the optional reader, *Case Studies in Computer Architecture,* which students can use to supplement their understanding of the text:

| | |
|---|---|
| Burroughs B1700 | ILLIAC IV |
| Burroughs B6700 | Intel 80*x*86 family |
| CDC 6600 and family | Intel iPSC/2 |
| CRAY-1 and family | MIPS R2000 |
| DEC PDP-11 family | Motorola 68000 family |
| DEC VAX-11 family | Sun SPARC |
| Goodyear MPP | Tandem/16 |
| IBM System/370 family | TIASC |
| IBM System/R6000 | Thinking Machine CM-2 |

Following is a more detailed description of the main text than given earlier, with suggestions for how to use the case studies to best advantage.

Chapter 1 describes computers in general and introduces their basic computational systems. It also gives a classification of computers based on how the CPU processes instructions and data. The chapter also covers a number of general characteristics governing a computer's quality and applicability for its intended audience, along with a number of common ways researchers measure the performance of a computer.

In Chapter 2 we describe the important features of instructions and instruction sets and how they relate to the underlying hardware components. The features of relevance are the register sets, types of instructions, addressing techniques, and the instruction-set qualities of completeness, orthogonality, and compatibility.

The *Case Studies* contains several examples of register sets and instruction sets, including those of the IBM System/360, the Digital Equipment Corporation (DEC) PDP-11, the Control Data Corporation (CDC) 6600, the MIPS R2000, the IBM RISC System/6000, and the Intel 8086 microprocessor.

While reading Chapter 2 a student would gain considerable insight into register-set and instruction-set design by studying the choices made by the architects of these prominent machines.

Chapter 3 focuses on two important subsystems of computers: the central processing unit and the input-output system. Our concern here is with the hardware-system architecture of the computer. Perhaps the best supporting material for this chapter is Chapter 5, where we describe the hardware-system architecture of the IBM PC family. In addition, we present various CPU designs in the *Case Studies.* For example, we describe the Intel 80x86 microprocessor family as well as the CPUs of the B1700 and the B6700 (both by Burroughs), the CDC 6600, and the IBM RISC System/6000 — all of which have considerably different design goals and philosophies.

The following machines illustrate and support the different I/O techniques discussed in Chapter 3: the IBM PC (Chapter 5), the IBM System/360, the PDP-11, the CDC 6600, and the Goodyear MPP.

Chapter 4 focuses on the design of the memory system, including interleaving techniques, cache memory, and virtual memory. Many historical machines used low-order interleaving, including the CDC 6600, the Texas Instruments (TI) ASC, the CRAY-1, and the ILLIAC IV; most of today's fastest processors use low-order interleaving as well. Many machines use cache memory in one form or another, including the ILLIAC IV, the CRAY-1, the MIPS R2000, and the IBM System/R6000. Many current machines provide virtual-memory hardware, including the Intel 80286 and 80386 microprocessors and two RISCs — the MIPS R2000 and the IBM RISC System/6000. Many historical machines used virtual memory as well, such as the PDP-11, the VAX-11, the IBM System/370, and the TI ASC.

Chapter 5 is the only chapter that presents a relatively complete picture of an entire computer, and we chose the IBM PC. The instruction-set architecture is not described in the text, but it is presented, along with descriptions of the central processing unit, in the *Case Studies* (see Case Study 12). Chapter 5 does describe the bus structure, the various serial and parallel I/O interface devices, the direct-memory-access (DMA) controller, and the interrupt controller. Chapter 5 also describes how the architects assigned addresses to the I/O and main-memory-address spaces. Finally, it describes how IBM architects extended the I/O bus architecture from the PC to the AT and how a consortium of industries further extended it to the EISA bus.

The final two chapters describe techniques for improving the performance of computers. Chapter 6 focuses on pipelining, while Chapter 7 focuses on parallel processing. In Chapter 6 we discuss both instruction pipelining and execution-unit pipelining, and we describe how current architects are using the principles of pipelining to design RISCs that lend themselves to pipelining. We also describe pipelined vector processing as an illustration of an important use of pipelining. The *Case Studies* describes a number of pipelined processors, vector processors, and RISCs, including the forerunner machines (the IBM System/360 Model 91 and the CDC 6600), the early vector processors (the CRAY-1 and the TI ASC), and current RISCs (the MIPS R2000, the Sun SPARC, and the IBM RISC System/6000).

In Chapter 7, the concluding chapter, we discuss parallel-processor architectures. These provide alternatives to pipelining (although they too may be pipelined). The two principle types of parallel processors are processor arrays, in which a single control unit regulates the activity of a large number of independent data processors (as many as 65,536 on the currently largest machine), and the multiprocessor computers. The latter tend to be either high-speed commercial multiprocessors, which are simply several CPUs sharing the same memory system, or systems designed specifically for fault-tolerant operation. The *Case Studies* describes several processor arrays (the ILLIAC IV, the Goodyear MPP, and Thinking Machine's CM-2 Connection Machine) and one historic fault-tolerant system, the Tandem/16.

Although we highly recommend using the text in conjunction with the *Case Studies,* we have written the text to stand alone. The exercises and problems given at the end of each chapter do not depend on the material in the *Case Studies,* in which we present separate, machine-dependent exercises.

The authors wish to thank our many colleagues and coworkers over the last quarter century who, in one way or another, have all contributed to this work. Some have offered specific suggestions, but all have influenced our way of thinking about computers and about how to present complex ideas. We would like to thank the many students at the University of Iowa who were forced to endure early manuscripts of this text, and Sukumar Ghosh who contributed several of the interesting problems. We wish to thank all of our many reviewers whose suggestions and corrections were invaluable. A partial list includes Bill Appelbe, Ken Breeding, Bill Carroll, Harvey Gragon, Jim Mooney, Howard Pollard, Harold Stone, and Frank Wagner. Any errors and shortcomings in this book remain the sole responsibility of the authors. We would like to thank Tom Robbins, our editor at Addison-Wesley, for more than a decade of encouragement in what must have seemed to be an interminable project, and the many other talented people at Addison-Wesley whose skill and effort led to this book in its final form. Two of them of particular note are Helen Wythe, the production supervisor, and Amy Willcutt, the production coordinator. Our special thanks go to Susan Middleton, whose superb developmental editing improved immeasurably the clarity and organization of the text, and ScotGraphics for the beautiful artwork. Connie Hulse was the art coordinator for the project, and Sally Bindari designed the book.

Finally, we would like to thank our wives, Linda and Rachel, for the patience they have shown throughout this project.

# Contents

*Foreword* iii
*Preface* vii

**1 Computer Architecture** 2
    **1.1 Historical Perspectives** 5
    **1.2 A Classification of Computer Architectures** 11
        1.2.1 Von Neumann Machines 11
        1.2.2 Non–von Neumann Machines 14
    **1.3 Measuring the Quality of a Computer Architecture** 20
        1.3.1 Generality 20
        1.3.2 Applicability 21
        1.3.3 Efficiency 21
        1.3.4 Ease of Use 22
        1.3.5 Malleability 22
        1.3.6 Expandability 23
    **1.4 Factors Influencing the Success of a Computer Architecture** 23
        1.4.1 Architectural Merit 23
        1.4.2 System Performance 25
        1.4.3 System Cost 30

**2 Instruction-set Architecture** 34
    **2.1 Data Representations** 36
        2.1.1 Units of Information 36
        2.1.2 Integers and Fractions 37
        2.1.3 Floating-point Numbers 40
        2.1.4 Data Structures 45
    **2.2 Data Precision and Datatypes** 48
        2.2.1 Precision of Basic Datatypes 49
        2.2.2 Provision of Variable-precision Data 51
    **2.3 Register Sets** 53

## 2.4 Types of Instructions  *57*
- 2.4.1 Operate Instructions  *59*
- 2.4.2 Memory-access Instructions  *63*
- 2.4.3 Control Instructions  *67*
- 2.4.4 Miscellaneous and Privileged Instructions  *70*
- 2.4.5 Vector Instructions  *72*

## 2.5 Addressing Techniques  *82*
- 2.5.1 Register Addressing  *82*
- 2.5.2 Boundary Alignment  *83*
- 2.5.3 Memory Addressing  *85*
- 2.5.4 Addressing Design Issues  *98*

## 2.6 Instruction-set Design  *102*
- 2.6.1 Completeness  *102*
- 2.6.2 Orthogonality  *103*
- 2.6.3 Compatibility  *103*
- 2.6.4 Instruction Formats  *107*

# 3 *Buses, the CPU, and the I/O System*  *118*

## 3.1 Buses  *120*
- 3.1.1 Types  *120*
- 3.1.2 Bus Transfers and Control Signals  *122*

## 3.2 Central Processing Unit  *124*
- 3.2.1 ALUs  *125*
- 3.2.2 Control Units  *126*
- 3.2.3 Exception-processing Hardware and Instructions  *143*

## 3.3 I/O System  *152*
- 3.3.1 CPU-controlled I/O  *154*
- 3.3.2 Multiprogramming Operating Systems  *155*
- 3.3.3 Multiported Storage  *156*
- 3.3.4 DMA I/O  *157*
- 3.3.5 Memory-mapped I/O  *164*
- 3.3.6 Physical I/O Devices  *165*

# 4 *Memory-system Architecture*  *174*

## 4.1 Memory-system Technology and Cost  *175*
- 4.1.1 Memory Organization  *179*
- 4.1.2 Types of Memory  *183*

## 4.2 Main-memory System  *189*
- 4.2.1 Program Relocation and Protection  *191*
- 4.2.2 Cache Memory  *196*
- 4.2.3 Virtual Memory  *204*
- 4.2.4 Memory Banking and Expanded Memory  *215*

## 4.3 Memory Design Issues  *218*
- 4.3.1 Memory Speed versus CPU Speed  *218*
- 4.3.2 Memory-address Space  *219*
- 4.3.3 Speed-Cost Tradeoffs  *221*

## 5 A Computer-family Architecture: The IBM PC  *230*

### 5.1 IBM PC Family and Its Descendants  *232*
- 5.1.1 IBM PC and PC AT  *233*
- 5.1.2 IBM PS/2  *235*
- 5.1.3 PC Clones  *236*

### 5.2 Basic Microcomputer Configuration  *237*

### 5.3 Components of the IBM PC  *238*
- 5.3.1 8088 CPU  *239*
- 5.3.2 Control Interface  *245*
- 5.3.3 PC Bus and Interrupt System  *248*
- 5.3.4 I/O System  *259*
- 5.3.5 Programmable Interval Timer  *268*
- 5.3.6 Floating-point Coprocessor  *269*

### 5.4 Software System  *272*
- 5.4.1 I/O Port-address Assignments  *273*
- 5.4.2 ROM BIOS  *273*
- 5.4.3 Memory-address Assignments  *275*

### 5.5 Architectural Merit of the PC Architecture  *279*

## 6 Pipelining and RISCs  *284*

### 6.1 Pipelining  *286*
- 6.1.1 Arithmetic-unit Pipelining  *289*
- 6.1.2 Instruction-unit Pipelining  *294*
- 6.1.3 Scheduling Functional Units  *298*

### 6.2 Pipelined Vector Processors  *304*

### 6.3 Reduced-instruction-set Computers  *306*
- 6.3.1 Historical Perspective  *308*
- 6.3.2 RISC-CISC Controversy  *309*
- 6.3.3 RISC Implementation Techniques  *312*

## 7 Parallel Processors  *320*

### 7.1 Interconnection Networks  *323*
- 7.1.1 Taxonomy  *324*
- 7.1.2 Interconnection Topologies  *327*
- 7.1.3 Application of Interconnection Networks for Parallel Processors  *338*

### 7.2 SIMD Machines  *341*
- 7.2.1 Types of SIMD Architectures  *341*
- 7.2.2 SIMD Operations  *344*

### 7.3 MIMD Machines  *364*
- 7.3.1 Running Processes on an MIMD Processor  *365*
- 7.3.2 Requirements for Multiprocessor Systems  *365*
- 7.3.3 Cache Coherence  *367*
- 7.3.4 Loosely Coupled Multiprocessors  *370*
- 7.3.5 Fault-tolerant Computers  *377*

**7.4 Alternate Architectures** *383*
    7.4.1 Dataflow Architectures *384*
    7.4.2 Neural Networks *389*

*Appendices 405*
*A Some Notational Conventions 405*
   **A.1 Octal and Hexadecimal Notation** *405*
   **A.2 Units of Time** *406*
   **A.3 Algorithmic Notation** *408*
   **A.4 Figure Conventions** *408*

*B Digital Components 411*
   **B.1 Circuit Components** *411*
       B.1.1 Buses *415*
       B.1.2 Gates *415*
   **B.2 Combinatorial Logic** *417*
       B.2.1 Encoders and Decoders *417*
       B.2.2 Multiplexors and Demultiplexors *419*
       B.2.3 Shifters *421*
       B.2.4 Adders *422*
       B.2.5 Arithmetic and Logic Units (ALUs) *424*
   **B.3 Sequential Logic** *424*
       B.3.1 Flip-flops *424*
       B.3.2 Clock Generators *424*
       B.3.3 Registers and Counters *426*
   **B.4 Devices That Combine Combinatorial and Sequential Logic** *429*
       B.4.1 Register Files *430*
       B.4.2 Hardware Stack *430*
       B.4.3 Multiplication Circuits *431*

*References and Suggested Readings 437*
*Suggested Answers to Selected Exercises and Problems 459*
*Glossary and Index 473*

# Computer Architecture

# 1
## Computer Architecture

- 1.1 Historical Perspectives  5
- 1.2 A Classification of Computer Architectures  11
  - 1.2.1 Von Neumann Machines  11
  - 1.2.2 Non–von Neumann Machines  14
- 1.3 Measuring the Quality of a Computer Architecture  20
  - 1.3.1 Generality  20
  - 1.3.2 Applicability  21
  - 1.3.3 Efficiency  21
  - 1.3.4 Ease of Use  22
  - 1.3.5 Malleability  22
  - 1.3.6 Expandability  23
- 1.4 Factors Influencing the Success of a Computer Architecture  23
  - 1.4.1 Architectural Merit  23
  - 1.4.2 System Performance  25
  - 1.4.3 System Cost  30

*In this chapter we begin our study of computer architecture. We start by describing what a computer architecture is and what a computer-family architecture is. Section 1.1 presents a brief historical overview of computer architecture development in the context of a rapidly changing technology. In Section 1.2 we discuss the basic categories of computer architectures. Sections 1.3 and 1.4 introduce the characteristics that can make a computer architecture a good one.*

> **Key Terms**
>
> **Architectural merit**  An assessment of the quality of a computer architecture based primarily on its applicability for intended users, its malleability, and its expandability.
>
> **Benchmark**  A standard program used for measuring the speed of a computer relative to the speeds of other computers that have run the same program.
>
> **Compatibility**  The ability of different computers to run the same programs.
>
> **Multiprocessor**  A computer having more than one processor, such as a processor array, an associative processor, or a multiple-processor computer.
>
> **Performance metric**  A measure of the speed of a computer; sometimes this is given in absolute terms, such as millions of instructions or per second (MIPS) or millions of floating-point operations per second (MFLOPS), and sometimes in terms relative to a standard computer, such as the VAX 11/780.
>
> **Pipelined processor**  A processor that achieves parallelism by overlapping the operation of several instructions, each one in a different stage of execution.
>
> **Register set**  The set of operational registers of a computer that the programmer can manipulate using the computer's instruction set.

**Computer architecture** is the design of computers, including their instruction sets, hardware components, and system organization. There are two essential parts to computer architecture: **instruction-set architecture (ISA)** and **hardware-system architecture (HSA)**. ISA includes the specifications that determine how machine-language programmers will interact with the computer. A computer is generally viewed in terms of its ISA, which determines the computational characteristics of the computer. In contrast, the HSA deals with the computer's major hardware subsystems, including its **central processing unit (CPU),** its storage system, and its **input-output (I/O) system** (which is the computer's interface to the world). The HSA includes both the logical design and the dataflow organization of these subsystems, and

computer architecture

instruction-set
 architecture (ISA)
hardware-system
 architecture (HSA)

central processing unit
 (CPU)
input—output (I/O)
 system

3

hence to a large degree the HSA determines how efficiently the machine will operate.

It is important to distinguish a computer's architecture from its implementation. An implementation is the realization of a computer in hardware and includes the choice of technology, speed, cost, and so forth. An architecture does not define an implementation, and vice versa; yet each influences the other. Note that, in general, two computers with the same ISA will run the same programs.

From a somewhat different perspective we may recognize that a computer is really just the implementation of an ISA. This implementation includes specifying both its HSA and its physical design.

There are many parallels between the study of building architecture and the study of computer architecture. In building architecture, one can study individual buildings, such as the Louvre and Westminster Abbey; historical periods, such as Roman and Greek; architectural classifications, such as French Renaissance and early Byzantine; and building components, such as stone and brick. In computer architecture the comparable areas of study are individual computers, such as the Control Data Corporation (CDC) 6600 and the ILLIAC IV; historical periods, such as the first, second, and third generations; architectural classifications, such as von Neumann machines, processor arrays, and multiple-processor architectures; and computer components, such as vacuum tubes and transistors.

A successful ISA generally has many implementations. Standard personal computers (PCs), for example, are available with a variety of performances, reliabilities, sizes, costs, and HSAs; yet all PCs (if based on the IBM PC) have essentially the same ISA. This leads us directly to the notion of a **computer-family architecture,** which is like a single computer architecture, except that its specification allows for a wider variety of implementations. To achieve this greater variety, the specification sometimes leaves some features of the HSA or implementation unspecified; generally these include the technology, logical flow of control, timing of operations, and size of memory—hence the implementation. A **computer family** is thus a set of implementations that share the same or similar ISA.

Here again there are parallels between building architecture and computer architecture. Developers often create a "family of houses" by repeating the same floor plan but with different materials and landscaping to alter the appearance of each house. Computer architects create a family of computers by using a variety of technologies, memory sizes, and speeds, thereby altering the performance of each model in a family.

International Business Machines Corporation (IBM) first introduced the notion of a computer family in the early 1960s, when it announced its System/360 family architecture. The family had a complete line of computers, including models 20, 30, 40, 44, 50, 65, and 91. Different computers in the family had different amounts of memory, used different technologies, had different bus structures, and had vastly different execution speeds; yet all the models could run the same programs.

Other computer manufacturers have also introduced families of computers. Digital Equipment Corporation (DEC), a pioneer in minicomputers, introduced the PDP-8 family in 1965, the PDP-11 family in 1970, and the VAX-11 family in 1978. CDC introduced the CDC 6000 family in the early 1960s, which evolved into the CYBER 170 series in the 1970s.[1]

Just like families in the animal kingdom, families of computers evolve and change. For example, although the IBM System/360 remained remarkably stable for many years, there were a few small changes and a few major ones. A major modification took place in the early 1970s resulting in the System/370 family, and again in 1988 resulting in the Enterprise System Architecture/370. There were also several minor (although notable) changes along the way.

**Compatibility** is the ability of different computers to run the same programs. Architects generally design for **upward compatibility,** which allows high-performance members of a family to run the same programs as do the lower-performance members. The converse ability, **downward compatibility,** is not always possible because high-performance family members often have features not available on lower-performance members. Upward compatibility preserves the user's investment in software while enabling a graceful switch to a higher-performance computer. **Forward compatibility** refers to software compatibility between one family and a later or descendant family of computers. Again, companies maintain forward compatibility to capitalize on their users' investments in software and thus keep their base of clients.

*compatibility*

*upward compatibility*

*downward compatibility*

*forward compatibility*

## 1.1 ■ Historical Perspectives

Computer technology has evolved rapidly since the late 1940s, when John Atanasoff of Iowa State University built the first special-purpose electronic digital computer, the ABC (Burks and Burks, 1988; Mollenhoff, 1988). **First-generation computers** were one-of-a-kind laboratory machines and included the ENIAC (Burks and Burks, 1981), the EDVAC, the EDSAC (Samuel, 1957), and the Mark-I, among others.[2] J. Presper Eckert and John Mauchly designed and built the ENIAC, which was not a stored-program computer, and they also worked on the design of the EDSAC, all at the Moore School of the University

*first-generation computers*

---

1. PDP stands for Programmed Data Processor; VAX stands for Virtual Address Extension.
2. ABC stands for Atanasoff-Berry Computer, ENIAC stood for Electronic Numerical Integrator and Calculator, EDVAC stands for Electronic Discrete Variable Computer, and EDSAC stands for Electronic Delay Storage Automatic Calculator.

of Pennsylvania. John von Neumann was a consultant to the ENIAC project and also contributed to the design of the EDVAC. Maurice Wilkes, another who worked on the EDVAC project, returned to England and designed the EDSAC, which he built at the Mathematical Laboratory at the University of Cambridge (Wilkes, et al., 1951). Meanwhile, Howard Aiken developed the Mark-I and its successors, the Mark-II, Mark-III and Mark-IV at Harvard University. In the mid-1940s, following the ENIAC project, von Neumann and his colleagues (Burks, et al., 1946) proposed many architectural innovations, and designers soon incorporated these ideas in newer machines, such as the IAS at Princeton's Institute of Advanced Studies (whence it got its name).

Although the Mark-I and Mark-II used electromechanical relays, most of these early machines used vacuum-tube technology. Transistors had not yet been invented, and vacuum tubes were the only nonmechanical switching elements then known. Even the first commercial machine, the Univac (Eckert, et al., 1951), used vacuum tubes. Vacuum tubes were fast, with switching times on the order of microseconds, but they consumed a great deal of power (watts rather than microwatts[3]) and consequently generated a great deal of heat. Early computers contained tens of thousands of vacuum tubes, but power requirements, heat generation, and reliability limited the practical size of such a computer to a few tens of thousands of switches. Thus vacuum-tube technology limited the potential growth of computers. The following statement, made by John von Neumann in 1951, illustrates how far computers have evolved to date:

> Two well-known, very large vacuum tube computing machines are in existence and in operation. Both consist of about 20,000 switching organs. One is a pure vacuum tube machine. (It belongs to the U.S. Army Ordnance Department, Ballistic Research Laboratories, Aberdeen, Maryland, designation "ENIAC.") The other is mixed—part vacuum tube and part electromechanical relays. (It belongs to the I.B.M. Corporation, and is located in New York, designation "SSEC.") These machines are a good deal larger than what is likely to be the size of the vacuum tube computing machines which will come into existence and operation in the next few years. It is possible that each one of these will consist of 2000 to 6000 switching organs. (The reason for this decrease lies in a different attitude about the treatment of the "memory," which I will not discuss here.) It is possible that in later years the machine sizes will increase again, but it is not likely that 10,000 (or perhaps a few times 10,000) switching organs will be exceeded as long as the present techniques and philosophy are employed. To sum up, about $10^4$ switching organs seems to be the proper

---

3. Appendix A describes standard unit prefixes (such as *mega, kilo, milli, micro,* and *nano*) and their use.

order of magnitude for a computing machine (von Neumann, 1951, pp. 12–13).

John Bardeen, Walter Brattain, and William Shockley of Bell Laboratories invented the transistor in 1948 (Leeds, et al., 1968). Although its advent was not a direct result of pressure by the computer industry, which was still very new, transistor technology soon played an essential role in computer development. Transistors use much less power than do vacuum tubes, are much smaller, and are much more reliable. By the early 1960s virtually all computers used transistor technology. Invention of the transistor abolished the practical limit imposed by vacuum tubes on the number of switching elements in a computer, and soon computer designers built computers containing many tens of thousands of switches. These were the **second-generation computers.**

If the transistor was the first needed breakthrough in computer technology, the second was **magnetic-core memory.** A magnetic-core memory is one that stores information in tiny doughnut-shaped magnetic elements, called cores. Although expensive, magnetic-core technology provided a reliability and speed that could not be matched at that time. Moreover, unlike vacuum tubes, core memories did not require power to hold their values because the cores are permanent magnets. Core memory and transistor technology were incorporated into computer design at about the same time, and they dominated the industry throughout the early 1960s. Still, magnetic-core memories had limited access times and were extrememly costly to manufacture. One megabyte (MB) of 1-$\mu$s magnetic core memory cost approximately $1 million.

Early computers cost hundreds of thousands to millions of dollars. A large part of the price came from the costs of design, engineering, and development along with basic research. The cost of manufacturing a computer also contributed, particularly the cost of manufacturing core memory. In contrast, in 1990, 1 MB of solid-state memory retailed for under $100 and is about eight times faster than magnetic-core memory, and an entire CPU chip costs about $20 to manufacture.

Because computers were initially expensive, a major design goal was to maximize their utility—to keep the CPU occupied as much of the time as possible—and several early developments resulted. Designers used special I/O processors to relieve the CPU from the burden of performing I/O operations. The use of **batch-processing operating systems** removed inefficiencies resulting from direct operator intervention. (A batch-processing operating system is one that automatically loads and executes programs, thus relieving the operator of that burden and speeding up program execution.) The introduction of **multiprogramming operating systems** resulted in better CPU utilization, since one program could be using the CPU while another was awaiting I/O operations. (A multiprogramming operating system loads two or more programs in memory at the same time, placing each program and its data in a different, nonoverlapping part of memory. When one program executes, the others remain idle.

*second-generation computers*

*magnetic-core memory*

*batch-processing operating systems*

*multiprogramming operating systems*

Special hardware allows the operating system to suspend an executing program and transfer control to one of the suspended programs.) The architectural innovations that were needed to support I/O processors and multiprogramming were efficient hardware for state swapping, interruption, memory protection, and program relocation. We shall discuss these topics in Chapters 2 and 3.

Major architectural innovations paralleled the technological evolution. In the early 1960s IBM introduced the notion of a computer-family architecture and established the effectiveness of microprogrammed control units (to be discussed in Chapter 2). Also during that time Burroughs introduced the **execution-stack architecture** and provided hardware support for high-level programming languages. (A stack is a storage device in which the last item stored is the first item removed; an execution-stack architecture uses a stack as an integral part of its CPU.) To increase execution speed, CDC introduced pipelining (assembly-line processing, to be discussed shortly) and multiple arithmetic units within its CPU. In the late 1960s researchers at the University of Illinois built a computer called the ILLIAC IV, which was a highly parallel computer.

All of these machines used **small-scale integration (SSI)**, solid-state or magnetic-core memories, and batch operating systems. (In small-scale integration, manufacturers fabricate several transistors on a single chip.) Together these attributes identify **third-generation computers,** which architects developed between about 1963 and 1975.

The 20-year period from 1965 to 1985 marked a rapid evolution in technology. Manufacturers first learned how to produce circuits using SSI. They next developed **medium-scale integration (MSI),** yielding circuits having hundreds of switches (transistors) on them. Progress was rapid, and by 1973 Intel Corporation had manufactured its first **microprocessor,** which consisted of an entire CPU on a single chip. Intel's first microprocessor contained several thousand transistors. By 1990, using **very-large-scale integration (VLSI),** Intel produced a CPU chip containing over a million transistors. Projections for the year 2000 place the transistor counts at over 100 million transistors per chip, which demonstrates how quickly the technology has evolved and is still evolving. Figure 1.1 plots the transistor count for several single-chip microprocessors in Intel's microprocessor family.

With the development of VLSI and a proliferation in solid-state technologies, large memories have also become reliable, fast, and inexpensive. Consequently, memory speeds have increased, and their costs and sizes have declined dramatically.

Current machines are **fourth-generation computers.** A number of features characterize them, including VLSI components, solid-state memories, time-sharing operating systems, virtual memory (to be discussed in Chapter 4), and support for many high-level programming languages. (A time-sharing operating system is one that divides available CPU time among a number of users so that each user appears to have exclusive use of the CPU.) As this partial list suggests, software technology, as well as hardware technology, has hastily evolved throughout the first three generations of computers. What about the future?

For a given CPU architecture, even assuming 100% utilization, technology limits the available computing power, measured in operations per second. The problem is that the demand for computation cycles always exceeds the attainable cycles for the current technology. (A **computation cycle,** also called a **clock cycle,** is a primitive unit of computation equal to one tick of the centralized clock, which synchronizes the events occurring inside a computer.) Special applications—such as simulations of complex physical systems, seismic prospecting, weather forecasting, molecular modeling, electronic design, large database systems, and image processing—are typical of those that require orders of magnitude more computation cycles than are available even on today's fastest machines. The speeds at which components can operate and signals can travel—and ultimately the speed of light—limit conventional (von

computation cycle
clock cycle

**FIGURE 1.1** *Logarithm of transistor count (vertical axis) as a function of time (horizontal axis) for key members of Intel's 80x86 microprocessor family. The numbers in parentheses under th CPU model number give the transistor count in thousands (K) and millions (M); the transistor count for model 80586 is projected.*

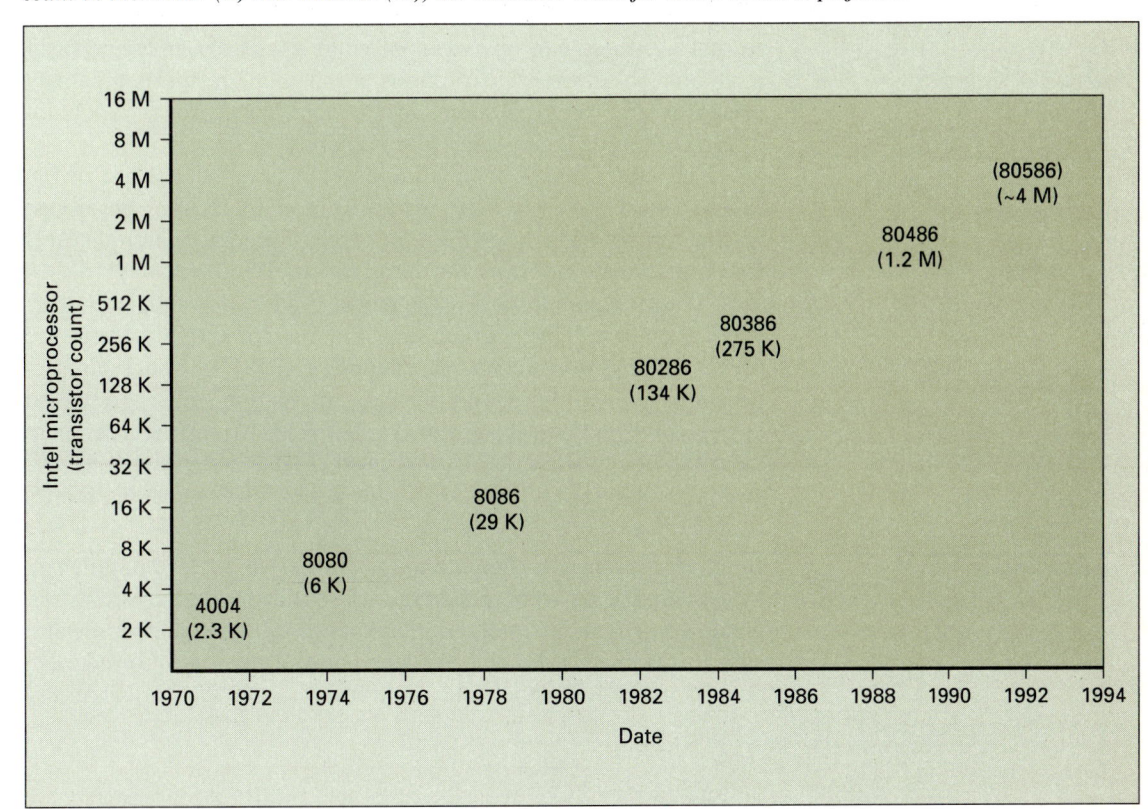

Neumann) architectures (discussed in Section 1.2.1). Yet these specialized applications continue to make more and more demands on computers. Hence there is a pressing need for faster computers.

There are two potential solutions: Change the technology or change the architecture. When the architecture remains the same but the technology differs, the result is a family of computers. Ultimately, this solution is of little help. What about changing the architecture? The fundamental way to extract more computation cycles from a given technology is to introduce parallelism into the design, and there are only a few known ways to do so:

processor arrays
processing elements (PEs)

1. Build **processor arrays,** computers that achieve parallelism by using many CPU components, or **processing elements (PEs).** One control unit controls the PEs, and the resulting speedup is proportional to the effective utilization of the PEs.[4] For these computers, effective utilization depends on the computation, which must consist of many replications of the same basic operations on different data elements. We shall briefly discuss these machines in Chapter 7.

pipelining

2. Build machines that achieve parallelism by using **pipelining**: Architects first decompose the instructions (or arithmetic operations) into sequences of short stages. They then provide specialized processors, one for each stage, which they **pipeline** (connect together), so that all stages can operate concurrently—in assembly-line fashion—only on different instructions or data. The resulting **pipelined processor** can perform many instructions concurrently, each instruction in a different stage of completion.

pipeline

pipelined processor

The effectiveness of pipelining depends on the nature of the ISA of the target machine. Recently architects have developed instruction sets with pipelining in mind. These new architectures differ in several important respects from their immediate predecessors: They use simple addressing modes, and mostly simple instructions; they have large register sets. The resulting architectures are called **reduced-instruction-set computers (RISCs),** and their predecessors, which have complicated instruction sets, are called **complex-instruction-set computers (CISCs)** to distinguish them from the newer RISCs. Chapter 6 will discuss pipelining and present a detailed examination of the issues distinguishing RISCs from CISCs.

reduced-instruction-set computers (RISCs)

complex-instruction-set computers (CISCs)

multiprocessor computers

3. Build **multiprocessor computers,** machines that achieve parallelism by using many separate processors. Here the speedup primarily depends on a fruitful interaction between software and hardware. The software must be able to decompose a process into independent or partially independent subprocesses, and the hardware and

---

4. A processing element resembles a CPU without a control unit. The term *processing element* will avoid any ambiguity with other types of ALUs or CPUs.

software must be able to distribute the subprocesses to different processors for execution. Finally, the communications and synchronization facilities must have manageable overhead (i.e., the cost of performing synchronization must not be too great). We shall briefly discuss these machines in Chapter 7.

4. Build computers using alternative architectures, such as neural networks, dataflow architectures, demand-driven architectures, and systolic arrays. Researchers are studying these alternative approaches, and some discussion of these will occur in the text.

## 1.2 ■ A Classification of Computer Architectures

Up to now, we have talked in generalities about computer architectures. In this section we categorize computer architectures and establish a basis for studying them later in this text. We begin by describing the characteristics of the simplest computers, called von Neumann machines, in honor of John von Neumann, computer pioneer and inventor. We then present a classification of computer architectures that covers almost all computers in existence today. We conclude by describing four architectural categories that are under investigation.

### 1.2.1 ■ Von Neumann Machines

Most, and perhaps all, of the computers with which you are familiar are **von Neumann machines,** but some of the machines described later in the book are not. In most contexts, the terms *computer* and *von Neumann machine* are synonymous. We shall call a computer a von Neumann machine if it meets the following criteria:

- It has three basic hardware subsystems:
    - a CPU,
    - a main-memory system,
    - an I/O system.
- It is a stored-program computer. The main memory system holds the program that controls its operation, and the computer can manipulate its own program more or less as it can any other data in memory.
- It carries out instructions sequentially. The CPU executes, or at least appears to execute, one operation at a time.
- It has, or at least appears to have, a single path between the main memory system and the control unit of the CPU; this is often referred to as the "von Neumann bottleneck."

Conventional von Neumann machines (Fig. 1.2a) provide one pathway for addresses and a second pathway for data and instructions. **Harvard architectures** (Fig. 1.2b) are a class of von Neumann machines similar to conventional computers except that they provide independent pathways for data addresses, data, instruction addresses, and instructions.[5] Harvard architectures allow the CPU to access instructions and data simultaneously.

The main parts of the CPU are:

control unit (CU)
- a **control unit (CU),** which controls the operation of the computer;

arithmetic and logic unit (ALU)
- an **arithmetic and logic unit (ALU),** which performs arithmetic, logical, and shift operations to produce results;

register set
- a **register set,** whichs holds various values during the computer's operation;

---

5. The name "Harvard architecture" stems from Howard Aiken's work at Harvard, where he built the Mark-I through Mark-IV computers. They had separate storage for data and instructions. Current Harvard architectures do not have separate main memories for data and instructions but only separate data paths and buffers.

FIGURE 1.2 *Main components of typical von Neumann machines. (a) A conventional von Neumann architecture. (b) A Harvard architecture.*

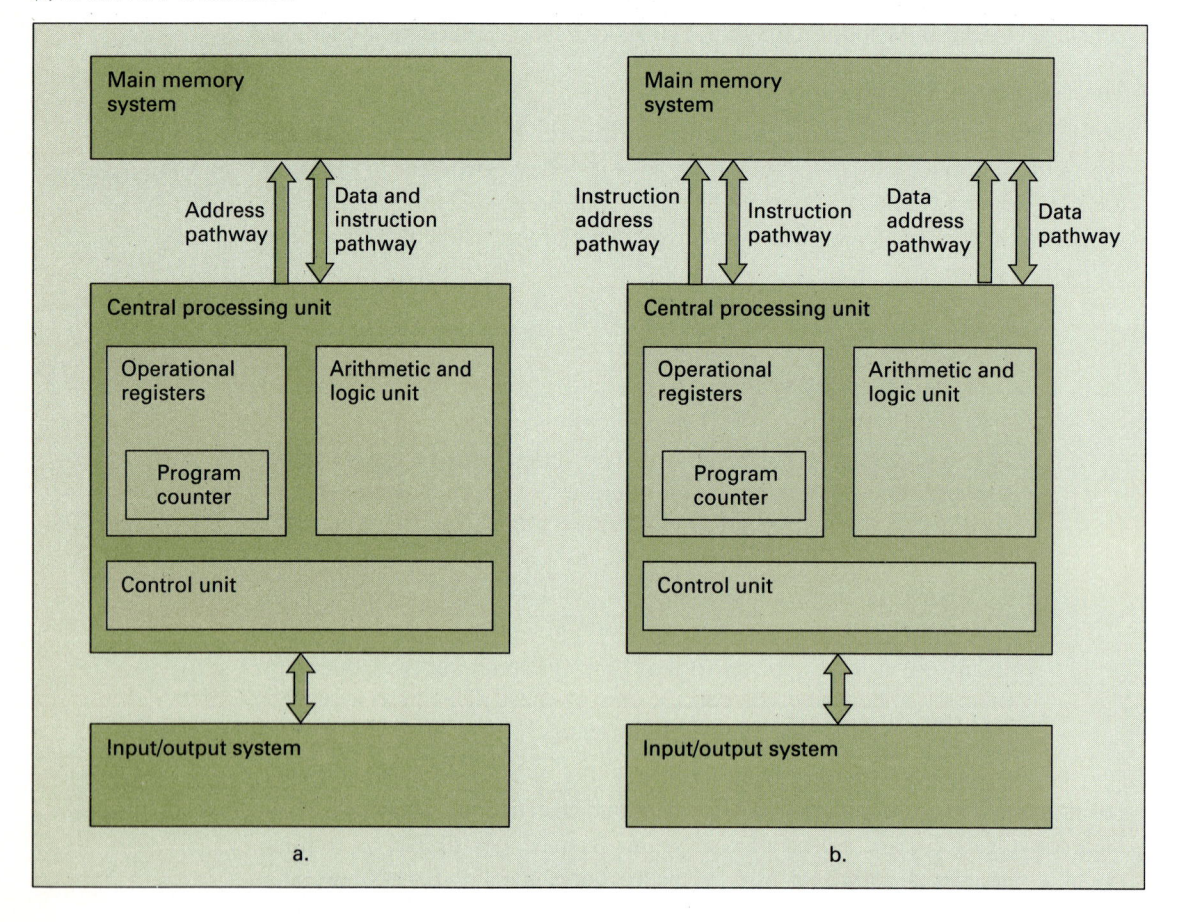

- a **program counter (PC)** (sometimes referred to as an **instruction counter**), which holds the main-memory address of an instruction.[6] The PC is part of the register set.

We can view a von Neumann machine as an abstract computer that executes **instructions**, values in memory that tell the computer what operation to perform.[7] Every instruction has a set of **instruction fields,** whose contents provide specific details to the control unit, and every instruction has its own **instruction format,** which is the way the fields are laid out in memory. The **instruction size** is the number of memory units (usually measured in bytes) that the instruction uses.

For instructions that operate on data (for example, arithmetic, logical, shift, character and string instructions), the data are the **operands** for the operation, and the sequence of data items on which the CPU operates is the **data stream.** The **instruction set** of a computer is the set of instructions that the computer is able to execute. Each computer has its own instruction set.

Every instruction has an **operation code (op code),** a numeric code usually found in the first field of the instruction that tells the computer what operation to perform. Other instruction fields tell the computer what registers to use, the number and datatypes of arguments (for example, for arithmetic and logical operations), and specifications for the operands' addresses. Instructions also tell the computer what processor status bits to test or set, and what to do if an error occurs. (Processor status bits, also called **flags**, are special 1-bit registers in the CPU.)

A **program** is a sequence of instructions for the computer to carry out. Each instruction has a logical ordering within the program, called its **logical address;** when a program is in main memory, each instruction also has a **physical address.** When a von Neumann machine executes a program, it executes the instructions one at a time, in sequence, except when one instruction tells the computer to break the sequence (for example a branch instruction).

The sequence of instructions that the computer executes is the **instruction stream.** To keep track of the instructions in memory, von Neumann machines use a PC. The PC "points to" (holds the address of) the next instruction to be executed.

During normal operation, the control unit performs a continuous sequence of two basic operations: **instruction fetch** and **instruction execution.** This sequence is called the **von Neumann machine cycle.** During instruction

---

6. The work of John von Neumann, H. H. Goldstine, A. W. Burks, J. P. Eckert, J. Mauchly, and others led to the use of the program counter. The term *von Neumann machine* came from this early work.
7. Machine instructions have names, and often the name for an instruction is the same as that for the operation resulting from its execution. For clarity we shall adopt the following convention in this text: instruction names will be printed in small caps, whereas operation names will appear in lowercase letters.

fetch, the control unit fetches the next instruction from main memory using the address held in the PC, and it increments the PC. After instruction fetch, therefore, the PC points to the instruction in memory following the one the CPU is about to execute.[8] The control unit then executes the current instruction, the one it just fetched. During execution, the CPU first decodes the instruction and determines what operation to perform. It then performs the operation. Finally, when it is finished with the current instruction, it starts the fetch-execute cycle over again by fetching the next instruction from memory.

Each computer implements an instruction set. The manuals that describe the computer instruction set are variously called "Principles of Operation," "Hardware References," "Architecture References," and "System References" by computer manufacturers.

To increase the speed of execution, architects often implement von Neumann architectures with pipelined processors. Architects also use multiple arithmetic units to increase the speed of the CPU, and they provide **buffers** (intermediate high-speed memories), to match the processor speed with the memory speed.

### 1.2.2 ■ Non–von Neumann Machines

Not all computers are von Neumann machines. Flynn (1966) classified computer architectures by a variety of characteristics, including number of processors, number of programs they can execute, and memory structure. His classification included the following categories (see also Fig. 1.3):

- *Single instruction stream, single data stream (SISD)* (Fig. 1.3a) The von Neumann architectures belong to this classification. SISD computers have one CPU that executes one instruction at a time (hence a single instruction stream) and fetches or stores one item of data at a time (hence a single data stream).

- *Single instruction stream, multiple data stream (SIMD)* (Fig. 1.3b). Processor arrays fall into this category. SIMD machines have a CU that operates like a von Neumann machine (i.e., it executes a single instruction stream), but SIMD machines have more than one PE. The CU generates the control signals for all of the PEs, which execute the same operation, generally in lockstep, on different data items (hence multiple data streams).

- *Multiple instruction stream, single data stream (MISD)* Logically, machines in this class would execute several different programs on

---

8. In practice, the instruction sets of most computers have instructions of more than one length. The op code of each instruction occupies the first few bits, frequently 1 byte, and indicates the operation and number of operands for the instruction. The CPU fetches the instruction in parts, each time incrementing the program counter (PC) to point to the next part of the instruction. Once the CPU has read the entire instruction, the PC points to the next instruction in memory.

the same data item. There are currently no machines of this type, although some MIMD systems may be used in this manner.

- *Multiple instruction stream, multiple data stream (MIMD)* (Fig. 1.3c). MIMD machines are also called *multiprocessors*. They have more than one independent processor, and each processor can execute a different program (hence multiple instruction streams) on its own data (hence multiple data streams).

**Multiple instruction stream, multiple data stream (MIMD) multiprocessors**

**FIGURE 1.3** *Flynn's classification of the three types of computers in existence. (a) SISD or von Neumann machine. (b) SIMD computer, or processor array. (c) MIMD, or multiprocessor system. (MISD, a fourth category of architectures, does not exist at present.)*

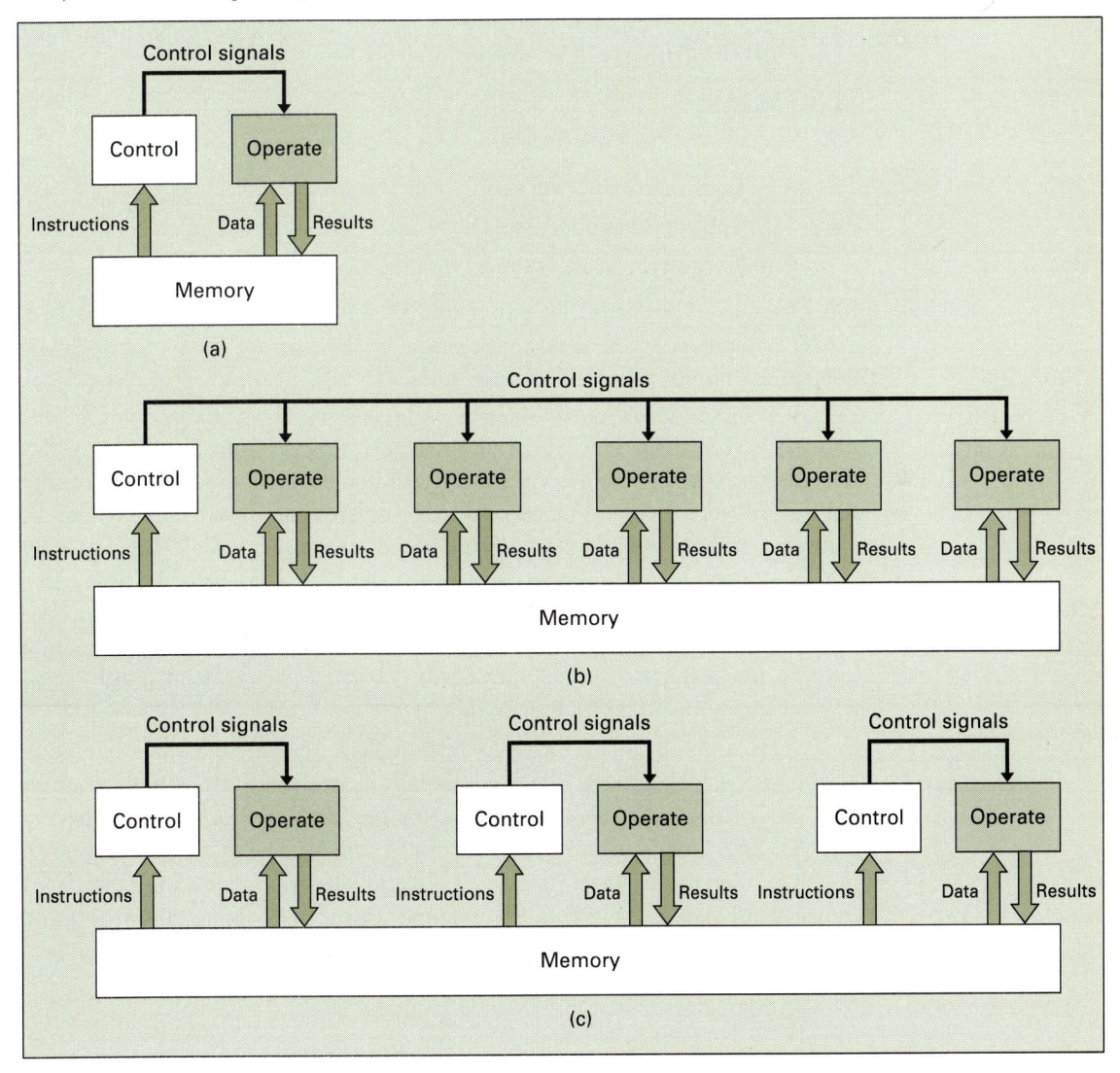

SIMD and MIMD machines are **parallel processors** because they operate in parallel on more than one datum at a time. Multiprocessor architectures can be divided into two categories based on the organization of their memory system:

- **Global memory (GM) system architectures.** One global memory system is shared by all of the processors. Current high-performance computer architectures are of this type and all three architectures in Fig. 1.3 are shown with global memory.

- **Local-memory (LM) system architectures.** Here one storage system exists for each processor. Multiprocessors with LM may also have GM and are also called **multiple processors.**

We now briefly consider the two kinds of parallel processors (SIMD and MIMD); Chapter 7 discusses these machines in greater detail.

### SIMD Machines

SIMD computers have the following characteristics:

- They distribute processing over a large amount of hardware.
- They operate concurrently on many different data elements.
- They perform the same computation on all data elements.

SIMD machines differ in the way their PEs access memory. The PEs of GM-SIMD computers share the same storage system, while those of LM-SIMD computers have independent storage systems.

Processor arrays are SIMD architectures. They have one CU and many PEs (Fig. 1.4). The CU generates control signals for all the PEs, which perform exactly the same computation simultaneously (or do nothing at all), but with different data. The term control unit in the SIMD context may be somewhat misleading and deserves additional comment. Usually the CU is itself a von Neumann computer in its own right, that is, a complete special-purpose computer with its own register set, ALU, and control unit of the type to be described in Chapter 2. This computer is referred to as a control unit because it was designed solely to control the PEs in a processor array, rather than to operate as a stand-alone computer.

Historically, SIMD architectures include several components in addition to the control unit and PEs. They usually include a **host computer** (or simply host) for loading programs, for configuring the array of PEs, and for supervising I/O. The host is usually a conventional computer with a well-established operating system. The architects may also provide specialized I/O devices for reformatting the arrays of data, for example, or for performing high-speed I/O.

### MIMD Machines

MIMD computers have the following characteristics:

- They distribute processing over a number of independent processors.
- They share resources, including main memory, among component processors.
- Each processor operates independently and concurrently.
- Each processor runs its own program.

**FIGURE 1.4** *An LM-SIMD processor array consisting of 16 PEs, and a single control unit. The PEs shown here, each with its own local memory, are organized in a 4 × 4 array; hence the name processor array.*

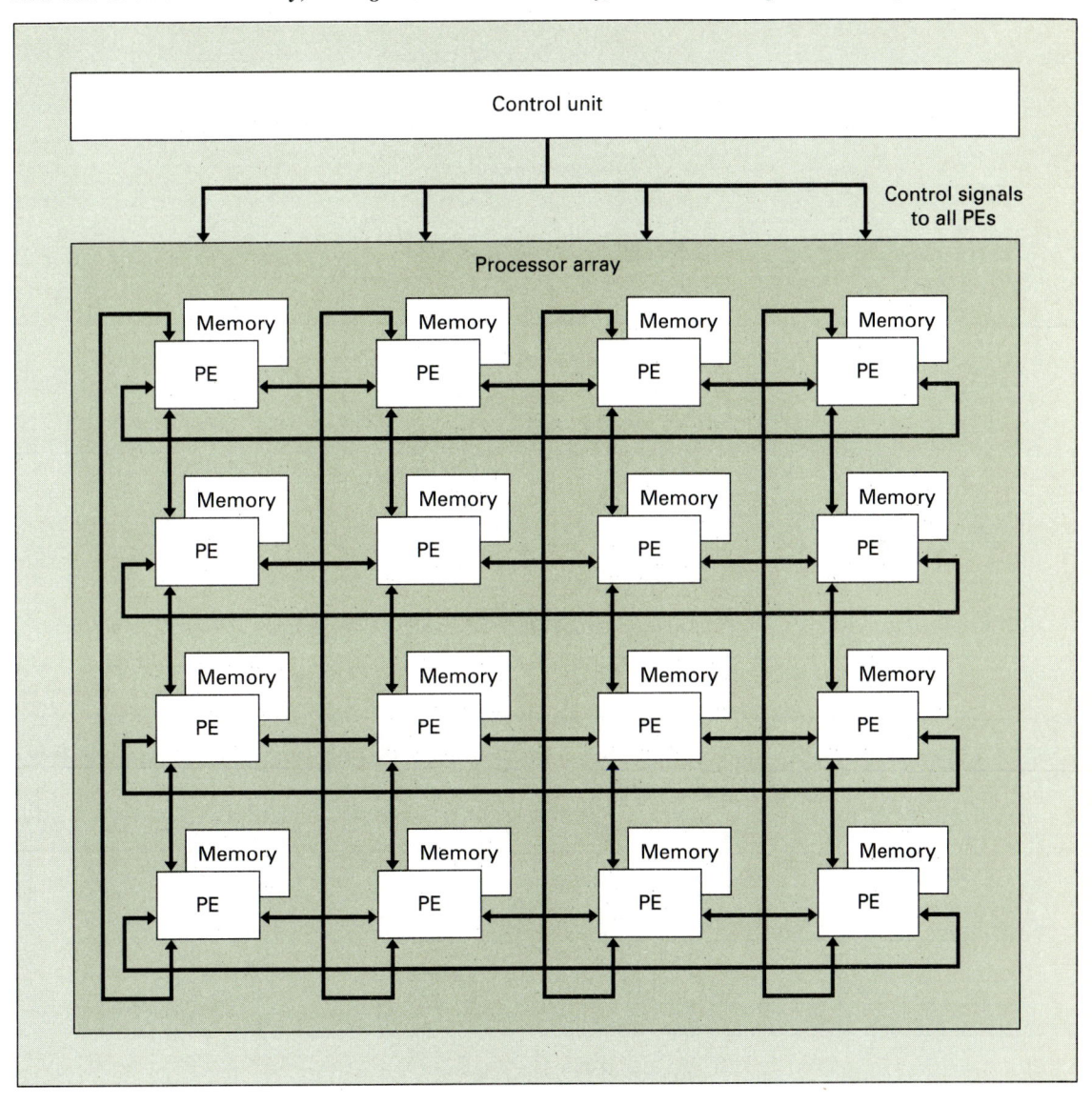

**Computer Architecture**

<u>interconnection networks</u>

<u>tightly coupled</u>

<u>loosely coupled</u>

Different MIMD architectures have different **interconnection networks,** different processors, different memory-addressing structures, and different synchronization and control structures. The interconnection networks allow the component processors to communicate with each other.

We can categorize multiple-processor computers as being either **tightly coupled** or **loosely coupled** (Figs. 1.5 and 1.6) depending on how the processors access each other's memory. The processors in a tightly coupled multiprocessor generally share one memory system. Those of a loosely coupled multiprocessor may also share a memory system, but each processor also has its own local memory and generally executes programs out of it. Thus, tightly coupled

FIGURE 1.5 *Architecture of a tightly coupled multiple-processor computer. M, memory systems; P, processors.*

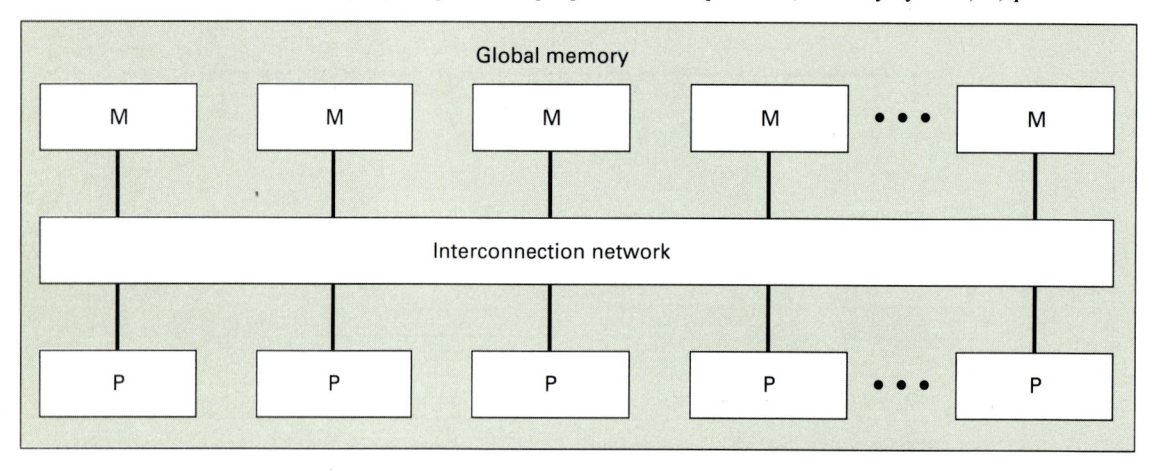

FIGURE 1.6 *Architecture of a loosely coupled multiple-processor computer. M, memory systems; P, processors.*

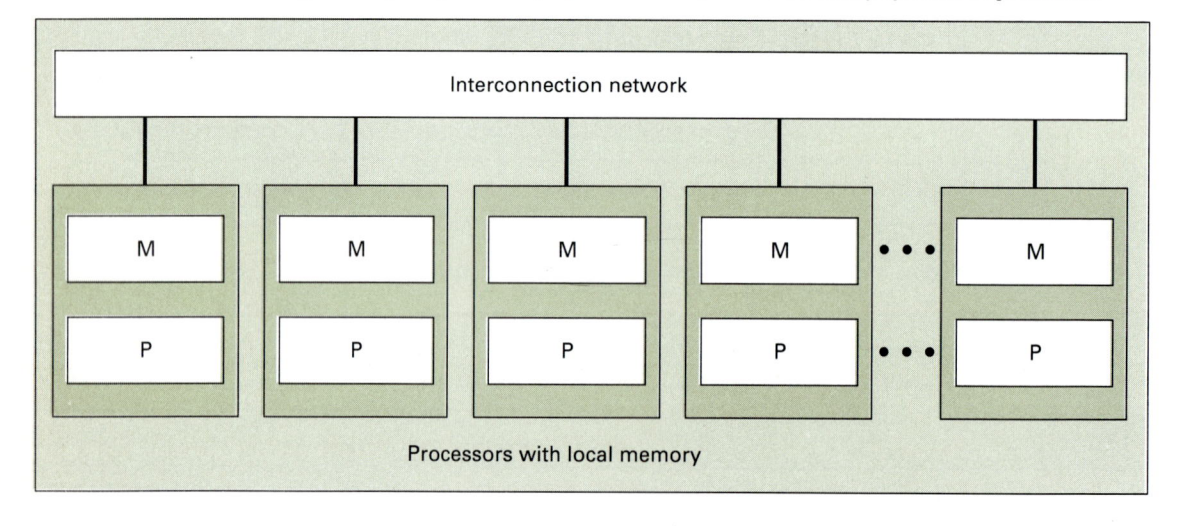

**Table 1.1**  Architectural categories

| Category | Common Name | Examples |
|---|---|---|
| SISD (CISC) | Uniprocessor | IBM PC, DEC PDP-11, DEC VAX-11 |
| SISD (RISC) | Uniprocessor | MIPS R2000, SUN SPARC, IBM System/R6000 |
| GM-SIMD | Processor array | Burroughs BSP |
| LM-SIMD | Processor array | ILLIAC IV, MPP, CM-1 |
| GM-MIMD | Multiprocessor | All existing tightly coupled (shared-memory) multiprocessors (DEC and IBM) |
| LM-MIMD | Multiple processor | Tandem/16, iPSC/2 |

and loosely coupled computers correspond approximately to the GM-MIMD and LM-MIMD classifications, respectively. Examples of GM-MIMD processors are the dual processor of the CDC 6600 series and the Cray XM-P. Examples of LM-MIMD processors are the Carnegie-Mellon Cm* and the Tandem/16.

Because most general-purpose computers include independent special-purpose I/O processors, we can logically view them as GM-MIMD architectures. However, their I/O processors generally play a role secondary to that of CPU. That is, the CPU starts them, stops them, and monitors their activity. Consequently we shall restrict our use of the MIMD classification to include only those computers that have independent processors of approximately equal stature.

Combining the various classifications discussed so far in Section 1.2.2 and RISCs yields the six architectural categories listed in Table 1.1. (The *Case Studies* discusses most of the computers listed in Table 1.1.)

**Other Architectures**

Computer designers and architects have introduced a number of alternatives to the architectures we have described, such as dataflow architectures and neural networks. In von Neumann machines programs determine the flow of control. In **dataflow architectures,** by contrast, the availability of data determines when the machines will perform operations. The computational models that dataflow processors implement, called **dataflow models,** are inherently parallel, and architects have designed dataflow machines to implement these models efficiently. A dataflow machine, like an MIMD computer, has many independent PEs, but these do not execute programs. When the supervising processor finds available data, it routes the data and an instruction to a PE, which performs the operation and forwards the result to memory. Because there is no program in the conventional sense, dataflow architectures are neither SIMD nor MIMD.

**Neural networks** are loosely based on biological systems. Like dataflow processors, they do not execute conventional programs and therefore do not fall into the SIMD or MIMD classifications. Current applications include signal processing and pattern recognition, and a number of manufacturers are developing special-purpose devices to implement them. At the present time the technology is in its infancy.

**special-purpose machines**

Finally, certain architectures are called simply **special-purpose machines** because of the specialized functions they perform. In general, they use conventional architectures that have been optimized for specific applications. All of them differ from conventional architectures because they are required to solve a particular equation or to handle specific applications, such as very large arrays, very large databases, or highly parallel algorithms. Included in this group are artifical intelligence machines, high-level-language machines, image-processing machines, three-dimensional display processors, and computers with embedded control.[9] Although they all have sufficiently large user bases to be economically feasible, we will not be examining them in this text.

## 1.3 ■ Measuring the Quality of a Computer Architecture

As with the architecture of a building, the excellence of a computer architecture is not easy to measure. Many computer architects use the attributes described in the following sections in their evaluation of excellence. Like the attributes that make for a good building architecture, most of these attributes are difficult to quantify. Indeed, an architecture that is good for one application may be poor for others, and conversely. In this section we shall discuss six attributes of architectural excellence: generality, applicability, efficiency, ease of use, malleability, and expandability. The chapter ends with a discussion of architectural merit, system performance, and system cost.

### 1.3.1 ■ Generality

**generality**

**Generality** is a measure of how wide the range of applications is for which an architecture is suited. For example, computers intended primarily for scientific and engineering applications use floating-point arithmetic (where numbers are stored with both a magnitude and an exponent) and those intended mainly for business applications use decimal arithmetic (where numbers are represented in terms of decimal digits). General systems provide both types of arithmetic.

Although the number of instructions in an instruction set is not a direct measure of a computer's generality, it does provide an indication of gener-

---

9. *Artifical intelligence* is the branch of computer science that endows computers with humanlike intelligence; architects design artificial intelligence machines to efficiently execute artificial intelligence programming languages like LISP. *Image processing* involves extracting information from images or enhancing the quality of an image. *Three-dimensional display processors* generally provide special-purpose hardware for displaying graphical images and find applications in computer-aided design (CAD), computer-aided manufacture (CAM), and animation. In *embedded control* the processors are included as integral parts of a machine of some type; for example, many printers have embedded processors to control the printing process.

ality. The diversity of addressing modes is also an indication of generality. Nonetheless, RISCs are quite general although they may have small instruction sets with few addressing modes. Instruction sets and addressing modes will be covered in Chapter 2, and CISC and RISC architectures will be examined in Chapter 6, where we also focus on pipelining.

One major discussion among computer researchers during the 1980s concerned whether generality was good. Currently the pendulum seems to have swung toward the opinion that it is not. Generality tends to increase the complexity of the implementations. For the large computer families of large manufacturers, this complexity makes it more difficult to design the machines. Generality also tends to make optimizing compilers more complex because they have more instructions to chose from when generating code. Also, generality tends to imply complexity, and the emphasis in the design of systems with computers has nearly always been to put most of the complexity into the software, where developers can more easily correct bugs (errors).

One commercial argument in favor of generality is that, because it makes designing computers more difficult, it reduces the number of companies that can clone (make copies of) a given computer. No large computer company wants to lose business to cloners of its designs.

## 1.3.2 ■ Applicability

**Applicability** refers to the utility of an architecture for its intended use. This book covers computers designed primarily for one of two major application areas: (1) scientific and engineering and (2) general commercial applications. Scientific and engineering applications are those that typically solve complex equations and make extensive use of floating-point arithmetic. They are **computation-intensive applications,** which means they have a much higher ratio of CPU operations to memory and I/O operations than most other applications (although many symbolic computations are also computation-intensive). General commercial applications are those supported by typical computer centers: compiling, accounting, editing, spreadsheet usage, and word processing, among many others. Other application areas—those pertaining to special-purpose machines—are important, but as mentioned earlier they will not be considered in this text.

*applicability*

*computation-intensive applications*

## 1.3.3 ■ Efficiency

**Efficiency** is a measure of the average amount of hardware in the computer that remains busy during its normal use. An efficient architecture permits (but does not ensure) an efficient implementation. Notice that a conflict exists between efficiency and generality. Also, because of the decreasing cost of computer components, efficiency is of much less concern now than it was early in the history of computer development.

*efficiency*

An efficient architecture, however, does tend to allow for both very high speed and very low cost implementations, and in a large computer family both types of implementation are important. One characteristic of efficient architectures is that they tend to be relatively simple. Because of the difficulty of designing complex systems correctly, most computers have a simple efficient core computer, the CU, with a layer of control around it that provides the complicated facilities that the architecture requires. We shall discuss CUs in Chapter 3.

### 1.3.4 ■ Ease of Use

*ease of use*

The **ease of use** of an architecture is a measure of how simple it is for a systems programmer to develop software, such as an operating system or a compiler, for it. Ease of use is therefore a function of the ISA and is closely related to generality. It should not be confused with how easy to use ("friendly") a user finds a computer to be, which is determined by the operating system and available software rather than the underlying architecture. We shall consider examples of some computers in which the lack of ease of use made it difficult for compiler designers to implement some high-level programming languages.

The instruction sets of early computers sometimes lacked instructions to do important operations. Consequently programmers were forced to use convoluted instruction sequences to implement those operations. Today instruction-set architects have had enough experience designing instruction sets that this type of shortcoming is rare.

### 1.3.5 ■ Malleability

*malleability*

These previous four measures—applicability, generality, efficiency, and ease of use—apply to computer family architectures. The next two measures—malleability and expandability—generally apply to the implementations of computers in a family. The **malleability** of an architecture is a measure of how easy it is for a designer to implement a wide range of computers having that architecture. The more specific an architecture, the more difficult it is to produce machines that differ in size and performance from others. By analogy, if one refers to the architecture of a house as colonial, say, then many sizes and styles are possible. If, on the other hand, the architecture specifies the floor plan, much less variety of implementation is possible.

Generally, the architecture includes many features at each level of detail. The floor plan of a colonial house includes many details, such as walls, doors, and electrical and plumbing fixtures. In the case of industry standard personal computers (PCs), the specification is loose, like that of the colonial house. In the case of the Apple Macintosh or the IBM PC AT, the architectural specification is much more complete, so all implementations are much more similar.

### 1.3.6 ■ Expandability

**Expandability** is a measure of how easy it is for a designer to increase the capabilities of an architecture, such as its maximum memory size or arithmetic capabilities. In general, a computer-family specification allows a designer to use a wide range of memory sizes in the family members. For example, because the DEC VAX architecture specifies the memory size only indirectly, and then only within wide limits, VAX computers have had memory sizes varying by more than a factor of 1000.

Designers can achieve expandability of external memory in a variety of ways: They can increase the number of devices, or they can increase the speed with which the devices move data to or from the external world. Many architectures leave some aspects of the I/O structure undefined. This lack of specification increases the expandability, but it may also increase the amount of reprogramming necessary for new family members.

Some computers have more than one CPU. In that case the expandability also relates to the number of CPUs the system can *effectively* use; the barriers to using large numbers of CPUs are generally not immediately obvious. If systems programmers find it difficult to synchronize CPUs, for example, synchronization will effectively limit the number of CPUs that a system can use.

## 1.4 ■ Factors Influencing the Success of a Computer Architecture

A number of factors influence the success of a computer architecture. The following sections discuss three of these: architectural merit, system performance, and system cost.

### 1.4.1 ■ Architectural Merit

When investigating a particular computer or computer-family architecture, one can apply all six measures given in Section 1.3 plus compatibility. In general, however, there are four primary measures that determine the success of an architecture, its **architectural merit**:

1. *Applicability.* The more appropriate the architecture is for its intended application, the better.
2. *Malleability.* The easier it is to build small systems, the better.
3. *Expandability.* The greater the expandability in computing power, memory size, I/O capacity, and number of processors, the better.
4. *Compatibility.* The more compatible with previous computers of the same family, the better.

The companion *Case Studies* reader, which presents specific architectures, does not mention any systems with serious shortcomings in the other three criteria mentioned in Section 1.3—generality, efficiency, or ease of use. We take these features as requirements, because virtually all successful architectures satisfy them.

One last word about computer-family architectures: Even though computer architects frequently try to design a complete family architecture, they generally leave some features unspecified in their initial definition of the family. Early implementations then serve to point up these missing aspects of the architecture. Similarly, initially specified features used rarely in early implementations may be omitted for later family members. Both of these situations occurred in the development of the two largest families of computers, the IBM System/370[10] and its descendants, and the DEC VAX family.

Having discussed the issue of architectural merit, it is worthwhile to look briefly at three other issues that influence the commercial success of a computer system:

- *Openness of the architecture.* An architecture is **open** when its designers publish its specifications; if they keep details proprietary, it is **closed.** Starting about 1980 the availability of standard software and application packages became important to the success of an architecture, perhaps the architecture's most important feature. By nearly any technological measure, the Macintosh is superior to the IBM PC, but it has had a relatively closed architecture for most of its life.

- *Availability of a compatible and comprehensible programming model.* Several of the highly parallel computers have proved so difficult to use that they have been much more interesting to analysts trying to find novel ways to use them than to users who wish to do something useful with them.

- *Quality of the early implementations.* There have been a number of computers that appeared to be good machines, with good software and good operational characteristics, but they were not successful. In many cases their commercial failure stemmed from the bad reputations they earned because their first models were unreliable and had many manufacturing defects.

Thus, those readers planning to start computer companies should pay attention to these issues, as well as to the quality of the architecture of their machine. Texts on computer architecture or engineering generally stress only architectural issues.

---

10. We shall use "IBM System/370" to denote either the System/360 or the System/370, unless we specify otherwise.

## 1.4.2 ■ System Performance

**System performance** is determined in part by the speed of a computer. It thus measures the merit not of an architecture, but rather of its implementation. Nonetheless, a good performance is crucial for many applications, and users spend a great deal of time and energy measuring system performance. To measure a computer's performance, architects run standardized batteries of programs, called **benchmarks**, on the computer. These benchmarks enable the architects to determine both the relative speeds of all computers that run the benchmarks and the absolute speed of each individual computer. Using the results, the architects report the system's performance using various **performance metrics,** which state the results either in absolute or in relative terms.

*system performance*

*benchmarks*

*performance metrics*

Measuring the performance of computers is a complex task. To illustrate its multidimensionality, consider an analogous but more familiar situation. Automobile performance can be measured in many ways, of which the following are only a few:

- for drag racers: the time to reach a quarter mile, or the speed at the end of a quarter mile;
- for race car drivers: the speed of acceleration, ability to corner, and top speed;
- for the *Guiness Book of Records:* top speed;
- for the average commuter: reliability (repair records);
- for the long-distance commuter: gas mileage.

To measure performance of a typical family car we might use a multidimensional conglomerate of criteria.

In this section, we shall list a number of ways that scientists measure computer performance, show how they differ, and indicate the breadth of the problem of making reasonable performance comparisons among computers. First, let us describe the general areas of measurement. Obviously the speed of the processor is important, but so are the speeds of the I/O and of system operations. In many cases the size of memory and the characteristics of the interconnection network are important.

Also, we shall make one other preliminary remark that applies to all these measures and to the hazards of trying to extract a single number from them. First imagine that there are five separate measures of the speed of the CPU. Then consider five computers, A through E, with the speeds shown in Table 1.2. Computer C would certainly be 10 times faster than computer A, but what about computer B? Its average speed is 600 times faster than A, but it cannot even do 40% of the problems. And what about D? It is 80 times as fast, on average, and can do 80% of the problems. Finally, what about computer E, whose average speed is 35 times faster than A?

The appropriate measure for any user is the average of the measures that are important for that user's work. Furthermore, the measures should be

**Table 1.2** Performance measurements of five hypothetical computers using five different metrics[a]

| Computer | A | B | C | D | E |
|---|---|---|---|---|---|
| Metric 1 | 1 | 1000 | 10 | 100 | 1 |
| Metric 2 | 1 | 0 | 10 | 100 | 5 |
| Metric 3 | 1 | 1000 | 10 | 100 | 10 |
| Metric 4 | 1 | 0 | 10 | 100 | 50 |
| Metric 5 | 1 | 1000 | 10 | 0 | 100 |

[a]Speeds in relative quantities per unit time.

weighted by how important they are to the user. We will discuss a common method of weighting shortly.

### CPU Performance Measures (Optional)

In this section we shall describe six ways to measure a CPU's performance. To evaluate a CPU's performance, however, it is important to average these measurements appropriately.

Probably the most common measurement of a CPU's performance is how many **millions of instructions per second (MIPS)** it can execute. Sometimes the MIPS rating of a computer is given by how fast the machine can operate, its **peak MIPS** rate. This is the speed that the salespeople guarantee the CPU cannot exceed, but it is as meaningless to the programmer as any other snake-oil claim. More interesting are the comparative numbers given by benchmarks. For example, **IBM MIPS** or **VAX MIPS** refer to average performance speeds relative to particular IBM or VAX computers. We can estimate a reasonable MIPS rating for a machine by computing the average time the computer takes to execute its instructions and weighting that average by how often each instruction is used.

For computers that perform scientific and engineering computation, MIPS is not the most useful measure of performance. This is because most such computers are **vector machines,** whose hardware has been optimized for executing vector instructions. (A **vector** is a linear collection of $N$ variables). A single instruction in a vector machine may initiate thousands of floating-point operations. Hence more appropriate measures for such computers measure how many **millions of floating-point operations per second (MFLOPS or megaflops)** or **billions of floating-point operations per second (GFLOPS or gigaflops)** they can perform.

Two common benchmarks measure a computer's speed in MFLOPS. (Of course, there are also peak MFLOPS and peak GFLOPS; like peak MIPS, these measures are often quoted in press releases but give unrealistic concepts of performance.)

*(margin notes: millions of instructions per second (MIPS); peak MIPS; IBM MIPS; VAX MIPS; vector machines; vector; millions of floating-point operations per second (MFLOPS or megaflops); billions of floating-point operations per second (GFLOPS or gigaflops))*

One of the earlier and most widely quoted benchmarks for evaluating MFLOPS is the **LINPACK benchmark.** Due to Jack Dongarra at Argonne National Laboratories, LINPACK measures the speed at which a computer solves a system of equations in a Fortran environment. The LINPACK benchmark operates on matrices of 100 × 100 to 1000 × 1000 elements. The second common MFLOPS measure is the **Livermore loops benchmark.** It consists (usually) of 24 Fortran loops that are assumed to reflect the types of computations common at the Lawrence Livermore National Laboratories. The loops operate mainly on data sets with 1001 or fewer elements.

An older CPU measure, which was quoted more commonly in 1980 than it is today, is the **Whetstone benchmark,** which H. J. Curnow and B. A. Wichmann introduced and named for the Whetstone Algol compiler. It is based on the time a computer takes to do several floating-point operations, including some common functions. The Whetstone benchmark results are normally quoted in units called **Whets** because of its structure, the Whetstone benchmark does not lend itself to vectorization. The advent of vector computing has caused the Whetstone benchmark to fall into disfavor. **Vectorization** is the compilation of programs to run efficiently on computers with vector instructions. Chapter 2 will discuss vector instructions, and Chapter 6 will introduce vector processors.

Another unit of performance that researchers often use is the **VAX unit of performance (VUP).** The VUP is a relative measure. It gives one system's performance relative to that of the DEC VAX 11/780. Because it assesses comparative performance, it is somewhat less open to exaggeration by salespeople than are the other measures. One VUP is approximately 0.5 IBM MIPS.

Two recent benchmarks are the SPEC Benchmark Suite[11] and the Perfect Club.[12] The **SPEC Benchmark Suite** consists of 10 real-world applications taken from a variety of scientific and engineering applications.[13] Many of these programs use double-precision floating-point arithmetic. Researchers using the SPEC Benchmark Suite report their results in units called **SPECmarks.** One SPECmark is approximately 1 VUP, but the correspondence between the two units is not linear.

---

11. SPEC stands for System Performance and Evaluation Cooperative. Four companies—Apollo, Hewlett-Packard, MIPS, and Sun Microsystems, founded SPEC, whose goal is to evaluate the performance of small computer systems, as opposed to large computers and vector processors.
12. Perfect is an acronym for PERFormance Evaluation for Cost-effective Transformations. David Kuck and Ahmed Sameh of the University of Illinois conceived the Perfect Club in the late 1980s. With several colleagues they developed this benchmark for supercomputers, which are the fastest-available machines at a given time.
13. The 10 applications are the GNU C (a C compiler), Espresso (optimization of programmable-logic arrays), Spice (analog circuit simulation), Dudoc (nuclear reactor simulation) Nasa7 (floating-point intensive kernels), LISP interpreter, Eqntott (integer-intensive parser generator), Matrix300 (matrix operations), Fpppp (quantum chemistry), and Tomcatv (vectorizable mesh generation).

**Perfect Club Suite**    The **Perfect Club Suite** constitutes 13 scaled-down, real-world programs taken from the sciences; they include studies of, among others, air pollution, supersonic reentry, structural dynamics, liquid water simulation, transonic flow, seismic migration, and circuit simulation. Like the SPEC Benchmark Suite, the Perfect Club Suite exercises all types of arithmetic and a variety of types of code, including vectorizable and nonvectorizable.

There are four often-quoted means used when averaging performance measurements over a number of trials. Let $\{X_i\}$ be a set of $N$ measurements, and let $\{W_i\}$ be as set of $N$ weights. Then the four means are as follows:

**arithmetic mean**   $$\text{arithmetic mean of } \{X_i\} = \frac{\sum_{i=1}^{N} X_i}{N},$$

**harmonic mean**   $$\text{harmonic mean of } \{X_i\} = \frac{N}{\sum_{i=1}^{N} \frac{1}{X_i}},$$

**weighted arithmetic mean**   $$\text{weighted arithmetic mean of } \{X_i\} = \frac{\sum_{i=1}^{N} (W_i \times X_i)}{\sum_{i=1}^{N} W_i},$$

**geometric mean**   $$\text{geometric mean of } \{X_i\} = \sqrt[N]{\prod_{i=1}^{N} X_i}.$$

The time it takes a computer to execute a set of programs, the total execution time, is the value a user generally wishes to know. Let $\{P_i\}$ be a set of $N$ programs whose execution times are $\{T_i\}$. Then the arithmetic mean of the execution times reflects the total execution time. When performance is expressed in MIPS or FLOPS, which are execution rates rather than execution times, the harmonic mean of the reciprocal rates for the $N$ programs reflects the total execution time.

The weighted arithmetic mean gives a way of factoring into the performance evaluation the workload distribution of a computing center. Suppose we have evaluated the execution times $T_i$ for a set of $N$ typical programs. If program $P_i$ represents $W_i$ percent of the workload, then the weighted arithmetic mean of the execution times reflects the total execution time for the programs.

Finally, when the performance of a new machine is expressed as a ratio, as in IBM MIPS or VUPs, we must multiply the execution times of the benchmark programs when run on the reference machine times the performance ratio $P$ of the new machine to reflect the new machine's total execution time. In this case the geometric mean of the products $T_i \times P$ is often used to reflect the execution time of the new machine.

People sometimes quote two other indications of computer performance. One is efficiency, which we discussed in Section 1.3.3. The other is the

**utilization ratio**    **utilization ratio,** which is the ratio between the time a computer spends on productive computations and the total time the system is operational. When computer hardware was relatively expensive, a machine's efficiency and utilization ratio were important considerations. Today, because hardware is relatively inexpensive, these measures are quoted much less often.

A useful metric during the design process is the number of **clock ticks per instruction (TPI),** which indicates the (average) time the CPU takes to execute an instruction. The higher the performance of the CPU, the smaller the TPI. Clearly the CPU performance is proportional to the product of the clock-cycle time times the TPI. When designers work on a CPU, they can determine the TPI from the execution times of the individual instructions and the probability of their occurrence. Notice that the TPI is independent of technology, whereas the clock cycle depends largely on technology.

clock ticks per instruction (TPI)

**Measures of I/O and System Performance**
There are two significant measures of I/O performance: bandwidth and I/O operations per second. Unlike the CPU measures noted in the previous paragraphs, these measures do not purport to measure the same thing. The **bandwidth** is the rate at which I/O can be performed, usually quoted in **megabytes per second (MBS).** Most I/O devices have specific transfer rates, and the I/O channels that connect to them have peak transfer rates that are often quoted in MBS. For applications where the transfers are very large, as is the case in many scientific and engineering applications, the I/O bandwidth is a meaningful measure of the performance of the I/O system.

bandwidth

megabytes per second (MBS)

For transaction processing, where the I/O blocks are quite small, a more significant measure of the I/O performance is the number of **I/O operations per second** the system can perform. We can illustrate the advantage of this measure by considering that typical slow disks have transfer rates of about 1 MBS and disk-block access times of about 0.1 sec. Thus, they cannot perform more than about 10 I/O operations per second. If each I/O operation transfers 512 bytes, then this slow disk can access at about 5 kilobytes per second (KBS). However, if the I/O block is 100 kilobytes (KB), the system may achieve the 1-MBS transfer rate, which is 200 times faster.

I/O operations per second

There is a measure of overall system performance that is far more comprehensive than any of the CPU performance or I/O performance measures so far examined. The number of **transactions per second (TPS)** that a system can perform reflects both CPU and I/O performance in a way that is meaningful for transaction processing. The transactions are typical of those required for a simple bank transaction, and the specific benchmark is the **debit/credit benchmark.** This measure includes all CPU and I/O operations necessary to perform a transaction: logging of the terminal keystrokes, updating of several single records in several large files, and so on. Although most real transaction-processing operations are far more complex than the debit/credit transaction, a computer's TPS rating does give a reasonable idea of that system's overall performance.

transactions per second (TPS)

debit/credit benchmark

### Other Performance Measures

*memory bandwidth*

*memory access time*

*memory size*

Three metrics are useful for the memory system. **Memory bandwidth** is the number of megabytes per second the memory can deliver to the processor. **Memory access time** is the average time the CPU requires to access memory, usually quoted in nanoseconds. **Memory size** is the volume of data the memory can hold, usually given in megabytes.

### 1.4.3 ■ System Cost

Like performance, cost in dollars is an important characteristic of a computer system; however, like most performance issues, cost reflects implementation more than architecture. Nonetheless, since cost determines the viability of a computer system, we shall discuss it here.

A major part of the cost of a computer system is the cost of the underlying logic, which can vary tremendously from one logic device to another. This variability does not appear likely to change. It is a law of nature that optimization in one direction (toward low cost, say) negatively influences optimization in other directions (such as high speed or reliability). Thus at any given time the availability of a wide variety of devices will allow any large family of computers to have a wide variety and number of devices. Also, device costs and speeds will probably always vary with time, so it is best for a computer family not to place implicit bounds on the number or speeds of devices.

Cost can be measured in many ways, and costs other than the purchase price of a hardware system are generally important. These other cost metrics also vary from system to system and from time to time. Other important metrics, and some applications where they are important, follow:

- *Reliability* is crucial in computers used for flight-critical control of aircraft, for safety-critical control of nuclear power plants, or wherever human life or safety is at stake.
- *Ease of repair* is particularly important for computers having a huge number of components.
- *Power consumption,* or equivalently heat generation, is especially critical in space-borne systems.
- *Weight* is especially critical in space-borne systems.
- *Ruggedness,* or the ability to withstand shock and unfriendly environments, is an essential consideration for military usage, which requires tolerance of all sorts of physical abuse and environmental extremes.
- *Software system interface quality,* measured by the user-friendliness and degree of standardization, is important for personal computers.

As with any optimization problem, good engineering practice suggests that cost can best be assessed by first defining the problem to be solved and then determining the appropriate metrics for judging the success of the solutions.

# Summary

This chapter introduced the notions of computer architecture and computer-family architecture. We presented a brief history of computers, describing how computer technology has evolved and how this rapid evolution has influenced computer architecture.

We then described the major categories of computer architectures. Considerable detail was given to explaining the components and operation of von Neumann machines, including the essential features of their machine cycle and the way they execute programs. Computer architectures were classified according to number of instruction streams, number of data streams, and type of memory (global or local). A number of specific architectural types were described, including processor arrays and multiple-processor systems.

We provided various measures of architectural merit, including generality, applicability, efficiency, ease of use, malleability, and expandability. Finally we delineated design factors influencing the success of a computer-family architecture. The chapter ended with a discussion of various measures of a computer's performance.

# Exercises

*1.1* Although architecture and implementation are separate tasks, they are not unrelated. For two historical buildings, describe how the technology of the time influenced the architecture. For two historical periods, describe how the architecture influenced the technology.

*1.2* A vector accelerator is a special CPU component that speeds up vector operations. Suppose that you have a choice of two vector accelerators for a scalar computer. One performs vector operations four times faster than scalar operations, the other 20 times faster. Plot the speed ratio of the machines as a function of the percent vectorization. (If the percent vectorization is 20%, then 20% of the instructions will run on the vector accelerator; the remaining 80% will run on the original machine, but without speedup.)

*1.3* As the architect for the Dynamic Graphics Corp. you are to build a new vector accelerator for a scalar computer. Plot the vector speedup required to achieve double the performance as a function of the old vector unit's speedup for 75% vectorization.

*1.4* A cache is a large buffer that speeds up a storage system. Consider two similar computers, one with a cache and one with a vector accelerator. Suppose the cache increases the general scalar performance by 50% and doubles the scalar performance on vectorizable loops of the cache computer. Plot the vector accelerator speedup required to make the performance of the noncache computer double the performance of the cache computer with no vector accelerator as a function of the percent vectorization.

*1.5* As president of the Huge Performance company you are faced with deciding how to allocate some R&D (research and development) funds. One choice is to improve your machine's compilers, which will increase performance for all users by 10% per year. The other is to add a cache, which will double the performance. (See Exercise 1.4.) How soon will the compiler improvement overtake the cache development in performance?

*1.6* Suppose that the cache in Exercise 1.5 will have to be redesigned every other year but that compiler development is stopped when the performance is doubled. When does the cache development cost overtake the compiler development cost?

*1.7* Evaluate the harmonic, geometric, and arithmetic means for the following set of measurements: 25, 40, 33, 16, 25, 27, 50, 44, 22.

*1.8* Derive a formula for the harmonic mean in terms of a weighted arithmetic mean.

*1.9* For two sets of $N$ measurements, $\{X_i\}$ and $\{Y_i\}$, show that the ratio of their geometric means,

$$\frac{\text{geometric mean of } \{X_i\}}{\text{geometric mean of } \{Y_i\}},$$

equals the geometric mean of the individual ratios,

$$\text{geometric mean of } \frac{\{X_i\}}{\{Y_i\}}.$$

*1.10* A memory system has two access speeds, A1 and A2. A1 holds for 20% of the accesses, while A2 holds for the remaining 80%. What is the average access speed?

*1.11* Many advertised benchmarks show performance values much greater than those achieved with real problems because the benchmarks are small and use small data sets. What are some of the reasons that they perform uncharacteristically well?

*1.12* Assume that you have four algorithms, A1 to A4, to sort $n$ data and that their sort times are as follows: $100n$ for A1, $10n \log 2n$ for A2, $3n^2$ for A3, and $2^n$ for A4. For what values of $n$ is each method best suited? If a pipelined machine takes $0.03n^2$ time using A3, perhaps because of vectorization, how do these regions of optimality change? If for $n = 100,000$ you incorrectly chose A3 instead of A1 or A2, how big is the penalty that you pay?

---

### Reference-needed Exercise

*1.13* Using the Case Studies manual that accompanies this text, manuals available from libraries, or Siewiorek, Bell and Newell (1982), evaluate a number of computers against the criteria given in Section 1.4.1.

---

### Discussion/Team Problem

*1.14* In large computer design projects, the technologists work on improving the semiconductor performance while the architects work on decreasing the number of clock cycles per instruction and finding new ways to exploit parallelism. Historically, currently, and in the future what are the relative speedups offered by the architects and the technologists?

---

# Chapter Index

applicability 21
architectural merit 23
arithmetic and logic unit (ALU) 12
arithmetic mean 28
bandwidth 29
batch-processing operating system 7
benchmark 25
billions of floating-point operations per second (GFLOPS or gigaflops) 26
buffer 14
central processing unit (CPU) 3
clock cycle 9
clock ticks per instruction (TPI) 29
closed architecture 24
compatibility 5

complex-instruction-set computer (CISC) 10
computation cycle 9
computation-intensive application 21
computer architecture 3
computer family 4
computer-family architecture 4
control unit (CU) 12
dataflow architecture 19
dataflow model 19
data stream 13
debit/credit benchmark 29
downward compatibility 5
ease of use 22
efficiency 21
execution-stack architecture 8
expandability 23

first-generation computer 5
flags 13
forward compatibility 5
fourth-generation computer 8
generality 20
geometric mean 28
global-memory (GM) system architecture 16
hardware-system architecture (HSA) 3
harmonic mean 28
Harvard architecture 11
host computer 16
I/O operations per second 29
IBM MIPS 26
input-ouput (I/O) system 3
instruction 13
instruction counter 13

instruction execution 13
instruction fetch 13
instruction field 13
instruction format 13
instruction set 13
instruction-set architecture (ISA) 3
instruction size 13
instruction stream 13
interconnection network 18
LINPACK benchmark 27
Livermore loops benchmark 27
local-memory (LM) system architecture 16
logical address 13
loosely coupled multiple processor 18
magnetic-core memory 7
malleability 22
medium-scale integration (MSI) 8
megabytes per second (MBS) 29
memory-access time 30
memory bandwidth 30
memory size 30
microprocessor 8
millions of instructions per second (MIPS) 26
millions of floating-point operations per second (MFLOPS or megaflops) 26

multiple instruction stream, multiple data stream (MIMD) 15
multiple instruction stream, single data stream (MISD) 14
multiple processor 16
multiprocessor computer 10
multiprocessor 15
multiprogramming operating system 7
neural network 19
open architecture 24
operand 13
operation code (op code) 13
parallel processor 16
peak MIPS 26
Perfect Club Suite 28
performance metric 25
physical address 13
pipeline 10
pipelining 10
pipelined processor 10
processing element (PE) 10
processor array 10
program 13
program counter (PC) 13
reduced-instruction-set computer (RISC) 10
register set 12
second-generation computer 7

single instruction stream, multiple data stream (SIMD) 14
single instruction stream, single data stream (SISD) 14
small-scale integration (SSI) 8
SPEC Benchmark Suite 27
special-purpose machine 20
SPECmarks 27
system performance 25
third-generation computer 8
tightly coupled multiple processor 18
transactions per second (TPS) 29
upward compatibility 5
utilization ratio 28
VAX MIPS 26
VAX unit of performance (VUP) 27
vector 26
vector machine 26
vectorization 27
very-large-scale integration (VLSI) 8
von Neumann machine 11
von Neumann machine cycle 13
weighted arithmetic mean 28
Whets 27
Whetstone benchmark 27

# 2

# *Instruction-set Architecture*

**2.1 Data Representations** *36*
    2.1.1 Units of Information *36*
    2.1.2 Integers and Fractions *37*
    2.1.3 Floating-point Numbers *40*
    2.1.4 Data Structures *45*

**2.2 Data Precision and Datatypes** *48*
    2.2.1 Precision of Basic Datatypes *49*
    2.2.2 Provision of Variable-precision Data *51*

**2.3 Register Sets** *53*

**2.4 Types of Instructions** *57*
    2.4.1 Operate Instructions *59*
    2.4.2 Memory-access Instructions *63*
    2.4.3 Control Instructions *67*
    2.4.4 Miscellaneous and Priviledged Instructions *70*
    2.4.5 Vector Instructions *72*

**2.5 Addressing Techniques** *82*
    2.5.1 Register Addressing *82*
    2.5.2 Boundary Alignment *83*
    2.5.3 Memory Addressing *85*
    2.5.4 Addressing Design Issues *98*

**2.6 Instruction-set Design** *102*
    2.6.1 Completeness *102*
    2.6.2 Orthogonality *105*
    2.6.3 Compatibility *105*
    2.6.4 Instruction Formats *107*

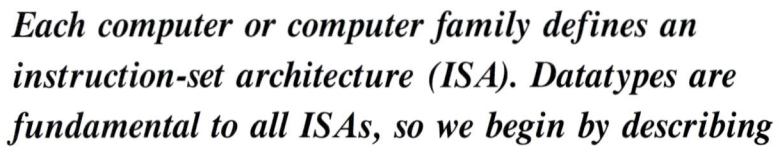

*Each computer or computer family defines an instruction-set architecture (ISA). Datatypes are fundamental to all ISAs, so we begin by describing them (Sections 2.1 and 2.2). Register sets form the operational basis of an ISA (Section 2.3). The third component of an ISA,*

## Key Terms

**Address specification**  The way an instruction specifies an address, such as absolute binary, register indirect, indexed, and base displacement.

**Complete instruction set**  An instruction set that does not lack any functionality, either in operations or control functions. Thus it includes instructions for all basic operations.

**Effective address**  The address generated by the CPU using the addressing modes available to the instructions, such as indexed addressing, base-displacement addressing, and segment-register addressing; the address before relocation or translation by virtual-memory hardware.

**Evaluation-stack architecture**  An architecture that uses an evaluation stack as an implied source for operands and an implied destination for results. Hence all operate instructions are 0-address instructions.

**Mutual exclusion**  In a multitasking environment, a control paradigm, often used for synchronization, that allows only one process at a time to access a critical resource (such as memory). When one process gains access to the resource, the system excludes all others from accessing it.

**Physical address**  The address in main memory of a memory reference, as opposed to the logical address of the reference.

**Vector operation**  An operation, specified by a vector instruction, that acts on one or more vectors to produce either a vector result or a scalar result (a vector-reduction operation).

*the instruction set, defines the operations the computer can perform and the techniques it can use for addressing values in memory. We therefore describe the types of instructions most computers provide and the addressing techniques instructions use for referencing memory (Section 2.5). The chapter ends with a look at some important properties of instruction-set design (Section 2.6).*

datatype
integer

A **datatype** is a set of values and the operations defined on them. For example, the datatype *integer* includes the set of integers together with the operations of addition, subtraction, multiplication, and truncated division (division in which the least significant digits are lopped off in the quotient).[1] The hardware of every computer implements one or more datatypes, and selecting datatypes is a crucial part of the design of the ISA of the computer. The choices made by the architect generally determine the usefulness of the computer for its intended audience (such as business or scientific).

register

operational registers

A **register** is a hardware device for holding a value. Every computer contains a variety of registers that may be used for holding the operands and results of arithmetic and other operations, memory addresses, control information, and other quantities. The registers that the programmer controls are called **operational registers.** All computers have registers that the programmer cannot control and thus are not part of the computer's operational registers. Computer scientists often refer to the operational registers as the computer's register set. As mentioned in Chapter 1, a machine instruction (or instruction for brevity) is a value in memory that controls one step in the operation of a computer. Each instruction specifies an operation, such as addition or subtraction, and the operands for the operation. The instruction set of a computer is the set of all instructions defined for that computer.

## 2.1 ■ Data Representations

This section discusses the major datatypes used by most computers, and indicates how the computer's hardware represents them.

### 2.1.1 ■ Units of Information

byte

Most computers use a byte as the basic unit of information. A **byte** is 8 bits and holds a single character or small integer. However, a byte is not adequate to represent large integers or floating-point numbers so computer hardware processes larger units to represent those quantities. (A **floating-point number** is a number expressed in scientific notation. We shall discuss floating-point numbers in greater detail in Section 2.1.3.)

floating-point number

word size

The **word size** of a computer is generally the size of its operational registers. A 16-bit computer, for example, has 16-bit registers, and a word consists of 2 bytes. For a 32-bit machine, a word consists of 4 bytes. For a 16-bit

---

1. Two other groups of operators could be included in this definition of *integer:* (a) comparison operations, such as < (less than), ≤ (less than or equal to), = , ≥ (greater than or equal to), and ≠ , which yield boolean values; (b) datatype conversion operations (e.g., integer to floating-point). However, we shall limit ourselves to this simple definition, which adequately illustrates the essential issues in specifying a datatype.

computer, a **doubleword** consists of 32 bits or 4 bytes; for a 32-bit computer, a doubleword consists of 64 bits or 8 bytes. Similarly, **quadwords** are four words long, and **octets** are eight words long, but the number of bytes depends on the word size of the computer.

When a computer's hardware processes numeric data, the precision of the data depends both on the number of bits in the representation and the way those bits represent the data. We shall discuss these issues in the following sections. In general, when a numeric representation uses a full word to represent a datum, the representation is **single precision.** When a representation requires two words, it is **double precision.** For a machine with 32-bit words, a double-precision floating-point representation would require 64 bits.

One byte of storage is usually sufficient to hold one **character.** The most common character representation is the American Standard Code for Information Interchange (**ASCII**). Personal computers (PCs) and minicomputers usually use ASCII, while IBM mainframes alone use IBM's **EBCDIC** Extended Binary Coded Decimal Interchange Code.

Numeric data usually use one of three representations: as a **binary-coded decimal (BCD),** where a byte or half-byte (4 bits) holds one decimal digit, and a sequence of bytes represents a number; as an integer, where several bytes hold the representation of the number; and floating-point numbers, where bit fields in several bytes represent the coefficient and exponent of the number. We shall review the most common representations here; manufacturer's manuals provide many additional examples.

## 2.1.2 ■ Integers and Fractions

**Unsigned-binary numbers** (also called **absolute-binary numbers**) represent only the positive integers and zero. The $n$-bit value $X_{n-1}X_{n-2}\cdots X_2X_1X_0$ represents the number

$$X_{n-1}2^{n-1} + X_{n-2}2^{n-2} + \cdots + X_2 2^2 + X_1 2^1 + X_0 2^0,$$

where each $X_i$ is either a 0 or a 1. $X_{n-1}$ represents the **high-order bit,** and $X_0$ the **low-order bit.** For example, $1010_2$ represents

$$1 \times 2^3 + 0 \times 2^2 + 1 \times 2^1 + 0 \times 2^0 = 10.$$

Note that the high-order bit carries the most significant value, while the low-order bit carries the least significant value.

Most applications require both positive and negative integers, and computers use a variety of binary patterns to represent them. We shall discuss four of the most common, shown in Table 2.1. We shall also discuss BCD numbers and fractions.

### Binary-coded Decimals (BCDs)

Some computers have special hardware for processing decimal numbers. One form of decimal encoding is the BCD format, in which 4 bits encode one decimal digit. The pattern $0000_2$ represents 0, $0001_2$ represents 1, and so forth up

**Table 2.1** Various 4-bit integer representations with their binary values.

| Decimal | Signed Magnitude | Ones' Complement | Two's Complement | Excess-3 |
|---|---|---|---|---|
| 12 | — | — | — | 1111 |
| 11 | — | — | — | 1110 |
| 10 | — | — | — | 1101 |
| 9 | — | — | — | 1100 |
| 8 | — | — | — | 1011 |
| 7 | 0111 | 0111 | 0111 | 1010 |
| 6 | 0110 | 0110 | 0110 | 1001 |
| 5 | 0101 | 0101 | 0101 | 1000 |
| 4 | 0100 | 0100 | 0100 | 0111 |
| 3 | 0011 | 0011 | 0011 | 0110 |
| 2 | 0010 | 0010 | 0010 | 0110 |
| 1 | 0001 | 0001 | 0001 | 0100 |
| 0 | 0000 | 0000 | 0000 | 0011 |
| −0 | 1000 | 1111 | — | — |
| −1 | 1001 | 1110 | 1111 | 0010 |
| −2 | 1010 | 1101 | 1110 | 0001 |
| −3 | 1011 | 1100 | 1101 | 0000 |
| −4 | 1100 | 1011 | 1100 | — |
| −5 | 1101 | 1010 | 1011 | — |
| −6 | 1110 | 1001 | 1010 | — |
| −7 | 1111 | 1000 | 1001 | — |
| −8 | — | — | 1000 | — |

to $1001_2$, which represents 9. The codes $1010_2$ through $1111_2$ are generally not allowed for representing digits (although they are sometimes used for such information as the sign, decimal point, and "$" symbol).

### Signed-magnitude Integers

Some computers represent integers as people do, in two parts, as **signed-magnitude integers.** The **sign bit,** usually farthest to the left, designates the sign of the number ($0_2$ for positive, $1_2$ for negative); the remaining bits designate its **magnitude.** The value of an $n$-bit signed-magnitude number can range between $-2^{n-1} + 1$ and $+2^{n-1} - 1$. Note that in signed magnitude the value 0 has both a positive and negative representation.

### Ones'-complement Integers

Some computers, such as some of the machines by Control Data Corporation (CDC), represent integers as **ones'-complement integers.** In this notation a positive integer has an absolute-binary representation, but the leading bit must be $0_2$. Thus it requires $n + 1$ bits to represent positive integers on the range $2^n$ to $2^{n+1} - 1$. For an $n$-bit positive number $N$, the representation of $-N$ is

$2^n - 1 - N$. This is obtained by **complementing the bits** of $N$ (converting zeros to ones and vice versa). For example, $0011_2$ represents 3 and $1100_2$ represents $-3$. An $n$-bit ones'-complement number can represent $2^{n-1} - 1$ positive values ($0000 \cdots 01_2$ through $0111 \cdots 11_2$) and $2^{n-1} - 1$ negative values ($1111 \cdots 10_2$ through $1000 \cdots 00_2$). The value 0, in ones'-complement notation, has two representations: $0000 \cdots 00_2$ for $+0$ and $1111 \cdots 11_2$ for $-0$. Notice that, as in signed-magnitude integers, the leftmost bit always indicates the sign of the number: $0_2$ for positive numbers and $1_2$ for negative numbers. However, the binary values of the negative ones'-complement numbers increase when moving from $-8$ to $-0$, while those of the signed-magnitude numbers decrease.

Ones'-complement representation allows for simpler addition, subtraction, and multiplication circuitry than is permitted by signed-magnitude representation. However, the fact that zero still has two different representations makes the next data representation, two's complement, the choice for most computers built today.

### Two's-complement Integers

**Two's-complement integers** use the same representation for positive values as do sign-magnitude and ones'-complement integers. A negative integer $N$ has the representation $2^n - N$. We therefore obtain the negative of a number by complementing its bits and adding 1. For example, we get $-3$ from 3 ($0011_2$) by complementing the bits ($1100_2$) and adding 1 ($1101_2$). Notice that, as in signed-magnitude and ones'-complement numbers, the leftmost bit always indicates the sign of the number, but that $-0$ equals $+0$ ($1111_2 + 1 = 0000_2$ because the carry is lost).

The pattern $1000_2$ in 4-bit two's-complement notation represents the value $-8$, which cannot be represented either as a 4-bit signed magnitude numbers or as a 4-bit ones'-complement number. An $n$-bit two's-complement integer can represent any value in the range $-(2^{n-1})$ to $2^{n-1} - 1$. The value $1000 \cdots 00_2$ always represents the negative number having the largest magnitude, $-(2^{n-1})$.

### Excess-$n$ Integers

The **excess-$n$ (bias-$n$)** representation of an integer $K$ is the binary representation of $n + K$, where $n$ is the **bias**. Numbers using an excess-$n$ representation are called **biased integers**. Table 2.1 shows the 4-bit excess-3 integers, which some calculators and 8-bit microprocessors use. Thus for an excess-3 representation, $11_2$ represents 0, $100_2$ represents 1, and so forth. For excess-8 numbers, $1000_2$ represents 0, $1001_2$ represents 1, and 0 represents $-8$.

### Fractions

A **fraction** is the quotient of two integers. Computers represent binary fractions having values between 0 and 1 by letting the leftmost bit of a number represent $\frac{1}{2}$, the next bit $\frac{1}{4}$, the third bit $\frac{1}{8}$, and so forth. The value $0.1001_2$ is equivalent to the decimal fraction 9/16, which is $\frac{1}{2} + \frac{0}{4} + \frac{0}{8} + \frac{1}{16}$. The period symbol in a binary fraction is properly called the **binary point.** An $n$-bit binary fraction can encode all values between 0 and $1 - 2^{-n}$ in steps of $2^{-n}$. In general, when a representation uses a base other than 2, the period is called a **radix point.** For example, a base 8 fraction has an octal point, while a base 16 fraction has a hexadecimal point.

Few machines process fractions as standard datatypes, but computers often use fractions to represent the mantissas of floating-point numbers, as we shall describe next.

### 2.1.3 ■ Floating-point Numbers

Computers represent floating-point numbers in a way that resembles scientific notation—in four parts: a **sign,** a **mantissa** (or **coefficient**), a **radix** (or **exponent base**), and an **exponent.** For some computers (for example, some Burroughs and CDC computers) the mantissa is an integer; for most computers, however, it is a fraction. Computers use various representations for exponents and radixes. However, since computers process binary numbers, their radixes are nearly always powers of 2, (e.g., 2, 8, or 16), whereas in scientific notation the radix is 10.

The bits of a word encode the sign, mantissa, and exponent, and the hardware assumes the radix. For a floating-point number $F$, let $S$ be the value of the sign bit ($0_2$ if positive, $1_2$ if negative), $M$ the mantissa, $E$ the exponent, and $R$ the radix. The value of $F$ is then $(-1)^S \times M \times R^E$.

Floating-point representations are not unique, because several representations can have equivalent values. Let the radix be $R$. Then we can group the bits of the mantissa into digits of $\log_2 R$ bits each (3 bits for octal and 4 bits for hexadecimal values). Shifting the mantissa by one digit corresponds to incrementing or decrementing the exponent by 1. For example, consider the octal floating-point number $0.0034_8 \times 8^4$, which represents the value 28.0 in base 10. The same number can also be represented as $0.0340_8 \times 8^3$ or $0.3400_8 \times 8^2$.

Among all representations having equivalent values, a computer obtains the one having highest precision by repeatedly decreasing the exponent by 1 and shifting the mantissa left by one digit until the most significant digit is nonzero. The result is a **normalized number,** and most computers normalize their floating-point numbers. Normalization also makes the representation unique.

In a computer with an exponent base of 2 and normalized floating-point numbers, the leading bit in the mantissa, called the **normal bit,** will always be $1_2$. Thus it is redundant to keep this bit physically present since its presence can be assumed by the hardware. Consequently, the computer can gain 1 additional bit of significance by **eliding** (omitting) it and extending the rest of the mantissa by 1 bit instead. When a computer operates on such data, it must restore this elided bit (conceptually, at least).

Over the years, computer manufacturers have used a number of different floating-point representations. Their choice depends on many factors, particularly the expected use of the computer. A number of factors influence their decision:

- For representations with the same radix, those with more bits in the mantissa have higher precision.
- For representations with the same radix, those with more exponent bits can represent a wider range of values.
- For representations with similar mantissas, the range of values increases with larger radixes, but the precision decreases.
- For similar hardware technology, the larger the representation, the slower the operations that use it.

Figure 2.1 illustrates the space of possibilities of floating-point representations. The horizontal axis gives the number of exponent bits, and the vertical axis gives the number of mantissa bits. The choices for a given word size fall above a staircase-shaped plot, as illustrated. Now let us look at some specific floating-point representations.

**Floating-point Numbers in the Burroughs Corporation B-5500**

We present the Burroughs B-5500 as an early example of a floating-point representation (Fig. 2.2). The B-5500 represented both the exponent and mantissa as signed-magnitude integers. Each word occupies 51 bits, but a number uses only 48 of them. The hardware uses the leftmost 4 bits of each word to indicate the datatype of the word and to regulate access to it. (The Burroughs hardware is described in the *Case Studies*.) The floating-point number occupies the remaining 47 bits. The exponent and its sign occupy 7 bits, and the mantissa and its sign occupy 40 bits. The radix is 8.

see Case Study 3

This floating-point representation has several notable features:

- Integers and floating-point numbers use exactly the same representation: Integers are simply floating-point numbers with a +0 exponent. As a result, there is no need for the hardware to convert from integer to floating-point representations.
- The use of integer mantissas and base 8 integer exponents enables the hardware to represent normalized floating-point values ranging from about $8^{-51}$ to about $8^{76}$. Integer mantissas give a greater range of numbers having extremely large magnitudes, where they were thought to be most often needed. (Representations that use fractional mantissas instead of integer mantissas have essentially the same range of positive and negative exponents).

**Floating-point Numbers in the CDC CYBER 170**

The CDC 6000 and 7000 series computers, as well as the more recent CYBER 170 family, represent floating-point numbers using an integer mantissa and a biased-integer exponent (Fig. 2.3). Each number is a 60-bit word. In these computers the leftmost bit is combined with the rightmost 48 bits to form a ones'-complement integer that is used as a mantissa. The remaining 11 bits are used as an excess-1024 integer exponent. The radix is 2. For negative numbers the hardware complements all the bits of a word, including the bits that represent the exponent.

---

**FIGURE 2.1** *Possible representations for floating-point number. Designers have used only a few of the infinite variety of representations. Radixes other than 2 decrease the effective precision of the mantissa and provide greater variation in effective mantissa length (precision).*

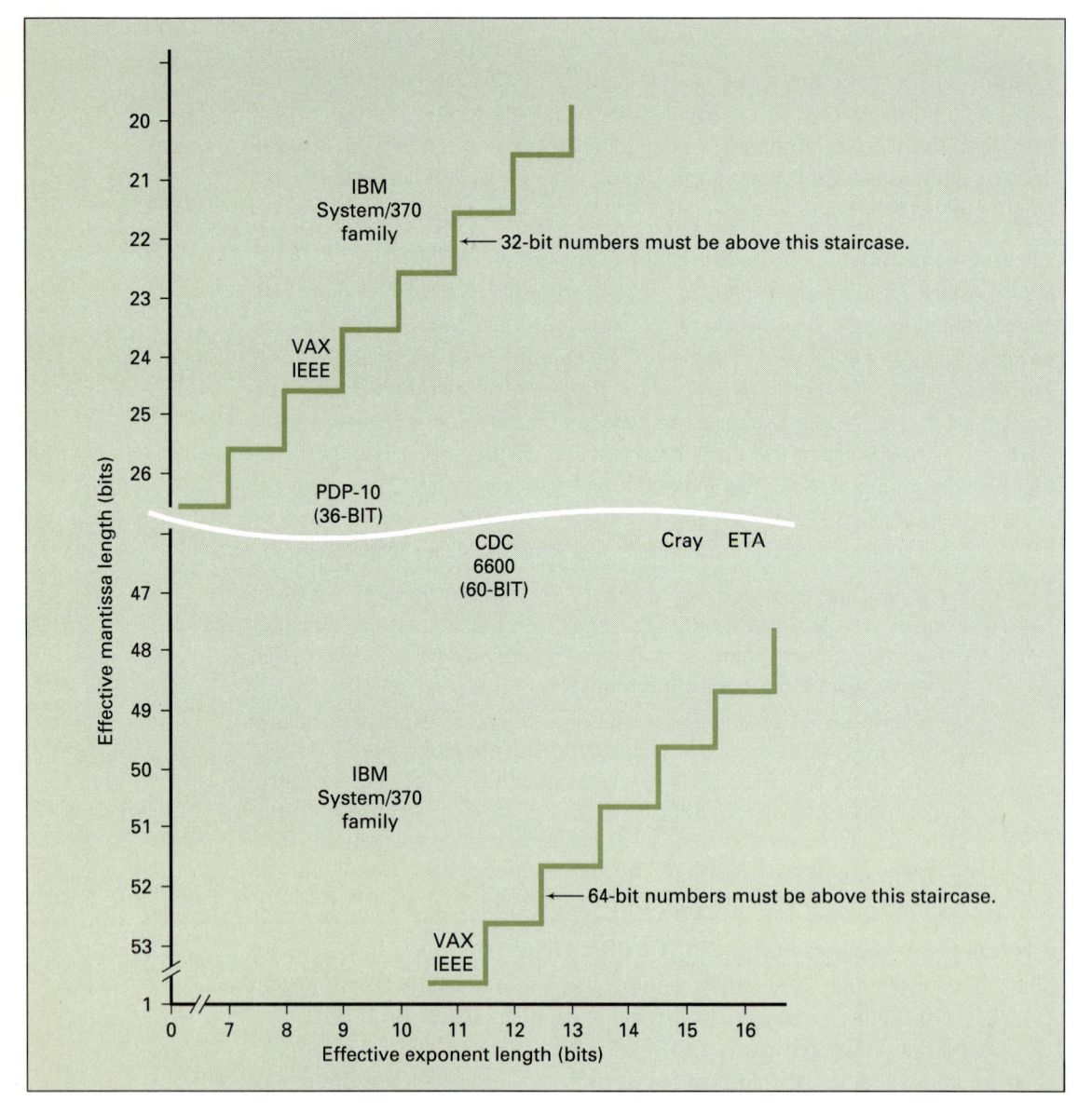

### Floating-point Numbers in the IBM Corporation System/370

The IBM System/370 single-precision floating-point representation is a 32-bit quantity, shown in Fig. 2.4. The mantissa is a normalized signed-magnitude hexadecimal (base 16) fraction. The sign occupies the leftmost bit, and the fractional part occupies the rightmost 24 bits. The exponent fills the remaining 7 bits and is an excess-64 integer. The radix is 16.

### Floating-point Numbers in the DEC PDP-11 and VAX

The DEC VAX computers use several floating-point representations, including one like the IEEE format described in the next section. We shall discuss only the single-precision F-floating-point datatype here. This representation uses 32

FIGURE 2.2  *B-5500 floating-point representation.*

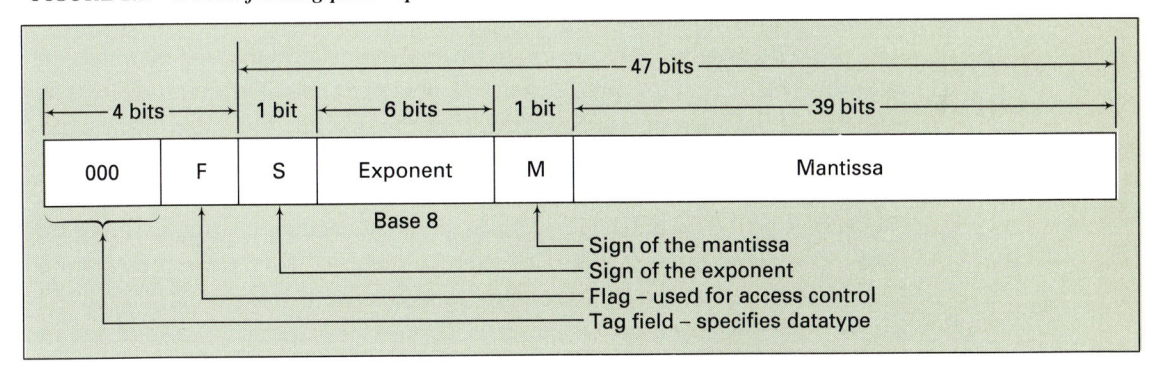

| 4 bits | 1 bit | 6 bits | 1 bit | 39 bits |
|---|---|---|---|---|
| 000 | F | S | Exponent | M | Mantissa |

- Base 8
- Sign of the mantissa
- Sign of the exponent
- Flag – used for access control
- Tag field – specifies datatype

FIGURE 2.3  *Floating-point representation for the CDC 6000, 7000, and CYBER systems.*

| 1 bit | 11 bits | 48 bits |
|---|---|---|
| S | Excess-1024 exponent | 1 | Mantissa |

- Base 2
- Normal bit
- Sign of the mantissa

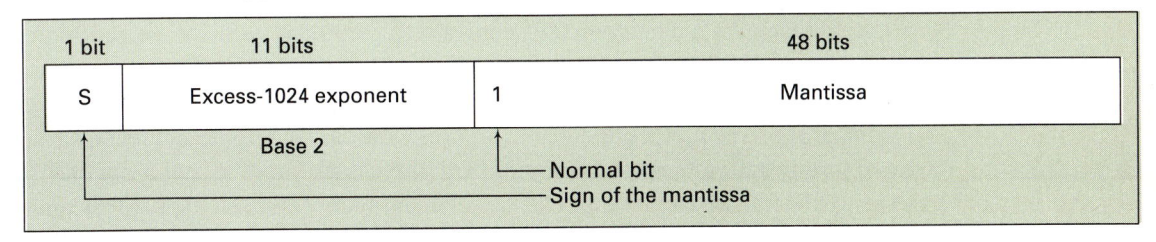

FIGURE 2.4  *Floating-point representation of the 32-bit IBM System/370*

| 1 bit | 7 bits | 24 bits |
|---|---|---|
| S | Excess-1024 exponent | Mantissa |

- Base 16
- Sign of the mantissa

bits, as shown in Fig. 2.5. Bit 0 is at the right and bit 31 is at the left. The mantissa is a normalized 24-bit signed-magnitude fraction that occupies bits 6 through 0 and 31 through 16. Its sign occupies bit 15, and its redundant high-order bit is elided. The exponent is an excess-128 integer that occupies bits 14 through 7. The VAX computers inherited this representation from the DEC PDP-11, which was a 16-bit machine; this legacy helps to explain the unusual field layout.

### IEEE Floating-point Standard

A committee for the Institute of Electrical and Electronics Engineers (IEEE) formulated a standard (ANSI/IEEE Standard 754-1985) for binary floating-point arithmetic. Most microcomputers have adopted this **IEEE floating-point standard** fully or partially.[2] The standard is comprehensive and includes roundoff, elementary functions, infinite and indefinite numbers, and unnormalized representations.

*IEEE floating-point standard*

The standard specifies four floating-point formats, two of which are shown in Fig. 2.6: single precision and double precision. The mantissa field assumes that the binary point is to the left of the first bit. The value of the exponent bias is 127 for 32-bit numbers (Fig. 2.6a) and 1023 for 64-bit numbers (Fig. 2.6b). The IEEE standard assumes a normalized mantissa with a value between $1.000\ldots0_2$ and $1.111\ldots1_2$; because the leading bit (representing the value 1) is always present, the IEEE standard elides it from the representation. As with other representations, a number is positive if its sign bit is $0_2$.

The IEEE format also reserves certain bit patterns for infinite and indefinite nonnumbers (resulting, for example, from dividing 0 by 0), and for small (unnormalized) numbers. The IEEE format represents $+\infty$ and $-\infty$ by a maximum exponent field ($377_8$ for single precision and $3777_8$ for double precision) and a 0 mantissa. (Readers not familiar with octal notation should consult Appendix A.) The computer generates an infinity, with the correct sign bit, whenever an arithmetic overflow occurs. (**Overflow** occurs when a number is too large for the intended representation. Similarly **underflow** occurs when a number is too small for the intended representation.) Indefinite numbers, such as those resulting from division of 0 by 0, are called NaN for "not a number"; the IEEE format represents NaN by a maximum exponent field ($377_8$ and $3777_8$) and a nonzero mantissa. The IEEE format represents the values $+0$ and $-0$ by a zero exponent, zero mantissa, and the appropriate sign bit, and it represents an **unnormal number,** one having the maximum exponent but too small to have a normalized representation, by a zero exponent and nonzero mantissa. Table 2.2 gives examples of various values expressed in the IEEE 32- and 64-bit representations.

*overflow*

*underflow*

*unnormal number*

---

2. The IEEE 754 Standard for Binary Floating-point Arithmetic. New York: IEEE, 1985.

The IEEE has also proposed a standard for nonbinary floating-point numbers that is specifically aimed at base 16 floating-point representations.

## 2.1.4 ■ Data Structures

Many computers provide hardware to help programmers implement character strings, stacks, arrays, and structures for parameter passage. This section will briefly describe each of these basic data structures.

**Character Strings**

A **character string** is a sequence of zero or more characters. Character-string operations (and their corresponding instructions) include finding the length of a string (LENGTH), testing for string equality (EQUAL), concatenating strings (CONCAT), searching for a substring (INDEX), and extracting a substring (SUBSTRING).

character string

FIGURE 2.5  *F-floating-point datatype representation of the 32-bit DEC system.*

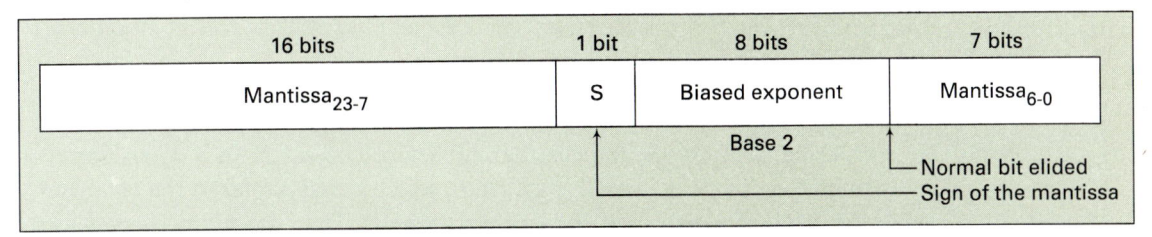

| 16 bits | 1 bit | 8 bits | 7 bits |
|---|---|---|---|
| Mantissa$_{23\text{-}7}$ | S | Biased exponent | Mantissa$_{6\text{-}0}$ |

Base 2 → Biased exponent
Normal bit elided → Mantissa$_{6\text{-}0}$
Sign of the mantissa → S

FIGURE 2.6  *IEEE floating-point formats. (a) Single precision. (b) Double precision.*

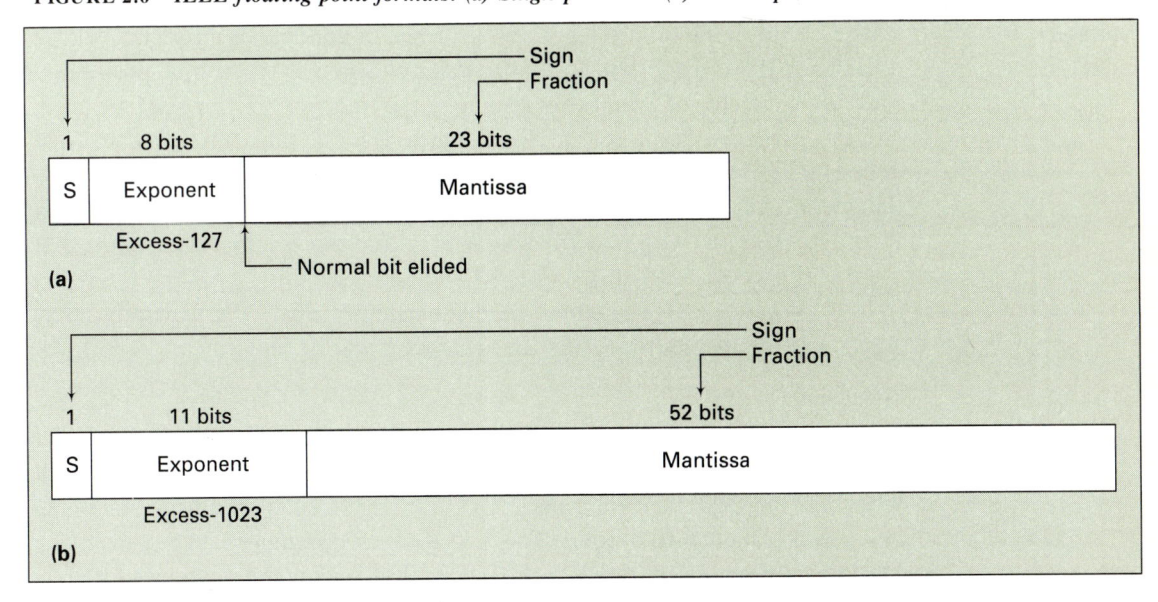

(a)
- Sign
- Fraction

| 1 | 8 bits | 23 bits |
|---|---|---|
| S | Exponent | Mantissa |

Excess-127
Normal bit elided

(b)
- Sign
- Fraction

| 1 | 11 bits | 52 bits |
|---|---|---|
| S | Exponent | Mantissa |

Excess-1023

**Table 2.2**  Various values represented in the IEEE single-precision (32-bit) and double-precision (64-bit) floating-point formats. The ? is a don't care value.

| Single-Precision (32-bit) Numbers | | | | Double-Precision (64-bit) Numbers | | |
|---|---|---|---|---|---|---|
| Examples | S[a] | E[b] | Montissa[c] | S[a] | E[b] | Mantissa[a] |
| NaN | ? | $377_8$ | Nonzero | 0 | $3777_8$ | Nonzero |
| ∞ | 0 | $377_8$ | $.0000\ 0000_8$ | 0 | $3777_8$ | $.0000\ 0000\ 0000\ 0000\ 00_8$ |
| 10.0 | 0 | $202_8$ | $(1).2000\ 0000_8$ | 0 | $2002_8$ | $(1).0400\ 0000\ 0000\ 0000\ 00_8$ |
| 1.0 | 0 | $177_8$ | $(1).0000\ 0000_8$ | 0 | $1777_8$ | $(1).0000\ 0000\ 0000\ 0000\ 00_8$ |
| 0.0 | 0 | $000_8$ | $.0000\ 0000_8$ | 0 | $0000_8$ | $.0000\ 0000\ 0000\ 0000\ 00_8$ |
| Unnormalized | 0 | $000_8$ | Nonzero | 0 | $0000_8$ | Non-zero |
| −0.0 | 1 | $000_8$ | $.0000\ 0000_8$ | 0 | $0000_8$ | $.0000\ 0000\ 0000\ 0000\ 00_8$ |
| −1.0 | 1 | $177_8$ | $(1).0000\ 0000_8$ | 1 | $1777_8$ | $(1).0000\ 0000\ 0000\ 0000\ 00_8$ |
| −10.0 | 1 | $202_8$ | $(1).2000\ 0000_8$ | 1 | $2002_8$ | $(1).0400\ 0000\ 0000\ 0000\ 00_8$ |
| ∞ | 1 | $377_8$ | $.0000\ 0000_8$ | 1 | $3777_8$ | $.0000\ 0000\ 0000\ 0000\ 00_8$ |

[a] Sign bit
[b] Exponent value
[c] The 1's in parentheses are elided values not stored in the representation.

For string S, LENGTH(S) returns the number of characters in S. Consider two strings, $S = s_1 s_2 \cdots s_k$ and $T = t_1 t_2 \cdots t_l$, where $s_i$ and $t_i$ refer to the characters in the *i*th position in each string; then CONCAT(S,T) returns the **concatenation** of S with T, which is the string $s_1 s_2 \cdots s_k\ t_1 t_2 \cdots t_l$ and is often denoted S|T. EQUAL(S,T) is a predicate that returns the value *true* if S equals T and *false* otherwise, where S equals T if S and T are the same length and $s_i$ equals $t_i$ for each *i*. A **substring** of a string is any sequence of contiguous characters within the string. If S is a substring of T, the **index** of S in T is the ordinal position of the first character of S in T. For example, the index of 'CD' in 'ABCDE' is 3. Given strings S and T, INDEX(S,T) searches T for a substring equal to S; if found, INDEX returns its index; otherwise it returns a failure flag, such as the value 0. Finally, given string S, SUBSTRING(S, $i, k$) returns the substring of length $k$ in S beginning with the *i*th character. SUBSTRING(S, $i, k$) is not defined if $i + l - 1$ exceeds LENGTH(S).

When a string is stored in main memory, the CPU generally references it using the address of its first character and its length.

### Stacks

A **stack** is any data structure that uses the **LIFO storage** policy: The last data item placed in the stack is the first item that can be retrieved from that stack ("last in, first out"). Within a stack, LIFO storage results in information being organized from top to bottom. The first (oldest) unremoved data item in the stack is on the bottom of the stack, and the last (youngest) unremoved item is on the top. A stack with no items in it is empty. An attempt to remove an item from an empty stack results in an error.

The stack operations generally include push, pop, top and empty. For stack S, PUSH(S,$v$) stores a new value $v$ in S, TOP(S) returns the most recently stored value, POP(S) returns the value most recently stored and also removes it from S, and EMPTY(S) returns *true* if S is empty and *false* otherwise. The operations TOP and POP are undefined for an empty stack (i.e., one for which EMPTY returns *true*).

**push operation**
**pop operation**
**top operation**
**empty operation**

### Arrays

**Arrays** are collections of data that have the same name. The individual data items in an array are **array elements.** When defining an array, the programmer assigns the name, the number of **subscript positions,** and the number of allowed **subscript values** for each subscript position. Suppose that an array whose name is A has $k$ subscript positions, and position $i$ has $N_i$ allowed values. Then A is a ***k*-dimensional array** with a total of $N_1 \times N_2 \times \ldots \times N_k$ elements. Let $n_1, n_2, \ldots, n_k$ be a set of valid subscripts for array A. Then A $(n_1, n_2, \ldots, n_k)$ designates the $(n_1, n_2, \ldots, n_k)$th element of the array. The list $(n_1, n_2, \ldots, n_k)$ is the **subscript list.**

**arrays**
**array elements**
**subscript positions**
**subscript values**

***k*-dimensional array**

**subscript list**

Two of the most frequently encountered kinds of arrays are vectors and matrices. A **vector** is one-dimensional array (i.e., $k = 1$). **Vector elements** are stored in memory in a regular pattern that can be expressed as locations $V$, $V + I$, $V + 2I$, $V + 3I, \ldots, V + (N-1)I$. The value $I$ is the **increment,** or **stride,** of the vector; $N$ is the **vector length;** and the $N$ individual data comprise the vector elements. We shall let $\vec{V}$ denote the vector and $V_i$ denote its elements. A **scalar** is a single value or a vector having only one element.

**vector**
**vector elements**

**increment**
**stride**
**vector length**

**scalar**

A **matrix** $\mathcal{M}$ is a two-dimensional array of data (i.e., $k = 2$). Each datum $m_{ij}$ is called a **matrix element,** and each matrix element is identified by its row and column position in the array. The first subscript designates the row number and the second the column number:

**matrix**
**matrix element**

$$\mathcal{M} = \begin{bmatrix} m_{11} & m_{12} & m_{13} & m_{14} \\ m_{21} & m_{22} & m_{23} & m_{24} \\ m_{31} & m_{32} & m_{33} & m_{34} \end{bmatrix}. \tag{1}$$

Most programming languages allow programmers to define arrays, and most programmers use arrays. Moreover, computations involving array elements often appear within deeply nested loops. Thus a computer must have efficient access to the array element. For that reason most computers provide special addressing hardware for speeding up computations of array subscripts.

### Parameter-passage Structures

Designers organize large and complex systems into modules, where each module has its own logical function within the system. Programs, which are software systems, are no exception. Programmers organize them into modules, such as subroutines, functions, procedures, and coroutines. We shall use the term **procedure** to designate any self-contained program module.

When one procedure calls another procedure, the procedure doing the calling is the **calling procedure** and the one being called is the **called procedure.** Any values that the calling procedure sends to the called procedure are **parameters** (or **arguments**), and any values that the called procedure sends back to the calling procedure are **results.**

Several questions on usage of procedures arise. How can the calling procedure pass parameters to the called procedure, and how can the called procedure return results to the calling procedure? How does the calling procedure know where to transfer control to when it calls a procedure, and how does the called procedure know where to return control when it finishes? We shall answer the first two questions here and the last two questions later in this chapter, when discussing subroutine-linkage instructions.

Programmers use several different methods for passing parameters to called procedures, the most common of which are as follows:

1. The calling procedure places parameters in a **parameter list** and passes the address of the parameter list to the called procedure.
2. The calling procedure places the addresses of the parameters in a **parameter-address list** and then passes the address of the parameter-address list to the called procedure.
3. The calling procedure pushes the parameters onto a stack before calling the called procedure.
4. The calling procedure pushes the parameters' addresses onto a stack before calling the called procedure.
5. The calling procedure passes parameters through the registers themselves.
6. The calling procedures creates the parameter-address list which it places in main memory immediately following the subroutine call.

Figure 2.7 shows the first, fourth, and fifth of these methods. The remaining three methods are left as exercises.

Note that parameter lists and parameter-address lists are data structures just as stacks are. Several computers, as we shall see later, provide special instructions for creating and manipulating stacks and parameter lists. For now, let us return to our general discussion of instructions.

## 2.2 ■ Data Precision and Datatypes

Most aspects of problems relating to data precision do not fall within the purview of the computer architect. Of those aspects that do, most interact strongly with the register width, which we shall discuss in this section. We will show a design method that allows for variability in the precision of data, and for an extensible instruction set, that is, one that allows additional datatypes to be added easily.

## 2.2.1 Precision of Basic Datatypes

It would be convenient if certain aspects of the precision of data could be tailored to the needs of users and customers. However, here we are mainly concerned with aspects of data precision that need to be varied over time or across

FIGURE 2.7  *Three of the six common methods of passing parameters to a called procedure. (a) Using a parameter list and passing its address to the called procedure; (b) pushing the parameter addresses onto the stack; (c) passing the parameters through the registers. R, register; SP, stack pointer.*

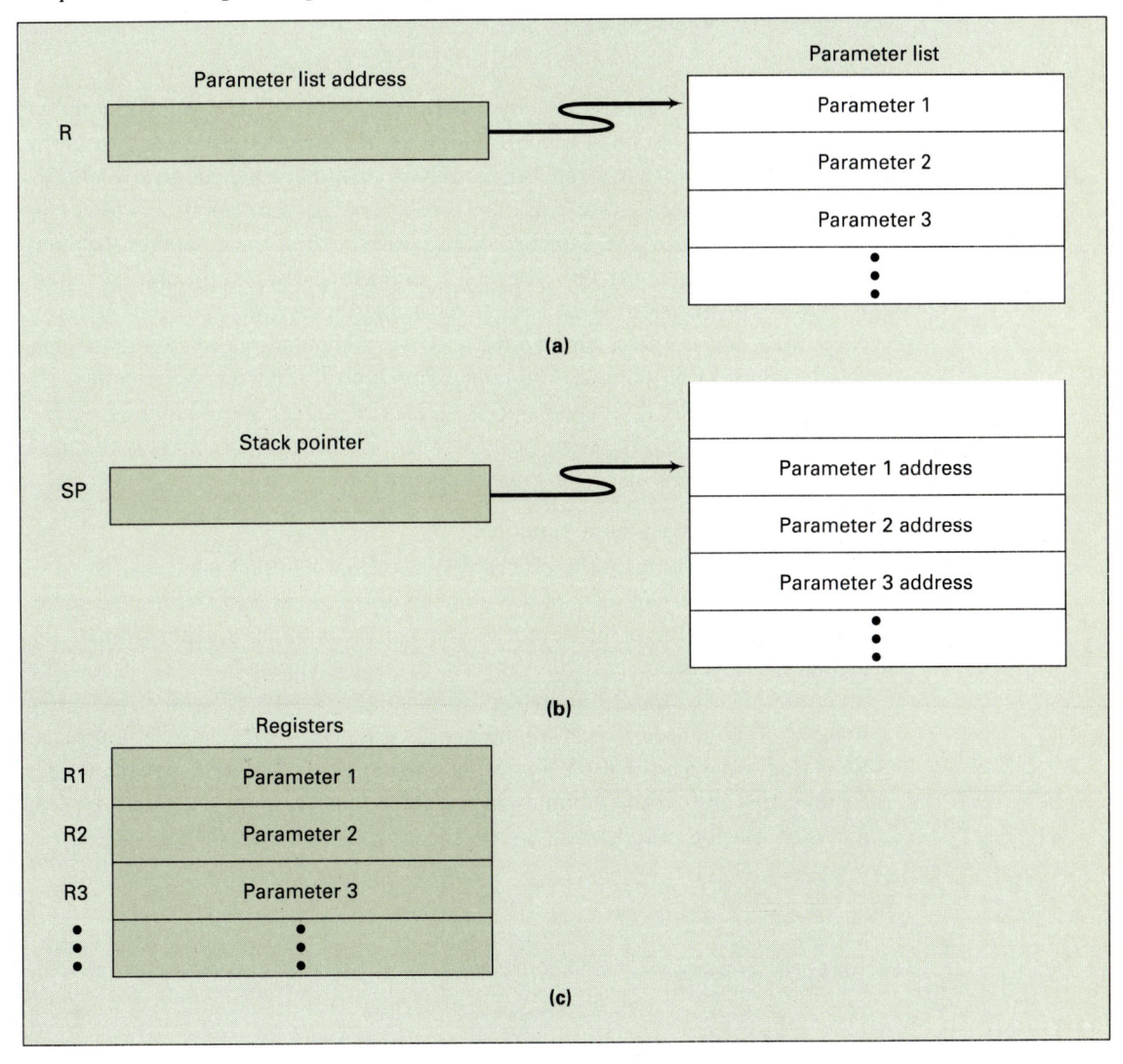

the models of a computer family, depending on the processor speed or major application area.

### Character Sets

Seven-bit ASCII is sufficient to describe all the commonly used characters in English, but as anyone who has used a typesetting word processor knows, authors use dozens of alphabets, several different fonts and faces, and various special characters. It is not at all rare to use several hundred different characters in a document, which suggests the usefulness of 10-bit bytes, for example. The Japanese, on the other hand, might well prefer a 12-bit character because they use more than 2000 characters.[3] Typical monotype machines provide in excess of 300 characters and separate face and font control. Chinese has tens of thousands of characters, of which thousands are in common use.

### Integer Range

The range or precision of integer data often depends on the application and so is fixed once a program is written. However, there are applications where the range of precision is not fixed. An example is **loop-iteration counts,** which give the number of times a program loop is to be executed or iterated. These may grow with the size of the database or with the speed of the computer. In many scientific and engineering programs, increasing the loop-iteration count increases the precision of the result. When these programs are used on supercomputers, whose speed allows more accurate computation or larger databases, the iteration count will often be larger than on a low-performance system. In weather forecasting, for example, finer grids (i.e., larger arrays) allow for more accurate predictions; the finer grids also require iteration counters with larger ranges, implying the need for greater integer range.

### Precision of Floating-point Numbers

Many algorithms control the precision of the floating-point numbers they use. For some iterative algorithms the number of iterations determines the precision of the floating-point numbers; the more iterations are performed, the greater the precision. For these algorithms, the computer's speed affects the precision. For example, many algorithms have roundoff errors that grow roughly as the square root of the number of data being processed. For applications that are performed for a specific amount of time, such as weather forecasting, this restricted computation indicates that the required floating-point precision may be proportional to the square root of the processor's speed.

---

3. Among the many characters used by the Japanese are 1945 standard Kanji symbols, 90 Kana symbols, 52 Latin letters, 10 numerals, and so on; well over 500 of these are used frequently. In addition, the Japanese use different faces and fonts also.

## 2.2.2 ■ Provision of Variable-precision Data

In this section we shall discuss techniques that are useful for providing variable precision or increased range of datatypes, to allow a computer family to address any concerns a user may have about the precision of the supported datatypes.

### Character Data

For representing more characters than there are different byte values (256 on most computers), **escape sequences** often are used. A special character value, such as the ASCII <ESC> = $27_{10}$, indicates that the following byte or bytes represent special, noncharacter information, usually in a different "alphabet." The new alphabet may be a change to a new font, some special characters, or some other special feature. Sometimes there are several escape characters and a number of ways to define the special information.

*escape sequences*

### Integer Data

Most computers support a variety of integer precisions: 8 bits, 16 bits, and 32 bits are common. Also, most computers provide access to the overflow bit (a bit set by the ALU when overflow occurs), frequently as a trap. (A **trap** is an alteration in the sequential flow of control of a program that the hardware initiates due to a program event.) Thus it is easy for programs to use a specific integer size and to let the **trap handler** (the program that processes a trap) increase the integer precision or range. (Section 3.2.3 describes traps and trap handlers.) Also, note that decimal datatypes sometimes represent integers (see Section 2.1), and those types frequently provide arbitrary precision or range.

*trap*

*trap handler*

### Floating-point Data

Most computers accommodate variable floating-point precision by providing double-precision hardware or software. Some systems offer more than two precisions. The IEEE Floating Point and VAX standards, for example, provide four. It should also be noted that most systems other than the IEEE standard do not increase the exponent range as the precision is increased. (A number of 32-bit computers, for example, provide for 32- and 64-bit, or 32-, 64-, and 128-bit floating-point numbers, all with an 8-bit exponent field.)

### Other Datatypes

There are many possible numeric representations; it would be arrogant to assume that today's typeless, character, integer, decimal, and floating-point representations are all that will ever be needed. We shall describe here a few novel data representations to show the types of data they may be deemed useful someday.

For general-purpose computers, wide acceptance of any of these other datatypes is probably dependent on the datatype's availability in some popular high-level programming language. Even then we would expect their support to be solely in software until their use increased to the point that would justify the expense of hardware support. However, special-purpose processors might find some of these useful for their specific applications.

**block floating-point**

A **block floating-point** representation may be used for arrays of floating-point numbers with a common exponent field. For the common 32-bit word size, block floating-point numbers might have one word for the exponent field and one full 32-bit word for each mantissa of the array. In many applications the data vary over only a small range of values, so the exponents are restricted to only a few values. In these cases this 32-bit block floating-point format would allow an increase of about 8 bits in the mantissa (and thus increasing the precision) if all the exponents were the same. For example, a weather-forecasting program might use block floating-point data for the temperature values, which would all lie between about 200 and 350 (degrees Kelvin), and so would allow 30- or 31-bit mantissas, with the exponent set to maximum precision for data in the range of 256 to 511 degrees.

**floating floating-point**

A block floating-point representation allows us to increase the precision for arrays of data where the values are of similar magnitude. A **floating floating-point** representation is at the other extreme. We can think of this representation as using two floating-point exponent fields to increase the range of exponent values (at the expense of reduced mantissa precision). Figure 2.8 illustrates this representation.

Many other representations are certainly easy to define. Many of these depend on abstruse mathematics like continued fractions and interval arithmetic and will not be discussed here.

The approach that all computers have used, and that computers will almost certainly continue to use, is to provide a few basic operations in hardware and to let the software provide as many more as are needed. One key factor in the hardware that is useful for many of these software implementations is high-precision integer operations. Sadly for the analysts who desire high-precision software support, few computers provide hardware for integer arithmetic of more than 32 bits.

FIGURE 2.8 *Floating floating-point Numbers. The value is given by the relationship* **value = mantissa × radix$^{exp}$**, *where* **exp = exp1 × radix2$^{exp2}$**. *Some bits allow the exponent to have a very large range. The hardware assumes both radix values.*

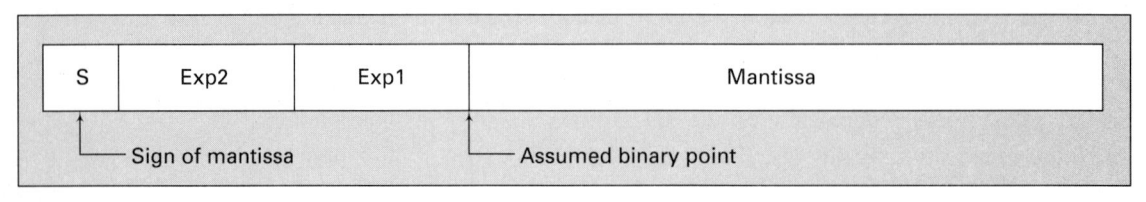

| S | Exp2 | Exp1 | Mantissa |
|---|------|------|----------|

Sign of mantissa — Assumed binary point

## 2.3 ▪ Register Sets

One of the chief differences between computers is the nature of their register sets. Some are large; others are small. Some have special-purpose registers; others have general-purpose registers. This section will focus on the differences and similarities among register sets.

All von Neumann machines have a program counter (PC), as mentioned in Chapter 1. In addition, most computers have one or more registers for holding the instruction that it is executing currently. When the computer uses a single register for holding the instruction, that register is called the **instruction register (IR)**. Generally the programmer cannot manipulate the IR, so it is not considered part of the register set of the machine.

When computers access memory, they hold the address for the reference in a programmer-invisible register called the **memory-address register (MAR),** and they either hold the data for a store operation or they receive the data during a load operation in another programmer-invisible buffer called the **memory-buffer register (MBR).** Neither the MAR nor the MBR is part of the register set of the machine.

Most computers provide registers that programmers can use as **index registers.** An index register is one that holds an **index,** which is an address displacement. When an instruction specifies both an operand address and an index register, the computer's addressing circuitry automatically adds the content of the index register, the index, to the operand address. The result is that the referenced word is displaced from the instruction-specified address by the index value. We shall discuss this method of address generation, called indexed addressing, later in this chapter.

Although the first computers did not have index registers, they have long been considered essential and are found on virtually all modern computers. They are used for numerous operations, such as accessing elements in an array or characters in a string. Their utility stems from the fact that indexing hardware is generally very fast and provides special instructions for incrementing, decrementing, and testing or comparing index-register contents.

Most computers have a set of bits called **processor-status bits,** or flags. Each processor-status bit has its own special purpose. Some hold result indicators for arithmetic and logical operations: positive result (P), zero result (Z), negative result (N), carry out (C), arithmetic overflow (V), and so forth. Various instructions tell the CPU when to set or clear these bits. Some hold information pertaining to interrupts or exceptions (which we shall discuss in Section 2.4.4 and Chapter 3). Some processor-status bits hold memory-protection information, and some hold information that describes the execution state of the processor—privileged or unprivileged. (These and other concepts are discussed in Section 2.4.4.) On some machines the processor sets the pattern, called the **condition code,** in several bits. Taken together, the condition-code bits are often called the **condition-code register;** they take the place of the individual processor status bits just described.

Some computers, notably the RISC machines, provide several sets of condition-code bits, and the instructions that use them specify which set to use. Providing several independent sets of condition-code bits enables the designer to increase the parallelism within the instruction execution unit.

In general, although each status bit has a different and independent function, the instruction set provides instructions for saving and restoring the entire set of processor-status bits. These instructions frequently manipulate the processor-status bits and other information, such as the PC contents, as a single quantity called the **program-status word (PSW).** We shall describe instructions that manipulate the PSW more fully when we review interrupt processing in Section 3.2.3.

### Register Operations

Most computers have several registers for holding operands and results, and the instructions may specify main-memory addresses, registers, or both to serve as operands. Instructions that access both main memory and a register or registers are **memory-to-register instructions.** Instructions that get their operands from main memory and place their results in main memory are **memory-to-memory instructions.** Instructions that operate on strings are often of this type. Instructions that get their operands from registers and place their results in registers are **register-to-register instructions.**

As an example, a register-to-register ADD instruction specifies two operand registers and one result register. Because of instruction size and other limitations, an instruction can often specify only one of two registers. In that case, one of them generally holds *both* an operand and the result of an arithmetic, logical, or shift operation.

Machines that provide more than one accumulator generally provide register-to-register instructions. When the CPU executes a register-to-register instruction, none of the operands comes from main memory. And because the CPU does not need to access memory when performing register-to-register instructions, it can perform them more quickly than it can their memory-to-register or memory-to-memory counterparts. The CDC 6000/7000 family of computers and all RISC machines are of this type: they have only register-to-register instructions (except for LOAD and STORE instructions, which read to memory or write to memory but do not operate on the data), and the resulting instruction sets are often called **load-and-store instruction sets.**

Many computers provide special registers, called **stack pointers,** to facilitate implementing stacks in memory. Some computers allow the programmer to use general-purpose registers in the same way. Stack pointers generally point to the top value in a stack, and the hardware automatically increments or decrements the stack pointer during a push or a pop operation. We shall discuss the stack pointers and the corresponding addressing modes in Section 2.5.3.

When computer architects choose register sets, they must consider a variety of factors; a partial list follows:

- The CPU can access registers more quickly than it can access main memory. Register-to-register operations generally execute faster than do register-to-memory or memory-to-memory instructions.
- Each instruction must designate the registers it will address. Hence an instruction must have $N$ bits to select among $2^N$ registers. A computer needs large instructions to select among a large number of registers.
- Machines with large register sets (RISCs are an example) can store more values close to the CPU. These computers often require fewer memory accesses and therefore operate more quickly.
- Compilers tend to use a small number of registers because larger numbers are very difficult to use effectively. Hence providing a large number will not necessarily improve the computer's performance.
- Registers are expensive but far less than they used to be.

The *Case Studies* describe the register sets of a number of current and historical computers.

### Register Architectures

A computer can be classified according to the number of operands each instruction specifies and how the ISA accesses and uses them. Instructions that have only implicit operands and results are **0-address instructions,** those that assume an accumulator and specify a single memory operand are **1-address instructions,** and those that specify $N$ operand addresses are **$N$-address instructions.** When instructions specify $M$ operands and $N$ branch addresses they are *(M + N)*-**address instructions.** Table 2.3 describes the addressing of a few instructions.

0-address instructions
1-address instructions
$N$-address instructions

$(M + N)$-address instructions

In this section we discuss various classifications of von Neumann architectures.

### Evaluation-stack Architectures

An **evaluation-stack architecture** is one that implicitly takes its operands from a stack and places the results in the stack. Thus most of the computer's instructions are 0-address instructions. For a machine of this type, an arithmetic instruction specifies an operation but not any operands. For example, an ADD instruction would simply specify addition; its operands would be implicit.

evaluation-stack architecture

The ALU of an evaluation-stack architecture would contain a stack, which could either be implemented in main memory, in hardware, or both. A PUSH instruction reads a value from memory and places it on the stack, and a POP instruction removes a value from the stack and stores it in memory. (The LOAD and STORE instructions are not 0-address instructions, as we shall see shortly.)

**Table 2.3** Number of explicit and implicit addresses for several instructions.

| Instruction | Explicit Operands | Implicit Operands | Items Actually Addressed |
|---|---|---|---|
| CLEAR CARRY | 0 | 1 | Carry register (1 bit) |
| JUMP L | 1 | 1 | Destination L of jump and the PC |
| BRANCH ON CONDITION L2 | 1 | 2 | Destination L2 of jump condition code register, and the PC |
| DADD2 R1, R2[a] | 2 | 1 | The two registers R1 and R2 and the condition code register |
| ADD3 R1, R2, R3[b] | 3 | 1 | The three registers R1, R2, and R3 and the condition code register |
| COMPARE STRINGS | 4 | 1 | Addresses and lengths of strings, and the condition code register |

[a] DADD2 stands for double-precision addition with two operands (register R1 for operand 1, register R2 for the result, and operand 2).
[b] ADD3 stands for three-register addition (result, operand 1, operand 2).

Once the stack holds a set of values, arithmetic instructions can operate on them. Arithmetic instructions implicitly reference the top elements in the stack. An ADD instruction, for example, would remove the top two stack elements, add them together, and place the sum back in the stack. A NEGATE instruction would simply change the sign of the top stack element.

Because 0-address instructions do not explicitly reference their operands, the op codes can be very short. Also, because the stack is within the CPU, the operands are close to the ALU. Hence 0-address instructions are generally very fast. However, although evaluation-stack architectures give excellent support for arithmetic processing and subroutine support, they are less general than other types of architectures and have been found to be more difficult to program for many common applications, such as text and string processing. Consequently they are not as common today as other types of machines. Nonetheless, a number of companies, including Burroughs Corporation, have successfully manufactured and sold them. We shall describe the Burroughs B6700 stack architecture in the *Case Studies*.

see Case Study 3

*Accumulator Machines*

accumulator machine
accumulator

An **accumulator machine** is a von Neumann machine that uses a single operational register, called an **accumulator,** to hold the result of an arithmetic, logical, or shift operation. The accumulator also holds one of the operands for the operation. In accumulator machines the instruction does not explicitly reference the accumulator, so the accumulator is an implicit operand of each operate instruction. Each operate instruction holds the specification for one memory address, and hence accumulator-machine instructions are mostly 1-address instructions.

As an example, an ADD instruction would have one address specification, the address in main memory of one operand. The computer fetches the datum from the specified address in memory, adds it to the value held by the accumulator, and places the result in the accumulator (replacing the operand value). For accumulator machines, LOAD instructions copy a value from memory to the accumulator, and STORE instructions copy the value from the accumulator to memory.

Many companies have manufactured accumulator machines, and they are common today. One-address instructions have some advantages. Because they specify a single memory address, they are shorter than 2- or 3-address instructions. Also, they do not need to make explicit reference to the accumulator. However, accumulator machines require frequent memory accesses and consequently do not perform as well as machines with several accumulators, which make fewer memory accesses.

*General-purpose Register-set Machines*
Some computers provide sets of registers called **general-purpose registers.** These registers may be used as accumulators, address registers, index registers, stack registers, and on some machines even the PC. Each instruction specifies how the registers will be used, and the computers are called **general-purpose register-set machines.** Computers in the IBM System/370 and DEC VAX families are examples of general-purpose register-set machines.

Instructions of general-purpose register-set machines may specify any number of register operands. Some have instructions of several types, such as register-to-memory instructions and memory-to-memory instructions. Others have only one or the other. If a machine has $2^N$ registers, then the architects assign $N$ instruction bits to specify each register. Because these machines generally have few registers, short instructions are possible.

*Special-purpose Register-set Machines*
In contrast, some computers provide sets of registers whose functions are restricted. One set may serve only as index registers, another set only to hold arithmetic operands, and so forth. These computers are **special-purpose register-set machines.** Computers in the CDC 6000/7000 family are of this type. Many machines fall on a continuum between general-purpose and special-purpose register-set machines, and the variety of register sets is limited only by the imaginations and design criteria of the architects who design them.

## 2.4 ■ Types of Instructions

Although the hardware components form the basis of a computer's capabilities, it is its instruction set that determines the machine's computational complexion. When architects design a computer, therefore, they carefully consider its ISA. They choose a set of datatypes, a set of operations on those datatypes, a set of techniques for addressing data in memory or in registers, and operations for controlling the run-time behavior of the programs—the logical flow of control. In addition, once they have defined the ISA, they specify the instruction formats, which determine how the hardware will represent each instruction. We shall discuss instruction formats briefly at the end of the chapter.

*operate instructions*

*character instructions*

*character-string instructions*
*string instructions*
*vector instructions*

*LOAD instructions*

*STORE instructions*

*process synchronization instructions*

*branch instructions*

*subroutine-linkage instructions*

*conditional branch instructions*

*I/O instructions*

Instructions can be loosely classified according to the operations they control. **Operate instructions** initiate arithmetic, logical, and shift operations on scalars or vectors; move or translate data; and manipulate stacks. Operate instructions that manipulate characters are **character instructions,** and those that manipulate strings are **character-string instructions** (or simply **string instructions**). **Vector instructions** manipulate vectors and are comprised of vector operate, vector LOAD, and vector STORE instructions.

Memory-access instructions include LOAD **instructions,** which load values from main memory into registers, and STORE **instructions,** which copy the contents of registers into main memory. Computers with more than one processor (e.g., non–von Neumann machines) require **process synchronization instructions** for regulating critical timing among executing processes.

Instructions that alter the logical flow of control of a program are **branch instructions.** Some branch instructions, called **subroutine-linkage instructions,** provide special hardware support for calling and returning from (linking) procedures. Instructions that compare or test values before branching are **conditional branch instructions.**

Finally, there is a miscellaneous group of instructions. I/O operations are initiated by **I/O instructions.** Most machines have a number of special instructions for controlling various hardware options, such as privilege level, interrupt hardware, and memory protection (all of which will be described in more detail later).

All these categories can be grouped together as follows:

1. Operate
    1.1. Arithmetic
    1.2. Boolean (logic)
    1.3. Shift
    1.4. Character and string
    1.5. Type conversion
    1.6. Stack and register manipulation
    1.7. Load immediate
    1.8. No operation
    1.9. Vector
2. Memory access
    2.1. Load and store
    2.2. Load address

2.3. Process synchronization
3. Control
   3.1. Branch
   3.2. Comparison and test
   3.3. Subroutine linkage
4. Miscellaneous and privileged
   4.1. I/O
   4.2. Interrupts and state swapping
   4.3. Privileged
   4.4. Halt

We shall look at different types of instructions throughout this text; Sections 2.4.1 to 2.4.5 follow the above classification approximately to describe some of the more common instructions that are shared by almost all computers.

## 2.4.1 ■ Operate Instructions

Operate instructions specify machine operations and therefore specify operands for those operations. An instruction may specify the operands implicitly or explicitly. Operands that are specified by the op code are **implicit operands;** they have no other specification. For example, a CLEAR CARRY instruction tells the control unit to clear the carry flag, which holds the carry bit of the last ADD instruction.[4] The CLEAR CARRY instruction has no other effect, and the carry flag is the instruction's implicit operand. **Explicit operands** are those that the instruction specifies in fields other than the op-code field. Most operands are specified explicitly.

    Most operands are data operands. These can be one of two principal types: immediate or addressed. **Immediate operands** appear in the instruction stream, generally in the instructions themselves. For example, the instruction AND(R1 ← R1 + #F7) tells the control unit to AND the bits of register R1 with the constant $F7_{16}$ and place the result in register R1.[5] The constant $F7_{16}$ is the immediate operand and appears within a field of the instruction.

    An operand that is not immediate is an **addressed operand;** the instruction must specify its address. In that case, the instruction holds an **address specification.** There are dozens of techniques for address specification, and we shall discuss many of them in the following sections. As one example, when an operand is held in a register, the register number is the address specification. In the instruction AND(R1 ← R1 + #F7), for example, "R1" is a reg-

*implicit operands*

*explicit operands*

*immediate operands*

*addressed operand*
*address specification*

---

4. Some computers use the carry flag in other ways—for example, as an extension bit during rotate and shift instructions.
5. This instruction clears the third bit of register R1 (numbering from the right and starting with bit 0) because $F7_{16} = 1111\ 0111_2$.

ister specification. In general, however, address specifications designate main-memory locations.

The remainder of Section 2.4.1 will describe the main operate instructions. Because of the complexity of the vector instructions, we defer our discussion of them until Section 2.4.5.

**Arithmetic, Logical, and Shift Instructions**

Arithmetic, logical, and shift instructions are available on virtually all computers and often come in several "flavors." Here we shall describe typical instructions from each of the three categories.

Computers provide arithmetic instructions, such as ADD, SUBTRACT (with and without carry), MULTIPLY, and DIVIDE for numeric operations. If the computer has more than one numeric format (e.g., integers, floating-point numbers, and BCD numbers) or multiple precisions, it may provide different instructions for each type.

Arithmetic instructions generally set the processor status flags or the condition code to indicate the outcome of the operation. Examples of such outcomes are that the operation generated a carry or a borrow, an overflow or underflow occurred, the result had the value 0, and the result was negative. Thus the condition code register is an implicit operand for most of these instructions. For RISC computers that have several independent condition code fields, the field specification is an explicit operand.

The product of two $N$-bit integers is $2N - 1$ bits long. As a consequence, some computers use two registers for the result of integer multiplication. Similarly, some computers use two registers for the result of an integer division—one for the integer quotient and one for the remainder.

Computers provide logical or boolean instructions that include bitwise AND, OR, NOT, and XOR (exclusive OR). These instructions set, clear, and extract specific groups of bits and perform many other operations. Logical operations frequently set condition codes but usually only for zero or nonzero results.

Shift instructions include circular shifts (ROTATE LEFT and ROTATE RIGHT), logical shifts (shifts that insert zeros in vacated bit positions, such as LOGICAL SHIFT LEFT and LOGICAL SHIFT RIGHT), and arithmetic shifts (an ARITHMETIC SHIFT RIGHT is a shift that replicates the value of the leftmost, or sign bit and an ARITHMETIC SHIFT LEFT checks for whether there has been a sign change). Shift operations sometimes use the carry flag as an extension bit to the specified register. On a SHIFT LEFT, for example, the hardware would insert the leftmost operand bit in the carry flag. On a ROTATE LEFT, the hardware would insert the leftmost operand bit in the carry flag after inserting the original carry flag into the rightmost bit position, as shown in Fig. 2.9.

Instruction-set architects provide the various shift instructions for a number of different reasons. Two illustrative uses are extracting fields from within words and extending the precision of integers.

Consider the operation of extracting the 3-bit field consisting of bits 4 through 6 from an 8-bit word, where the bits are numbered from the left (bit 0 is the leftmost bit). A programmer can accomplish the desired field extraction by shifting the word to the left by 4 bits and then shifting the word to the right by 5 bits. If $X_0X_1X_2X_3\,X_4X_5X_6X_7$ is the original content of the word, then SHIFT LEFT 4 produces $X_4X_5X_6X_7\,0000$ and SHIFT RIGHT 5 produces $0000\,0X_4X_5X_6$. Notice that the instruction inserts zeros in the vacated bit positions.

To convert an 8-bit two's-complement integer into a 16-bit two's-complement integer, one must copy the sign bit of the original number into each bit position of the 8 high-order bits of the new word. For example, $0001\,0010_2$ ($18_{10}$) becomes $0000\,0000\,0001\,0010_2$ and $1001\,1101_2$ ($-99_{10}$) becomes $1111\,1111\,1001\,1101_2$. One can easily accomplish the desired result by placing the original number in a 16-bit register (right justified), shifting left by 8 bits, and then shifting right by 8 bits using an ARITHMETIC SHIFT RIGHT operation.

**Character- and String-processing Instructions**

Character strings are particularly useful for processing textual information. Consequently, although boolean and shift instructions can manipulate character strings, most computers provide special instructions for manipulating them. Character instructions include MOVE CHARACTER, MOVE STRING, COMPARE CHARACTERS, and COMPARE STRINGS. MOVE CHARACTER and COMPARE CHARACTERS are byte-oriented instructions. MOVE STRING specifies two main-memory addresses and a length. The main-memory addresses of the two operands are called the **source address** and **destination address.** When executed, MOVE STRING moves a block of contiguous bytes that begin at the source address to a block of contiguous bytes that begin at the destination address. Figure 2.10 illustrates how a MOVE STRING instruction works. COMPARE STRINGS is similar but returns the character number of the first character mismatch. There are several ways different computers specify addresses and lengths, and most computer architectures leave unspecified the result when the source and destination strings overlap.

source address
destination address

**Stack and Register Manipulation**

Stack instructions operate on stacks. In general, a register holds the address of the top of a stack in memory, and a stack instruction either alters the contents

FIGURE 2.9  *A* ROTATE LEFT *that includes the carry flag, c.*

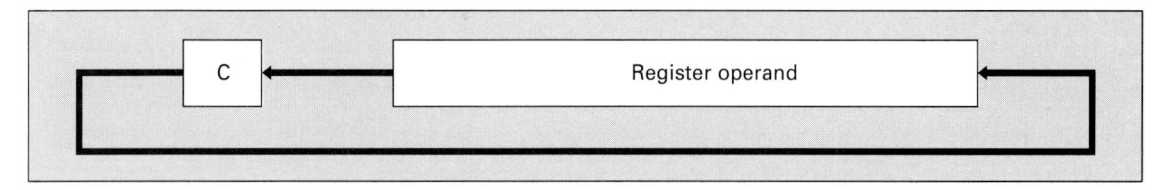

of the stack or performs a test on its contents. Section 2.1.4 described the most common stack operations: push, pop, top, and the predicate empty.

Instructions that operate on the contents of registers and place their results in registers are register-manipulation instructions. They include most of the types we have already described, such as arithmetic, logical, and shift instructions. For example, a shift instruction that shifts the content of a register is a register instruction, and one that complements the bits of a register is a register instruction. Register instructions also include register-to-register manipulations.

The LOAD IMMEDIATE instruction is another example. It loads a register with a value contained within the instruction itself, and thus is an immediate operand. Some register instructions operate on the contents of registers using immediate operands.

Most instructions include a NO OP instruction, which does nothing. Instruction sets often include the NO OP instruction to allow compilers to align subsequent instructions on specific types of memory boundaries (see Section 2.5.2), and some RISC instruction sets require them because of the way they process branch instructions (see Section 6.3.3).

**FIGURE 2.10** *MOVE STRING instruction (MOVE). This instruction copies the string of length L, starting at source address and ending at source address + L − 1 to destination address. (Notice that the string length L, appears within the instruction.)*

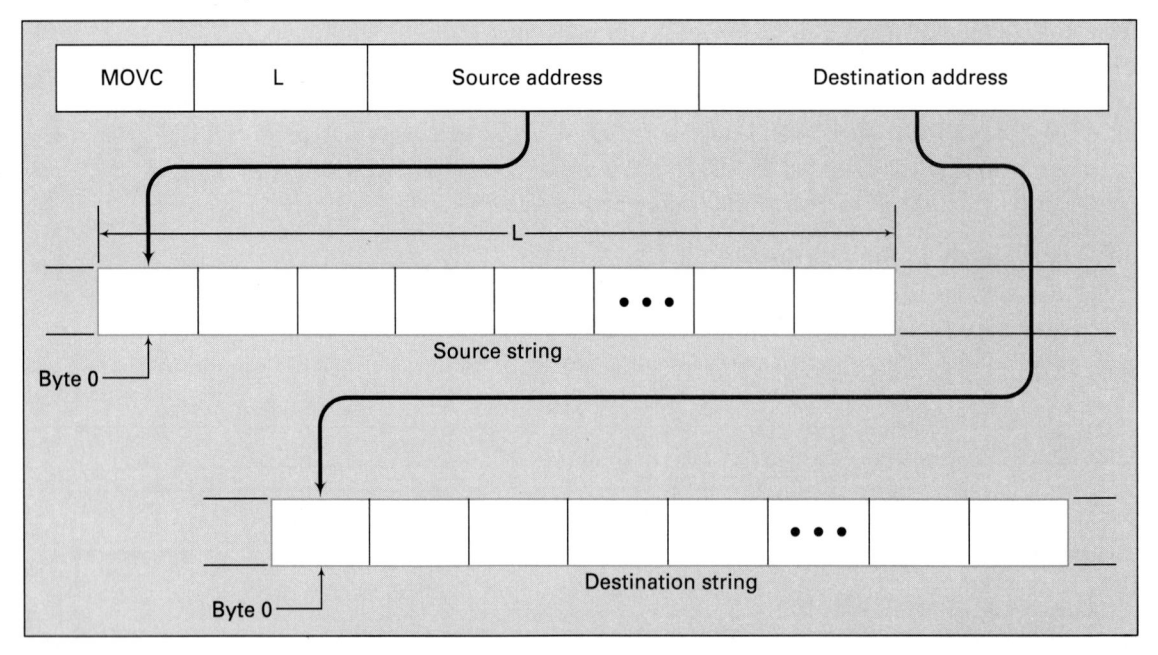

## 2.4.2 ■ Memory-access Instructions

### LOAD and STORE Instructions

Computers provide a number of instructions for loading registers and for storing the contents of registers into main memory. These LOAD and STORE instructions specify the size of the operand (e.g., byte, word, or doubleword) and the type of operation (e.g., LOAD POSITIVE, LOAD NEGATIVE). Instructions that perform an operation in addition to a load, such as LOAD POSITIVE and LOAD NEGATIVE, are operate instructions as well as load instructions.

### LOAD ADDRESS Instructions

Many computers provide a LOAD ADDRESS instruction for getting the effective address of a datum or the instruction itself. Unlike a LOAD instruction, however, the LOAD ADDRESS instruction does not access memory at all. Computers that use base-displacement addressing (described later in this chapter) also have LOAD ADDRESS instructions. Programmers can then use the LOAD ADDRESS instructions to place the address of the instruction itself in a base register.

### Process Synchronization Instructions (Optional)

Systems that support multitasking (the execution of two or more programs at a time) need instructions for supporting four types of activities:

1. synchronization,
2. interprocess communication,
3. task initiation,
4. task termination.

The only instructions that we shall discuss here are synchronization instructions, because many computers provide them in hardware. Synchronization instructions, also called **synchronization primitives,** are widely used in operating systems and in user multitasking.[6]

In the following discussion it is crucial to distinguish between *processes* and *processors*. Processes are the programs or procedures executed by processors, whereas processors are the computers that execute processes. A multiprocessor can execute several processes concurrently. Also, because of multitasking, a uniprocessor can also execute several processes, although only one controls the CPU at any given time. The CPU executes them by sharing cycles among them. Indeed, many of the problems that arise on multiprocessor systems are also found in multitasking uniprocessor systems. These problems occur because a process generally can be interrupted between any two instructions.

*sychronization primitives*

---

6. Any good text on operating systems will discuss the methods and hazards of multitasking; here we focus on machine instructions that allow a programmer to synchronize processes.

Processes can be either active or inactive. An **active process** is one that a processor is currently executing, even if the processor does not control the CPU at the moment. An **inactive process** is one that no processor is currently executing. An active process can **suspend a process,** either another active process or itself; once a process is suspended, the CPU no longer executes its instructions. An active process can also **resume a process,** one that has been suspended, which allows the CPU once again to execute its instructions.

A **shared variable** is a data item in memory that several processes can access. Similarly, a **shared data set** is a data set that several processes can access. All the variables in a shared data set are shared variables.

Whenever several processes attempt to update a shared variable, the final outcome depends on the order of the accesses to it. This concept can be illustrated by a simple example. Assume that two processes are incrementing a shared variable X:

|  | Process A |  |  | Process B |  |
|---|---|---|---|---|---|
| A1 | LOAD | $R1 \leftarrow X$ | B1 | LOAD | $R1 \leftarrow X$ |
| A2 | INCREMENT | $R1 \leftarrow R1 + 1$ | B2 | INCREMENT | $R1 \leftarrow R1 + 1$ |
| A3 | STORE | $X \leftarrow R1$ | B3 | STORE | $X \leftarrow R1$ |

The final value of X can be either $X + 1$ or $X + 2$, depending on the order in which the instructions are executed. If either process completes all three of its instructions before the other process starts, the final value will be $X + 2$. However, if the sequence is, say, A1, B1, A2, B2, A3, B3, then the value will be $X + 1$.

Because the outcome depends on the execution order, sections of code that update shared variables are called **critical sections.** The goal is to synchronize critical sections so that their outcomes are known. In general, an operating system synchronizes critical sections by allowing at most one process to execute a critical section at a time. This method of synchronization is called **mutual exclusion.** In the previous example, all three statements of each process form a critical section. If the operating system enforces mutual exclusion, then the final value of X will always be $X + 2$.

Operating systems usually enforce mutual exclusion by enabling each process to exclude all other processes from executing their critical sections when it is about to execute its own. How does one process prevent other processes from executing their critical sections? Several mechanisms that various systems use for implementing mutual exclusion are presented here in order of increasing complexity. The first ones (TEST AND SET, CLEAR, and MATCH AND REPLACE) are more likely to be implemented in the hardware of a computer; the others (FETCH AND INCREMENT, FETCH AND ADD, SEND, and RECEIVE) are more likely to be implemented in software by complex operating systems for synchronization.

First a couple of definitions are necessary. An **atomic instruction** (also called an **indivisible instruction**) is one that meets these two criteria: (1) It proceeds to completion in an operation that cannot be interrupted, and (2) other processes cannot access its operands or its result until it is finished. A process that blocks all other processes from accessing an entire data set that it is using is **locking the data set**.

Now let us look at several typical synchronization primitives that many computers provide. The first is TEST AND SET, which operates on a boolean variable in memory. In one atomic operation, TEST AND SET loads the (old) value of the variable into a register, for example, and sets the value in memory to *true* regardless of the previous value. A companion instruction, CLEAR, simply sets the value to *false*. Systems programmers generally use TEST AND SET and CLEAR to manipulate special shared variables called **semaphores**. A semaphore is a datatype with two allowed values, *true* and *false*, and the two defined operations, TEST AND SET and CLEAR.

Another synchronization primitive is MATCH AND REPLACE. It operates on three variables—say C, R, and S (for comparand, replacement value, and semaphore). Two of them, C and R, are within the processor. The other, S, is in a memory location. The MATCH AND REPLACE instruction compares C to S and returns the result of the comparison to the processor, which may, for example, set the condition code. In addition, if C and S are equal, MATCH AND REPLACE stores the value of R in S. However, if C and S are unequal, MATCH AND REPLACE takes no further action. Notice that MATCH AND REPLACE is a generalization of TEST AND SET and is an atomic operation, like all synchronization primitives. Therefore MATCH AND REPLACE prevents all other processes from accessing the location holding S from the time it reads the stored value until it finishes updating the stored value. For a multiprocessor the storage system must contain the locking logic. For a single processor with multitasking the operating system must allow the instruction to run to completion without interruption.

Another synchronization primitive is FETCH AND INCREMENT. It, too, is an atomic operation. First, it loads the value of a variable into a register. It then adds 1 to the value in memory (ending with the old value in the register and the incremented value in memory). Another primitive, FETCH AND ADD, is probably more common than FETCH AND INCREMENT. FETCH AND ADD allows the programmer to specify the value to be added to the variable in memory, instead of always incrementing it.

The synchronization primitives SEND and RECEIVE are just like the ordinary STORE and LOAD instructions, except that they check the memory cell that they reference before (logically) accessing it. The memory cell holds information telling the processor whether the cell it is *empty*.[7] A memory cell is empty

---

7. Generally, computers with SEND and RECEIVE instructions have 1 extra bit for each memory cell to denote whether it is empty or full.

until it is filled by a SEND operation; it then becomes *full*. If a process executes a RECEIVE instruction on an empty cell, the CPU suspends that process until an active process executes a SEND operation and fills the cell. There are many variations on how to empty cells and suspend processes. We shall explore some of them in the problems.

Many processors provide one or more of these synchronization primitives. The TEST AND SET primitive is probably the most common, although it usually accesses 1 byte of memory rather than a single bit. For example, the IBM System/370 family transfers the high-order bit of the referenced byte to the condition-code register (effectively testing it), and then sets the byte to $FF_{16}$ in one indivisible and uninterruptible operation. The IBM System/370 family also has two MATCH AND REPLACE instructions, which are called COMPARE AND SWAP and COMPARE DOUBLE AND SWAP.

To illustrate the use of the synchronization operations, we shall consider the following problem. Several processors are to be used to execute a single loop. Each processor will execute its own process, and each process will perform one or more of the loop iterations. For example, if there are three processors and the controlled loop variable, say I, runs from 1 to 10, then the first process, executing on processor P1, might execute the loop for I = 1. The second process, executing on processor P2, might execute the loop for I = 2, 3, and 4. The third process, executing on processor P3, might execute the loop for I = 5 and 6. Then, the first process would execute the loop for I = 7, the second for I = 8 and 9, and finally the third for I = 10. The problem here is that each process would be updating the shared variable I, and each one must get its own unique value and increment I.

In a parallel Fortran, the code might be as follows:

**do all** (I = 1, N)
<loop body>
**repeat**

What kind of code must the compiler generate to execute the loop? Specifically, since copies of the same code will execute on several independent processors, how will they synchronize their accesses to the shared variable I? In the remainder of Section 2.4.2 we will show several ways a programmer or compiler might use synchronization primitives to implement the loop.

*Using* TEST-AND-SET *and a Semaphore*

In this example, FLAG is a semaphore that is initially *false,* and TEST AND SET returns the previous value of its argument (FLAG). All critical sections use a similar **if** statement to protect their critical sections, and they all test the same shared variable, FLAG. The first process to execute the TEST AND SET instruction sets FLAG to *true*. Since TEST AND SET is an atomic operation, no other process can access or update FLAG at the same time. Once a process sets FLAG to *true,* any other process that attempts the TEST AND SET operation will loop at the SPINLOCK statement, that is, it will loop until the process that is executing its critical section clears FLAG.

SPINLOCK:  **if** TEST AND SET FLAG **goto** SPINLOCK
  LOAD       $R1 \leftarrow I$      ⎫
  INCREMENT  $R1 \leftarrow R1 + 1$ ⎬ critical section
  STORE      $I \leftarrow R1$      ⎭
  CLEAR      FLAG

  <loop body>

  **goto** SPINLOCK

Note that <loop body> includes such things as testing the value of I to determine whether to execute the loop.

Because MATCH AND REPLACE is a generalization of TEST AND SET, a programmer can use MATCH AND REPLACE instead of TEST AND SET. For MATCH AND REPLACE, the programmer must explicitly specify the comparand, which is *false* in this example, and also the replacement value, which is *true* in this example.

*Using* FETCH AND INCREMENT

  FETCH AND INCREMENT $R1 \leftarrow I$
    <loop body>

Since FETCH AND INCREMENT is itself an atomic operation, only one process can execute it at a time. Thus each process is guaranteed to get a unique value for I.

For a critical data-set implementation, I is put in a critical data set. Notice that the problem of determining when I can be released is nontrivial if the load-increment-store operation requires more than one instruction.

*Using* SEND *and* RECEIVE *with the Variable* FLAG

  RECEIVE    FLAG                   Empties FLAG
  LOAD       $R1 \leftarrow I$      ⎫
  INCREMENT  $R1 \leftarrow R1 + 1$ ⎬ Critical section
  STORE      $I \leftarrow R1$      ⎭
  SEND       FLAG                   Fills FLAG

Note that the RECEIVE operation empties FLAG. However, RECEIVE causes the processor to wait if FLAG is already empty. Used in this way, FLAG is really just a semaphore. Its value is immaterial; its *full* or *empty* status is all that matters.

## 2.4.3 ■ Control Instructions

Control instructions include branch instructions and subroutine-linkage instructions. The following five sections describe these instructions and techniques for specifying and evaluating the branch tests.

### Conditional and Unconditional Branch Instructions

As we mentioned earlier, von Neumann machines execute instructions sequentially unless explicitly told to do otherwise. If there were no branch instructions at all, the CPU would execute instructions in strictly sequential order. But because computations often depend on the results of previous operations, conditional branches are necessary. Conditional branches initiate a branch only if certain test conditions are satisfied. Instructions that always branch, **unconditional branches,** are also useful but not strictly necessary, since conditional branches that always succeed can be used in their stead.

Branch instructions generally specify one address, the **branch address.** The branch address is the address of the next instruction for the CPU to execute, called the **branch-target instruction.** The branch address is therefore an operand of the branch instruction. To carry out a branch instruction, the control unit simply resolves the branch-target address and places it in the program counter.

Instructions specify branch addresses in a variety of ways, such as relative, absolute, indirect, and register indirect. We shall discuss these techniques when we discuss addressing techniques in general.

### Branch Test

The **branch test** is an operand for conditional branch instructions. A branch test is a test whose outcome determines whether the branch in question should occur. If it should, the CPU places the branch-target address in the PC. If the branch should not occur, the CPU does not alter the content of the PC, and the instruction "falls through" to the next instruction. As an example, the instruction BRANCH **if** $X \geq 0$ would test the content of the X register and would branch if that value were nonnegative. The check for $X \geq 0$ is the branch test.

Conditional branch instructions often test the values of one or more processor status bits (e.g., bits in the condition-code register) and branch only if these values form a certain pattern. The simplest conditional branch instructions test a single processor status bit to see whether it is set or clear. For example, a BRANCH ON NEGATIVE instruction branches only if the negative flag is set. More complex branch instructions test several processor-status bits.

When branch instructions test processor-status bits, the outcome of the branch depends on the results of earlier instructions in the instruction stream. Instructions that modify the processor-status bits are **condition-code-setting instructions,** and most arithmetic and logical instructions, as well as many SHIFT and ROTATE instructions and some LOAD and STORE instructions, modify the condition-code register or the processor-status bits. In general, a program can execute many instructions that do not alter the status bits before executing a conditional branch instruction. In that case, the outcome of the branch depends on the outcome of the most recent instruction to set the status bit or bits that the branch instruction tests.

For von Neumann computers, which execute instructions serially, it does not matter than many instructions can intervene between a condition-code-setting instruction and a branch instruction that tests the condition code. However, we shall look at some computers that can execute several instructions concurrently. For them the architects must build appropriate interlocks into the hardware to guarantee that the CU will wait for the final condition-code-setting instruction to finish executing before evaluating the branch test for a conditional branch instruction.

**Subroutine-linkage Instructions**

We have described why one procedure might like to call another procedure, and why the second procedure would like to return control to the calling procedure. Most computers provide at least two subroutine-linkage instructions for that purpose, one for branching to a procedure and one for returning from it. We shall use JSR (jump and save register) as a typical branch-to-procedure instruction, and RET (return) as a typical return-from-procedure instruction.

The JSR instruction is like an ordinary branch instruction except that it saves the content of the PC before branching (Fig. 2.11). Because the PC holds the address of the next instruction during execution of the current instruction, the saved value is the address of the instruction following the JSR instruction. The RET instruction is also a branch instruction. However, its branch-target ad-

FIGURE 2.11  *Relationships between calling and called procedures. RA, the return address; EPA, the called procedure's entry-point address;* JSR, *the calling instruction;* RET, *the return instruction. The computer saves RA when it executes* JSR. *It executes the instruction labeled "entry point" immediately after it executes* JSR, *and it executes the instruction labeled "continuation point" immediately after it executes* RET.

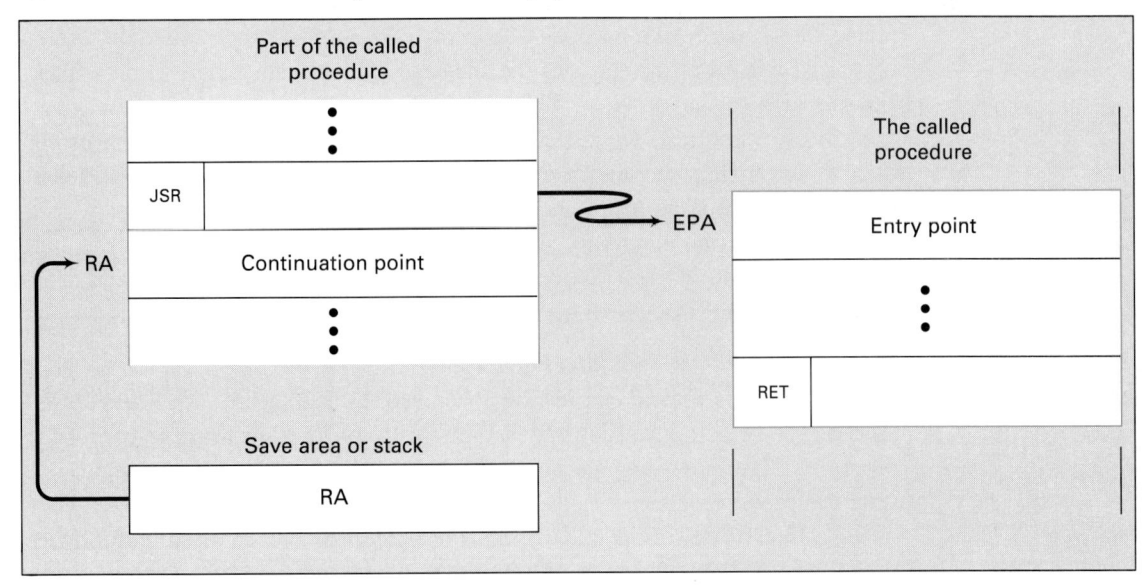

dress is the address saved by the most recently executed JSR instruction. The next instruction the CPU executes after RET is therefore the instruction immediately following the JSR instruction in memory. When using the JSR and RET instructions, the branch-target address must be the address of the first instruction of the called procedure. This address is called the **entry-point address** of that procedure. The saved address is called the **continuation-point address** or **return address.**

<small>entry-point address</small>
<small>continuation-point address</small>
<small>return address</small>

There is no standard policy specifying where a computer should save the PC content when it executes a JSR instruction; some computers save it on a stack, others at an instruction-specified address, and still others in a predetermined area in main memory. The choice depends, in part on the nature of the procedures being implemented. For recursive procedures (those that call themselves, either directly or indirectly), a stack-based mechanism is appropriate. For nonrecursive procedures, the use of a stack may not be important and may have disadvantages.

### 2.4.4 ■ Miscellaneous and Privileged Instructions

In this section we describe instructions that do not fit into the previous three categories, including I/O instructions, interrupts, state-swapping instructions, and instructions that alter the privilege level, among others.

#### I/O Instructions

Many computers do not have any I/O instructions at all, and Section 3.3.5 describes how such computers perform I/O. When computers do have I/O instructions, the I/O instructions initiate the control signals that control the I/O devices. Typical I/O instructions specify an **I/O device address** (a number that selects the I/O device) and a code that tells the device what operation to perform. Alternatively, the op code of the instruction may specify the device operation. Typical I/O instructions include INPUT, which reads a byte of data from the specified device; OUTPUT, which writes a byte of data to the specified device; TEST DEVICE, which tests for a specified condition and sets a processor-status bit depending on the outcome of the test, and CONTROL DEVICE, which specifies a device-specific operation for the device to perform.

<small>I/O device address</small>

Some computers have simple I/O processors called I/O channels, and for them typical I/O instructions include START I/O, HALT I/O, TEST I/O, and TEST CHANNEL. We shall discuss these instructions more fully in Section 3.3.4.

#### Interrupts and State-swapping Operations

Hardware events may alter the flow of control of a program. An **interrupt** is an example of a hardware-initiated branch. When the hardware interrupts a program, it preserves enough information about the state of the program to restart the program later.

<small>interrupt</small>

Interrupts are one of two kinds of **exceptions,** which are alterations in the sequential flow of control of a program. The other kinds of exceptions are

<small>exceptions</small>

traps, which, as mentioned earlier, are initiated by program events. Unlike branches and subroutine calls and returns, which the program initiates, the hardware initiates exceptions. Furthermore, it may initiate them without regard to the state of execution of the interrupted program. Although the hardware initiates an exception, software processes it and may return control to the interrupted program. A special instruction, such as RETURN FROM INTERRUPT or RETURN FROM TRAP, completes the process. Instructions that initiate software traps go under the names INTERRUPT or SUPERVISOR CALL.

In addition to exceptions, some computers provide mechanisms for swapping the entire register set of one program with another. These mechanisms enable an operating system to swap control rapidly between different programs. Instruction sets often provide instructions that initiate interrupts and then branch to a user-specified routine. The exception hardware therefore performs the required state saving. We shall discuss exceptions (including interrupts), exception hardware, and exception-processing instructions in Section 3.1.4.

### Privileged Instructions

Most large computers have special instructions, called **privileged instructions,** that enable system software to protect itself from manipulation by user software. Today many personal computers (PCs) also have privileged instructions, although the original microprocessor-based computers, such as the IBM PC, did not.

An operating system consists of the programs that are necessary for the efficient operation of a computing system. There is one significant difference between the execution of an operating-system program and the execution of user software: The operating system must have privileges and responsibilities that user programs do not. To support this difference, most computers have at least two modes of operation, of which at least one is a **privileged mode.** For example, IBM System/370 computers have both a **problem mode** (for unprivileged instructions) and a **supervisor mode** (for privileged instructions).[8] DEC VAX family has four modes: a **user mode** and three privileged modes—**executive mode,** supervisor mode, and **kernel mode.** An IBM CPU executing in supervisor state, or a VAX CPU executing in kernel mode, can execute all instructions in the computer's instruction set. An IBM CPU executing in problem state, or a VAX executing in user mode, however, can execute only some of the instructions. Instructions that the CPUs can execute only when in a privileged mode are privileged instructions, and any attempt by a program to execute a privileged instruction when the CPU is operating in an insufficiently privileged mode causes an interrupt (see Section 3.2.3).

*privileged instructions*

*privileged mode*
*problem mode*
*supervisor mode*
*user mode*
*executive mode*
*kernel mode*

---

8. IBM calls these the problem state and supervisor state, respectively.

Much of the operating system runs in privileged mode, and before it transfers (or as it transfers) control to a user program, it places the CPU in an unprivileged mode. Instructions that cause the CPU to switch states are themselves privileged, and it is by this mechanism that the hardware and operating system together protect a user program from interfering with the operating system and other programs.

Various other kinds of instructions are privileged besides the already-mentioned instructions that switch the mode of the machine. I/O instructions are privileged to protect files; instructions that protect and allocate memory are privileged, as are instructions for setting clocks and timers. In general, instructions that control the hardware interface between the computer and its attached devices are privileged. Usually only a small percentage of all the instructions are privileged.

When a computer is started, it automatically begins execution in its privileged mode. The startup routine then loads and executes the operating system. From then on the operating system controls the mode of the machine.

### 2.4.5 ■ Vector Instructions

Although not available on most computers, vector instructions are found in supercomputers and many high-performance computers, including several RISC machines. In addition, many computers allow the addition of special vector hardware for speeding up vector and matrix operations. Because of their increasing importance in many scientific applications, we shall describe a number of typical vector, matrix, and vector-scalar operations in considerable detail in this section.

Two properties of vector operations are crucial: (1) they use regular patterns for accessing memory, and (2) they perform identical operations on sequences of operands. Both properties are essential for their efficient implementation, which we shall discuss in Chapter 6.

#### Vector LOAD and STORE Instructions

Vector LOAD and STORE instructions are similar to scalar LOAD and STORE instructions, except that the former specify a vector stride and they load or store multiple values into vector registers. A **vector register** is a set of registers that a vector instruction can reference individually or as a unit. The values referenced by these vector instructions occur at a fixed number of memory locations apart.

#### Vector Operate Instructions

There are four basic types of **vector operations** (on vectors $\vec{U}$ and $\vec{V}$ and a scalar $S$):

1. **Monadic vector operations.** These operations have only one vector operand: Element $W_i$ of the result $\vec{W} \leftarrow \text{op } \vec{V}$ is given by $W_i = \text{op } V_i$ for each $i$. Examples are SQUARE, SQUARE ROOT, RECIPROCAL, and NEGATE.

2. **Vector-scalar operations.** Element $W_i$ of result vector $\vec{W} \leftarrow \vec{U}$ op $S$ is given by $W_i = U_i$ op $S$ for each $i$. Examples are arithmetic, boolean, and shift operations.

3. **Vector-vector operations.** Element $W_i$ of result vector $\vec{W} \leftarrow \vec{U}$ op $\vec{V}$ is given by $W_i = U_i$ op $V_i$ for each $i$. Examples are arithmetic, boolean, and shift operations.

4. **Vector-reduction operations.** Reduction operations are those that operate on a vector and produce a scalar by some procedure more complicated than indexing. The op reduction of $\vec{V}$ is given by $V_1$ op $V_2$ op $V_3 \cdots$. Examples are sum reduction (column addition), ANY (OR reduction) and ALL (AND reduction).

## *Monadic and Vector-scalar Operations*

The simplest vector operations are monadic and vector-scalar operations, which perform the same computation on a sequence of consecutive variables in memory or in registers and place the results in a second sequence of consecutive memory locations. Vector instruction sets typically include a number of monadic operations:

| | |
|---|---|
| COPY | Copies the elements of one vector to another, or copies a single scalar into all elements of a vector. |
| NEGATE | Replaces the value of each vector element $V_i$ by $0 - V_i$. |
| COMPLEMENT | Replaces the value of each vector element $V_i$ by NOT($V_i$). |
| RECIPROCAL | Replaces the value of each vector element, $V_i$, by $1/V_i$. |

Vector-scalar operations typically include arithmetic, comparison, logical, and shift operations. Figure 2.12 illustrates the vector-scalar addition of the constant 5 to each element of a 10-element vector.

## *Vector-vector Operations*

Vector-vector operations are just slightly more complex than vector-scalar operations: The sum of two vectors is formed by adding their corresponding elements and placing the results in a third vector. Also, the sum operator can be replaced by any binary arithmetic or logical operator. See Fig. 2.13.

## *Vector-reduction Operations*

The most common reduction operations are listed below. All of these operations can be defined for any type of array, but here we shall describe them for vectors only.

| | |
|---|---|
| Sum reduction | This is the same as column addition: Sum reduction adds all of the elements in the vector. |
| AND/OR reduction | The AND reduction of a logical vector is formed by performing AND on all of its elements together; similarly, the OR reduction is effected with the OR instruction on all elements together. Thus the AND reduction of a vector |

**FIGURE 2.12** Vector-scalar addition of the constant value 5 to each element of a 10-element vector array, $\vec{V1}$. The results form a second 10-element vector array, $\vec{V2}$.

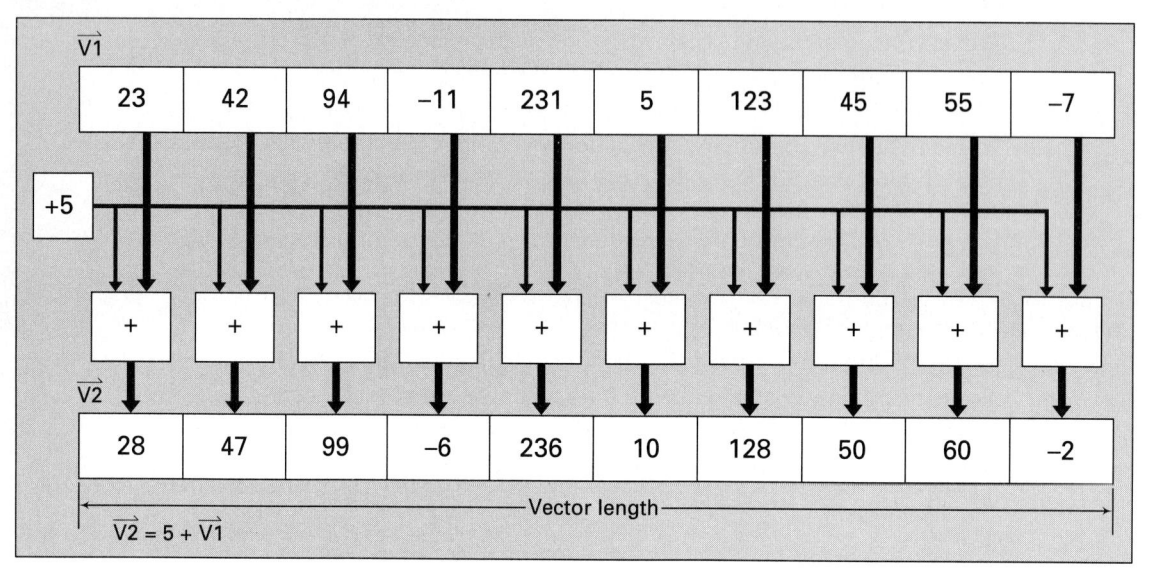

**FIGURE 2.13** Vector product of two vectors. The result is a third vector.

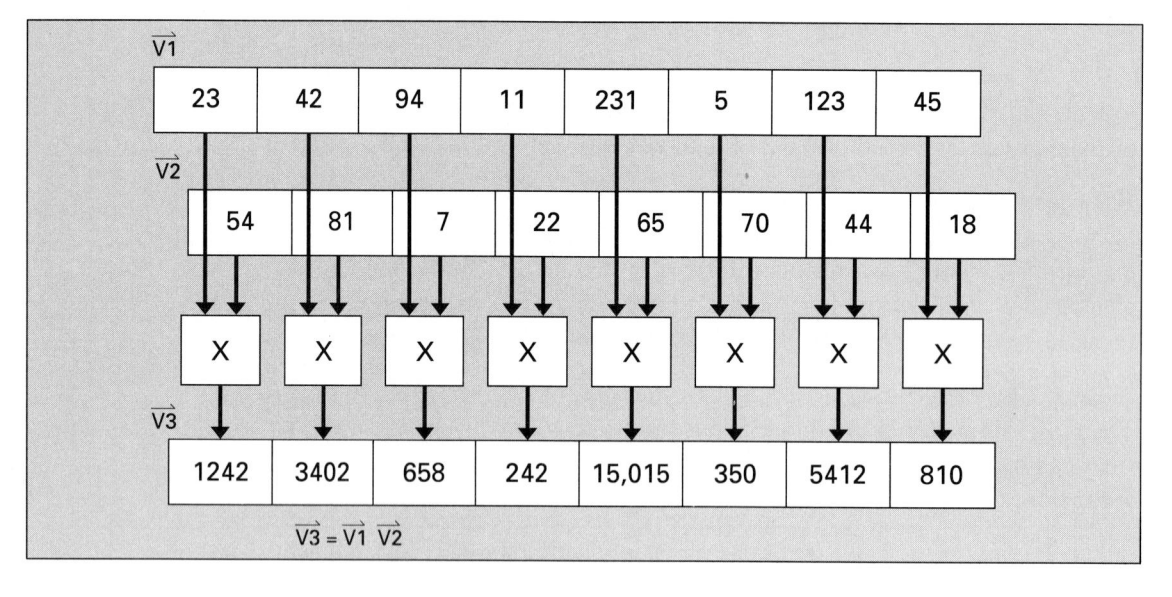

yields *true* only if all elements are *true*, and the OR reduction yields *true* if any element is *true*.

Extremal reduction  The extremal reduction instruction finds the maximum or minimum of the elements of a vector (or sometimes the index of the maximum or minimum element).

An example of a vector operation that combines a vector-vector operation with a vector reduction is the **dot product,** also called **scalar product,** of two vectors. The dot product of two *N*-element vectors is the sum reduction of their vector product. Figure 2.14 illustrates the dot product of two 8-element vectors.

dot product
scalar product

It is a rather straightforward exercise to implement each of these operations in hardware. In each case the address of each vector element differs from the previous address by a constant amount. Hence standard address circuitry that uses index registers can easily compute the addresses of successive elements, given the base address of the vector and the address increment. The address circuitry computes the addresses of the results the same way. For vector-scalar operations, the arithmetic computation circuitry only needs to access the scalar operand once, and likewise for a scalar product, it only needs to store a single value.

*Selection Operations*

Many programs require vector operations on selected vector elements. For example, a procedure may need to find the reciprocal of every element of a vector whose initial value is not zero. Similarly, many operations require the selection of elements based on a test, such as the selection of all positive elements.

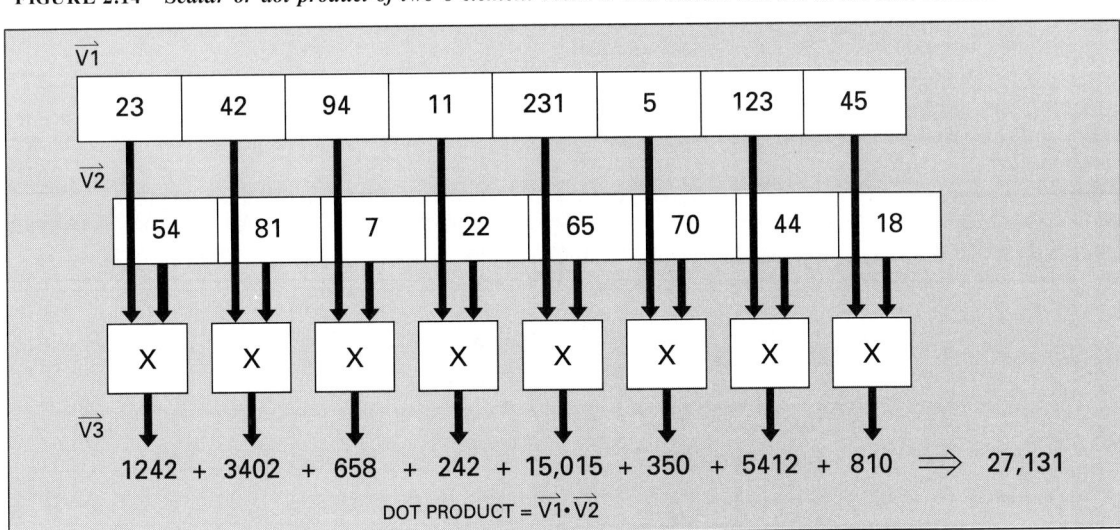

**FIGURE 2.14**  *Scalar or dot product of two 8-element vectors. The bottom line shows the sum reduction.*

$\vec{V1}$: 23, 42, 94, 11, 231, 5, 123, 45

$\vec{V2}$: 54, 81, 7, 22, 65, 70, 44, 18

$\vec{V3}$: 1242 + 3402 + 658 + 242 + 15,015 + 350 + 5412 + 810 $\Rightarrow$ 27,131

DOT PRODUCT = $\vec{V1} \cdot \vec{V2}$

**vector mask**
**test vector**
**logical vector**

A number of vector operations act on selected vector elements, and most of these instructions use a **vector mask,** also called a **test vector,** to control the selection. A vector mask is a **logical vector,** that is, a vector whose elements are *true* or *false*. A vector mask is sometimes represented by a bit string whose bits correspond to elements of a vector. Operations for creating vector masks include vector comparisons.

In this section we shall describe a number of common vector operations: comparison for creating vector masks, MERGE for controlling operations on individual vector elements, compression and expansion for eliminating selected elements from vectors and for inserting selected elements into vectors, and GATHER and SCATTER for using an index array for selecting vector elements.

**vector comparison**
**test-vector operation**

*Comparison* A **vector comparison** or **test-vector operation** checks each element of a vector to see if it satisfies a specified test condition, and if so it sets the corresponding bit (or element) of a mask. Figure 2.15 illustrates a vector-scalar comparison for equality. The scalar constant is 1.

**merge operation**

*Merge* Merging is the vector analog of conditional branching interior to a loop. A **merge operation** takes selected elements of one vector and inserts them in another vector. A mask generally selects the elements to merge. The following code illustrates a merge operation by comparing a scalar loop with the corresponding vector code:

| Fortran Loop Body | Vector Code |
|---|---|
| **if** (M(I).NE.0)Y(I) = X(I) | $\vec{Y} \leftarrow$ MERGE($\vec{X}, \vec{Y}$) **where** $\vec{M}$ |

The merge operation replaces an element of Y by the corresponding element of X only when the corresponding mask element is *true*.

FIGURE 2.15 *Using a 16-element vector, a comparison operation produces a 16-element mask. The bits of the mask indicate which vector elements satisfied the test. The figure illustrates a vector-scalar test for equality to the scalar value 1.*

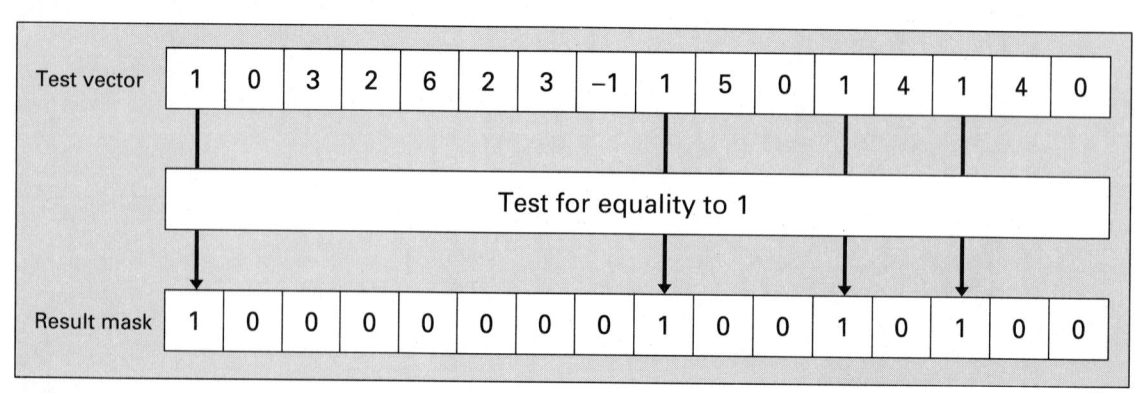

| Test vector | 1 | 0 | 3 | 2 | 6 | 2 | 3 | −1 | 1 | 5 | 0 | 1 | 4 | 1 | 4 | 0 |

Test for equality to 1

| Result mask | 1 | 0 | 0 | 0 | 0 | 0 | 0 | 0 | 1 | 0 | 0 | 1 | 0 | 1 | 0 | 0 |

***Compression and Expansion*** A **vector compression** operation squeezes out the "bad" elements of a vector as specified by a mask, and **vector expansion** is the inverse of vector compression. The following two loops describe these operations, where $\vec{X}$ is a vector, $\vec{CX}$ is the compressed vector, $\vec{EX}$ is the expanded vector, and $\vec{M}$ is the mask:

vector compression
vector expansion

  Scalar code for compression:
    K ← 1
    **do** (I = 1, N)
     **if** (M(I)) **then**
      CX(K) ← X(I)
      K ← K + 1
     **endif**
    **repeat**
    CX_LENGTH ← K − 1
  Scalar code for expansion:
    K = 1
    **do** (I = 1, N)
     **if**(M(I)) **then**
      EX(I) ← X(K)
      K ← K + 1
     **endif**
    **repeat**

Notice that $\vec{CX}$ only has as many elements as there were *true* elements in $\vec{M}$. Also, we have not defined the elements of $\vec{EX}$ that were left undefined by the expansion of $\vec{X}$. Various implementations are reasonable, such as leaving the unspecified values unchanged, or setting them all to a constant, for example 0. Figure 2.16 illustrates vector compression. Since 5 bits of $\vec{M}$ are set, the result of the compression operation is the creation of a vector of length 5.

**FIGURE 2.16** *Vector compression. The resulting vector consists of the elements of the operand whose corresponding mask bits are set.*

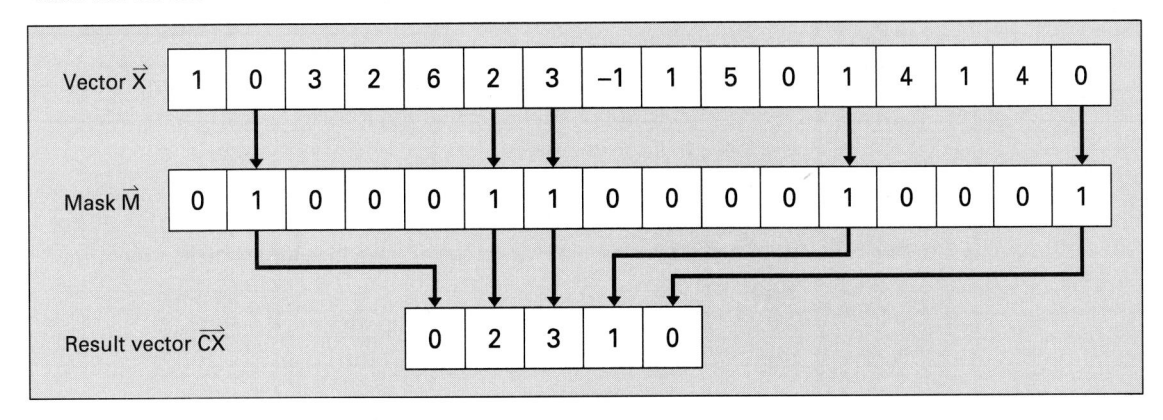

| Vector $\vec{X}$ | 1 | 0 | 3 | 2 | 6 | 2 | 3 | −1 | 1 | 5 | 0 | 1 | 4 | 1 | 4 | 0 |
| Mask $\vec{M}$ | 0 | 1 | 0 | 0 | 0 | 1 | 1 | 0 | 0 | 0 | 0 | 1 | 0 | 0 | 0 | 1 |
| Result vector $\vec{CX}$ | | | | | | 0 | 2 | 3 | 1 | 0 | | | | | | |

To see the utility of these operations, we first show a scalar loop and then the corresponding vectorized loop:

**do** (I = 1, N)
    **if** (X(I) ≠ 0) **then** Y(I) ← 1.0/X(I)
**repeat**

In the vectorized loop, all the variables denote vectors, not scalars, as above:

| | |
|---|---|
| T      ← COMPARE(X, 0.0) | Elementwise compare X(i)s to 0.0, creating a test vector T. |
| TEMP ← COMPRESS X **using** T | Create a temporary vector without 0 elements. |
| TEMP ← 1/TEMP | Get reciprocals only of good data (element ≠ 0). |
| TEMP ← EXPAND TEMP **using** T | Put reciprocals where they belong. |
| Y     ← MERGE(TEMP, Y) **where** T | Depending on definition of EXPAND, this could expand directly into Y. |

**gather**
**scatter**

*Gather and Scatter*    The third selection operation is **gather,** which has **scatter** as its inverse. Using an index vector $\vec{IND}$, gather collects selected elements from a vector $\vec{X}$ and places them in a target vector $\vec{GC}$ (Fig. 2.17). Gather corresponds to the subscripted-subscript operation below. Scattering from $\vec{X}$ spreads element vectors out again, as Fig. 2.18 shows.

Here are the scalar definitions of gather and scatter:

Gather:
    **do** (I = 1, N)
        GC(I) ← X(IND(I))
    **repeat**

Scatter:
    **do** (I = 1, N)
        SX(IND(I)) ← X(I)
    **repeat**

In this code, $\vec{GC}$ is gathered from vector $\vec{X}$, and $\vec{X}$ is scattered to vector $\vec{SX}$.

**Matrix Operations (Optional)**

Although matrix operations are extremely important for a large number of scientific and engineering applications, few computers have instructions that directly implement them. Nonetheless, vector operations provide an effective tool for implementing them. The following examples show that vector LOAD and STORE instructions with specifiable stride provide an efficient way of transposing a matrix, and the DOT PRODUCT instruction provides an efficient way of multiplying two matrices.

Consider the following 3 × 4 matrix whose elements are $m_{11} = 5$, $m_{12} = 0$, $m_{13} = 7$, $m_{14} = 1$, $m_{21} = -3$, and so forth:

$$\mathcal{M} = \begin{bmatrix} 5 & 0 & 7 & 1 \\ -3 & 9 & 2 & -1 \\ 6 & 4 & 0 & 2 \end{bmatrix}.$$

There are any number of ways to organize the elements of a matrix in the computer's memory, but when working with matrix operations, the choice may be crucial. The two most common ways are called **row-major order** and **row-minor order**. When stored in row-major order, as done by some compilers, the

row-major order
row-minor order

**FIGURE 2.17** *An illustration of* $\vec{GX} \leftarrow$ GATHER$(\vec{X}, \vec{IND})$

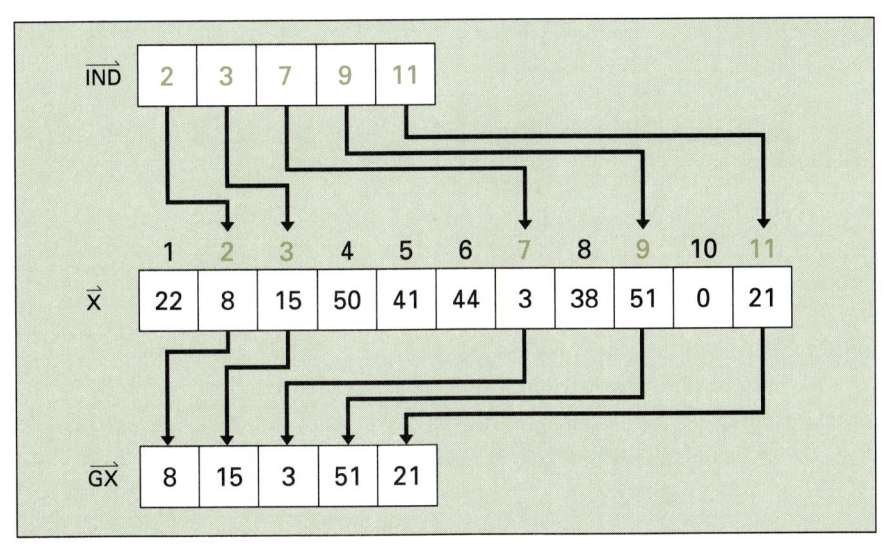

**FIGURE 2.18** *An illustration of* $\vec{SC} \leftarrow$ SCATTER$(\vec{X}, \vec{IND})$

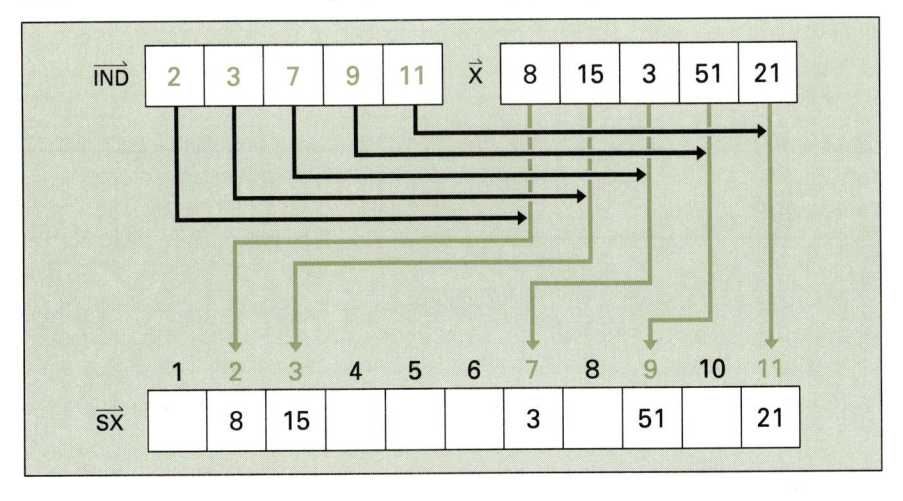

elements of the first row are stored in sequence followed by the elements of the second row and so forth until the entire matrix is stored (Fig. 2.19a). When stored in row-minor order, as Fortran generally does, the elements of the first column are stored in sequence, followed by the elements of the second column, and so on until the entire matrix is stored (Fig. 2.19b).

**transpose**

The **transpose** of a matrix $M$ is the matrix $M^T$ whose columns are the rows of the untransposed matrix. That is, each element $m_{ij}$ of $M^T$ is element $m_{ji}$ in $M$:

$$M = \begin{bmatrix} 5 & 0 & 7 & 1 \\ -3 & 9 & 2 & -1 \\ 6 & 4 & 0 & 2 \end{bmatrix} \qquad M^T = \begin{bmatrix} 5 & -3 & 6 \\ 0 & 9 & 4 \\ 7 & 2 & 0 \\ 1 & -1 & 2 \end{bmatrix}.$$

Suppose a programmer or compiler has stored a $K \times L$ matrix $M$ in row-major order. Then vector transpose can be done as follows:

    **do** (I = 1, K)
       Read row I of $M$ (with stride 1)[9]
       Write column I of $M^T$ (with stride $K$)
    **repeat**

Figure 2.20 illustrates this process.

Our next example is multiplication of two matrices to produce the **matrix product**. Let $M$ be an $m \times n$ matrix and let $N$ be an $n \times k$ matrix. The product of $M$ and $N$, denoted $MN$, is an $m \times k$ matrix. Let $P$ be $MN$. Each element of $P$ is given by

**matrix product**

$$p_{ij} = \sum_{k=1}^{n} m_{ik} n_{kj}.$$

As an illustration, here are two matrices and their product. Note that each element of the product matrix $P$ is the dot product of a row of $M$ and a column of $N$. We have highlighted row 2 of $M$, column 3 of $N$ and the resulting element, $p_{23}$, in $P$.

$$\begin{bmatrix} 5 & 0 & 7 & 1 \\ -3 & 9 & 2 & -1 \\ 6 & 4 & 0 & 2 \end{bmatrix} \begin{bmatrix} 1 & 6 & 1 & 4 \\ 0 & 2 & 5 & 1 \\ 3 & 3 & 0 & 4 \\ 2 & -1 & 1 & 0 \end{bmatrix} = \begin{bmatrix} 28 & 50 & 6 & 48 \\ 1 & 7 & 41 & 5 \\ 10 & 42 & 28 & 28 \end{bmatrix}$$

Let us consider two implementations of matrix multiplication. First suppose that $M$ and $N$ are stored in row-major order and that the product is

---

9. On a byte-addressed machine, the stride is the number of bytes per element.

also to be stored in row-major order. Figure 2.21 illustrates that the matrix product requires the evaluation of 12 dot products and their storage in 12 consecutive memory locations. It also shows that the vector strides for the second vectors of each product are $k = 4$, the row length of the second matrix.

Now suppose that $M$ is stored in row-major order but $N$ is stored in row-minor order. Also suppose that the product is to be stored in row-major order. Again the product requires evaluation of 12 dot products and storage of their results in 12 consecutive memory locations. However, Fig. 2.22 illustrates that the strides for the second vectors of each dot product are now 1, just as they are for the first vectors. Thus having the second matrix stored in row-minor order makes the product more amenable to vector hardware.

**FIGURE 2.19** *Order representations of a matrix $M$. (a) Row-major order and (b) row-minor.*

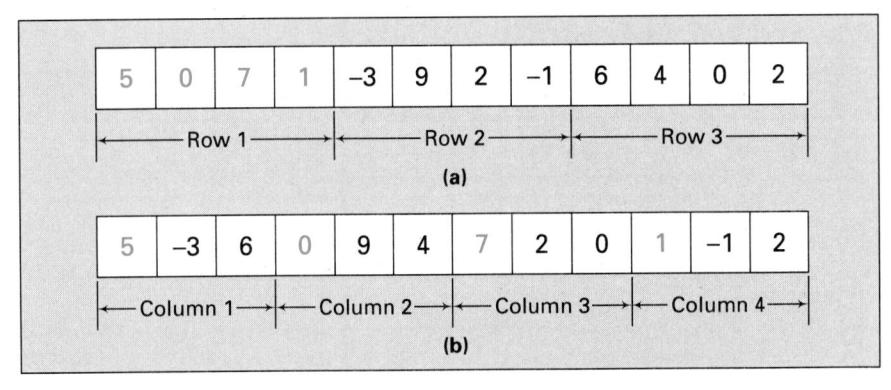

**FIGURE 2.20** *Transposing matrix $M$ using vector operations.*

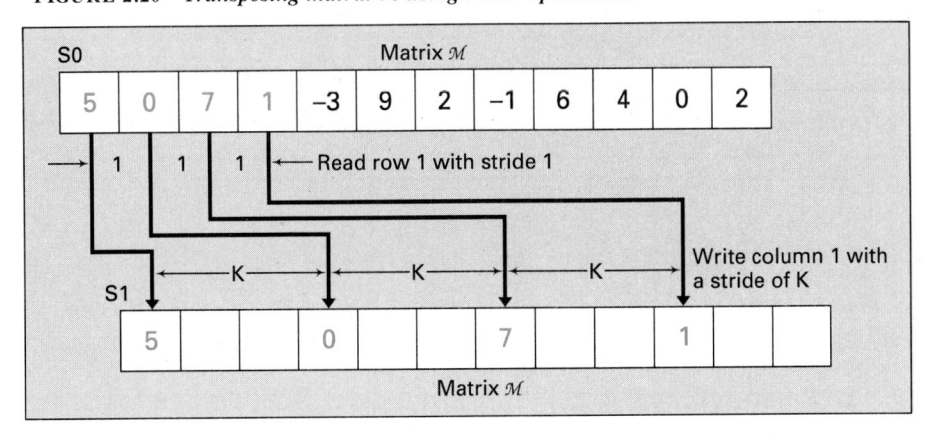

## 2.5 ■ Addressing Techniques

This section focuses on addressing techniques, which are the ways instructions reference their operands. We begin by discussing register addressing. Next, we describe boundary alignment, a method of placing variables in memory to comply with the way storage systems access data. The remainder of the section elaborates the prominent ways instructions specify main-memory addresses. Architects have developed these addressing techniques to provide efficient hardware support for string, array, stack, and procedure processing.

### 2.5.1 ■ Register Addressing

When instructions specify operands, the operands may reside either in the instruction itself, in main memory, or in one or more operational registers. Operands held by the instructions are immediate operands, as discussed previously.

FIGURE 2.21 *Formation of the product of two matrices $\mathcal{M}$ and $\mathcal{N}$ by using inner products. The strides of $\vec{M1}$ to $\vec{M3}$ are 1, while the strides of $\vec{N1}$ to $\vec{N4}$ are each 4.*

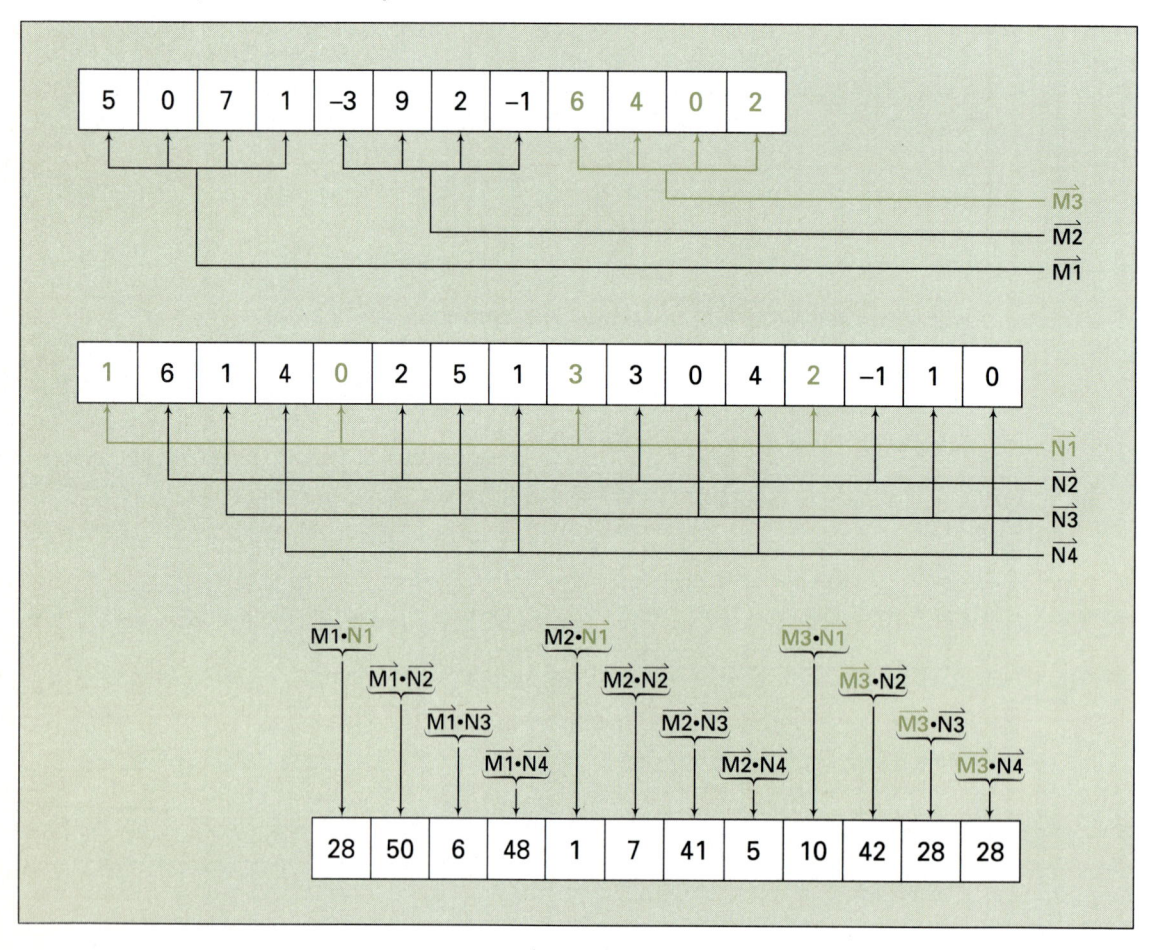

Operands that reside in registers are **register operands**, and those that reside in memory are **memory operands.** In this section we describe how instructions specify register operands.

register operands
memory operands

As discussed earlier, accumulator machines have just one, implicit register operand, which the instructions never specify. When a computer has more than one register of a given type, certain instruction bits select the register for the CPU to use. Register numbers within the instructions select the registers, and these register numbers are called *register designators* or *register addresses*. Computers typically have about 16 (and usually no more than about 64) registers of any given type, so register designators require about 4 to 6 bits each.

## 2.5.2 ■ Boundary Alignment

The CPUs of most computers specify main-memory addresses as byte addresses, rather than word addresses. The storage systems, on the other hand,

**FIGURE 2.22** *Formation of the product of two matrices, $M$ and $N$ by using inner dot products.*

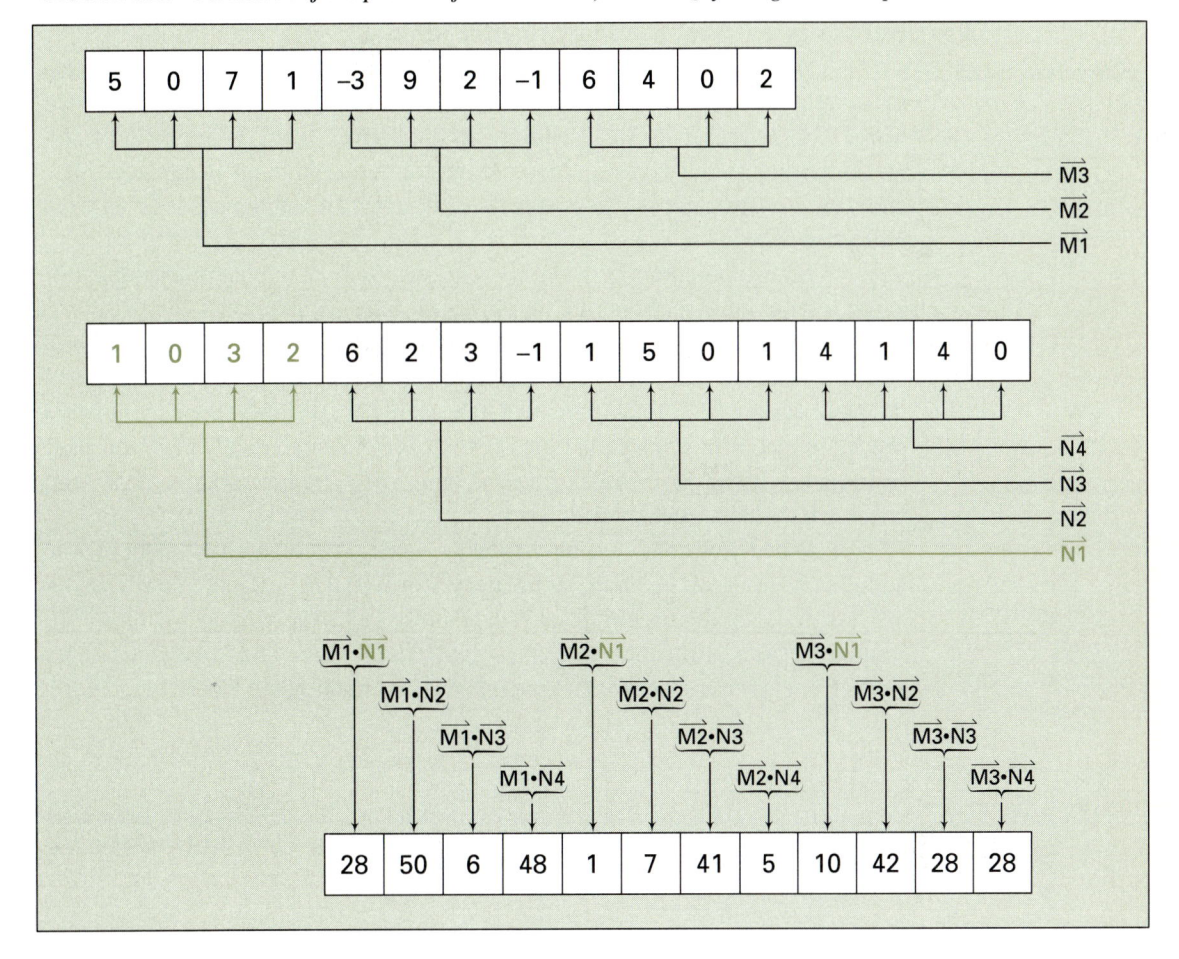

generally use word addresses and store and recall words. Consequently the storage system or CPU requires special circuitry for byte operations.

For example, consider a 32-bit computer that uses byte addresses. Word 0 contains bytes 0, 1, 2, and 3; word 1 contains bytes 4, 5, 6, and 7; and so forth. In this case the word address is simply the byte address divided by 4, which is the same as the byte address with the low-order 2 bits truncated. During a byte-load or byte-store operation, the CPU gives the storage system the word address, which is the byte address with the low-order 2 bits truncated, and the storage system fetches the desired word. The CPU now uses the 2 low-order bits to select the desired byte within the word. For a load operation, the CPU simply extracts the selected byte. For a store operation, the CPU inserts the new byte into the word and returns the modified word to the storage system for storage.

Because storage systems load and store words using word addresses, these addresses are called **word boundaries.** For words that are 4 bytes long, these addresses are 0, 4, 8, and so on. By analogy, **byte boundaries** fall between the bytes of memory. If the memory system uses 8-bit words, then byte boundaries and word boundaries are the same.

Words that begin on word boundaries are **aligned words.** The processor's access to aligned words is generally faster than its access to unaligned words for several reasons. Reading an unaligned word from memory requires reading to adjacent words, selecting the required bytes from each word, and concatenating those bytes together. Writing an unaligned word is even more complex.

Many computers provide instructions, such as double-precision arithmetic instructions, that operate on blocks of data. Doublewords comprise two consecutive words of data, quadwords four words and octets eight words. For a computer whose words contain 4 bytes each, the byte addresses for aligned doublewords are 0, 8, 16, 24, and so forth, as Fig. 2.23 shows. Some computers process memory in units called **pages,** and pages must generally begin on **page boundaries.** If the pages are 512 words long, then the byte addresses of valid pages are 0, 2048, 4096, and so forth.

When a storage system stores a value, it stores that value in one addressable unit of memory, a memory word. Large computers with byte-addressing generally access 4- or 8-byte units from the storage systems.[10] In summary, the significance of byte, word, doubleword, and page boundaries stems from the way specific machine instructions manipulate blocks of memory.

---

10. Some microprocessor-based computers, such as the IBM PC, use storage systems that process bytes. The processor, however, operates on 16-bit (2-byte) words. The computer, therefore, is a 16-bit-word machine that accesses memory in bytes.

## 2.5.3 ■ Memory Addressing

All computers have instructions that reference memory, and we shall describe some of the common memory-addressing techniques in this section. In general, architects develop addressing techniques for a variety of reasons. Some provide efficient hardware support for accessing the elements of an array. Some provide support for passing parameters. Some enable small address specifications to generate large addresses. In general, addressing techniques provide support for more than one function.

**Address Spaces**

When programmers develop programs, they generally use statement labels to refer to instructions and the names of variables or expressions (e.g., an array name with a subscript list) to refer to the variables themselves. Programmers rarely work directly with addresses. When **compilers** convert the programs into machine instructions, they assign addresses to the instructions and variables. These addresses are called **logical addresses,** and they appear within a potentially infinite address space called the **logical-address space. Compilation** is the process of converting the original program into machine instructions, and during compilation the compilers convert the logical addresses into **instruction addresses,** which are specifications for the addresses in terms of the addressing techniques supported by the computer's hardware.

compilers

logical addresses

logical-address space
compilation

instruction addresses

FIGURE 2.23  *Boundaries for a byte-addressed 32-bits-per-word storage system.*

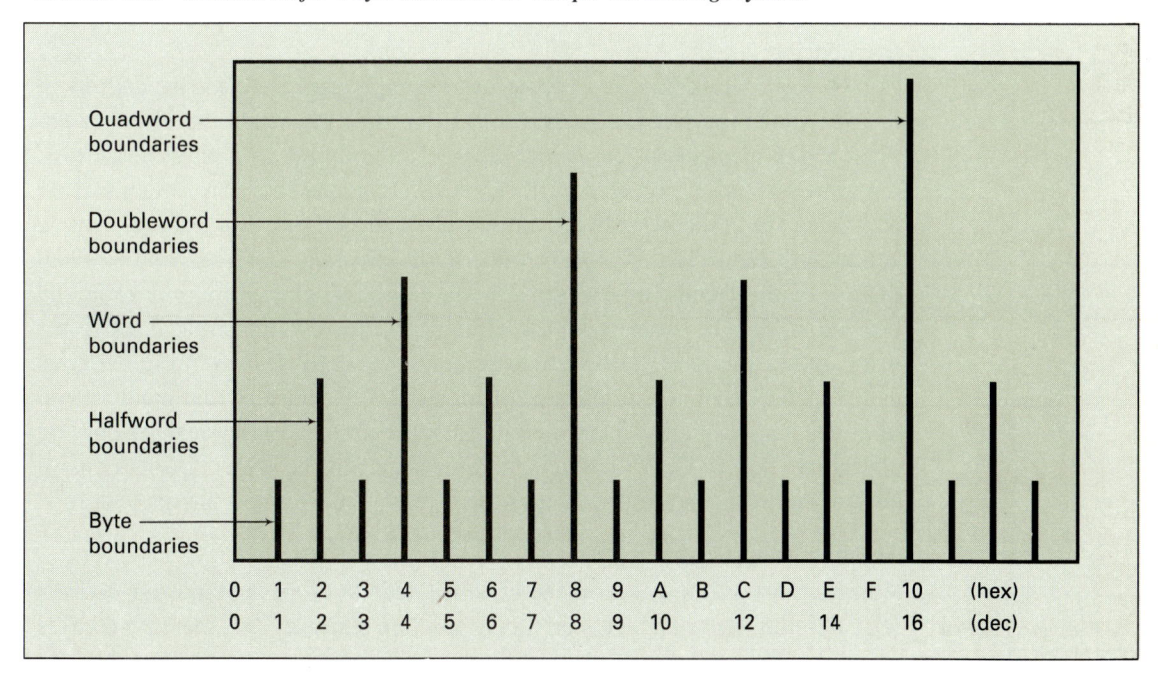

Within a computer, each word in the main memory system has a **physical address,** which is the address that the hardware system uses to access that word, and the space of addresses for a given computer is its **physical-address space.** The physical-address is also called the **main-memory address.** The number of bits in the computer's addressing hardware limits the size of the physical address space, and for a computer that uses byte addresses, an $n$-bit address accommodates a $2^n$-byte physical-address space. For example, a computer that has 20-bit addresses has a $2^{20}$-byte or 1 MB physical-address space. A given computer may have less physical memory, however. Note that there is generally no implied relationship between the logical addresses assigned by a compiler and the physical addresses in main memory.

To execute a program, the operating system first allocates physical memory for the program; that is, it decides where to place the program in the computer's main memory. A **loader,** which is part of the operating system, then loads the compiled program into memory. When loading a program, the loader may need to alter parts of the compiled program, a process called **linking,** so that the instructions' address specifications properly refer to locations where the loader places the program in memory.

During program execution the addressing hardware converts the instructions' address specifications into **effective addresses.** These are the addresses that the CPU uses when referencing an instruction or variable, and in general they agree with the compiler's logical addresses. The process of converting an instruction's address specification into an effective address is called **address resolution,** and the addressing hardware is said to resolve the effective address.

For many computers the hardware simply uses the effective address of a reference as the physical address. That is, the CPU sends the effective address to the memory system, which uses it, unmodified, as a physical address. On some systems, however, additional hardware comes into play, which further translates the effective address into a physical address. For example, some computer systems add a constant value to all effective addresses, and we shall discuss these systems in Section 4.2.1 when discussing program relocation and protection. Some systems map the effective addresses into physical addresses using rather complex hardware maps, and we shall discuss these systems, called **virtual-memory systems,** in Section 4.2.3. Because virtual memory systems can run programs that are larger than the amount of physical memory on a machine, they are said to have **virtual memory.** For the present discussion, we shall assume that the computer uses the effective address as a physical address.

### Absolute Addressing

When an instruction contains the effective address of an operand, the address is an **absolute-binary address** or simply **absolute address.** This memory-address specification is clearly the simplest form of addressing and requires $N$ bits for total access to $2^N$ units of storage. For example, assuming byte addressing, an instruction needs 24 bits to reference 16 MB of memory with absolute addressing. Note that 24 bits is larger than the word size of 16-bit computers.

A closely related technique is **register-indirect addressing,** sometimes called **register-deferred addressing.** For register-indirect addressing the instruction specifies an operational register, which holds the absolute-binary address of the operand. The operational register may be an implicit operand of the instruction or an explicit operand. Figure 2.24 illustrates absolute-binary addressing and register-indirect addressing.

When a computer allows register-indirect addressing, the program generates the address of the operand and places it in an operational register for later use. That address is then available for subsequent LOAD and STORE instructions; therefore the CPU does not need to recompute it each time the program uses it. For these reasons RISC computers often use this technique.

*register-indirect addressing*
*register-deferred addressing*

**FIGURE 2.24** *Absolute addressing. (a) Absolute-binary addressing. (b) Register-indirect addressing.*

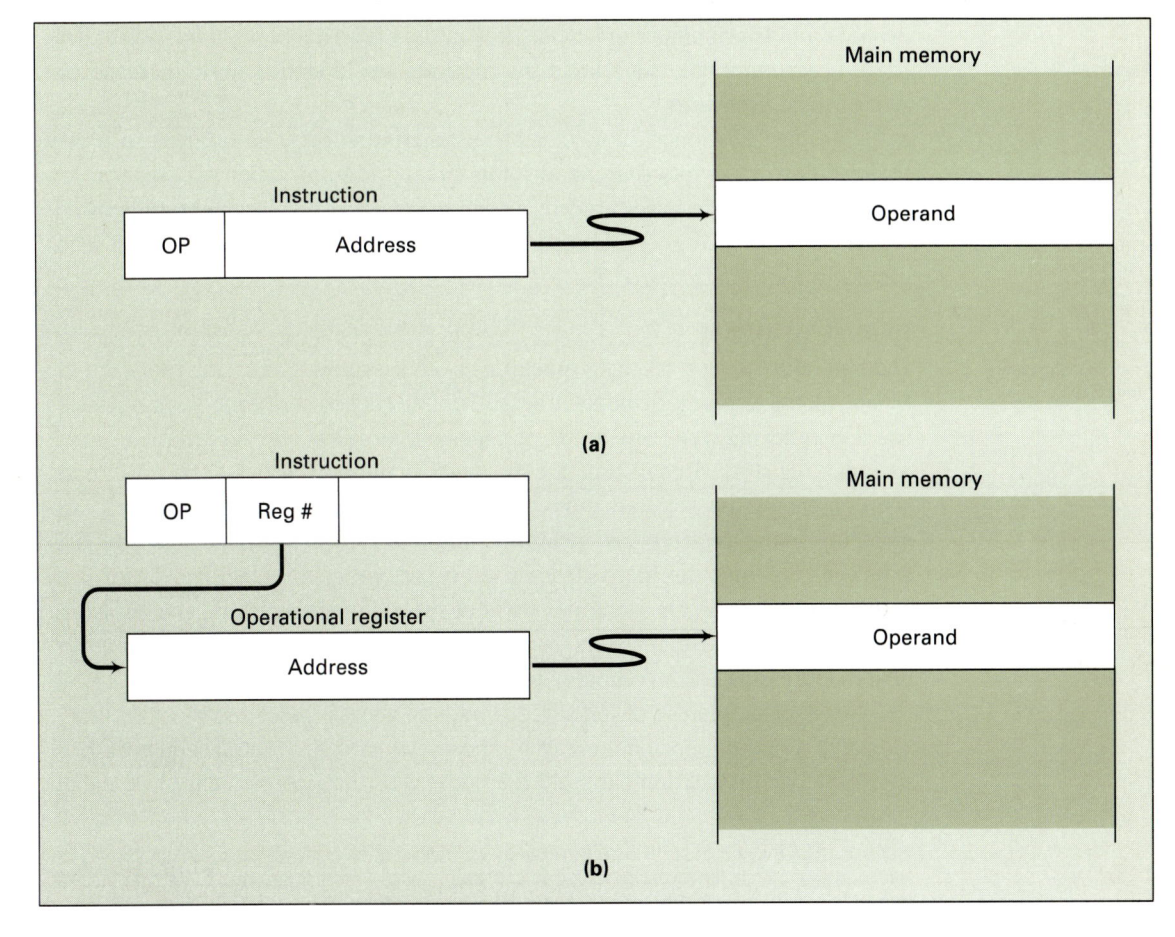

Many small computers have special short instructions that have only enough bits to address part of main memory. An 8-bit address field within the instruction is typical, and the instruction can therefore reference only the low-order 256 bytes of memory (bytes 0 to 255) when using absolute-binary addressing. On these small machines, memory is logically divided into 256-byte pages, such that the low-order 8 bits of an address give the word number on the page and the high-order bits give the page number. Addresses from 0 through 255 are all on page 0, addresses from 256 through 511 are on page 1, and so forth. Because the short instructions can only reference data on page 0, they are called **page-0 instructions.** In general page-0 instructions are 2 bytes long, the first byte is for the op code and the second is for the address.

Current computers typically have at least 1 MB of main memory, so the absolute-binary addresses of memory operands are generally at least 20 bits long. Further, except for a few of the smaller PCs, current designs allow 16 MB or more, commonly several gigabytes (GB) of memory. Thus main-memory addresses tend to be between 20 and 32 bits long. Let us suppose an instruction holds the absolute-binary address of its operands. If it had an 8-bit op code and two memory operands, it would have to be 48 to 70 bits wide. The need to accommodate such large instructions would significantly increase the size of most programs.

The question is, how can an instruction specify an address in a way that requires fewer bits than an absolute-binary address? There are several answers. One is to use page-0-indirect addressing, base-displacement addressing, segmented addressing, or PC-relative addressing. We shall explore these techniques in the remainder of Section 2.5.3.

**Indexed Addressing**

**Indexed addressing** (or simply **indexing**) is an essential addressing mode for efficient access to array elements, and all computers provide some form of indexing. For indexing, the register set provides one or more registers that can serve as index registers. Recall that for an indexed memory access, the CPU adds the content of the selected index register to the address specified in the instruction. Index registers are generally numbered from 1 to $N - 1$, where $N$ is a power of 2, and the instructions use an index-register specification of 0 to specify no indexing. On machines without special index registers, the hardware uses general-purpose registers as index registers. Figure 2.25 illustrates indexed addressing for a computer with eight index registers.[11]

A principle use of index registers is to access the elements in an array. Consider a one-dimensional array A whose elements are stored sequentially in memory. The instruction can hold the address of the first element of A, called

---

11. Note that the index register 0 cannot serve as an index register. However, most machines that have index registers have one because it can hold index values temporarily. Programs must move the value into another index register, however, for use.

the address of the array, and an index register, say I, can hold the subscript of the array element. Indexing hardware then computes the address of A(I) automatically.

**Indirect Addressing**

Many computers have instructions that use memory cells to hold the addresses of operands. In this case the effective address specifies a cell in memory, and that memory cell holds an **indirect address.** The indirect address is the operand address, so this type of addressing is called **indirect addressing** (Fig. 2.26). Note how similar indirect addressing is to register-indirect addressing. When using indirect addressing, the CPU must read and resolve the indirect address to get the address of the operand. This requires an extra main-memory access and is therefore slower than the other addressing techniques mentioned earlier.

Branch instructions sometimes use indirect addressing. An indirect branch through address 123, for example, would not branch to the instruction at address 123; instead, it would branch to the instruction whose address is held by memory location 123, as Fig. 2.27 shows.

indirect address
indirect addressing

FIGURE 2.25  *Indexed addressing. One field of the instruction, labeled I, holds an index-register designator. The computer adds the value in the selected index register (register 4 in the figure) to the address in the instruction to obtain the effective address of the operand. In this figure the effective address is also the physical address.*

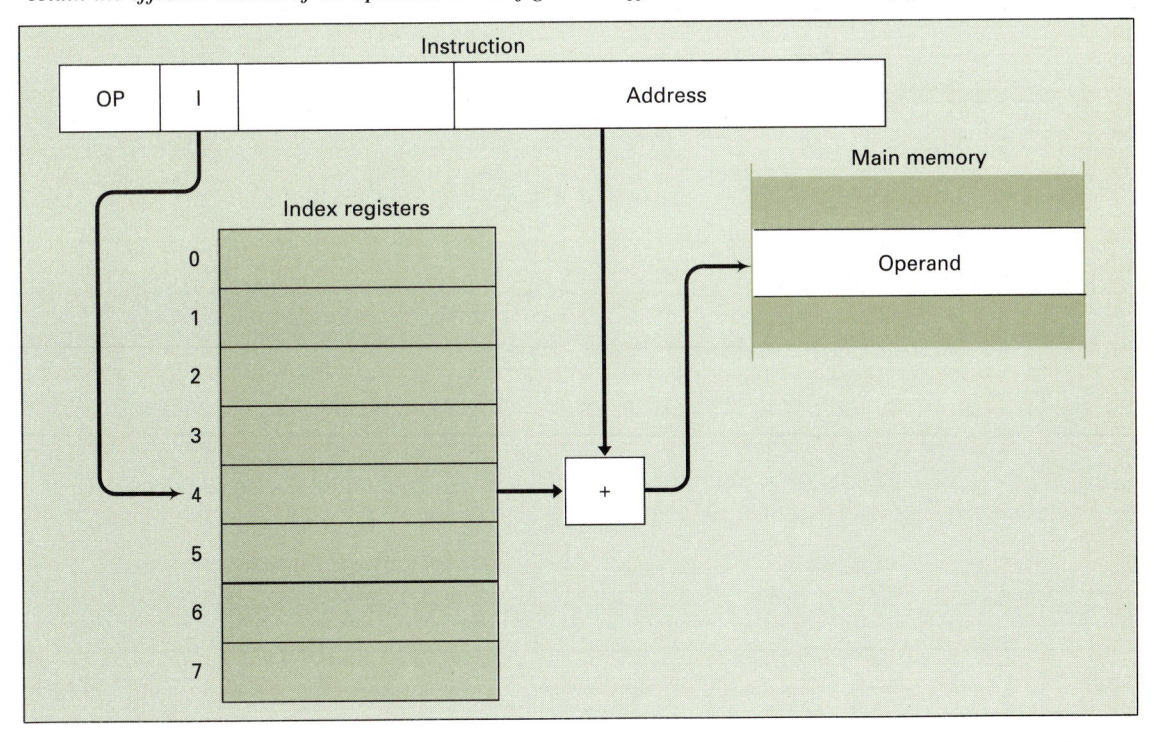

**FIGURE 2.26** *Indirect addressing.*

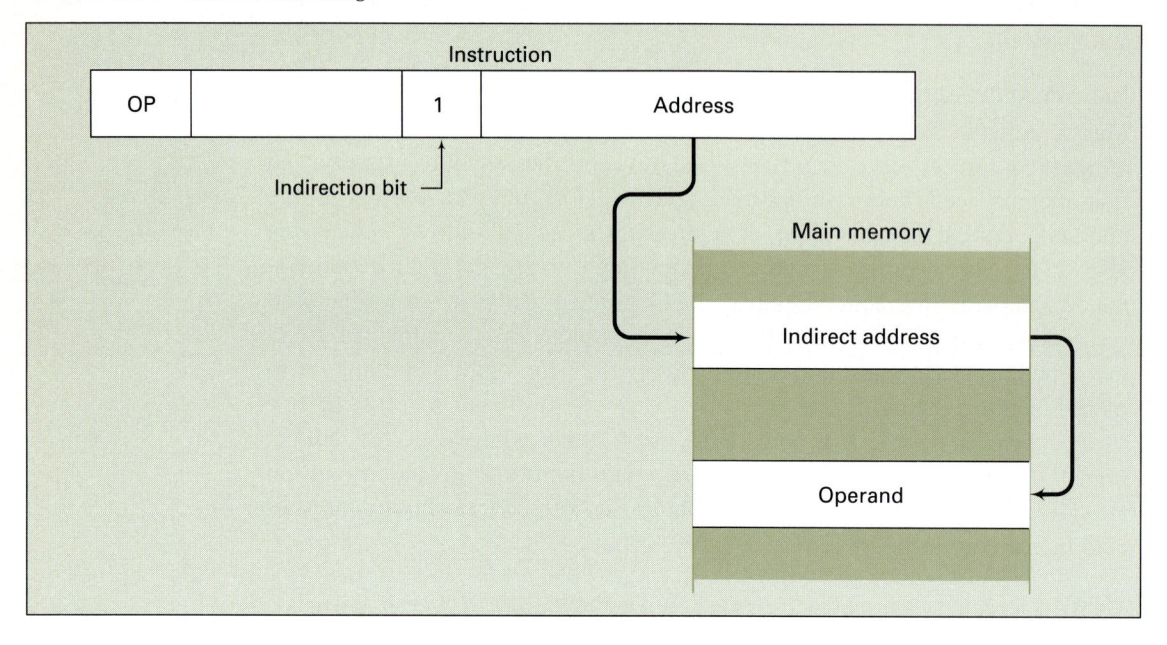

**FIGURE 2.27** *An indirect branch through address 123.*

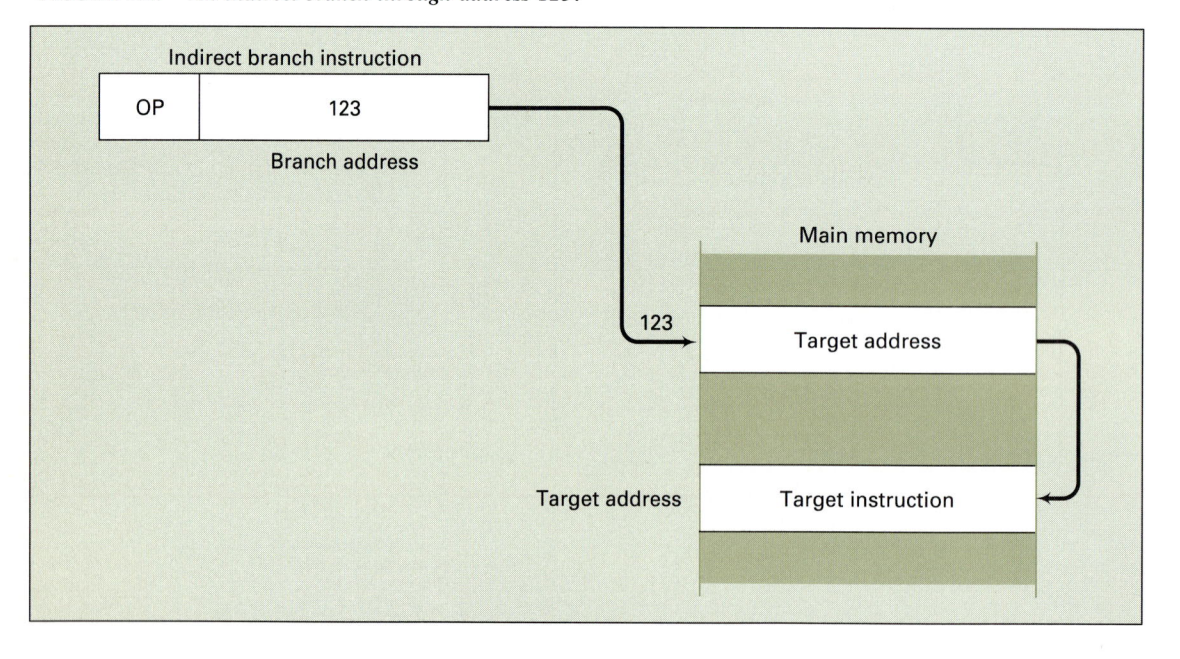

Most computers allow at most one indirect address in a given branch operation; however, some computers allow any number of indirect addresses. When a computer allows **multiple levels of indirection,** a bit in each address specification indicates whether this address is the final address in the indirection chain. For indirect referencing, each address specification might be absolute, indexed, or some other type. Architects now consider indirect addressing with multiple levels of indirection to be obsolete because of the inefficiency.

*multiple levels of indirection*

Many early 8- and 16-bit microprocessors had special instructions, called **page-0-indirect instructions,** for referencing operands indirectly. These instructions were limited; they could specify only the words on page 0 as indirect addresses. Those page-0 words could then hold a full 16-bit address and reference all of main memory. Since an address specification within page 0 requires only 8 bits, a 16-bit page-0-indirect instruction can access 64 KB of main memory if one assumes an 8-bit op code.

*page-0-indirect instructions*

### Indexed-indirect Addressing

**Indexed-indirect addressing** combines both indexed addressing and indirection. For indexed-indirect addressing, the CPU may hold the indirect address in a register or in main memory (Fig. 2.28). Indexing may precede (**preindexed indirect addressing**) or follow (**postindexed indirect addressing**) the indirect referencing. When indexing precedes indirection, the instruction specifies an

*indexed-indirect addressing*
*preindexed indirect addressing*
*postindexed indirect addressing*

**FIGURE 2.28** *Preindexed-indirect referencing. Compare with Fig. 2.25 and 2.26.*

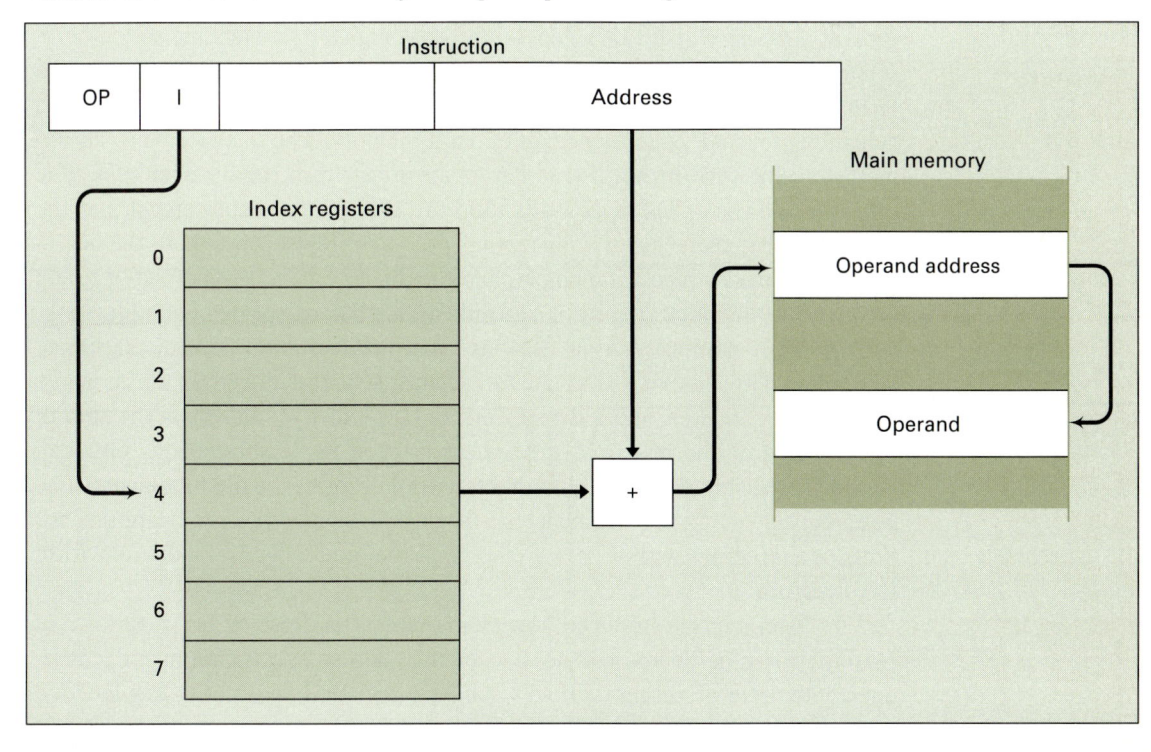

index register and an address. The CPU adds the content of the index register to the address in the instruction to get the operand address. When indexing follows indirection, the CPU resolves the indirect address and then adds the content of the index register to it to get the operand address.

Systems often use indexed-indirect addressing for branching to exception handlers, and the exceptions are then called vectored exceptions. (An exception handler is a program that assumes control after an exception and processes the exception. See Chapter 3.) The operating system assigns each exception handler a number, say $N$. It also maintains a branch-address table and places the address of procedure $N$ at offset $N$ within the table. (An **offset** value is a displacement of a word within a page, or other data structure.) A program wishing to branch to an exception handler references it by number. For example, suppose the operating system placed the branch-address table at address $A$ in main memory. Further suppose that the address of procedure $N$ is $AN$, which is also the $N$th entry in the table. A program wishing to jump to procedure $N$ would execute an indirect jump to $A$ indexed by $N$.

Many RISC machines support register-indirect and indexed register-indirect addressing, which is similar to indexed-indirect addressing except that a register holds the indirect address, for the reasons described earlier. A related form of addressing is base-displacement addressing, which we describe next.

**Base-displacement Addressing**

**Base-displacement addressing** resembles indexed addressing. A **base register** holds an effective address, called a **base address.** The base register may be a general-purpose register on a general-purpose register-set machine. A memory-referencing instruction specifies both a base register and a **displacement.** The term *displacement* is used rather than *address* because, unlike an address, it is generally too small to reference all of main memory. The displacement, an immediate value within the instruction, is an offset from the base address. The effective address of the operand is then the sum of the displacement and the content of the base register. Conceptually the base register points to the beginning (or base) of a block of memory, and the displacement is the offset of a data area within the block. Figure 2.29(a) illustrates base-displacement addressing.

Most computers that use base registers combine base-displacement addressing with indexing (Fig. 2.29b). Each instruction specifies a base register, an index register, and a displacement. The effective address is the sum of the contents of the base and index registers and the displacement. One can view base registers as dividing main memory into pieces, called **segments.** The base register points to a segment, the displacement specifies the beginning address of a structure within the segment, and the index specifies a datum within the structure.

Architects introduced base-displacement addressing for a number of reasons. First, it decreases the size of an address specification and consequently the size of an instruction. Each base register can point to any location

FIGURE 2.29  *Base-displacement addressing. (a) Without indexing. (b) With indexing. B = base register, I = index register, D = displacement.*

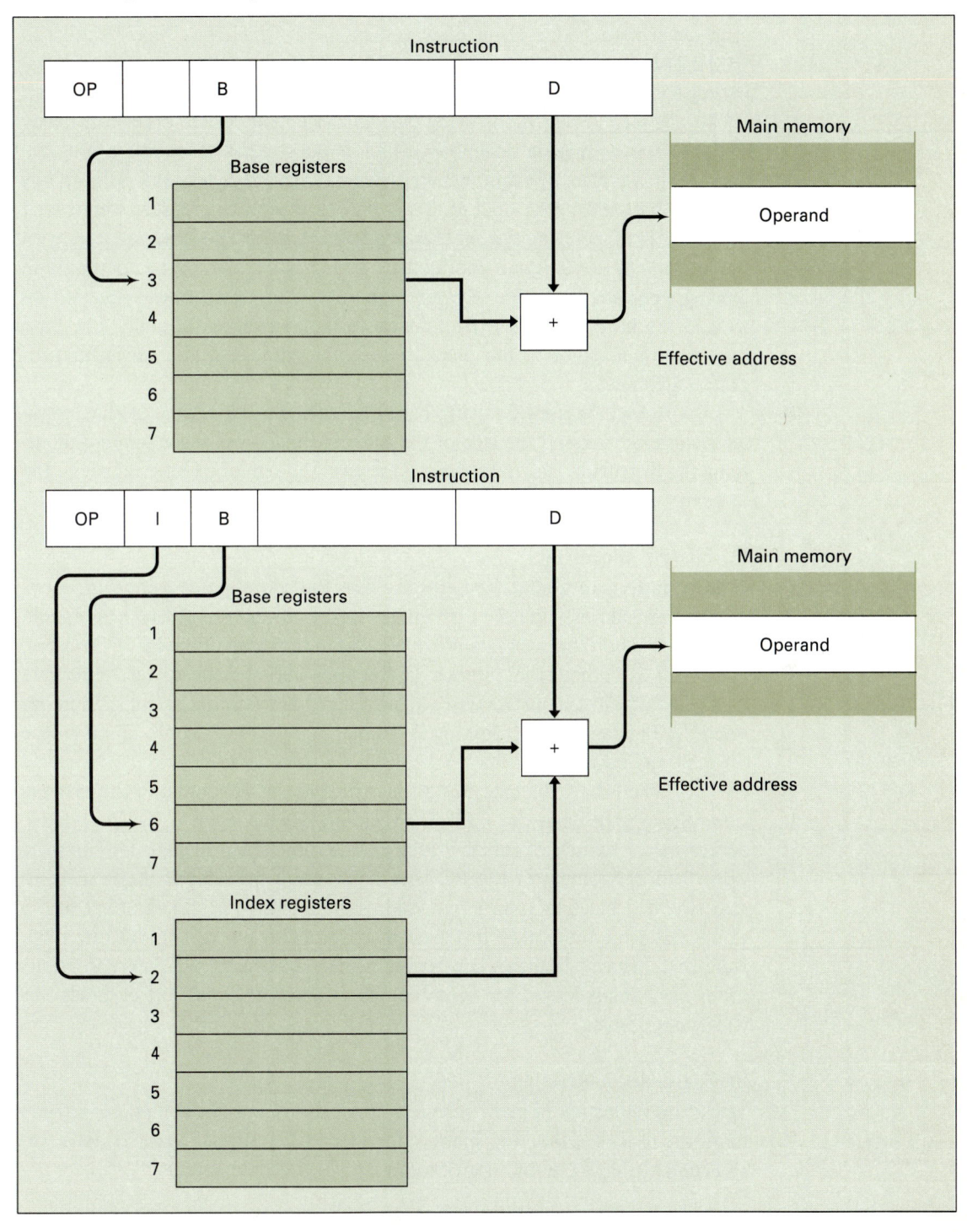

in memory. Using a base register, a given instruction can access any word in memory regardless of how large or small the displacement is. For example, when IBM first introduced base-displacement addressing with its System/360, each instruction had a 12-bit displacement field, which was small relative to IBM's 24-bit addresses. Most RISC machines use base-displacement addressing for the same reason.

A second reason for using base-displacement addressing is to provide initial or **static program relocation,** which is the process of loading a program at an arbitrary place in main memory. Because base registers can point to any location in memory, the operating system can place the program wherever it needs to. The operating system then loads the appropriate base registers with the location of the program and its data, and transfers control to the program. During program execution the program uses the LOAD ADDRESS instruction to load the base registers with pointers to its own pieces of code. The base registers, then, point to the blocks in memory that hold the executing program segments.

A final reason for using base-displacement addressing is that architects can easily extend the size of the computer's address space without modifying the instruction set. They simply increase the size of its base registers. the longevity and success of the IBM System/360 is a tribute to this fact.

### PC-relative Addressing

In **PC-relative addressing** the hardware uses the address in the program counter as a base address, and the instuction specifies its operand (usually a branch-target instruction) by giving its offset relative to the value in the PC. PC-relative addressing is common for branch instructions and sometimes for immediate data (data within the instruction stream), but this technique is considered obsolete for data addressing: Mixing code and data makes program maintenance difficult and costly.

When the CPU executes an instruction, the PC points to the instruction *following* the one the CPU is executing. Hence when using PC-relative addressing, a branch offset of 0 implies that no branch occurs. (Adding the value 0 to the content of the PC does not cause a branch.) If the branch instruction is 3 bytes long on a byte-addressed machine, a branch offset of −3 would reexecute the branch instruction and probably result in an infinite loop. Note that, because branches are generally made to nearby locations (programs often have small loops, for example), branches with small offset fields are widely applicable.

### Stack-register Addressing

Stacks are important in many software applications, but few computers provide hardware stacks. However, many computers have special **stack-register instructions** to facilitate the use of main memory to hold stacks.

When a computer's hardware has a stack register, or has general-purpose registers with stack instructions, the stack register holds a main-memory address. A STORE instruction that uses the stack register implies a PUSH operation. A LOAD operation that uses a stack register implies a POP operation. Figure 2.30 illustrates these concepts.

FIGURE 2.30 *The* PUSH *and* POP *operations on a stack in memory. (a) The initial situation for a* PUSH *operation. When the computer executes* PUSH *A, it first decrements the S register (b) and then copies the value in A into memory (c). (d) The initial situation for a* POP *operation. When the computer executes* POP *A, it first copies the value from memory into A (e) and then increments S (f). The shaded area shows the extent of the stack in memory, and $V_i$ designates the ith value in the stack.*

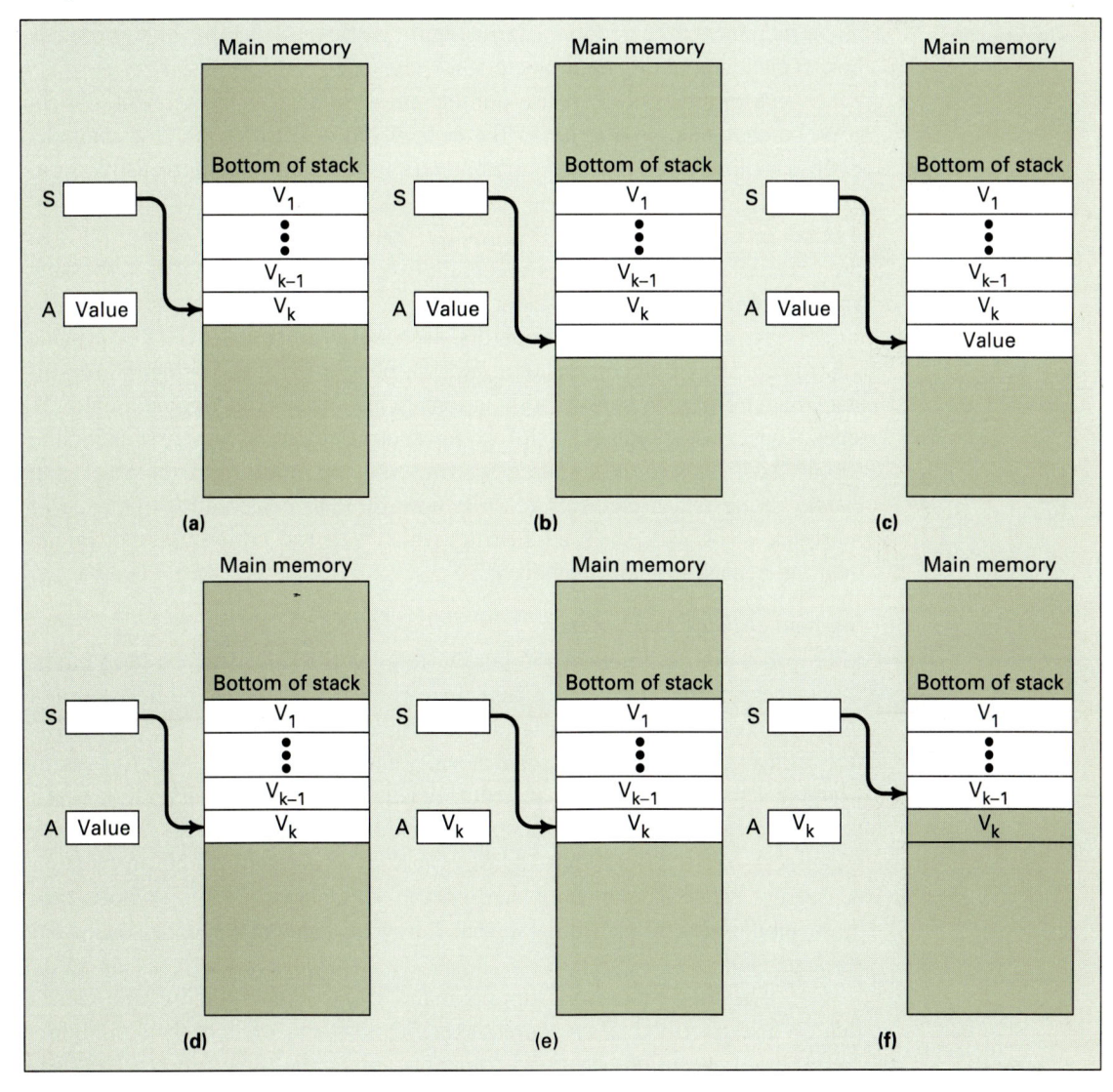

Notice that **stack-register addressing** is a form of register-indirect addressing: except during stack addressing, the hardware automatically increments or decrements the indirect address. The following addressing modes support this concept.

### Autoincrement and Autodecrement Addressing

Some computers provide special addressing modes that automatically increment or decrement the indicated index register. **Autoincrement** and **autodecrement addressing** help the programmer implement stacks in main memory and to sequentially access the elements in linear structures, among other uses. Most frequently the autodecrement addressing mode decrements the register address before using it (**predecrementing**), and the autoincrement addressing mode increments the address after using it (**postincrementing**). That is exactly how typical computers manipulate stack registers.

A programmer can use autoincrement addressing to sequentially access the characters in a string or the elements in a vector or list. For example, when a calling program passes parameters to a called procedure using a parameter list, it usually sends the address of the parameter list to the called subroutine in a register, called the linkage register. The called subroutine can then reference the parameters sequentially by using autoincrement addressing and specifying the linkage register.

As an aside, some computers, such as the Burroughs B-1700, provide a hardware stack that consists of a fixed number of registers. Using the top-of-stack register (tos) as a destination automatically pushes the argument onto the stack, causing other values to shift to lower stack registers. Similarly, using the top-of-stack register as a source removes the top value from the stack and causes deeper stack elements to shift upward. (Do not confuse this type of hardware stack with stack addressing, which aids the programmer in implementing a stack in main memory.)

### Segment-register Addressing

Microprocessors in Intel's 80x86 family (refer to the *Case Studies*) have modified somewhat the technique of base-displacement addressing and introduced a technique called **segment-register addressing.** (Segment-register addressing differs from segmentation, a virtual-memory technique that we will discuss in Chapter 4.) Intel introduced segment-register addressing for several reasons: (1) to increase the size of the physical-address space from 64 KB (16-bit addresses) to 1 MB (20-bit addresses), (2) to maintain 16-bit instruction addresses, which is the word size of the CPU, and (3) to promote program modularity by providing special hardware support for code, data, and stack segments.

The Intel processors support many of the standard addressing modes that we just described. Each address specification selects one of them, and during program execution, the CPU computes an address, now called a **CPU ad-**

**dress,** just as it would an effective address if it did not use segment-register addressing. The CPU then converts the CPU address into an effective address as follows.

Each processor has four special-purpose registers, called **segment registers,** which hold the base addresses of four segments. The addressing circuitry selects a segment register based on the type of memory access (e.g., instruction fetch, operand fetch, or stack access) and determines the effective address by adding to the CPU address a quantity equal to 16 times the content of the selected segment register (Fig. 2.31). Because multiplication of a binary value by 16 is equivalent to shifting it to the left by 4 bits and inserting $0000_2$ on the right, the final effective address is a 20-bit address instead of a 16-bit address.

segment registers

The difference between segment-register addressing and base-displacement addressing lies in the fact that the processor *automatically* selects a segment register and pads its content with $0000_2$ on the right. The effective address is a 20-bit address, which can accommodate a 1-MB address space, 16 times bigger than what a 16-bit address alone can accommodate. In essence, a 16-bit segment register holds a 20-bit base address, which is always divisible by 4 (i.e., it has four low-order 0 bits).

One chief difference between segment-register addressing and base-displacement addressing stems from the fact that segments are much larger

**FIGURE 2.31** *Segment-register addressing. The instruction contains a 16-bit address. The CPU adds the content of a segment register (the third one in this figure), extended to 20 bits by padding on the right with $0000_2$, to the instruction address to form a 20-bit main-memory address.*

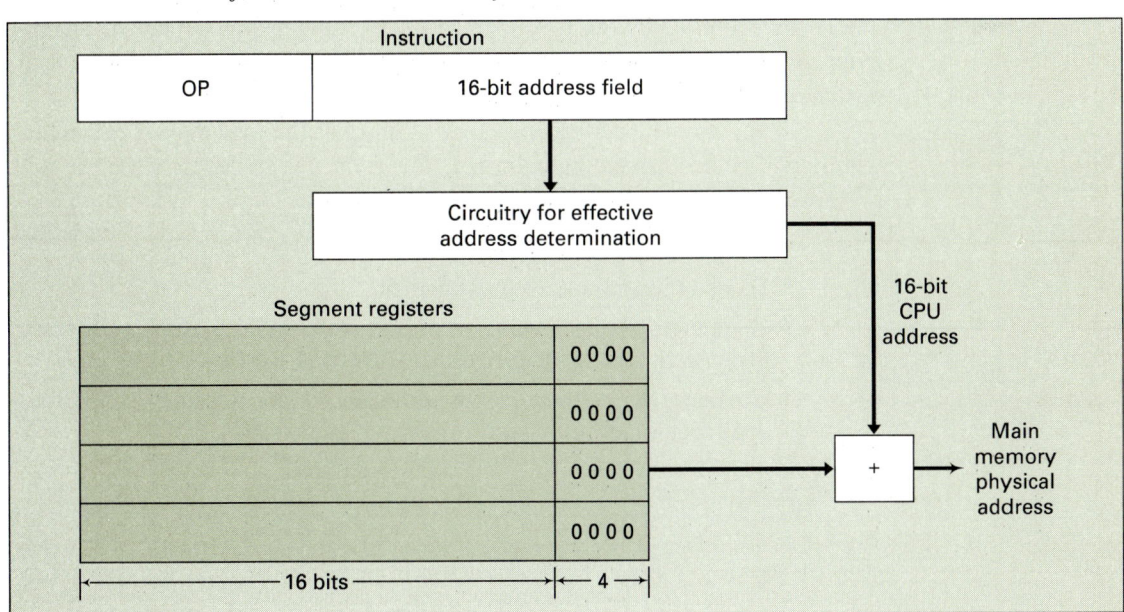

than the segments of memory that base registers reference. Consequently programmers have tended to use different programming techniques when working with segment-register addressing systems than when working with base-register systems.[12] In particular, 64 KB of memory was large enough for many programs, so programmers (or more accurately, old compilers) often used segment registers to relocate the programs in memory. In particular, they viewed memory as having a 64-KB program segment, a 64-KB data segment, a 64-KB stack segment, and an extra 64-KB segment. If a program grew larger than 64 KB, the programmers were forced to alter them in nonuniform ways.

In contrast, when programmers started to use systems with base registers, there was little chance that a program could fit within the address space spanned by one base register. Thus the programmers and compilers were forced at the outset to view memory as one large uniform address space and to use the base registers in a systematic way to reference all of main memory.

### 2.5.4 ■ Addressing Design Issues

Architects consider many features of addressing when designing computers or computer families. We shall discuss three of them here: addressing range, addressing homogeneity, and addressing efficiency.

**Physical-Addressing Range**

One key parameter of a computer family's expandability, and hence of its architectural merit, is its **physical-addressing range.** This refers to the maximum size of memory that the computers of a family can have, which is limited by the number of bits in the physical address. In contrast, **virtual-addressing range** refers to the maximum number of logical addresses a user can specify, and hence is limited by the ISA. The actual physical-memory space of a computer can be larger than the virtual-addressing range if the computer uses various virtual-memory techniques (discussed in Section 3.2.2).

If the physical-addressing range is limited, the longevity of the architecture will be correspondingly limited. The following trends increase the importance of having a large physical-addressing range.

- Programs are becoming larger and more sophisticated.
- Databases continue to grow in size.
- Computers are increasing in power, which allows users to increase array sizes and strive for results with finer resolution.
- Computer users tend to buy as much memory as they can afford and, over time, to expand it as much as possible.

*physical-addressing range*

*virtual-addressing range*

---

12. This situation has changed, in part because programs have grown so complex that 64 KB simply is not adequate for them. Newer compilers now use segment registers the way previous compilers used base registers, and the programs view the address space as a large uniform block.

- The unit cost of memory continues to decrease as technology improves.

For these and other reasons the amount of physical memory in computers is expected to continue growing. It follows that a large physical-addressing range is important for the survival of a family architecture.

Historically the inhibiting factors to having a large physical-addressing range have been cost and expandability. In contrast, current large computers have on the order of 250 MB of main memory and an addressing range of a few gigabytes. Thus there is still some room to grow. However, the usefulness of the memory depends on how easily programs can access it, and larger physical-addressing ranges bring with them increased problems in access. Thus you can see that the addressing range is also an issue in ease of use.

With base-displacement addressing (or relocation-register addressing, as described in Section 3.2), it might appear that an architect can make the physical-address space arbitrarily large by merely increasing the width or precision of the base registers. There are, however, some hidden limits that are worth exploring. Most computers with base-displacement addressing depend on an operating-system utility to move programs that are already in memory to other memory locations in order to make room for other programs, as shown in Fig. 2.32. However, if for any program the computer has only one register for address relocation, then there is no way for the operating system to move programs to arbitrary places in memory. This inability effectively limits the types of useful memory-allocation policies, and hence the program mix, that the operating system can support.

With paged memory-management systems (see Chapter 4), the page-table output, which provides the high-order bits of the address, can be made arbitrarily large and can, clearly, span all of any memory, so the difficulty we noted would not arise. However, here too there are problems. Page-table entries contain a variety of information in addition to the physical-page number. Typically, they include "dirty" bits, protection bits, use bits, and a program identifier. For many computers, page-tables entries are over 20 bytes long for each page of main memory. The operating system must have access to the entire page table at certain times, which places a hard limit on the maximum size of main memory.

### Addressing Homogeneity

A uniform, or homogeneous, address space is one of the major ease-of-use features of a computer's instruction set (see Section 1.3.4). In **homogeneous addressing,** all addresses are preferred equally, whereas in **inhomogeneous addressing,** some addresses are preferred over others. When an address space is inhomogeneous, programmers and compilers must adapt the addressing they generate to the inhomogeneities in the address space. Special cases of this sort increase the complexity of compilers.

homogeneous addressing

inhomogeneous addressing

What factors affect addressing homogeneity? We shall first look at an example. Most computers have an indexed-addressing mode (see Fig. 2.25). The CPU adds the instruction displacement to the content of an index register to obtain the effective address of the operand. If the displacement is small—say, on the order of a few bytes—then compilers will attempt to use it only as an offset into a small data structure (much smaller than a segment). For example, the compiler may use it to point to a specific character in a short string, or to point to the low-order part of a multiple-precision quantity.

FIGURE 2.32 *Memory map. The shaded areas represent programs that are in some state of execution, and the blank areas are free. Notice the three small programs in the middle that could be moved to make room for another large program. One could be moved to the top of physical memory, and two could be moved to the bottom. However, the operating system, like all single programs, cannot reference a region of memory larger than the virtual-address span, so without using external storage, it cannot move the small programs to make room for a large program.*

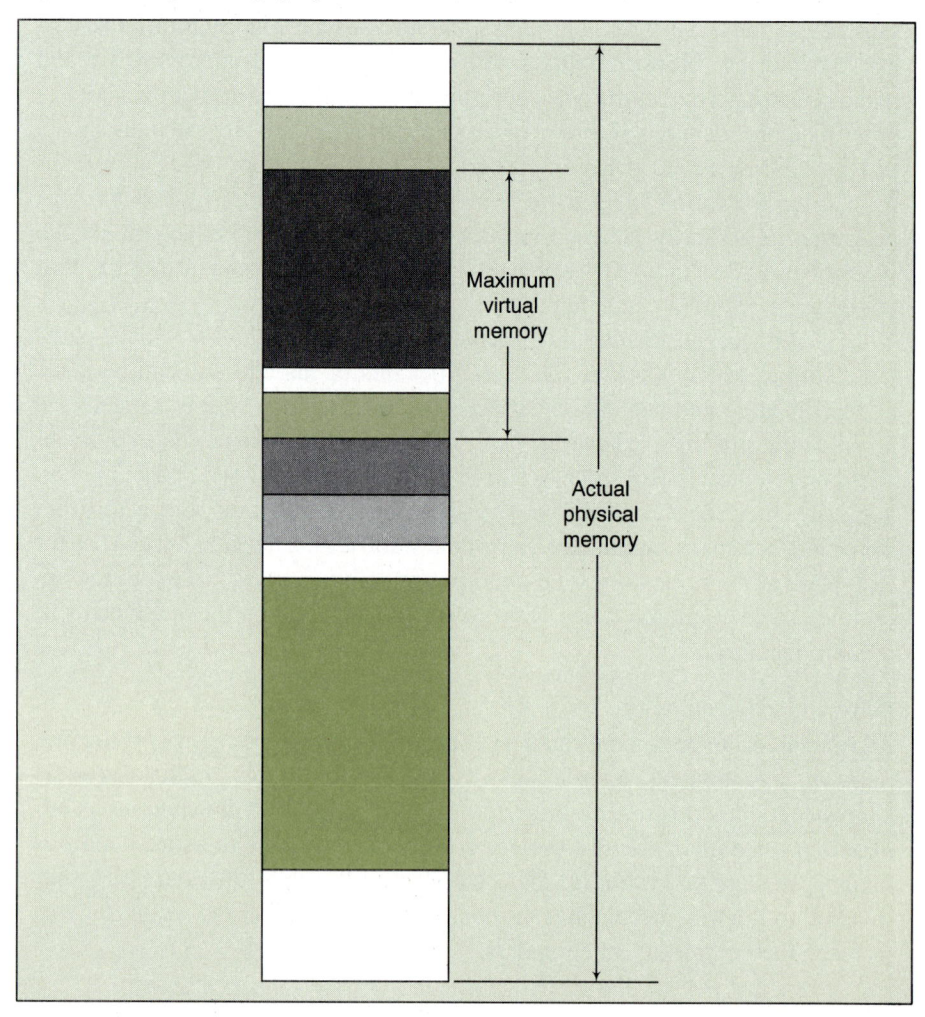

If, on the other hand, the displacements are big enough to reference large blocks of data or entire programs, then compiler writers may try to use the displacements as addresses (i.e., without using an index register at all), rather than as displacements. This use of displacements for general addressing creates problems when programmers use blocks of data or programs that exceed the size of the displacement. For example, some computers have 16- to 22-bit displacements. These displacements are large enough to serve as base addresses for small programs. As the programs grow, however, the compiler writers are faced with the onus of modifying the addressing scheme to allow for arbitrary-size (or at least larger) blocks.

As another example, suppose the instruction set provides instructions with small displacements, say 8-bit displacements, and the compiler uses them to reference the bytes in a string. If the programming language allows strings to have more than 256 characters, the compiler must use an addressing scheme for the strings that exceed 256 (i.e., $2^8$) characters that differs from the one used for smaller strings.

When designing an ISA that has instructions with large displacements, the architect should design the instructions so that the displacement is large enough that the memory size cannot outgrow it. Otherwise the architect should move the displacement from the instruction to a register and have the instruction designate the register. The displacement will then be the same size as all other parts of the address. Alternatively, at the expense of some minor inefficiency, the architect can provide instructions that have displacements of several sizes. The compiler can then use the largest displacements unless told to optimize, in which case it can easily check for the smallest instruction that will hold the required displacement.

In both cases the compiler writer is presented with a difficulty because there are hidden inhomogeneities in the address space. The small-displacement case is not so severe because small displacements can span many types of variables and the compiler writer should recognize its limitations. Moderately sized displacements are insidious because some compilers can overlook them, but they present definite limitations in any case.

### Addressing Efficiency

**Addressing efficiency** refers to how effectively a programmer or compiler can use the addressing modes specified for an ISA. RISC architectures provide a few simple addressing modes, while CISC architectures provide many, often complex, addressing modes. In this section we discuss design tradeoffs an architect must consider when choosing addressing modes for an ISA.

*addressing efficiency*

An architect must consider two issues from an implementation standpoint: ease of implementation, and cost of implementation with a concern for overall machine performance.

As the control units of computers became more sophisticated, architects tended to include more and more addressing modes with each new ISA.

The VAX family, for example, includes almost every addressing mode so far discussed, and others: indirect, register indirect, autoincrement, autodecrement, autodecrement deferred (indirect), indexed, indexed deferred, and others. These addressing modes provide the user with adequate means of referencing data, but the resulting instructions require many clock cycles to execute, and several of them require multiple memory accesses. Furthermore, compilers rarely use the more complex addressing modes; moreover, programmers can implement them in software if they are truly needed. Often they are redundant: a programmer can use many different addressing modes to achieve the same result.

As speed becomes important, an architect must consider how costly an addressing mode is with respect to overall machine performance. When an addressing mode takes many clock cycles to execute, or it requires several memory accesses, it may be difficult to implement in a pipelined processor. If an addressing mode is used only occasionally, it may be more efficient to let the software implement it, rather than the hardware. Architects of the fastest RISC machines have found that a few addressing modes are adequate, and they usually include direct, register indirect, and base-displacement addressing (which substitutes for indexed addressing). We shall discuss these and related issues more fully in Chapter 6, when we discuss pipelining.

## 2.6 ■ Instruction-set Design

Architects consider many features of instruction-set design when they develop computers or computer families. For an initial design, a primary concern is that the instruction set be complete—that there be no missing functionality. A second concern is that the instructions be orthogonal, that is, not unnecessarily redundant. For a new computer in an existing family, a primary concern is compatibility—that programs used by one computer be able to run on another. For architectural longevity, expandability of the physical-addressing range and homogeneity of the address space (discussed in Section 2.5.4) are both important design issues. Finally, we conclude this chapter with a brief look at some issues related to the instruction format, which plays an important role in the ease of implementation of the ISA.

### 2.6.1 ■ Completeness

complete instruction set

What makes for a **complete instruction set** is not well defined, and there are many degrees of completeness that we shall describe. At the most basic level, because NAND gates are sufficient to implement all boolean and arithmetic operations, they suffice for all computer operations.[13] Correspondingly, a conditional branch instruction that also saves the PC content suffices for all con

---

13. See Appendix B for a discussion of NAND gates and other digital components.

trol flow in a computer. Thus it is possible to design a complete instruction set with a single instruction that combines a NAND, a conditional branch, and a program counter (PC) save operation. Generally, however, completeness implies that the CPU can complete each basic operation with a single instruction or short sequence of operations. This implies that the set of datatypes is rich enough to accomplish all the operations that are required of a general-purpose computer and that the instruction set includes instructions for all the basic operations.

It is probably more eluciating to give some examples of incompleteness than to try to define completeness more precisely. Architects targeted the CDC 6600 for floating-point number crunching, so it has no instructions for string operations or for decimal arithmetic. From this point of view the CDC 6600 does not have a complete instruction set. For its targeted use, however, the lack of string and decimal instructions probably would not render the instruction set incomplete in the minds of most architects.[14]

This computer's instruction set can be considered incomplete in the area of subroutine linkage as well. Following is a specific example. The single CDC 6600 subroutine linkage instruction is RETURN JUMP TO EPA, where EPA is the entry-point address of the called subroutine. (Refer to the Case Studies for a general discussion of the CDC 6600.) The RETURN JUMP TO EPA instruction operates as follows. Let RA be the return address—that is, the address of the instruction following RETURN JUMP TO EPA (Figure 2.33). Upon executing RETURN JUMP TO EPA, the control unit stores an unconditional branch instruction (GO TO RA) at EPA. It then fetches the next instruction from EPA + 1. When it finishes executing, the called subroutine returns to the calling procedure by executing an unconditional branch to its own entry point address (i.e., GO TO EPA). Figure 2.33 shows the return statement as the last statement in the called subroutine. Since the RETURN JUMP TO EPA instruction modifies the called procedure's code, programmers cannot use it to implement reentrant or recursive subroutine linkages. Yet it is the only subroutine linkage instruction that the CDC 6600 provides. In the view of most computer architects, the lack of an easy way to build a recursive subroutine renders the instruction set incomplete.

see Case Study 2

Incompleteness is a serious problem for a computer, but is one that admits a number of interesting solutions. For example, many early computers provided an EXECUTE instruction, a special type of instruction that has now fallen into disfavor. EXECUTE causes the computer to execute a single instruction at a specified memory address (or perhaps in a specified register). If the executed instruction is a successful branch, the program branches to the target of the branch. Otherwise it executes the instruction and then proceeds with

---

14. For applications requiring character strings there are a number of ways to implement them on the CDC 6600. Thus the lack of string-processing instructions represents an ease-of-use issue more than a completeness issue. Refer to Section 1.3.4.

the one following EXECUTE. The usual use of EXECUTE was to allow programmers to incorporate into their programs any unimplemented instructions, that is, instructions the designer chose not to, or forgot to include in the instruction set.[15]

Most computers today use a trap for unimplemented instructions (see Section 3.2.3). If the trap branches to a user procedure, then the user can write routines that implement those operations that are unavailable in the machine's instruction set. In this way the user can make a program think the computer has more instructions than are actually available. Few computers provide a trap to the application program; most make the trap pass through the operating system, which adds so much time as to make this technique suitable on only rare occasions.[16]

Computer architects today regard EXECUTE as obsolete. Architects now have enough experience in most areas to be sure that their instruction sets are complete. On occasion, however, we note that architects may intentionally

---

15. As an example use of EXECUTE, the shift instructions on some computers required the shift count to be in the instruction itself. If the shift count was not known at the time of compilation, the programmer had to build in memory a SHIFT instruction with the correct shift count, and then use EXECUTE on it.
16. The IBM PC (refer to Chapter 5), for example, supports a floating-point coprocessor, which extends the instruction set to include floating-point instructions. Computers without a floating-point coprocessor can still execute the code by trapping the instructions and transferring control to software procedures that implement the floating-point operations. However, the resulting execution is slower than that for code that does not assume the existence of the floating-point coprocessor in the first place. Moreover, programs that can run with or without the coprocessor must be designed with that option in mind, and consequently they run more slowly than do similar programs without that option.

---

**FIGURE 2.33** *Subroutine linkage used by the CDC 6600.*

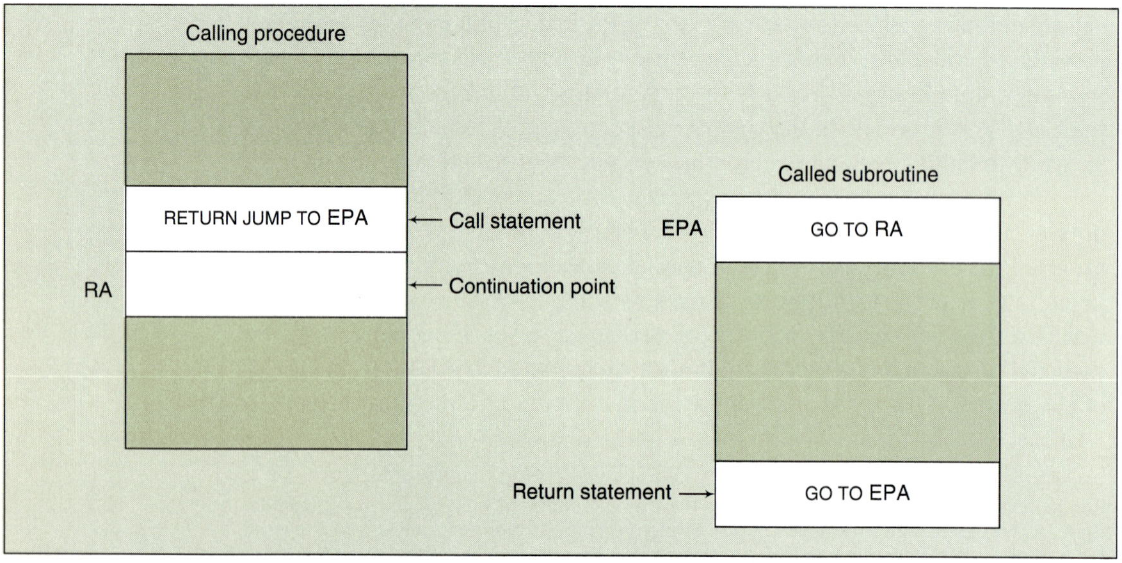

omit instructions if they would be too costly or inefficient to implement in hardware, or they would be used so infrequently that a software implementation would be acceptable.

## 2.6.2 Orthogonality

Related to completeness is **orthogonality**, which is the property of instruction independence. More explicitly, an instruction set is orthogonal if there is only one easy way to do any operation. For example, programmers can use the basic boolean operations to implement arithmetic operations, but the execution time for the resulting operations would be very great. Consequently the existence of arithmetic instructions in addition to boolean operations does not violate orthogonality. Similarly, programmers can implement floating-point operations with integer and shift operations, but for the same reason the presence of both floating-point operations and integer operations does not violate orthogonality. As an aside, most large computers allow the addition of floating-point hardware to support floating-point instructions.

*orthogonality*

As before, examples of nonorthogonality will help to clarify this concept. Many computers have multiple addressing modes, and generally there are a number of ways a program can address any given datum. For example, a program can use indexing, indexing with postincrementing, or indexing with preincrementing on a machine with those addressing modes. The proper choice depends on the type of optimization (space or time) and degree of optimization that the programmer desires for the program.

Completeness and orthogonality influence compilers in many areas and also affect the architectural merit of the computer (see Sections 1.3 and 1.4). If an instruction set is not complete, the compiler must insert sequences of code instead of single instructions for common operations. Although this is not difficult for a compiler, it presumably does slow execution and increase code size. Lack of orthogonality in an instruction set means that the compiler has a number of ways to generate code for common operations. If optimization is requested, it must check all the possibilities and select the best. Thus, a good optimizing compiler must have tables of all the alternatives for these common sequences so that it can select the optimal one for the situation at hand.

From a computer designer's standpoint, lack of orthogonality means that there are more instructions to implement and check. In addition, these extra instructions generally slow the computer, because they require extra hardware, so the machine is at least a bit larger and thus slower. We shall discuss this issue further in Section 6.3, where we shall examine RISC machines.

## 2.6.3 Compatibility

Like orthogonality or completeness, compatibility has many degrees; to a large extent it is in the eye of the beholder. Figure 2.34 shows a model for the steps required to generate a result on a computer, beginning with an idea and ending

**source-code compatibility**

**object-code compatibility**

with the execution of a program. A computer system can achieve compatibility of computation at many levels in the model. With **source-code compatibility** programs will execute on different computers provided the programs are recompiled, relinked, and reloaded for the target machine (the particular machine on which the programs are to run). With **object-code compatibility** programs will execute on different machines without being recompiled or relinked. However, it is important to understand that user programs generally start much farther to the right in this model (requires fewer steps) than do operating-system programs.

As an example, some families, such as the VAX and IBM System/370 families, can generally move executable code from one family member to another; other families require varying degrees of reprocessing, starting at earlier or farther-left points in Fig. 2.34.

As mentioned in Chapter 1, the machines of a family are upward compatible if programs that run correctly on one family member also run correctly on more advanced members of the same family. They are forward compatible if programs that run on one family generation also run on a later family generation (the reverse is not necessarily true). Nearly all IBM System/360 programs run on IBM System/370 computers, for example.

**portability**

As a final note, compatibility and **portability** are similar concepts. Portability refers to the property of a program that enables a user to run it on different (incompatible) hardware systems. If a program depends on specific characteristics of a computer's hardware, it will not be very portable. With reference to Fig. 2.34, portability requires recompilation of the source code (and everything to the right of compilation). The goal of standardizing high-level languages is to provide a platform for writing portable software, but ultimately portability depends on how faithfully the compilers for the language adhere to the language standard and how well the programmers avoid hardware-dependent features of the language, if indeed there are any.

Some features that affect portability are the availability of consistent datatypes and the availability of standardized operating systems for maintain-

FIGURE 2.34 *Generation of results by a computer. A designer can achieve compatibility at many levels. Source-code compatibility requires recompilation and execution of all operations illustrated to the right of "Compile" to move a program from one computer to another. Object-code compatibility requires only reloading of the program. User programs generally fall farther to the right on this diagram than operating system programs.*

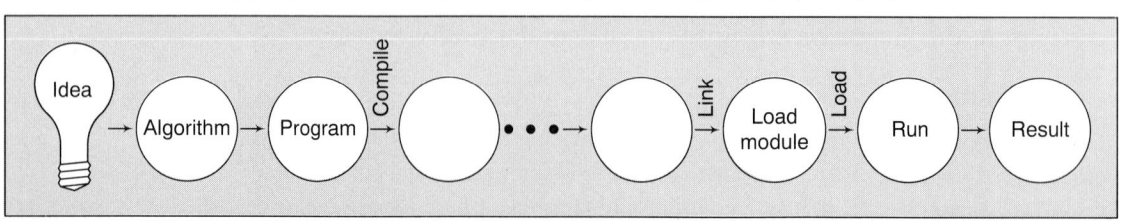

Idea → Algorithm → Program →[Compile]→ ... → [Link]→ Load module →[Load]→ Run → Result

ing the data files. The use of a common numeric representation, such as the IEEE floating-point standard, makes the job of writing portable numeric software much simpler, and the acceptance of a common operating-system environment, such as UNIX, generally simplifies the process of sharing data files.

### 2.6.4 ■ Instruction Formats

An **instruction format** refers to the way the fields within the instructions appear in memory and how they encode the op codes and operands. We shall briefly discuss these issues here.

*instruction format*

Instruction-set architects must weigh a number of factors when designing instruction formats, including the use of more than one instruction length. Short instructions require less memory, but they also provide fewer bits for encoding op codes, immediate operands, and address specifications. One can provide instructions of several lengths to reduce the demands on memory, but the result is an increased complexity within the control unit, which must analyze and execute the instructions.

The op code generally appears first in the instruction. For instruction sets with several instruction sizes and formats, the op code specifies the instruction size and format. Thus, the control unit first analyzes the op code and then interprets the remaining fields. For small instructions, in particular, architects often use special coding techniques for reducing the number of op code bits, thus providing the maximum number of remaining bits for other essential information.

Consider a 16-bit instruction format with a 4-bit op code. With 4 bits, the designer can specify 16 op codes, a number that is too small for most instruction sets. However, using a 4-bit op code, the designer can assign 15 op codes to those instructions that require the largest number of remaining bits for other information (e.g., immediate operands and absolute addresses), and use a single op code, say $F_{16}$, to indicate that the next 4 bits give additional op code information. If there are less than 31 instructions in the ISA, the second 4 bits are enough, but for larger instruction sets, the designer can again use 15 op codes to specify instructions and a single op code to specify that the following 4 bits contain additional op code information. Using this technique, a 16-bit instruction word can specify 61 op codes.

When instructions must select registers for operands and results, there is little choice in the method of encoding the register number. For a machine that has $2^N$ general-purpose registers, an instruction requires an $N$-bit register specifier. If the instruction specifies two source registers and one destination register, the designer must provide $3 \times 2^N$ instruction bits for those specifications. However, the placement of those fields within the instruction may be an important design consideration. If a large number of instructions have similar register specifications, the architect can simplify the design of the control unit by placing them all in the same relative field positions. The control unit can then use those bits to control the register-select circuitry. Most instruction-set designers use this technique in some form or another.

see Case Study 5

Instructions in CISC computers often need to specify thousands of combinations of op codes and addressing modes. The VAX is the extreme case. It specifies op codes in a uniform way, and each op code indicates the operation and number of operands for the operation. However, the op code does not specify the addressing modes of the operands. Rather, the address specification for each operand begins with a field that indicates whether it uses indexing. The next field, a mode specification, indicates what the addressing mode is for that operand. Several fields may follow the mode specification for each operand address, depending on the mode. The result is that the control unit must sequentially analyze each instruction field, because the op code no longer specifies the length or organization of the instruction. The instruction decoding process therefore takes many clock cycles, and consequently, architects have found it difficult and costly to pipeline the instruction decoding process.

# Summary

This chapter has focused on the instruction sets of simple computers. First we described data representations, precision, and datatypes followed by the basic machine concepts of register sets and instructions. We then described types of instructions, addressing techniques, and the flow of control of a program. We concluded with a brief general discussion of instruction-set design.

All instructions have an op code and most specify one or more operands. The types of instructions reflect structure and usage. Instructions can be classified according to the number and types of operands they specify (0-address, 1-address, 2-address instructions, etc.). They can also be classified according to their usage: operate (arithmetic, logical, shift, character and string processing, vector operations), memory-access instructions, control instructions (including branch instructions), and privileged instructions.

The addressing techniques provided the programmer with alternative ways of specifying the operands of an operation. Some addressing techniques, such as autoincrement and autodecrement, in addition provide support for implementing stacks in memory. Others (indexed and indexed indirect) provide efficient ways of accessing items in data structures, such as arrays.

Branch instructions provide the programmer with mechanisms for implementing loops and for structuring programs. Simple conditional branches provide a variety of mechanisms for loop control; branch instructions that save the content of the PC provide the basic facility needed for subroutine linkage. Moreover, hardware mechanisms for swapping the runtime state of a program provide the operating system with important facilities for interrupt and task management.

The design of an instruction set is an important part of the ISA of a machine, and three properties give a measure of the effectiveness of the design: completeness, orthogonality, and compatibility. Completeness measures how easily programmers can specify all basic operations; orthogonality measures how many ways they can do so; and compatibility gives a measure of how similar different computer's instruction sets are.

Another design dimension is addressability, and two properties of importance are addressing range and addressing homogeneity. The expected life of a computer family architecture depends on how large the memory can be and how easily a program can address all of that memory. Families with large maximum address ranges should outlive families with smaller ones.

The feature that is important for applicability is completeness. Generality also requires completeness, but usually contradicts orthogonality, generally requiring multiple nuances of many instructions. For efficiency, orthogonality is commonly required, because excess and complex instructions tend to slow a system, as well as making very small systems difficult to use. Ease of use is the same as completeness, as the terms are used in this text.

# Exercises

*2.1* With 8-bit bytes, how can you represent more than 256 characters? More that 512 characters?

*2.2* The EBCDIC character representation does not represent the letters in one continuous binary sequence. For example, the representations for the letters I and J are not adjacent. State two ways this might affect software design.

*2.3* Which of the following three representations for the value of $28.0_{10}$ has the greatest precision? Explain your choice.
- a. $0.0034_8 \times 8^4$
- b. $0.0340_8 \times 8^3$
- c. $0.3400_8 \times 8^2$

*2.4* What is the scientific-notation analog of an unnormalized number?

*2.5* Why might computer architects choose floating-point notations that separate the sign bit of the number from the rest of the mantissa?

*2.6* What are the values of the following B-5500 floating-point numbers (flag and tag fields omitted)?
- a. $202\,0000000005120_8$
- b. $376\,0000000000001_8$
- c. $001\,0000000000001_8$

*2.7* What are the values of the following Cyber 170 floating-point numbers?
- a. $3777\,0000000000000001_8$
- b. $1772\,0000000000000001_8$
- c. $7777\,7777777777777777_8$
- d. $4000\,0000000000000000_8$

*2.8* What are the values of the following 32-bit IBM floating-point numbers?
- a. $\text{7F FFFFFF}_{16}$
- b. $40\,100000_{16}$
- c. $\text{BF}\,100000_{16}$
- d. $\text{BF FFFFFF}_{16}$

*2.9* Show how DEC would represent the following values using the F-floating-point datatype:
- a. $+1$
- b. $-1$
- c. $653 \times 2^{65}$
- d. $-17 \times 2^{-43}$

*2.10* Suppose that you are supposed to design a floating-point number system for a 32-bit computer for the Marketeers Information Processing System Co. that is required to have 8 decimal digits of accuracy and a numeric range of $10^{-25}$ to $10^{25}$. What representation would you use? How much worse than the marketing department's requirement is your choice?

*2.11* What are the advantages and disadvantages of using radixes other than 2 for floating-point numbers?

*2.12* Why is the IEEE excess-1023 exponent representation preferable to an excess-1024 exponent representation when the mantissa is fractional (between $\frac{1}{2}$ and 1)? (*Hint:* Consider what happens when small numbers underflow and when large numbers overflow.)

*2.13* How big is the alphabet that can be represented on an old standard IBM card, in which each column has 12 positions for holes to be punched but only two holes can be punched in any single column?

*2.14* Draw figures like those in Fig. 2.7 for the following additional parameter-passage methods:
   a. Use a parameter-address list and pass the list's address to the called procedure.
   b. Push the parameters in the stack.
   c. Use a parameter-address list and place it in memory immediately following the subroutine call instruction.

*2.15* Typewriters typically have 45 to 50 keys. Design a 6-bit typewriter code, and define the escape sequences.

*2.16* PC ATs generally have 101 keys of which seven are shift keys of one sort or other (Left Shift, Right Shift, SHIFT Lock, Alt, Ctrl, Num Lock, and Scroll Lock). Given that keyboard I/O is 8 bits wide, define a keyboard code for I/O on a PC AT.

*2.17* Assume that the IEEE 32-bit floating-point format is extended to a floating floating-point format with the 4 extra exp2 bits taken from the mantissa and that the value of radix2 is 16. Although Fig. 2.8 does not show the exponent biases, both exponents must have them. Assume that the exponent biases give approximately the same exponent range above and below zero. What is the range of exponents and what is the largest value that exponents can represent?

*2.18* Describe one way to make the floating floating-point representation unique. In other words, give an analog of normalization for this representation.

*2.19* Using the following instructions, write a program to compute $AX^2 + BX + C$ and put the result in the accumulator. Assume A, B, C, and X are stored at addresses with the same names. You may use memory location T to hold a temporary value.

| 1 LOAD Acc ← M | Load the accumulator with the content of memory location M. |
| 2 STORE M ← Acc | Store the content of the accumulator at memory location M. |
| 3 ADD Acc ← Acc + M | Add the content of the accumulator to the content of memory location M, and put the result in the accumulator. |
| 4 MULT Acc ← Acc × M | Multiply the content of the accumulator with the content of memory location M, and put the result in the accumulator. |

*2.20* Using the following two instructions, show how to set and clear arbitrary bits of register R without altering any other bits (#N indicates an immediate constant whose value is $N$).

| 1 AND R ← R AND #N | Register R gets the logical AND of the content of register R with the value $N$ (probably expressed as a hexadecimal). |
| 2 OR R ← R OR #N | Register R gets the logical OR of the content of register R with the value $N$ (probably expressed as a hexadecimal). |

*2.21* Show how to use MATCH AND REPLACE instead of TEST AND SET.

*2.22* Show how to use FETCH AND ADD instead of MATCH AND REPLACE.

*2.23* Show how to use SEND and RECEIVE instead of FETCH AND ADD.

*2.24* There are many ways architects might define and implement SEND and RECEIVE. In particular, they must specify what the CPU should do when SEND attempts to store a value in a full cell and when RECEIVE attempts to read a value from an empty cell. Define a set of instructions that allows several variations, and show how they can be useful for detecting various programming errors.

*2.25* Using IBM's COMPARE AND SWAP (CS) synchronization primitive, show how to synchronize processors so that no two of them can execute critical sections at the same time. The CS instruction specifies two registers (R1 and R3 in this example) and a memory location using base-displacement addressing. The assembler format of a CS instruction is
   CS R1, R3, (B2, D2)   or   CS R1, R3, <loc>,
where <loc> designates a memory location. CS compares the fullword value in memory with the value in register R1. If they are equal, the comparison succeeds, in which case the CPU replaces the prior value in memory with the value in R3 and sets the condition code to 0. Otherwise the comparison fails, in which case the CPU loads the memory value into register R1 and sets the condition code to 1.

*2.26* When different iterations of the same loop are independent of one another, it is possible on a multiprogramming system to let different processors execute them. These are called parallelizable program loops. Here is an example:

**do** (I = 0, 99)
  A(I) ← B(I) + C(I)
**repeat**

This loop assigns B(I) + C(I) to A(I) for each of the 100 values of I. Assuming A, B, and C designate nonoverlapping blocks of memory, each loop iteration is independent of the others. Show how to use FETCH AND ADD to implement this multiprocessing program loop. Your code should not depend on the number of processes.

*2.27* Give two advantages to using a stack instead of a save area (an area in memory for saving values) for subroutine linkage.

*2.28* Write a loop to compute X!, which is defined as $X \times (X-1) \times (X-2) \times \cdots \times 1$ using a conditional branch instruction. Assume that register R1 holds the initial value of X.

*2.29* Suggest how to use the same stack for passing parameters and for holding return addresses.

*2.30* Describe addressing modes that would facilitate having stacks grow from low addresses to high addresses in memory.

*2.31* Suppose a stack grows from high addresses to low addresses. What is the lowest address that the stack can start at if it is to have at least 256 entries?

*2.32* What facilities do users need in order to prevent stack overflow and to prevent the reading of an empty stack?

*2.33* How many instruction bits are required to specify two operand registers and one result register in a machine that has 16 general-purpose registers?

*2.34* How many instruction bits are required to specify three memory addresses in a machine with 64 KB of main memory? Articulate your assumptions.

*2.35* Von Neumann designed one of the earliest computers, the IAS. The IAS was an accumulator machine that had no index registers, but it did have instructions for modifying the address fields (bits 8 to 19) of instructions in memory. Words were 40 bits long. Instructions were 20 bits long; thus two instructions fit in each word. Instructions consisted of an 8-bit op code and a 12-bit absolute-binary address as illustrated:

| 0 | 7 8 | 19 20 | 27 28 | 39 |
|---|---|---|---|---|
| OP | Address | OP | Address |  |

Write a program that adds the elements of one array to those of a second array and places the results in a third array. You may use the following IAS instructions, where X is the absolute address in the instruction, X[a:b] designates the field of X from bit *a* to bit *b*, where bit 0 is on the left, and Acc is the accumulator:

| | | |
|---|---|---|
| LOAD | Acc ← [X] | [X] designates the content of memory location X, |
| STORE | [X] ← Acc | |
| STORE | X[8:19] ← Acc[28:39] | These instructions modify the address fields of word X in memory. |
| STORE | X[28:39] ← Acc[28:39] | |
| ADD | Acc ← Acc + [X] | This is one of eight arithmetic instructions. |
| GO TO | PC ← X, LOW | This is an unconditional branch to the low-order instruction at the branch-target address. |
| GO TO | PC ← X, HIGH | This is an unconditional branch to the high-order instruction at the branch-target address. |
| GO TO IF | Acc ≥ 0 PC ← X, LOW | These are the two conditional branch instructions. |
| GO TO IF | Acc ≥ 0 PC ← X, HIGH | |

*2.36* List three uses of the indexed-indirect addressing technique shown in Fig. 2.28. List three uses for postindexed-indirect addressing.

*2.37* Draw a figure similar to Fig. 2.28 that illustrates postindirect indexing.

*2.38* Refer to Fig. 2.30, and note that PUSH decrements register S before it stores A, and POP increments register S after it accesses A. Describe how to perform PUSH using a procedure that stores A before decrementing S and describe how to perform POP using a procedure that accesses A after incrementing S. Explain how these differences affect stack management.

2.39 Show how to implement parameter passage using a parameter list.

2.40 Show how to implement parameter passage using a parameter-address list.

2.41 Show how to implement parameter passage using a stack to hold the parameter list.

2.42 Show how to implement parameter passage using a stack to hold a parameter-address list.

2.43 Base-displacement addressing is the normal adressing mode on the IBM System/370 family. Describe how compilers for a System/370 computer should use the base registers and the displacements for accessing data. (*Hint:* Consider how a program might access items of data in blocks that are larger that $2^N$ elements, where $N$ is the number of bits in the displacement field of an instruction.)

2.44 Let A be a three-dimensional array, and let registers R1, R2, and R3 hold the subscripts of an array element. Suggest a way to arrange the elements of A in main memory, and give an algorithm for computing the index of element A(R1, R2, R3).

2.45 Classical von Neumann machines allow users to modify their own programs. Give four reasons why this is not a good idea.

2.46 In the design of a new 32-bit computer, International Electronics decides that its new machine must conserve op-code space. It has decided to reserve 1000 op codes for the machine but wants most of the op codes to be only 6 bits long. Describe an op-code format for this new machine.

2.47 To handle opinion data, which so often asks for a "yes," "no," or "don't care," the Galloping Computer Company is building a computer with ternary (base-3) logic. Each memory *tryte* holds $N$ *trits*, whose values are 0, 1, or 2. How big should $N$ be so that each tryte can hold at least 256 different values?

2.48 Name three typical uses and three typical restrictions of the following forms of constants. Name three advantages of each.
  a. immediate constants
  b. constants in ROM memory
  c. constants in memory that the loader stores there

2.49 Some early microprocessors could only afford to provide a shift by a single bit position. How long could it take to normalize the result of a floating-point multiplication? How long for the result of a floating-point addition?

2.50 The MAX instruction puts the maximum of registers $R_1$ and $R_2$, say, into $R_3$. How useful would a MAX instruction be? What types or uses of branch instructions might it replace in actual programs?

2.51 Show how to implement floating-point instructions using only integer arithmetic. (Thus floating-point instructions are not strictly necessary for a complete instruction set.)

2.52 Show how to implement integer instructions using only boolean operations. (Thus integer instructions are not strictly necessary for a complete instruction set.)

2.53 Using a load-and-store instruction set and a machine with general-purpose registers, show how to implement stack operations using only simple operations. (Thus stack instructions are not strictly necessary for a complete instruction set.) Carefully define your stack characteristics.

2.54 Consider a simple load-and-store instruction set that includes both JSR (R, SUB) and RET (R), where JSR (R, SUB) saves the content of the next PC in register R before branching to SUB, and RET (R) branches to the address in register R. Show how to implement subroutine-linkage instruction for recursive subroutines using only simple instructions plus JSR and RET. Assume that the subroutines can have up to $N$ arguments. (Thus complex subroutine linkage instructions are not necessary for a complete instruction set.)

2.55 This problem illustrates how a word-oriented CPU might implement a MOVE STRING operation. Use the following word-operand instructions (and others) to write a program that places in register R the 4-byte field beginning at the third byte of the word at address A. Note that the desired field overlaps a word boundary.

| | |
|---|---|
| LOAD   R ← [A] | Load register R with the content of memory location A. |
| STORE [A] ← R | Store the content of register R at memory location A. |
| AND   R ← R AND #N | Register R gets the logical AND of the content of register R with the value $N$ (expressed as a hexadecimal). |

OR  R ← R OR #N | Register R gets the logical OR of the content of register R with the value N (expressed as a hexadecimal).

**2.56** Some early computers had shift instructions that used the instruction's displacement field to specify the shift amount. For such a machine, give three ways to program a shift operation where the shift amount is not known until execution time.

**2.57** The original IBM PC had no hardware for memory protection. How does this omission make the instruction set incomplete?

**2.58** What are the key differences between a trap and a subroutine call?

**2.59** The various types of addressing that one can imagine include:

1. absolute binary (the code contains the address)
2. indexed
3. indexed with preincrementing of the index register
4. indexed with postincrementing of the index register
5. indexed with predecrementing of the index register
6. indexed with postdecrementing of the index register
7. base displacement
8. base displacement with indexing
9. PC relative
10. indirect
11. preindexed indirect
12. postindexed indirect
13. multilevel indirect
14. multilevel preindexed indirect
15. multilevel indirect with postindexing
16. register-indirect
17. autoincrement
18. autodecrement

a. Give one application for each addressing mode.
b. How small a set of addressing modes is sufficient?

**2.60** What should op code 0000 be used for, and why?

## Reference-needed Exercises

**2.61** What is the value of the negative number having the largest magnitude that each of the following machines can represent, and what is the value of the normalized negative floating-point number with the smallest magnitude?

a. B-5500
b. CYBER 170
c. IBM System/370, 32-bit representation
d. VAX using F-floating point

**2.62** What is the value of the largest positive floating-point number and smallest positive normalized floating-point number each of the following machines can represent?

a. B-5500
b. CYBER 170
c. IBM System/370
d. VAX, using F-floating point

## Computer Exercise

**2.63** Is the floating-point arithmetic on your own computer commutative? associative? distributive? Consider the various arithmetic options available. Explain how you arrived at your answers.

# Problems

**2.64** An EXECUTE instruction executes the instruction at a specified address and then continues with the instruction following the EXECUTE instruction (unless the executed instruction is a branch instruction). Thus EXECUTE (A) executes the instruction at address A (acting like a single-instruction subroutine). Why might architects consider this instruction to be obsolete? Would EXECUTE be obsolete if a register could hold the executed instruction?

**2.65** Exercise 2.28 requested that you use a loop to program X!. Now write a program for X! using a recursive subroutine. Be careful how you manage the stack. Check for overflow and underflow, and use the stack for argument and result passing, as well as for other functions.

**2.66** An operating system on the VAX has a data space of $2^{30}$ bytes, and the entire page table must be accessible to any operating system. (See Fig. 2.32.) Each VAX instruction provides a 9-bit byte offset. The VAX page tables can occupy one-fourth of the 4-GB virtual memory, and each page-table entry uses 20 bytes. Explain why the VAX is limited to $2^{34}$ bytes of main memory. What limitations would result if a machine could not access part of the page table? What does this page-table-size limitation imply about the maximum memory size of a paged-memory-management system in general? (Consulting the VAX architecture manual may help.)

*2.67* Some computers do not use a program counter but store the address of the next instruction within each instruction. Identify two types of instructions that would be superfluous on these machines. Identify two applications for this type of control.

## Challenging Problems

*2.68* Identify at least two advantages and two disadvantages of using a stack for parameter passage.

*2.69* One of the few good ways to evaluate computer design alternatives (called *optimizing a design* by engineers who do not know what *optimizing* means) is to collect traces of instructions, which are lists of instructions that are executed. Traces allow the design team to compare various alternatives and evaluate their relative performance. Suggest two methods for collecting reasonably comprehensive instruction traces.

*2.70* A machine has an accumulator Acc, an index register N, a program counter PC, and a 1-bit condition-code register CCR. The ALU sets the CCR when the result of the previous operation is negative and clears it when the result is not negative. The instruction set has five instructions:

| | | |
|---|---|---|
| LOAD | Acc ← [M(N)] | M is the instruction address, M(N) is M indexed by the content of N, and [M(N)] is the content of M(N). |
| STORE | [M(N)] ← Acc | |
| SUBTRACT | Acc ← Acc − [M(N)] | |
| COPY | N ← Acc | |
| JUMP | if CCR = 0, then PC ← X, else PC ← PC + 1 | |

Assuming that memory locations 0 and 1 always store the constants 0 and −1, explore the possibility of implementing a subroutine call on this machine. Do not feel frustrated about the crudeness of the mechanism, but determine feasibility and point out any limitations in the call mechanism. Requirements for the subroutine call: saving the current PC, pointing to some locations for arguments, and branching to the subroutine. You may need to assume that the compiler and/or the linker has saved the PC at some location(s) for you.

*2.71* Give three examples of instructions that are difficult to implement with a very wide range of technologies, and explain why they are difficult to implement. That is, what are some instructions that are either very expensive to implement (bad for microcomputers) or make very high speed execution difficult (bad for supercomputers)?

*2.72* Consider a hypothetical computer with an instruction set of only three *N*-bit instructions. The first 2 bits specify the op code, and the remaining bits, X, specify a word in main memory. The three instructions are:

| | | |
|---|---|---|
| SUB | Acc ← Acc − [X] | Subtract the contents of location X from the accumulator, and store the result in location X and the accumulator. |
| ADD | Acc ← Acc + [X] | Add the contents of location X to the accumulator, and store the result in location X and the accumulator. |
| JUMP | PC ← X | Place address X in the program counter. |

A word in memory may contain either an instruction or a binary number in two's-complement notation. Examine whether you can perform the following operations on this hypothetical computer:

    a. a subroutine call
    b. an I/O operation

You may assume that locations 0 and 1 in main memory always contain the constants 0 and 1, respectively. Check feasibility only (do not bother about the efficiency).

*2.73* Suppose the Diminutive Electronics Company has asked you to design an 8-bit microprocessor that will use instructions with 3-bit op codes. What eight instructions would you implement? Try to demonstrate (informally) the completeness of your instruction set.

## Discussion/Team Problems

*2.74* Summarize the major alternatives an instruction-set architect must consider in the design of a future high-performance computer family. Indicate the influences that each alternative will have on the others, and describe how they will affect the performance of the various family members.

*2.75* As team leader for the Inormously Big Machine Company, you are considering the following five methods of passing parameters to a called procedure:

1. Pass the parameters on a stack.
2. Pass the parameters in registers.
3. Place the parameter addresses in a stack.
4. Place the parameters in a list, and pass the address of the list to the called procedure in a register.
5. Place parameters addresses in a list, and pass the address of the list to the called procedure in a register.
   a. Discuss these five methods with reference to parameter passage by value and parameter passage by reference.
   b. Discuss these five methods with reference to the types of parameters being passed (e.g., simple variables, multiword variables, arrays, and structures).

*2.76* A function can return its result to its calling procedure in several ways. Discuss the advantages and disadvantages of each of the following methods:

a. Place the result in the stack before returning.
b. Place the result in the register before returning.
c. Place the result in memory, and return the memory address by using one of the first two methods.

*2.77* A new instruction-set architecture has the following numbers and types of instructions:

   7    3-address instructions
  92    2-address instructions including 28 memory-referencing instructions
  60    1-address instructions
  20    0-address instructions

The machine will have 16 16-bit registers and use 16-bit register-to-register instructions for all but the LOAD, STORE, branch, and other memory-referencing operations. Outline a scheme for encoding the instructions.

*2.78* Discuss why architects introduced each of the following addressing modes:

a. indexed
b. 0-page indirect
c. base displacement
d. segment register

*2.79* As a new member of a team of instruction-set architects for the Huge and Large Computer Company, you have been asked to examine two additional instructions for inclusion on the 9000. Identify the factors you would consider in making your report.

*2.80* Why are index registers so important? Describe a common use of index registers that is very difficult or impossible to carry out without them.

*2.81* Gibson of IBM performed one of the early studies of the usage of computers. In general terms, he and others since then have found that instructions are distributed roughly as shown below. This obviously depends heavily on the programs and types of applications, but this sort of guide helps designers of computers decide where to spend their design time.

  50%   LOAD/STORE instructions
  15%   branch instructions
  10%   floating-point arithmetic
  10%   integer arithmetic
  10%   boolean
   5%   miscellaneous

How do you expect this breakdown to vary with application load? Consider, for example, compiling, scientific and engineering software, commercial data processing (banking or airline reservation), games, and any three other applications of your choice.

*2.82* With reference to Exercises 2.51 to 2.54, what can you say about the definition of completeness? What can you say about the definition of orthogonality?

*2.83* Ivan's Basic Machines recently proposed a RISC machine with 16-bit instructions and 6-bit addresses (64 registers). (A RISC machine has only register-to-register operate instructions. In other words, the only instructions that reference memory are LOAD, STORE, and branch instructions. Chapter 6 describes RISCs in more detail.) In the best spirit of glasnost you are offering to help with the design. What reasonable distributions of 0-, 1- and 2-address instructions can this design accommodate? Carefully articulate your assumptions.

*2.84* Perestroika has led to a competitor for Ivan. You are now working on the design of a similar machine for Igor's Better Machines. This one uses 32-bit instructions and has 7-bit register designators. For this new machine answer the same question as in the Problem 2.83 but here you expect to provide 0-, 1-, 2-, 3-, and 4-address instructions (the fourth "address" is generally used as a small immediate constant rather than as a register designator). Be careful to articulate your assumptions.

# Chapter Index

0-address instruction 55
1-address instruction 55
absolute address 86
absolute-binary address 86
absolute-binary number 37
accumulator 56
accumulator machine 56
active process 64
address resolution 86
address specification 59
addressed operand 59
addressing efficiency 101
aligned word 84
American Standard Code for Information Interchange (ASCII) 37
argument 48
array 47
array element 47
atomic instruction 65
autodecrement addressing 96
autoincrement addressing 96
base address 92
base-displacement addressing 92
base register 92
bias 39
biased integer 39
binary-coded decimal (BCD) 37
binary point 40
block floating-point number 52
boundary alignment 83
branch address 68
branch instructions 58
branch test 68
branch-target instruction 68
byte 36
byte boundary 84
called procedure 48
calling procedure 48
character 37
character instruction 58
character string 45
character-string instruction 58
coefficient 40
compiler 85

compilation 85
complementing the bits 39
complete instruction set 102
concatenation 46
conditional branch instruction 58
condition code 53
condition-code register 54
condition-code-setting instruction 68
continuation-point address 70
CPU address 96
critical section 64
datatype 36
destination address 51
displacement 92
dot product 75
double precision 37
doubleword 37
effective address 86
elision 40
empty operation 47
entry-point address 70
escape sequences 51
evaluation-stack architecture 55
exception 70
excess-$n$ integer 39
executive mode 71
explicit operand 59
exponent 40
exponent base 40
Extended Binary Coded Decimal Interchange Code (EBCDIC) 37
floating floating-point representation 52
floating-point number 36
fraction 39
gather operation 78
general-purpose register 57
general-purpose register-set machine 57
high-order bit 37
homogeneous addressing 99
IEEE floating-point standard 44
immediate operand 59
implicit operand 59

inactive process 64
increment 47
index 46, 53
indexed addressing 88
indexed-indirect addressing 91
indexing 88
index register 53
indirect address 89
indirect addressing 89
indivisible instruction 65
inhomogeneous addressing 99
instruction address 85
instruction format 107
instruction register (IR) 53
integer 36
interrupt 70
I/O device address 70
I/O instruction 58
$k$-dimensional array 47
kernel mode 71
LIFO storage 46
linking 86
loader 86
load-and-store instruction set 54
LOAD instruction 58
locking a data set 65
logical-address 85
logical-address space 85
logical vector 76
loop-iteration count 50
low-order bit 37
($M + N$)-address instruction 55
magnitude 38
main-memory address 86
mantissa 40
matrix 47
matrix element 47
matrix product 80
memory-address register (MAR) 53
memory-buffer register (MBR) 53
memory operand 83
memory-to-memory instruction 54

memory-to-register instruction 54
merge operation 76
monadic vector operation 72
multiple levels of indirection 91
mutual exclusion 64
N-address instruction 55
normal bit 40
normalized number 40
object-code compatibility 106
octet 37
offset 92
ones'-complement integer 38
operate instruction 58
operational register 36
orthogonality 105
overflow 44
page 84
page-0 instruction 88
page-0-indirect instruction 91
page boundary 84
parameter 48
parameter-address list 48
parameter list 48
PC-relative addressing 94
physical address 86
physical-addressing range 98
physical-address space 86
pop operation 47
portability 106
post decrementing 96
postindexed-indirect addressing 91
preincrementing 96
preindexed-indirect addressing 91
privileged instruction 71
privileged mode 71
problem state (or mode) 71
procedure 48
processor-status bits 53
process synchronization instruction 58

program-status word (PSW) 54
push operation 47
quadword 37
radix 40
radix point 40
register 36
register address 87
register-deferred addressing 87
register-indirect addressing 87
register operand 83
register-to-register instruction 54
results 48
resume a process 64
return address 70
row-major order 79
row-minor order 79
scalar 47
scalar product 75
scatter operation 78
segment 92
segment-register addressing 96
segment register 97
semaphore 65
shared data set 64
shared variable 64
sign 40
sign bit 38
signed-magnitude integer 38
single precision 37
source address 61
source-code compatibility 106
special-purpose register-set machine 57
stack 46
stack pointer 54
stack-register addressing 96
stack-register instructions 94
static program relocation 94
STORE instruction 58
stride 47
string instruction 58

subroutine-linkage instruction 58
subscript list 47
subscript position 47
subscript value 47
substring 46
supervisor mode (or state) 71
suspend a process 64
synchronization primitive 63
test vector 76
test-vector operation 76
top operation 47
transpose 80
trap 51
trap handler 51
two's-complement integer 39
unconditional branch instruction 68
underflow 44
unnormal number 44
unsigned-binary number 37
user mode 71
vector 47
vector comparison 76
vector compression 77
vector element 47
vector expansion 77
vector instruction 58
vector length 47
vector mask 76
vector operation 72
vector-reduction operation 73
vector register 72
vector-scalar operation 73
vector-vector operation 73
virtual-addressing range 98
virtual memory 86
virtual-memory system 86
word boundary 84
word size 36

# 3
# Buses, the CPU, and the I/O System

> 3.1 **Buses** *120*
>   3.1.1 Bus Types *120*
>   3.1.2 Bus Transfers and Control Signals *122*
> 3.2 **Central Processing Unit** *124*
>   3.2.1 ALUs *125*
>   3.2.2 Control Units *126*
>   3.2.3 Exception-processing Hardware and Instructions *143*
> 3.3 **I/O System** *152*
>   3.3.1 CPU-controlled I/O *154*
>   3.3.2 Multiprogramming Operating Systems *155*
>   3.3.3 Multiported Storage *156*
>   3.3.4 DMA I/O *157*
>   3.3.5 Memory-mapped I/O *164*
>   3.3.6 Physical I/O Devices *165*

*This chapter focuses on three hardware subsystems of a computer: buses, CPUs, and I/O systems. Section 3.1 describes buses, which convey information from one device to another and from one component to another. Section 3.2 discusses CPUs, which contain the computer's register set, control unit, operational logic, and interrupt-processing hardware. Section 3.3 focuses on I/O processing and describes three standard techniques for I/O processing: CPU-controlled, memory-mapped, and direct-memory-access (DMA).*

> **Key Terms**
>
> **Central processing unit (CPU)** That part of a computer consisting of the control unit, an arithmetic and logic unit (ALU), and a register file; not part of the CPU are the main memory and I/O systems.
>
> **Control unit** That part of the CPU that generates the control signals for itself, the ALU, the register file, and other CPU buses and components.
>
> **Exception** A hardware-initiated branch that transfers control from the executing program to an exception handler. Exceptions whose origins are external to the program are interrupts; those triggered by software events are traps.
>
> **Microprogrammed control unit** A control unit that generates control signals by reading microinstructions stored in read-only memory (ROM), and decoding and issuing them, rather than by using sequential logic circuits.
>
> **Multiprogramming** A technique for increasing the utilization of the CPU by allowing several tasks to reside in memory at the same time. The operating system can keep the CPU busy by transferring control from one memory-resident program to another when one of them awaits I/O or other services.
>
> **Processor context** The state of the CPU, including all operational registers, the PC, the processor status bits, and any other registers whose contents affect the execution of the program.
>
> **System bus** A bus that has its own control circuitry and arbitrates among the various components, including the CPU, that wish to use it.

As we emphasized in Chapters 1 and 2, the instruction-set architecture (ISA) specifies a computer from a programmer's point of view, while the implementation and the hardware-system architecture (HSA) determine its organization and performance. That is, the ISA specifies a computer's behavioral characteristics; the HSA specifies its structural characteristics. Moreover, programmers and compilers are seldom immune to differences in features of machines having the same ISA but different implementations. By utilizing features specific to the hardware subsystems of high-performance models, for example, programmers can often optimize the performance of their programs.

## 3.1 ■ Buses

Buses carry information between the components of one device or between subsystems. Buses can be divided into two major groups based on their control: local buses and system buses. A hybrid group, expanded local buses, combines features of the other two. The following sections describe buses and their control.

### 3.1.1 ■ Bus Types

**Local Buses**

The simplest buses consist of set of wires (or traces when they are manufactured as part of a circuit board). These buses are **local buses,** because they are part of the device that uses and controls them.

Within the CPU, local buses can generally be divided in three types: address buses, data buses, or control buses. **Address buses** tend to be specialized in purpose and are usually unidirectional: They most frequently transfer addresses from the program counter (PC), stack register, or address-computation circuitry to memory but not the reverse. **Data buses** tend to be more general in purpose and are bidirectional. They may carry data, instructions, and also addresses, and they convey the data to and from the main memory system, attached I/O devices, and the ALU. **Control buses** carry signals from the control unit to other components of the computer and back to the control unit. The control signals they carry, in turn, control the operations of the components that receive them.

**System Buses**

Unlike local buses, **system buses** are independent functional components of many computers. Each system bus has its own control circuit, called a **bus controller,** and within each bus controller is an **arbiter**, which processes requests to use the bus (Fig. 3.1). The bus controller may be distributed among the devices that use the bus. A device that wishes to use a system bus must request permission to do so from the bus arbiter. System buses generally connect system components together, such as the CPU, the I/O system, and often the main-memory system, and designers often optimize system buses for transferring data between I/O devices and main memory.

A key distinction between system buses and local buses is that system buses tend to have well-documented and stable definitions, so that designers can attach a wide variety of devices to them; local buses, in contrast, are processor-specific and not widely documented. They tend to be proprietary. Examples of system buses are the DEC UNIBUS, the S-100 bus, and the Apple NuBus.

## Expanded Local Buses

**Expanded local buses,** found mostly in microcomputer systems, are local buses with special extensions for use outside the CPU (see Fig. 3.2). They are similar to system buses in that they provide standardized control signals in addition to the data and address pathways; yet they are local in the sense that the CPU's clock and timing circuits regulate them and hence, they are processor-specific.

*expanded local buses*

FIGURE 3.1 *Typical system bus with two attached devices.*

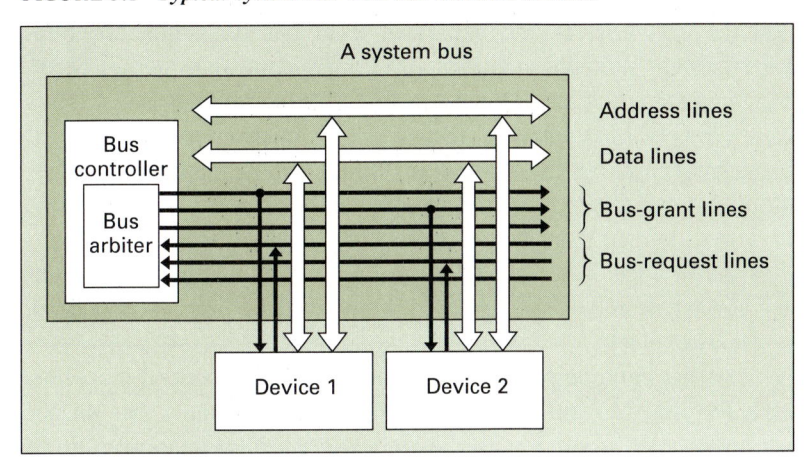

FIGURE 3.2 *A CPU bus and an expanded local bus. The CPU delivers status signals to the bus-control unit, which then generates the bus-control signals. The bus-control unit may also latch (hold) the addresses and data.*

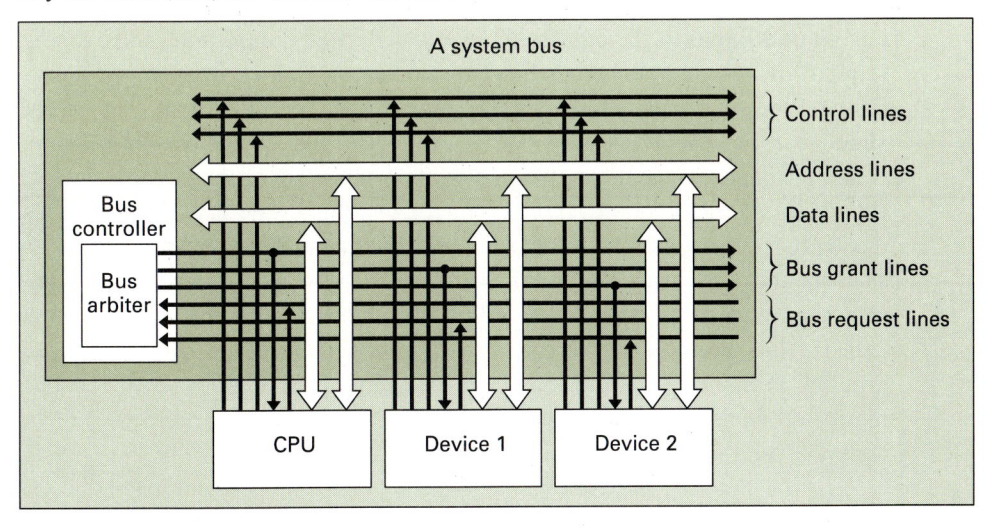

**status signals**

The CPU may send **status signals** to the bus controller to tell it what type of bus cycle to execute. Status signals simply describe the state of the CPU to the bus controller.

Expanded local buses are flexible operationally and provide a platform for system expansion. Examples are the IBM PC I/O Channel Bus and the IBM Micro Channel Architecture (MCA).

### 3.1.2 ■ Bus Transfers and Control Signals

**bus transfer**

A **bus transfer** is the transmission of one or more items of information across a bus. Although each system and expanded local bus is slightly different, devices use relatively standard methods for transmitting data across them. There are many different types of bus transfers, and each type is called a **bus cycle**. Typical types of bus cycles are **memory read, memory write, I/O read, I/O write,** and **interrupt**, but there are many others depending on the bus.

**bus cycle**
**memory read cycle**
**memory write cycle**
**I/O read cycle**
**I/O write cycle**
**interrupt cycle**
**bus states**

A bus transfer takes place in stages, called **bus states,** and a bus cycle consists of a well-defined sequence of bus states. A clock regulates the bus states. For expanded local buses, the CPU generates the clock signals that control the bus. For a system bus, the bus controller may either have its own clock or use a systemwide clock.

**bus masters**

Devices that can compete for use of a system or expanded local bus, such as the CPU and I/O interfaces, are called **bus masters.** A bus master wishing to transfer data across a system bus must request permission to do so from the bus arbiter. Other devices, such as memory, are passive and can only respond to requests from bus masters. These are called **slaves**. Some devices may be bus masters for some data transfers and serve as slaves for other data transfers.

**slaves**

**bus-request signal**
**bus-request line**

A device requests to use a system or expanded local bus by sending a **bus-request signal** to the bus arbiter over a dedicated control line called a **bus-request line.** (A number of bus lines are dedicated, that is, reserved for a particular kind of signal.) If the arbiter grants the request, it sends an **accept signal** back to the requesting device over a second dedicated control line, called a **bus-grant line.** Once the bus arbiter grants use of the bus to a device, the chosen device becomes bus master for one bus cycle; it controls the bus during that cycle. Only the bus master, along with the device it selects to be its slave for that cycle, may send information to the bus. The convention of a device requesting permission to use a bus and then being granted permission is called a **bus protocol.** Different buses use different bus protocols, such as granting permission for one bus cycle or granting permission until the bus master relinquishes it. Many standard system buses and bus protocols are in common use today.

**accept signal**

**bus-grant line**

**bus protocol**

To illustrate the use of a bus, we shall describe a typical read cycle for an expanded local bus (Fig. 3.3). At the beginning of the read cycle (Fig. 3.3a) the CPU sends a signal on the read-control line R, which indicates that a read

Buses, the CPU, and the I/O System   123

**FIGURE 3.3**  *Typical read cycle using an expanded local bus.*

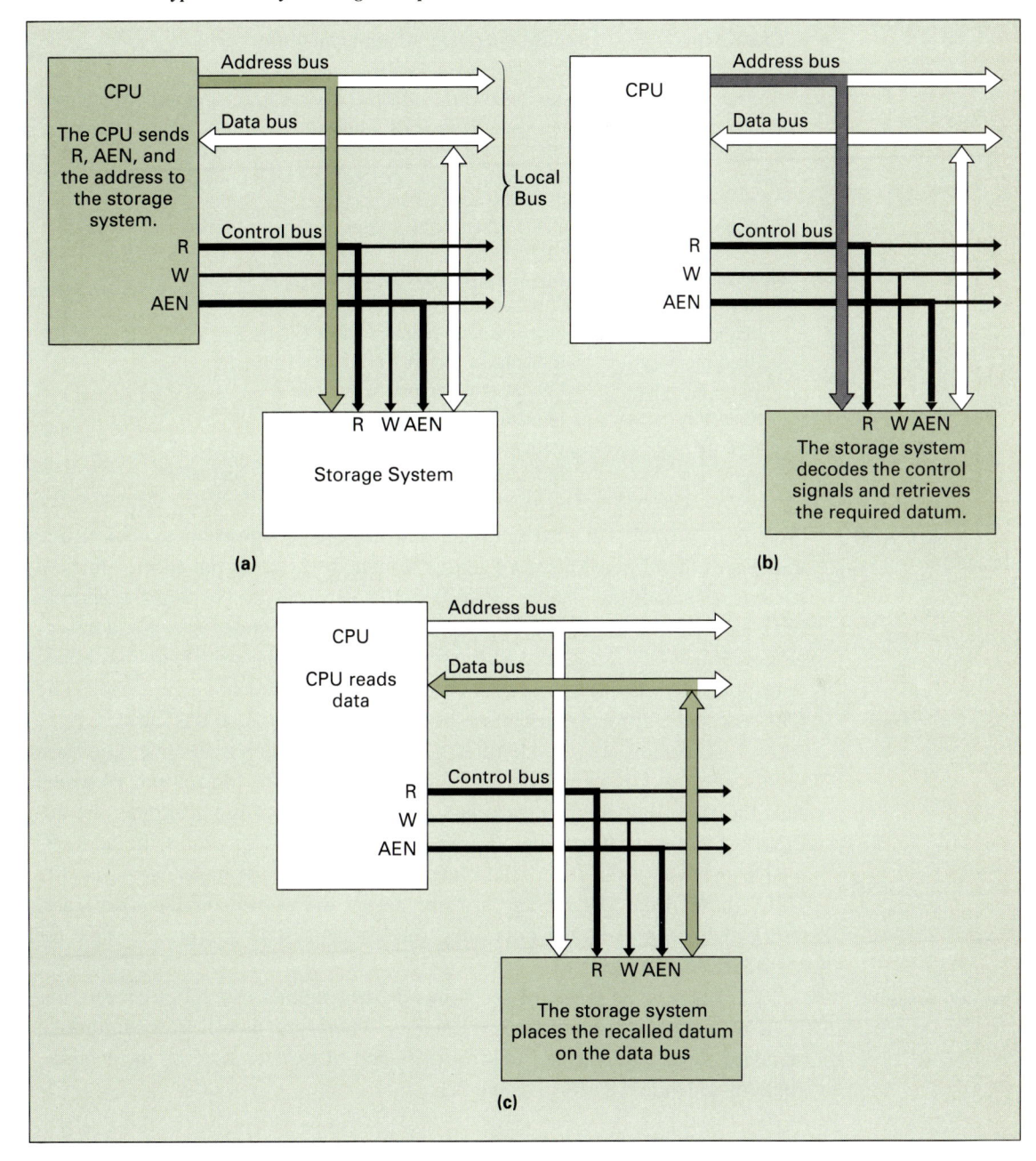

**Table 3.1** Typical bus-control lines

| Control line | Typical operation definition and use |
|---|---|
| Bus request | Lines used by the attached devices to request use of the bus |
| Bus grant | Lines used by the bus arbiter to give permission to be bus master to one requesting device |
| Address enable | Indicates that a bus master is placing an address on the address lines |
| Data enable | Indicates that a bus master or slave is placing valid data on the data bus |
| Bus-cycle type | Status lines that indicate the type of bus cycle: |
|   Read/write | Distinguishes read from write cycles |
|   Memory/IO | Distinguishes memory from I/O cycles |
|   Read memory | Indicates a memory read cycle |
|   Write memory | Indicates a memory write cycle |
|   Read/IO | Indicates an I/O read cycle |
|   Write/IO | Indicates an I/O write cycle |
|   Interrupt | Indicates an interrupt acknowledge sequence |

*address-enable signal*

cycle is in progress. It also sends an **address-enable signal** on the AEN line and places the physical-memory address for the transfer on the address lines of the bus. (The address-enable signal tells the attached devices that the address lines have an address on them.) Next the storage system decodes all addresses (Fig. 3.3b). When one of the addresses is for a word the storage system holds, it responds by placing the requested datum on the data bus (Fig. 3.3c). The CPU accepts a copy of the datum at or near the end of the bus cycle.

A memory write cycle differs only slightly from a read cycle. During a write cycle, the CPU sends a control signal on the write control line W, which tells the slave that the bus cycle is a write cycle. The CPU generates the address, which it places on the address lines, and it also generates the address-enable signal as it did for a read cycle. During the data transfer, however, the CPU, rather than the storage system, places the datum on the data lines. While the datum is on the data lines, the storage system accepts the value for the addressed storage cell.

*bus-control signals*

There is no standard set of **bus-control signals** that all buses use, nor is there a standard set of bus-cycle types. There are, however, a number of standard types of dedicated control lines and bus cycles used by most buses, some of which are listed in Table 3.1.

## 3.2 ■ Central Processing Unit

*central processing unit (CPU)*

The **central processing unit (CPU)** of a simple computer has three major components: a register set, an ALU, and a control unit. (Chapters 1 and 2 introduced these components, and Chapter 2 examined register sets in some detail.) These components usually communicate among themselves using local buses, and they communicate with the storage system and I/O system using one or more system buses, local buses, or expanded local buses. In this section we shall describe the CPU components and the various ways they communicate with each other.

### 3.2.1 ■ ALUs

All computers have **functional units** that perform the arithmetic, logical, and shift operations demanded of the computer's instruction set. Some computers have a single functional unit, the ALU, but some have several independent functional units. Figure 3.4 illustrates an ALU that has two functional units: a

*functional units*

FIGURE 3.4  *The ALU of a simple computer, showing the functional units, data pathways, and control pathways. The control signals operate the individual gates, registers, and functional units; the status signals convey the values in the C, V, N, and Z flags.*

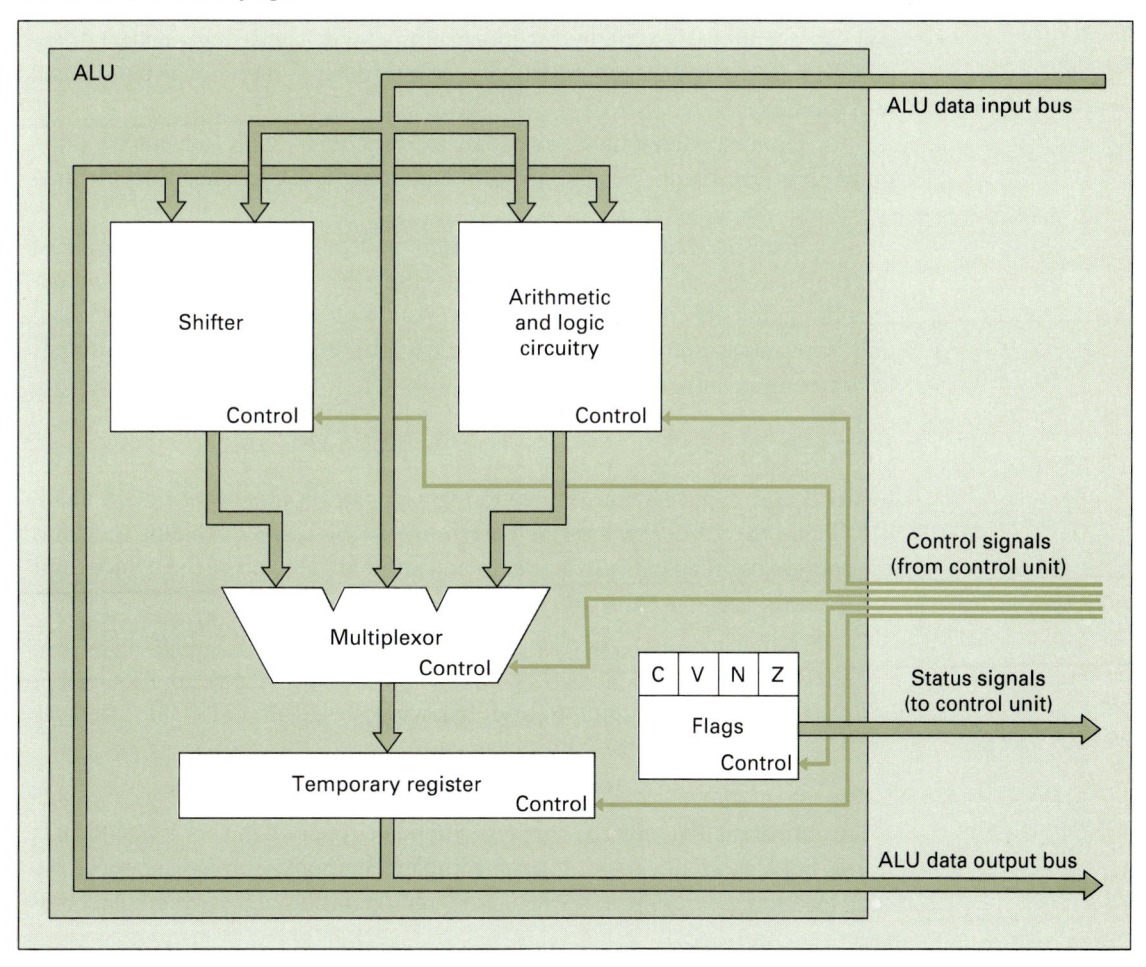

shifter and an arithmetic and logic unit. It also has a multiplexor, a temporary register, and a set of flags with their control circuits. Notice that functional units may in turn contain functional units, as with the ALU.

**status register**

The ALUs of most computers have a **status register** and associated logic. The status register usually has a carry flag (C), an overflow flag (V), a negative-result flag (N), and a zero-result flag (Z). A dedicated control bus carries control signals from the control unit to the ALU, and a dedicated status bus carries status signals from the ALU to the control unit. The input and output data buses carry data to and from the CPU's register file (not illustrated). They are local data buses.

Some computers use special floating-point coprocessors to implement complex arithmetic operations. (We shall explore the use of coprocessors in Chapter 5.) Some computers, such as reduced-instruction-set computers (RISCs), use two or three independent functional units to implement different types of operations, such as branch processing, arithmetic and logical operations, and floating-point operations. Some computers, such as the CDC 6600 and Cray families, use many functional units, and having independent functional units was a necessary first step in introducing operational parallelism into the CPU.

Computers that have more than one functional unit often employ pipelining to utilize them. We shall explore pipelining and the scheduling of functional units in Chapter 6.

The speed of a von Neumann machine depends largely on the speed of its computational circuitry, so the designers spend a great deal of time and energy designing efficient functional units. Although the design of a functional unit is an important part of any computer implementation, the details are left to books and courses on logic design.

### 3.2.2 ■ Control Units

Figure 3.5(a) depicts a von Neumann machine with a program in main memory. While the CPU executes the current instruction, the PC points to (holds the address of) the next instruction to be executed. The job of the control unit is to control the von Neumann machine cycle:

1. Fetch from memory the next instruction to be executed, place it in the instruction register (IR) (Step 1 in Fig. 3.5b), and increment the PC to point to the following instruction in main memory (Step 2 in Fig. 3.5b).
2. Decode and execute the instruction just fetched.

In actuality, only the simplest computers operate in this way, and later in this book we shall explore alternate implementations. For now, however, we shall look more carefully at the structure and operation of a conventional computer's control unit.

The control unit generates the control signals that regulate the computer. For a very simple computer, the control unit may send **microorders**, individual signals sent over dedicated control lines, to control individual components and devices.[1] An example would be a control signal that sets or clears a status flag. The control unit would generate such a control signal to implement a CLEAR CARRY instruction, for example.

microorders

It is much more common for the control unit to generate sets of microorders operating concurrently than to issue individual microorders. To illustrate, suppose the control unit is executing a MOVE A TO X instruction. To do so it must copy the datum from register A to register X using a data bus. The control unit generates one microorder to tell register A to place its contents on the data bus and, after a small delay, when the data have stabilized, it generates a second microorder to tell X to read the datum from the bus. These signals appear to be almost simultaneous. See Fig. 3.6. The control unit issues

---

1. This terminology comes from the literatue on microprogrammed control units. We shall use it for both conventional and microprogrammed control units to avoid ambiguity.

---

FIGURE 3.5 *A simple von Neumann machine with a program in memory. (a) While the CPU executes the current instruction, the PC points to the next instruction to be executed. (b) During the fetch cycle, the CPU fetches the instruction pointed to by the PC (1) and then increments the PC (2). IR, instruction register.*

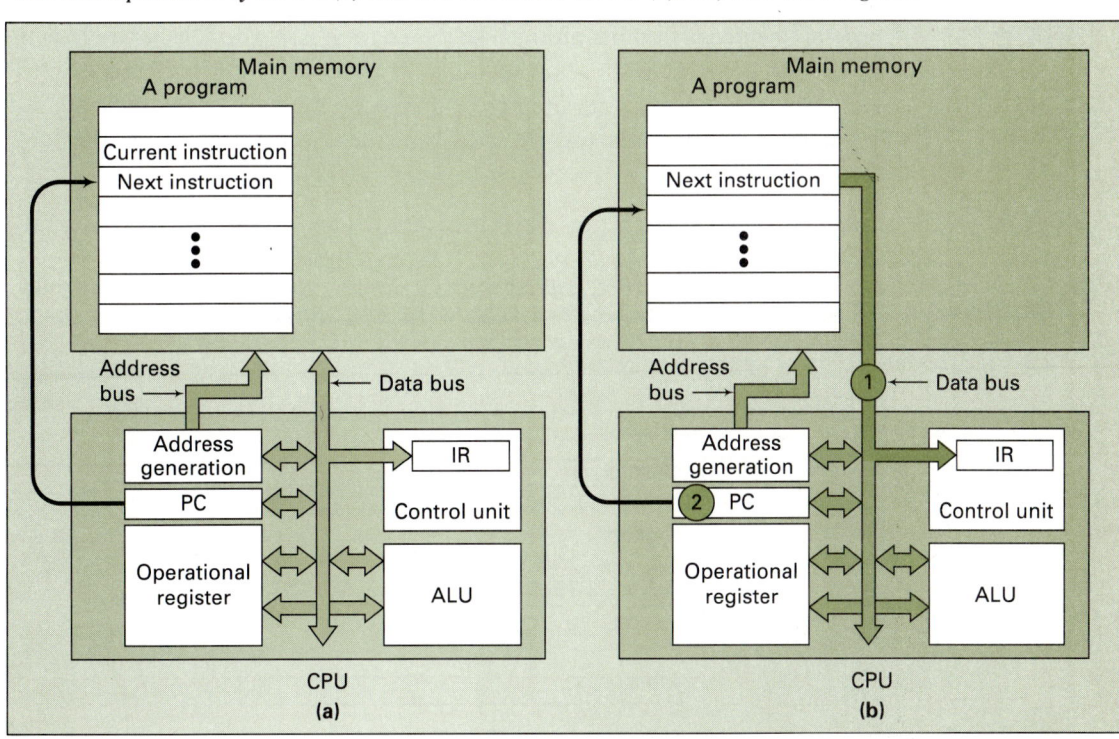

both microorders to effect the desired data transfer. The set of microorders issued by the control unit at one time is a **microinstruction**.

Whenever a computer executes a machine instruction in its instruction set, the control unit issues a sequence of microinstructions. The sequence that implements a single machine instruction is a **microprogram**. Although a microprogram may consist of a single microinstruction, it usually consists of a sequence of microinstructions. For example, when an accumulator machine executes an ADD instruction, the control unit issues microinstructions for computing the address of the memory operand, for reading memory and transferring the operand from the storage system to the ALU, for transferring the second operand from the accumulator to the ALU, for adding the two values, and for transferring the result from the ALU to the accumulator. Note that the control unit might issue a sequence of microinstructions for address computation and, in contrast, it might issue a single microinstruction for transferring both operands to the ALU. The details depend on the complexity of the address computation and on the availability of buses in the machine. In addition, the control unit might issue microorders for incrementing the PC and for setting or clearing processor status bits depending on the result of the addition.

There are basically two different types of control units: microprogrammed and conventional. Most computers built during the 1970s and 1980s have **microprogrammed control units,** whereas high-performance computers and RISCs have **conventional** (also called **hard-wired**) **control units.** Microprogrammed control units are relatively easy to design, they enable architects to develop complex instruction sets at very little cost, and they are easy to manufacture. However, they are slower than conventional control units; consequently it is difficult to use them to generate the control signals that are

---

FIGURE 3.6  *Implementing the* MOVE *A* TO *X machine instruction. The control unit issues two microorders (*ENABLE TO *A, and* CLOCK TO *X), shown in boldface, to transfer data from register A to register X.* ENABLE *tells a register to place its content on the bus, while* CLOCK TO *X tells register X to accept a new value from the bus.*

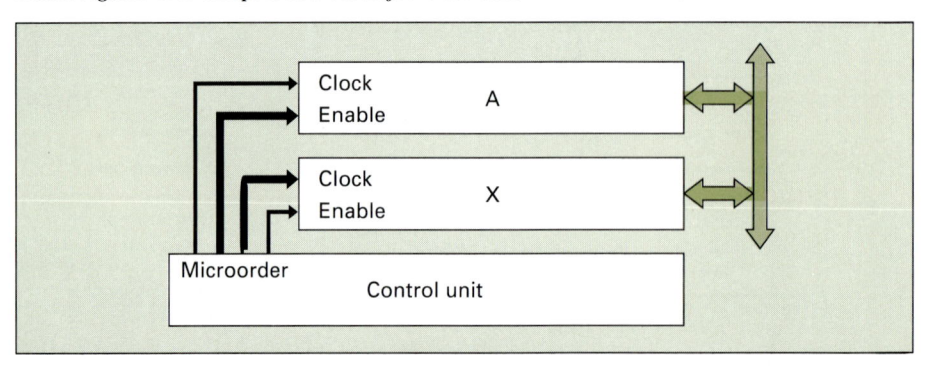

needed for the highest-performance computers of each family or for current RISC machines. That is why high-performance computers use conventional control units.

Now we describe in principle how the control unit of a computer regulates its operation and implements its instruction set.

**Microprogrammed Control Units**

Figure 3.7 illustrates a conceptual model for microprogrammed machine control. The control unit first fetches an instruction from memory. It then converts the instruction into a series of microinstructions. To do so it uses a microprogram translator, a device that does table look-up, to translate the instruction's op code into a microinstruction address. Using that address the microinstruction processor fetches the first of a sequence of microinstructions from its own memory, or sometimes from main memory. After fetching each microinstruction, the processor issues it by sending the proper microorders over the control bus lines. Both the microprogram translator and the microinstruction processor are part of the control unit.

A real microprogrammed control unit is somewhat more complex, and Fig. 3.8 illustrates the principal components of a prototypical one. The IR holds the machine instruction to be executed (or perhaps just its op code). The **control store,** sometimes implemented in ROM and generally not part of the computer's main memory, contains the microprograms for all of the machine's instructions as well as for machine startup and for interrupt processing. The **address-computation circuitry** determines the address in the control store of the next microinstruction to be executed, and the **microprogram counter ($\mu$PC)** holds the address of the next microinstruction. The control unit recalls microinstructions from the control store and places them in the **microinstruction buffer,** which holds them during execution. The **microinstruction decoder**

control store

address-computation circuitry
microprogram counter ($\mu$PC)

microinstruction buffer
microinstruction decoder

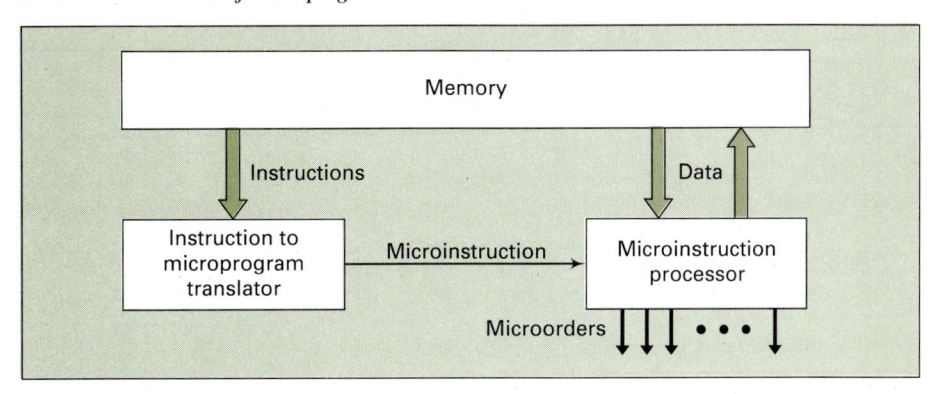

FIGURE 3.7  *Basics of microprogrammed machine control.*

sequencer

generates and issues microorders based on the microinstruction and the op code of the instruction being executed. Finally, the **sequencer** synchronizes the activities of the components of the control unit.

The sequencer is the heart of the control unit. It has two distinct modes of operation: ordinary operation and machine startup.

*Ordinary Operation*

During ordinary operation the sequencer generates the control signals that regulate the control unit. These control signals are the microorders that the control unit obeys. Using a clock generator for timing, the sequencer generates signals that initiate the following repeating sequence of actions. The numbers in braces refer to control signals issued by the sequencer as identified in Fig. 3.8.

1. The sequencer causes an address to be placed in the $\mu$PC, either by sending a clock signal to the $\mu$PC {5} thereby loading a new

FIGURE 3.8  *Main components of a microprogrammed control unit. C, clock; CL, clear, EN, enable; INC, increment; IR, instruction register; $\mu$PC, microprogram counter; 1 − 10, control signals — see text for explanation.*

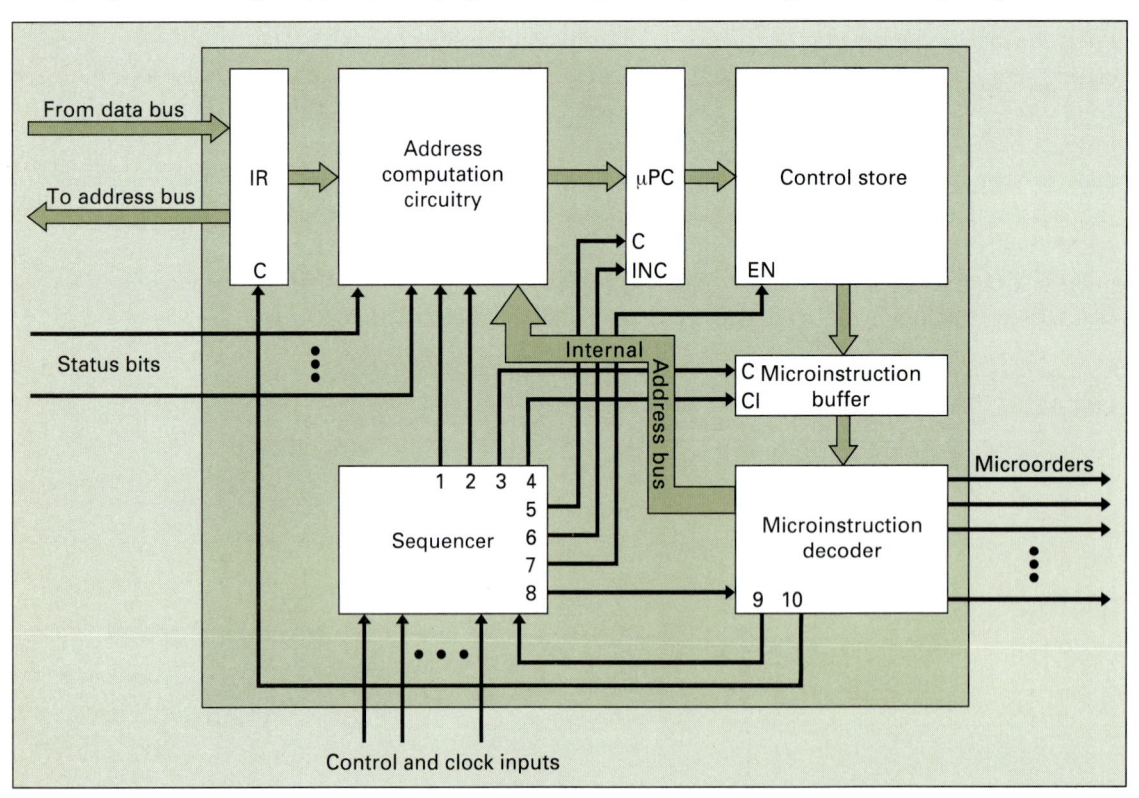

value from the address-computation circuitry, or by incrementing the value in the μPC {6}. It may also clear the microinstruction buffer {4}.

2. The sequencer initiates a control-store read {7} for the addressed microinstruction and transfers it into the microinstruction buffer {3}.
3. The sequencer causes the microinstruction decoder to issue the microinstruction {8}.

Once the control unit finishes executing the microprogram for one machine instruction, it must fetch the next machine instruction from main memory. After the control unit fetches the machine instruction, the microinstruction decoder, not the sequencer, issues the microorder {10} to load the machine instruction into the IR.

*Machine Startup*
During machine startup the control unit initializes various registers (by either clearing them or placing specified values in them). It then loads a hardware-generated address in the PC (not the μPC) and begins running. For some machines the hardware-loaded address is a **reset vector,** which is the address of the first instruction the machine is to execute after starting. For machines that use a reset vector, the control unit immediately begins normal operations after loading the reset vector in the PC. See Fig. 3.9(a).

    For other machines the hardware-generated address points to the address of the first instruction the machine is to execute after starting. Figure 3.9(b) illustrates this situation. For these machines, the initial address is the **reset-vector address.** Now the control unit must fetch the reset vector and place it in the PC before it begins ordinary operation. The advantage

reset vector

reset-vector address

**FIGURE 3.9** *Two mechanisms for referencing the initial startup program in memory. (a) Using a hardware-generated reset vector. (b) Using a hardware-generated reset-vector address.*

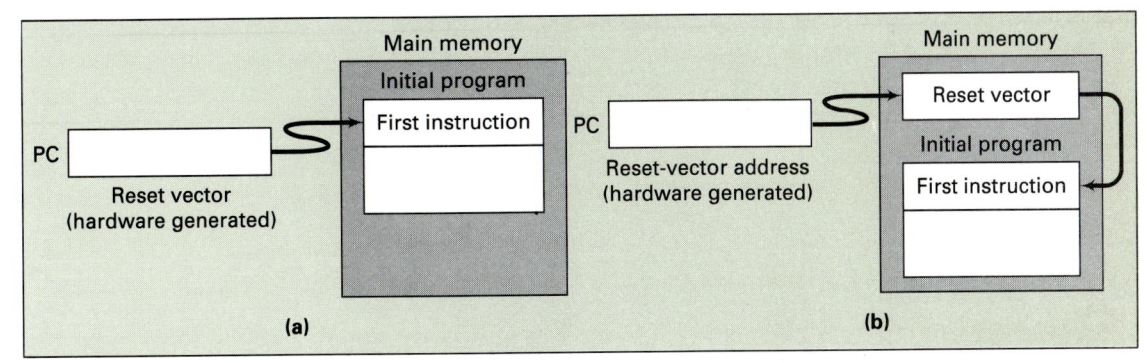

of introducing this extra complexity is that it allows increased design generality: Machine architects do not need to assign the address of the initial program in memory. They only need to assign the address of a single value—the reset vector.

### Organization of Microprograms in the Control Store

There are many ways to organize microprograms in a control store. One way, illustrated in Fig. 3.10, is to place the microinstructions sequentially in memory. Each machine instruction, then, has its own sequence of microinstructions in the control store. Additionally, the control store contains the microinstructions for instruction fetch, interrupt initiation, and any other activities it controls.

Let us assume this organization. After the control unit fetches a machine instruction from main memory and places it in the instruction register, it must generate the **entry-point address** for that op code, that is, the address of the first microinstruction of the microprogram. For example, if the control unit fetches a microinstruction with op code 1, it must generate the address A1 shown in Fig. 3.10. Generating an entry-point address is one responsibility of the address-computation circuitry. After the control unit generates the entry-point address, the sequencer increments the μPC to get the address of each following microinstruction.

**entry-point address**

**FIGURE 3.10** *One organization for microcode in a control store.*

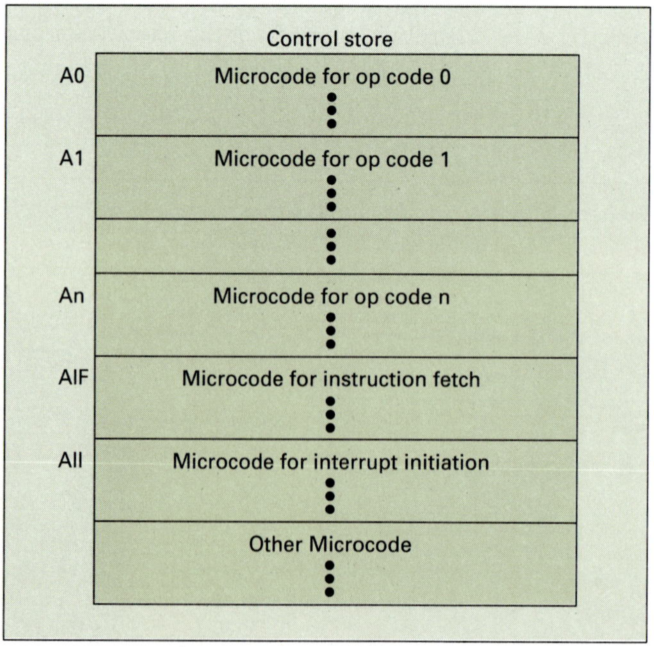

| | Control store |
|---|---|
| A0 | Microcode for op code 0 |
| A1 | Microcode for op code 1 |
| | |
| An | Microcode for op code n |
| AIF | Microcode for instruction fetch |
| AII | Microcode for interrupt initiation |
| | Other Microcode |

After executing the last microinstruction in a microprogram (i.e., after finishing the execution of one machine instruction), the sequencer must once again execute the microcode for the fetch sequence; it must fetch the next instruction. Referring to Fig. 3.10, it must branch to address AIF in the control store. The question now is, how can the sequencer control branching within the microcode of the control store? Figure 3.8 illustrates one way. Microinstructions are either branching or nonbranching (not to be confused with branching and nonbranching *instructions*). We have only described execution of **nonbranching microinstructions** so far. **Branching microinstructions** hold branch addresses and microorders for the address-computation circuitry, possibly in addition to some microorders for the rest of the computer. The sequencer, together with the address-computation circuitry, uses the control signals provided by the branch microinstruction for determining the address of the next microinstruction.

nonbranching microinstructions
branching microinstructions

To control branching, every microinstruction, both branching and nonbranching, generates one microorder, shown at {9} in Figure 3.8, that the sequencer analyzes. This microorder tells the sequencer whether the current microinstruction is a branching microinstruction. If it is a branching microinstruction, the sequencer notifies the address-computation circuitry to generate the next address, and it signals the $\mu$PC to accept the address from the address-computation circuitry {5} (instead of incrementing the address in the $\mu$PC). If the microinstruction is a nonbranching microinstruction, the sequencer simply signals the $\mu$PC {6} to increment its content.

Now let us focus on the address-computation circuitry. After an instruction fetch, the address-computation circuitry must decode the op code of the machine instruction and generate the entry-point address of the microinstruction for that op code. During a microprogram branching instruction, however, it must generate the address of the next microinstruction based on the address it receives over the internal address bus (refer to Fig. 3.8) and the control signals it receives from the microinstruction decoder. Based on control microorders it receives from the branch microinstructions (not shown in Fig. 3.8), the sequencer generates control signals at {1} and {2} that tell the address-computation circuitry which way to proceed. When the sequencer sends control signal {1}, the address-computation circuitry uses the op code to generate the next microinstruction address. When the sequencer sends control signal {2}, the address-computation circuitry uses the address it receives over the address bus from the microinstruction decoder. For an unconditional branch, the address bus may transmit the actual branch-target address. For conditional-branch instructions, the address bus transmits an address that the address-computation circuitry may modify based on the status signals it gets from the ALU.

Suppose the machine instruction is a conditional-branch instruction, such as BRANCH ON NEGATIVE. Our prototypical control unit receives the status bits from the ALU and uses them to modify the microprogram control flow. It works as follows. A BRANCH ON NEGATIVE instruction causes a program branch (not a microprogram branch) when the negative flag N is set (by an earlier operation, for example). If the N flag is set, the control unit places the branch-target address, usually specified in the machine instruction, in the PC by executing a sequence of microinstructions. However, if the N flag is clear, the control unit ignores the branch address; that is, it executes a different sequence of microinstructions. For the BRANCH ON NEGATIVE instruction, then, the address-computation circuitry analyzes the status bits as well as the microinstruction branch address. It generates one control-store address when N is set and a different address when N is clear. (One typical way an address-computation circuit modifies the address it gets is to OR a value with it. The value to which OR is applied is often the result of a branch-condition test—$1_2$ if the branch succeeds and $0_2$ if it fails, for example. If the branch address is $10110_2$, for example, and the branch test fails, the result of the OR operation will be $10110_2$, whereas if the branch test succeeds, it will be $10111_2$. See Fig. 3.11.

In general, microprogrammed control units are somewhat more complex than the one we just illustrated. Nonetheless, the principles are the same.

Historically, microprogrammed control units have been classified as horizontal or vertical (Fig. 3.12). The difference lies in how they code microinstructions. In **horizontal control** the individual bits in the microinstruction correspond to individual microorders (Fig. 3.12a). Each bit directly controls a single bus or perhaps a gate in the machine. For this design the microinstruction decoder is not needed. These microinstructions are very wide, perhaps hundreds of bits wide; hence this microprogramming is often called horizontal.

**horizontal control**

FIGURE 3.11  *Organization of a microprogram for* BRANCH ON NEGATIVE. *N, negative flag.*

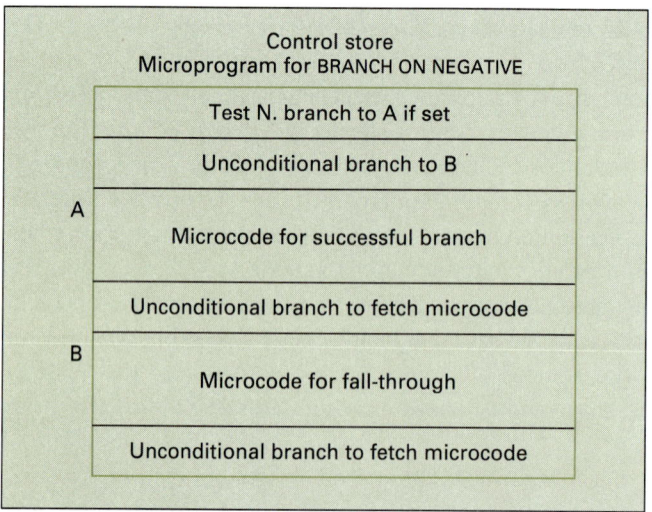

```
                Control store
       Microprogram for BRANCH ON NEGATIVE
   ┌─────────────────────────────────────────┐
   │        Test N. branch to A if set       │
   ├─────────────────────────────────────────┤
   │        Unconditional branch to B        │
A ─┼─────────────────────────────────────────┤
   │       Microcode for successful branch   │
   ├─────────────────────────────────────────┤
   │   Unconditional branch to fetch microcode│
B ─┼─────────────────────────────────────────┤
   │         Microcode for fall-through      │
   ├─────────────────────────────────────────┤
   │   Unconditional branch to fetch microcode│
   └─────────────────────────────────────────┘
```

**FIGURE 3.12** *Microinstruction organizations. (a) Horizontal control. (b) Vertical control using decoders. (c) Vertical control using a demultiplexor. Vertical arrows to the multiplexor in (c) represent dual-use bits — able to hold microinstruction-branch addresses during branch microinstructions and ordinary microinstructions during nonbranch microinstructions. Lines without arrowheads between the microinstruction and the demultiplexor represent bits that control the demultiplexor.*

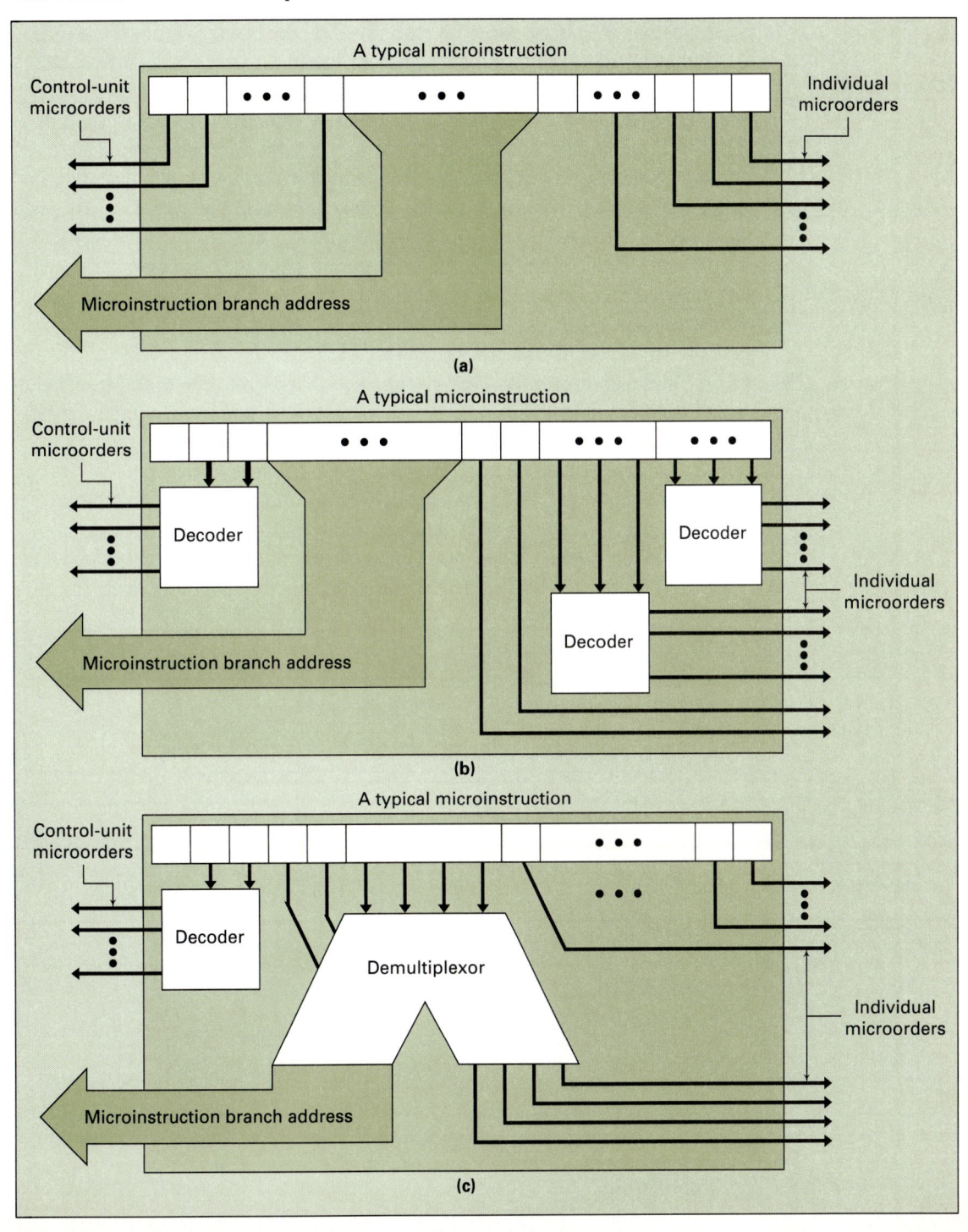

**vertical control**

In **vertical control,** microorders are coded into the microinstruction bits, usually in specific fields (Fig. 3.12b). For example, a microinstruction may use a 4-bit field to control one of 16 ALU operations, or it may use a 5-bit field to select one of 32 registers. Decoders within the microinstruction decoder (see Fig. 3.8) or elsewhere within the CPU decode the bits of these fields to get the individual microorders. Another method of vertical control uses a demultiplexor, a device that can send a value to one of two or more places, to route selected bits to one place or another within the CPU. For example, Fig. 3.12(c) illustrates a control unit that uses a 4-bit microinstruction field as a microinstruction branch address during branching microinstructions and as a source for four individual microorders during nonbranching microinstructions. The control unit uses two microinstruction bits to control the 4-bit demultiplexor, 1 bit to tell it where to send the output (the address-computation circuitry or the CPU) and 1 bit to enable the output. Various combinations of these techniques are also possible. In general, vertical microinstructions are typically on the order of a few dozen bits wide.

Some control units use several levels of control. For example, a field in the machine instruction, or a field in a microinstruction, may hold the address of the word in a secondary control ROM that holds the microorders. Figure 3.13 illustrates such an organization. The secondary control ROM could also hold large address constants, such as exception-branch addresses.

Clearly a designer must consider many tradeoffs when designing a microprogrammed control store. Horizontal control is fastest but requires wide instruction words. Vertical control requires decoders or demultiplexors to gen-

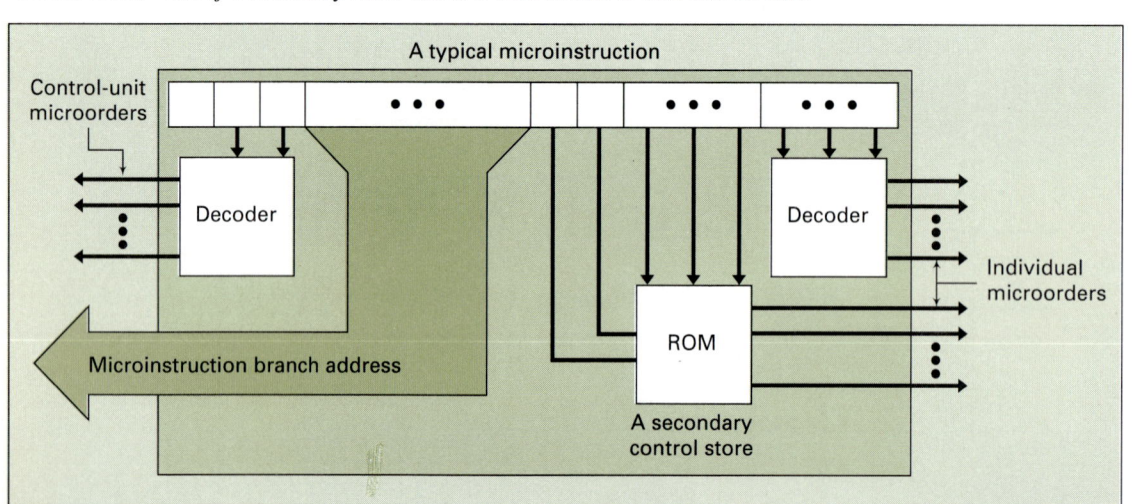

**FIGURE 3.13** *Use of a secondary ROM within a control unit to hold microorders.*

erate the microorders, but it allows shorter control words and hence less control ROM. Most real systems fall somewhere between being purely horizontal and purely vertical. Multilevel control stores also allow for small microinstructions, but they require additional control ROM and hence additional complexity.

### *Microprogramming (Optional)*

In a trivial sense, **microprogramming** is the art of writing microprograms for a control unit. At a somewhat deeper level, microprogramming is the process of specifying the control signals that implement the computer's instruction set. Regardless of the computer, control signals always regulate a computer's activity, and whether a conventional control unit or a microprogrammed control unit generates the control signals, the sequences of control signals are the same.

*microprogramming*

In this section we shall focus on how the control signals of a computer regulate its activity. Our goal is not to teach microprogramming but rather to illustrate the relationships between a computer's control unit and its ISA. The control unit's microprograms define the instruction set, and this section illustrates the mechanism of that definition.

Figure 3.14 shows part of the HSA of a very simple computer. The computer has two user registers (A and PC), two internal registers (IR and X), and four buses: an address bus (A-bus), a data bus (D-bus), a control bus (C-bus), and a local bus (L-bus). It is an accumulator machine. Thus the A register holds the first operand of every arithmetic, logical, and shift instruction, and also gets the result. The memory system supplies the second operand of all binary operations.

Using the demultiplexor (DEMUX) the PC can send its content to the D- and A-buses, and using the multiplexor (MUX), the PC can get values from the A- and D-buses.

The functional unit can perform four binary operations: addition (ADD), subtraction (SUB), logical AND, and logical OR. It can also perform three unary operations (operations with a single operand): bit complement (NOT), LOGICAL SHIFT LEFT (LSL), and ARITHMETIC SHIFT RIGHT (ASR). The details are not important for this discussion.

We must make a few additional assumptions. First, register A always sends its value to the L-bus, so that the functional unit knows what value the A register holds. Second, when the functional unit performs an operation, it puts the result into its internal register X. Third, the enable (EN) input {13} to the functional unit causes it to send the contents of X to the D-bus. Finally, the control unit must never instruct more than one device at a time to place a value on a bus. For example, the control unit must not send the EN signal {11} to the A register and the EN signal {13} to the functional unit simultaneously. (The numbers in braces refer to the control signals illustrated in Fig. 3.14.)

Some of the control lines that regulate the machine are numbered in the figure, which shows 22 of them. Microorders activate these control lines.

**FIGURE 3.14** *Components of a simple accumulator machine. See text for explanation.*

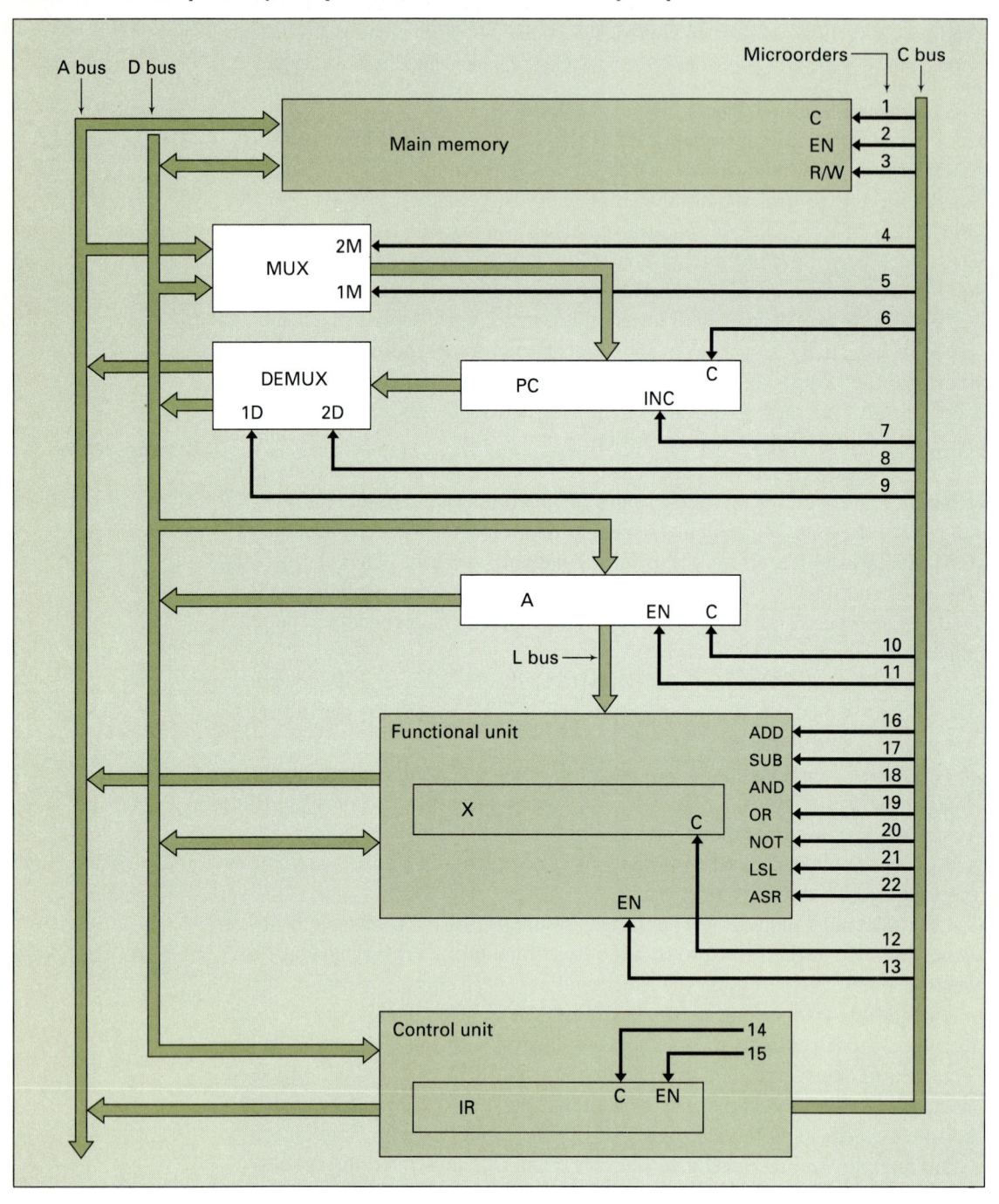

For example, a signal on control line {11} instructs register A to place its content on the D-bus, a signal on control line {22} instructs the functional unit to perform an ARITHMETIC SHIFT RIGHT operation, and a signal on control line {7} increments the PC. The microorders, then, are the signals these control lines carry. Except for the clock and enable inputs to the IR, Fig. 3.14 does not show the control lines that regulate the control unit. (Note that the clock signal to the IR is {10} in Fig. 3.8 and {14} in Fig. 3.14.)

The **microinstruction format** is the way that microinstructions are laid out in the control store. In our example, the microinstructions are 20 bits wide, and the bits are numbered from 19 to 0 (Fig. 3.15). Bit 0 distinguishes between branching and nonbranching microinstructions, and corresponds to control signal {9} in Fig. 3.8. In nonbranching microinstructions bits 1 through 15 generate microorders for the control lines numbered {1} through {15} in Fig. 3.14. Within the control unit, bit 14, which corresponds to control signal {10} in Fig. 3.8, tells the IR to read the value from the D-bus; the IR then receives a copy of the instruction. Bit 15 instructs the IR to send its address field to the A-bus. Bit 16 is unused. Bits 17 through 19 (the FOP field) vertically encode the functional unit operations.

*microinstruction format*

For branching microinstructions, bit 16 through 3 hold the branch addresses and branch control microorders for the address-computation circuitry. For branch microinstructions (when bit 0 is set), bits 13 to 16 hold the control signals while bits 3 through 12 hold the branch address. When bits 0 and 16 are both set, the address-computation circuitry decodes the op code in the IR to determine the entry-point address for the corresponding microprogram. When bit 0 is set and bit 16 is clear, the address-computation circuitry uses the branch address in bits 3 through 12. The remaining details are unimportant for this discussion.

Our next step is to define a few machine instructions. We shall consider only five of them:

| | |
|---|---|
| LOAD | A ← (ADDR) |
| STORE | (ADDR) ← A |
| ADD | A ← A + (ADDR) |
| COMPLEMENT | A ← $\overline{A}$ |
| JUMP | to ADDR |

Instruction format: | OP | Address |

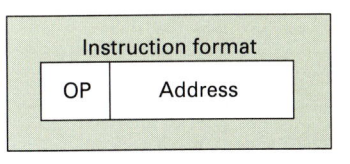

For each instruction, ADDR is the absolute address of a memory location. Instructions have a 4-bit op code; the remaining bits hold the absolute address of the operand. The COMPLEMENT instruction does not use its operand field.

Now let us consider some example microprograms.

## Example 1. *Instruction Fetch*

During instruction fetch the control unit must do three things: (1) fetch the instruction, (2) increment the PC, and (3) branch to the proper microprogram.

**FIGURE 3.15** *Microinstruction formats and control signals for the computer illustrated in Fig. 3.14.*

**Nonbranch microinstruction format:**

| 19 | 17 | 16 | 15 | 14 | 13 | 12 | 11 | 10 | 9 | 8 | 7 | 6 | 5 | 4 | 3 | 2 | 1 | 0 |
|---|---|---|---|---|---|---|---|---|---|---|---|---|---|---|---|---|---|---|
| FOP | | | IA | CI | UD | CX | AD | CA | 1D | 2D | IP | CP | 1M | 2M | RM | MD | CM | 0 |

| | | | |
|---|---|---|---|
| 0 | 0 | 1 | ADD |
| 0 | 1 | 0 | SUB |
| 0 | 1 | 1 | AND |
| 1 | 0 | 0 | OR |
| 1 | 0 | 1 | NOT |
| 1 | 1 | 0 | LOGICAL SHIFT LEFT |
| 1 | 1 | 1 | ARITHMETIC SHIFT RIGHT |

This bit distinguishes between branch and nonbranch microinstructions

| Microorder Number | Code | Microoperation |
|---|---|---|
| 1 | CM | Clock memory |
| 2 | MD | Memory to D-bus |
| 3 | RM | Read/write memory |
| 4 | 2M | Control 2 to multiplexor |
| 5 | 1M | Control 1 to multiplexor |
| 6 | CP | Clock PC |
| 7 | IP | Increment PC |
| 8 | 2D | Control 2 to demultiplexor |
| 9 | 1D | Control 1 to demultiplexer |
| 10 | CA | Clock A register |
| 11 | AD | A register to D-bus |
| 12 | CX | Clock X |
| 13 | UD | Functional unit to D-bus |
| 14 | CI | Clock IR |
| 15 | IA | IR to A-bus |
| 16 | | ADD |
| 17 | | SUB |
| 18 | | AND |
| 19 | | OR |
| 20 | | NOT |
| 21 | | LOGICAL SHIFT LEFT |
| 22 | | ARITHMETIC SHIFT RIGHT |

**Multiplexor**

| 1M | 2M | Operation |
|---|---|---|
| 0 | 0 | Disabled |
| 0 | 1 | D-bus to PC |
| 1 | 0 | A-bus to PC |
| 1 | 1 | 0 to PC |

**Demultiplexor**

| 1D | 2D | Operation |
|---|---|---|
| 0 | 0 | Disabled |
| 0 | 1 | PC to D-bus |
| 1 | 0 | PC to A-bus |
| 1 | 1 | 0 to A-bus |

**Branch microinstruction format:**

| 19 | 17 | 16 | 15 | 14 | 13 | 12 | 11 | 10 | 9 | 8 | 7 | 6 | 5 | 4 | 3 | 2 | 1 | 0 |
|---|---|---|---|---|---|---|---|---|---|---|---|---|---|---|---|---|---|---|
| | | | Branch-control microorders/Branch address | | | | | | | | | | | | | | | 1 |

To fetch an instruction, the control unit must do four things simultaneously:

- Place the content of the PC on the A-bus (1D).
- Enable memory to the D-bus (MD).
- Signal a read operation (RM).
- Transfer the resulting value into the IR (CI).

These four things cause the memory system to read the instruction and place it on the D-bus and they cause the IR to get a copy from the D-bus.[2] The first microinstruction, consisting of these four microorders, looks like this:

| FOP |   |   |   | IA | CI | UD | CX | AD | CA | 1D | 2D | IP | CP | 1M | 2M | RM | MD | CM | B |
|---|---|---|---|---|---|---|---|---|---|---|---|---|---|---|---|---|---|---|---|
| 0 | 0 | 0 | 0 | 0 | 1 | 0 | 0 | 0 | 0 | 1 | 0 | 0 | 0 | 0 | 0 | 1 | 1 | 0 | 0 |

Next the control unit must increment the PC. The second microinstruction, consisting of one microorder, therefore looks like this:

| FOP |   |   |   | IA | CI | UD | CX | AD | CA | 1D | 2D | IP | CP | 1M | 2M | RM | MD | CM | B |
|---|---|---|---|---|---|---|---|---|---|---|---|---|---|---|---|---|---|---|---|
| 0 | 0 | 0 | 0 | 0 | 0 | 0 | 0 | 0 | 0 | 0 | 0 | 0 | 1 | 0 | 0 | 0 | 0 | 0 | 0 |

After incrementing the PC, the control unit must branch to the microprogram whose op code is in the IR. Thus the control unit must execute a branch microinstruction with bit 16 set. The final microinstruction looks like this:

| 19 | 18 | 17 | 16 | 15 | 14 | 13 | 12 | 11 | 10 | 9 | 8 | 7 | 6 | 5 | 4 | 3 | 2 | 1 | 0 |
|---|---|---|---|---|---|---|---|---|---|---|---|---|---|---|---|---|---|---|---|
| 0 | 0 | 0 | 1 | 0 | 0 | 0 | 0 | 0 | 0 | 0 | 0 | 0 | 0 | 0 | 0 | 0 | 0 | 0 | 1 |

For this machine, the microprogram for the instruction fetch consists of three microinstructions.

### Example 2. COMPLEMENT

We now suppose that during an instruction fetch the control unit loaded a COMPLEMENT instruction into the IR. We also suppose that the address-computation circuitry of the control unit has generated the entry-point address of the COMPLEMENT microprogram and loaded it in the $\mu$PC. The microprogram must do the following two things to implement COMPLEMENT (bullets represent individual microorders):

---

2. In general, the timing of control signals is crucial. We shall assume for this discussion that the microinstruction decoder, using signals from the clock generator, sends the control signals at the proper times.

1. First microinstruction:
   - Have the functional unit perform a NOT operation (the value of FOP must be $101_2$).
   - Transfer the result into X (CX).
   - Instruct the functional unit to send X to the D-bus (UD).
   - Transfer the result into A (CA).
2. Second microinstruction:
   - Branch to the fetch microprogram.

Since COMPLEMENT does not require a memory operand, the D-bus is available to carry the result to the A register. A microprogram for a COMPLEMENT consists of the following two microinstructions:

| FOP | | | IA | CI | UD | CX | AD | CA | 1D | 2D | IP | CP | 1M | 2M | RM | MD | CM | B |
|---|---|---|---|---|---|---|---|---|---|---|---|---|---|---|---|---|---|---|
| 1 | 0 | 1 | 0 | 0 | 1 | 1 | 0 | 1 | 0 | 0 | 0 | 0 | 0 | 0 | 0 | 0 | 0 | 0 |
| 0 | 0 | 0 | \multicolumn{13}{c}{Address of fetch microprogram} | 0 | 0 | 1 |

*Example 3.* ADD

The microprogram for addition is only slightly more complex. Since ADD is a binary operation, it requires an operand from memory. Consequently the control unit must initiate a memory-read access, which ties up the D-bus temporarily. The control unit must therefore wait for one microinstruction before having the functional unit send the result across the D-bus to the A register. Here is what the control unit must do:

1. First microinstruction:
   - Send the address field of the IR to the A-bus (IA).
   - Signal a read-memory operation (RM).
   - Send the data from the memory unit to the D-bus (MD), which in turn makes it available to the functional unit.
   - Instruct the functional unit to perform an add operation (the value of FOP must be $001_2$).
   - Store the result in X (CX).
2. Second microinstruction:
   - Send the functional-unit result to the D-bus (UD).
   - Store the result in A (CA).
3. Third microinstruction:
   - Branch to the fetch microprogram.

Here is a microprogram for ADD:

| | | FOP | | IA | CI | UD | CX | AD | CA | 1D | 2D | IP | CP | 1M | 2M | RM | MD | CM | B |
|---|---|---|---|---|---|---|---|---|---|---|---|---|---|---|---|---|---|---|---|
| 0 | 0 | 1 | 0 | 1 | 0 | 0 | 1 | 0 | 0 | 0 | 0 | 0 | 0 | 0 | 0 | 1 | 1 | 0 | 0 |

| 0 | 0 | 0 | 0 | 0 | 0 | 1 | 0 | 0 | 1 | 0 | 0 | 0 | 0 | 0 | 0 | 0 | 0 | 0 | 0 |
|---|---|---|---|---|---|---|---|---|---|---|---|---|---|---|---|---|---|---|---|

| 0 | 0 | 0 | Address of fetch microprogram | 0 | 0 | 1 |
|---|---|---|---|---|---|---|

**Conventional Control Units**

The alternative to a microprogrammed control unit is a conventional or hard-wired control unit. As with microprogrammed control units, when executing a machine instruction in the computer's instruction set the conventional control unit issues a sequence of microinstructions. The difference lies in the fact that logic gates generate all of the microorders resulting in faster execution. Conventional control units are mostly used in supercomputers and more recently RISCs. We shall explain why in more detail in Chapter 6. Mixtures of control design, where some key instructions have hard-wired control and others use microcode are common in high-performance computers. High-performance mainframe computers frequently use conventional control for the simple arithmetic, logical, shift, and memory access instructions and microcode for exception handling, decimal arithmetic, character instructions, and other complicated instructions.

Although the internal circuitry in a conventional control unit differs substantially from that in a microprogrammed control unit, its outputs are just the same: the proper sequence of control signals to operate the circuitry of the machine.

### 3.2.3 ■ Exception-processing Hardware and Instructions

**Exceptions** are branches initiated by special exception-processing hardware. During an exception the CPU performs the branch in such a way that it can restart the interrupted program at the point of interruption as though nothing had happened.[3] This section will describe both the motivations for exceptions and the underlying exception-processing hardware.

*exceptions*

There are two types of exception. **Interrupts** are asynchronous branches triggered by events external to the program. They are asynchronous because the computer's clock does not control them. The primary examples are timer interrupts, I/O interrupts, and console interrupts: A timer interrupt

*interrupts*

---

3. Most computers have time-of-day clocks (run by the central clock) whose values are not saved on exception. A program can therefore tell if it has been interrupted if it checks the clock before and after the exception. In our discussion of exceptions we shall assume for simplicity that a computer has no time-of-day clock.

discontinues the operation of a program that exceeds its time allocation; an I/O interrupt tells the operating system that an I/O device has completed or suspended its operation and needs service, such as additional work to do; and a console interrupt is a way for the operator to halt the flow of the program using the console keyboard.

*traps*

**Traps** are very similar to interrupts except that program events trigger them. Hence they are synchronous. Examples are arithmetic overflow, illegal op codes in instructions, and memory-protection violations. Multiprogramming systems need traps to prevent one program from modifying another program's memory, for example. Traps have numerous other uses, as we will see later in the text. Most computers have instructions that go under a variety of names, including SUPERVISOR CALL and INTERRUPT, that allow programs to trigger traps. Programs use these traps to communicate with the operating system.

Exception-processing facilities that are not dependent on the operator are essential for a modern computer system. Without them, the executing program would maintain absolute control over the operation of the computer. If a program got into an infinite loop, for example, the only way to recover would be to reset the computer. (In fact, resetting a computer is really a type of exception.) On early computers an operator could only reset the computer from the console or by turning off the power entirely and then restarting the machine. On a personal computer (PC), the keyboard is the console; in most PCs the console interrupt or reset is triggered by pressing the Control, Alt, and Delete keys simultaneously.

*exception handlers*
*trap handlers*
*interrupt handlers*

Exceptions are processed by special routines called **exception handlers**—called, appropriately, **trap handlers** for traps and **interrupt handlers** for interrupts. Although traps and interrupts are initiated by different kinds of events (software versus hardware), this distinction is crucial only from the point of view of the program software; to the system's hardware (CPU), traps and interrupts look alike, and it initiates both kinds of exceptions the same way.[4]

*run-time behavior*
*program context*
*run-time state*
*processor context*

The conception underlying how exception processing works derives from the fact that the **run-time behavior** (the activity of a program during its execution) is completely determined by its context. The **program context,** also called the **run-time state,** consists of two parts: processor context and memory context. The **processor context** is the state of the CPU's program-visible registers—those registers whose contents affect the execution of the program; these include the program counter (PC), the processor status bits, and other operational registers. The **memory context** is the state of the program's memory. See Fig. 3.16.

*memory context*

---

4. Notice an important distinction in our discussion of exception initiation. Although traps and interrupts are *initiated* (caused or triggered) by different kinds of events, in both cases, once the CPU receives signals calling for an exception, it is the hardware that *initiates* (begins processing) the exception.

The responsibility of the hardware during exception processing is to preserve as much of the processor context as possible. (In general, during exception processing, only the processor context is affected; the memory context remains untouched.) When the CPU starts processing an exception, special exception-processing hardware saves some essential processor context information, minimally the PC and processor status flags, but often much more. Some computers, such as the CDC 6600 when executing an EXCHANGE JUMP instruction, swap the entire register set, thereby saving the entire processor context. To save the processor context, the hardware either pushes it into a stack or puts it in a special **save area** in main memory. It then loads the PC with the entry-point address of the exception handler. That causes a branch to the exception handler. The exception handler than saves any additional state information it needs in order to completely restore the context of the interrupted program.

When the exception handler finishes processing the exception, it may return control to the interrupted program. To do so it first restores as much of the processor context as it can. It then uses a special RETURN FROM INTERRUPT instruction to return control to the interrupted program.[5] The RETURN FROM INTER-

save area

---

5. Although this instruction is used in processing traps as well as interrupts, it is conventional to call it a RETURN FROM INTERRUPT, rather than, say, RETURN FROM EXCEPTION.

---

FIGURE 3.16 *Program context (shaded areas) in relation to the system.*

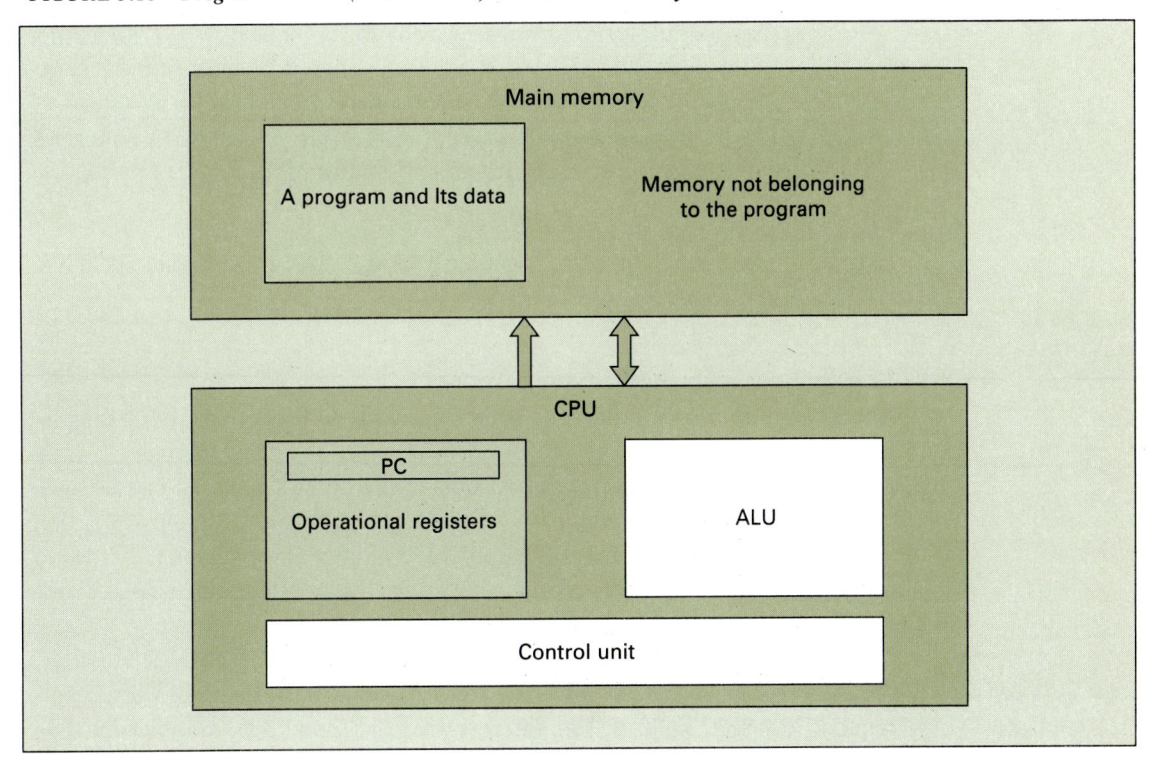

RUPT instruction restores the remainder of the processor context and branches back to it. In that way the hardware restores the exact processor context of the interrupted program at the point of interruption. Provided the exception handler does not modify the program's main memory, the program then continues executing as if it had never been interrupted in the first place. We shall describe the RETURN FROM INTERRUPT instruction in more detail at the end of Section 3.2.3.

Now suppose that an exception caused the CPU to save the processor context of a program. If the exception handler starts a second program executing that does not modify the memory context or saved processor context of the first program, the operating system can later restore the context of the original program, which will then continue executing as though it had never been interrupted. Notice that if the CPU interrupts the second program and saves its context without destroying the context of the first program, the exception handler can pass control between these programs simply by storing and restoring their contexts. (We assume, of course, that the sets of memory locations used by the two programs do not overlap.)

The requirements for exceptions are these:

- The CPU needs special hardware, operations, and instructions to save and restore key registers.
- The hardware must include a way of invoking these operations and instructions.
- The operating system must provide an organized way of allocating and deallocating memory for the interrupted programs, and it must provide the programs with save areas for their processor contexts.
- The hardware must know where to transfer control when an exception occurs and where to return control at the end of exception processing.

Exception-processing hardware together with the operating system (including the exception handlers) does these things.

**Priority Exceptions and Exception Vectors**

As a general rule, more than one source can initiate exceptions. For example, I/O devices, interval timers, and the power supply can raise interrupts, while memory-protection hardware, the ALU, and the control unit can cause traps. To maintain software modularity, systems generally use different exception handlers to process different types of exceptions. The exception hardware must therefore be able to generate the proper exception-handler address for each type of exception.

Most systems prioritize exceptions. For interrupts, each device requesting an interrupt raises an interrupt-request signal on a dedicated **interrupt-request line.** See Fig. 3.17. The interrupt-request signal sets an **interrupt-code**

**flag** indicating that a device of that priority has requested an interrupt. All interrupt-code flags taken together form the **interrupt-code register (ICR)**. Because interrupts are asynchronous, any device can request an interrupt at any time, including while the software is processing a previous interrupt. To prevent the hardware from initiating a second interrupt before the software finishes saving the appropriate context information from a previous interrupt, the

interrupt-code register

---

FIGURE 3.17  *Hardware for priority interrupts. Logical* OR *is applied to all interrupt request signals of the same priority. They set a single bit in the interrupt-code register (ICR). If interrupts are not disabled by the interrupt-disable (I) flip-flop, the interrupt signal sets the interrupt-pending (IP) flip-flop, which informs the control unit of the impending interrupt. The four microorders (colored circles) for this circuitry are clear I, clear IP, clear ICR, and EN to the priority address encoder.*

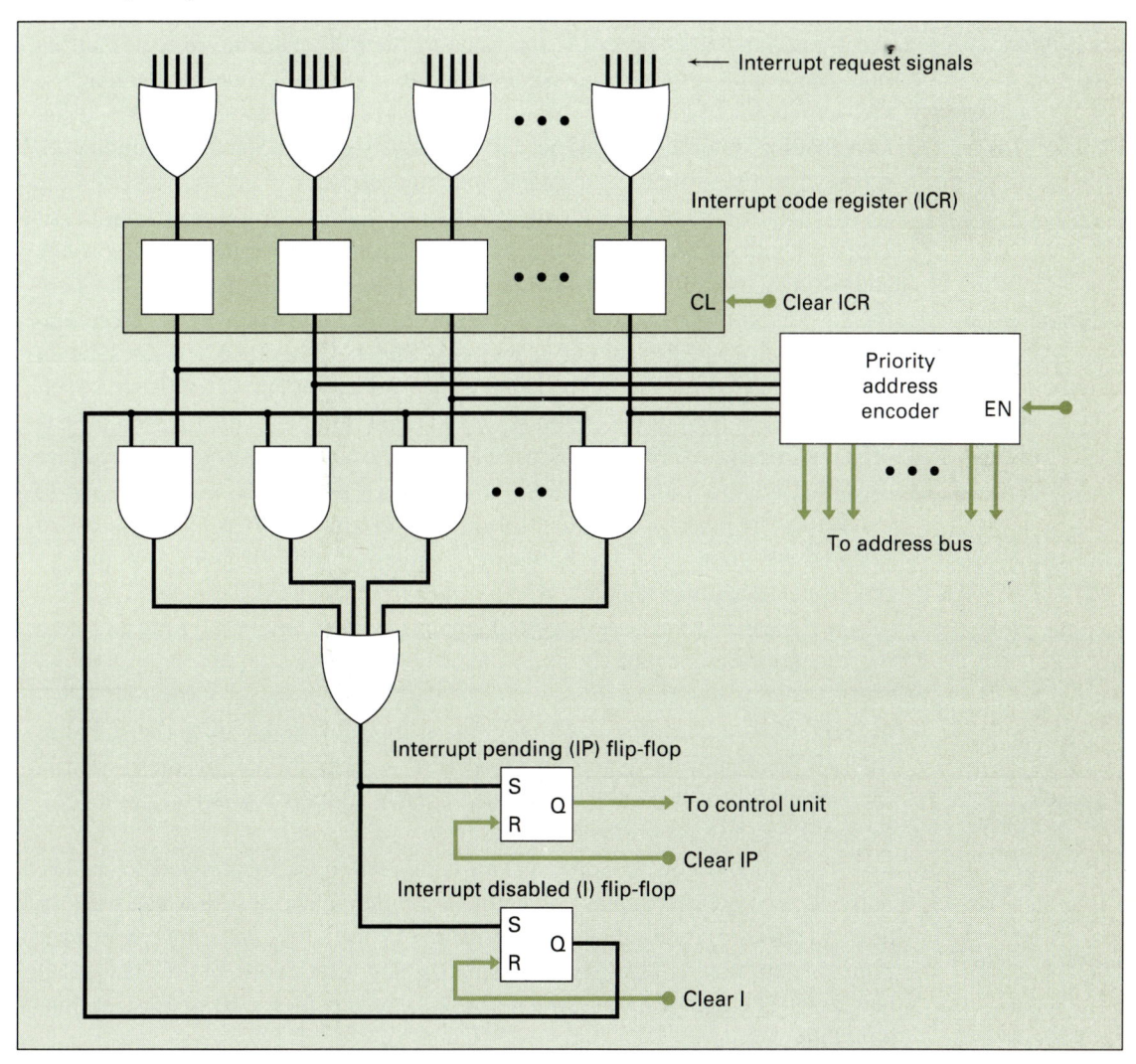

exception hardware also generally sets an **interrupt-disable flip-flop.** Finally, the exception hardware sets an **interrupt-pending flip-flop,** which sends a signal to the control unit to initiate the exception.

After the exception hardware transfers control to the exception handler (as will be described in the following paragraphs), the exception handler must determine which device of the given priority actually requested the interrupt. A technique used by many systems is called **interrupt polling,** in which the exception handler asks each device of the given priority, in turn, whether it requested the interrupt. Another technique is for the device to place a device-specific code in a register that the interrupt handler can interrogate.

To transfer control to the correct interrupt handler, the exception-processing hardware must determine an address for each exception. Some systems automatically generate the absolute address for the first instruction of the exception handler by decoding the value in the ICR. During exception initiation, the control unit simply loads that address into the PC before fetching the next instruction, which is the first instruction of the exception handler. It follows that for systems of this type, the hardware fixes the exception-handler addresses and the number of available interrupt classes.

Many computers use indexed-indirect addressing for branching to exception handlers, which is a somewhat more general technique than absolute addressing. (Indexed-indirect and absolute addressing were described in Chapter 2.) The computers hold all exception-handler addresses in an **exception-vector table,** a specific block of memory that may be ROM. Each type of exception has one entry in the table, called an **exception vector.** Also associated with each type of exception is an **exception number,** which represents the offset within the exception-vector table of the exception vector. The hardware uses the exception number to find the address of the exception handler and to determine the priority of the exception. The exceptions themselves are called **vectored exceptions,** and the hardware executes an indirect jump to branch to the proper exception handler.

When systems use vectored exceptions, the operating system places the exception-vector table in main memory. For some systems the exception-vector table always resides in the same place—for example, beginning at address 0—so the hardware can easily find it. Some systems allow the software to place the exception-vector table anywhere in memory, and for these systems the hardware provides an **exception-vector-table address register** to point to it. Figure 3.18 illustrates this organization.

It should now be apparent why computers use exception-vector tables. Although the architects may determine exception addresses, they generally do not write the exception-handling software. In fact, they may not know what types of software a given system will use nor what types of I/O devices it will have. The use of an exception-vector table provides a flexible exception-handling paradigm.

**Exception Initiation**

As we emphasized earlier, the control unit initiates interrupts and traps in much the same way. Consider the microprogrammed control unit illustrated in Fig. 3.8. The last microinstruction of each microprogram is a branch to the fetch microcode. To process interrupts, the control unit simply performs a conditional branch to the fetch microcode, where the condition is a test for the interrupt-pending signal. When the interrupt-pending signal is *true*, the address-computation circuitry modifies the branch address and branches to the interrupt-initiation microcode instead of the fetch microcode.

In general, the only time a control unit initiates an interrupt is between instructions, not during them, and there is no overhead in term of clock cycles for the interrupt-pending test. A control unit initiates traps in much the same way. When it detects an invalid op code or an arithmetic error condition, for example, it executes a branch to the appropriate microcode to begin trap processing. The same is true for reset processing: The control unit branches to the reset microcode, instead of to the fetch microcode.

The microcode for exception initiation is similar to any other microcode. Let us assume that the computer uses an exception-vector table. The control unit first saves the key registers (the PC and the status flags, for example) in a save area or stack (depending on the computer). It then clears the interrupt-pending flip-flop, but it does not clear the interrupt-disable flip-flop, which is a responsibility of the interrupt handler (see Fig. 3.17). Using the exception number, the control unit computes an offset into the exception-vector table, and finally it reads the exception vector and copies it into the PC. The result is a branch to the proper exception handler.

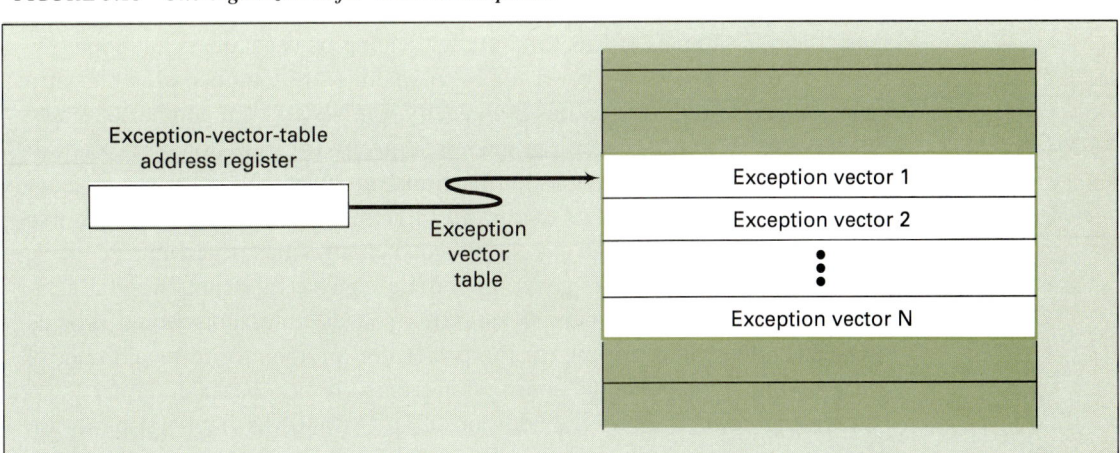

**FIGURE 3.18**  *One organization for vectored exceptions*

Because most computers initiate interrupts only after they finish executing the current machine instruction, it is not necessary for them to save any intermediate values used by the functional units (such as the value in the X register of the functional unit in Fig. 3.14). However, initiating interrupts only after instructions finish executing also means that there may be a significant delay between the request for an interrupt and the initiation of that interrupt, especially for computers with long and complex instructions. Computers that cannot tolerate such delays allow interrupts to be initiated during instructions. To do so they must provide special hardware for saving the state of the CPU in the middle of an instruction, for restoring that state after interruption, and for continuing execution of the interrupted instruction.

### Exception Masking

Many computers use an interrupt mask to prevent certain types of interrupts from occurring automatically. An **interrupt mask** is a value held by an **interrupt-mask register (IMR)** that indicates which interrupts are allowed. When the hardware masks an exception, the CPU either ignores the exception signal or queues it (holds it for later processing).

Maskable interrupts are useful because they provide an efficient mechanism for branching to an exception handler when a hardware-detectable condition arises. Examples of maskable exceptions include I/O interrupts, arithmetic exceptions, and memory-bounds exceptions. For example, some software may need to know when a division by zero occurs. If the hardware provides a trap for division by zero, the software can use the exception-processing hardware to branch to the division-by-zero handler. Other software may wish to ignore the fact that a division by zero occurs and simply mask the interrupt, which saves time.

Not all interrupts can be masked. Catastrophic hardware errors occur very infrequently and must always be processed, so designers choose not to mask them. Examples of this kind are impending power failures and memory-parity errors. **Parity** in general refers to whether the number of 1 bits in a value is even or odd; a value has even parity if it has an even number of 1 bits, for example. Memory-system designers use parity to check for corruption of bit values due to cosmic rays and other transient events. To check for memory parity, they add extra bits to each word in memory so that the hardware can detect when a parity change (i.e., a bit value change) has occurred.

Likewise, operators generally initiate console interrupts when a catastrophic software error occurs, so masking console interrupts would provide no means, other than turning off the power, for an operator to regain control of the system. Consequently, console interrupts are not maskable either.

Figure 3.19 shows the addition of an IMR to the interrupt hardware described earlier and illustrated in Fig. 3.17. Exception masking works as follows. Logical AND is performed on the bits of the IMR and with those of the

Buses, the CPU, and the I/O System 151

FIGURE 3.19 *The addition of an interrupt mask register allows an interrupt system to disable interrupts of selected priority. The circuitry requires two microorders in addition to those shown in Fig. 3.17: clear IMR and read IMR. (All microorders are shown as colored circles.)*

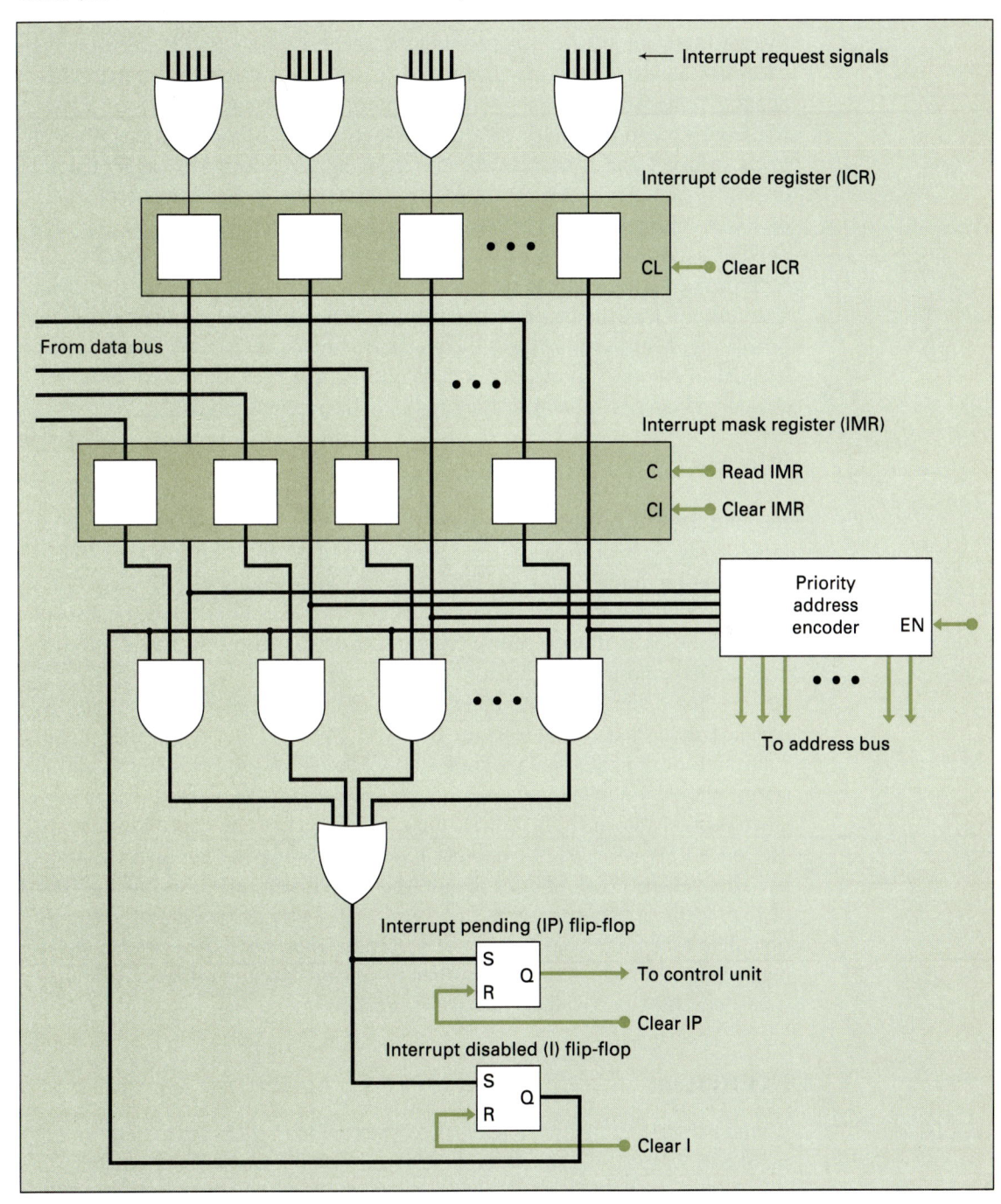

ICR. Consequently, if an IMR bit is clear, the corresponding ICR bit is masked, that is, prevented from initiating the interrupt. Note the addition of two micro-orders to this circuitry: one for loading the IMR and one for clearing it.

In systems that prioritize their exceptions, when an exception occurs, the hardware automatically masks all maskable exceptions and branches to the exception handler of the specified priority. If several exceptions occur simultaneously, some systems branch to the exception handler having the *lowest* priority. Each exception handler sets the IMR to mask all possible exceptions of lower priority, and it enables exceptions of higher priority to occur. Consequently if two or more exceptions occur simultaneously, the exception handler of lowest priority gains control first but is immediately interrupted by the pending exception of higher priority. In like manner each exception waiting to be processed is interrupted until the one with the highest priority is reached. The result is that the highest-priority exception is first to be processed. After processing, control returns to the exception handler of the next highest priority, and so on down through the queue until all the exceptions have been processed and control returns to the originally interrupted program.

**Returning from Exceptions**

A RETURN FROM INTERRUPT instruction does several things. First, using values in the save area, it restores the registers that the exception-initiation hardware initially saved. It also clears the interrupt-pending flip-flop, which initiated the exception in the first place. Since the interrupt-pending flip-flop is a CPU flag, the control unit saved its value during exception initiation. If the control unit did not clear it upon return from interrupt, the flip-flop would immediately initiate another exception.

Some computers use an exception procedure that is simpler than the one just described. Computers in the IBM System/370 family (IBM mainframes), for example, use a program status word (PSW) to hold the PC, all the status bits, the interrupt-code register, the interrupt mask register, and miscellaneous other information. When an exception occurs, the control unit swaps the active PSW with one of five other PSWs, depending on the exception priority. This has the effect of branching to the appropriate exception handler (one of five) while at the same time saving the status bits and exception information. The exception handler, not the hardware, then saves the contents of the registers it uses and restores them when it finishes executing. Figure 3.20 illustrates how IBM mainframes manage exceptions.

## 3.3 ■ I/O System

I/O system

A vital component of any computer architecture is its **I/O system.** This is the set of all I/O devices in the system, including both physical I/O devices and I/O interface devices. Physical I/O devices are those that actually perform I/O,

**FIGURE 3.20** *IBM System/360 interrupt structure. When an interrupt occurs, the CPU copies the old (current) program status word (PSW) into one of five fixed doubleword areas in main memory (depending on the type of exception) and loads a new PSW from one of five corresponding doubleword areas. Because the PSW contains the PC, swapping PSWs automatically causes a branch to the interrupt handler. Since the PSW also contains the interrupt mask, another effect is the automatic masking of additional interrupts.*

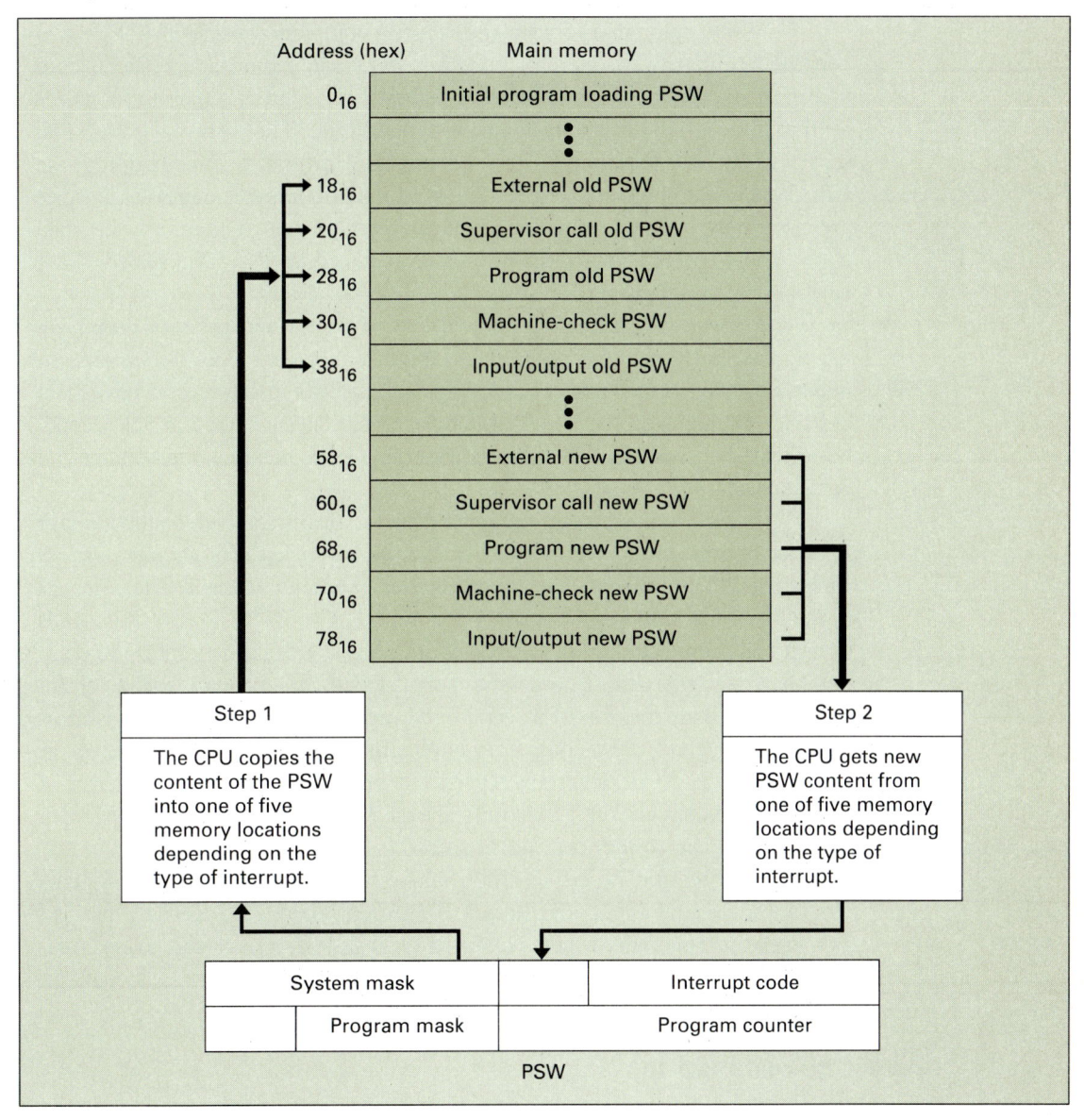

such as line printers, video displays, and consoles. We shall describe some of these in Section 3.3.6. I/O interface devices communicate with the CPU on the one hand and the physical I/O devices on the other. Thus they control the physical I/O devices while isolating the CPU from the specific characteristics of these devices.

When companies first manufactured computers, physical I/O devices consisted primarily of operator consoles, card and paper-tape readers, card and paper-tape punches, magnetic tapes, and line printers. Operator consoles at that time were electromechanical typewriters. They had switches that sensed which keys the operator pressed and transmitted the information to the CPU, and electromagnets actuated the keys under computer control. Consoles are used only by the computer operator: Cost precluded their use for data entry. Users entered data indirectly using punched cards (often called "IBM cards") or punched paper tape.

Printers take signals generated by computers and produce output on paper. Fast early printers could print about a thousand lines per minute or about 1300 characters per second. High-speed laser printers can now print close to one hundred pages per minute or about 8000 characters per second, but even these speeds are slow relative to the speeds at which a computer can generate data.

There are now numerous input devices. Terminals, personal computer (PC) keyboards, computer mouses, trackballs, joysticks, and scanners are all widely used. The amount of data that a user can enter through a terminal is limited to a few hundred characters per minute. Even with tens of thousands of terminals connected to a single computer, the aggregate data rates are comparable to a single disk. By way of contrast, video cameras can digitize entire images in a small fraction of a second and produce millions of bytes of information per second. Few computers have either the computational power or enough memory to perform any significant processing of digitized images at these rates. Later we shall explore some of the reasons for this, along with steps being taken to improve the situation.

This section describes three major techniques that current systems use for processing input and output: CPU-controlled I/O, memory-mapped I/O, and direct-memory-access (DMA) I/O. It also describes the corresponding I/O interface devices. We shall begin with a brief historical account of their need, their introduction, and their evolution.

### 3.3.1 ■ CPU-controlled I/O

The architects of early computers paid little attention to I/O processing, and the CPU directly controlled the I/O devices using very simple I/O instructions, such as WRITE A TO DEVICE N or READ A FROM DEVICE N. In these statements, A designates or implies a register and N designates an I/O device number (e.g., 1 for card reader, 2 for printer, and so on). These instructions transfer 1 byte or word of data at a time. The computers ran one program at a time, and each program executed its own instructions for input and output.

By the mid 1950s computers had become readily available, but their cost was still prohibitive for all but the government and very large companies. One of the primary goals of the computer architect was to design computers with the greatest-possible CPU utilization. I/O devices are mechanical, and their speeds are limited by mechanical components (usually on the order of milliseconds). This is much slower than the electronic components that comprise the CPU and buses (microseconds to nanoseconds). Thus the challenge was to find ways to increase the CPU utilization even though I/O devices were extremely slow.

Several different solutions have emerged, all based on three underlying developments:

1. **Multiprogramming operating systems.** The operating system loads several different programs into memory at the same time. The CPU can execute one program while another waits for an input or output operation.

    *multiprogramming operating systems*

2. **Multiported storage systems.** These devices either allow several processors to access memory simultaneously, or they arbitrate requests for memory cycles. I/O devices and the CPU can then share the same storage system.

    *multiported storage systems*

3. **I/O processors.** These special I/O interfaces, which include devices called DMA channels, and peripheral processing units (PPUs), can control the I/O devices without CPU intervention.

    *I/O processors*

The ideal is to have the CPU busy executing programs 100% of the time, while the I/O devices perform I/O. This ideal is rarely achieved, however.

## 3.3.2 ■ Multiprogramming Operating Systems

A multiprogramming operating system partitions memory, loads each program into a different partition, and restricts programs to their own partitions, perhaps using the relocation and protection techniques described in Section 4.2.1. When a program wants information from an external device (input), or it wants to send information to an external device (output), it requests an I/O service from the operating system. It makes the request by placing appropriate I/O request parameters in a prespecified place (a mailbox) and calling the operating system (for example, by generating a trap with a SUPERVISOR CALL instruction). The operating system then suspends the program that requested the I/O, initiates the I/O operation, and starts a different program executing. After the I/O processor services the I/O request, the operating system suspends the second program and resumes operation of the original program that was waiting for I/O. We described how the operating system can resume programs in Section 3.1.4, where we discussed exception-processing hardware.

### 3.3.3 ■ Multiported Storage

The earliest computers had an integrated CPU and storage system, and only the CPU could access memory. However, with the demand for multiprogramming and the need for independent I/O processors, designers have developed various types of hardware that allows more than one device to access the same storage system. A system bus is one example. A comparable device is a **memory-traffic controller,** which is also called a **memory-port controller.** A memory-port controller in essence is a switching circuit that accepts requests for memory from several competing devices, prioritizes the requests, and connects to memory the device with the highest priority.

    In general, whenever two different devices wish to share the same resource, the hardware must use a switch and an arbiter to decide which device will gain access to the resource. For system buses the arbiter is in the bus controller and the switches are within the bus masters; for main memory the arbiter and switches are within the memory-port controller. When a CPU or I/O controller wants to access memory, it sends a **service-request signal** (a read request or a write request) on a dedicated request line to the memory-port controller (see Fig. 3.21). When making a request, the requesting device must be ready to send the address of the datum to the address bus. It must also be ready to send a datum to the data bus (during a write cycle) or read a datum

*memory-traffic controller*
*memory-port controller*

*service-request signal*

FIGURE 3.21 *Use of a memory-port controller for connecting several devices to the same memory system. The control lines appearing between the devices and the memory-port controller include service-request lines and service-grant lines. R, read request; W, write request; G, request grant.*

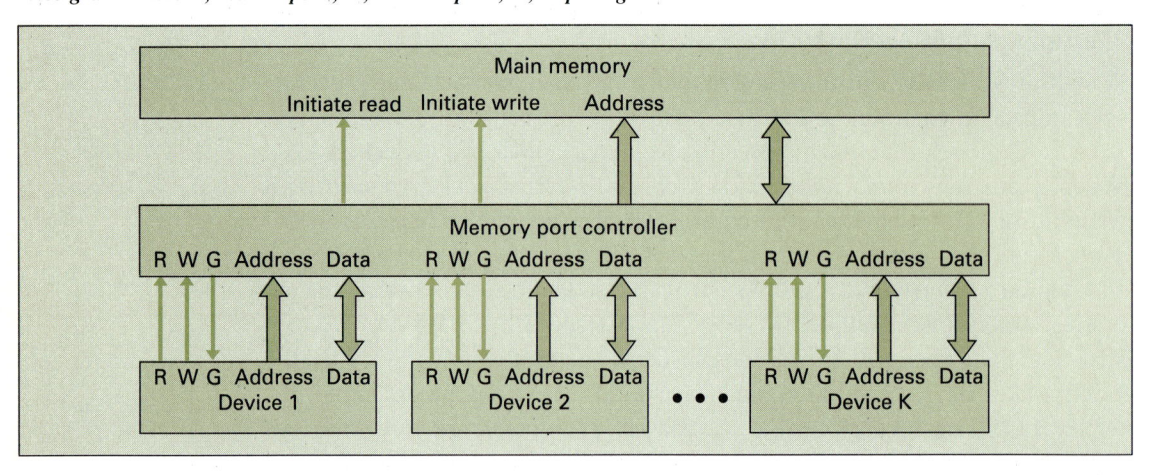

from the bus (during a read cycle). In either case, after sending the service-request signal to the port controller, the requesting device waits for a **service-grant signal** to arrive before proceeding.

*service-grant signal*

Request flags within the memory-port controller record the requests. At the start of each memory cycle an **arbitration network** or arbiter within the memory-port controller decides which device it will grant service to, and it connects that device to the storage system for one memory cycle. The memory-port controller also informs the connected device, with a service-grant signal, that it is connected to the memory system for one memory cycle. At the end of the memory cycle the memory-port controller clears the request flag of the device it just serviced.

*arbitration network*

There are many ways to select which I/O devices in Figure 3.21 will be granted access to the memory. Some of the prioritization algorithms, or protocols, are:

- *Fixed by device number.* The memory-port controller selects the device with the lowest device number N, say, when several devices simultaneously request service.
- *Round robin.* The memory-port controller selects the next device in order, restarting with the first device only after servicing the last device.
- *Time multiplexed.* The memory-port controller gives each device a fixed time slot. If there are 10 devices, for example, each device has access to memory one-tenth of the time.

You have now seen what it takes to connect several different devices to the same storage system. The following sections focus on I/O controllers, devices that transfer data between physical I/O devices, such as terminals and line printers, and main memory.

### 3.3.4 ■ DMA I/O

Hardware devices that directly control the transfer of data to and from main memory are called **direct-memory-access (DMA) controllers.** Some computers use relatively simple DMA controllers. For each transfer of data, the CPU sends the DMA controller the memory address for the block of data, the number of bytes to transfer, and the direction of transfer (input or output). The DMA controller performs the transfer without CPU intervention and interrupts the CPU when it is finished. For single-bus systems, such as typical microcomputers, the DMA controller is bus master during the transfer and therefore generates all bus control signals during the process. While the DMA controller is bus master, the CPU may have to wait to use the bus. The DMA controller is said to steal bus cycles from the CPU. **Cycle stealing** refers to any

*direct-memory-access (DMA) controllers*

*cycle stealing*

situation in which an I/O device causes the CPU to wait because it has exclusive access to a shared resource, such as a system bus or storage system. For some systems the DMA controller has an independent port to memory. Section 5.3.2 describes a simple DMA controller and its use.

*channels*

Some systems, notably IBM machines, use simple I/O processors called **channels**, which perform DMA I/O under the control of a very simple program called a channel program. Early channels had little or no memory of their own and very simple instruction sets. We shall describe channels in more detail later in this section. Current channels may have large cache memories for buffering data. (Cache memory will be discussed in detail in Chapter 4.)

*single-cycle DMA*

DMA controllers and channels that share system buses with the CPU and other devices often provide several modes of operation. One mode is **single-cycle DMA.** In this mode the DMA controller or channel requests use of the bus for each item it wishes to transfer. Other devices, including the CPU, can then access the bus during a transfer, thus not being blocked from memory for long periods of time. A second mode is **burst-mode DMA.** In this mode the DMA controller does not relinquish the bus until it completes an entire block transfer. DMA controllers that do not have local buffering use this mode for transferring blocks of data from or to I/O devices that can operate at main-memory speeds. For example, hard disks can usually transfer entire sectors at main-memory speeds.

*burst-mode DMA*

*peripheral-processing units (PPUs)*

Some computers, notably CDC computers, use relatively sophisticated I/O devices called **peripheral-processing units (PPUs),** which also perform DMA I/O. PPUs are complete although simple computers, and they have their own local memory. They also may perform computations in addition to I/O, such as data formatting, character translating, and buffering. Other computers use DMA devices of various intermediate levels of sophistication.

The remainder of this section shall enlarge upon many of the concepts pertaining to DMA I/O that we have introduced here in this summary introduction—DMA controllers, cycle stealing, channels and channel programs, and PPUs.

**DMA Channels**

DMA channels, used chiefly by IBM, resemble simple von Neumann machines in that they have their own PCs and register sets, but they differ in that they use the CPU's main memory. Architects design them primarily to control physical I/O devices, such as tape drives, disk drives, line printers, and so forth. As such, they have extremely simple instruction sets. Channel memory on early channels was generally limited to control registers and I/O buffers, which the channels used for assembling words of input data before transferring them to main memory, or for holding words of output data while preparing them for transfer to the output devices.

Figure 3.22 shows the major hardware components of a computer that uses DMA channels. It also shows typical control lines that pass between the CPU and one of the channels. I/O instructions activate the control lines, labeled SIO, HIO, TIO, and TCH in Fig. 3.22. The control lines start, stop, and test the channel. The channel uses the lines labeled CC and INT to contact the CPU. A channel raises an I/O interrupt request by sending a signal on INT, and it passes status information to the CPU by sending values on the condition-code lines, labeled CC. The CPU and the channel transfer all other information through specific main-memory locations, which they both can read and write, and they obey a strict **channel protocol,** which we shall discuss shortly.

channel protocol

For a computer that uses channels, the CPU generally has I/O instructions for starting them (START I/O), stopping them (HALT I/O), and testing their

**FIGURE 3.22** *Typical control lines (color) connecting a DMA channel to a CPU.*

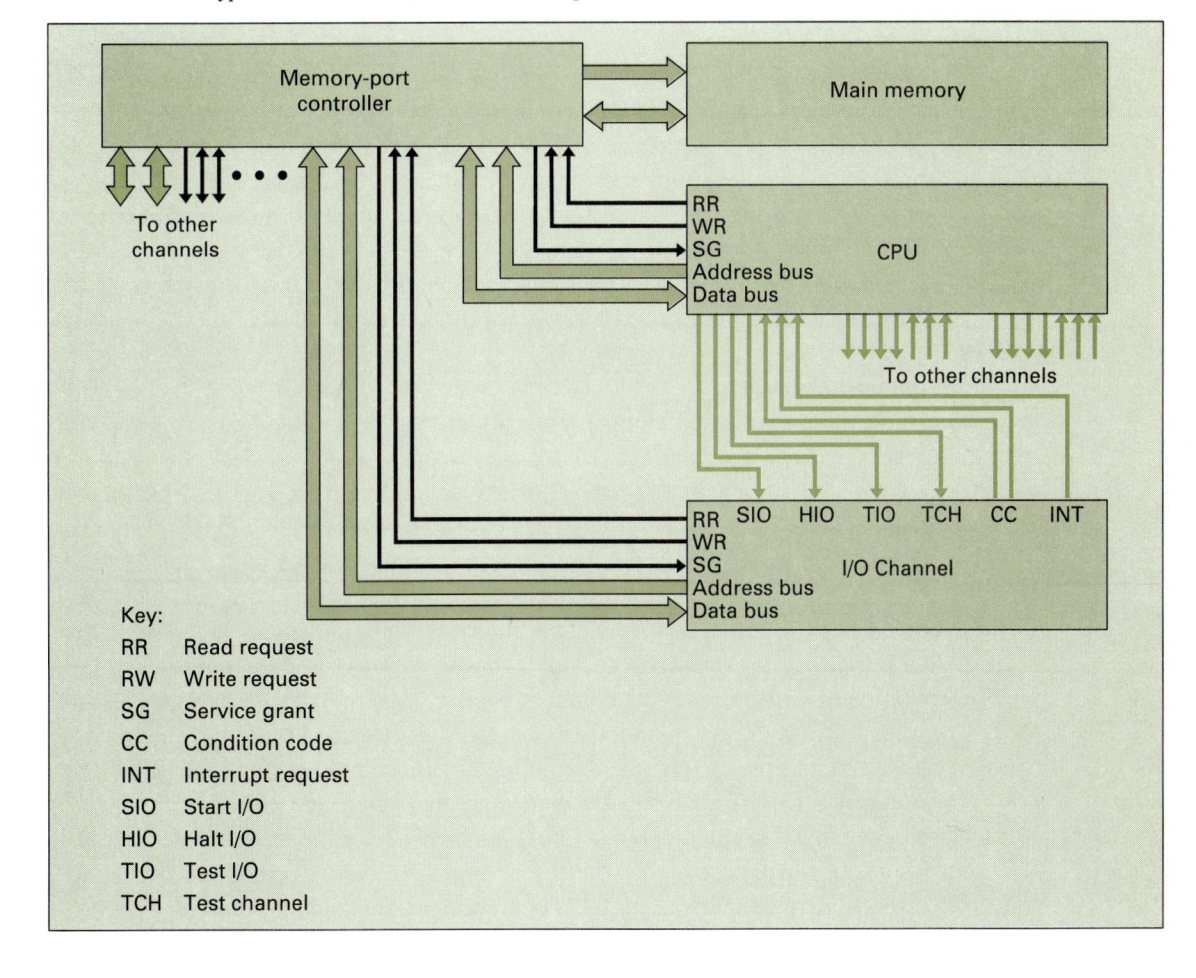

Key:
- RR    Read request
- RW    Write request
- SG    Service grant
- CC    Condition code
- INT   Interrupt request
- SIO   Start I/O
- HIO   Halt I/O
- TIO   Test I/O
- TCH   Test channel

progress (TEST CHANNEL and TEST I/O). These I/O instructions activate the control lines just described. After the CPU starts a channel, both the CPU and the channel operate independently. However, the CPU can stop the channel or check on its progress, and the channel can interrupt the CPU and request service, for example, if it senses an I/O error or finishes doing what the CPU requested it to do.

**channel commands**

Each channel controls itself and any attached I/O devices by executing instructions called **channel commands.** The nature of the commands depends on the devices the channel can control. For example, for a magnetic-tape device, the channel commands include SENSE, READ, WRITE, REWIND, WRITE TAPE MARK, BACKSPACE BLOCK, and so forth. The set of channel commands, which is sufficient for controlling all a computer's I/O devices and all physical I/O operations, defines a channel's ISA in the same way that a computer's instruction set defines its ISA. A CPU cannot execute channel commands, as they are not part of the CPU's instruction set; similarly, a channel cannot execute a CPU's instructions.

### Channel Programs

**channel programs**

Programmers organize channel commands into **channel programs.** A channel program is simply a sequence of channel commands for a complete I/O operation. Most channel commands control I/O devices, but some, such as TRANSFER IN CHANNEL, are branch instructions. Thus a channel can branch from one part of a channel program to another, loop, or execute conditional branches depending on the outcome of an I/O operation. The principles are the same as for ordinary computers, and we will not discuss them further.

### Channel Hardware

As we have seen, each channel has its own control unit, its own register set, and its own instruction set. Its registers include a PC, an IR, one or more counters, a data-address register, buffers for holding data, and additional control registers for memory protection or other services. See Fig. 3.23. Channel registers go under various names, such as command-address register (instead of PC) and command-code register (instead of instruction register). Nonetheless, the PC and IR serve the same functions for channels as they do for the CPU. The data-address register holds the main-memory address of the word or byte being transferred. The counters hold the total number of bytes the channel is to transfer and the number of bytes already transferred, and the buffers hold the data the channel is assembling or disassembling. For example, if the storage system processes doublewords and and I/O device processes bytes, the channel must assemble 8 bytes into a doubleword for input, and it must disassemble a doubleword into 8 bytes for output. Since the principles of channel operation are the same as for CPU operation, we shall not discuss them further.

## Channel Protocols

We shall now describe how channel I/O works. Suppose a program requires 100 bytes of data from tape drive T, which it wants in main memory beginning at address A. It therefore makes a request to the operating system for input. The request includes the following information: (1) the device name (tape drive T), (2) the byte count (100), (3) the direction of transfer (input), and (4) the starting main-memory address for the data (A). The program places this information in a preassigned place, such as on a stack, and it calls the operating system, often by initiating a trap (e.g., through a SUPERVISOR CALL). In response, the operating system generates a channel program to satisfy the request, and it places the channel program in main memory at some address, say P. (See Fig. 3.24.) It then starts the channel (by executing a START I/O instruction), and tells the channel where in main memory to find the channel program.

The channel now executes the channel program without CPU intervention. When the channel is done with one command, it fetches the next one from main memory, increments its PC, and continues in this way until either it finishes executing the entire channel program or it senses an abnormal condition. The last command in the channel program, END I/O in the Fig. 3.24, tells the channel to raise an I/O interrupt to inform the CPU that it is done.

**FIGURE 3.23** *Register set of a typical channel.*

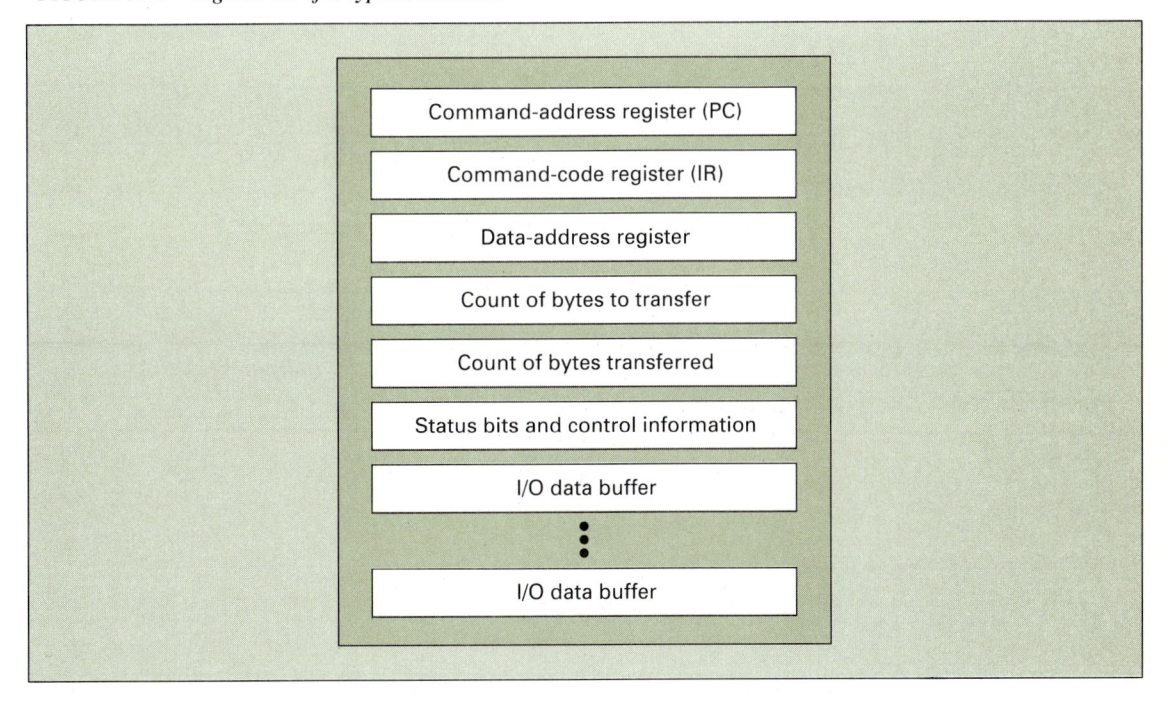

Following is a summary of the actions in the channel protocol. The numbers here correspond to the numbers circled in Fig. 3.24.

1. The operating system (CPU) creates a channel program and loads it into memory at address P.
2. It then issues a START I/O instruction to the channel and gives it the channel-program address, P. The CPU is now free to attend to other tasks unrelated to the channel program until Step 5.
3. The channel loads its PC with the value P and executes the channel program without CPU intervention.
4. The channel program controls the I/O device, which transfers the required data directly from the tape drive to main memory.
5. When finished, the channel interrupts the CPU to inform it that the channel program is done. The CPU may now assign a new task to the channel and restart the program that had requested the I/O operation in the first place.

When a channel interrupts the CPU, the I/O interrupt handler must determine which attached device requested the interrupt. To do so it checks

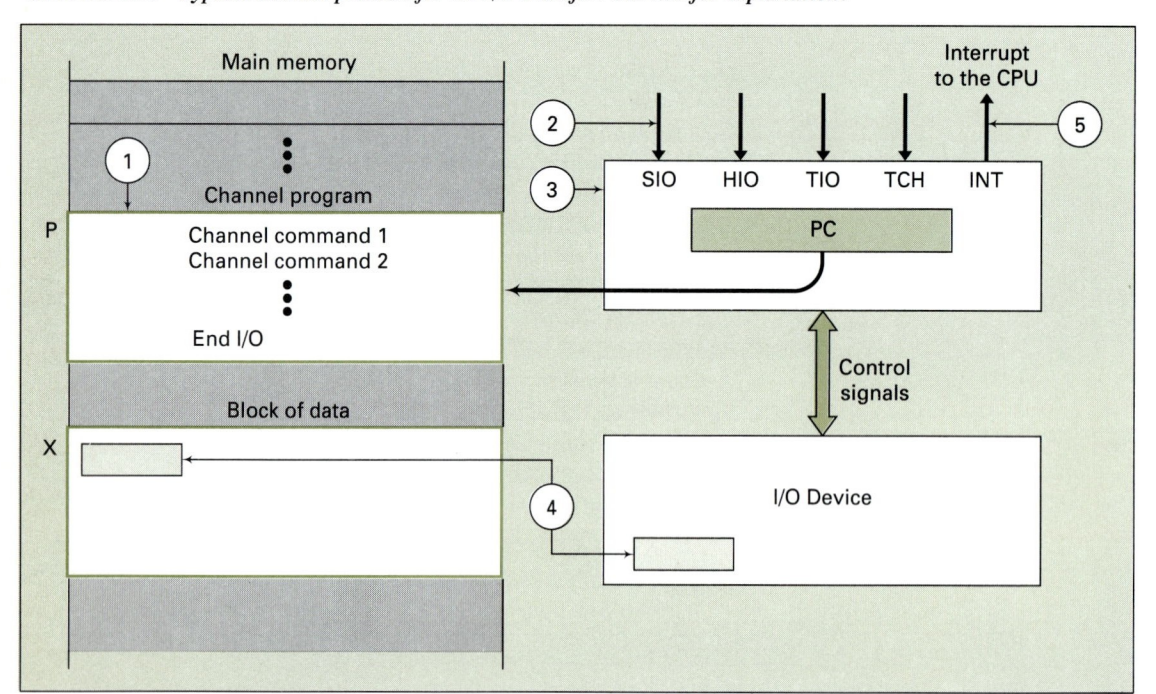

FIGURE 3.24  *Typical channel protocol for an I/O transfer. See text for explanation.*

the status of each device by issuing a TEST I/O instruction to it. In response, the tested channel sets the condition code and may also store additional status information in memory, where the CPU can read it. Once the interrupt handler determines which device requested the interrupt, it services that device. Details are beyond the scope of this discussion.

### Cycle Stealing
Whenever two devices simultaneously request a memory access, one of them must wait. If one of the devices is the CPU and the other is a channel, the memory-port controller generally gives higher priority to the channel for different reasons. For slow devices, the number of memory accesses is extremely small compared with the number of CPU memory accesses. Hence, a channel's stealing a memory cycle from the CPU will not have much affect on the CPU's performance. For fast devices, such as a disk, if the channel cannot transfer the data to or from the disk and free its buffer for the next item, it may be forced to miss a read or write access and have to wait for an entire disk revolution. Having a channel miss disk accesses can thus degrade system performance (i.e., reduce the system's efficiency) much more than holding up the CPU for a few cycles.

  Channels do not necessarily need to steal CPU cycles when they access main memory. Many memory-port controllers have several **ports** (independent data paths) to memory. Also, many memories have independent banks that are connected through different ports to the memory-port controller. When a system provides this hardware, different devices can access independent banks of memory simultaneously. For example, a channel can load a program into one bank of memory while the CPU simultaneously executes a program out of a different bank. In practice, however, there are always some points of contention, and channels steal cycles from the CPU.

                          ports

### Peripheral Processing Units
Control Data Corporation (CDC), as an example, has taken a different approach to I/O processing. Rather than using DMA channels, it uses relatively complex PPUs to perform I/O. The two features that most distinguish PPUs from channels are that (1) their programs are stored in their own memory rather than in the computer's main memory, and (2) their instruction sets are much more general and complete. Hence they can perform a greater variety of operations on the data they transfer, including formatting, conversions between datatypes (for example, ASCII characters into integers or floating-point numbers), and validity checking (i.e., assuring that the I/O device has transferred data without errors). For some computers, such as the CDC 6600, the PPUs may even hold and run part of the operating system. PPUs are generally slower and less powerful than the CPU, however, and consequently are much

less expensive. Also, intermediate configurations between extremely simple channels and sophisticated PPUs are possible and do exist.

PPUs transfer data between the physical I/O devices and their own memories, and they assemble the data into an appropriate format for the CPU. They also transfer the assembled data to main memory through a memory-port controller in much the same way that channels transfer data to and from main memory. In general, however, the memory-port controller gives the PPUs low priority for access to memory because the PPUs have sufficient buffering to continue performing I/O operations while awaiting access to main memory.

### 3.3.5 ■ Memory-mapped I/O

Many computers have I/O instructions for controlling the I/O devices. These computers generate special signals that differentiate I/O operations from memory-access operations. When executing an I/O instruction, these computers issue a signal indicating an I/O operation, and they generate the address of the I/O device, which they place on the address bus. Because the addresses are either I/O-device addresses or memory addresses, the I/O devices operate in one address space, called the **I/O-address space,** and memory-access instructions operate in an independent address space, called the **memory-address space.**

*I/O-address space*
*memory-address space*

*memory-mapped I/O*

Not all computers have I/O instructions, however. Many microcomputers and minicomputers use an I/O control technique called **memory-mapped I/O.** Rather than having explicit I/O instructions, these computers reserve specific addresses within the memory-address space, which they use for controlling the I/O interface devices. In essence the interface devices take the place of a portion of the physical main memory, and the CPU controls them using standard instructions that read and write to memory. For example, if the physical-address space of a computer is 64 KB, the designer may reserve the upper 16 KB for I/O interface devices. Like main memory, the I/O interface devices decode the addresses that appear on the address bus. Each I/O interface device responds to one or more specific **I/O port addresses.** The ports may be **control ports, status ports, input ports,** or **output ports,** depending on how the I/O device uses them. I/O port addresses are actually main-memory-location addresses and are mutually exclusive; that is, no other I/O interface device or memory responds to the same port addresses.

*I/O port addresses*

*control ports*
*status ports*
*input ports*
*output ports*

A processor that uses memory-mapped I/O requires no special I/O instructions. A store operation to an output port sends data to the attached I/O interface device, and a load operation from an input port receives data from the interface device. In fact, the CPU cannot distinguish between a memory access and an access to an I/O interface device. A store operation to a control port sends an I/O command to the interface device, and a load operation from a status port gets status information from it. To output a value, then, the CPU simply stores the output value in the correct output-port address, and to input a value the CPU loads it from the correct input-port address.

CPU-controlled I/O and memory-mapped I/O are not exclusive concepts, and computers that have I/O instructions may use memory-mapped I/O as well. The IBM PC is an example. We describe in Chapter 5 how it uses its I/O-address and memory-address spaces.

There is a large number of I/O interface devices, including DMA controllers, programmable parallel interfaces, and universal asynchronous receiver-transmitters. We shall describe several of them in Chapter 5, when we describe the architecture of the IBM PC.

## 3.3.6 ■ Physical I/O Devices

As technology changes, the characteristics of peripheral devices also change, and these changes frequently affect the I/O interface. Although a computer's architecture can be relatively independent of technology, as much of this text will show, peripheral devices have not achieved such technology independence. Partly this is due to their great diversity. Some address large blocks of data, some address individual bytes of data, and some access data sequentially; some use permanent storage media (e.g., fixed disks), while others use removable storage media (tapes and floppy disks); and transfer rates differ by orders of magnitude for each of these varieties of devices. Even when considering the parameters of one specific medium—disks—the range is enormous: the number of bytes per sector, sectors per track, tracks per cylinder, and cylinders per disk vary by orders of magnitude between devices. In addition, systems can be configured with a wide variety of printers, mouses, monitors, keyboards, communications devices (modems, facsimile machines), and so on.

**Intelligent peripheral devices**—those with controllers that hide the device-specific characteristics from the CPU and frequently buffer the data as well—are beginning to provide architects with one sort of device independence. For example, computers address some disks by sector number only, instead of by sector number, track number, and cylinder number. The following sections present brief descriptions of a few common I/O devices.

*intelligient peripheral devices*

### Peripheral Storage Devices

Many devices provide the CPU with a large amount of **external storage** (storage outside of main memory), and the CPU accesses these devices using the I/O system. Two examples are tape drives and disk drives, which store data on magnetic tapes and magnetic disks, respectively. The CPU accesses a datum (or a block of data) by presenting the I/O system with a description of the I/O medium (e.g., tape name or disk name), the number of words or bytes to transfer, the direction of transfer (input or output), and the address of the first word or byte on the storage medium. The program requesting the data may also need to describe the organization of the data on the storage medium.

*external storage*

Here we will briefly describe two common storage devices: tape drives and disk drives.

### Tape Drives

Tape drives store their data on magnetic tapes, which resemble tapes used in popular audio systems. Some tape drives use reel-to-reel tapes; others use tape cassettes. A physical transport mechanism moves the magnetic tape across a read/write head, which can read or write only the datum that is physically beneath the head. Some tape drives can read or write a single bit at a time; others have several adjacent read/write circuits and can read or write several bits (e.g., a byte) simultaneously. In either case, the tape drive must process successive bits or bytes serially, so these devices are considered **sequential-access devices.**

For data stored on tape, the access time depends both on where the item is on the tape and on the state of the tape in the tape drive. If the tape is rewound (to the beginning), the time required to access a word is proportional to its (linear) position on the tape. Access time may be as long as several minutes. Once an item is located under the read head, the **transfer rate,** which is the time it takes to transfer sequential words of data, approaches processor speeds.

### Disk Drives

A magnetic disk is a storage device that resembles a phonograph record in appearance. The surface of a disk is smooth, however, and is covered with magnetic material resembling the material that coats magnetic tapes. Inflexible magnetic disks are called hard disks; flexible magnetic disks are called floppy disks. The devices that hold and process them are **disk drives.**

A disk drive may hold a single disk or several. Floppy drives generally hold a single disk; hard drives with nonremovable disks generally hold several disks called **platters**. The platters are all on the same spindle and rotate together. See Fig. 3.25(a). Each platter has a top and bottom surface, but disk drives often do not use all of the surfaces. **Read-write heads** within the disk drive read and write the data on the platters. Each usable disk surface may have one head, a few heads, or as many as one head for each track (see below), and a given disk drive may have several heads for each surface. The disk drive illustrated in Fig. 3.25(a) has three platters and three read-write heads. When a disk drive has a single read-write head for each surface (the most common case), a single mechanical head assembly holds all the read-write heads and positions them simultaneously.

Disk drives generally organize their data into **tracks**, which are circular paths of data (see Fig. 3.25(b)). Notice that this concentric-circle arrangement differs from the way data on one side of a phonograph record is organized into a single spiral track. Disks may have hundreds of tracks on them. For multiple-platter disks, the set of tracks on all platters at a given distance from the spindle is a **cylinder**. Frequently a disk drive organizes each track into **sectors** of 256 bytes to 4 KB, and many disks write the sector numbers on each track at the beginning of each sector. This is **soft sectoring,** and when using soft sectoring the software or hardware must search for the required sector. A program specifies the address of a word by giving its platter number, track number, sector number, and word number.

The **disk access time,** the time it takes for a disk drive to access a single word, depends on several factors. To begin with, if the device has fewer than one head per track, the head assembly must physically position the heads above the desired track. The time it takes a disk drive to position the heads is the **seek time,** which depends on the speed of the head-positioning mechanism and the initial position of the heads relative to the desired track. Once the read head has reached the correct track, it must be positioned over the desired word. Since the heads cannot move around the track, the disk must rotate into position under the head. The time this takes is the **rotational delay** or **rotational latency.** Disk access time is therefore a combination of four factors: initial configuration of the device, seek time, rotational delay, and the speed of the circuitry. Once a word is accessed, disks can transfer blocks of sequential items at relatively high speeds. Frequently disk drives can transfer blocks of data at processor speeds, where **block** here refers to a sequence of contiguous words contained within one disk sector. Disk drives are therefore examples of **block-oriented memories.**

**disk access time**

**seek time**

**rotational delay**
**rotational latency**

**block**

**block-oriented memories**

FIGURE 3.25 *A typical hard disk. (a) Basic hardware. (b) Organization of a single disk or platter.*

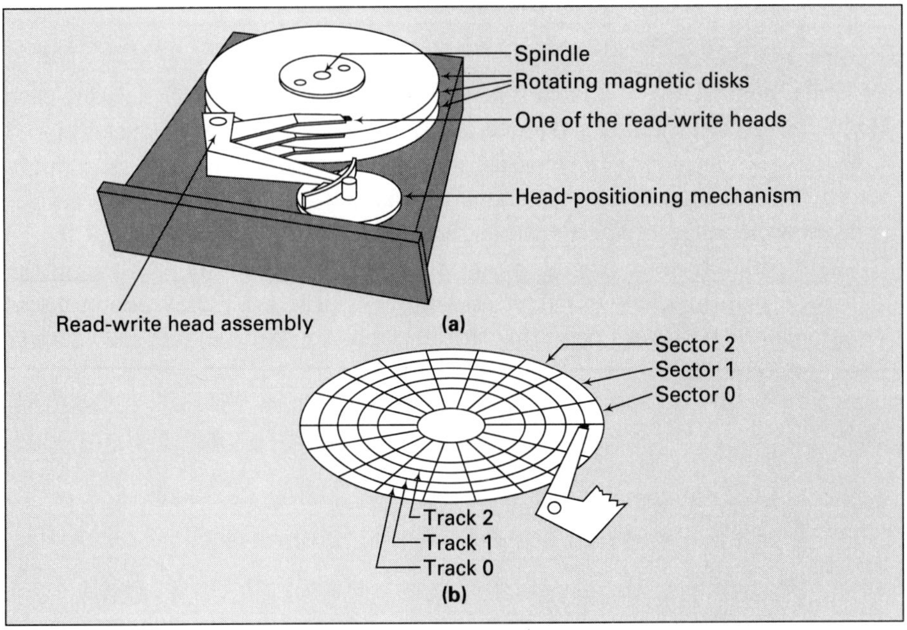

The average access times for single items from disks range from a few milliseconds for very fast devices to 100 ms or more for slow devices. In 1990 transfer rates varied from a few score kilobytes per second (slow floppy disks) up to about 25 MB/S (supercomputer disks).

The access times for disks are much shorter than for tapes. This stems from the fact that both seek time and the rotational delay are limited: Rotational delay is generally less than $16\frac{2}{3}$ ms (3600 rpm or 1/60 second per revolution), while seek time, although device-dependent, rarely exceeds 100 ms, even for slow devices. That is why disks are sometimes called pseudo-random access. They are also sometimes called **block-oriented, random-access devices.**

### Printers

Printers are output devices, and, as we said earlier, they are relatively slow. A CPU or I/O interface controls a printer by sending it two types of information: control information and data to be printed. The control information is printer-specific but typically tells the printer what to do: eject a page, move to the next line, advance the page a fixed number of millimeters, change the typeface, change the type size, and so forth. The data tell the printer what to print, frequently using a character code such as ASCII to specify the characters. Many printers can print graphic images as well as text.

Although from the point of view of a user program a printer is strictly at output device, most printers send status information to the CPU or I/O interface devices that control them. The status information tells the CPU about the outcome of a printer operation, such as, that is was successful, that a paper jam occurred, or that the paper tray was out of paper.

### Other I/O Devices

Device manufacturers currently produce a wide variety of I/O devices, each with its own I/O interface characteristics. Input devices range from slow-speed devices, such as mouses, keyboards, track balls, and digitizing tablets, to high-speed devices, such as video cameras and page scanners. Output devices also have a range of speeds, from relatively slow dot-matrix printers to the faster-operating voice synthesizers, plotters, and monitors. Although the characteristics of their I/O interfaces differ widely, a CPU can control and communicate with each one using the relatively standard I/O interface devices so far described.

# Summary

This chapter focused on the hardware-system architecture of von Neumann computers, with major emphasis on the bus system, the central processor, and the I/O system.

We first discussed buses, distinguishing between local, system, and expanded local buses, and we described a typical bus transfer protocol.

The CPU consists primarily of the control unit and the functional units that perform arithmetic, logical operations, and shift operations. The components of a functional unit were briefly described. We took a brief look at microprogramming, discussing the difference between a microprogrammed control unit and a conventional or hard-wired control unit. We then described exception-processing hardware (usually part of the control unit), demonstrating how the hardware initiates interrupts and restores the program state after returning from them.

The I/O system is a major component of all computers. The chapter described three ways of organizing I/O: CPU-controlled I/O, DMA I/O, and memory-mapped I/O. The primary focus was on DMA I/O, because that is how most systems manage I/O. Personal computers, for example, use DMA controllers, which are essentially very simple channels; these will be examined in greater detail in Chapter 5. Some systems use PPUs, a more complex form of DMA, for processing I/O.

# Exercises

*3.1* Describe a technique for decreasing the microinstruction size in a control unit that uses horizontal control. (*Hint:* The control unit will issue only a few microorders at a time.)

*3.2* Describe how a computer manufacturer can correct a design error that a user discovers in a microprogram.

*3.3* Describe circuitry that would allow a computer to execute microinstructions whose execution time is variable or unknown. (For example, a memory access may take an unpredictable amount of time if the memory is shared by several devices.)

*3.4* For the hypothetical computer described in the optional section on microprogramming, show microcode for interrupt initiation.

*3.5* Determine how long the delay can be between a request for an interrupt and its initiation. Assume there is a MOVE STRING instruction that can move strings of up to 16 K characters.

    a. In a mainframe computer that moves 16 characters with each memory access and with a memory cycle time of 40 nsec.

    b. In a microcomputer that moves 2 bytes at a time and has a 125-nsec memory cycle.

State clearly any additional assumptions you need to make for your computations, such as to how the control unit implements the MOVE STRING instruction.

*3.6* Describe two special machine instructions that a computer with masked and prioritized interrupts would need.

*3.7* Refer to Fig. 3.17. Describe how the circuitry to handle vectored interrupts differs from that used with nonvectored interrupts.

*3.8* Explain how a microprogrammed control unit can handle invalid op codes.

*3.9* Describe the events that would follow a RETURN FROM INTERRUPT if the control unit did not clear the exception flag when executing the RETURN FROM INTERRUPT instruction.

*3.10* Describe the events following a RETURN FROM

interrupt when there is a lower-priority exception pending.

*3.11* If a CPU receives multiple requests for exceptions at about the same time, it should service all of them before returning control to the interrupted program. What type of mechanism should it use for holding the interrupt requests: a queue, a stack, or something else? Explain.

*3.12* Describe advantages and disadvantages of using (1) a stack, (2) a queue, and (3) a save area for saving the processor context when an interrupt occurs.

*3.13* Some computers have special traps, often used for unimplemented instructions, that do not invoke the operating system. Explain why such traps might be useful. (For example, the VAX has "emulation exceptions" that operate this way.)

*3.14* Operating systems generally place data for I/O into a specific area of memory, called an I/O buffer. How does the size of the I/O buffer affect I/O performance?

*3.15* What is the relationship between a memory-port controller and a bus controller? Show how to connect several devices to one memory system using a single system bus.

*3.16* Consider a computer that uses DMA channels. Suppose the transfer rate to main memory is 1 MHz and that each transfer consists of 1 word (4 bytes). Also suppose that an I/O device operates at 1000 bytes/s (about 9600 baud). Finally, suppose the channel has a memory conflict with the CPU during every access and therefore steals cycles from the CPU at every opportunity. How many cycles can it steal in 1 min? What percentage of the CPU's memory accesses does that amount to if the CPU would normally access memory at the rate of 1 word/$\mu$s?

*3.17* Operating systems frequently use circular buffers for I/O: A DMA device puts data into the buffer at one end while the operating system removes it from the other. What are the consequences if the operating system does not remove data fast enough from a circular buffer? From a circular character buffer for a terminal?

*3.18* Why does DMA I/O generally have priority over the CPU for access to memory? (*Hint:* Consider disk I/O.)

*3.19* What types of instructions can systems with memory-mapped I/O use for I/O?

*3.20* Assume that your computer executes on the average 500 K instructions per second and has a bus bandwidth of 5 MBS. If each instruction requires on average 4 bytes of information for operands and the instruction itself, what I/O bandwidth is available for DMA I/O? If the CPU performs the I/O itself and each byte of I/O requires two instructions, what I/O bandwidth is available? In the latter case, what bus bandwidth is available for DMA I/O?

## Reference-needed Exercise

*3.21* Explain why the designers of the IBM System/360 computer might have assigned the addresses they did to the doublewords in main memory that hold the old and new PSWs during interrupts. (*Hints:* For each type of interrupt, consider how the old PSW and new PSW addresses differ. Some System/360 family members did not have hardware registers but used main memory instead. What locations in main memory would you expect those systems to use for the registers?)

# Problems

*3.22* For the hypothetical computer described in the optional section on microprogramming, write a microprogram for the JUMP instruction and show its microcode. The JUMP instruction copies the address field of the instruction into the PC.

*3.23* For the hypothetical computer described in the optional section on microprogramming, describe the circuitry that would be needed for a conditional branch instruction, such as BRANCH ON CARRY SET, and show the microprogram for it. You may want to assume that the addresses of certain microinstructions are even numbers.

*3.24* Describe three ways that the replacement of a functional unit in a microprogrammed computer might affect its microprograms.

*3.25* For the hypothetical computer described in the optional section on microprogramming, write a microprogram for the STORE instruction and show its microcode.

*3.26* Describe how a control unit can overlap the execution of one instruction with fetching the next instruction. Explain what the control unit must do if the executing instruction is a conditional branch instruction.

*3.27* Describe some uses for a MAX instruction. (MAX puts the maximum of R1 and R2, say, in R3 where R1, R2 and R3 are registers.) What instructions might MAX replace in actual programs?

*3.28* Some computers include a NORMALIZE(R1, R2) instruction, which shifts the value in register R1 left by $n$ bits (where $n$ is the number of leading zeros in the mantissa field of R1) and then places the value $n$ in register R2. Illustrate two nontrivial uses of this NORMALIZE instruction. Describe how to get the same result with other instructions.

*3.29* Many microinstruction formats allow for immediate constants. Describe three uses for such constants.

*3.30* If a computer does not vector its interrupts to specific interrupt handlers, how can it accommodate multiple interrupts? That is, how can it handle multiple interrupts if they all cause it to store its program context at one location?

*3.31* Compare the execution times, hardware complexity, and software complexity of an interrupt system that uses vectored interrupts with one that swaps PSWs.

*3.32* Explain how a designer might add power-failure detection to a computer, and show how power-failure hardware could raise an interrupt. Under what circumstances would such an interrupt be useful?

*3.33* Some computers can initiate traps in the middle of long instructions, such as MOVE STRING. Some initiate traps, such as machine-fault traps, the moment they occur. Under what conditions can a computer restart an interrupted instruction after the instruction has started executing? Consider both simple and complex instructions, and consider a variety of types of exceptions.

*3.34* Generally, when a program wants to perform an I/O operation, it makes a request to the operating system. The operating system usually issues those requests to an available I/O device. For a complex system any number of I/O requests may be waiting for service by an I/O device. One way for the operating system to manage the I/O requests is to build queues in memory that hold them. Each queue holds requests for one controller, and each queue entry holds one I/O request. The operating system inserts requests at the end of the queues, while available I/O devices remove requests from the front. What special instructions might be necessary for a system of this type to maintain its integrity? Describe the design of such an I/O system.

*3.35* Assume that memory is divided into two banks. Design a memory-port controller that has two ports to main memory, one to each bank, and can service four devices. Design it so that it can simultaneously connect any two devices to memory, provided the devices do not request the same bank.

*3.36* Justify with numbers the fact that system performance can suffer if a high-speed disk misses a read or write access and is forced to wait for an entire revolution of the disk. Assume that a high-speed disk rotates at about 90 revolutions per second and that each track can hold 75 KB.

## Challenging Problem

*3.37* Designers of several large computer families have expended great effort to make all the exceptions precise, in the sense that the programs can always be backed up to exactly the point of the exception and reexecuted from that point, perhaps after fixing the exception-causing condition. What features of computers make precise exceptions difficult? Are there computer architectures that make precise exceptions unnecessary? In other words, are there architectures that allow aborting any job that causes a trap?

## Discussion/Team Problems

*3.38* A conventional (hard-wired) control unit follows the same general control principles as a microprogrammed control unit. Would you expect to find vertical or horizontal control in a conventional control unit? Explain.

*3.39* Nearly all computer systems use interrupts to allow peripheral equipment to request service from the CPU. An alternative is to use polling, where the CPU checks the peripheral equipment at specific intervals. If an interrupt requires 100 $\mu$s of overhead time (typical for a fast computer), and polling requires 10 $\mu$s per device (about right for simple devices that are close to the computer), what are some of the situations where each seems preferable? (*Hint:* Remember to consider "impatient" peripheral equipment, like disks and DMA transfers, that require only CPU notification and initiation.)

**3.40** Gene Amdahl formulated a useful rule of thumb that a computer should be able to do 1 byte of I/O per instruction. In other words, if a computer executes at the rate of 1 MIPS, it should have an I/O transfer rate of 1 MBS. For what types of programs does this seem to be a useful rule of thumb, and for what types does it appear to be unreasonable? Explain.

**3.41** My favorite computer (favorite every Tuesday evening when my manuscript is on a prime page number) has just added vector instructions, which quadruple the effective speed of the computer. How can you increase the speed of the disks by a factor of 4 (i.e., increase their bandwidth or decrease their access time by a factor of 4)?

**3.42** Why do virtually all computers use interrupts to awaken the operating system for I/O rather than polling the I/O devices at some time that is convenient for the operating system?

# Chapter Index

accept signal 122
access time (disk) 167
address bus 120
address-computation circuitry 129
address-enable signal 124
arbiter 120
arbitration network 157
block 167
block-oriented memory 167
block-oriented random-access device 168
branching microinstruction 133
bus arbiter 120
burst-mode DMA 158
bus controller 120
bus-control signal 124
bus cycle 122
bus-grant line 122
bus master 122
bus protocol 122
bus-request line 122
bus-request signal 122
bus state 122
bus transfer 122
central processing unit (CPU) 124
channel 158
channel command 160
channel program 160
channel protocol 159

control bus 120
control port 164
control store 129
conventional control unit 128
cycle stealing 157
cylinder 166
data bus 120
direct-memory-access (DMA) controller 157
disk access time 167
disk drive 166
entry-point address 132
exception 143
exception handler 144
exception number 148
exception vector 148
exception-vector table 148
exception-vector-table address register 148
expanded local bus 121
external storage 165
functional unit 125
hard-wired control unit 128
horizontal control 134
I/O-address space 164
I/O port address 164
I/O processor 155
I/O read cycle 122
I/O system 152
I/O write cycle 122
input port 164

intelligent peripheral device 165
interrupt 143
interrupt-code flag 146
interrupt-code register (ICR) 147
interrupt cycle 122
interrupt-disable flip-flop 148
interrupt handler 144
interrupt mask 149
interrupt-mask register (IMR) 149
interrupt-pending flip-flop 148
interrupt polling 148
interrupt-request line 146
local bus 120
memory-address space 164
memory context 144
memory-mapped I/O 164
memory-port controller 156
memory read cycle 122
memory traffic controller 156
memory write cycle 122
microinstruction 128
microinstruction buffer 129
microinstruction decoder 129
microinstruction format 139
microorder 127
microprogram 128
microprogram counter ($\mu$PC) 129
microprogrammed control unit 128

microprogramming 136
multiported storage system 155
multiprogramming operating system 155
nonbranching microinstruction 133
output port 164
parity 149
peripheral processing unit (PPU) 158
platter 166
port 163
processor context 144
program context 144
read-write head 166

reset vector 131
reset-vector address 131
rotational delay 167
rotational latency 167
run-time behavior 144
run-time state 144
save area 145
sector (disk drive) 166
seek time 167
sequencer 130
sequential-access device 166
service-grant signal 157
service-request signal 156

single-cycle DMA 158
slave device 122
soft sectoring 166
status port 164
status register 126
status signal 122
system bus 120
track 166
transfer rate 166
trap 144
trap handler 144
vectored exception 148
vertical control 136

# 4
# Memory-system Architecture

**4.1 Memory-system Technology and Cost** *175*
    4.1.1 Memory Organizations *179*
    4.1.2 Types of Memory *183*

**4.2 Main-memory System** *189*
    4.2.1 Program Relocation and Protection *191*
    4.2.2 Cache Memory *196*
    4.2.3 Virtual Memory *204*
    4.2.4 Memory Banking and Expanded Memory *215*

**4.3 Memory Design Issues** *218*
    4.3.1 Memory Speed versus CPU Speed *218*
    4.3.2 Memory-address Space *219*
    4.3.3 Speed—Cost Tradeoffs *221*

*This chapter focuses on memory. We begin in Section 4.1 by describing memory technology and the characteristics of various types of memory components. Section 4.2 indicates how designers combine memory components to form memory systems. After discussing the characteristics of a typical one-level memory system (Section 4.2.1), we focus on multilevel storage systems. Cache memory (Section 4.2.2), virtual memory (Section 4.2.3), and memory banking (Section 4.2.4) are discussed, along with the relationships between these memory-system components. As in Chapter 3, this chapter ends with a focus on design issues (Section 4.3).*

> **Key Terms**
>
> **Cache memory**  A high-speed random-access memory (RAM) positioned between a memory system and its user to reduce the effective access time of the memory system. All memory requests go to cache. When the cache holds a copy of the requested datum, the cache quickly processes the request (a cache hit). Otherwise, the cache forwards the request to main memory (a cache miss).
>
> **Dynamic random-access memory (DRAM)**  Memory that requires periodic refreshing to keep the data active.
>
> **Memory banking**  A technique for increasing the amount of high-speed RAM available to a computer. The memory banking system consists of a number of physical banks of memory and a bank-select register. The memory banking hardware maps a specific range of physical addresses, called a window, to addresses within this selected memory bank.
>
> **Memory hierarchy**  The hierarchy of storage devices within a computer, comprising primary memory (internal components such as the CPU registers, cache memory, and main memory) and secondary memory (any external storage devices such as disks or tapes).
>
> **Virtual memory**  A memory system used to increase the effective size of the computer's physical memory. Virtual memory maps the user's logical addresses to physical addresses, so parts of the program may reside at physical addresses that differ from the logical addresses.

## 4.1 ■ Memory-system Technology and Cost

Two technologies have dominated the central or main memory industry: magnetic-core memory during the 1960s, and solid-state memory since then. However, designers have tried many other technologies along the way.

The first commercially manufactured computer was the Univac. Its CPU used vacuum-tube technology and performed decimal arithmetic. It had a 1000-word main memory, where each word was 60 bits wide and held 12 five-bit characters. Because vacuum tubes were too costly to use for main memory, Univac's designers used 100 memory modules consisting of mercury delay lines. Each memory module was a shift register that could hold 10 words. Within each module the circuitry introduced electrical pulses at one end of the delay line and detected them 404 $\mu$s later at the other end. After the circuitry detected the pulses, it amplified, cleaned, and reinserted them at the beginning of the delay line. The average access time for a word was 202 $\mu$s, or half the total time for a word to pass through the delay line.

During the 1960s the dominant main-memory technology was magnetic core, and as a result people often referred to main memories as *core memories*. Today we sometimes use the expression *core memory* to mean main memory, but it rarely presumes any particular technology. The storage cells in a core memory were manufactured out of doughnut-shaped ferrous elements called **magnetic cores** or simply **cores**, hence the name. The circuitry could magnetize them in either of two directions. When magnetized in one direction, a core held the value $0_2$; when magnetized the other way it held the value $1_2$. Manufacturers organized cores in a variety of ways to form **core planes,** and they organized core planes, together with other required circuits, into **memory banks.** Core planes correspond to the memory chips in today's solid-state memories, and manufacturers often organize memory chips into banks just as they once did core planes.

Memory systems that were previously manufactured out of magnetic cores, and cost millions of dollars, can now be manufactured out of integrated circuits (ICs) for a few hundred dollars. Moreover, memory speeds were once limited by relatively long **cycle times,** the time it took to read and write a magnetic core (1000 to 2000 ns being typical). Memory speeds are now limited by the switching times (gate delays) of the ICs; 60 to 150 ns cycle times are common today.

Except for mercury-delay-line memory, all of the memory circuits we shall describe are **random-access memories (RAMs).** RAMs are able to access every word in essentially the same amount of time because they use switching circuits to select words to be accessed. In this respect they differ from other kinds of memory that must first physically move the data to the read circuitry. Shift-register memory (such as magnetic bubble memory and charge-coupled devices) and magnetic tapes and disks are all forms of memory that use the latter form of access; hence the access time depends on how long it takes the device to move the data to the read head.

Figure 4.1 illustrates the major external connections to a typical RAM chip. The data bus serves both as an input and an output bus for data, although some chips use separate input and output buses. The address bus delivers addresses to the RAM chip, and the control lines control its operation. Designers usually use a number of RAM chips when building memories, as Fig. 4.4 shows.

Addressed memories are by far the most common type; any references made in this text to memory systems will assume them to be addressed memory systems unless otherwise stated.

The cost of memory has decreased exponentially or nearly exponentially, and it appears likely that it will continue to do so for a long time because of the rapid increase in density of integrated circuits and the demand for larger memories. Larger RAMs, lower-cost packaging, and lower-power technologies promise continued cost declines during the rest of the 20th century. Furthermore, speeds are slowly increasing as memory sizes grow, so there is little reason to assume a drastic change will occur in the trends in memory cost and size.

The rapidly decreasing unit cost of memory implies that main-memory sizes will continue to grow. Eventual, practical upper bounds on the size of main memory will be dictated by applications and solutions. We predict that in time all memory used for nonarchival purposes will become part of the central memory of the computer. In other words, disks and similar devices now used to hold databases and intermediate results will be relegated to archiving, backup, and other kinds of long-term storage.

A related question is whether there is an upper limit on the size of memory for programs. We cannot answer that in general, but we can at least determine the sizes of very large databases and very large scientific and engineering data sets. What are the largest problems run on computers today? What are the largest databases? The answer appears to be on the order of $2^{40}$ to $2^{50}$ bytes, a terabyte (TB) to petabyte (PB). There are on the order of 1 TB of characters in the books of the Library of Congress or 1 TB of pixels in one day's worth of high-definition TV (HDTV) or a feature-length movie. A typical 1990 supercomputer could reference its memory at the rate of about 1 PB/day or generate output at the rate of about 1 PB per year.

Figure 4.2 shows the historical and extrapolated trends in memory-device sizes. From this figure one can extrapolate the expected minimum memory sizes if one assumes that designers will organize memories so that each memory word uses 1 bit per chip. This last assumption may not be at all well founded, but one can also assume that memory interleaving (to be discussed in Section 4.1.1) will increase to offset multibit chip organizations. For

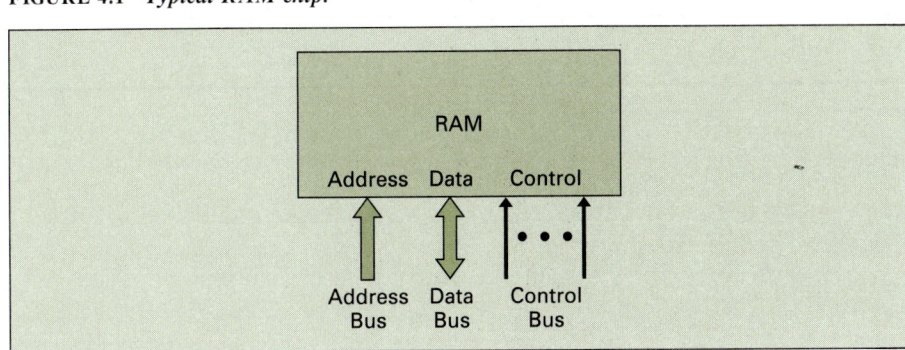

**FIGURE 4.1** *Typical RAM chip.*

example, computers of a given cost and family tend to use about the same number of memory chips from one model to the next. The point of this extrapolation is to show that computer architects should not limit the size of the physical-address space of a computer to less than about 1 PB, and that individual programs should be able to reference about that much memory for some applications.

Figure 4.3 shows the historical trend in memory sizes for supercomputers and minicomputers. From this figure one can show that maximum memory sizes for minicomputers roughly fall on the curve

$$M_m = 2^{[2(Y-1979)/3]} \text{MB}, \tag{1}$$

where $Y$ is the year. Similarly, maximum supercomputer memory sizes fall roughly on the curve

$$M_s = 2^{[Y-1966/2]} \text{MB}. \tag{2}$$

The functions in Eqs. 1 and 2 already span two technologies, magnetic cores and silicon ICs. Clearly these relationships cannot be expected to hold indefinitely, because then minicomputer memory sizes would overtake supercomputer memory sizes, a rather unlikely event.

FIGURE 4.2  *Evolution of memory and device sizes. Notice that growth has been nearly exponential despite the fact that computer-memory technology has varied from magnetic core to integrated circuit. Static RAM (SRAM) and dynamic RAM (DRAM) are two RAM implementations described in Section 4.1.2.*

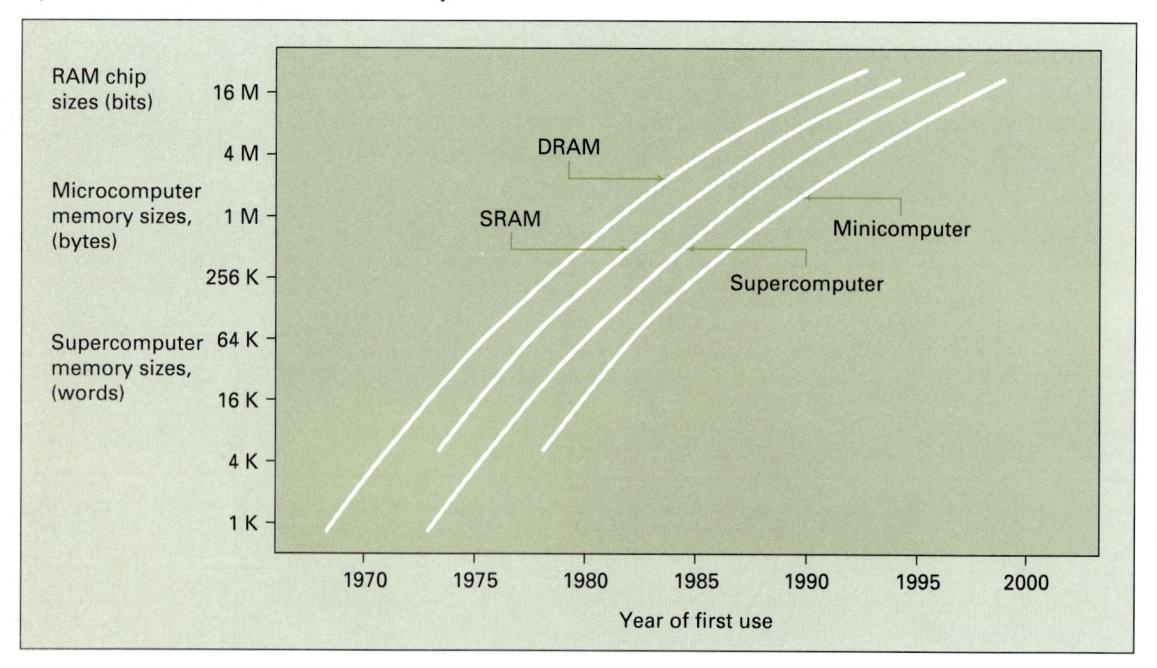

### 4.1.1 ■ Memory Organizations

Figure 4.4 shows the design of a 2-MB memory system whose circuit uses an organization called **high-order interleave**. Each word is 1 byte wide. The RAM chips can store 256-K 4-bit words, so the memory system requires eight pairs of chips. Note that each chip has 18 address lines ($2^{18}$ = 256 K), while the entire memory system requires 21 address lines. In this organization the high-order address bits select a particular pair of memory chips while the 18 low-order address bits select the same word from each pair of chips. Consecutive words lie on the same set of chips (chip-pairs in Fig. 4.4). When the address changes from 256 K − 1 to 256 K, 512 K − 1 to 512 K, 768 K − 1 to 768 K, and so on, the next word is on the next chip-pair.[1]

As a design alternative, the circuits could send the 18 high-order bits to all chips and the three low-order bits to the selector. The resulting organization would then be **low-order interleave**. In this organization, the first word

*high-order interleave*

*low-order interleave*

---

1. Large numbers—whether addresses or numbers of bits or bytes—are frequently expressed in condensed form using abbreviations indicating powers of 2. 1 K = $2^{10}$ = 1024, so 256 K = $2^8 \times 2^{10}$ = $2^{18}$ = 256 × 1024 = 262,144. Similarly, 512 K = $2^{19}$ = 524,288, and 768 K = 156 K + 512 K = 786,432. Appendix A gives a description of the units used in computer science.

**FIGURE 4.3** *Memory sizes for supercomputers and for minicomputers.*

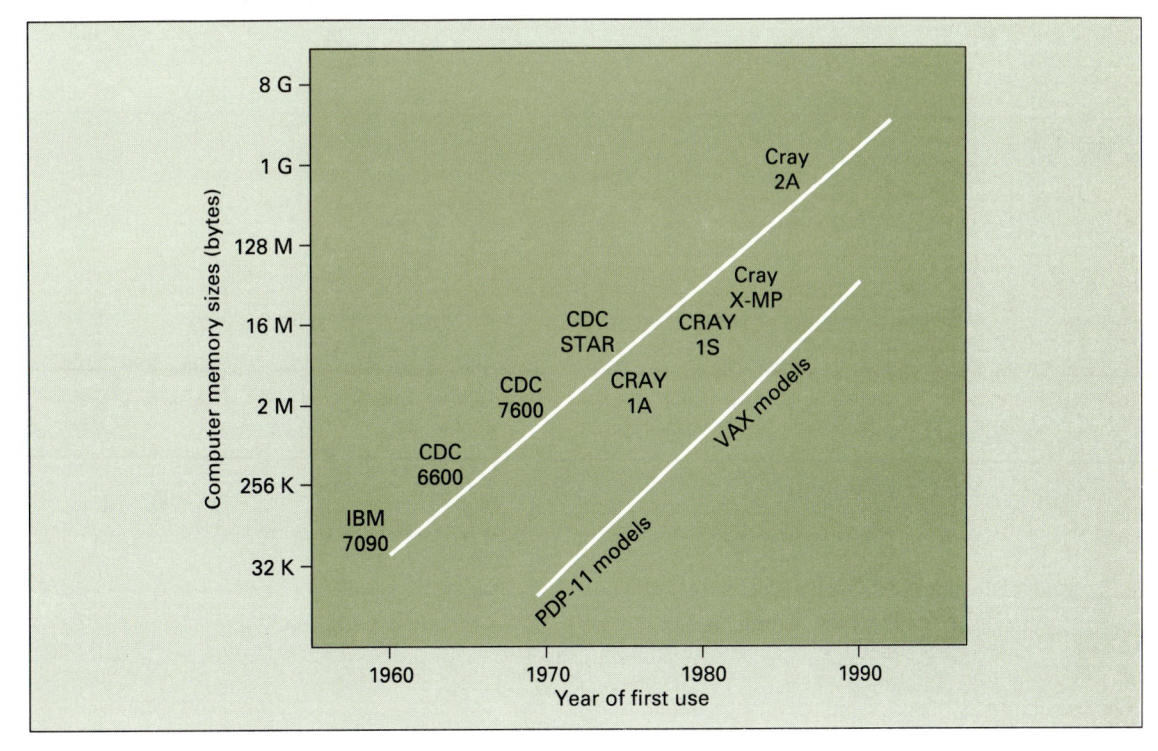

is on chip-pair 0, the second word is on chip pair 1, the third word is on chip-pair 2, and so forth. If there are $k$ chip-pairs, then the $(k + 1)$st word is on chip-pair 0, the $(k + 2)$nd word is on chip-pair 1, and so forth.

Designers use interleaving to increase the speed of accessing large storage systems. In general, a large storage system consists of several independent banks of memory that the CPU and I/O devices access through a

**FIGURE 4.4** *A 2-MB memory assembled using 16 256-K-by-4-bit RAM chips. Each pair of chips, highlighted in color, represents 256 KB. The figure shows only the major address and data paths. Sel, chip select.*

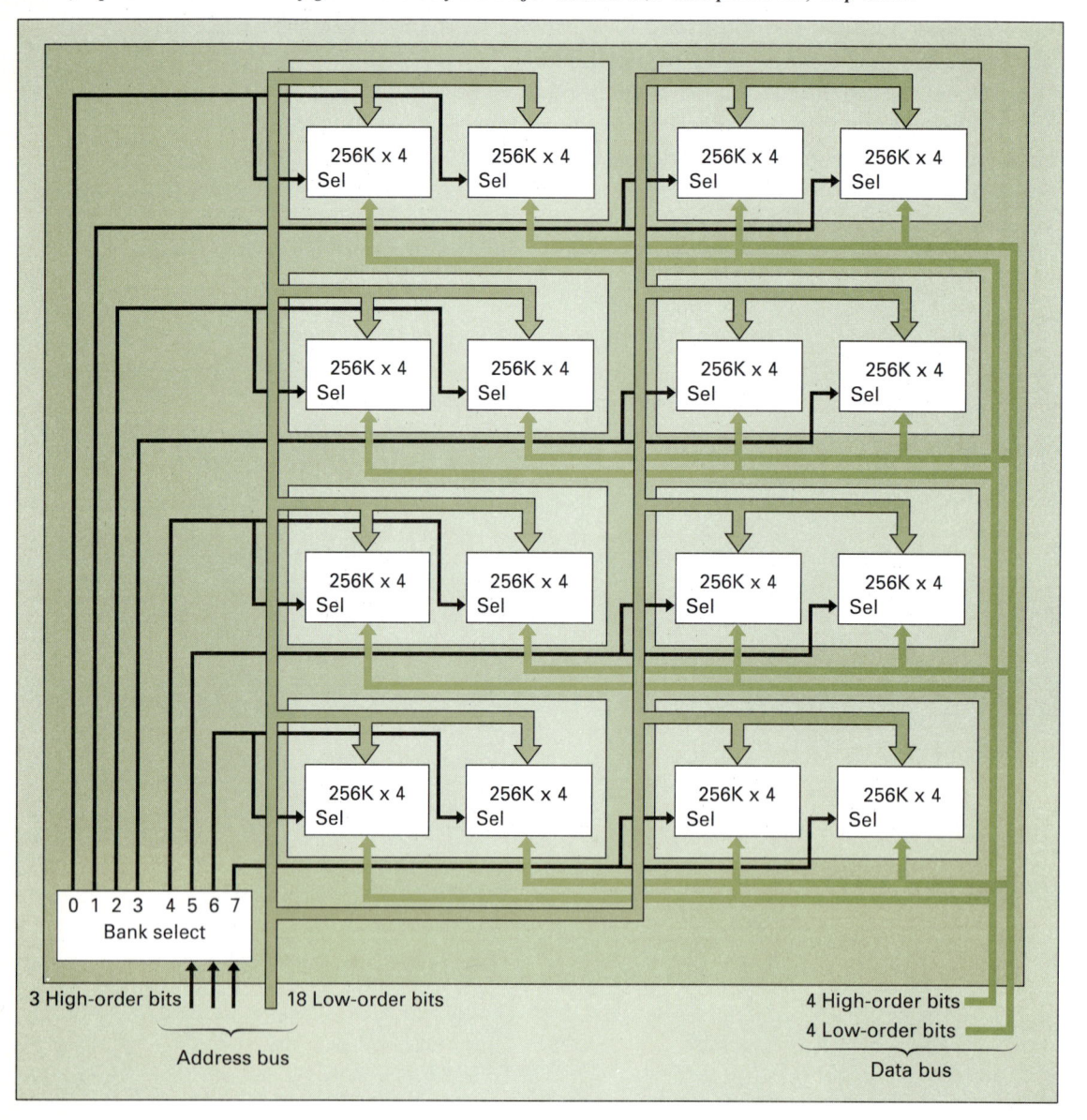

memory-port controller (see Section 3.3.3), such as a crossbar switch. Figure 4.5 illustrates a storage system that uses a four-port memory-port controller and consists of four banks of memory.

When a storage system uses high-order interleave, each bank contains a block of consecutive addresses. If it happens that each device, including the CPU, uses a different bank of memory for its programs and data, then all the banks can transfer data simultaneously. Figure 4.6 shows a situation where the CPU is executing a program in bank 0, channel 1 is transferring data to a block of memory in bank 2, and channel 3 is transferring data to a block of memory that spans banks 2 and 3. All three active processors can access memory simultaneously provided channel 2 accesses bank 3 rather than bank 2.

Figure 4.7 shows the same programs in memory, only now the storage system uses low-order interleave. With low-order interleave, consecutive addresses are in alternate banks, so each device will need to access all four banks as it executes its program or transfers data. This will result in a memory conflict whenever two devices request simultaneous access to the same bank of memory.

Low-order interleave does not always degrade memory performance, as this example might suggest. Consider the situation where the memory cycle time is much longer than the CPU cycle time. If the CPU wished to access a sequence of words, and word sequences were stored in the same bank, the CPU would have to wait for an entire memory cycle between consecutive accesses, resulting in inefficient use of the CPU. For such systems, designers often use low-order interleave to increase the access rate. When consecutive

**FIGURE 4.5** *System with a CPU, three channels, four banks of memory, and a memory port controller with four ports to memory.*

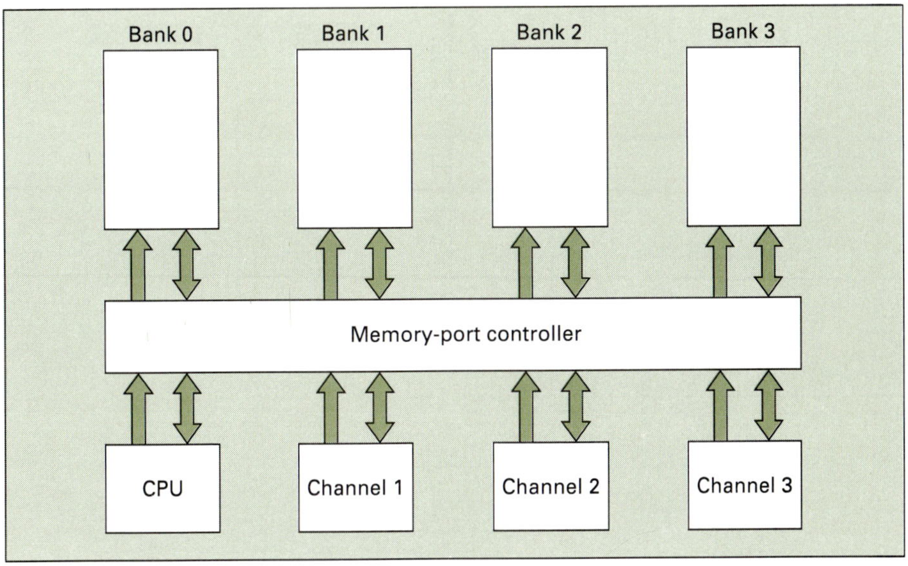

**FIGURE 4.6** *The storage system shown in Fig. 4.5 using four-way high-order interleave.*

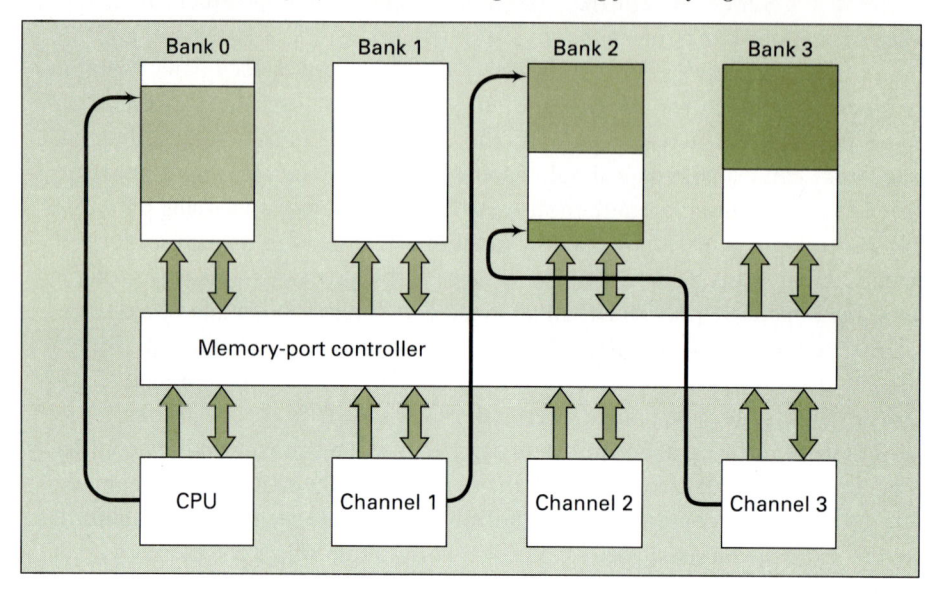

**FIGURE 4.7** *The storage system shown in Fig. 4.5 using four-way low-order interleave.*

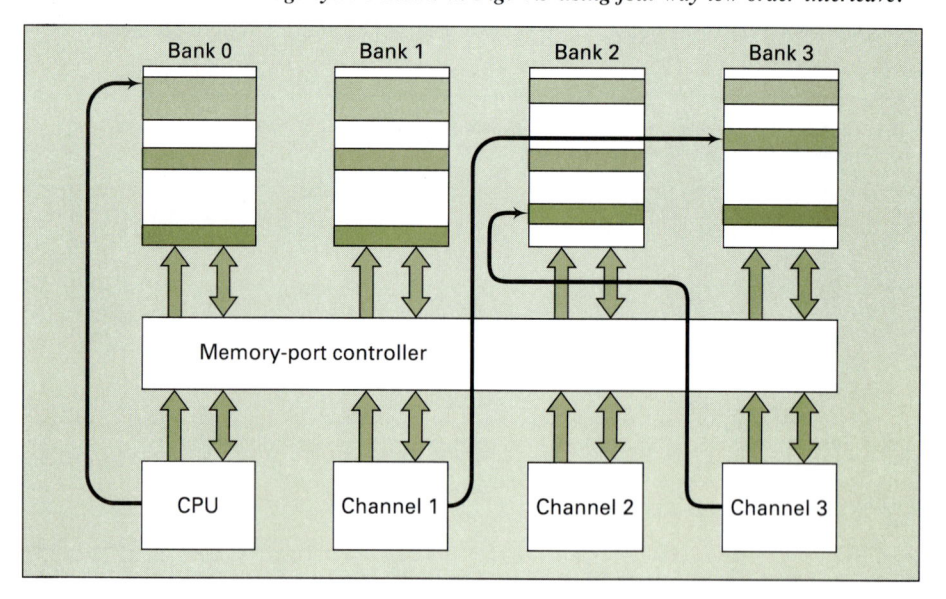

words are in different banks, the storage system, if provided with suitable circuitry, can overlap consecutive memory accesses. In other words, after the CPU has requested access to the first word stored in one bank, it can move to the second bank and initiate access of the second word while the storage system is still retrieving the first word. The CPU continues in like manner from one bank to the next. By the time the CPU returns to the first bank, the storage system will ideally have already completed accessing the first word and be ready for access again. Many high-performance computers use low-order interleave for this very reason.

Here is an example to show that a computer designer must take into account the physical characteristics of the memory chips when designing a storage system. Manufacturers usually specify a chip's speed in nanoseconds by giving the time it takes the chip to respond to requests for data. Suppose that a CPU has a 16-MHz clock and requires access to data in 2 clock cycles or 125 ns. Designers can use 125-ns memory chips, in which case the memory chips will operate fast enough to supply the CPU with data in the required two clock cycles. Alternatively, they can use slower chips, such as 150-ns memory chips, in which case the CPU will have to wait for the data. A CPU waits for memory by remaining idle for one or more clock cycles (called **wait states** for microprocessors).

*wait states*

## 4.1.2 ■ Types of Memory

Manufacturers produce a number of different types of memory devices having a variety of technologies. The technology affects not only the operating characteristics, such as power consumption, size, and speed, but also the manufacturing cost. Thus designers must weigh the tradeoffs between cost and performance in their selection of chips for a particular application. In this section we shall describe some of the major types of memory devices in current use.

### Read-only Memory[2]

**Read-only memories (ROMs)** are memory devices that the CPU can read but cannot write. Mechanical switches are an example, and computers use them for holding constants that specify the system's configuration (e.g., the amount of main memory). Many ROMs are factory programmed, and there is no way to alter their contents. (The term *programming* here means writing values into a ROM.) These devices are denser and cheaper to manufacture in large numbers than other types of ROM.

*read-only memories (ROMs)*

Field engineers can program **programmable ROMs (PROMs)** by using special high-current devices to destroy (burn) fuses that were manufactured

*programmable ROMs (PROMs)*

---

2. Note that we are considering ROMs to be a form of RAM, which they are, since memory can be accessed at random; however, common usage distinguishes RAMs and ROMs as if they were mutually exclusive.

into the devices. The result of **burning a PROM** is that certain bits are always $0_2$ and the rest are always $1_2$. These values cannot be altered once written.

A number of types of ROMs are alterable, although not during ordinary use. A technician can program an **erasable PROM (EPROM)** off line, later completely erase its contents by using ultraviolet light, and then reprogram it. **Electrically alterable ROMs (EAROMs)** are ROMs that the computer can program using special high-current operations, but programming them many times (in excess of 1000) tends to destroy them. Thus designers use them to hold information that rarely changes such as configuration information.

### Read/Write Memory

We can classify read/write memories (as opposed to read-only memories) in a variety of ways depending on their operating characteristics. The following is a partial classification:

1. Physical Characteristics
   - static versus dynamic
   - volatile versus nonvolatile
   - destructive read versus nondestructive read
   - removable versus permanent support
2. Logical Organization
   - addressed
   - associative
   - sequential access

*Physical Characteristics*

*Static versus Dynamic Memory* In **static random-access memories (SRAMs)**, the individual words, once written, do not need to be further addressed or manipulated to hold their values. These devices are composed of flip-flops that use a small current to maintain their logic level. SRAMs are used mostly for the CPU registers and other high-speed storage devices, although some computers use them for caches and main memory. (Cache will be discussed later in Section 4.2.2.) SRAMs are currently the fastest and most expensive of the semiconductor memory circuits.

The most common type of device used for main memory is actually a capacitor (a device for holding an electric charge) together with a single transistor. This pair of devices is far smaller than the two or more gates required for each flip-flop in an SRAM, and a charged capacitor represents a 1 bit. Unfortunately, the capacitors slowly lose their charges due to leakage, so computers that use them must use refresh circuits to maintain the charges representing 1 bits. The refresh circuits must refresh the charges about every 4 ms (1990 timing). Because the charges change over time, these memories are called **dynamic random-access memories (DRAMs).** The DRAM cycle time, the actual time necessary between accesses, is typically about twice the **read-access time,** which is the time necessary to retrieve a datum from the device. The longer cycle time results from using the capacitor's charge to see if it held a $1_2$ (see discussion of destructive read below).

Though much cheaper than SRAMs, DRAMs are also slower. By the later 1980s, chips with 1M ($2^{20}$) bits were widely available, and 16M-bit ($2^{24}$-bit) chips had already been made in laboratories. As Fig. 4.2 shows, approximately every two years the capacity of the latest commercially available chips quadruples.

*Volatile versus Nonvolatile Memory*  A memory device is **volatile** if it requires a continuous source of power to hold its values; otherwise it is **nonvolatile.** Most magnetic-core memories were nonvolatile as are ROMs. Most static and dynamic RAMs are volatile.

*Destructive-read versus Nondestructive-read Memory*  A memory has **destructive read** in the case where the process of reading a word also destroys its value. Current DRAMs are of this type: Reading a DRAM cell discharges the capacitor. In practice, the circuitry on the chip always rewrites the original value back into the cell.

In contrast, circuitry can read SRAMs and ROMs without destroying their values. They are **nondestructive read** memories.

Memories with destructive read have a two-phase operation: (1) a **read cycle,** and (2) a **restore cycle.** During a read access, the storage system first reads the word (driving all bits to $0_2$) and then rewrites the bits that were initially $1_2$. During a write access, the storage system first reads the word (driving all bits to $0_2$) and then write the bits that should be $1_2$. As a consequence, the read-access time, is shorter than the cycle time.

*Removable versus Permanent Memory*  Memories whose active elements can be removed from the system hardware are **removable memories.** In contrast, **nonremovable memories** are comprised entirely of components that are not physically removed. Main memories are nonremovable. In most computers, floppy disks ("floppies") and tape cartridges are removable, while the RAM and hard disks are nonremovable.

Table 4.1 shows a number of different types of memory devices and their physical characteristics.

*Logical Organization*

*Addressed Memory*  **Addressed memories** use addresses to select the cells being read or written. Therefore when a device accesses the memory, it must supply both address and transfer direction—read or write—to the memory system. Nearly all memories are of this type, including the RAMs and ROMs

**Table 4.1** Characteristics of common storage devices, based on sample technologies.

| Memory Type | Destructive Read | Data Life | Write Time | Read Time | Number of Write Cycles Allowed | Volatility (Power Required) |
|---|---|---|---|---|---|---|
| ROM | No | Decades | Once | 100 ns | 1 | No |
| PROM | No | Years | Hours | 100 ns | Many | No |
| EPROM | No | Years | ms | 100 ns | 1000s | No |
| SRAM | No | While power is on | 10 ns | 10 ns | Infinite | Full |
| DRAM | Yes | 4 ms | 100 ns | 200 ns | Infinite | 10% |
| Magnetic core | Yes | Decades | 1–2 ms | 0.5–1 ms | Infinite | No |

described in the previous section, and the disk memories described in Section 3.3.6. Two exceptions are associative memories and sequential-access memories, which we describe shortly.

RAMs and ROMs, as mentioned earlier, can access all words in essentially the same amount of time. Some addressed memories, such as disks, charge-coupled devices, and magnetic bubble memories, are addressed memories but cannot access all words in the same amount of time.

*charge-coupled devices (CCDs)*

**Charge-coupled devices (CCDs)** have arrays of cells that can hold packets of electrons (charge packets). In these arrays, sets of charge packets represent the words, where the presence of each charge packet indicates a $1_2$ bit. Unlike RAMs, where fixed circuits hold words, the charge packets do not remain stationary: The cells pass them along to neighboring cells with each clock tick. Designers organize the cells into tracks, one for each bit position in a set of words, and place circuitry at the beginning of each track to generate or "write" the charge packets and circuitry at the end of each track to detect or "read" the charge packets. Logically these tracks may be viewed as loops, because the read circuits pass the information to the write circuits, which regenerate the bit values in the tracks (unless, of course, they write new data.) If there are $N$ cells in each of $M$ tracks, the device can hold $N$ $M$-bit words. The access time on average for a word is $(N/2) \times C$, where $C$ is the clock time. **Magnetic bubble memories (MBMs)** are similar, but they use magnetic bubbles (local regions of magnetism in a magnetic crystalline substrate) instead of charge packets to represent $1_2$ bits.

*magnetic bubble memories (MBMs)*

Because these devices must wait for the requested datum to reach a read head (for disks), a circuit for detecting charges (for CCDs), or a circuit for detecting magnetic bubbles (for MBMs), the access time depends on the position of the desired datum relative to the read circuit. The access time is relatively short in the worst case, so these devices are considered **pseudo-random access memory.**

*pseudo-random access memory*

Another form of addressed memory is **orthogonal memory,**[3] which can access data either by word or by bit-slice. A **bit-slice** is the set of all bits from the same bit position of all words. A user presents the memory with the word address and a read-word or write-word request, in which case the memory reads or writes the desired word; alternatively, the user presents the memory with a bit number and a read-bit-slice or write-bit-slice request, in which case the memory reads or writes the desired bit-slice. With reference to the four-word array shown in Fig. 4.8, word 2 is $b_{20}b_{21}b_{22}b_{23}$ and bit-slice 2 is $b_{02}b_{12}b_{22}b_{32}$.

**orthogonal memory**

**bit-slice**

***Associative Memory*** **Associative memories** use the contents of part of the memory words to select the cells being read or written. Hence they are also called **content-addressable memories (CAMs).** An example of an access request in an associative memory might be "to search for all words whose highest-order 8 bits contain the value $1101\ 1110_2$, and return the value in the first word that matches." The value $1101\ 1110_2$ is the argument, the specification "highest-order 8 bits" is the mask, and the directive "return the value in the first word that matches" is the procedure for **conflict resolution,** what to do when several words satisfy the search criteria.

**associative memories**

**content-addressable memories (CAMs)**

**conflict resolution**

Figure 4.9 shows the components of an associative memory. The **argument register** holds the argument for an associative search, the **mask register** specifies the fields of each word that the memory should match, and the bits of the **match register,** called **match bits,** indicate which words match the search criterion. There is 1 match bit for each word in the associative memory. The **any-match bit** indicates whether any match bits are set, and the **memory buffer register** holds the value to be stored or the value just recalled.

**argument register**
**mask register**

**match register**
**match bits**

**any-match bit**
**memory buffer register**

Associative memories are active storage devices. Each storage location has circuitry for comparing the argument with the value the location holds,

3. Shooman developed the idea of orthogonal memory in 1960. Around 1972 Goodyear incorporated an orthogonal memory into the STARAN computer.

**FIGURE 4.8** ***A four-word memory consisting of 4 bits per word. Word 2 (Row 2) and bit-slice 2 (Column 2) are highlighted in color.***

| | Column 0 | Column 1 | Column 2 | Column 3 |
|---|---|---|---|---|
| Row 0 | $B_{00}$ | $B_{01}$ | $B_{02}$ | $B_{03}$ |
| Row 1 | $B_{10}$ | $B_{11}$ | $B_{12}$ | $B_{13}$ |
| Row 2 | $B_{20}$ | $B_{21}$ | $B_{22}$ | $B_{23}$ |
| Row 3 | $B_{30}$ | $B_{31}$ | $B_{32}$ | $B_{33}$ |

and each storage location has circuitry to indicate a successful search. In addition, the memory system has circuitry for performing conflict resolution (or at least detection). An associative store may have address decoders as well. Because associative memories have more circuitry than RAMs, large associative memories are expensive and uncommon. (Although uncommon in computers, humans do seem to have extremely large associative memories.)

Although small associative memories are used in the control hardware of many virtual memory and cache memory systems (these will be described later in this chapter), they are not yet used as main memories in general-purpose computers. That situation may change when they become inexpensive and programming-language designers learn to take advantage of their computational power.

### Sequential Access

Magnetic tapes generally access data sequentially. A user requests a datum by specifying its offset from the current position of the read/write head (i.e., the

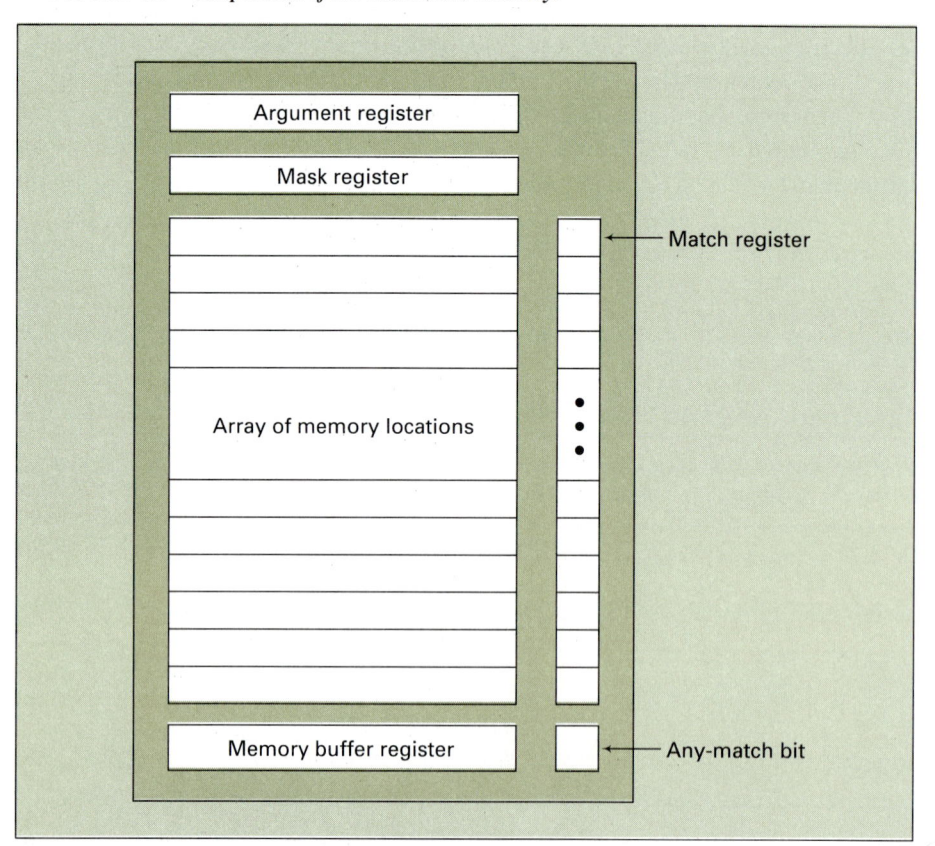

**FIGURE 4.9** *Components of an associative memory.*

next word, the previous word, the hundredth word forward), and the tape device obtains the datum by counting forward or backward from the current position to the required datum. If the desired datum is the last one on a tape and the read/write head is at the beginning of the tape, the user must wait for the tape device to scan the entire tape to get the desired word. Hence the device is a sequential-access device.

Pseudo-random access devices also access data sequentially. However, they organize the data so that they never need to move a required datum very far before it reaches the read head or read circuits. Furthermore, designers generally build these devices to access data by address, so they appear to operate as slow random-access devices rather than sequential-access devices.

**Archival Memory**

**Archival memories** are nonvolatile memories that can hold a lot of data at very little cost for a very long time. Tapes and disks are currently the most common types and are used for virtually all very large systems. Optical disks are also becoming popular but are not yet as common as tapes or disks. Optical disk drives store data by thermally altering the reflective properties of small domains on the disks and read data by visually detecting the altered domains. Some optical disks can only be written once and are called **WORM memories** (write once, read many times). WORM memories seem ideal for archival storage, since once they are written they are functionally ROMs.

archival memories

WORM memories

## 4.2 ▪ Main-memory System

Early in the computer era, when programs were small and the hardware provided few address lines, physical memories were often as large as the computer's logical-address space. However, the cost of memory (dollars per bit) steadily decreased, and the need for memory steadily increased. In the early 1960s, systems programmers developed multiprogramming operating systems, which benefit greatly from having very large main memories. Some manufacturers built machines with more physical memory than logical. Architects now design machines with large logical-address spaces (32-bit machines can address 4 GB), but few have been built with comparable amounts of physical memory. If current trends continue, starting in the 1990s physical memories will not only increase in size but will also commonly exceed the sizes of the logical-address space.

In general, programmers and compilers view programs as having one large continuous logical-address space. Within each program, logical addresses range from 0 to some maximum value, which depends on the size of the program. The size of a computer's logical-address space usually limits the size of the programs the computer can execute easily.

When computers without special memory-management hardware execute programs, the operating system loads them entirely into main memory be-

**overlays**

fore executing them. For these computers the amount of physical memory limits the size of the programs they can execute. Programmers can use a variety of techniques to overcome the logical-address-space size limitation. For example, they can partition a program into **overlays**, where two or more program overlays have the same logical addresses. These overlays consist of independent blocks of code, typically subroutines. When one overlay executes, the other remains on an external storage device. The programmer inserts statements in the program requesting the operating system to load a required overlay before transferring control to it.

**program relocation**
**relocation offset (*RO*)**

**relocation address (*RA*)**

Most computers are able to execute programs even when the operating system relocates them in memory, as it must do in multiprogramming. In **program relocation,** a program is loaded at physical addresses that differ by a constant amount, called a **relocation offset (*RO*),** from the logical addresses used by the program. When the logical address for the beginning of a program is zero, the relocation offset is equal to the **relocation address (*RA*),** which is the address of the beginning of the program; otherwise they differ. See Fig. 4.10. Simple program-relocation techniques and their associated hardware will be described in Section 4.2.1. The use of base registers for program relocation was described in Chapter 2. For computers that relocate programs, the

**FIGURE 4.10** *Relocation offset. The operating system has relocated a program in memory by an amount RO. Since the logical addresses began with 0 before relocation, here RO = RA (relocation address).*

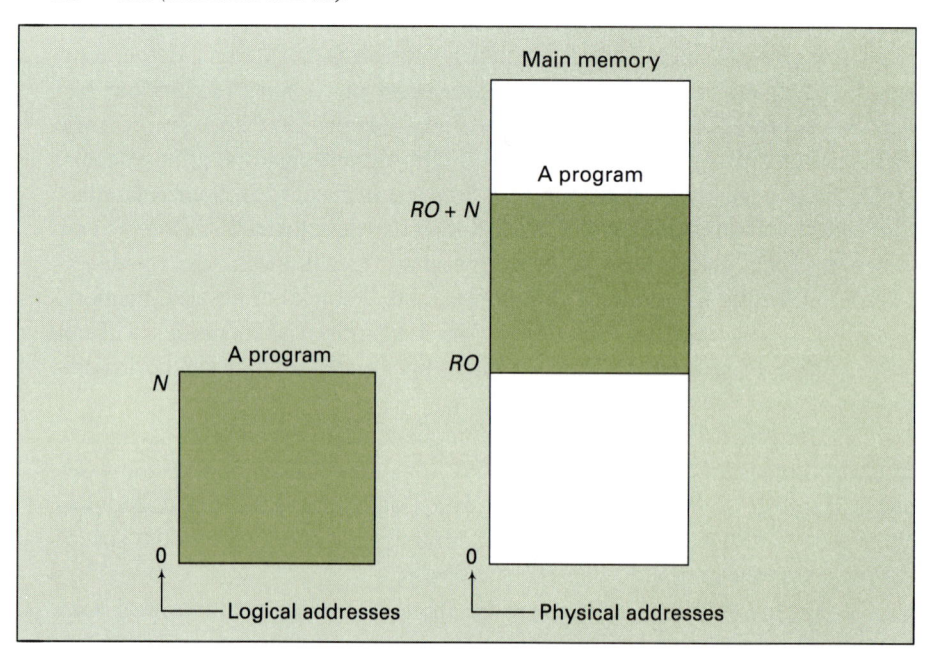

relocation hardware *maps* the program's effective addresses to physical addresses by adding the relocation offset to each effective address. Still, the computer must have enough main memory to hold an entire program before it can execute the program.

Many modern computers do not need to load an entire program into memory before executing it. Instead, the operating system, together with a special map for address-translation, keeps the program on an external device, such as a hard disk. The operating system then loads the program into main memory in parts, as demanded for execution. The operating system maintains special tables that keep track of where each part of the program resides in main memory and in external storage. During program execution, the program's logical addresses no longer correspond to the physical addresses. The CPU uses the map to translate the program's effective addresses into their corresponding physical addresses. Computers that operate in this way are said to have **virtual memory,** a name that comes from the fact that the storage system *appears* to have a large amount of physical memory even though it does not; the memory is not real. Computers with virtual memory can run programs that are larger than the computer's physical memory. Indeed, the size of a program is limited only by the size of the logical-address space of the computer. Section 4.2.3 will cover virtual-memory systems.

virtual memory

Computers that have only a single main-memory system are said to have a **one-level storage system.** Most computers, especially those with virtual memory, use a **multilevel storage system.** We can think of the central (internal) memory components—including main memory and the CPU registers—as being **primary memory,** and any external storage devices, such as magnetic disks and tapes, as being **secondary memory.** The entire set of storage devices and components comprises the **memory hierarchy.** For example, a computer may use an intermediate high-speed buffer called a **cache memory** (or simply **cache**) that resides between the external devices and main memory or between main memory and the CPU. Cache memories speed up the apparent access times of the slower memories by holding the words that the CPU is most likely to access. We shall focus on cache next in Section 4.2.2.

one-level storage system

multilevel storage system

primary memory

secondary memory

memory hierarchy

cache memory

cache

Some microprocessors use a technique called expanded memory for increasing the amount of high-speed memory available to programs. We present a brief introduction to that technique in Section 4.2.4.

## 4.2.1 ■ Program Relocation and Memory Protection

Multiprogramming is an important way of increasing CPU utilization, and computer professionals developed it long before the advent of virtual memory. Four architectural features are crucial for multiprogramming: program relocation, memory protection, privileged modes of operation, and timer interrupts. We have already discussed the latter two features; we shall focus on the first two here.

First, as mentioned earlier, the operating system must be able to relocate programs by placing them anywhere in memory. Consider a simple example of program relocation. Suppose a program uses logical addresses that range from 0 to 2K, and also suppose the operating system loads the program into main memory at addresses ranging from 10K to 12K. The relocation offset is 10K. During program execution, the addressing hardware must translate each effective address into the proper physical address by adding 10K to it. The process of relocating a program when the operating system first puts it in memory is called **initial program relocation.** Sometimes the operating system can move a program from one place to another in main memory after the program has already started executing; this process is called **dynamic program relocation.**

Second, the computer must be capable of performing **memory protection,** that is, prevent one program from accessing memory that the operating system has assigned to another program. Special memory-protection hardware performs this function.

Modern virtual-memory systems provide for both program relocation and memory protection, and we shall discuss them in detail later in this section. Historically, however, some early computers such as the IBM System/360 and the CDC 6600 used simpler techniques, which we shall describe next.

### Program Relocation and Memory Protection in the IBM System/360

Computers of the IBM System/360 family use base registers for program relocation. When the loader initially places the program in memory, it also loads some base registers with certain key data addresses. This serves to relocate the data in memory. The instructions use base-displacement addressing with displacements measured relative to those key addresses. Programs use the LOAD ADDRESS instruction to load the addresses of the program statements in the base registers. This serves to relocate the programs in memory. Because the addressing hardware adds a base-register content to each displacement, it automatically maps each effective address to the correct physical address. Consequently, the memory references do not depend on where the operating system initially loads the program. However, because programs use base registers, once a program begins executing, the operating system cannot relocate it. The reason is that the program can store the contents of its own base registers in memory. If the operating system were to move the program, it would also need to update the stored base-register values. But it has no way of knowing where the program stored those values in memory, so there is no way for it to update them. Computer systems of this type thus use initial but not dynamic program relocation.

The IBM System/360 uses **key-controlled memory protection.** The operating system assigns to each executing program a value, called an **access key,** which the hardware holds in the program status word (PSW) during program execution. When the operating system allocates memory to the program, it associates the access key with each bank of memory it assigns to the program. These memory banks hold a fixed number of words, called pages. When a device initiates a memory access, the memory-protection hardware compares the access key of the requesting program to the access key associated with the physical bank holding the reference. If the two values disagree, the memory-protection hardware raises a memory-protection exception.

**Program Relocation and Memory Protection in the CDC 6600**
The CDC 6600 has a special register, a **relocation-address register (RA)**,[4] to enable dynamic program relocation. Only the operating system, using privileged instructions, is allowed to modify the RA, and the executing program is totally unaware of its presence. Before the operating system loads a program in memory, it allocates a block of memory, called a **field**, to that program. The amount of memory it allocates is called the **field length** (*FL*). It then places the address of the field, which is the program's relocation address, in the RA and loads the program in memory. Whenever the CPU generates an effective address (either an instruction address or an operand address), the addressing hardware automatically adds the relocation address to it. Thus all memory references are linearly relocated by the relocation address; hence references do not depend on where the operating system loads the program in memory. This mechanism provides both initial and dynamic relocation.

In addition to RA, the CDC 6600 provides a **field-length register (FL)**, which holds the field length of the executing program and is part of the memory-protection hardware. Only the operating system is allowed to modify its content, which it loads with the field length when it allocates memory to the program. The memory-protection hardware also includes a comparison circuit that checks whether each effective address is within the allocated bounds. If not, the hardware raises a memory-protection exception. In essence, the program views memory as a single block with addresses ranging from zero to *FL*. See Fig. 4.11.

*relocation-address register (RA)*

*field*
*field length (FL)*

*field-length register (FL)*

**Security**
Having focused on memory-protection hardware, in our discussion of the IBM System/360 and the CDC 6600, we now turn to some more general security issues.

There are many techniques to provide protection to programs, both from themselves and from other programs. Most of these techniques rely on software and, as hackers have shown, are none too secure for many systems.

---

4. It is also frequently called a base register. We shall not use this term in order to avoid confusion with the concept of programmer-visible base registers, as described in Section 2.5.3.

Here we discuss some of the architectural features required to provide security. This discussion will focus on the basic requirements and functions that a multiuser (multiprogramming) operating system needs to have in order to provide security to its users. Some of the requirements are as follows:

- It must be able to distinguish between operating-system software and user programs so it can protect the operating system from corruption.
- It must provide facilities so different procedures can share code, but it must also be able to prevent one procedure from accessing another procedure's private code.
- It must provide protected, secure, and efficient I/O. That is, the system must maintain protection during traps, interrupts, and error recovery. Thus the hardware must distinguish user traps (those triggered by user programs) from system traps (those triggered by system programs).

FIGURE 4.11 *A storage system with a relocation-address register (RA) for program relocation and a field-length register (FL) for memory protection. The hardware adds the relocation address to the effective address (EA) to get the physcial address of the reference.*

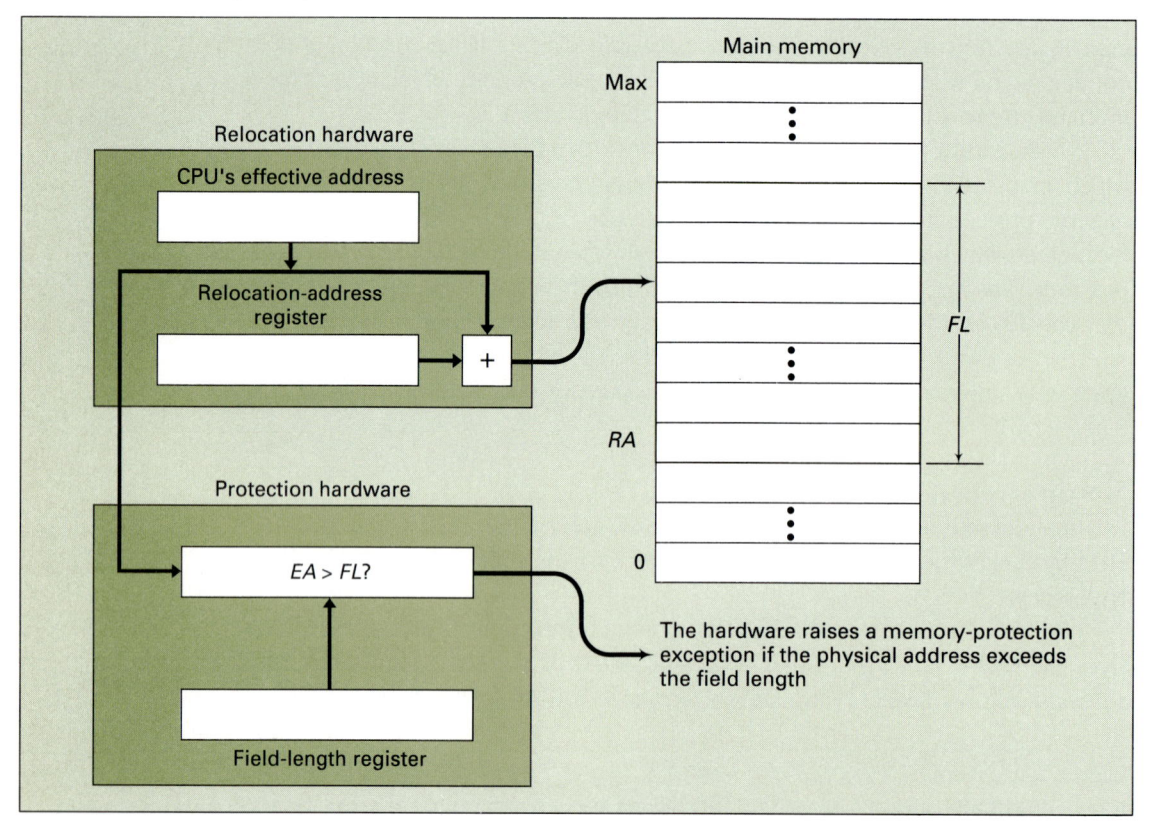

- For highly pipelined operations (see Chapter 6), the system must respond efficiently when it detects an illegal condition during pipelined operation.

All computers that can reasonably support multiuser operating systems have multiple modes of execution, which we discussed in Section 2.4.4. The hardware provides one or more mode bits, which set the privilege level. Using a privileged instruction, the operating system sets the privilege level to an unprivileged mode whenever it transfers control to a user and to a privileged mode when it regains control from the user. Once the operating system reduces the privilege level, the user has no access to privileged operations (including those that set the privilege level). Most modern systems provide three or four modes with intermediate stages of privilege for some tasks. Multiple modes allows the operating system to keep the fully privileged code small and hence easier to verify and test.

One basic method of sharing information is for tasks to send data to each other by placing the data in an area of memory where both tasks can access it. Sending data allows for security because the sender can decide what to send and what not to send, and the receiver can decide what to accept and what not to accept. The problem is that sending data is very inefficient for large data sets. For paged-memory systems (to be discussed in Section 4.2.3) the operating system can make individual pages available to multiple users. This puts the burden of sharing data both on the operating system and on the users, who must avoid putting any data in the shared pages that other tasks should not see. With relocation-address registers, there is no way to share data securely. However, designers can easily extend such a system to provide multiple relocation-address registers, so that some parts of the address space can be shared and other parts kept private (i.e., the virtual-address space can be segmented).

When an external event occurs, the hardware must transfer control to the operating system to verify that the new task is allowed to do whatever it is supposed to do. When traps occur, however, the situation is trickier. Most systems call the operating system for traps as well as interrupts, but calling the operating system means that certain classes of traps, such as unimplemented-instruction traps, would be much less efficient than is desirable.

To see why, assume that a team of architects is implementing a computer for use in space. They wish to maintain compatibility with existing software and have selected the ISA of the VAX-11, say. Finally, noting that the software rarely uses either floating-point or complex operations, they have eliminated those instructions (and corresponding hardware) from the space-borne computer model. When the new CPU encounters a floating-point or complex instruction, it will generate an unimplemented-instruction trap. If this trap goes directly to a user routine to perform the floating-point or complex operation, there is only the cycle-time overhead of the trap, about the same as an ordinary subroutine call. If, on the other hand, the trap invokes the operating system, then processing it may require thousands of cycles of overhead.

A security breech that illustrates how difficult it is to design secure systems occurred many years ago. On a specific computer model, when an instruction accessed data on a page that was not in memory, the operating system brought the demanded page into main memory (as usual for demand paging). The executing task could then see this page (even if it did not belong to the executing task) by requesting a **dump** of its memory space, which is a listing of all values currently in memory. By dumping memory repeatedly, a person intent on violating the system could see many pages of memory and perhaps find system tables, thereby facilitating breaking the system's security.

This "war story" illustrates how easy it is to inadvertently put traps in the hardware that make secure software almost impossible. Current supercomputers tend to have traps like this, some documented, others not, that are a direct result of the designers' desire to provide the highest performance possible.

Recapitulating, to allow for secure, multiprogramming operating systems, the hardware needs the following features:

- Multiple privilege levels, so it can restrict certain capabilities to the operating system. Research suggests that systems need at least three privilege levels for efficient and secure operation.
- Multiple regions, each with its own protection, to allow tasks to share some data and code but not other parts of their data and code.
- Exception handlers that invoke the operating system for all external events. In addition, efficiency suggests that the hardware should provide traps that branch directly to user procedures, but only for specific trappable (internal) exceptions.
- No hidden *trap doors* (i.e., ways for an unprivileged program to circumvent the protection mechanisms). There is no way to guarantee that there are no such holes in the architecture, but a widely used family of machines is less likely to have trap doors than a narrowly used one. In addition, the hardware must detect and handle faults in a way that does not compromise security.

### 4.2.2 ■ Cache Memory

Generally, the least expensive memory is slower than all but the slowest CPUs. System performance suffers when a fast device must wait for a memory system to access data. The device may be an I/O device or the CPU, and the memory system may be main memory or an external device. Because computer users always seem to want larger memories, computer designers must carefully weigh the tradeoffs between memory cost and performance. One way to reduce the performance degradation due to slow memory is to incorporate a cache memory into the system. Cache memories are high-speed buffers for holding recently accessed data and neighboring data in main memory. By adding a cache memory between the fast device and the slower memory system, a designer can provide an apparently fast memory system. This section summarizes several principles of the organization and operation of cache memories, focusing on those that speed up main-memory systems.

Some caches are invisible to the architecture: the hardware regulates them without software control. Other caches, notably those within RISC systems, are an integral part of the architecture: the instruction set includes instructions for invalidating specific cache entries, for loading and clearing cache contents, and for preventing the cache from mapping specific ranges of addresses.

The utility of a cache stems from a general characteristic of programs, which is that they tend to access data and code that were recently accessed or are located in nearby memory locations. This tendency is called the **principle of locality of reference.** The reasons are simple:

- Programs tend to execute instructions in sequence and hence in nearby memory locations.
- Programs often have loops in which a group of nearby instructions is executed repeatedly.
- Most compilers store arrays in blocks of adjacent memory locations, and the programs frequently access array elements in sequence. Hence array accesses tend to be localized.
- Compilers often place unrelated data items in data segments. Hence accesses to these unrelated data also tend to be localized within segments. This is especially true for local variables in stacks.

Each cache consists of a number of **cache entries,** and each cache entry consists of two parts: some cache memory and an **address tag.** The cache memory is usually high-speed SRAM, and the data it holds are either copies of selected current main-memory data or newly stored data that are not yet in main memory. The tag indicates the physical addresses of the data in main memory and perhaps some validity information.

The way a cache works is simple. Whenever the CPU initiates a memory access, the storage system sends the physical address to the cache. The cache compares the physical address with all of its address tags to see if it holds a copy of the datum. If the operation is a read access and the cache holds the given datum, the cache reads the requested datum from its own high-speed RAM and delivers it to the CPU. This is a **cache hit,** and it is usually much faster than reading the same value directly from main memory. If the cache does not hold the datum, however, a **cache miss** occurs and the cache passes the address to the main-memory system to read the datum. When the datum arrives from main memory, both the CPU and the cache receive a copy. The

*principle of locality of reference*

*cache entries*
*address tag*

*cache hit*

*cache miss*

cache then stores its copy with the appropriate address tag. While the CPU executes the instruction or processes the data, the cache concurrently reads additional data from nearby main-memory cells and stores them with their address tags in its high-speed memory.

There are two reason why caches work so well. First, because the cache operates in parallel with the CPU, the additional words it loads after a cache miss occurs do not penalize the CPU's performance. These new data become immediately available for the CPU at cache speeds. Second, because of the principle of locality of reference, the CPU is likely to request these new data soon. Cache-hit rates exceeding 90% are common for current cache memories.

When a cache is present, the apparent speed of the memory is the weighted average of the cache speed and the main-memory speed. Suppose the memory delay is 100 ns, the cache delay is 30 ns, and cache hits occur 90% of the time. The apparent speed of main memory is then $(0.9 \times 30) + (0.1 \times 100)$ or 0.37 ns.

Two different things can happen during a write operation. If the location being written in memory has an image in cache, then a cache hit occurs and the cache updates its copy of the value. The cache may also forward the datum to main memory for an immediate update, or it may wait until some later time before forwarding the datum. A cache that forwards data immediately is a **write-through cache;** one that holds data is a **write-back cache,** and the write-back is called a **posted write.** For example, a write-back cache may wait until it needs to write an entire block of data before sending it to main memory. A **dirty cell** is a cell in main memory that has an updated image in cache, but which itself has not yet been updated; it awaits a posted write, for example.

If the location being written in memory does not have an image in cache, then the cache can do one of several other things. Some caches, called **write-around caches,** simply send the datum to memory and do nothing else. Alternatively, if there is a block in cache for the datum that has no dirty cells, the cache may store the datum there. It would then either post the write (if it is a write-back cache) or send the datum to memory (if it is a write-through cache). For a write-back cache, if the only locations for the datum are in dirty blocks, the cache can use the same two strategies, but now it must write the dirty block to memory before it can store the new datum.

A cache memory enhances system performance because its speed is faster than that of main memory, and its utility increases with the ratio of CPU speed to main memory speed. For example, microprocessor CPU chips operating at 25 MHz are much faster than the least expensive DRAMs available with 1990 technology. Coupled with the demand for very large main memories, cache memories provide an acceptable cost-to-performance ratio, even though they use expensive, high-speed SRAMs. Several chip manufacturers now produce entire cache control units on a single chip, and some microprocessors, such as Intel's 80486, include cache memories on the same chip.

## Cache Structure and Organization

Now let us look in more detail at how architects structure cache memories. Every cache has two major subsystems: a **tag subsystem,** which holds the addresses and determines whether there is a match for a requested datum, and a **memory subsystem,** which holds and delivers the data.

  Both main memory and cache are divided into **refill lines,** whose sizes are all equal and generally contain $n$ words, where $n$ is a power of 2. Cache lines typically have between 4 and 64 bytes. Refill lines are the only unit the cache processes, and it places them so they do not cross natural refill-line boundaries. (A refill-line boundary is any address that is an integral multiple of the refill-line size.) When the storage system transfers units smaller than a refill line, such as a word or quadword, the cache initiates several main-memory accesses to read or write an entire refill line. The cache will request the demanded word first, followed by the neighboring data.

  Cache memories use different mapping techniques for mapping main-memory addresses into its own local addresses. There are four common organizations: associative, direct, set-associative, and sector, which we shall describe briefly here.

*Associative Cache*

An **associative cache** (also called **fully associative cache**) holds its tags in an associative memory or a functionally equivalent memory. The cache can place any refill line in memory into any of its own refill lines, and during a memory access it compares the given address with all the addresses it holds. For a main memory that has $N$ refill lines, refill-line addresses require $\log_2 N$ bits. With a cache that uses an associative memory, all comparisons occur simultaneously, but the associative memory is very costly for a large system. With a cache that does not use an associative memory, $\log_2 N$-bit comparisons tend to take too much time or hardware for a large memory, which degrades cache performance. Figure 4.12 shows the associative organization.

*Direct-mapped Cache*

A **direct-mapped cache** partitions main memory into $K$ columns of $N$ refill lines per column. By using low-order interleaving, for example, the resulting partitioning may place consecutive main-memory words into different refill lines and allow faster cache refill. In any event, the cache has a single column of $N$ rows, and each row can hold one refill line. The $N$th row in the cache can hold the $N$th refill line from any column of memory, and the address tag for that row holds the column number of the current refill line. The cache does not need an associative memory. For a given main-memory address, the cache uses the row number as an offset into its tag memory. It then compares the indexed value with the column-number field of the reference to see if it holds the required refill line. See Fig. 4.13.

tag subsystem

memory subsystem
refill lines

associative cache
fully associative cache

direct-mapped cache

### Set-associative Cache

**set-associative cache**

A **set-associative cache** combines the associative and direct organizations and is equivalent to a multiple-column, direct mapping. A set-associative cache organizes both main memory and its own memory into columns of $N$ refill lines. The cache can map refill line $i$ from any column in main memory into refill line $i$ of any column in its own RAM. (A set is a collection of items without duplication. The term set-associative stems from the fact that a given cache line can hold any main-memory refill line from a restricted set of them, but

**FIGURE 4.12**  *A fully associative cache. Any cache refill line can hold any main-memory refill line. Address tags have $\log_2 N$ bits each, where memory comprises $N$ refill lines.*

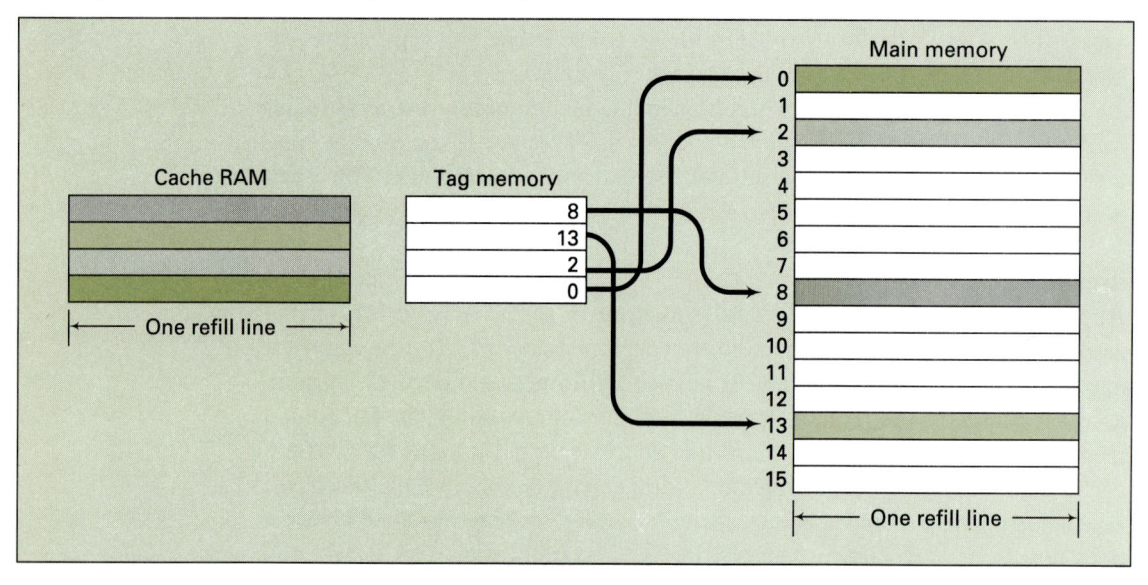

**FIGURE 4.13**  *A direct-mapped cache. The cache will only place a refill line with refill-line number M in main memory in refill line M in cache. Hence the tag memory only needs to hold the column number.*

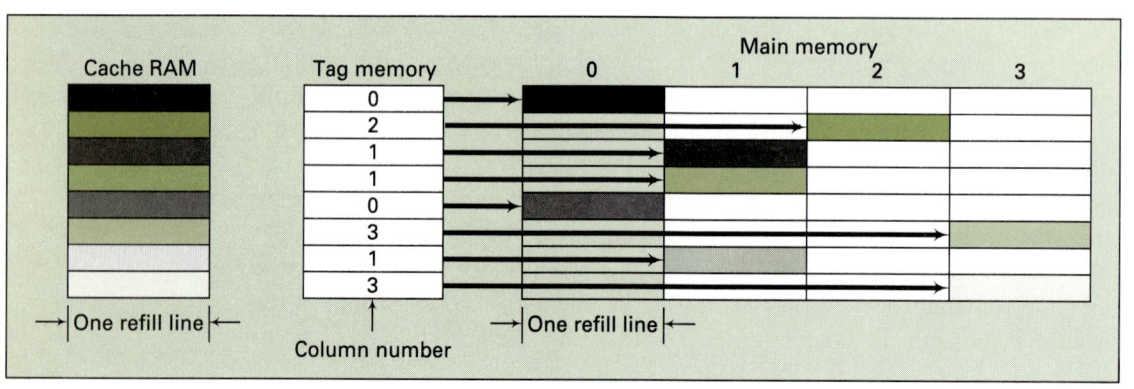

no others.) Each cache refill line has an associated tag address that specifies the main-memory column number of the refill line it holds. See Fig. 4.14. As you can see, a set-associative cache with one set is equivalent to a direct-mapped cache.

*Sector-mapped Cache*

Sector mapping is a modification of associative mapping. In **sector-mapped cache** main memory and cache refill lines are grouped into **sectors**, also called **rows**. The cache can map any main-memory sector into any cache sector, and the cache logically uses an associative memory to perform the mapping. Because refill lines always preserve their ordering within sectors, the associative memory only maps sector addresses. The cache uses **validity bits,** one for each refill line, to keep track of the refill lines that are present in cache RAM. See Fig. 4.15.

There is an important difference between a sector mapping with a single cache sector and a direct mapping. In the latter organization, each refill line in cache can hold the corresponding refill line from a different column in main memory. In sector mapping with a single sector, each refill line in cache can only hold the refill line from the main memory sector the cache is currently mapping.

**Design Alternatives**

Direct-mapped cache and fully associative cache can be thought of as special cases of set-associative cache, with the number of sets equal either to 1 (direct-mapped) or to the number of lines in the cache (fully associative). Thus in some sense, set-associative cache is the general case.

In practice, designers do not use fully associative caches because they require too much hardware and barely outperform two-way set-associative

sector-mapped cache
sectors
rows

validity bits

**FIGURE 4.14**  *A two-way set-associative cache. Cache RAM consists of 8 sets having two refill lines each; main memory consists of 8 sets having four refill lines each.*

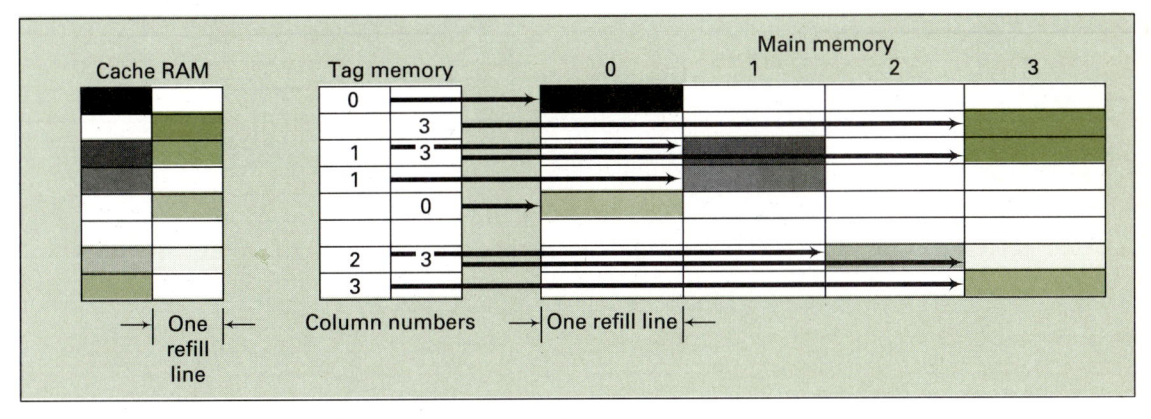

caches. Fully associative caches are, however, easy to analyze mathematically, so researchers frequently mention them in the literature and use the term *set-associative cache* (as we have here) to mean caches that are not at either design extreme. In other words, a set-associative cache has at least two sets but not as many sets as cache lines.

Accessing a direct-mapped cache is faster than accessing a set-associative cache because the hardware does not need to select among sets. However, for a fixed cache size and line size, increasing the associativity (i.e., increasing the number of sets) increases the hit rate, because there are more places to put a given refill line. If one fixes the size of the cache and the length of the cache line, then increasing the associativity increases the amount of hardware. If one fixes the amount of hardware approximately and the cache size, then increasing the associativity decreases the line length. Thus it is reasonable to say that a direct-mapped cache has lines that are twice as long as a two-way set-associative cache and four times as long as a four-way set-associative cache. We assume this relationship in the next paragraph.

Because the pattern of accesses to instructions tends to be regular and sequential, direct-mapped caches with long refill lines have the highest performance for instruction caches. Furthermore, direct-mapped caches are the easiest to implement and, therefore, generally the least expensive. In contrast, the pattern of data accesses is relatively irregular, and two-way or four-way set-associative caches with refill lines of about 64 bytes tend to be the best for data or mixed data-and-instruction caches. However, their advantage in hit rate

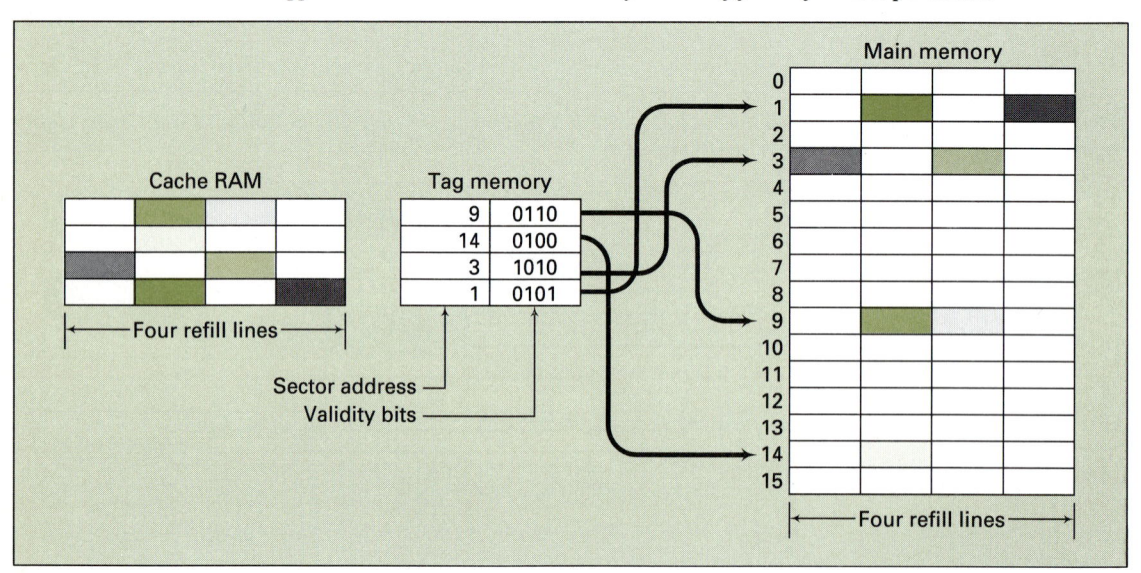

**FIGURE 4.15** *A sector-mapped cache. Both cache and memory consist of four refill lines per sector.*

peaks at about 2:1 near a 32-KB cache size and drops off rapidly for both larger and smaller caches.

**Cache-address Processing**

Here is a summary of how cache memories check their address tags. Associative caches check all tags to see if any one matches the requested address. Caches with sector organization also simultaneously check all address tags. However, the tags hold sector addresses rather than refill-line addresses, so they are $N$ bits shorter, where $2^N$ is the number of refill lines in a sector. The remaining $N$ bits select a validity bit to complete the check. Direct-mapped caches use some address bits to index into the tag table to check cache addresses. Each cache access requires checking only a single cache entry. Set-associative caches directly index into the tag memory with part of the address to get a set of tags. They then compare the remaining high-order address bits to all the tag entries in the set. Hence a two-way set-associative cache uses part of the address as an index into the tag memory to select a set of two tags and then checks to see if either tag is correct for it. Figure 4.16 shows how each cache handles the address for the three primary cache organizations. (We do not include sector-mapped cache because of its special use of validity bits.)

**FIGURE 4.16** *Cache address manipulation. Here the cache is assumed to have $2^L$ refill lines of $2^K$ bytes each. Notice that if $N = 0$, then (b) and (c) are the same. Also, if $N = L$, then (a) and (c) are the same.*

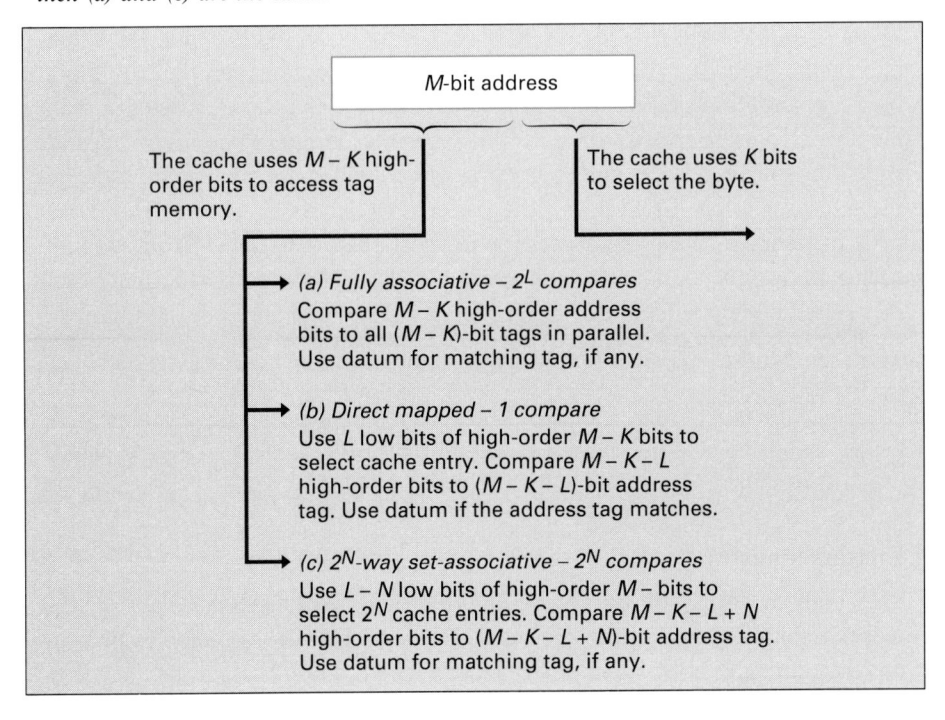

$M$-bit address

The cache uses $M - K$ high-order bits to access tag memory.

The cache uses $K$ bits to select the byte.

(a) Fully associative – $2^L$ compares
Compare $M - K$ high-order address bits to all $(M - K)$-bit tags in parallel. Use datum for matching tag, if any.

(b) Direct mapped – 1 compare
Use $L$ low bits of high-order $M - K$ bits to select cache entry. Compare $M - K - L$ high-order bits to $(M - K - L)$-bit address tag. Use datum if the address tag matches.

(c) $2^N$-way set-associative – $2^N$ compares
Use $L - N$ low bits of high-order $M -$ bits to select $2^N$ cache entries. Compare $M - K - L + N$ high-order bits to $(M - K - L + N)$-bit address tag. Use datum for matching tag, if any.

### Cache Performance

There are several ways of evaluating the performance of a cache, and here we shall focus on the one that is useful for a computer architect. The instruction decoders in most computers hold a few instructions, just as their registers hold a few data. We shall refer to the average time to execute instructions when the instructions and their data are both in the CPU as the base time per instruction ($TPI_{base}$). The actual time per instruction of a computer is

$$TPI = TPI_{base} + time_{memory\ access},$$

where the second term is the average time to fetch operands and data. Now, when there is a cache, this second term can be decomposed:

$$Time_{memory\ access} = hit\ rate \times time_{cache\ access} + miss\ rate \times time_{memory\ access}.$$

Many factors affect the hit rate of the cache (or its miss rate, which is $1 - hit\ rate$), such as the workload on the computer, the operating system strategies, the compilers, and the structure of the cache. We are only concerned with those factors that are under control of the computer designer, such as cache size, structure, and organization. At this time, we shall only observe that the size of the cache is the dominant factor in determining the miss rate. Other factors, such as the replacement strategy and the refill line length, do not affect the miss rate much, provided they are well chosen. Modifying the size, on the other hand, changes the miss rate and directly affects the cost.

### Specialized Caches

Designers sometimes provide separate caches for code and for data. RISC machines that use Harvard architectures are an example; however, they are based on the assumption that the operating system separates code from data in main memory. Knowing this in advance simplifies the design of the cache because the CPU will read the memory holding the code but not write into it during program execution. In addition, the patterns of access to memory that holds code differ from those that access the memory that holds data. Using separate caches allows the designer to put each one close to its user (the instruction processing unit versus the execution unit) for faster response, and to tailor the refill and replacement strategies for the application. For example, instruction caches perform better with larger refill lines than those optimal for data caches.

Although we have focused on caches that speed up main-memory accesses, designers also use caches to speed up disk accesses. Because the principles are similar, we shall not elaborate on them here.

### 4.2.3 ■ Virtual Memory

Most computers provide storage media other than main memory. Disks are the most common because of their low cost, but tapes are also common, especially on large computers. Because programs can be stored on these secondary storage devices, the size of a program is limited not by the size of main memory but rather, by the size of the computer's logical-address space.

In practice, the logical-address space of many computers is much larger than their physical-address space. For example, if a byte-addressed computer uses a 32-bit address, its logical-address space has $2^{32}$ memory locations, which is 4 GB. Few computers of the 1980s had that much physical memory, even though many of them use 32-bit addresses. Consequently, until the advent of virtual memory, either the operating system restricted the size of a program to the size of physical memory, or the programmer had to use overlays to reduce the program's maximum physical size.

Earlier we presented an overview of virtual-memory systems. In them, the operating system loads only part of a program, the currently active part, in main memory at one time. When the active part of the program requests a memory reference, the CPU resolves the effective address exactly as it would if the computer did not have virtual memory. However, it does not send the effective address directly to the main-memory system. Instead, it sends it to a **memory map,** which is part of the virtual-memory hardware. The memory map is the conceptual system that translates virtual addresses into physical addresses. The memory map checks to see if the reference is active, that is, present in main memory. If so, the memory map translates the CPU's effective address into the proper physical address, and the program executes just as if it were on a system without virtual memory. However, if the required word is not in main memory, the memory map interrupts the CPU. The operating system then loads the demanded part of the program into main memory, updates the memory map, and returns control to the instruction that raised the fault in the first place. Refer to Fig. 4.17.

<small>memory map</small>

Virtual-memory systems generally use one or both of two techniques for mapping effective addresses into physical addresses: paging and segmentation. We shall describe both techniques shortly. Although most people refer to these systems simply as virtual memory, it would be more accurate to distinguish between **demand-paged virtual memory** and **demand-segmented virtual memory** because the operating system loads the pages or segments on demand. (Sometimes the term *virtual memory* is used to describe any system in which the effective addresses differ from the physical addresses. This is unusual usage, and we shall avoid it here.)

<small>demand-paged virtual memory<br>demand-segmented virtual memory</small>

### Paging

**Paging** is a hardware-oriented technique for managing physical memory. Architects introduced paging so that large programs could run on computers with small physical memories. In essence, the computer loads into main memory only those parts of the program that it currently needs for execution. The remainder of the program resides in external storage until needed. Paging is unrelated to the logical structure of the program, and the entire program must be

<small>paging</small>

created as a single unit (i.e., within a single logical-address space) for this technique to work.

In a paging system, the virtual-memory hardware divides logical addresses into two parts, a **virtual-page number** (or simply **page number**) and a **word offset** within the page. The hardware makes this division by partitioning the bits of the address: The high-order bits are the page number, and the low-order bits are the offset. When the system loads a page into memory, it always places the page beginning at a page boundary. The units of physical memory that hold pages are called **page frames** (or sometimes **blocks**) to distinguish them from virtual pages. For current systems, page frames tend to range from 512 to 4096 bytes.

In a demand-paged virtual-memory system, the memory map is called a **page map.** As part of the page map, the operating system maintains a **page table,** which holds various pieces of information about the program's pages. A page table consists of a number of **page-table entries,** and each page-table entry holds information about a specific page. The virtual page number serves as an offset into the page table. A typical page-table entry includes a validity bit, which indicates whether the page is in memory; a **dirty bit,** which indicates

*Margin terms:* virtual-page number, page number, word offset; page frames, blocks; page map, page table; page-table entries; dirty bit

**FIGURE 4.17** *Components of a virtual-memory system.*

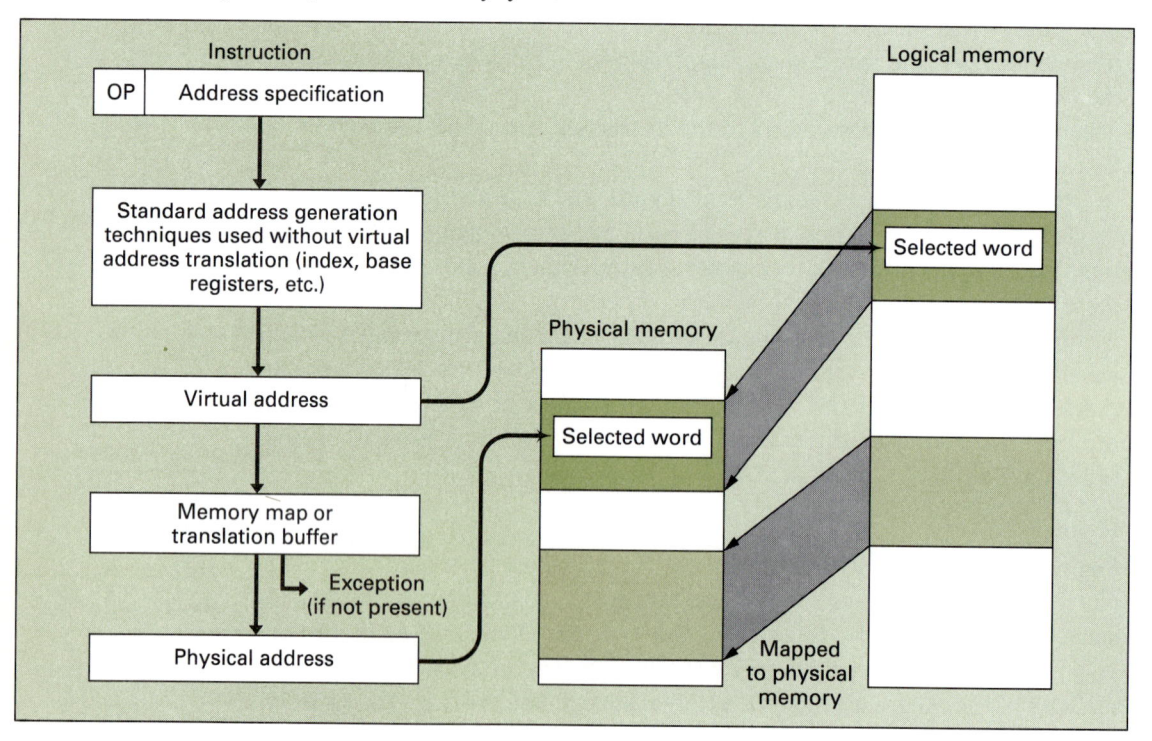

whether the program has modified the page; **protection bits,** which indicate which users may access the page and how (e.g., to read only or to read and write); and the **page-frame number** for the page (if the page is in memory).

Most paging systems keep their page tables in main memory, and the hardware has a **page-table base register** that points to the page table in memory. The operating system alters the page-table base register using privileged instructions. When the page table is in main memory, each main-memory access potentially requires the overhead of a second memory access: The addressing hardware must consult the page table to get the page-frame number for the reference. To avoid the additional overhead, some hardware systems maintain, as part of the page map, a small cache called a **translation lookaside buffer (TLB),** which holds essentially the same information as part of the page table. In addition, it holds the virtual-page number so it can map the virtual-page number into the page-frame number. In general, a TLB holds entries only for the most recently accessed pages and only for valid pages, that is, pages that have an image (exact copy of the data) in main memory. (Note that the hardware uses the TLB strictly for page-table entries.) Figure 4.18 shows the components of a paging system.

For a paging system, whenever the CPU generates an effective address, the CPU sends it to the TLB, which produces the page-frame number if

*protection bits*

*page-frame number*

*page-table base register*

*translation lookaside buffer (TLB)*

FIGURE 4.18 *Components of a paging system. The hardware uses the virtual-page number in two ways: as an offset into the page table, and as a key when searching the translation lookaside buffer (TLB). The page-table entry holds the page-frame number of the page, the validity bit (V), the dirty bit (D), and protection information.*

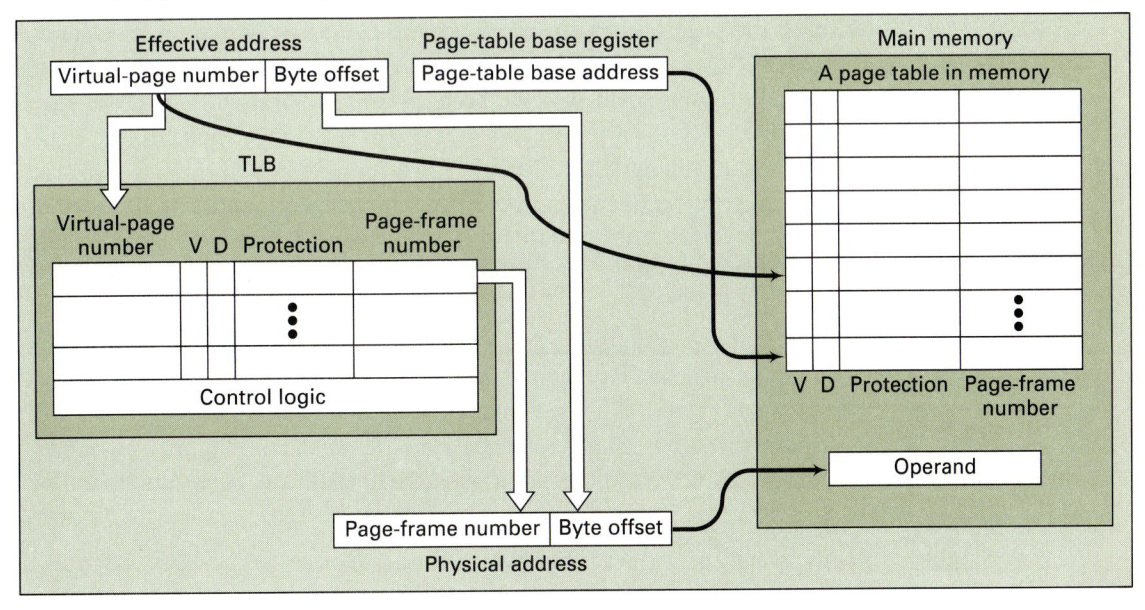

it holds an entry for the page. If the TLB has no entry, the hardware consults the page table in main memory by using the page number as an offset into the page table. If the validity bit indicates the page is in memory, the hardware uses the page-frame number to access the memory and simultaneously copies the page-table entry into the TLB. Otherwise the hardware initiates a trap called a **page fault,** at which point the operating system intervenes to load the **demanded page** in memory and update the page table.

page fault<br>demanded page

Because of the principle of locality of reference, for most programs memory accesses tend to be to pages already in memory, so page faults are relatively infrequent. That is the basis for a successful paging system. Some programs, however, cause frequent page faults and need to be rewritten to operate efficiently on a paging system. For example, suppose a paging system uses pages of 1024 bytes and a program defines a 1024 × 1024 character array whose elements are stored in row-major order. If the program accesses the array elements in row-minor (column) order, each successive element will lie on a different page. Consequently, almost every access will cause a page fault, a situation called **page thrashing.**

page thrashing

Some computers with paging, instead of using page tables in main memory, implement the memory map as an associative memory in hardware. In this case, when the CPU requires a memory access, it sends the effective address directly to the page map. The output of the page map is either the page-frame number (if the page is in memory) or a page fault.

For all types of paging systems, whenever a page fault occurs the operating system must decide in which page frame to put the demanded page. The operating system will choose an empty page frame whenever possible. However, if all the page frames are occupied, the operating system must delete an existing page to make room for the new page. Operating systems use several different **page-replacement policies,** such as **first in, first out (FIFO)** or **least recently used (LRU).** To support various page-replacement policies, the hardware may need to maintain information that indicates when the page was last referenced.[5] After removing an active page, if necessary, and perhaps copying it to external storage, the operating system loads the demanded page into main memory, updates the page map or page table, and returns control to the interrupted program.

page-replacement policies
first in, first out (FIFO)
least recently used (LRU)

When a program modifies a page that is in main memory, the corresponding page in secondary memory (e.g., on the disk) will have stale (i.e., no longer current) values. It follows that if the operating system removes a modified page from main memory, it must update the image of that page in secondary memory. However, if the program never modifies a page, the operating

---

5. The reader should consult any good book on operating systems for details on page-replacement policies.

system does not need to update its image in secondary memory, a considerable time savings. The dirty bit is present to reduce the update time. The operating system clears the dirty bit when it first loads a page into memory. Whenever a program modifies any part of a page, the hardware automatically sets the dirty bit for that page. When the operating system later removes the page from memory, it first checks the dirty bit and only copies the page back into secondary memory if the dirty bit is set.

In addition to the dirty bit, most page maps also provide protection bits and other information, such as usage bits, for each page. Protection bits may indicate if the page is a read-only page, an execute-only page, or an unrestricted page, for example. These protection mechanisms replace the lock-and-key protection used by the IBM System/360 family and the relocation address-field length protection used by the CDC 6000 family.

A difficult implementation issue arises when a computer has complex instructions, such as vector instructions or string-processing instructions, and the designer wants to implement demand paging. For complex instructions, the hardware can raise a **delayed page fault,** which is one that occurs during the middle of an instruction execution. For simple instructions, instructions whose operands are single words, delayed faults will not occur because the paging hardware will raise the fault during the operand fetch. However, an instruction whose operands span several pages, as can occur with a MOVE STRING instruction, may cause a delayed page fault. If the page holding the beginning of the string is valid but a page holding another part of the string is invalid, the hardware will not discover the page fault until it has processed part of the string.

*delayed page fault*

There are a number of possible ways to handle delayed page faults. One technique is for the hardware to check for the validity of every page that the instruction will use before starting execution of the instruction. If any pages are invalid (i.e., not in memory), it loads them into memory to validate them before starting the instruction. A second technique, called **roll back,** is for the hardware to record enough information during the execution of the instruction so that if a page fault occurs, it can restore the system to the state that existed prior to instruction execution. After processing the page fault, the hardware can then restart the instruction at its beginning. A third technique is to provide enough interrupt hardware so the system can interrupt the instruction in the middle of execution. For this solution the hardware must be able to preserve all intermediate values that the instruction uses during its execution, such as address pointers and loop counters. The interrupt system can then restart the interrupted instruction at the point of interruption. A fourth technique is for the hardware to use the operational registers to hold intermediate values. When a page fault occurs, the usual interrupt hardware will be adequate to save the required context information so the hardware can resume the interrupted instruction.

*roll back*

Current systems use all of these techniques. The practicality of a given solution for a particular instruction set depends on many factors, including the complexity of the instructions, the number of operations the instructions initiate, the cost of implementing a particular solution, and the resulting delay that the solution might cause. For example, if a string-processing instruction operates on long strings, say in excess of 10,000 characters, it may be too time-consuming to check whether every page is present before starting the instruction. It also may be impractical to preserve enough information to allow roll back. For this situation, the simplest solution may be to use the existing operational registers for holding temporary values during instruction execution, and interrupt the instruction whenever a page fault occurs. (Note that the control unit or software system must save the contents of any registers the instruction uses and restore them after the instruction finishes executing.)

**Segmentation**

segmentation

Like paging, **segmentation** is a virtual-memory technique introduced by architects so that large programs could run on a computer with a small physical memory. However, segmentation is not an alternative to paging; systems with segmentation often use paging as well, as we shall discuss later in the section.

Segmentation differs from paging in a number of ways. The most important is that, while paging is hardware-oriented, segmentation reflects the logical structure of a program. Instead of dividing logical addresses into pages of a fixed size and main memory into fixed-size page frames, the hardware divides logical addresses into **segments** of arbitrary size (although any given system will have some maximum segment size), and the processor treats main memory as a single block. Segments that contain only procedure code are called **code segments,** and those with only data are **data segments.** Some systems contain segments that combine procedures and data.

segments

code segments
data segments

Another difference between segmentation and paging is that segments tend to be much larger than pages (frequently as large as 64 KB); moreover, segments can usually range in size, whereas pages are always one size for a given system. Segment sizes are chosen to reflect the sizes of the corresponding code or data they contain. For example, segment 0 might contain only the main program and be 25 KB long, segment 1 might hold several independent procedures and be 64 KB long, and segment 2 might be a 20-KB data segment containing a single large array.

Also unlike paging, in segmentation the entire program does not need to be created as a single module to be loaded into memory as a unit. Thus different programs can share subroutines, such as I/O routines and scientific subroutines. However, unless a segmentation system also provides paging, it must load an entire segment in memory at a time, which places a practical limit on the maximum size of a segment.

Figure 4.19 illustrates the main components of a segmentation system. As the figure shows, a **segment map** replaces the page map and an adder now appears where there was none for paging. The valid (V), dirty (D), and protection bits play the same role for segmentation as they do for paging.

segment map

In a segmentation system, logical addresses have two parts: a **segment number** and a **byte offset.** As with paged systems, the CPU determines each operand's effective address, which it now views as a segment number and a byte offset. It sends only the segment number to the segment map, which translates it into the base address of the segment in memory. The adder adds the byte offset to the base address to get the physical address of the reference.

segment number
byte offset

If an address-computation results in a segment number that is not present in main memory, the segment map raises a **segment fault.** A segment fault, like a page fault, is an exception that instructs the operating system to load into main memory the requested or **demanded segment** and to update the segment map. Because segments can be placed anywhere in memory, the operating system now has even more responsibility than it did for a paged system. It must now determine where to place the demanded segment in memory, and it must allocate space for it, a process that may require the removal of some segments already in memory. Placing a segment in memory can leave **splinters,**

segment fault

demanded segment

splinters

**FIGURE 4.19**  *Components of a segmentation system.*

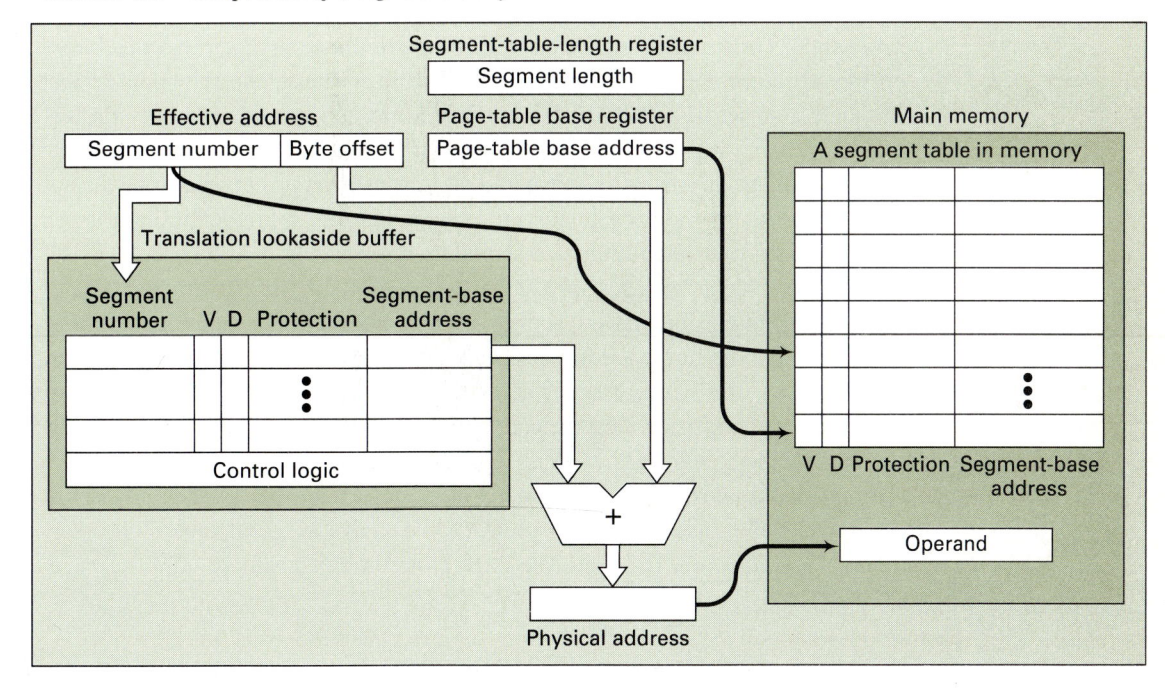

small blocks sandwiched between other allocated blocks that are too small to be used by other segments.[6]

**segment tables**

As with paging, the operating system usually maintains its **segment tables** in main memory and the hardware provides one or more registers for accessing the segment tables. One register is the **segment-table base register,** which holds the beginning address in memory of a segment table. A second register is the **segment-table length register,** which holds the size of the segment table. The hardware accesses a segment-table entry in the same manner described earlier for accessing a page-table entry, and it uses the segment length to prevent a program from attempting to access a segment-table entry that is out of bounds. As with paging, the hardware may also provide a cache or TLB for holding the most recently used segment-table entries.

**segment-table base register**

**segment-table length register**

To change segment tables, the instruction set provides instructions, usually privileged, for loading the segment-table registers.

Finally, most systems that support segmentation keep separate segment tables appropriate for each privilege level of operation. When the CPU operates in privileged mode, the hardware uses a **system segment table,** and when operating in unprivileged mode, the system uses the **user segment table.** In either case, instructions that alter the segment registers are generally privileged.

**system segment table**

**user segment table**

### Segmentation with Paging

Architects introduced demand paging primarily to allow large programs to run on systems with limited-size main memory. They introduced segmentation to satisfy the needs of the software: Since compilers organize data or procedures into data or code segments, the operating system must manage programs based on the structures of their segments. In addition, because the segments reflect the logical structure of the programs, hardware can provide memory protection when using segmentation more easily than it can when using paging alone. However, many problems arise when a system uses only segmentation, including difficulties in memory allocation, fragmentation, and the limitations on program sizes that maximum-size segments impose.

To take advantages of the hardware and software characteristics of both paging and segmentation, some systems combine them. See Fig. 4.20. For these systems, the hardware divides the logical address into a segment number, page number, and word offset. The operating system creates a page table for each segment, and it divides segments into pages that it can load individually. It treats the segment number as an offset into a segment table, whose entries are page-table addresses (and perhaps other information). Systems often use a segment-table base register to point to the active segment table. The page number specifies an offset into the page table for that segment, and the page-

---

6. Consult the references for listings of textbooks that provide additional details about the memory-management responsibilities of the operating system in a system with segmentation.

**FIGURE 4.20** *Segmentation with Paging. The effective address of a word now has three parts: segment number, page number, and the offset. The segment number is an index into the segment table. The segment-table entry gives the address of the page table for the page holding the word. The page number is an index into the page table for the segment. The page-table entry gives the page-frame number of the page frame holding the word. The offset is the distance from the beginning of the page to the word. The ○ symbol indicates concatenation.*

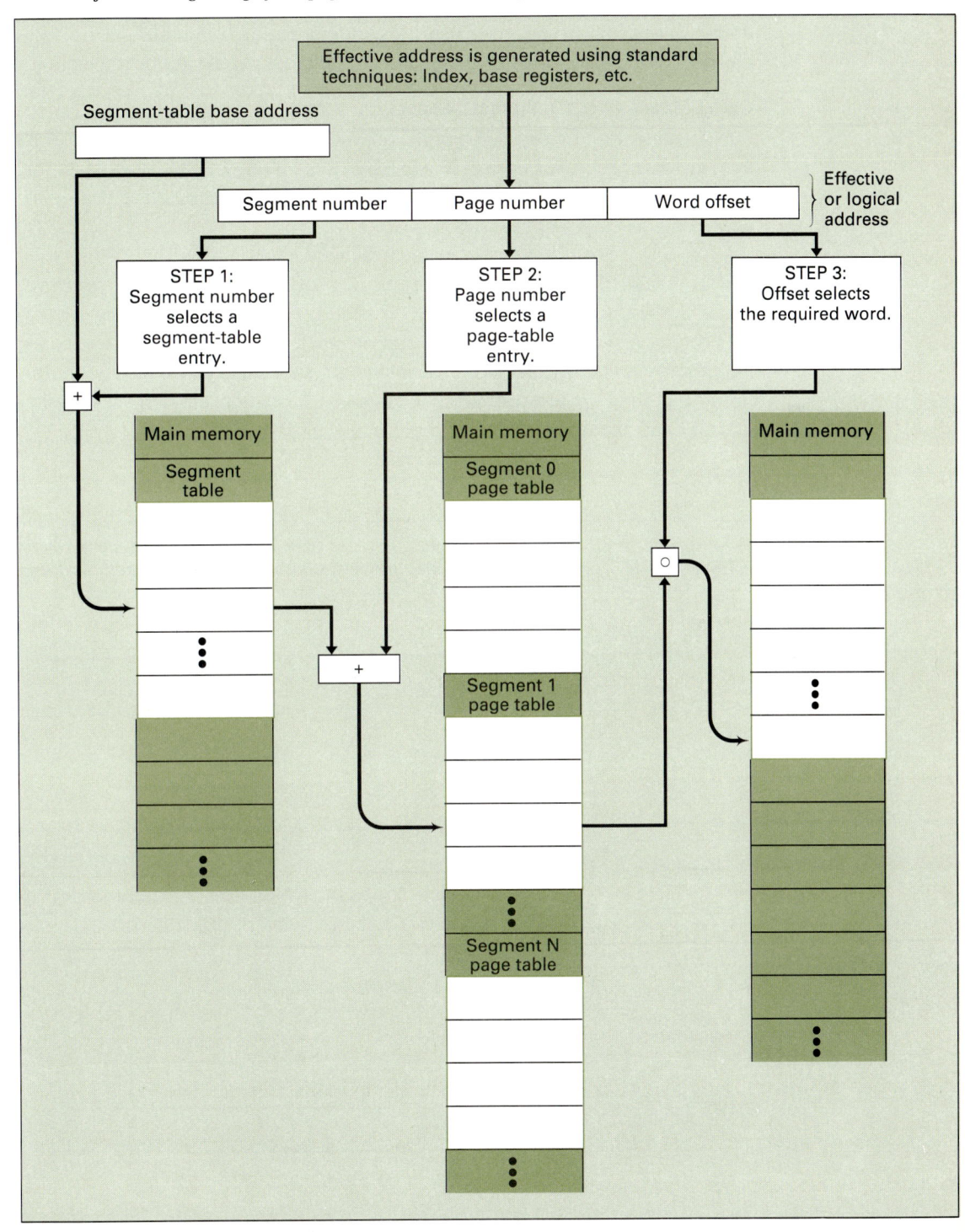

table entry gives the page-frame address. The physical address is the page-frame address concatenated with (appended to) the word offset. Like a paging system, a paged-segmented system divides physical memory into page frames, and it loads pages into page frames using a standard paging technique. Figure 4.20 illustrates the components of a system that combines paging and segmentation.

**Cache Memory versus Virtual Memory**

Cache memory and virtual memory share a number of features. Both systems use hardware that maps one set of addresses to another, and both hold data for the CPU. Finally, both operate on a demand basis, replacing older data with newer data as the CPU requests it.

There are differences between cache memory and virtual memory as well as similarities. The most important is a difference in purpose. As mentioned earlier, architects use caches to speed up memory systems and virtual memory to allow large programs to run on small computers. It is not uncommon for systems to include both cache and virtual memory in their configurations. Figure 4.21 illustrates the conceptional relationship between cache memory and virtual-memory hardware in a typical system that uses both.

FIGURE 4.21 *Typical system incorporating both virtual-memory and cache memory. Data buses appear in color; while address buses are not colored. This system uses segmentation for virtual memory but could equally well use paging or both.*

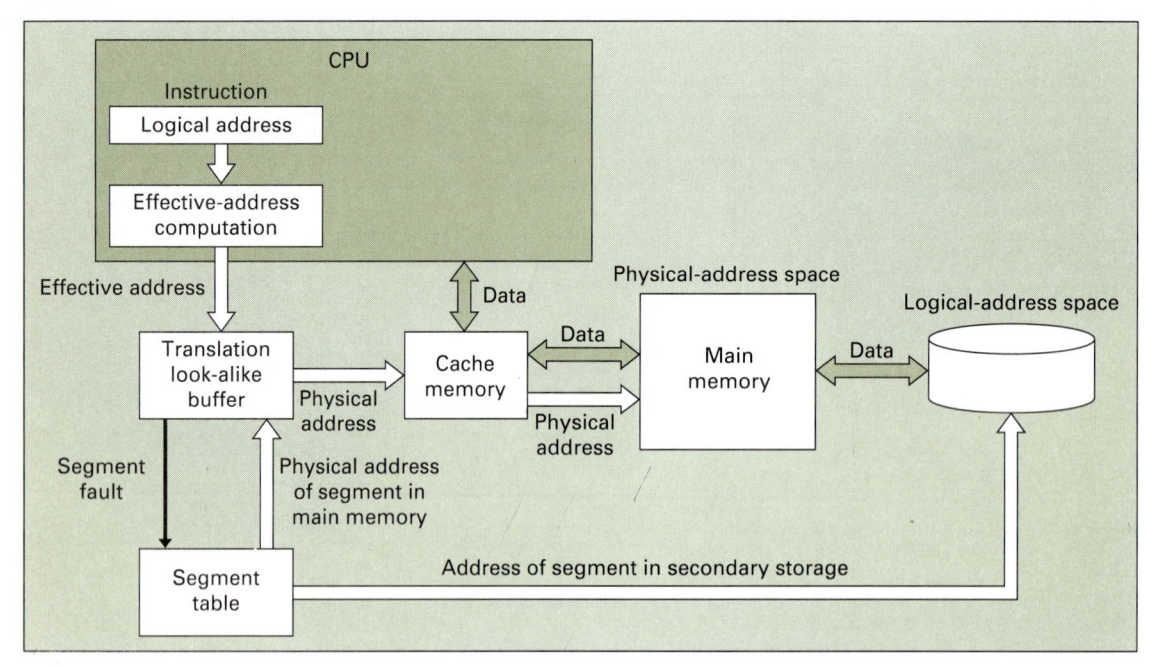

A second difference lies in faults and how they are processed. Cache misses occur much more frequently than do segment or page faults. For example, if a cache has a 90% hit rate, then a cache miss will occur about once every 10 memory accesses. In contrast, a segment fault, depending on its size, may not occur for thousands of memory accesses.[7] Cache performance would degrade dramatically if the operating system intervened every 10 or so memory accesses, so cache memories are hardware-controlled devices. A third difference is that cache refill lines are much smaller than pages or segments, so that processing a cache miss is much faster than processing a page or segment fault.

When a computer uses a cache to speed up main memory, the address the CPU sends to the cache is the physical address of the required datum. Consequently, if a cache miss occurs, the cache can forward the address to main memory without additional processing. In contrast, in a system using segmentation, the CPU forwards the virtual addresses to the segment map. If a segment fault occurs, the operating system must consult its segment tables to determine where to find the demanded segment. Consequently, the operating system has a greater responsibility in processing a segment fault than a cache does in processing a cache miss.

A closer comparison exists between paging and cache memory than between segmentation and cache memory. All pages are the same size as are all cache refill lines, but pages tend to be much longer than cache refill lines: Pages are typically 512 to 2048 bytes long, while cache refill lines tend to be under 64 bytes. Finally, paging systems often use hardware-replacement algorithms, as do caches.

### 4.2.4 ■ Memory Banking and Expanded Memory

The first personal computers, such as the Apple and Atari, used 8-bit CPUs that supported 16-bit addresses. These small computers had a limited, 64-KB physical-address space, which programs quickly used up. The IBM PC (Chapter 5) supported 20-bit physical addresses and hence provided a 1-MB physical-address space to its users. This, too, proved to be too small for large programs. To alleviate the problem, several manufacturers developed a technique, called **memory banking,** as a way of supplementing a computer's main memory by providing additional high-speed memory to the computer. It is external memory, much like a magnetic disk. However, the computer does not access banked memory using I/O operations as it would with a disk. Instead, the CPU accesses banked memory in the same way it accesses main memory. Thus from

memory banking

---

7. For a system with 64-KB segments, entire procedures often fit within one segment, and they may execute without a single segment fault. However, it is always possible to create a situation where segment faults occur frequently. For example, if a programmer stores a large array in row-major order and accesses the elements in row-minor order, and if the segments are the same size as the array rows, then segment faults may occur on every element access.

the CPU's point of view, banked memory is indistinguishable from main memory. Figure 4.22 illustrates the idea.

Internally, memory-banking hardware has a number of banks of memory and a **bank-select register,** which selects one of the banks. Whenever the CPU references a word in banked memory, the memory-banking hardware picks the corresponding word from the selected bank.

To use banked memory, a user replaces a block of the computer's physical memory with the memory-banking hardware. The physical addresses of the memory that the user replaces define a **window** into the banked memory. Any reference to an address within that window becomes a reference to the corresponding word in the selected bank. The user also assigns an I/O port address to the memory-banking hardware. The user changes the content

bank-select register

window

FIGURE 4.22  *Memory banking. (a) Hardware of a simple system before banking. (b) Hard-ware after the user replaces one RAM chip with four banks. The hardware shown here maps a single block of addresses into a selected bank of memory.*

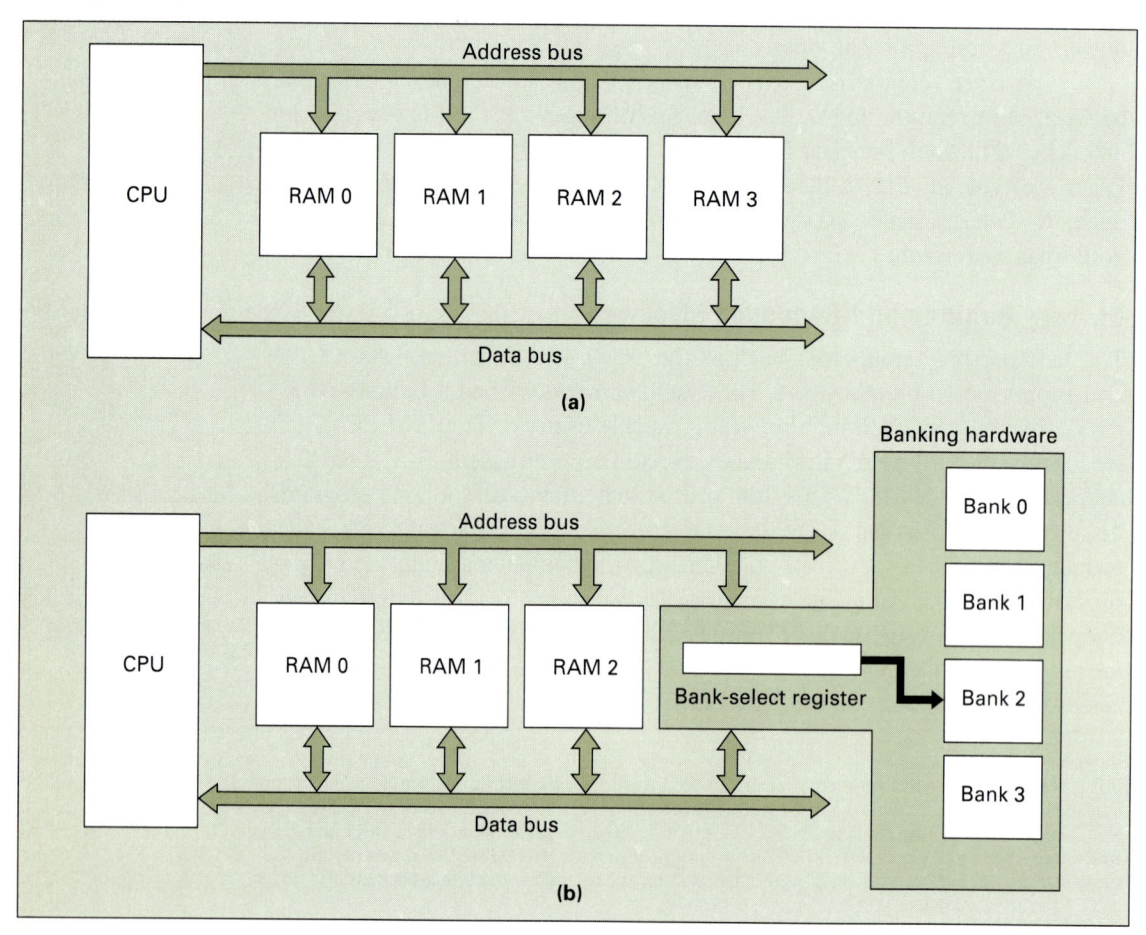

of the bank-select register by writing the desired bank number to that register's port address.

As a specific example, suppose a computer uses 16-KB RAM chips (Fig. 4.23a), and the user replaces one RAM chip with a memory-banking device that has four 16-KB RAM chips on it (Fig. 4.23b). Further, suppose that the replaced RAM chip responded to the 16-KB block of addresses on the range 49,152 to 65,535. From the CPU's point of view, a single 16-KB RAM chip still responds to addresses on the indicated range. However, if the CPU references address 52,153, which is within the window, and the bank-select register points to bank 2, the reference will be to word 3001 (52,153 − 49,152) of memory bank 2.

Notice that memory banking does not alter the size of the computer's physical-address space. Rather, it enables the program to access a number of additional banks of memory by changing the content of a single register, the bank-select register. But it can only access those banks one at a time. Notice also that memory banking is not like virtual memory, because it is unrelated to the computer's memory-addressing hardware. The CPU is unaware of any memory-banking hardware.

**Expanded memory** is a method of memory banking that Lotus, Intel, and Microsoft standardized for the IBM PC. Fig. 4.23 illustrates the idea, showing an expanded-memory device with four registers to select different banks of memory. The device divides a 64-KB window into a number of 16-KB windows. One may view expanded memory as comprising up to 512 16-KB banks, for a total of 8 MB of memory. For the PC the addition of expanded

*expanded memory*

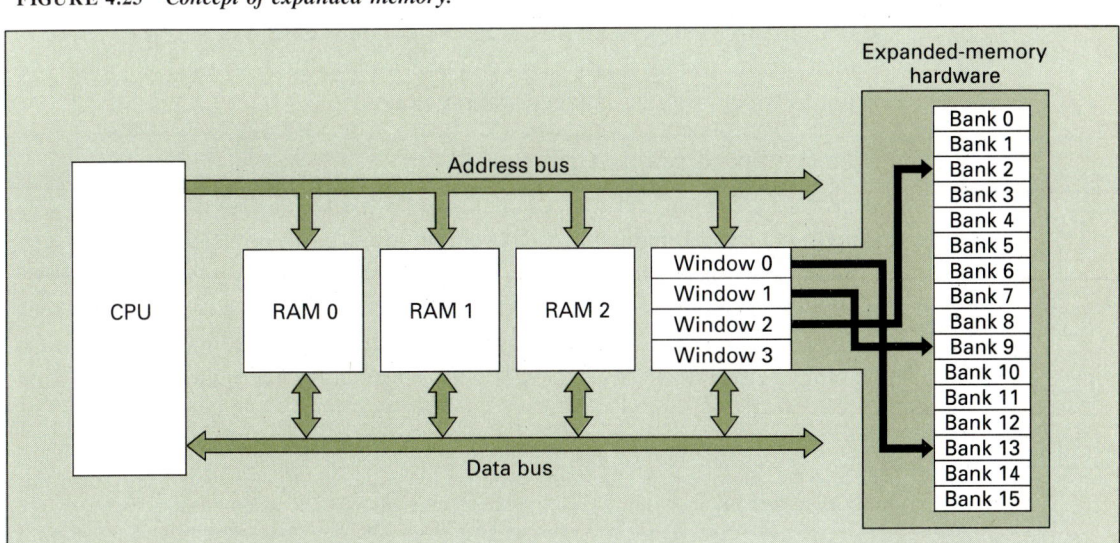

FIGURE 4.23  *Concept of expanded memory.*

memory provides additional storage for data but not for programs: programs are still strictly limited to the 640-KB size imposed by the PC architecture (see Chapter 5).

In addition to special hardware, a program wishing to use expanded memory must use a standard software interface, called an **expanded-memory manager.** The expanded-memory manager allocates blocks of expanded memory to requesting programs by controlling the bank-select registers. When a program requests a bank of expanded memory, the expanded-memory manager reserves a bank, tells the program the address of the 16-KB window, and sets that window's bank-select register to point to that allocated bank. Similarly, if a program wishes to switch banks or relinquish a bank of expanded memory, it makes the request to the expanded-memory manager.

There are two main differences between expanded memory and virtual memory. The first is that the user's program controls the use of expanded-memory hardware by calling the expanded-memory manager. In contrast, the user's program is unaware of the presence of virtual memory because the operating system controls the virtual-memory hardware. The second difference is that the user is free to use expanded memory in any way at all. The operating system does not put information in expanded memory, or remove information from it; the user does those things. The operating system has no control of expanded memory, although it may use it.[8]

## 4.3 ■ Memory Design Issues

A number of issues have bearing on the design and use of memory components and systems. Many of these—such as cost, technology, address-space size, protection, virtual memory, and cache—have already been covered earlier in the text from different perspectives. Here we explore these issues as they relate to limitations on the plasticity of a computer architecture, which is its ability to adapt to widely varying implementation technologies.

### 4.3.1 ■ Memory Speed versus CPU Speed

A particularly clear example of changing device technology that affects CPU design is the small high-speed RAMs that are used to implement the registers of many machines. These devices, like the RAMs used for memory, are slowly increasing in speed and rapidly decreasing in cost. Thus it is reasonable to seek architectural features that take advantage of them. Multiple register sets, overlapping register sets, large register sets, large stores for microprograms, and

---

8. In practice, any program, including the operating system, can request memory from the expanded-memory manager. Hence, programs tend to share expanded memory. However, the expanded-memory manager will not alter an allocated block of expanded memory, or assign it to another program, unless the program that originally requested it relinquishes it.

large high-speed caches are possible applications for large amounts of high-speed RAM.

Between the early 1960s and the early 1980s, both memory and CPU speeds increased, but the overall ratio between them held relatively steady, with memory speeds generally about 10 times slower than CPU speeds. For supercomputers like the CDC 6600, CDC 7600, CRAY 1, and Cray X-MP, memory access times were 10 to 14 times the CPU cycle time, and in minicomputers like the VAX 11/780, 8600, and 8700, the memory access times ranged from 4 to 7 CPU cycles. However, since the mid-1980s this trend has changed. CPU speeds are now generally increasing at a faster rate than memory speeds. (For example, the Cray-2 has a memory access time more than 50 times its CPU cycle time.) There are several reasons to expect this new trend to continue:

- Large memories generally require special hardware for detecting and correcting errors, adding to the effective memory access time.
- The fastest CPUs are pipelined, so they operate much faster than a memory of comparable technology. Designers provide adequate memory bandwidth for the CPU by using interleaved memory, but this slows access time even though it increases memory bandwidth. (Recall from Chapter 1 that memory bandwidth is the rate at which the memory can send or receive bytes to or from the processor, usually in megabytes per second.)
- Users will demand that memories always get larger, so it is difficult for computer designers to use the smaller, faster memory devices that may be available.

The proliferation of cache memories, large register sets, and sophisticated compilers points to the utility of maintaining memory that is substantially slower than the CPU. We have already discussed many of the techniques for matching slow memories to fast CPUs. Designers have tried a number of other techniques in the past, some only a few times, and we shall not be concerned about them here. In summary, because of decreasing memory cost, it appears that computers will need memory space on the order of $2^{45}$ bytes for single users, for a reasonably large number of applications. Users may require much larger memories for some applications, such as image processing, and archival memory systems will be substantially larger than this figure.

## 4.3.2 ■ Memory-address Space

Earlier we discussed limits on the physical-address space of a machine. As we have seen, there is need for very large virtual-address spaces so that single jobs can reference large databases. Historically, surpassing the limits on the virtual-address space of computers has been one of the most difficult problems to overcome. When IBM extended the System/360 to the System/370 and increased the address space from 24 to 31 bits, it had to include a compatibility mode (in essence, to operate as a System/360) so old programs could run on the new system. In the early 1960s, when IBM first designed the System/360 family, the 24-bit address seemed huge, just as the 31-bit address did in the early 1980s for both the IBM and the Digital VAX families. Now we see that much larger memories will be available on both of these systems.

If the historical trend in the near-exponential increase in memory sizes suggested by Fig. 4.2 were to continue, no memory size would last for long. As noted earlier, there do appear to be reasonable limits on the useful address-space size, even if memory were free. However, in addition to the large size of the databases in use today, the existence of inexpensive memory encourages the use of algorithms and coding techniques that increase system performance at the expense of requiring more memory. For example, increasing the sizes of I/O buffers for today's database programs allows more of the database to be memory-resident, a step on the way to putting the entire database in main memory. Expanding programs by loop unrolling (to yield fewer loop iterations) increases the code size and speed. Saving more temporary and intermediate results in memory can increase the speed of many programs, but it also increases their memory requirements.

What are some of the simplest ways of providing for much larger address spaces without making enormous changes in computer architectures? For systems that have base-displacement addressing, one step looks especially easy. The architects can increase the lengths of the base registers. Using the IBM System/360 as a model, extending the base registers to 64 bits would allow referencing memories of arbitrary size (for all time, as far as we can see). In real life there are many problems with trying to increase the base-register width. Some of those problems and possible actions to surmount them are as follows:

- Programs load base registers from memory, and loading a 64-bit value would place garbage (undefined values) in the high-order half of the register. This means that the instruction set would need new instructions for loading 64-bit values from memory into the base registers, so old programs could continue using the registers as before.

- Base registers may be used for other purposes because they are not physically separate from index registers, for example. Again, new instructions could be introduced to use the new base registers. Alternately, the hardware could treat them as 64-bit registers only when they serve as base registers. Few architectures can distinguish a register's usage sufficiently well for this technique to work smoothly. There are bound to be a number of surprises here.

- Having base registers that are twice as wide as index registers allows referencing all of memory, but it introduces inhomogeneity in the address space (see Section 3.3.4). A 32-bit computer cannot reference any array of more than 4 GB using a single base register. Today this is not viewed as a severe restriction, but in 10 years it may be.

### 4.3.3 ■ Speed–cost Tradeoffs

There are two key characteristics of memory technology:

1. Its unit price (price per bit) is decreasing very rapidly, while its speed is slowly increasing.
2. There is a great variety of speeds and costs in memory devices.

Generally speaking, there have been three uses of RAM technology in computer systems to take advantage of these variations:

1. slow, inexpensive devices for main memory;
2. fast devices for cache;
3. very fast, expensive devices for registers and the control store.

Cache memory allows systems to run as though much or nearly all of their memory is the fast expensive type when in fact most of it is slow and inexpensive. Virtual memory is useful when many applications require more memory than is economically available. Unfortunately, because memories are growing so fast, few large programs take advantage of the large memories that are now available. And those that do, such as image processing, need a large amount of space are likely to need more virtual-address space than the systems provide.

## Summary

This chapter focused on the storage-system architecture of computers. We looked both at single-level and multilevel storage systems.

Most computers provide support for initial program relocation and memory protection, which are necessary for multiprogramming and effective CPU utilization. High-performance systems may use multiported, interleaved storage systems to provide adequate memory bandwidth, and many have cache memory as well to provide adequate speed. We described four cache organizations (associative, sector, direct, and set-associative) and presented a simple method for evaluating cache performance. In addition to cache, many computers provide hardware for virtual-memory mapping, using either paging, segmentation, or both. These techniques provide users with an adequate environment for running large programs on computers with limited main memory.

Memory-system technology has changed quickly, and large main memories are becoming commonplace. We examined memory banking, which provides a way to add high-speed physical memory to an existing architecture; however, because it does not increase the size of a computer's logical-address space, it is a stopgap to the availability of large systems. We also discussed techniques for increasing the size of an existing architecture's logical-address space. The chapter ended with a discussion of some of the tradeoffs between speed and cost.

# Exercises

*4.1* Within an order of magnitude, carefully estimate the number of bytes in the following very large databases. Articulate your assumptions.

   a. The collective "phone book" for the United States.
   b. The number of pixels required to photograph the whole word at the current resolution of our satellites, purported to be 1 pixel per 10 cm$^2$. (This is presumed to be a desirable daily task for them in times of crisis.)
   c. The number of bytes in an airline reservation system.

*4.2* If you restrict your view of the data in Fig. 4.3 to include only the time period up to 1980, what mathematical functions describe the supercomputer memory sizes?

*4.3* When do extrapolated supercomputer memory sizes reach the sizes of the very large databases described in Exercise 4.1?

*4.4* Describe three advantages of low-order interleaving. Describe three advantages for high-order interleaving.

*4.5* Actual memories have a pair of internal registers, the memory address register (MAR) and the memory data register (MDR). Most memory devices require the CPU to load the MAR before sending data on a write operation, and, naturally, data and addresses go in opposite directions on read operations. Explain why using the same data paths for addresses and data is thus very sensible for low-cost systems.

*4.6* Modify Fig. 4.4 so the memory uses low-order interleave.

*4.7* Suggest how you might build a storage system that uses DRAM chips if you want to overlap the refresh operation with ordinary memory accesses.

*4.8* Identify four applications of ROMs in computers.

*4.9* Registers are more flexible than arithmetic stacks, because programs can access many registers at any time. On the other hand, stacks can hold more data because they have conceptually unlimited size. One technique for combining some of the virtues of each approach is to add a single operational stack to a register computer. For what types of applications would you recommend this design, and why?

*4.10* When accessing a memory of $W$ words of $B$ bits each made from $w \times b$ devices, the address must be sent to $B/b$ devices for each word and is generally sent to all $W/w$ banks of memory and to a decoder that selects the correct bank. If the time for a signal to propagate through the gates that transmit the signal to the memory is fixed and each gate is only allowed to be connected to $f$ devices, how long does it take the address to reach the memory devices?

A fan-out tree for the addresses, illustrated here, shows why memory-access time is longer for large memories than for small ones. This system uses gates with a fan-out of $f = 4$ to create enough copies of the address for the full memory. At the $n$th level there are $f^n$ devices accessible; shown here is $n = 3$. Typical $f$ values for fan-out are 2 to 6, but this depends on many factors. (Actually, memories have

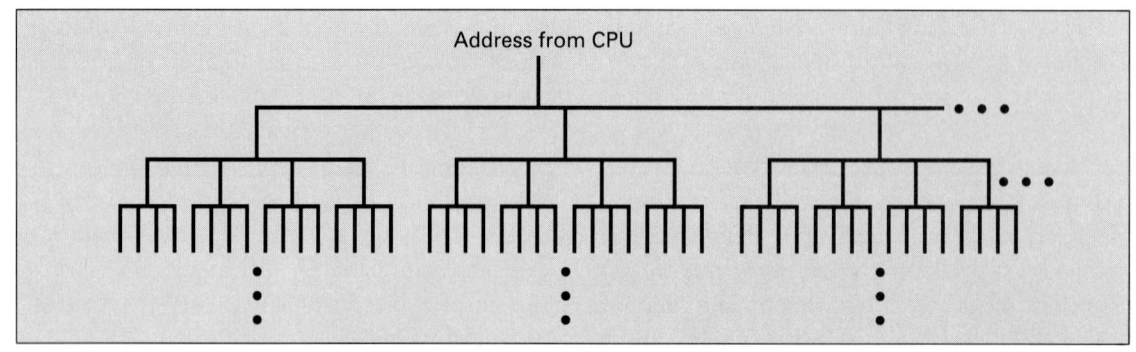

*Exercise 4.10*

tended to be faster as they get larger because each new IC generation is so much faster than the last that the technology change overwhelms the increased number of gate delays. These faster gates are, of course, also used in the CPUs, which increases their speeds even more.)

**4.11** In base-address/field-length memory-protection systems, instead of using the field length for memory protection, some computers use the highest address. Note that field length corresponds to the largest logical address, whereas the highest address corresponds to the largest physical address. What are the timing implications of using a largest physical address instead of a largest logical address?

**4.12** What are the major differences between key-controlled protection and field-length protection? (*Hint:* What system notes the exception, and when?)

**4.13** Compare the differences in memory utilization between systems that use key-controlled protection and those that use field-length protection. That is, what granularities can each system provide?

**4.14** Assuming equivalent refill-line sizes, why does a direct-mapped cache allow the fastest access, and why does a fully associative cache have the highest hit rate?

**4.15** Why is a long refill line more useful for an instruction cache than for a data or mixed instruction and data cache?

**4.16** What advantages would there be to using separate caches, one for the operating system and for the users' programs, rather than using a single cache?

**4.17** Verify that for a single-bus system, snoopy caches maintain cache coherence only if they are write-through caches. (A system with several CPUs may have several caches, and cache coherence refers to the situation where all caches that map a given main-memory word hold the same current value. A snoopy cache monitors the address bus and invalidates any cache entry that maps to a monitored address.)

**4.18** What is the effective access time of a memory system that has a cache access time $c$, a hit ratio $h$, and a main-memory access time $m$? Typical values for these parameters are $c = 3$, $h = 90\%$, $m = 15$. Access times are in clock cycles.

**4.19** Elaborate the analysis in Exercise 4.18 for a two-level cache system. Typical values in this case might be $c_1 = 2$, $h_1 = 85\%$, $c_2 = 12$, $h_2 = 98\%$, and $m = 40$.

**4.20** Some of the most quoted standard engineering benchmarks are the Livermore loops benchmark and the LINPACK benchmark. Discuss how representative these benchmarks are, in terms of cache size, refill-line size, and cache organization, for predicting the performance of large programs that operate on large data sets. (The benchmarks typically operate on data sets that hold a few kilobytes to a few tens of kilobytes.)

**4.21** Levesque's law states that it is always possible to make one computer run slower than another. Illustrate this principle with two code sequences for machines that are identical in all respects except for the organization of their cache. Assume that both have 16-KB caches, one direct-mapped with a 256-byte refill line and the other four-way set-associative with a 256-byte refill line. Make each machine look as much faster than the other as you can. To make answers comparable, assume that all instructions in your machine take 1 clock cycle in the CPU. When a cache miss occurs, loads and stores take 10 cycles if their operands are not in cache, and the memory can only satisfy one request at a time.

**4.22** Cache memories of 1 MB will soon be common if not already by the time you read this. Many benchmarks will fit entirely in such a cache. Describe how to force these small benchmarks to be representative of the performance on large programs.

**4.23** Before caches were in use, many compiler writers had found that compiling for minimum size tended to produce faster-running code and conversely. Do caches increase or decrease the likelihood of this correlation? Explain your answer.

**4.24** As president of the Huge Performance Company you are faced with deciding how to allocate some research and development (R&D) funds. One choice is to improve your machine's compilers, which will increase performance for all users by 15% per year. The other option is to add a cache, which will double the machine's performance. If the only increase in speed is due to the improved compilers, how many years will it take for the performance of the computers without caches to match the performance of the computers with caches?

**4.25** Suppose the cache described in Exercise 4.24 has to be redesigned every other year but compiler development is stopped when the initial performance is doubled. Assuming that the development cost of a new cache version equals the development cost of the 15% compiler boost, when does the cache development cost overtake the compiler development cost?

**4.26** If the speed of the primary memory were to exceed the speed of the CPU, then cache memory would be useless. True or false? Justify your answer.

**4.27** The Dualsys Computer Company is now building computers with caches, shown here schematically. $M_1$ is the cache and $M_2$ is the main memory. There are three parameters that determine the apparent access time of memory: the access times to $M_1$ and $M_2$, and the probability that $M_1$ will satisfy the memory access. ($M_2$ satisfies all requests that $M_1$ does not satisfy.) If $M_1$'s access time is 50 ns, $M_2$'s is 500 ns, and the probability that $M_1$ will satisfy a request is 95%, what is the actual apparent access time of memory?

**4.28** Find the unit cost of the Dualsys memory system described in Exercise 4.27 if main memory costs $0.05/KB and the cache costs $10/KB. Assume there is 32 KB of cache but varying sizes of main memory.

**4.29** Virtually all small computers use a single system bus that interconnects the CPU, the memory, and the I/O devices. Suppose each bus transfer uses the bus for 100 ns and the receiving device takes the information immediately and relinquishes the bus.
  a. How fast can the computer store data into memory if there is one memory module with a 500-ns cycle time?
  b. How fast can the computer store data into memory if there are $N$ memory modules, each with a 500-ns cycle time, and successive stores go to different memory modules?

**4.30** Consider a computer with 24-bit addressing, a 64-KB cache, and refill lines of 32 bytes.
  a. How many bits are there in the tags
    1. for a direct-mapped cache?
    2. for an $n$-way set-associative cache?
  b. How are main-memory addresses mapped onto cache addresses
    1. for a direct-mapped cache?
    2. for an $n$-way set-associative cache?
  c. Does the replacement policy affect the mapping?
  d. Does the replacement policy affect the tags?
Justify your numbers.

**4.31** Typical 1990 computers have caches that are about 10 times faster than main memory (30-ns and 300-ns access times, respectively) and have hit rates of about 95%. What is the apparent access time of these memory systems?

**4.32** One way of speeding up read accesses in a memory system with a cache is to start reading the data from main memory in parallel with reading it from cache. If the requested datum is in cache, the value from main memory is then ignored. What are two disadvantages of this system? If the cache hit rate is 95% and is 10 times faster than main memory, how much gain is there by using this simultaneous read? (Assume the simultaneous read reduces the access time to main memory by 20%.)

**4.33** In a paged system, how does the computer determine the page-frame number when given the page number?

**4.34** There are many ways to do table look-up. Describe three techniques that are suitable for hardware implementation of page tables.

**4.35** What are the main differences between segments and pages?

**4.36** A computer system supporting virtual memory uses a main memory that has an access time of 500 ns. Each page is 512 bytes, and the system can transfer a page from disk to memory or from memory to disk in 50 ms. Estimate the maximum permissible page-fault rate so that the effective memory-access time does not increase to more than 800 ns. Make any realistic assumptions you want to about other factors that affect the system's performance, but state clearly any assumptions you do make.

*Exercise 4.27*

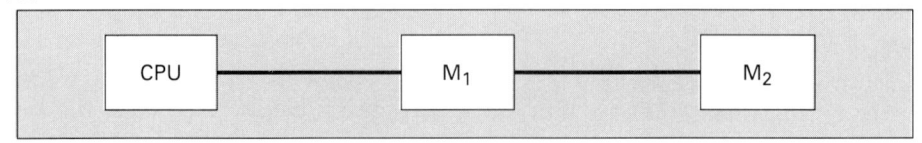

**4.37** In the implementation of a demand-paged virtual-memory system, 0.2% of the memory references will result in a page fault. The access time of main memory is 200 ns, the time to copy a page to or from external memory is 20 ms, and the time to run the page-replacement algorithm is 1 ms. Estimate the effective cycle time of the main memory. State clearly any assumptions you make in doing your calculations.

**4.38** Having the system responsibility for a new computer for the Turtle Computer Company, your task is to provide a mechanism for dumping the state of the machine to disk whenever there is a power failure. Assume the following system characteristics:

  a. Software overhead to detect the interrupt and store the CPU state in memory is 0.1 ms.
  b. The memory size ranges from 1 MB to 16 GB on a given system.
  c. The CPU can write to the system disks at the maximum disk-transfer rate.
  d. Disks rotate in 10 ms, have 100 1-KB sectors per track and 10 tracks per cylinder. Each disk has 1000 cylinders. Cylinder seek time is 15 ms, but the disk can switch from one track to another of the same cylinder in less time than the time between sectors (i.e., the track switch time is essentially zero).

Determine the amount of time that the system must remain working after the CPU receives the power-fail interrupt.

**4.39** Repeat Exercise 4.38 for the Hare Computer Company. Assume that you have an unlimited number of disks that can all be written at the same time, but that each access to a new disk takes an additional 1 ms of disk-controller overhead.

**4.40** The Dualsys Computer Company (DCC) builds computers with virtual memory. See figure for Exercise 4.27. $M_1$ is now the main memory and $M_2$ is now a paging device. Three parameters determine the apparent access time of memory: the times to access $M_1$ and $M_2$, and the probability that $M_1$ will satisfy the memory request. ($M_2$ satisfies all requests that $M_1$ does not satisfy.) If $M_1$'s access time is 500 ns, $M_2$'s access time is 50 ms, and the probability of an access being satisfied by $M_1$ is 99.99%, what is the actual apparent memory-access time?

**4.41** Find the unit cost of the Dualsys memory system described in Exercise 4.40 if the main memory costs $0.05/KB and the paging device costs $10/MB. Assume that the system has varying amounts of main memory and the paging device has a capacity of 300 MB.

**4.42** Assume that a computer has eight pages of virtual memory, four pages of physical memory, a fully associative cache, and the following sequence of unduplicated page references (i.e., with successive references to the same page omitted):
1 4 6 1 5 7 1 0 3 2 7 3 2 6 3 2 3 1 4 6 1 5 7 1 7 3 2 5 4 2 6 4 2 3 6 1 5 3
For each of the following page-replacement policies, determine (1) the sequence of pages loaded, and (2) the number of page faults.

  a. LRU—The CPU replaces the least recently used page.
  b. FIFO—The CPU replaces the oldest (least recently loaded) page in the set.
  c. Random—The CPU replaces a random page.
  d. Optimal—The CPU replaces the page not needed for the longest time in the future. (The optimal policy clearly cannot be implemented, but it can be used on an address trace as a standard for comparison.)

**4.43** In what ways is expanded memory similar to paging? How does it differ from paging?

**4.44** Why do memories with multiple ports and multiple attached devices steal some cycles from the CPU?

**4.45** Identify three reasons for not restricting virtual addresses to 32 bits in a system with 64-bit physical addresses. Identify three reasons for providing only 32-bit virtual addresses in a 64-bit system.

## Reference-needed Exercises

**4.46** Describe the components, cost, and operation of a magnetic-core memory system. You may need to consult an old computer-hardware textbook.

**4.47** Do the principles that underlie 2-D, $2\frac{1}{2}$-D, and 3-D organizations used for core-memory systems pertain as well to solid-state memory systems?

**4.48** Identify 10 different technologies that computer designers have used for ROMs. You may need to consult a digital-systems textbook.

## Exercises for Electrical Engineers

**4.49** Give an example of a volatile nonrandom-access memory.

**4.50** How do MBMs differ from CCD memories?

**4.51** Innovative Business Machines has recently developed an optical disk (having both read and write capability) with a block size of 1024 bytes, a total capacity of 256 MB, an average latency of 10 ms, and a transfer rate of 10 MBS. Assume that this disk is much cheaper than current DRAM. Design a main memory that uses this optical disk instead of conventional RAM. Because of cost, you may only use 32 KB of high-speed (20-ns-cycle-time) SRAM in your design.

# Problems

**4.52** Describe the operation of a CCD or MBM storage system that has 16 storage tracks of 1-K bits each and operates at 1 MHz (magnetic bubbles or charge packets move from one storage site to the next every $10^{-6}$ s). The array has circuitry for detecting signals (i.e., charges or magnetic bubbles) at the end of each track, and it has circuitry for inserting signals at the beginning. It also has a 10-bit resetting counter that the input clock increments as it shifts data along the tracks. All 16 tracks operate in parallel. Where do the addresses come from?

**4.53** At the logical level, both demand-paged virtual memory and cache are the same: Both are programmer-invisible techniques for increasing the size of fast memory or increasing the speed of low-cost memory. Explain why virtual memory is usually managed by software and cache is usually managed by hardware. Why is the disparity in hit rates suggested in Exercises 4.27 and 4.40 not a severe performance problem?

**4.54** Describe how to implement a least recently used (LRU) algorithm for replacing blocks in a two-way set-associative cache using a single bit for age in each tag. Can you find a comparably efficient scheme for a four-way set-associative cache?

**4.55** How should a disk cache differ from a main-memory cache? Consider cache-RAM size, refill-line size, and cache-update policy.

**4.56** One apparent drawback to a write-back cache is that writes that miss in cache must wait for the cache write-back. How can you improve on this apparent slowdown?

**4.57** Suppose that to increase the speed of a computer, the architects wish to use multiple ports between the memory and the memory control unit. How can they design the system to maintain the appearance of a single port? In other words, how can they guarantee that the memory stores and retrieves data in order, as though it has a single port?

**4.58** Give three reasons for separating the program memory from the data memory. How do compilers and loaders for these machines differ from those of conventional von Neumann machines?

## Challenging Problems

**4.59** Name an alternative interleaving strategy to low-order and high-order interleaving. Of what use might it be?

**4.60** In a virtual-address machine, is the cache tag checked against the virtual address or the physical address? Which is better, when, and why? (*Hint:* There is no unique answer.)

**4.61** Generally speaking, caches discard blocks based on a least recently used (LRU) criterion, although designers have also used circular replacement and other tactics. One way to implement an LRU scheme for an *n*-way set-associative cache is to have an $n \times n$ binary matrix (all entries are single bits) to give the age for the blocks of each line of the cache. Whenever the *n*th block of the line is referenced, the *n*th row of the matrix is set to ones and then the *n*th column is set to zeros. The least recently used set at any time is the set whose row is all zeros.
  a. Show that this technique works for $n = 1$ (direct-mapped caches), $n = 2$, and $n = 3$.
  b. Prove that this technique does in fact always find the LRU set of the cache.
  c. Describe simpler schemes that can be used for $n = 1$ and $n = 2$.
  d. Find a corresponding simplification for $n = 3$.

## Discussion/Team Problems

**4.62** When do the memory-size functions illustrated in Fig. 4.3 suggest that minicomputer memories will be larger than supercomputer memories? Why might this actually happen? (*Hint:* Mainframe disks storage systems frequently hold more memory than supercomputer disk storage systems.)

**4.63** My favorite computer has just offered a vector accelerator that quadruples the effective speed of the computer. How can you increase the speed of the memory system by a factor of 4? Which is more important, memory bandwidth or read-access time? In what cases?

**4.64** When might designers choose high-order interleave? Low-order interleave?

**4.65** Based on the observation that microinstructions execute faster than machine instructions, a computer architect at the Delightfully Engineered Computer Company (DECC) came up with the following design of a computer system, which is intended primarily for supporting the execution of high-level language operations.

The processor will use vertical microprogramming and have only two 48-bit microinstruction formats. There will be nothing equivalent to the classical machine-language instructions. (The compiler will generate only microcode.) The control unit will have a ROM with 64K 48-bit words with a cycle time of 50 ns, and it will have a 256-KB RAM with a cycle time of 300 ns to hold the compiler-generated microcode. The computer will also have a 300-MB hard disk, which will support a virtual-address space of 4 MB per user.

Describe in detail the potential performance impact of these architectural choices.

**4.66** Qualitatively compare the performances of virtual-memory computers that use paging, segmentation, and paging with segmentation. Consider the frequency of page faults or segment faults, memory utilization, and so forth.

**4.67** Discuss the necessity of each of the following features in the implementation of a practical demand-paged virtual-memory system:

a. a hardware timer
b. relocatable code
c. a page dirty bit set by the hardware
d. a cache memory

**4.68** Suppose you have a machine design with the following characteristics:

1. disk with 50-ms average access time to hold program and data pages
2. 1 MBS I/O transfer rate
3. 500-ns average access time to the memory system

Describe three techniques for reducing the average memory access time to 200 ns.

**4.69** The bandwidth between the CPU and memory is typically orders of magnitude higher than disk transfer rates. Describe four techniques for reducing the apparent performance imbalance.

**4.70** One of the continuing problems at the Delightfully Efficient Computer Company (DECC) is reducing the latency of disk accesses. Because the reduction of disk-access latency is so difficult, DECC decided instead to increase the I/O bandwidth. What advice would you offer them about these tradeoffs?

**4.71** In a computer with two processors, there are two choices for positioning cache: (1) a local cache to each processor, and (2) a cache shared between the two processors (i.e., a cache logically within the memory system).

a. Which has a higher hit rate: two local caches, or one shared cache equal in size to the two local caches combined?
b. Why might so many commerical multiprocessors have a local cache for each processor? What advantages can you find for local caches versus a single large shared cache?

**4.72** What is the magnitude of the effect on the hit rate of the following changes to a cache's parameters? Guess small, medium, or large; rationalize your guesses; and elaborate the question in any way you see fit.

a. separating the instruction and data streams and caches.
b. doubling the cache size.
c. doubling the cache-refill line size.
d. changing from a direct-mapped to an *n*-way set-associative cache.
e. changing the cache replacement policy.
f. changing the cache write-through, write-back, or write-around policy.

**4.73** When a computer with a cache has instructions, like string instructions, that access large blocks of memory, there are several ways the CPU can handle the memory accesses:

a. It can divide (segment) the memory access into several requests with each request aligned on a cache refill-line boundary.
b. It can send the request to the cache and require that the cache have the segmenting capability.
c. It can send the request to main memory, bypassing the cache altogether.

Identify two advantages of each technique. Is one technique superior for most computer architectures? If so, which one, and why?

**4.74** Some of the most-quoted standard benchmarks are the Livermore loops, which comprise a set of small loops that mostly operate on data sets with at most 1001 elements, and the LINPACK benchmark, which operates on a matrix of $100 \times 100$ to $1000 \times 1000$ elements. With reference to any machines for which you can find the cache size, how representative are these "toy" benchmarks for predicting the performance of large programs that operate on large data sets? (If you are too lazy to check the sizes of caches, you may be interested to know that $10^4$-word caches are common today and that $10^6$-word caches would be very large. No cache that large had been built when this text was published.

**4.75** Some studies have shown that the improvement in hit rate of a four-way set-associative cache over a direct-mapped cache peaks at sizes of about 32 KB and drops off sharply for either larger or smaller caches. Why is this plausible?

**4.76** One apparent drawback to a write-back cache is that writes that miss in cache must still wait for the posted write to occur. How can you ameliorate this apparent slowdown?

**4.77** Describe two advantages and two disadvantages of write-through cache versus write-back cache. Consider both disk caches and main-memory caches.

**4.78** Show that memory delay for an $N$-word memory is greater than $2 \log_2 N$ gate delays and therefore the ratio of CPU speed to memory speed should increase "indefinitely."

**4.79** The Macho Computer Company (MCC) has just proposed a new architecture in which it plans to use its new ultrafast memory. The CPU can access any word in memory as quickly as it can access its registers. Write a critique on whether MCC should abandon registers entirely.

# Chapter Index

access key 192
addressed memory 185
address tag 197
any-match bit 187
archival memory 189
argument register 187
associative cache 199
associative memory 187
bank-select register 216
bit-slice 187
block (in paging) 206
block (on a disk) 206
burning a PROM 184
byte offset 211
cache 191
cache entry 197
cache hit 197
cache memory 191
cache miss 197
charge-coupled device (CCD) 186
code segment 210

conflict resolution 187
content-addressable memory (CAM) 187
core 176
core plane 176
cycle time 176
data segment 210
delayed page fault 209
demanded page 208
demanded segment 211
demand-paged virtual memory 205
demand-segmented virtual memory 205
destructive read memory 185
direct-mapped cache 199
dirty bit 206
dirty cell 198
dump 196
dynamic program relocation 192
dynamic random-access memory (DRAM) 185

electrically alterable ROM (EAROM) 185
erasable PROM (EPROM) 184
expanded memory 217
expanded-memory manager 218
field 193
field length (*FL*) 193
field-length register (FL) 193
first in, first out (FIFO) 208
fully associative cache 199
high-order interleave 179
initial program relocation 192
key-controlled memory protection 192
least recently used (LRU) 208
low-order interleave 179
magnetic bubble memory (MBM) 186
magnetic core 176
mask register 187
match bit 187
match register 187

memory bank  176
memory banking  215
memory buffer register  187
memory hierarchy  191
memory map  205
memory protection  192
memory subsystem  199
multilevel storage system  191
nondestructive read memory  185
nonremovable memory  185
nonvolatile memory  185
one-level storage system  191
orthogonal memory  187
overlays  190
page fault  208
page frame  206
page-frame number  207
page number  206
page map  206
page-replacement policy  208
page table  206
page-table base register  207
page-table entry  206
page thrashing  208
paging  205
posted write  198
primary memory  191

principle of locality of reference  197
programmable ROM (PROM)  183
program relocation  190
protection bit  207
pseudo-random-access memory  186
random-access memory (RAM)  176
read cycle  185
read-only memory (ROM)  183
read-access time  185
refill line  199
relocation address ($RA$)  190
relocation-address register ($RA$)  193
relocation offset ($RO$)  190
removable memory  185
restore cycle  185
roll back  209
row  201
secondary memory  191
sector  201
sector-mapped cache  201
segment  210
segment fault  211
segment number  211

segmentation  210
segment map  211
segment table  212
segment-table base register  212
segment-table length register  212
set-associative cache  200
splinter  211
static random-access memory (SRAM)  184
system segment table  212
tag subsystem  199
translation lookaside buffer (TLB)  207
user segment table  212
validity bit  201
virtual memory  191
virtual memory system  311
virtual page number  206
volatile memory  185
wait state  183
window  216
word offset  206
WORM memory  189
write-around cache  198
write-back cache  198
write-through cache  198

# 5
# A Computer-family Architecture: The IBM PC

| | |
|---|---|
| 5.1 | **IBM PC Family and Its Descendants** *232* |
| | 5.1.1 IBM PC and PC AT *233* |
| | 5.1.2 IBM PS/2 *235* |
| | 5.1.3 PC Clones *236* |
| 5.2 | **Basic Microcomputer Configuration** *237* |
| 5.3 | **Components of the IBM PC** *238* |
| | 5.3.1 8088 CPU *239* |
| | 5.3.2 Control Interface *245* |
| | 5.3.3 PC Bus and Interrupt System *248* |
| | 5.3.4 I/O System *259* |
| | 5.3.5 Programmable Interval Timer *268* |
| | 5.3.6 Floating-point Coprocessor *269* |
| 5.4 | **Software System** *272* |
| | 5.4.1 I/O Port-address Assignments *273* |
| | 5.4.2 ROM BIOS *273* |
| | 5.4.3 Memory-address Assignments *275* |
| 5.5 | **Architectural Merit of the PC Architecture** *279* |

*In this chapter we show how architects put together the components of a computer. The IBM PC is our example, but the principles apply equally to most other computers. Section 5.1 gives an overview of the IBM PC family (including the PC AT), its descendant family the PS/2, and PC clones. Then we examine in detail the hardware-system architecture (HSA) of the PC (Sections 5.2 and 5.3). We also present several of the PC's support chips and the interface between the hardware and software systems. We describe how the architects assigned addresses to various system components, such as random-access memory (RAM), ROM, the exception-vector table, and memory-mapped I/O*

## Key Terms

**Coprocessor**  A special-purpose processor designed to operate closely with a central processing unit (CPU) to provide it with additional functionality, such as floating-point arithmetic.

**Enhanced Expanded Memory Standard (EEMS)**  A type of expanded memory out of which the IBM PC (International Business Machines Corporation's Personal Computer) can directly execute programs; also called LIM 4.0 expanded memory.

**PC I/O (input-output) Channel Bus**  The IBM PC's expanded local bus. It has eight data lines, 20 address lines, and a large number of power and control lines.

**PC AT I/O Channel Bus**  An extension of the IBM PC I/O Channel Bus used by the PC AT (Advanced Technology) computer. The AT bus provides 16 rather than eight data lines, 24 rather than 20 address lines, and support for additional interrupt and direct-memory-access (DMA) controllers.

**Programmable parallel interface (PPI)**  A programmable device that provides an interface between the PC I/O Channel Bus and a parallel I/O device, such as disk drive or printer.

**ROM BIOS**  Basic I/O System for the PC that resides in read-only memory (ROM) and provides direct (hardware) control of the I/O devices and timer. At power up, it checks the hardware, programs the dynamic RAM (DRAM) refresh circuits, programs the I/O devices, and loads the operating system.

**Universal asynchronous receiver-transmitter (UART)**  A device that provides an interface between the PC I/O Channel Bus and an attached I/O device that sends and receives information in bit-serial fashion, such as a modem.

**Wait state**  A dummy bus cycle that a CPU executes when an attached device (including memory) cannot deliver the requested datum within the required amount of time.

*ports (Section 5.4). Also in our discussion of the PC's software system is a look at the responsibility of the ROM BIOS. The chapter ends with an assessment of the PC's architectural merit (Section 5.5).*

This is the only chapter where we present in detail the HSA of a computer, and we describe many specific architectural details that we do not mention again for any other machine. We chose to use the IBM PC as our example because it revolutionized the computer industry in a number of ways. Prior to the PC, a large computer family consisted of perhaps 10 models and tens of thousands of individual computers. Today there are well over 60 million PCs in common uses. The PC introduced the public to serious computing, as opposed to the hobbyist outlook of games and small applications programs that existed before. This change in approach profoundly altered both the software and hardware industries. Before the advent of the PC a software product was considered successful if its authors sold tens of thousands of copies. Today software houses like Microsoft Corporation, Lotus Development Corporation, Ashton-Tate Corporation, and Borland International, are multimillion dollar corporations whose best-selling products sell from hundreds of thousands to millions of copies. Finally, the PC is the parent of many of today's advanced personal computers, including the PS/2 (Personal System/2) family. We expect that virtually all readers will have had some contact with a personal computer. Clearly, its historical significance is uncontested.

## 5.1 ▪ IBM PC Family and Its Descendants

The computer industry has evolved rapidly since its inception in the late 1940s. In the early years the least expensive computers cost hundreds of thousands of dollars, and costs continued to increase as computers increased in size and complexity. However, with the advent of large-scale integration in the 1970s, prices of computers dropped markedly, and by the late 1970s, computers that were inexpensive enough for individual use reached the marketplace. These became known as **personal computers;** their prices were typically under $5000.

*personal computers*

*mainframes*

Before the introduction of personal computers, users often classified computers as being mainframes, minicomputers, or supercomputers. **Mainframes** are the workhorses of business and industry. They are designed to meet the needs of large corporations, support thousands of terminals, provide gigabytes of storage, and supply the resources to manage large databases; however, they also cost hundreds of thousands to millions of dollars. **Minicomputers**, generally smaller than mainframes, are designed to meet the needs of small companies, laboratories, and departments. These machines can support from a few users to roughly 100 users and generally cost from $50,000 to $1 million. **Supercomputers** are the fastest and largest machines available at the time and are therefore also the most expensive. Clearly individuals could not afford minicomputers, mainframes, or supercomputers.

*minicomputers*

*supercomputers*

Personal computers first appeared after the advent of the **microprocessor**, a single-chip CPU that includes the register set, ALU, and control unit of a computer. Intel Corporation introduced the first microprocessor, a 4-bit calculator chip called the 4004, in 1971, followed in 1975 by the 8080, an 8-bit general-purpose CPU chip. Other companies, such as Rockwell and Motorola, introduced competing microprocessors at about the same time. Computer manufacturers can easily build an inexpensive personal computer using a microprocessor as a CPU, combined with other off-the-shelf components. The other components include a power supply, a main-memory system, a system bus, a keyboard, a video-display terminal, and an I/O system.

The first personal computers to reach the marketplace included MITS's Altair 8800, Radio Shack's TRS-80, and Commodore's PET PC (Personal Electronic Transacter), all around 1977. These were targeted at hobbyists. Although the personal computer revolution had begun, it was not until 4 years later, August 1981, that IBM introduced the IBM PC. IBM, already a giant of the computer industry, brought to bear both manufacturing and marketing resources unavailable to its personal-computer competition. It also introduced the MS DOS operating system (Microsoft Corporation's Disk Operating System), which quickly became the industry standard.

The original intended use of the PC was small business and hobby applications. At the time IBM introduced the PC, the pattern of use of personal computers was very different from what we see today. Spreadsheets and word processors, two major applications of personal computers today, were rudimentary and not widely used. Graphics applications, such as computer-aided design and desktop publishing, were only available on mainframes and minicomputers. The major business uses that manufacturers foresaw at that time were running small versions of programs that were run on mainframes and minicomputers, such as small-firm accounting and tax programs. This intended market guided several important decisions IBM made concerning the PC's configuration. We shall examine these in more detail in the sections that follow.

## 5.1.1 ■ IBM PC and PC AT

Unlike its best-known predecessor, the Apple II by Apple Computer, which uses an 8-bit CPU, the IBM PC uses a 16-bit CPU. In 1981, Intel's **8086 microprocessor** was one of the most widely-used 16-bit microprocessors in the world, and hence many programmers were familiar with it. However, rather than choosing the 8086 microprocessor, which uses a 16-bit data bus, IBM chose for the PC Intel's **8088 microprocessor,** a less expensive version of the 8086 that uses an 8-bit data bus instead of a 16-bit bus. (See the *Case Studies* for details of the Intel microprocessor family.) The advantages of using the 8088 microprocessor were (1) that it had the same instruction-set architecture (ISA) as the 8086 and so could run all of the 8086-based software, and (2) because it used an 8-bit bus, designers could keep the initial cost of the PC low by using 8-bit rather than 16-bit peripheral devices. As cost was a major obstacle to the success of the PC project, the price of the PC had to be low enough to attract a large new audience, and yet the PC's perfomance had to rival its minicomputer competitors.

The IBM PC is a single-bus architecture. If the brain of the PC is the 8088 microprocessor, its nervous system is its expanded local bus, which IBM calls the **PC I/O Channel Bus** (or simply **PC Bus**). The PC Bus provides the PC with eight data lines, 20 address lines, and numerous control and power lines for flexibility. The PC's physical-address space is 1 MB.

One of IBM's key decisions that led to the success of the PC was to market it as an open architecture, one whose components, bus structure, and operating system are openly documented by the manufacturer. Component manufacturers can therefore design new or replacement components, which users can easily add to their original system. A number of manufacturers have marketed computers with open architectures, including Apple (but not the Macintosh), and there is now an abundance of bus-compatible devices for these computers. Available devices include memory boards, graphics adapters, disk drives, communications interfaces, modems, and even replacement CPUs.

Finally, the success of a system depends on the reliability and availability of its component parts, and IBM chose to base the PC on a well-established and reliable family of components. The components include not only the microprocessor, but also a bus controller, interrupt controller, timer, DMA controller, and parallel and serial I/O interfaces. Later sections in this chapter will describe these components and show how IBM assembled them into a high-performance microcomputer.

In 1983 Intel advanced the 8086/8088 family when it introduced the **80286 microprocessor,** and almost immediately IBM incorporated it into the PC family to capitalize on its added speed and memory-protection capabilities: In 1984 IBM introduced the **PC AT,** the first major performance enhancement to the IBM PC. The 80286 has essentially the same ISA as the 8086 and 8088, but with additional hardware support for segmentation and memory protection. It can operate in **Real Address mode,** which is an 8088 compatibility mode, and it can run all of the original 8088-based software (in addition to software that supports segmentation). In addition, the 80286 uses a 16-bit I/O path rather than an 8-bit path, and it has 24-address lines and hence a 16-MB physical-address space.

With the introduction of the AT, IBM needed to upgrade the PC Bus. IBM called the new bus the **PC AT I/O Channel Bus** (or simply **PC AT Bus**). The bus structure is a major difference between the PC and PC AT, and we shall discuss the differences later in the chapter.

In addition to establishing bus standards for the personal computer industry, IBM's PC family also set standards for video displays. The IBM PC came with a standard **Monochrome Display Adapter (MDA),** which has one foreground color and one background color, such as green on black. The IBM PC also had an optional color display adapter, called **Color Graphics Adapter (CGA).** However, CGA had such a low resolution (320 × 200 pixels with four colors) that most businesses relied on the higher resolution of MDA (720 × 350 pixels). With the IBM PC AT came the **Enhanced Graphics Adapter (EGA),** with a resolution of 640 × 350 pixels and 16 colors.

*Monochrome Display Adapter (MDA)*

*Color Graphics Adapter (CGA)*

*Enhanced Graphics Adapter (EGA)*

### 5.1.2 ■ IBM PS/2

In 1987 IBM introduced a new family of personal computers, the PS/2 family, to replace the PC family. The PS/2 family differs from the PC family in a number of ways; two of the most important are that is uses a redesigned bus called the **Micro Channel Architecture (MCA),** and it uses a higher-resolution video display, called **Video Graphics Array (VGA).** (Many PCs now use VGA). VGA has a resolution of 640 × 480 pixels with 16 colors.[1] Nonethelsss, the PS/2 family uses the same family of Intel CPU chips and runs virtually all of the same software. (The converse is not true; software developed for the PS/2 will not necessarily run on a PC.)

*Mirco Channel Architecture (MCA)*
*Video Graphics Array (VGA)*

The PS/2 family includes a number of models with different component configurations that reflect the rapid growth of microcomputer technology in the 1980s and 1990s. Models 25 and 30 used the 8086 CPU chip and the PC AT Bus (not yet the MCA bus). Models 50 and 60 use 80286 CPUs and a 16-bit MCA bus, and Model 80 uses an **80386 microprocessor** and is the only original PS/2 family member to use a full 32-bit MCA bus. Intel introduced the 80386 microprocessor in 1987. It is a 32-bit CPU and supports a 32-bit data bus, a 32-bit address bus, and a 48-bit virtual-address space. Like the 80286, it also has a Real Address mode of operation, which makes it compatible with programs designed to run on 8086 and 8088 CPUs; thus it can run all the software intended for the PC family.

*80386 microprocessor*

In 1988 Intel announced the **80386SX microprocessor,** which is essentially an 80386 chip with a 16-bit data bus (instead of a 32-bit data bus). The 80386SX chip enabled developers to produce 32-bit computers at a substantially reduced cost because they could use 16-bit memory chips and 16-bit I/O devices, like hard disks. In the same year IBM introduced a less expensive PS/2 family member, the Model 70, which uses the 80386SX CPU and a 16-bit MCA bus. In 1989 Intel introduced the **80486 microprocessor,** which is similar to the 80386 but includes an internal cache and circuitry for calculating floating-point arithmetic. (Some earlier personal computers included external cache memories and floating-point processors, but these were not part of the CPU

*80386SX microprocessor*

*80486 microprocessor*

---

1. Some manufacturers also produce a super-VGA mode (800 × 600 with 256 colors) or an enhanced VGA mode (1024 × 768 with 256 colors).

chip.) In 1991 IBM introduced Models 90 and 95, which use the 80486 microprocessor and a new video standard, called the **Extended Graphics Array (XGA).** XGA supports two resolutions: 1024 × 768 with 256 colors, or 640 × 480 with 65,536 colors and is essentially the same as enhanced VGA.

### 5.1.3 ■ PC Clones

Soon after IBM began producing the IBM PC, and in part because it was an open architecture, other manufacturers began to make PC clones. A **PC clone** is simply a computer that is software- and hardware-compatible with the IBM PC.

To be compatible with the PC or PC AT, a clone must support the entire 8086 (or 80386) instruction set[2] and have essentially the same interrupt hardware. It must also have an I/O structure that uses system calls compatible with the PC's **basic input-output system (BIOS).** However, if a clone uses a different I/O system than that of the PC, it might not be able to run software that performs its own hardware-level I/O (rather than calling the BIOS routines). Many high-performance programs avoid BIOS calls, and as a result some of these programs do not run on particular PC clones. Many PC clones are therefore not 100% PC-compatible, even though they may run the vast majority of software currently available for the PC.

The PC family, which we take to include clones as well as IBM machines, continues to follow the state of the art in technology. Presently, dozens of companies produce PC clones based on each of Intel's CPU chips: 8088, 8086, 80286, 80386, 80386SX, and 80486.

When IBM announced the PS/2 family, it made a decision regarding PS/2 configuration that affected the clones. IBM decided not to extend the AT Bus to 32 bits, but rather to redefine the architecture and introduce the MCA-based PS/2. Yet by this time other manufacturers had already produced PC clones boasting the 80386 CPU. Even with Intel's subsequent releases of the 80386SX and 80486 CPUs, many manufacturers continue to produce PC clones with AT-compatible buses. Because the 32-bit PC clones use a 32-bit processor, manufacturers generally include proprietary 32-bit memory buses.

When IBM discontinued manufacturing PC AT Bus machines, the industry was left without a 32-bit bus standard. In fact, IBM never published detailed specifications of the PC AT Bus. To overcome the lack of a 32-bit PC standard, in 1988 a consortium of companies[3] standardized a 32-bit extended AT bus, calling it the **Extended Industry Standard Architecture (EISA) bus.** The EISA specification includes all the timing characteristics of the new bus.

---

2. For example, Nippon Express Computer (NEC) produces a CPU chip, called the V80, that is plug-compatible with the 8088: A user can simply remove the 8088 microprocessor from its socket and replace it with a V80 chip.
3. Wyse Technologies, AST Research, Tandy Corporation, Compaq Computer Corporation, Hewlett-Packard Company, Zenith Data Systems, Olivetti, NEC, and Epson America.

In contrast, the PC AT Bus is now known as the **industry standard architecture (ISA) bus.** The EISA bus appears to be an accepted standard for future 32-bit PC family members, and both the MCA architecture and the EISA architecture appear to be standards for the PC industry of the 1990s. As of 1991 the majority have ISA buses, some have MCA buses, and some have EISA buses.

  It is worthwhile to mention that dynamic RAM (DRAM) speeds have not been able to keep pace with increasing CPU speeds. As a result, several PC manufacturers incorporate relatively large cache memories or use interleaved storage systems to speed up the slower main-memory accesses. The caches use high-speed static RAMs (SRAMs) and have a variety of organizations as discussed in Section 4.2.2. A typical cache has 8-K 32-bit words and a posted write-through policy that maintains cache coherence by monitoring the bus and invalidating any cache entry whose image in memory is modified by a store operation. Some PCs use SRAMs instead of DRAMs, but SRAMs are more expensive, so the resulting computers cost more.

*industry standard architecture (ISA) bus*

## 5.2 ■ Basic Microcomputer Configuration

A **microcomputer,** like the PC, is a computer based on a microprocessor. Microcomputers use buses in much the same way that other computers do. The computer generally consists of a chassis that contains a power supply and a **system board,** also called a **mother board.** The system board frequently holds the CPU and its primary support chips, such as a clock, data and address buffers, a bus controller, an interrupt controller and some main memory. The system board also has **slots,** connectors with many individual connections in them. The slots hold **cards** (or **daughter boards**) which themselves hold circuitry, such as additional memory, hard disks, controllers for floppy and hard disks, monitor controllers, mouse controllers, and numerous other options. Designers standardize the slots and wire them in parallel on the mother board. With this configuration a user can purchase a new card and simply plug it into any vacant slot. The new device immediately becomes an integral part of the computer.

  With the integrated circuit technology of the late 1970s and early 1980s, chip manufacturers could not build one single chip that supported all the desired functionality of a computer system (although they now come quite close). They therefore produce **chip sets,** which are sets of compatible support chips that implement a wide variety of specific functions, such as interrupt controllers, bus controllers, and timers. Computer manufacturers can freely and easily use these chip sets when designing a computer. In general, the chips within a set obey the same timing constraints and have compatible logic. Designers simply select the required components and connect them together

*microcomputer*

*system board
mother board*

*slots*

*cards
daughter boards*

*chip sets*

using a suitable bus. It is even possible for a designer to lay out an entire computer without ever designing a single logic circuit. Architects and designers of mainframe computers, in contrast, usually specify each of the individual circuit components, which manufacturers then produce to specifications. Nonetheless, the results are very similar, as you will soon see.

**coprocessors**

Chip manufacturers often manufacture special chips, called **coprocessors**, which operate in conjunction with a CPU to extend its functionality. Some coprocessor chips perform high-speed arithmetic, others provide mapping hardware for virtual memory, and others provide high-speed graphics. Coprocessor chips differ from support chips mostly in the way they communicate with the CPU, and we shall describe Intel's 8087 floating-point coprocessor and its communications protocol in Section 5.3. Intel also manufactures coprocessor chips for its other CPU chips, and PCs based on the newer and faster CPU chips often use the corresponding coprocessor:

| CPU | Corresponding Floating-point Coprocessor |
| --- | --- |
| 8088 and 8086 | 8087 |
| 80286 | 80287 |
| 80386 and 80386SX | 80387 |
| 80486 | None—the 80486 has internal floating-point circuitry. |

## 5.3 ■ Components of the IBM PC

The IBM PC family architecture is defined not only by its microprocessor, but also by the details of its system bus, display adapter, keyboard, printer, video display, and BIOS. In this section we first take a detailed look at the 8088 microprocessor (Section 5.3.1) followed by a description of the microprocessor's control interface (Section 5.3.2). Then we describe the PC Bus, the PC AT Bus, and the interrupt system (Section 5.3.3). Sections 5.3.4 and 5.3.5 consider the I/O system and discuss several programmable I/O support chips that efficiently perform many I/O tasks, thus relieving the CPU of that responsibility. Finally we shall describe the floating-point arithmetic coprocessor (Section 5.3.6).

In the following sections we shall discuss the PC's circuit components in considerable depth. Our reason is to demonstrate the kinds of detailed considerations that architects and designers must weigh while designing a computer. Nothing can be left to chance, and the choice of components is a major design factor in any implementation. This is the only computer in which we describe circuit components in detail, but we feel it is instructive to do so, particularly because of their influence on the utility of the PC architecture. Three primary goals of this section are to illustrate the use of an expanded local bus, DMA-controlled I/O, and vectored interrupts.

Figure 5.1 shows the major components of the IBM PC. The bus-control system includes a bus controller as well as data buffers and address latches (**Latches** are simple registers that hold valves and place them on the buses.) The interrupt-control system (INTR control) consists primarily of an interrupt controller. The RAM- and ROM-control systems include RAM and ROM chips, address decoders, and buffers. The DMA-control system consists mainly of a DMA controller. The timer is a programmable interval timer, and the I/O-control system includes a programmable parallel interface (PPI). The figure shows the CPU, but it does not show an 8087 floating-point coprocessor.

latches

### 5.3.1 ■ 8088 CPU

Following is a brief overview of the ISA of the Intel 8088 microprocessor. Because the 8088 and 8086 have the same ISA, what we say here pertains equally to the 8086. Also, with the exception of instructions for managing a segmentation and memory protection, the 80286 also has the same ISA and the following description holds. Case Study 12 presents additional details.

see Case Study 12

**Datatypes**

The 8088 supports the following datatypes:

- 8-bit and 16-bit unsigned binary integers;
- 8-bit and 16-bit two's-complement integers;

**FIGURE 5.1**  *Major components of the IBM PC. The figure does not show most of the control lines or bus connections. NMI, nonmaskable-interrupt; INTR, interrupt request. The numbers in parentheses indicate the Intel part numbers for each component.*

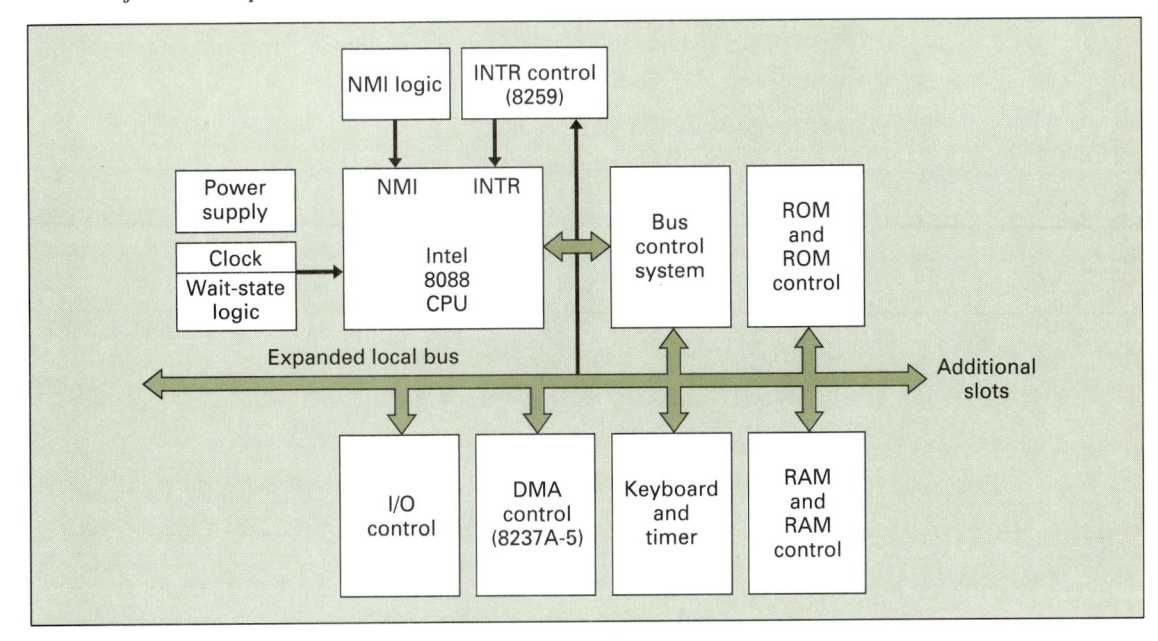

- Packed decimals (two BCD digits per byte);
- Unpacked decimals (one BCD digit per byte; the high-order 4-bits are 0s.

**Register Set**

The 8088 is a 16-bit microprocessor. Its register set, summarized in Fig. 5.2, consists of thirteen 16-bit special-purpose registers and a set of nine flags.

Each data register has a special purpose: AX is the accumulator, BX is a base register, CX holds a count (used during certain data transfer instructions), and DX holds temporary data. The CPU can address each data register or each 8-bit half of a data register.

The 8088 has four segment registers and uses segment-register addressing (Section 2.5.3) both to increase the size of an effective address from 16 to 20 bits and to provide the software a means of independently relocating each of four different segments, which we shall describe when we discuss effective-address formation.

The four index registers provide offsets into the various segments. For example, during string operations, the source-index register (SI) and the destination-index register (DI) give the offsets of the current character in the source and destination strings, and the direction flag (DF) specifies whether the operation will increment or decrement SI and DI.

Finally, the CPU can individually set or clear many of the flags. It can also treat the set of flags as a 16-bit quantity (with 7 unused bits).

**Instruction Set**

The 8088 has a full set of instructions. Many instructions manipulate data and have both 8-bit and 16-bit variants. The AX register is the accumulator for most arithmetic and logical instructions. The following list summarizes the instruction types:

- arithmetic (integer, decimal);
- SHIFT and ROTATE (with or without carry flag);
- logical (AND, OR, XOR, NOT);
- string (MOVE, COMPARE, SCAN);
- control transfer (JUMP, LOOP, REPEAT, CALL, RETURN);
- interrupt (INITIATE INTERRUPT, RETURN FROM INTERRUPT, SET and CLEAR IF flag);
- stack (PUSH, POP, PUSH FLAGS, POP FLAGS);
- load, store, and exchange (byte, word);
- processor control (ESCAPE, HALT, LOCK, TEST, WAIT, NO OP);
- input (IN) and output (OUT) (byte or word);
- miscellaneous (ADJUST, CONVERT, TRANSLATE).

*A Computer-family Architecture: The IBM PC* 241

**FIGURE 5.2** *User-visible registers of the Intel 8088 microprocessor. (Flags: OF, overflow flag; DF, direction flag; IF, interrupt flag; TF, trap flag; SF, sign flag; ZF, zero flag; AF, auxiliary carry flag; PF, parity flag; and CF, carry flag. Dashes indicated unused bits.*

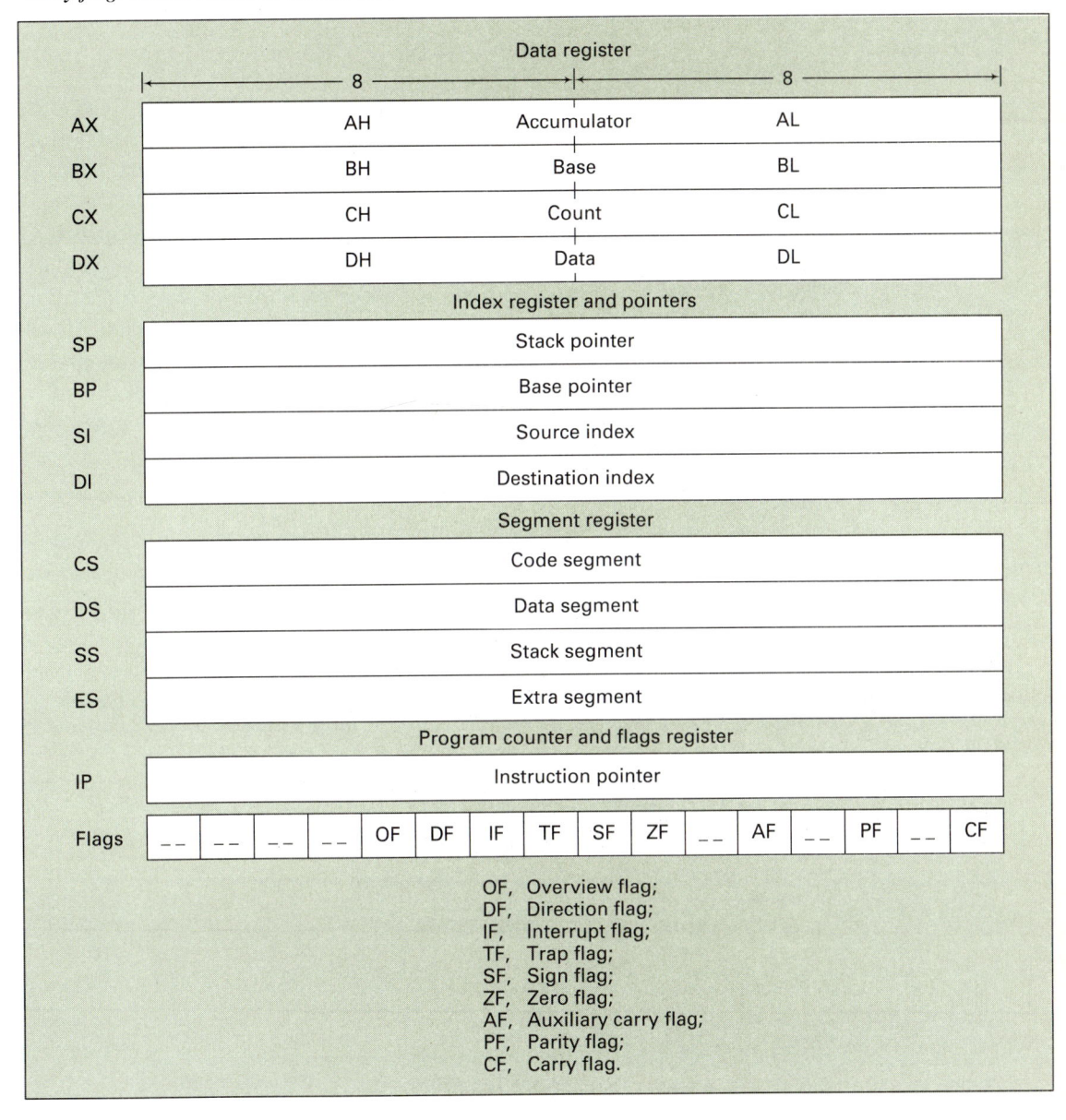

```
                         Data register
             |←———— 8 ————→|←———— 8 ————→|
    AX       |     AH      | Accumulator |     AL      |
    BX       |     BH      |    Base     |     BL      |
    CX       |     CH      |    Count    |     CL      |
    DX       |     DH      |    Data     |     DL      |

                   Index register and pointers
    SP       |              Stack pointer               |
    BP       |              Base pointer                |
    SI       |              Source index                |
    DI       |            Destination index             |

                         Segment register
    CS       |              Code segment                |
    DS       |              Data segment                |
    SS       |              Stack segment               |
    ES       |              Extra segment               |

              Program counter and flags register
    IP       |            Instruction pointer           |
    Flags    |__|__|__|__|OF|DF|IF|TF|SF|ZF|__|AF|__|PF|__|CF|
```

OF, Overview flag;
DF, Direction flag;
IF, Interrupt flag;
TF, Trap flag;
SF, Sign flag;
ZF, Zero flag;
AF, Auxiliary carry flag;
PF, Parity flag;
CF, Carry flag.

*see Case Study 12*

Since most of the instructions are standard (and many have been discussed in earlier chapters), we shall not elaborate on them here. Readers interested in additional details of the 80x86 family might like to read the appropriate sections in the Case Studies.

### Instruction Format

*op-code byte*

Every instruction has a mandatory **op-code byte.** Implied-operand instructions consist of the op-code byte alone. Some instructions have either 8 or 16 bits of immediate data, that follow the op-code byte. Instructions that access memory have several bytes for each address specification. Each address specification consists of an **address-mode byte** followed by one or two **displacement bytes.** When present, the address specification indicates the addressing mode, address length, displacement, and base and index registers, as described in the following section. The CPU usually selects a segment register by default. However, a programmer can precede an instruction with a **segment-override-prefix byte,** which specifies which segment register to use. The following section also describes how the CPU selects segment registers. Figure 5.3 illustrates the 8088 instruction components.

*address-mode byte displacement bytes*

*segment-override-prefix byte*

### Addressing

*CPU address*

The CPU computes the 20-bit effective address in two parts. First it computes a 16-bit **CPU address** using one of the standard addressing modes indicated in the following description. Second, it computes the effective address using

---

**FIGURE 5.3** *Components of an 8088 instruction. The value of rr in the segment-override byte indicates the following segment registers: ES (00), CS (01), SS (10), and DS (11); Disp, displacement (offset); Mod, reg, r/m; see text for explanation.*

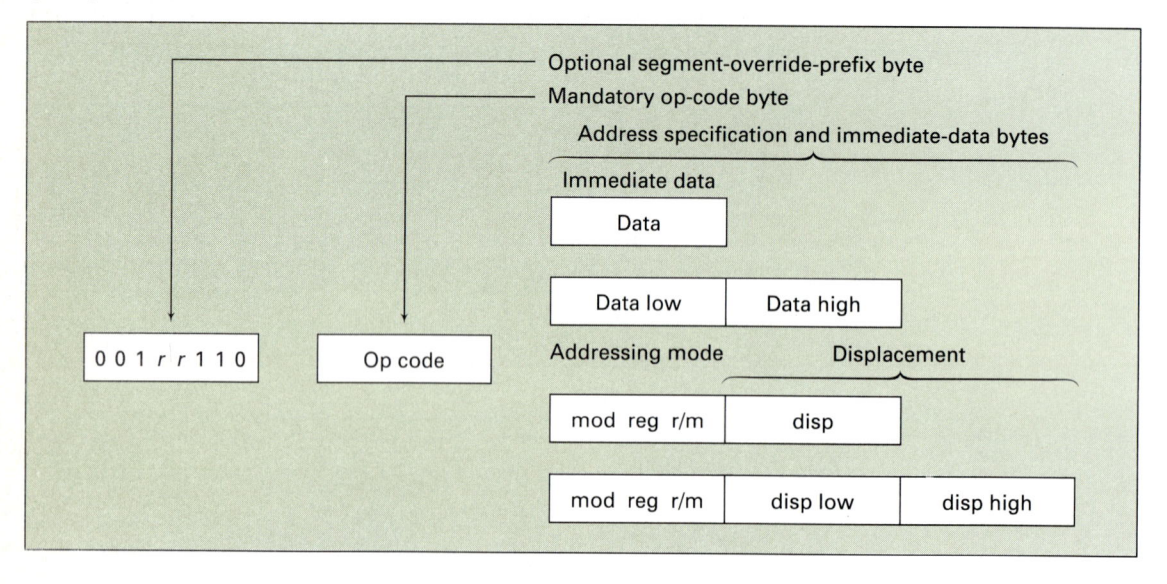

**Table 5.1** Standard addressing modes of the Intel 8088 instructions.

| Mode | Computation[a] | r/m | mod |
|---|---|---|---|
| Implied | *SI* | 100 | 00 |
|  | *DI* | 101 | 00 |
| Direct | Direct address | 110 | 00 |
| Direct, indexed | *SI* + *disp* | 100 | 01, 10 |
|  | *DI* + *disp* | 101 | 01, 10 |
| Base relative | *BX* | 111 | 00 |
| Base relative direct | *BX* + *disp* | 111 | 01, 10 |
| Base relative indexed | *BX* + *SI* | 000 | 00 |
|  | *BX* + *DI* | 001 | 00 |
| Base relative indexed stack | *BP* + *SI* | 010 | 00 |
|  | *BP* + *DI* | 011 | 00 |
| Base relative direct stack | *BP* + *disp* | 110 | 01, 10 |
| Base relative direct indexed | *BX* + *SI* + *disp* | 000 | 01, 10 |
|  | *BX* + *DI* + *disp* | 001 | 01, 10 |
| Base relative direct indexed stack | *BP* + *SI* + *disp* | 010 | 01, 10 |
|  | *BP* + *DI* + *disp* | 011 | 01, 10 |

[a]displacement (offset); the two-letter abbreviations refer to the values in the corresponding registers.

segment-register addressing as described in Section 2.5.3. Because the 8088 does not support virtual memory, the physcial address is the same as the effective address. During instruction fetch, the CPU gets the 16-bit CPU address of the instruction from the program counter (IP). During stack accesses it gets the CPU address from the stack pointer (SP). During instruction execution, the CPU uses the addressing-mode byte and the displacement field of the instruction to determine the operand's CPU address. The addressing-mode byte has three fields (**mod**, **reg**, and **r/m**) which, taken together, specify the registers and addressing mode:

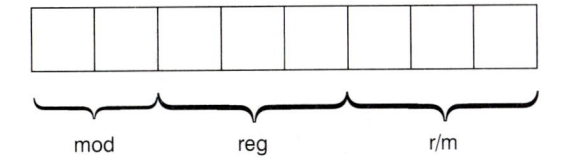

mod
reg
r/m

```
         mod    reg    r/m
```

When mod ≠ $11_2$, the CPU uses one of the standard addressing modes listed in Table 5.1. For the standard addressing modes, the CPU gets the displacement, *disp*, from the instruction itself. (Offsets are usually called displacements in the PC literature.) When mod = $11_2$ the CPU uses register addressing, in

**Table 5.2** Register selection for mod = $11_2$ addressing.

| reg | $w = 0^a$ | $w = 1$ |
|---|---|---|
| 000 | AL | AX |
| 001 | CL | CX |
| 010 | DL | DX |
| 011 | BL | BX |
| 100 | AH | SP |
| 101 | CH | BP |
| 110 | DH | SI |
| 111 | BH | DI |

$^a$The *w* bit comes from the op code.

which case the reg field of the addressing-mode byte and 1 bit of the op code (w) select the register. Table 5.2 summarizes how the 8088 selects a register for register addressing.

*Effective-Address Formation*

The 8088 uses segment-register addressing to convert the CPU address into a 20-bit effective address. The segment registers always point to four 64-KB segments of main memory called the **data segment, code segment, stack segment,** and **extra segment.** (Throughout our discussion the segment registers pointing to these four segments will be abbreviated DS, CS, SS, and ES, respectively; see Fig. 5.2.) In general, the data segment and the extra segment hold data, the code segment holds part of the executing program, and the stack segment holds the system stack.

When forming an effective address, the CPU selects a default segment register based on the type of memory access:

- During an instruction fetch the CPU gets the effective address from IP and *always* selects CS.
- During a stack operation the CPU gets the effective address from SP and *always* selects SS.
- For other operations the CPU uses the following defaults, which the programmer may override:
  - When it forms the effective address using the base pointer (BP), it selects SS.
  - When it forms the effective address using the destination index (DI), which occurs during string operations, it selects ES.
  - For all other operations it selects DS.

**I/O**

The 8088 has two I/O instructions, IN and OUT, which transfer data between the accumulator (AL for byte transfers or AX for word transfers). The CPU supports a 16-bit I/O address space and can therefore accommodate 64-K 8-bit ports or 32-K 16-bit ports. During I/O operations, the CPU takes the port address either from the instruction itself as an immediate operand or from DX.

### 5.3.2 ■ Control Interface

The 8088 is a single-chip device that has a number of external connections, called pins, for connecting it to other devices and to memory. Some pins are address pins, others are data pins, and the remainder are power and control pins. The 8088 uses **bidirectional pins,** for input and for output (although obviously not at the same time). The 8088 also uses some pins for both addresses and data and some pins for both addresses and status information (although again not at the same time). Pins with different uses at different times are called **time-division-multiplexed (TDM) pins.**

     The 8088 microprocessor is housed in a 40-pin package. Intel's designers based their choice of 40 pins on cost and in part on limitations imposed by the packaging technology in 1980. The consequences were considerable. Several pins must serve more than one function and hence require time-division multiplexing. Then, since pins have different uses at different times, the PC must provide latches for holding temporary values. A related design decision was for the CPU to send and receive data by bytes rather than by words. This decision was made partly to make the PC easier to use with 8-bit external devices and partly for economic reasons. A 16-bit data path, such as that used by Intel's 8086 microprocessor, uses eight additional time-division-multiplexed pins, which require additional data latches and data-bus lines, hence added cost.

     The 40 pins of the 8088 define its interface to the external world, which for our purposes is the remainder of the PC. However, it is not essential to understand each of the pins to understand the general principles of a PC's operation. Table 5.3 gives an overview of the 40 pins and their uses.

**CPU Bus Control**

The 8088 uses bus cycles that take a minimum of 4 clock cycles; each clock cycle defines one bus state. During a memory or I/O bus cycle, the CPU places the memory address or I/O-device address on the bus during the first bus state. The 8088 divides the address into three parts (bits 19-16, bits 15-8, and bits 7-0), which it sends over pins A19/S6 to A16/S3, A15 to A8, and AD7 to AD0. The reason the CPU sends an address only during the first bus state is that it uses pins A19/S6 to A16/S3 for status information and AD7 to AD0 for data during the other bus states. Because 1 clock cycle is not long enough for the storage or I/O systems to decode addresses, the bus circuitry includes address

**Table 5.3** Summary of Pin Function in the 8088 microprocessor.

| Pin Name | Function |
| --- | --- |
| AD7–AD0 | These eight pins are time-division-multiplexed. They serve as both address-output pins and bidirectional data pins. |
| A15–A8 | These eight pins function only as address-output pins. |
| A19/S6–A16/S3 | These four pins are time-division multiplexed. They serve both as address-output pins and as status-output pins. |
| GND, Vcc | These three pins (there are two GND pins) connect the chip to the power supply. (GND, ground; Vcc, voltage) |
| CLK | This pin, a clock input, accepts a 4.77 MHz signal from an external clock (an 8284A Clock Generator) and regulates the 8088's timing. The clock signal regulates the CPU's speed. The 4.77 MHz is based on the operating characteristics of all system components. Some PC clones run at higher speeds because *all* the components are faster. |
| RESET | A signal to this pin causes the 8088 to initialize various registers and begin operation. The PC issues a RESET signal at power up or in case of a system crash. The RESET signal causes the CPU to initialize its segment registers and instruction pointer, and it sets its code-segment register to $FFFF_{16}$, the reset-vector address. As a result, execution begins at the routine whose address is in location $FFFF_{16}$. |
| Control | The other 15 pins carry additional control signals; some will be discussed individually. |

latches for holding the addresses and placing them on the bus while the storage and I/O systems decode them (see Figs. 5.1 and 5.4).

During a memory or I/O bus cycle, the address selects a memory location or I/O device. After the CPU sends the address, it either sends data (during a write bus cycle or an output bus cycle) or reads data (during a read bus cycle or an input bus cycle). During a write bus cycle or an output bus cycle, the CPU places the datum on pins AD7 to AD0 during the second, third, and fourth bus states, and the receiving device (either the selected memory location or the selected I/O device) reads the CPU-generated datum during the fourth bus state. For a read bus cycle or an input bus cycle, the selected memory location or I/O device places the datum on the data lines, and the processor reads the datum (by reading the values on pins AD7 to AD0) during the fourth bus state.

Finally, the selected external device logically disconnects itself from the bus, and the CPU prepares for the next bus cycle by logically disconnecting itself from the address bus. Other devices can now request use of the bus.

### *Wait States*

Not all devices can respond to an input request within the required four bus states. When a device is unable to respond, it informs the CPU of that fact by sending a not-ready signal to the CPU's READY input, which is one of the control inputs.[4] The CPU tests the READY input at the end of the second bus state. If READY is *false*, the CPU inserts a wait state in the bus cycle. A **wait state** is a dummy bus state executed by the CPU when an attached device or memory cannot deliver the requested datum in the required amount of time. The CPU rechecks READY at the end of the wait state and repeats the process until READY is *true*. It then reads the datum from the data bus. Note that, because of wait states, a bus cycle may be longer than 4 clock cycles.

wait state

### CPU Status Signals

The CPU has seven pins that deliver status information to the bus controller: S2 to S0 and A19/S6 to A16/S3. Status pins S2 to S0, which are three of the control pins, always send status information from the CPU; TDM pins A19/S6 to A16/S3 send status information only at specified times during a bus cycle. Using the status pins the CPU makes the following information available to the bus controller:

> segment register used to form the address;
>
> state of the interrupt flag;

---

[4]. The device actually sends the signal to wait-state logic (shown in Fig. 5.1), which relays the signal to the CPU.

---

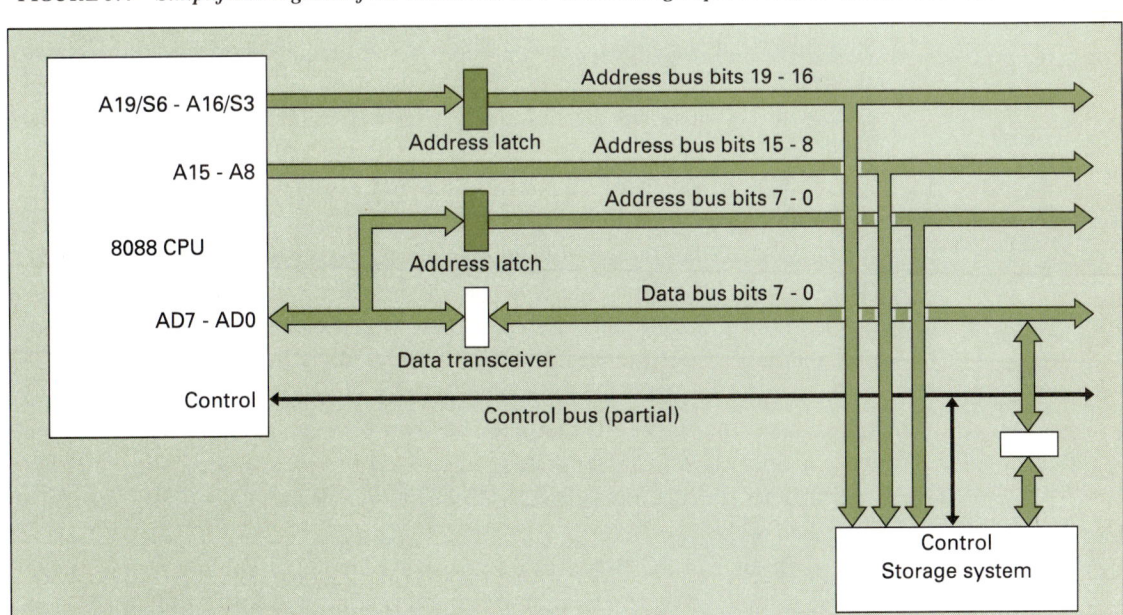

**FIGURE 5.4** *Simplified diagram of the Intel 8088 CPU bus showing required address latches and data transceiver.*

**248** Computer Architecture

The bus-cycle type:
    code-segment access,
    memory read,
    memory write,
    no bus operation,
    interrupt acknowledge,
    I/O read,
    I/O write,
    halt;

instruction-queue status:
    The CPU is executing the first byte of an instruction.
    The CPU is emptying the instruction queue.
    The CPU is taking the next instruction byte from the queue.

In addition, the CPU provides the following control signals:

    bus-request and bus-grant signals for coordinating coprocessors;
    bus-control signals for locking the bus with the LOCK instruction;
    interrupt-control signals.

### 5.3.3 ■ PC Bus and Interrupt System

In Chapter 3 we described local, expanded local, and system buses. This and the following section illustrates the use of an expanded local bus.

The PC Bus is an expanded local bus. Its developers designed it so a user could easily attach a large number of different I/O devices to it. The PC Bus is similar to the 8088 local bus but uses slightly different control signals. (The 8088 local bus appears in Fig. 5.4 between the CPU and the address latch and data transceiver. Also see Fig. 5.5.) It also provides a number of additional services to the attached devices, such as power, interrupt-request lines, and DMA-control lines.

The PC Bus uses a bus controller, address latches, and data transceivers (bidirectional data buffers) as part of its circuitry. The bus controller, which we describe in the following section, generates the control signals. These signals differ from those of the CPU local bus; the differences are not important for this discussion except to note that they include separate memory read, memory write, I/O read, and I/O write control lines, to distinguish I/O read and write bus cycles from memory read and write bus cycles. (Using two control lines, the 8088 CPU distinguishes only between read and write, and between memory and I/O.) Separate memory and I/O control lines allow a DMA controller to transfer data directly from an I/O device to memory during a single bus cycle.

In all, the PC Bus uses 62 lines, of which 20 are address lines, eight are bidirectional data lines, eight are power and ground lines, and 26 are control lines. The control lines include DMA-request lines, DMA-acknowledge lines, interrupt-request lines, an I/O-channel-ready line, a high-frequency clock line, and several other special-purpose control lines.

### Intel 8288 Bus Controller

The 8288 bus controller converts CPU status and clock signals into bus-control signals. Figure 5.5 shows the relationship between the CPU, the bus controller, the CPU local bus, and the PC I/O Channel Bus.

### Interrupt Processing

The processor architects provided the Intel 8088 with a general mechanism for processing interrupts. When an external device requests an interrupt, the CPU initiates a special sequence of bus cycles, called an **interrupt-acknowledge sequence.** External devices recognize the interrupt-acknowledge sequence by decoding the bus control signals, and the requesting device responds by placing its interrupt-vector number on the data bus for the CPU to read. The CPU uses the interrupt-vector number, multiplied by 4, as an offset into the interrupt-vector table, and it then branches to the appropriate interrupt handler.

*interrupt-acknowledge sequence*

**FIGURE 5.5** *Clock, power, and bus circuitry used by the IBM PC.*

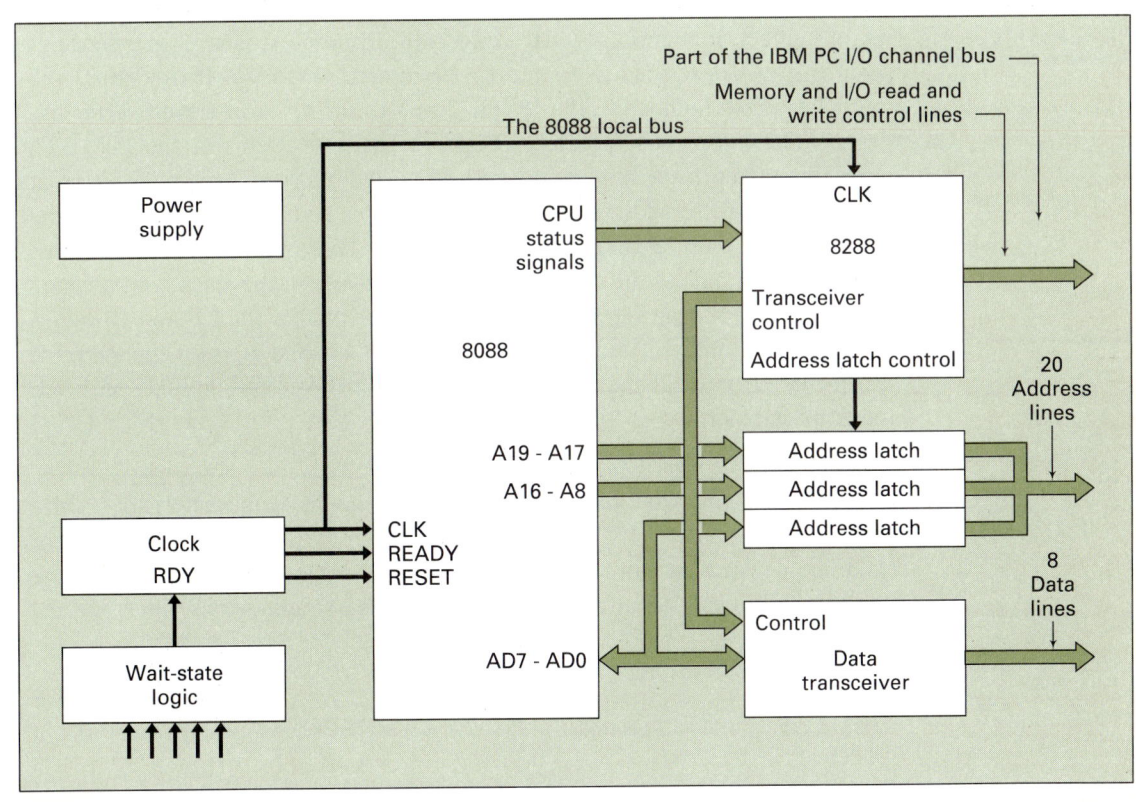

Because the IBM PC uses an interrupt controller, external devices do not communicate directly with the CPU. Instead, they send their interrupt requests to the interrupt controller (to be described shortly). Only the interrupt controller directly requests interrupts of the CPU, and only the interrupt controller responds to the CPU's interrupt-acknowledge sequence. It responds by sending the interrupt-vector number of the requesting device to the CPU.

If the CPU enables interrupts and the interrupt controller requests an interrupt, the CPU begins interrupt processing. The exact time the processing begins depends on several factors, including whether the bus-interface unit is fetching an instruction, whether a processor-synchronization instruction (an instruction with a LOCK prefix) is executing, or whether a bus HOLD request is pending.[5] In any event, once the CPU begins to process the interrupt, the CPU-generated status signals inform the bus controller of that fact.

The CPU begins interrupt processing with the interrupt-acknowledge sequence, which includes adequate time for the CPU to receive 1 byte of data, the interrupt-vector number, from the interrupt controller. The CPU controls the bus during the entire interrupt-acknowledge sequence. This prevents the bus controller from honoring a HOLD request and giving control of the bus to another device, such as a coprocessor.

### Interrupt Initiation

After the CPU acknowledges the interrupt request and gets the interrupt-vector number, it begins a standard **interrupt-initiation sequence.** In essence, it performs an indexed-indirect jump to the interrupt handler. It first shifts the interrupt-vector number to the left by 2 bits to form the **interrupt-vector address.** (The interrupt-vector table begins at address $0000_{16}$ in the IBM PC; hence the offset in the table is the address of the interrupt vector.) Starting at the interrupt-vector address, the first 2 bytes are a code-segment value and the next 2 bytes are an IP value. The CPU fetches these bytes using ordinary bus cycles. Next, it pushes the content of the flag register in the stack, and it clears the interrupt and trap flags (IF and TF). It then pushes the CS and IP values in the stack. Finally, it replaces the contents of CS and IP with the values it just fetched from the interrupt vector. Execution therefore continues with the interrupt handler.

### Intel's 8259A Interrupt Controller

The 8088 has only two interrupt-control inputs, nonmaskable interrupt (NMI) and interrupt request (INTR). If a system, such as the IBM PC, uses more than one device that can raise interrupts of the same type, that system must provide additional circuitry to arbitrate among simultaneous interrupt re-

---

5. External devices (the bus controller in the PC) generate HOLD requests to gain control of the bus.

quests. It must also provide circuitry to inform the CPU of the interrupting device's interrupt-vector number, which it does by sending that number to the data bus during the interrupt-acknowledge sequence. Intel's 8259A interrupt controller is a special-purpose chip designed for these purposes.

Figure 5.6 illustrates how the IBM PC uses the interrupt controller. It also shows the interrupt connections for the keyboard logic and for the timer, which we shall discuss shortly.

The interrupt controller has several functions:

- It receives interrupt requests from up to eight different sources.
- It prioritizes the interrupt requests.
- It masks interrupt requests.
- It processes the CPU's interrupt-acknowledge signal by sending an

FIGURE 5.6  *IBM PC's interrupt controller. NMI, nonmaskable interrupt; INTR, interrupt request; CS, chip select.*

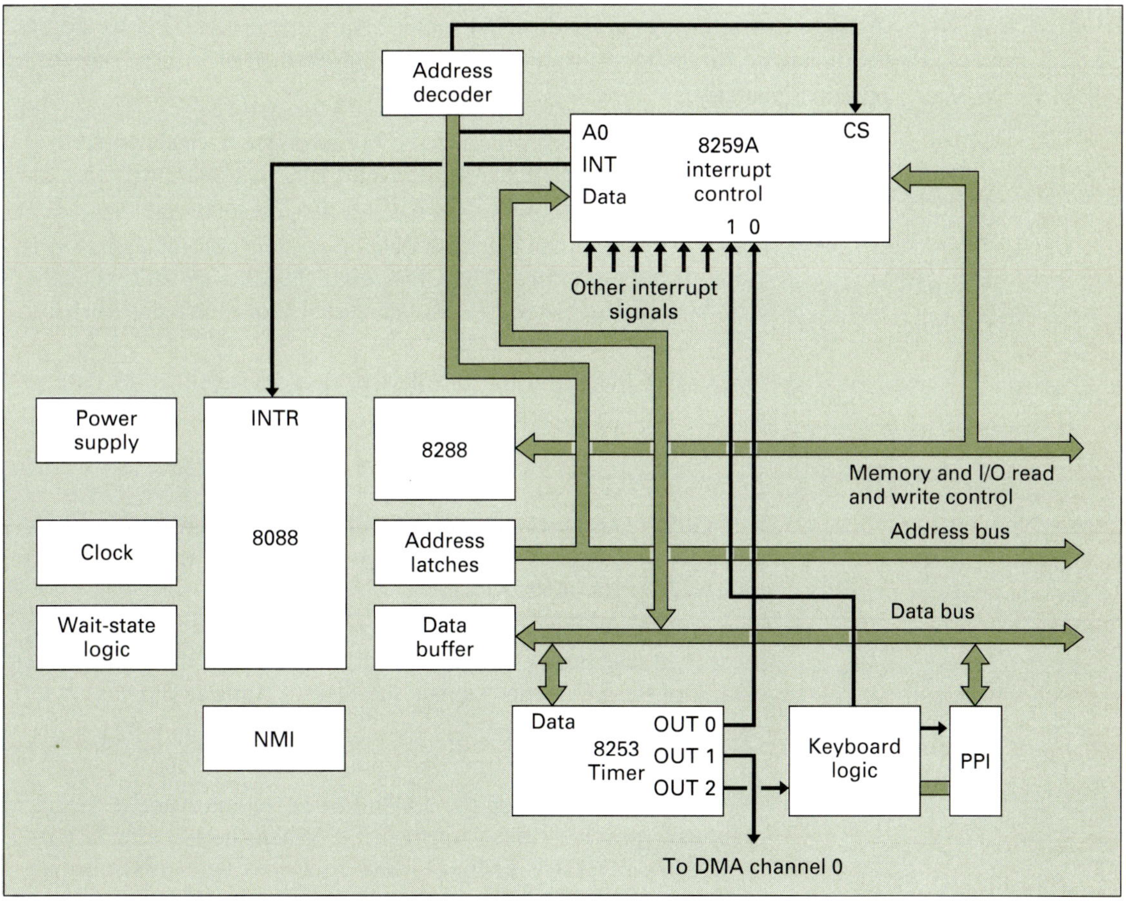

interrupt-vector number to the CPU, which it bases on the interrupt source and a programmed value.

If other interrupt requests occur while the PC is processing an interrupt, the interrupt controller queues them for the CPU.

**DMA Controller**

The CPU can control all I/O by directly writing data and control words to the I/O interfaces (using OUT instructions) and by reading data and status information from them (using IN instructions). However, for the CPU to control each data transfer would be an inefficient use of the CPU. To provide efficient I/O services to the user, the PC uses a DMA I/O controller. Before describing the PC's DMA I/O controller and its use, let us first see what the CPU would have to do if there were no DMA controller.

As a general rule, I/O devices process data in blocks. For example, when reading data from a floppy disk, the CPU may require the transfer of an entire sector of data from the disk to a buffer in memory, or vice versa. When the CPU transfers a file across a telephone line, it may send a sequence of hundreds of characters to the serial I/O interface. In general, the CPU would do the following things to transfer a block of input data from a disk, say, to a buffer in memory:

1. The CPU would first program the I/O interface device as described in Section 5.3.4. (In general, the ROM BIOS software will have already instructed the CPU to program the I/O interface device.)
2. The CPU would then start the disk by sending control signals to it using the I/O interface. The CPU sends the starting address of the first byte of the block as well as a signal requesting that the disk drive start reading the data.
3. Once the CPU starts the I/O device, that device transfers data to the I/O interface one byte at a time.
4. The I/O interface interrupts the CPU when it receives a datum from the disk.
5. The CPU reads (using the IN instruction) the datum into its accumulator byte register (AL), which simultaneously readies the I/O interface for the next byte.
6. The CPU now checks whether there is more data to transfer. If there is, it tells the I/O device to continue on to get the next byte of data, and the I/O device signals the disk to transfer the next byte.
7. Meanwhile the CPU transfers the previous byte from its AL register to memory and increments its pointer into memory.
8. The CPU now waits for the I/O interface to interrupt it. It may proceed with other tasks while waiting. When the I/O interface interrupts it, it returns to Step 5 and continues with this sequence until there is no more data to transfer (Step 6).

The purpose of a DMA controller is to perform the equivalent of Steps 5, 6, and 7 (signaling the I/O device to transfer the next byte of data, transferring the datum to the next memory location, and checking whether there are any more data to transfer), thus freeing the CPU of these repetitious tasks. The DMA controller does not program the I/O interface, nor does it process interrupts. However, when it is finished transferring data, it will notify the CPU by requesting an interrupt.

Notice that to transfer data from the I/O device to memory, the DMA controller must take control of the bus for each transfer. That is, it must send the correct addresses to the PC Bus, and it must initiate the proper I/O and memory bus cycles. It does these things while the CPU is busy doing other things, but it and the CPU must observe a suitable bus protocol, so that both of them do not try to use the bus at the same time.

### Intel's 8237 DMA Controller

A DMA controller, then, is a special-purpose processor designed to transfer blocks of data between memory and I/O interface devices. The PC uses Intel's 8237 DMA controller. The 8237 has four independent I/O channels and hence can control four independent data transfers at the same time. Of course, only one at a time can use the bus. During a data transfer, the DMA controller becomes the bus master: it generates the memory addresses and informs the I/O interface of when to place data onto or when to take data from the bus, depending on the direction of the transfer. If the CPU needs the bus while the DMA controller is bus master, the CPU must wait until the DMA controller relinquishes the bus.

The 8237 has 27 registers. Twenty of them are channel-specific (five different registers for each channel), while seven are systemwide. The channel-specific registers consist of four 16-bit registers and one 6-bit **DMA mode register** per channel. The 16-bit registers hold the starting or **DMA base address** of the block of data in main memory, the **DMA current address** (the address of the byte being transferred), the total or **DMA base count,** and the **DMA current count** (the remaining number of bytes to be transferred) for the data transfer. The bits of the mode register specify various transfer parameters, including whether to increment or decrement the current address after each transferred byte, whether the transfer is a read or write transfer, whether to automatically reset the current address and count registers to their starting values when the current count reaches zero (**DMA autoinitialization**), and what the transfer mode is. Autoinitialization is useful for channels that perform the same operation to the same addresses time after time, such as refreshing DRAM or video screens.

There are four transfer modes:

1. *DMA single mode,* where the DMA controller requests the bus independently for each byte it wishes to transfer;

DMA mode register
DMA base address
DMA current address
DMA base count
DMA current count




DMA autoinitialization




DMA single mode

2. *DMA block mode,* where the DMA controller does not relinquish the bus until it finishes tranferring the entire block of data;

3. *DMA demand mode,* where the DMA controller remains bus master for as long as the attached I/O device tells it to;

4. *DMA cascade mode,* where a second DMA controller controls the bus and the transfer. Cascading (linking together) controllers is referred to as **daisy chaining**.

The seven systemwide registers are a 16-bit **DMA temporary address register,** a 16-bit **DMA temporary count register,** an 8-bit **DMA status register,** an 8-bit **DMA command register,** an 8-bit **DMA temporary register,** a 4-bit **DMA mask register,** and a 4-bit **DMA request register.** The status register has 2 bits for each channel: a request bit that indicates whether a request is pending, and a terminal count bit (TC) that indicates whether the current count has reached zero. The command register controls the DMA controller's operation and specifies, among other things, whether a memory-to-memory transfer is to occur (which requires two DMA channels), the timing mode, and the priority for servicing I/O requests. The bits of the mask register disable I/O requests for the corresponding channel. When a channel completes a transfer, it sets its mask bit and goes inactive. The bits of the request register, which the program can set, initiate DMA-controller service. The DMA controller clears them when the transfer is complete. The temporary register holds data during memory-to-memory data transfers, and the temporary address and temporary count registers hold addresses and counts while the DMA controller increments or decrements them.

The CPU can write each channel's base-address register, base-count register, command register, request register, and mode registers. It can read each channel's current address and current count, the status register, and the temporary 8-bit register. Finally, the CPU can set and clear various mask register bits and initiate the master clear operation; which initializes all DMA registers. (A hardware reset does the same thing.)

Data transfers proceed roughly as follows. Before a transfer begins, the CPU programs the transfer operation: It sends the base address, base count, and transfer parameters to the desired channel in the DMA controller. The DMA controller automatically loads the current-address and current-count registers with the base address and base count. The CPU transfers all 16-bit quantities to the same device address using two OUT instructions. It always transfers the low-order byte first and then the high-order byte. The CPU then finishes programming the channel by sending the proper control information to the command and mode registers. Finally, it activates the DMA controller by clearing the channel's mask bit. That puts the DMA controller in charge of the data transfer and frees the CPU for other tasks.

For a memory-to-I/O transfer, the DMA controller immediately transfers the first byte. For an I/O-to-memory transfer, the DMA controller waits for the I/O interface to indicate that a byte is available; it then transfers the first byte. In either case, after the byte is transferred, the DMA controller decrements the current count and either increments or decrements the current address, depending on the transfer mode. When the current count finally reaches zero, the transfer is complete. The DMA controller sends the value *true* on an end-of-process line (EOP) and sets the terminal-count bit in the status register.

The DMA controller maintains control of the bus during block-mode transfers. It maintains control of the bus according to the demands of an attached I/O interface during demand-mode transfers, and it relinquishes control of the bus after it transfers each byte during single-mode transfers. Finally, like the CPU, it inserts wait states if the attached I/O interface is not ready. Because the DMA controller can generate an address and send data on the bus simultaneously, it can transfer a datum in five clock periods as compared with a minimum of 29 for the CPU. Under ideal circumstances it can transfer data at the rate of nearly 1 MBS, whereas the CPU's maximum transfer rate is about 170 KBS.

The optimal transfer mode depends on the characteristics of the I/O interface. Single mode is best for slow devices, such as keyboards, which transfer 1 byte at a time. Demand mode is best for devices that buffer their data, such as disk controllers. During demand transfers, the external device continually requests the bus until its buffer is empty. When it stops requesting the bus, the DMA controller relinquishes the bus to the CPU. Block mode is best when the device can transfer data at, or nearly at, DMA-controller speeds as for video-screen refresh.

Figure 5.7 shows the general connections between the 8237 DMA controller, the PC I/O Bus, and the I/O devices, as well as the details of the DMA request and acknowledge lines. For the IBM PC, channel 1 of the timer connects to channel 0 of the DMA controller. The PC's BIOS programs channel 0 of the DMA controller to refresh DRAM and channel 1 of the timer to tell the DMA when to refresh memory. Within the PC, channel 1 of the DMA connects to a **programmable parallel interface** (PPI), which serves as an interface between the PC I/O Channel Bus and a parallel I/O device such as a disk drive or printer. Channel 2 connects to a floppy disk controller (the righthand PPI in the figure). Channel 3 connects to a **universal asynchronous receiver-transmitter (UART),** which serves as an interface between the PC I/O Channel Bus and an attached I/O device that sends data in bit-serial fashion (e.g., a modem). The UART is not shown in the figure. Both PPIs and the UART will be described later in Section 5.3.4.

The 8237 DMA controller operates in conjunction with an external 8-bit latch. During ordinary operation the 8237 outputs 8 bits of a 16-bit address on its address lines. The external 8-bit latch provides the remaining 8 bits of

**FIGURE 5.7** *DMA Controller circuits of the IBM PC. Also see Fig. 5.5 and 5.6. Notice that the interrupt (INT) outputs from the PPIs and channel 1 of the timer are DMA service-request signals. Key: DRQn, DMA request line n; DACKn, DMA acknowledge line n; ACK, acknowledge; INT, interrupt request; NMI, nonmaskable interrupt; PPI, programmable parallel interface.*

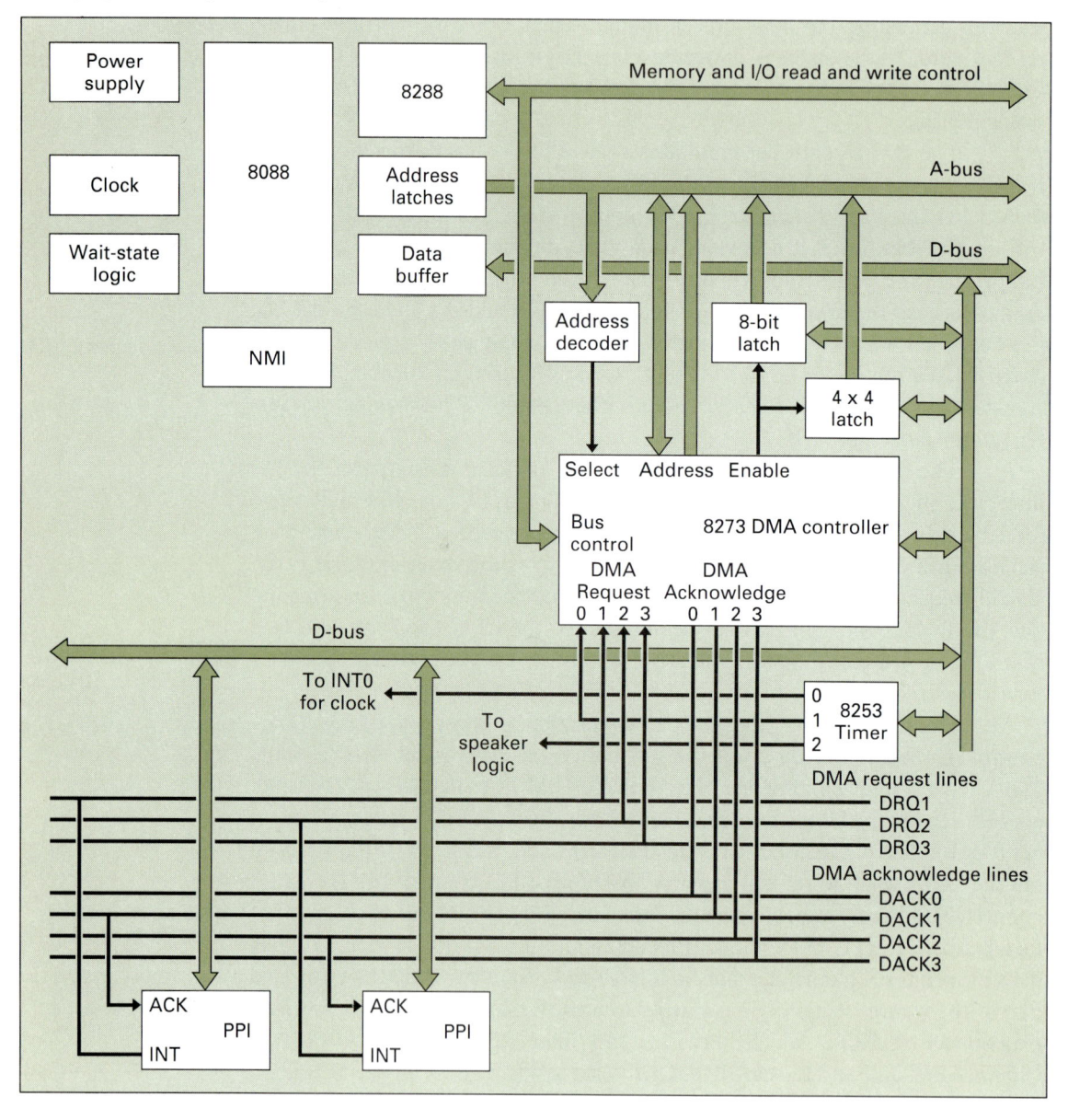

the 16-bit address. The 8237 controls the 8-bit latch and sets its value when needed. Because the PC uses 20-bit addresses, circuitry external to the 8237 must provide the additional 4 address bits, which are the 64-K segment number. The 4 × 4 latch illustrated in Fig. 5.7 supplies one 4-bit segment number for each of the 8237's four independent channels.

**IBM PC AT I/O Channel Bus**

When IBM designed the AT, it redesigned the system bus to accommodate 16 data bits (rather than 8) and a number of additional control lines. Rather than completely redesigning the bus, however, it did so in such a way as to make the PC AT Bus an extension of the PC Bus. First, to maintain compatibility with PC hardware, IBM kept the same basic 62-pin I/O channel slots that it used in the PC. IBM renamed some of the pins as will be described shortly. Then it added a 36-pin auxiliary slot, which it placed in line with the standard PC slot. Consequently, a single card can use both slots simultaneously. The auxiliary bus has eight additional data lines, seven additional address lines, five additional interrupt-request lines, four additional DMA request and acknowledge lines, and eight power and control lines.

Reasons for most of the changes should be clear from the following observations: The PC AT uses an 80286 processor. The PC AT added an additional DMA controller, an additional interrupt controller, and special memory-refresh circuits, thereby freeing up DMA channel 0 (now seen on the auxiliary bus). To indicate that a memory refresh is taking place, IBM added to the AT Bus a special line, called REFRESH, which replaced the function of the channel 0 DMA acknowledgment line on the PC. The AT uses interrupt request 2 to cascade the second interrupt controller, and it uses interrupt request 9 to take over the previous function of interrupt request 2. When the 80286 operates in Real Address mode (hence behaves like an 8088), the address space is small—restricted to 1 MB. When the AT runs its CPU in Real Address mode, it uses the original 62 bus lines just as the PC does; the AT behaves like a PC, so to speak. When not operating in Real Address mode and the AT generates large addresses, it uses special memory read and write control lines, which are new to the PC AT Bus, to indicate the large addresses. It follows that devices assigned to addresses within the first megabyte do not need to decode the high-order address lines at all, and cards that were plugged into PC slots can just as easily be plugged into PC AT slots.

Although the PC AT can use cards designed for the PC, the AT has a 16-bit data bus. Devices that can transfer 16 bits at a time should be able to do so, and the AT Bus has special control lines for that purpose. One added control line, the zero-wait-state line (0WS), eliminates wait states within the CPU. IBM placed this line in an unused position on the original PC Bus so that device manufacturers can produce fast 8-bit cards as well as 16-bit cards. One special control line indicates that a device is initiating a 16-bit transfer. This line allows the PC to distinguish between 8-bit and 16-bit cards. Because the DMA controller of the PC latched the high-order address lines, IBM placed unlatched copies of these three lines on the AT Bus. This allows high-speed boards to operate considerably faster than they would otherwise have been able to because of the propagation delay of the latching process. As a final note, an external device, such as an alternate CPU, can become bus master by using the MASTER control line.

**EISA Bus**

Designers must solve many problems when extending a given architecture, and the EISA consortium did a remarkable job extending the PC AT Bus. As of 1991, Intel had manufactured an EISA chip set, which includes an 82358 Bus Controller, an 82357 Integrated System Peripheral, and an 82355 Bus Master Interface Controller. Several companies now produce EISA bus-based PCs.

When IBM extended the PC Bus to the PC AT Bus by adding data, address, and control lines to it, the designers maintained downward compatibility: A user could use any 8-bit PC device with it. The EISA designers extended the PC AT Bus in a similar way:

- The EISA bus is downward-compatible with the PC and PC AT buses. That is, the EISA slots accept 8-bit PC and 16-bit PC AT cards as well as 32-bit EISA cards.
- Any bus master using the bus can transfer data to and from any memory or attached peripheral, regardless of widths of their data transfers (8, 16, or 32 bits).
- The EISA bus supports cycle-by-cycle translation for different widths of data and for different types of transfers, such as single transfers and burst transfers (high-speed synchronous data transfers).
- The EISA bus allows devices to share interrupt lines, although only EISA devices are designed to use this facility. (On the PC and PC AT buses only one device can use a given interrupt line.)
- The EISA bus controller guarantees bus access to all high-priority bus masters. For example, the DRAM-refresh circuitry is guaranteed access to memory.

The PC AT Bus consists of two slots containing 98 connections. The EISA bus adds an additional 88 contacts to the EISA slots and 59 new lines to the bus. (Several contacts have duplicated functionality.) The EISA bus has a total of 157 lines. EISA slots are deeper than PC AT and PC slots. In addition, EISA cards have special notches in them, which allows them to go deeper into the EISA slots than PC and PC AT cards can go. Hence EISA cards can contact the new EISA bus lines while the slots prevent PC and PC AT cards from contacting the new bus lines. This design results in plug compatibility between EISA slots and PC and PC AT cards.

The new bus lines include 16 data lines, 30 address lines (which excludes the 2 low-order address bits), and 13 power and control lines. The control lines specify, among other things, which byte or bytes are being transferred, whether the bus cycle is an EISA bus cycle (and hence can transfer 32 bits), what type of EISA bus cycle (memory or I/O) is involved, whether the attached board is an EISA board, what is the bus-master number of the attached board, and what is the number of the bus master currently controlling the bus. The EISA bus has facilities that allow EISA devices to configure themselves automatically and facilities that allow the CPU or any attached bus master to read or write any memory or I/O device.

How are EISA and non-EISA devices integrated in a PC clone? EISA devices indicate their presence by placing appropriate control signals on the bus. A non-EISA device does not generate these signals. By interpreting the PC and PC AT Bus signals, both the bus controller and the bus master can determine the type of attached device. Now suppose a 32-bit EISA device wishes to write to a non-EISA device, say an 8-bit device. During the initial bus cycle, the bus controller and the EISA device monitor the bus control signals. When the responding device indicates that it does not support 32-bit data transfers, the EISA bus controller reads the data and address and takes control of the bus; the original bus master relinquishes control. The EISA bus controller now generates the control signals for four 8-bit data transfers using the appropriate protocol (PC or PC AT) of the attached device, and it sends the data a byte or 2 bytes at a time, as needed.

We shall now return to our discussion of the IBM PC.

### 5.3.4 ■ I/O System

The 8088 microprocessor has two I/O instructions: IN and OUT. When executing an IN instruction, the CPU initiates an I/O read cycle. Either the instruction or the DX register holds the I/O port address, which the CPU sends to the address bus. The CPU then loads the AL register with the value placed on the data bus by the external device whose port address it transmitted. When executing an OUT instruction, the CPU initiates an I/O write cycle. Either the instruction or the 8088's DX register holds the I/O port address. The CPU sends the port address to the address bus, and it sends the content of the 8088's AL register to the data bus. The addressed external device accepts the data from the data bus.

The I/O port-address decoders on the PC decode only the 10 low-order address lines during I/O instructions. Thus the PC architecture limits the number of I/O port addresses to $2^{10}$, or 1024. Because some applications, such as video-display buffers, require more addresses than that, the PC architects reserved several blocks of main-memory addresses for those purposes. Thus some I/O devices use memory-mapped I/O while others use I/O instructions. We shall describe the reserved main-memory addresses later in this chapter.

### I/O Interface Adapters

Most microcomputers, including the IBM PC and PC AT, support both parallel and serial I/O. Devices that transmit 1 or more bytes of data at a time use **parallel I/O.** Disks and printers are examples. Devices that use **serial I/O** transmit data 1 bit at a time over a single data line (instead of all the bits in a byte concurrently over independent bus lines). For example, many PCs use telephone lines for long-distance communications, and telephone lines require serial data transmission.

To support both serial and parallel I/O, chip designers have produced a variety of programmable I/O interfaces for serial and parallel I/O. These interfaces satisfy a large number of requirements and support a variety of I/O protocols.

The IBM PC has one parallel interface on the mother board, which it uses for a variety of applications. In addition, a user can add both serial and parallel I/O interfaces as optional equipment by plugging appropriate option cards into available slots. For example, a communications adapter is an option card that has a serial interface for a modem, while a printer adapter and many mouse adapters are option cards that have parallel interfaces for printers and mouses. These I/O interfaces become integral parts of the computer once the user adds them.

Serial and parallel devices use standard I/O interface chips. Two typical I/O interface chips, mentioned earlier, are the 8255A PPI, which is used in the standard interface on the IBM PC for parallel I/O, and the 8250 UART, which the IBM PC uses for serial I/O. There are differences between these interface chips and those used in other microcomputer families, as well as between these and the corresponding devices used in 80286 and 80386 machines, but the differences are minor. Optional sections within Section 5.3.4 describe the functional architectures of these two chips in greater detail. First, however, we show how designers add I/O interface circuits to a computer.

Each I/O interface must have its own address-decoding circuitry for determining its I/O port addresses. The system architects assign those port addresses, and we shall discuss them later. Connecting a device to the PC Bus, then, is a matter of connecting the device's chip-select inputs to the address-decoding circuitry, connecting its control and power pins to the control and power lines of the bus, and connecting its data lines to the data lines of the bus. After that, the designer connects the interface's I/O ports to the I/O device of choice, for example a modem or floppy-disk-drive controller. Figure 5.8 illustrates how to connect an 8255A PPI to the PC Bus.

### 8255 Programmable Parallel Interface (Optional)

In this section we describe the 8255A PPI's operation and its functional capabilities and indicate the CPU's responsiblity in programming it. The level of detail presented in this section is far greater than that required for many architects. We have included it to show how a complete I/O system works, for any architect needs to know this when designing a system.

Internally the 8255A contains four registers: a control register, and three data registers, one for each of its three ports. The data registers hold data to be sent by the port (if the CPU programs the port for output) or data to the port is to receive (if the CPU programs it for input). The control register specifies the mode of operation of the 8255A. The CPU programs the 8255A by writing a value into the control register. However, the CPU cannot read the content of the control register since the control register is write-only.

When the CPU executes an IN or OUT instruction that selects the PPI, two address pins specify which of the four registers the CPU will access. One may therefore view the CPU as directly addressing the three data buffers and the control register.

**FIGURE 5.8** *Connecting an 8255A PPI to a PC Bus. The dashed line outlines devices on boards that can be placed on an option card and plugged into a PC slot.*

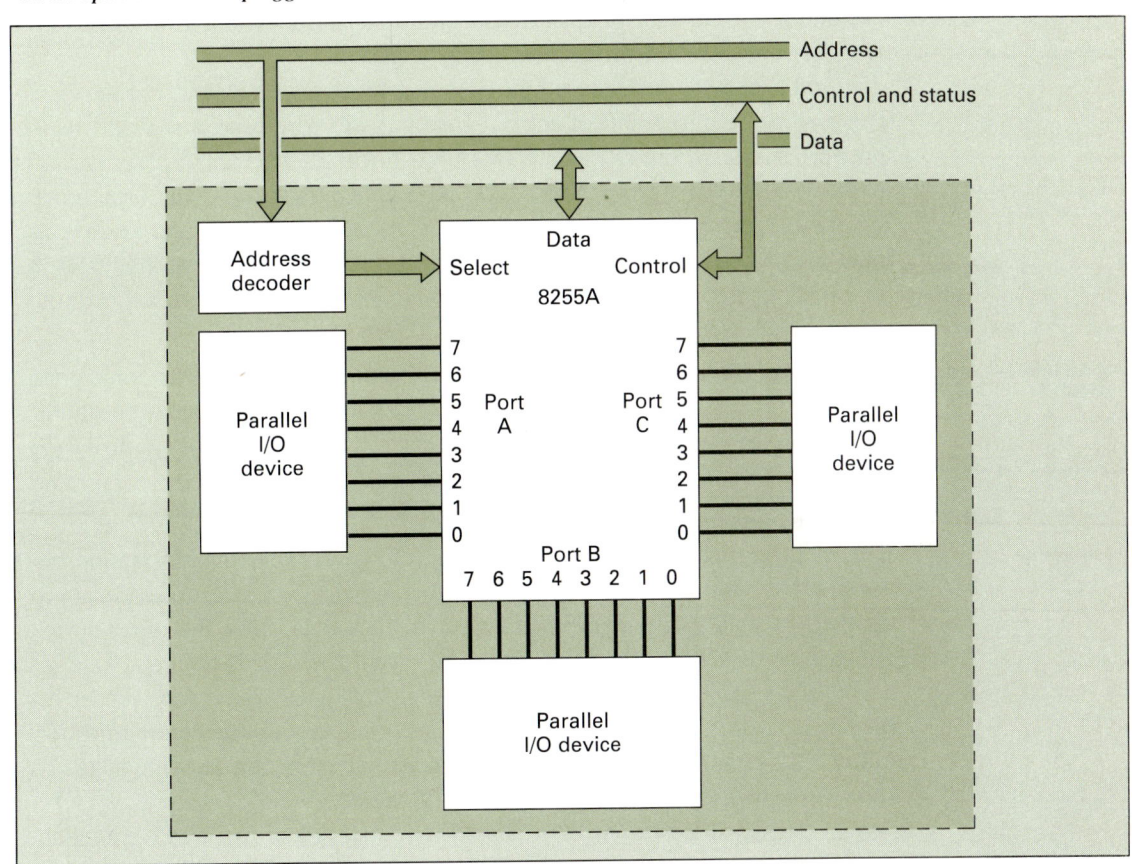

### Modes of Operation

The 8255A has three basic modes of operation: basic I/O, strobed I/O, and bidirectional bus. Here is a brief summary of the basic I/O and strobed I/O modes of operation.

**basic I/O mode of PPI**

***Basic I/O Mode*** The basic mode is the default mode, with all three ports initialized for input. In this mode the ports latch all outputs: When a port is programmed for output and the CPU writes a value into its data register, the port holds the value—latches it—and sends it to its output pins until the CPU writes a new value into the data register. The PPI does not latch its inputs. Thus the CPU can only read a value while the external device actively sends it. The CPU reads a value by reading the port's data register.

**strobed mode of PPI**

***Strobed Mode*** During strobed operation the hardware divides the ports into two groups. For the first group, port A operates as an input or output data port, and the upper half of port C operates as a control port for port A. We shall describe what that means shortly. For the second group, port B operates as an input or output data port, and the lower half of port C operates as a control port for port B. Both groups operate independently and in a similar fashion, and the CPU can program each group separately. Hence we shall only describe the operation of the first group's registers.

During strobed operation, port A latches all input and output data. The bits in the upper half of port C, together with the control register, regulate port A's operation. In particular, 1 bit determines whether port A operates as an input or output port. If the CPU programs port A to be an output port, the parallel interface uses the bits of port C to raise interrupts and to serve as input-acknowledge and output-buffer-full flags. If the CPU programs port A for input, it uses the bits of port C to raise interrupts, to serve as an input strobe, and to serve as an input-buffer-full flag.

**bidirectional bus mode of PPI**

***Bidirectional Bus Mode*** In this mode, Port A functions as a bidirectional port, and the bits of Port C's data register perform a handshake protocol in a similar manner to the one described next. In addition, the CPU can program Port B either as an input port or as an output port.

### Parallel Communications Using Handshaking

**handshaking**

**Handshaking** is a general method of controlling the flow of information between two communicating processors. When one device wishes to send data to another, it requests permission to do so. It then waits until the other device grants it permission to send the data. The sender then sends the data. The receiving device may then send an acknowledgment signal back to the sender indicating that it has received the information, thus ending the communication protocol. A communications protocol is much like to people shaking hands to show agreement on a transaction, hence the name.

We shall now analyze a simple output protocol for a PPI and show what the bits of the control register do. Assume that the PPI initially sends the following information: INT = *false* (i.e., the PPI is not requesting an interrupt) and OBF = *false* (the output buffer is not full); assume also that the I/O device sends back ACK = *false* (acknowledging no receipt of data). When it wishes to send a datum to the I/O device, the CPU executes an OUT instruction with the PPI's port address as the operand. The OUT instruction sends the datum in AL to the PPI. The PPI automatically reads the datum and sends it to the I/O device. The PPI also sends *true* for OBF to tell the I/O device that the datum is available and valid. As soon as the I/O device senses that the OBF has changed state, the I/O device reads the datum and sets ACK to *true*, which tells the PPI that it has received the datum. The PPI may now change the value in its data register. The PPI informs the CPU that it is ready to send more data by raising an interrupt (setting INT = *true*). Figure 5.9 summarizes this output protocol.

The input protocol is very similar to the output protocol (see Fig. 5.10). When the CPU wants to read data, it programs the port for input. Let us assume that the CPU has already programmed the PPI for input and has notified the PPI to read some data. Initially the PPI sends IBF = *false* (indicating that the input buffer is not full), and the I/O device sends STB = *true* (strobe input). (When STB goes from *true* to *false*, the PPI actually reads the input data.) As soon as the I/O device gets the datum, it sends it to the PPI on its output port. It then sets STB = *false*, which tells the PPI to read the datum. The PPI reads the datum and immediately sets IBF = *true* to tell the I/O device that it is not ready to receive any more data. The I/O device must not send

**FIGURE 5.9** *A standard output handshake protocol.*

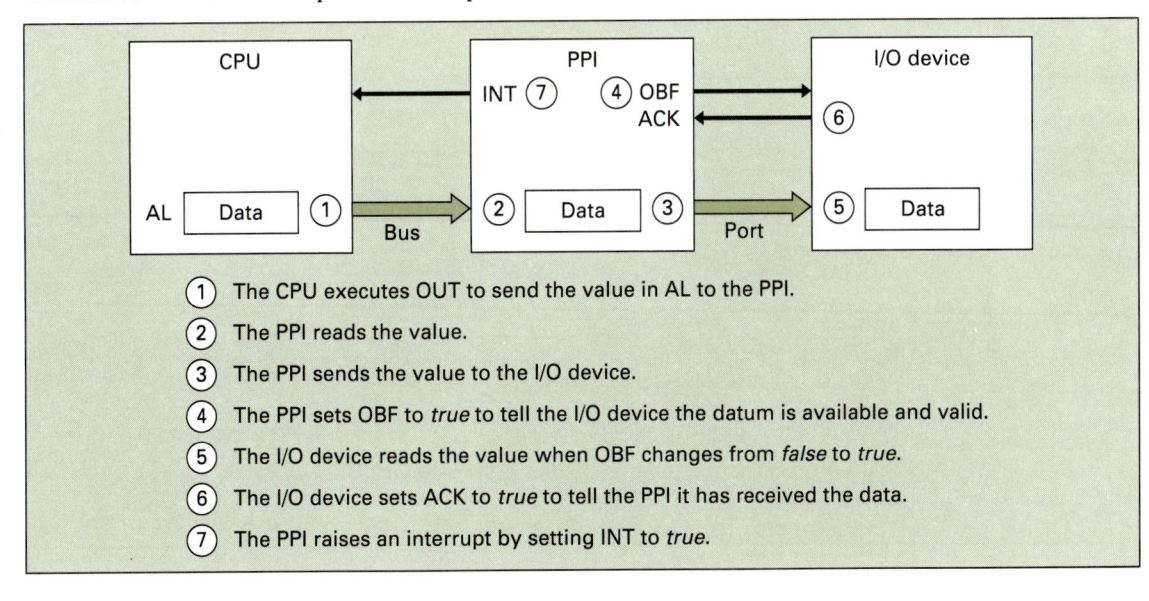

①  The CPU executes OUT to send the value in AL to the PPI.
②  The PPI reads the value.
③  The PPI sends the value to the I/O device.
④  The PPI sets OBF to *true* to tell the I/O device the datum is available and valid.
⑤  The I/O device reads the value when OBF changes from *false* to *true*.
⑥  The I/O device sets ACK to *true* to tell the PPI it has received the data.
⑦  The PPI raises an interrupt by setting INT to *true*.

more data on its output port until the PPI sends IBF = *false*. The PPI now notifies the CPU that it has the data by requesting an interrupt (setting INT = *true*). The CPU reads the data into AL by executing an IN instruction, which also clears the buffer, and the PPI responds by setting INT and IBF equal to *false*.

This in principal is how the CPU can communicate with an I/O device using an 8255A. The bits of the C register provide the control functions. In addition the PPI must tell the I/O device to start reading or writing the data, and that is how the PPI uses the remaining bits of the C register. The CPU can send control signals to the I/O device (by programming bits of the C register for output), or it may receive status signals from the device (by programming bits of the C register for input). If the CPU programs the port for output, it writes output values in Port C's data register. If it programs the port for input, it reads the values from Port C's data register. Readers interested in additional details, may consult the 8255A specifications.

An 8255A can serve many functions. The PC mother board uses one to read status information, keyboard information, configuration-switch settings, and to control various devices. The PC programs ports A and C for input and port B for output, and it connects the ports to specific external devices.

Although our discussion has assumed that communication takes place between the CPU and the 8255A, there are really no direct connections between them. All control signals and data pass through the PC Bus. If a device other than the CPU were to initiate an I/O read or write cycle and send the 8255A's address on the bus, the 8255A would respond just as if the CPU had

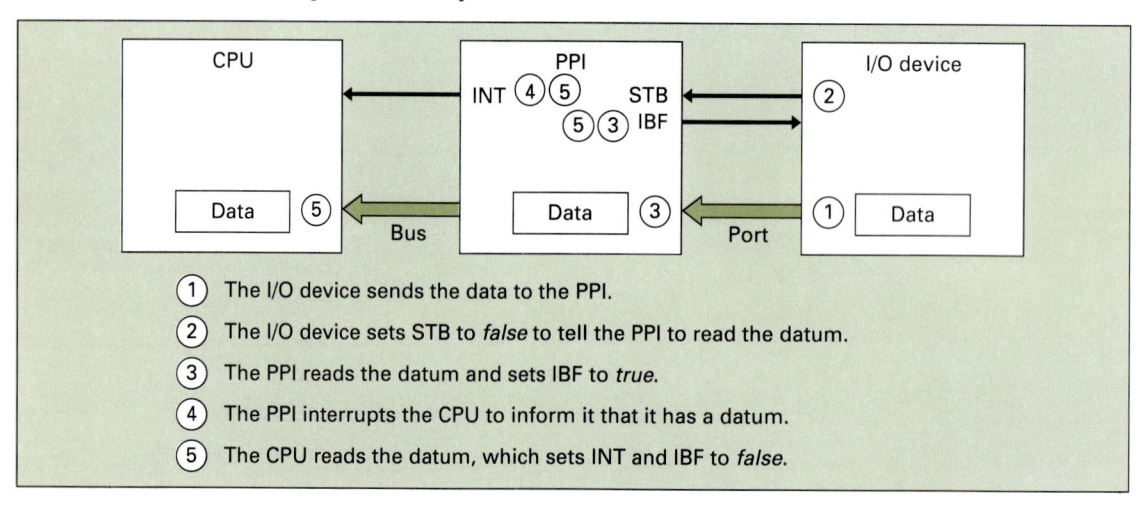

**FIGURE 5.10** *A standard input handshake protocol.*

① The I/O device sends the data to the PPI.
② The I/O device sets STB to *false* to tell the PPI to read the datum.
③ The PPI reads the datum and sets IBF to *true*.
④ The PPI interrupts the CPU to inform it that it has a datum.
⑤ The CPU reads the datum, which sets INT and IBF to *false*.

initiated the read or write bus cycle. Later we will show that DMA controllers do just that—they initiate I/O read and write bus cycles to transfer data between the I/O interface chips and main memory without CPU intervention. First let us look at the operation of a serial I/O interface adapter.

**Techniques of Serial I/O**

For devices requiring serial transmission of data, like modems, component manufacturers provide special interface circuits to convert parallel data sent over the PC Bus into a serial format suitable for transmissions, and vice versa. The IBM PC uses the 8250 UART for that purpose, and we shall focus on it shortly. But first we present a very brief overview of serial transmission. Keeping in mind that designers can make many other choices for serial communications, this description is for a typical serial communications line.

For our example of a serial transmission, the sending device sends *true* (higher voltage, usually) on the transmission line when it is **idle** or not transmitting data. A transmission begins when the sending device changes the line signal to *false* (lowers the voltage). After that the sending device sends the individual bits by changing the signal for a fixed length of time, called a **bit time**. A *false* signal means it is sending a zero bit; a *true* signal means it is sending a one bit. The transmission rate, called the **baud rate,** specifies the number of changes in voltage per second. At low speeds this is effectively equivalent to the number of bits the sending device sends per second, and the bit time is the inverse of the baud rate.

The first bit the sender transmits after it begins a transmission is called a **mark bit;** it contains no data but simply alerts the receiver that a transmission is beginning. Following the mark bit, the sender sends a fixed number of **data bits.** After that it sends a parity bit. The I/O interface devices use the parity bit to check for transmission errors. The sender then terminates the transmission by sending a fixed number of **stop bits.** Figure 5.11 shows a sample serial transmission.

idle

bit time

baud rate

mark bit

data bits

stop bits

**FIGURE 5.11** *A serial data transmission of the value $1000101_2$ using 7 data bits, 1 parity bit, and 2 stop bits.*

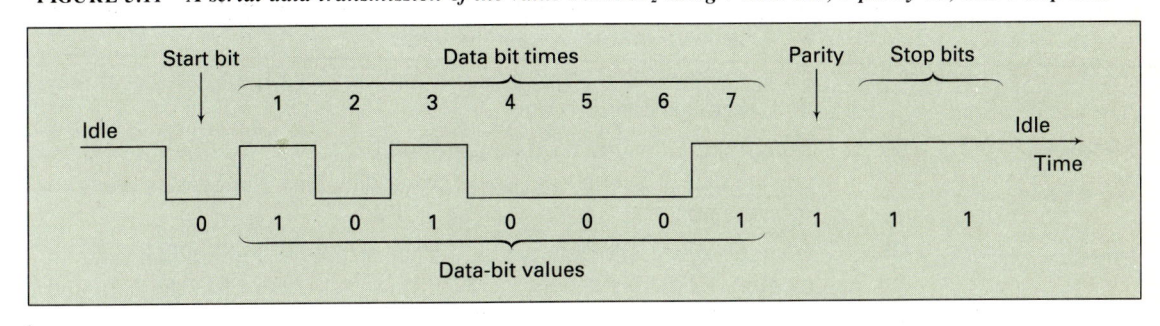

## 266  Computer Architecture

Standard communications devices use a number of standard combinations of baud rate, parity bits, data bits, and stop bits. In general, the communicating devices are not synchronized by the same clock, so this is **asynchronous transmission.** When the receiver detects the start of a serial transmission, it reads (checks the voltage on) the I/O line in the middle of each bit time. It records a 1 if the line is high and a 0 if it is low. This sampling procedure negates any small differences between the clock frequencies of two communicating devices. However, it requires a high-frequency clock, the **receiver clock.** Likewise, the transmitter uses a low-frequency clock, the **transmitter clock,** to regulate the bit time.

Errors of several types sometimes occur. In an **overrun error** the sending device continues to send data while the receiver is not ready to receive a transmission. Sometimes the differences between the clock frequencies cause the receiver to sample the transmission line at the incorrect time. This is called a **framing error.** If the devices are using parity bits to detect errors and the receiver gets an incorrect parity bit, the result is a **parity error.**

### 8250 Universal Asynchronous Receiver-transmitter (Optional)

We now describe the 8250 UART in some detail. Its designers developed it to interface computers with telephone lines, and the attached serial I/O device is often a **modem** (short for modulator-demodulator). A modem converts digital signals into audio signals suitable for telephone line transmission, and vice versa.

The 8250 has eight control signals that regulate its interface to the bus. Four are read input signals. They enable the 8250 to capture its input or send its output data. One control signal enables the 8250 to capture its address and chip-select pin values. The two output signals inform external devices when the CPU has selected the 8250 and when the CPU is reading its data. The 8250 uses its interrupt output to request a CPU interrupt.

Eight handshake lines, of which six have assigned uses, regulate communications between the 8250 and the attached serial I/O device. We assume the device is a modem for the following discussion. Here are the six assigned functions:

RTS  *Request permission to send.* This output tells the modem that the 8250 has data that it is ready to send.

CTS  *Clear to send.* This input from the modem tells the 8250 that it may now begin sending its data.

DTR  *Data terminal ready.* (A **data terminal** is a device for sending and receiving data.) This output tells the modem that the 8250 is ready to receive data.

DSR  *Data set ready.* (A **data set** is a data structure for holding data in memory.) This input tells the 8250 that the modem has the data and is ready to send it.

RI     *Ring indicator.* The modem has detected the telephone ring signal.

RLSD   *Received line signal detect.* The modem has now detected the transmitter carrier frequency and can begin data communications.

Following is a description of a typical handshake that takes place during data communications with a modem. In this discussion the 8250 is the data terminal and the modem is the data set. Numbers in braces refer to steps illustrated in Fig. 5.12.

If the modem has data that it wishes to send to the 8250, it performs an analogous handshake. When the 8250 has data it wishes to send to the modem, it requests permission from the modem by sending it an RTS = *true* signal {1}. The RTS signal tells the modem that the 8250 is ready to send data. When the modem is ready to receive data it sends DSR = *true* {2} and hence informs the 8250 that it is ready to receive the data. The 8250 now sends the data {3} on its serial output port (SOUT). The data is generally a sequence of bytes, each byte framed with a start bit and the correct number of parity and stop bits. When the 8250 has no more data to send, it sends DTR = *false* {4}. If, during a transmission, the modem is unable to accept data, it can send DSR = *false* {5}, which tells the 8250 that the modem is no longer able to receive data.

The CPU programs the 8250 by sending data (using OUT instructions) to the 8250's control registers. The CPU determines the status of the 8250 by reading the 8250's status register. One of the control registers regulates the transmit and receive clock frequencies; a second control register regulates parity, the number of stop bits, and the number of data bits. The status register holds the status of the transmission (full receive data register, empty transmit

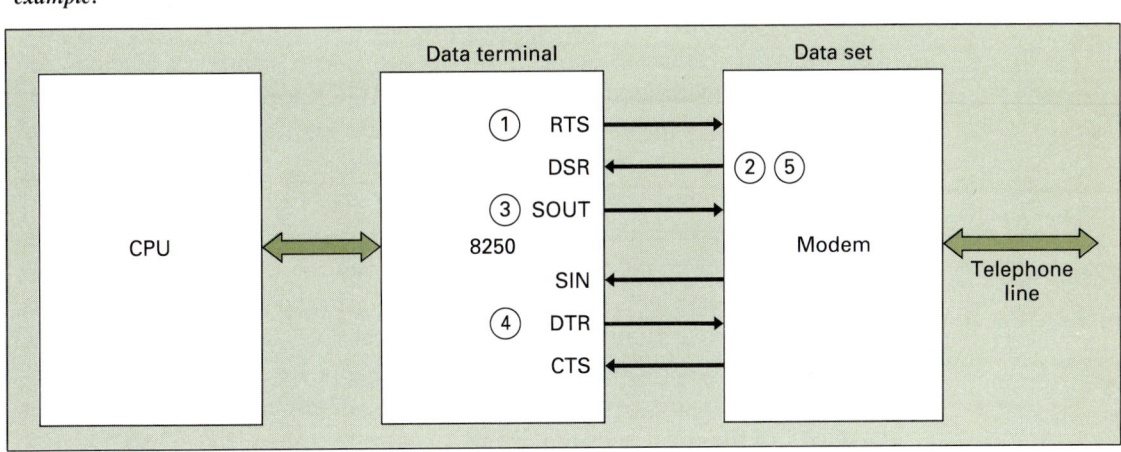

**FIGURE 5.12** *Typical connections between a UART and a modem. The 8250 initiates the transmission in this example.*

data register, framing error, parity error, overrun error, etc.). To summarize, the 8250's control register controls the states of the output handshake signals, while its status register, when read by the CPU, gives the status of the input handshake signals.

### 5.3.5 ■ Programmable Interval Timer

Many devices, as well as applications, need timer signals to activate them. For example, the memory must be refreshed every so often, the speaker needs periodic signals to generate its sounds (beeps, warning signals, tones), and programs that keep track of the time of day need to be told when the seconds pass. In this section we describe the 8253 Programmable Timer, which the PC uses. We also show how the PC uses it to initiate DRAM-refresh operations.

**8253 Programmable Interval Timer**

*interval timer*

*mode register*

*initial-count register*

*terminal count*

An **interval timer** is a special-purpose circuit for generating timing signals for application devices. The 8253 contains three independent counters, labeled channels 0 to 2. Each channel has its own external clock input, a 6-bit **mode register,** a 16-bit **initial-count register,** a gate input, and an output. A counter begins its count with the value held in its initial-count register. It then decrements the count with each tick of its input clock. **Terminal count** occurs when the count reaches zero. When the counter reaches terminal count, the timer generates an output as determined by the value of its mode register. We shall summarize the 8253's modes shortly.

Programming the interval timer means writing values to the three initial-count registers and three mode registers. Because of the timer's design, the CPU can only write values to the mode registers, but it can read and write the count registers. Programming each counter consists of two parts: (1) writing a byte to its mode register, and (2) writing a count to its count register.

The 6 mode-register bits specify a read-write operation, a mode, and whether the timer will use binary-coded-decimal (BCD) or binary arithmetic. The read-write-operation bits specify how the CPU will write values into the count register: (1) most significant byte only, (2) least significant byte only, or (3) both bytes (with least significant byte first). Once the CPU sets the read-write operation, it *must* read or write the count register exactly as the mode register specifies. For example, if a counter expects to get or send a 16-bit value, the CPU must send 2 bytes of data or read 2 bytes of data from it.

The PC uses its own 4.77-MHz (210-ns period) clock signal with a divide-by-4 circuit to clock the timer. It then uses the timer's outputs to regulate its time-of-day clock, to initiate DRAM refresh, and to activate the speaker.

The output from channel 0 of the timer goes directly to the interrupt controller to request a type-0 interrupt (See Fig. 5.7.) A type-0 interrupt informs the CPU to increment its (software) time-of-day clock. The output from channel 1 of the timer goes to the DMA controller's channel 0. The CPU uses channel 0 of the DMA controller to refresh DRAM. The output from channel 2 of the timer goes to the speaker circuits. Various programs load values in the timer to control the speaker's sound frequency and duration.

**Dynamic RAM Refresh**

The IBM PC uses DRAM chips for main memory. They must be refreshed every 2 ms to retain their values. The PC does this by reading data from 128 consecutive memory locations within every 2-ms period. When the system first starts, the CPU programs channel 0 of the DMA controller to read from 64-K consecutive memory locations using single mode and autoinitialization. (It is just as easy to program the DMA controller to read from 64-K consecutive memory locations as it is to program it to read from 128 consecutive locations. Autoinitialization mode tells the DMA controller to repeat the previous operation, i.e., use the same parameters.) The CPU also programs channel 0 of the timer to request DMA channel 0 service every 15 $\mu$s. When the DMA controller gets a request, it reads the next memory location. When it finishes reading from 128 consecutive memory locations, it has refreshed all of DRAM. However, it continues to read consecutive memory locations, one every 15 $\mu$s, until it reads from 65,536 consecutive memory locations. It then starts the process over again.

### 5.3.6 ∎ Floating-point Coprocessor

The Intel 8088 microprocessor does not support floating-point numbers, nor does it have floating-point operations of its own. Applications programs that require floating-point arithmetic, such as graphics design software, generally provide subroutines for that purpose. The subroutines emulate floating-point operations using standard integer, logic, and shift operations. For many programs software emulation is acceptable, but for floating-point-intensive applications, the PC provides a faster alternative: a math coprocessor. A math coprocessor is a special-purpose processor designed to operate in conjunction with a CPU and perform mathematical operations for it. Intel designed the **8087 coprocessor** to enhance the 8088 and 8086 microprocessors, and users can easily add an 8087 to their PCs by inserting it in the prewired chip socket (not a slot) provided for that purpose. In this section we describe the relationship between it and the 8088 CPU.

*8087 coprocessor*

Software that does little floating-point arithmetic may ignore a coprocessor, even if present, and do all arithmetic using the 8088's instruction set. Some software checks for the presence of an 8087 and uses it if available; otherwise it uses software for floating-point. Other software requires the 8087 to be present.

The 8087 provides arithmetic instructions for several categories of data: 16-bit word, 32-bit short integers, 64-bit long integers; 32-bit short floating-point numbers, 64-bit long floating-point numbers, 80-bit temporary floating-point numbers, and 80-bit packed decimal numbers. It thus extends the natural data types of the 8088 CPU. The 8087 is compatible with the IEEE Floating-point Standard 745. The 8087 represents all integers in two's-complement notation. Figure 5.13 summarizes the floating-point representations. The 8087 always reads and writes data 1 byte at a time, lowest-order byte first. It converts all data into temporary floating-point values when it reads them, and it converts them back into their specified types when it writes them. Except for integer add, subtract, multiply, and divide on two-integer operands, all of which produce integer results, the 8087 performs all floating-point arithmetic using the 80-bit temporary floating-point representation.

Unlike the 8088 CPU, the 8087 coprocessor will not operate alone. It requires the support of an 8088 or 8086. Intel manufactures the 8087 in 40-pin DIP package which is pin-compatible with the 8088, and on the PC the pins are wired in parallel.

The 8087 has its own register set, which we shall describe shortly, and a full set of arithmetic instructions (including ADD, SUBTRACT, MULTIPLY, DIVIDE, ABSOLUTE VALUE, CHANGE SIGN, SCALE, ROUND, $LOG_2$, $LOG_e$, SQUARE ROOT, TAN, and ARCTAN). It also provides a variety of support instructions (loads, stores, comparisons, tests, and examinations) and processor-control instructions (INITIALIZE PROCESSOR, ENABLE and DISABLE INTERRUPTS, LOAD and STORE CONTROL WORD, STORE STATUS WORD, LOAD and STORE ENVIRONMENT, SAVE and RESTORE STATE, INCREMENT and DECREMENT STACK POINTER, NO OP, and WAIT). It does not, however, do any address computations, nor does it process interrupts; those are the responsibility of the CPU.

FIGURE 5.13  *8087 (or IEEE) floating-point numbers. The floating-point representations supported by Intel's 8087 numeric coprocessor and the IEEE floating-point standard 745 have the binary point to the left of F1 for short and long reals and between F0 and F1 for temporary reals (as shown). For short and long reals, F0 has an implicit value of 1, which has been elided.*

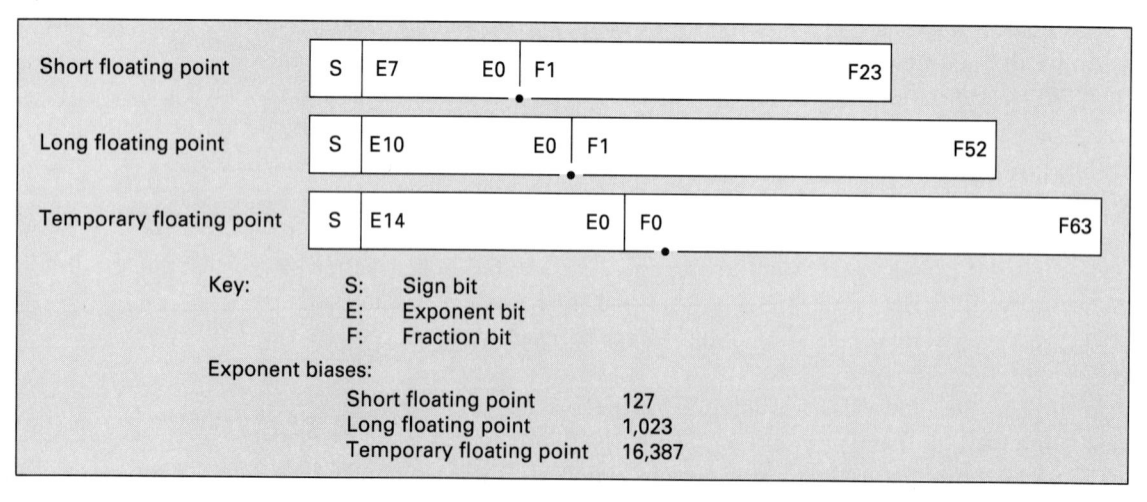

|  |  |
|---|---|
| Short floating point | S \| E7 ... E0 \| F1 ... F23 |
| Long floating point | S \| E10 ... E0 \| F1 ... F52 |
| Temporary floating point | S \| E14 ... E0 \| F0 ... F63 |

Key:
- S: Sign bit
- E: Exponent bit
- F: Fraction bit

Exponent biases:
- Short floating point: 127
- Long floating point: 1,023
- Temporary floating point: 16,387

## 8087 Operation

Following is a brief description of how the coprocessor and the CPU cooperate. During normal operation the 8087 is continually "watching" the bus. Whenever the CPU fetches and decodes an instruction, the 8087 also decodes it. The 8087 can tell when an op code is present by analyzing the CPU's status outputs, and it can tell which byte it is decoding by analyzing the instruction-queue status outputs. The 8087 ignores all instructions except ESCAPE. (See Fig. 5.14.) When an ESCAPE instruction occurs, the CPU and the coprocessor operate in parallel, each responding to ESCAPE with different actions.

When the CPU executes an ESCAPE instruction, it determines the addressing mode (based on the r/m and mod bits in the instruction), generates the address, and fetches the operands. The CPU then ignores these items and proceeds to its next instruction.

When the 8087 executes an ESCAPE, it first determines the instruction's addressing mode by analyzing the CPU's control signals, and then it captures the CPU-generated addresses and operands from the bus. Finally it decodes 6 bits in the ESCAPE instruction that tell the 8087 which operation to perform. (The CPU, however, ignores these 6 bits; from its point of view, ESCAPE is one instruction not two.)

The TEST signal synchronizes the coprocessor. When the CPU executes a WAIT instruction, the hardware checks the TEST input. If TEST = *true*, the CPU stops until TEST = *false*. Whenever the 8087 executes ESCAPE, it initially sets TEST to *true*. When it is done, it changes TEST to *false*. It follows that a programmer can force the CPU to wait for the 8087 to finish executing by placing a WAIT instruction in the program at any point where coprocessor timing is critical, such as prior to using an 8087 result. In addition, a good programming practice is to insert WAIT instructions prior to all ESCAPE instructions to make sure that the coprocessor finishes executing each instruction before giving it a new one.

## Bus Control

The 8087 must get control of the bus when it wants to read or write to memory. (If you recall, the CPU earlier provided the 8087 with the operand and result addresses.) The 8087 then requests to be bus master, and when the CPU can

**FIGURE 5.14** *Format of the* ESC *instruction.*

| 15 | | | | | | | | 8 | 7 | | | | 0 |
|---|---|---|---|---|---|---|---|---|---|---|---|---|---|
| 1 | 1 | 0 | 1 | 1 | X | X | X | mod | X | X | X | r/m | |

give up the bus it responds and relinquishes it. The 8087 recognizes the acknowledgment and takes over as bus master. When the 8087 is done, it returns bus control to the CPU.

Note that the 8087 has no access to the CPU's register set. As a consequence, it can operate only on operands that are stored in memory. (Even though the CPU accesses the operands for the ESCAPE instruction, it ignores them.) Likewise the CPU does not have access to the 8087's registers. Thus the 8087 must place values in memory before the CPU can use them. Although the 8087 can interrupt the CPU, it must place in memory any values it wishes to communicate to the CPU. This includes status information.

**Register Set**

The 8087 has an eight-word register stack, with 80 bits per word. Each stack word has a 2-bit tag that indicates whether it is empty, whether it contains a valid number, 0, or an erroneous result (such as the result of division of zero). The 8087 can read values from memory and push them in the stack, and it can pop values from the stack and store them in memory. Memory operations are subject to the type conversions mentioned earlier. The 8087 can also generate and push several constants onto the stack ($\pi$, $+1$, $-1$, $e$, etc.). It can operate either on stack operands or on memory operands, and it can either push the results on the stack or place them in memory. In addition, individual registers in the stack can serve as operand and result registers.

The 8087 has four additional registers: a control register, a status register, an instruction pointer, and a data pointer. The control register has several functions. It enables or masks 8087-generated interrupts. It specifies arithmetic precision (24, 53, or 64 bits), how the 8087 should round off numbers, and how the 8087 should process invalid results such as division by zero. The status register consists of exception flags, an interrupt-request flag, a condition code, the stack-top pointer, and a busy flag. Finally, the instruction pointer holds the address of the current instruction, and the data pointer holds the address of the operand. The 8087 can write the contents of all these registers to memory (for example, to determine what instruction caused an interrupt), and it can load the control register from memory.

The 8087 coprocessor clearly gives the CPU great performance for numeric processing. Any reader who wishes to explore further should consult one of the manufacturers' reference manuals on the 8087.

## 5.4 ■ Software System

The HSA architects of a computer furnish it with essential physical components—a CPU, a storage system, an I/O system, a timer, and various attached devices. These alone, however, do not define the architecture. Programs must be able to communicate with the hardware devices, so the system architects must assign known I/O port addresses to the hardware devices. The hardware and software together must also provide a suitable execution environment for the software. For example, when the hardware initiates an interrupt and branches to an interrupt handler, the software must not only be able to deal with the source of the interrupt and the interrupt hardware, but it must also be able to return to the interrupted program as though nothing had happened.

Another architectural responsibility is to assign main-memory addresses to special software components of the system, such as the BIOS, that control the hardware. Because BIOS code in the PC is in ROM, it is often called **ROM BIOS** for that reason. Among the responsibilites of BIOS are to initialize the system when the power is first turned on, to program the various support chips, and to control the hardware devices, such as the keyboard, printer, and video screen display.

*ROM BIOS*

This section discusses the software organization of the PC family, including I/O port-address assignments, interrupt-vector assignments, ROM BIOS, and main-memory assignments. We hope that you will gain a deeper understanding of the scope of an architectural family definition by studying these assignments.

## 5.4.1 ■ I/O Port-address Assignments

Table 5.4 shows the I/O port-address assignments made by the PC architects. Although IBM modified several of them when introducing the PC AT, the modifications were generally additions, such as assigning some of the previously unassigned addresses (e.g., 22–2F and 44–5F).

## 5.4.2 ■ ROM BIOS

When a user first turns on the power of a PC, the hardware automatically resets, which begins the process of **system initialization.** The RESET signal goes to all programmable circuits. In response, these circuits initialize certain essential registers. The 8088 microprocessor, for example, clears its segment registers, instruction pointer, and flags register. Circuits that can send data to the buses, such as I/O interfaces and timers, clear the data direction and the control registers. This initializes their bidirectional pins as input pins and prevents them from placing spurious data on the buses.

*system initialization*

After hardware initialization the CPU loads its code-segment register with the value $FFFF_{16}$ and starts executing. As a result, it fetches the first instruction from $FFFF0_{16}$. (Recall that the hardware automatically shifts the content of the segment register 4 bits to the left during address formation.) In the PC, $FFFF0_{16}$ is the beginning of the ROM BIOS initialization code. This software, which finishes the process of system initialization, has a number of general responsibilities:

1. check the reliability of the hardware system:
    - test the first 16 KB of RAM;

**Table 5.4** Standard IBM PC I/O port addresses.

### System Board Components

| | |
|---|---|
| 0–F | 8237A-5 DMA controller |
| 20–21 | 8259A interrupt controller |
| 40–43 | 8253-5 programmable interval timer |
| 60–63 | 8255A-5 programmable parallel interface |
| 80–83 | DMA page registers |
| A0 | NMI mask register |
| C0–DF | Reserved |
| E0–FF | Reserved |
| 100–1FF | Not usable |

### I/O Channel Components

| | |
|---|---|
| 200–20F | Game I/O adapter |
| 210–217 | Expansion unit |
| 220–24F | Reserved |
| 250–277 | Not used |
| 278–27F | Printer controller (secondary parallel port, or LPT2) |
| 2F0–2F7 | Reserved |
| 2F8–2FF | 8250 UART (secondary serial port, or COM2) |
| 300–31F | Prototype card |
| 320–32F | Fixed-disk controller |
| 378–37F | Printer controller (primary parallel port, or LPT1) |
| 380–38C | Synchronous data link control (SDLC) communications or secondary binary synchronous interface |
| 390–39F | Not used |
| 3A0–3A9 | Primary binary synchronous interface |
| 3B0–3B9 | Monochrome display adapter (MDA) and parallel printer port |
| 3C0–3CF | Reserved |
| 3D0–3Df | Color/graphics display adapter (CGA) |
| 3E0–3EF | Reserved |
| 3F0–3F7 | $5\frac{1}{4}''$ floppy-disk controller |
| 3F8–3FF | 8250 UART (primary serial port or COM1) |

- test the processor flags;
- test the processor registers;
- test the ROM containing BIOS;
- test the timer.

2. check and program the programmable devices:
    - program the timer and DMA controller to refresh DRAM;

- test and initialize the interrupt controller;
- test, initialize, and start the video controller;
- test the keyboard;
- test the diskette controller.

3. load the operating system and transfer control to it, after which the operating system enables interrupts.

Aside from system initialization, the primary purpose of ROM BIOS is to provide users with support for performing I/O while relieving them of the responsibility of dealing directly with such hardware as I/O devices, interrupt controller, timer, DMA controller, and keyboard. The ROM BIOS procedures that drive this hardware are meant to be activated through interrupts in a manner to be described shortly. The user does not need to program the DMA controller or even know its port address to write to the disk. Moreover, when a user replaces a hardware device, the only necessary change is to upgrade the ROM BIOS routine that controls that device or to provide RAM BIOS for that purpose.

Once the operating system is in charge, the user software uses BIOS only for performing low-level operations. It invokes the ROM BIOS code by requesting an interrupt and supplying the system with an interrupt-vector number. Recall from Section 5.3.3 the CPU translates an interrupt-vector number into an interrupt-vector address by shifting it to the left by 2 bits (i.e., multiplying it by 4). This implies that the interrupt-vector table is located in main memory at addresses ranging from 0 to $3FF_{16}$. Each interrupt vector within the table is the address of the interrupt handler for that type of interrupt, and some of the addresses are in ROM BIOS. We include Table 5.5 to show the scope of the interrupts. Note that interrupts $19_{16}$ is a call to the bootstrap loader, which is also the final procedure executed during system initialization.

### 5.4.3 ■ Memory-address Assignments

Main memory, also called **conventional memory,** refers to the storage locations that the CPU can reference during an ordinary memory-read or memory-write bus cycle without special hardware. Because the architects who designed the PC selected the 8088 microprocessor as its CPU, they limited the amount of main memory a PC could directly address to 1 MB ($2^{20}$ bytes).

*conventional memory*

The PC architects divided the address space of conventional memory into a number of blocks, which they allocated for various software components. They allocated the largest block, with addresses ranging from 0 K to 640 K, to program memory, which they implemented with DRAM chips.[6] They

---

6. Initially the PC architects only allocated 512 KB to user RAM. However, they allocated an additional 128 KB to user RAM shortly after they released the PC.

**Table 5.5** IBM PC interrupt-vector table.

| Address | Function |
| --- | --- |
| 0 | Divide by zero |
| 1 | Single step |
| 2 | Nonmaskable interrupt (NMI) |
| 3 | Breakpoint instruction |
| 4 | Overflow |
| 5 | Print screen |
| 6, 7 | Reserved |
| 8 | Time-of-day hardware interrupt |
| 9 | Keyboard hardware interrupt |
| A | Reserved |
| B, C | Serial communications hardware interrupts |
| D | Fixed-disk hardware interrupt |
| E | Diskette hardware interrupt |
| F | Printer hardware interrupt |
| 10 | Video I/O call |
| 11 | Equipment-check call |
| 12 | Memory-check call |
| 13 | Diskette I/O call |
| 14 | RS232 I/O call |
| 15 | Cassette I/O call |
| 16 | Keyboard I/O call |
| 17 | Printer I/O call |
| 18 | ROM basic entry code |
| 19 | Bootstrap loader |
| 1A | Time-of-day call |
| 1B | Get-control-of-keyboard break |
| 1C | Get-control-of-timer interrupt |
| 1D | Pointer-to-video initialization table |
| 1E | Pointer-to-diskette parameter table |
| 1F | Pointer-to-graphics character generator |
| 20 | DOS program terminate |
| 21 | DOS function call |
| 23 | DOS CTRL-BRK exit address |
| 24 | DOS fatal-error vector |
| 25 | DOS absolute disk read |
| 26 | DOS absolute disk write |
| 27 | DOS terminate, fix in storage |
| 28–3F | Reserved for DOS |
| 40–5F | Reserved |
| 60–67 | Reserved for user software interrupts |
| 68–7F | Not used |
| 80–85 | Reserved for BASIC |
| 86–F0 | Used by BASIC interpreter while running |
| F1–FF | Not used |

reserved the remaining block, with addresses ranging from 640 K and 1024 K, for ROM BIOS and other system components. Table 5.6 summarizes the allocation of addresses within conventional memory.

Notice the location of the interrupt-vector table. A program clearly cannot occupy that space. Nor can it occupy the 512 bytes between $400_{16}$ and $5FF_{16}$, which the architects allocated to other system software. However, the user can modify the tables and software residing in these addresses and install special software modules. Many programs take advantage of that fact and modify the interrupt-vector table, for example, so an interrupt will branch to the user's routine rather than the predefined system routine. That is how users can add special device handlers to the system.

Notice also that the architects have reserved large blocks of addresses for the monochrome and color graphics adapters. The 8088 does not provide a large enough I/O address space to handle the video-screen buffers (video-display RAM) or the video-display and hard-disk-control ROMs, so the PC simply uses part of the conventional memory-address space for those purposes.

**Expanded Memory**

The area labeled "LIM data area" in Table 5.6 deserves special note. As we mentioned earlier, the maximum address-space size of conventional memory is 1 MB, although the user can use only 640 KB of it. However, by adding special expanded-memory hardware to a PC, the user can increase the amount of available memory to up to 16 MB. We described expanded memory in Section 4.2.4.

In 1984 Lotus, Intel, and Microsoft (LIM) introduced an **Expanded Memory Specification (EMS),** also called **LIM 3.2 EMS.** This standard uses the otherwise-unused block of 64-K conventional addresses for accessing data that is labeled "LIM data area" in Table 5.6. Note that in the 8088 PC these addresses range between 816 K and 880 K, whereas in 80286 and 80386 PCs the LIM data area comprises addresses 784 K to 848 K. The hardware maps those addresses into expanded memory and therefore allows, in addition to the full 640 KB of conventional memory, an additional 64 KB of memory addresses for accessing data. By swapping banks of memory, an EMS card can supply a user with up to 16 MB of expanded memory.

The same hardware can also usually map a block of addresses between 64 K and 640 K into expanded memory, provided there are no RAM chips in the PC that respond to those addresses. (If two devices, e.g., RAM and the expanded memory board, respond to the same address and both assert data on the bus at the same time, they would short circuit and burn out the bus circuits.) However, the PC cannot run programs from expanded memory (only data), so most computers that use EMS memory usually provide the full 640 KB of conventional memory as well. For users with less than 640 K of main memory, many EMS cards allow the user to use up to 640 K of the card's memory as additional main memory and to use the remainder of the card's memory for EMS memory.

*Expanded Memory Specification (EMS) LIM 3.2 EMS*

**Table 5.6**  Reserved memory on the IBM PC, PC AT, and PC clones including those with 80386 CPUs.

| Address[a] | PC Usage | PC AT and 80386 PC Usage |
|---|---|---|
| 960 K–1024 K | ROM BIOS | ROM BIOS |
| 880 K–960 K | Unused | Extra ROM |
| 896 K–960 K | Unused | Extra ROM |
| 880 K–896 K | Unused | Unused |
| 848 K–880 K | LIM data area | Unused |
| 816 K–848 K | LIM data area | LIM data area |
| 800 K–816 K | Hard-disk ROM | LIM data area |
| 784 K–800 K | Unused | LIM data area |
| 768 K–784 K | EGA ROM | EGA ROM |
| 752 K–768 K | Unused | Unused |
| 736 K–752 K | CGA | CGA |
| 720 K–736 K | Unused | Unused |
| 704 K–720 K | MDA | MDA |
| 640 K–704 K | EGA or VGA | EGA or VGA |
| 1536–640 K | User RAM | User RAM |
| 1152–1535 | BASIC, special system RAM | BASIC, special system RAM |
| 1024–1151 | RAM BIOS | RAM BIOS |
| 0–1023 | Interrupt-vector table | Interrupt-vector table |

[a]Addresses below 640 K are available to users; those above 640 K are reserved for system use.

**LIM 4.0 EMS**

**Enhanced Expanded Memory Specification (EEMS)**

### Enhanced Expanded Memory

More recently (1987), Lotus, Intel, and Microsoft adopted an expanded memory standard called **LIM 4.0 EMS** which AST Research, Quadram, and Ashton-Tate originally introduced as **Enhanced Expanded Memory Specification (EEMS)**. LIM 4.0 EMS (EEMS) differs from LIM 3.2 EMS in several important ways. First, it supports more expanded memory—up to 32 MB. Second, it provides a more flexible address-mapping technique. Rather than using only the LIM-data-area addresses, it can map conventional-memory addresses, those within the first 640 K of main memory, into expanded-memory addresses. As a consequence, the PC can run programs directly out of EEMS. An EEMS board can load many programs into expanded memory and almost instantaneously swap between them. Still, the system must not have RAM chips at the same addresses used by the EEMS board. And since most PCs have a minimum of 512 KB of conventional memory, there is a practical limit on the size of a program that it can run in EEMS memory. Nonetheless, EEMS has several important advantages over EMS, including the facts that (1) EEMS can map several nonadjacent conventional memory areas into enhanced memory, (2) the user program can modify the mapped addresses, and (3) the PC can run programs directly out of EEMS memory. Note that programs are still absolutely limited to 640 KB of memory, and in practice they must be considerably smaller.

## 5.5 ∎ Architectural Merit of the PC Architecture

The success of the PC in expanding beyond its originally intended market is a tribute to its designers, who crafted a competent, low-cost computer using the technology at hand. The cost constraints were so severe in 1980 that they had to make many compromises to reduce cost. We shall discuss some of them here.

The PCs were applicable to their target users and were sufficiently general for the intended applications programs. Indeed, a quick look in a software shop will show that their applicability and generality has been sufficient for a much wider range of programs than the original designers could have envisioned. There was little thought of running major scientific programs, so the lack of integral support for floating-point arithmetic then was not a major burden. The fact that the designers included a socket for the floating-point coprocessor even though Intel had not yet manufactured one showed remarkable foresight indeed. It is perhaps unfortunate that Intel did not design its processor to directly support floating-point arithmetic through a mechanism such as a trap on an unused op code, which would have speeded up the interface and improved applicability at little or no extra cost.

When IBM introduced the PC in 1981, memory was expensive and existing personal-computer applications were small; it was hard to imagine a PC requiring more than 640 KB of main memory. Nonetheless, mainframe computers had main memories many times that size, and the PC designers could easily have foreseen that the 640 KB main-memory restriction would be a severe constraint on future applications. However, increasing the address space would have increased the cost and, as a trip to any software store will show, the restricted address space has not prevented the proliferation of software. In fact, the limited address space has actually helped to control the cost of PC hardware, because virtually all pre-1990 programs were designed to run with no more than 640 KB of memory. (In contrast, because the Macintosh has always supported more memory, many Macintosh programs required over 1 MB.)

As IBM demonstrated when it left the low end of the PC business to others, the PC architecture allows low cost implementations and is easy to design. However, because of the small address space the narrow memory access of only 1 byte, it is not possible to build high-performance PCs. Applications requiring high performance have awaited the extensions introduced by the PC AT, the 80386 and 80486 PC clones, and other newer machines.

The issues of ease of use, malleability, and expandability have largely been described already for the memory space and system speed. The PC has allowed evolution to newer, higher-performance designs and expansion to larger systems. It could not directly support those desirable features itself.

In assessing the architectural merit of the PC, a proverbial expression comes to mind: You can recognize the Pioneers—they are the ones with arrows in their backs. Most of the personal computers that preceded the PC have died, stuck full of arrows. The PC had enough merit and a big enough name plate to evolve into a good design and establish a number of microcomputer standards, even though it lacked many of the desirable features of a computer architecture.

On system performance the PC was better than adequate when IBM introduced it. As applications grew in complexity, the major performance bottleneck for most users turned out to be the disk storage system. Thus, when users added hard disks to PCs, most of them saw tremendous improvements in speed. Many applications now require the newer, higher-performance personal computers, but many PC users cannot see the extra CPU speed offered by the fastest 80286 chips, nor by the 80386 and 80486 chips.

For all but the most casual users, a hard disk is now essential. Part of the importance, we must point out, stems from the relatively small PC memory. In many applications, faster disks substitute for more main memory.

# Summary

Using the IBM PC as an example, this chapter presented an overview of a complete computer system. We described the CPU, its instruction set, and its operation. We described a number of support chips, including a bus controller, a programmable interrupt controller, a DMA controller, two I/O interfaces, and a floating-point coprocessor. Finally, we described the software-hardware interface, including the responsibilities of ROM BIOS, the I/O port-address assignments, and the memory-address assignments.

The IBM PC uses the Intel 8088 microprocessor, a 16-bit microprocessor with an 8-bit data bus and a 20-bit address bus, and it uses an expanded local bus called the PC I/O Channel Bus. The CPU generates status signals, which the bus controller translates into bus control signals. In addition to address, data, and power lines, the bus includes interrupt-request lines, DMA request and acknowledge lines, and independent memory and I/O control lines. The bus circuitry includes address latches and data transceivers.

The 8088 CPU recognizes two types of interrupt requests, maskable and nonmaskable. The PC interrupt controller manages maskable interrupt requests, which arrive from the keyboard logic, a timer, and the DMA controller. The interrupt controller prioritizes interrupts, masks them, acknowledges them, and generates interrupt-vector numbers, which it sends to the CPU when requested.

The PC uses a programmable DMA controller to transfer data between the serial and parallel I/O interfaces and memory, and it uses a flexible PPI for communicating with I/O devices. Programmability gives the user or operating system versatile control over the DMA controller and PPIs. The PPIs, for example, support a variety of I/O options and handshakes, which the PC uses to read configuration switches, the keyboard, RAM parity, and the I/O channel status, and to control several devices, including the speaker.

The PC uses a programmable interval timer to initiate DRAM refresh, to control the speaker's tone, and to drive a time-of-day clock. It uses a UART for serial communications with a modem, for example.

The CPU communicates with system devices by reading or writing to their port addresses, and we presented the PC's I/O port address assignments. Similarly, the hardware and software communicate with BIOS by raising specific types of interrupts, and we showed the PC's interrupt-vector table. Finally, the system architects reserved various main memory addresses for the interrupt-vector table, RAM BIOS, BASIC, user RAM, and other system options, such as the video-display memory and hard-disk ROM.

The PC family has grown or evolved to include a wide variety of computers and a large number of clones. Newer family members include 80286-, 80386-, and 80486-brand machines-ATs. The PC I/O Bus uses an 8-bit data path, while the PC AT I/O Bus uses a 16-bit data path. Although IBM never standardized a 32-bit PC bus, an independent consortium of PC manufacturers recently introduced the EISA bus, which promises to extend the life of the PC family.

## Exercises

*5.1* For a two-way set associative cache with 8K 32-bit words, how many bytes of SRAM are in each bank of cache memory?

*5.2* Explain why address buses on PCs are unidirectional while data buses are bidirectional. Explain why the CPU chip uses some pins for both data and addresssses.

*5.3* Explain why DMA I/O is faster than CPU-controlled I/O for the PC.

*5.4* How many milliseconds does it take the DMA controller to read 128 consecutive storage locations if it accesses one every 15 $\mu s$? Assuming the DMA controller reads from 65,536 consecutive memory locations before it autoinitializes, how many times does it refresh memory before it autoinitializes?

*5.5* Suppose a 16-bit PC executes at the rate of 1 MIPS. Its disk rotates at 3600 rpm, has a head seek time averaging 30 ms, and has a transfer rate of 500 KBS. How many instructions can the PC execute during the average rotational latency? How many instructions can it execute during the average delay in positioning the head?

*5.6* With reference to the system described in Exercise 5.5, what are the advantages and disadvantages of DMA I/O? If the data are stored in a 2-byte I/O buffer, can the CPU keep up with the disk (assuming two instructions are required to move each byte pair from the buffer to memory)?

*5.7* Name four applications where adding the following devices would substantially improve the performance of a PC:

    a. a math coprocessor,
    b. a higher-performance disk system,
    c. a higher-performance CPU chip.

**5.8** How would adding a cache affect the performance of a 4.77 MHz PC (like the original 8088-based IBM PC)? How might it affect the performance of a 20, 25, or 33 MHz 80386- or 80486-based PC? State clearly your assumptions.

**5.9** What advantage is there in having separate memory-read, memory-write, I/O-read, and I/O-write control lines on the PC I/O Channel Bus?

## Reference-needed Exercises

**5.10** Refer to an Intel 8088 microprocessor manual. Based on the values in the segment-override prefix, what op codes are disallowed for instructions?

**5.11** Using a manual for the Intel 8088 or the IBM PC, work through an interrupt and return-from-interrupt sequence to show that after being restored to execution, an interrupted program will run as though it had not been interrupted in the first place.

**5.12** Identify as many reasons as you can that limit the size of a program that can execute out of EEMS (LIM 4.0) memory.

**5.13** Consult an Intel 8088 manual and determine what happens when address addition overflows. [Adding the largest segment address to the largest effective address, $(2^{20} - 16) + (2^{16} - 1)$, yields more than a 20-bit value for the physical address.]

**5.14** Find the I/O port addresses for the registers of the system board DMA chip. Do the same for the system board 8253 interval timer.

## Discussion/Team Problems

**5.15** How would adding virtual memory affect the following?
   a. a PC that runs MS-DOS;
   b. a PC that runs Windows.

**5.16** The interrupt controller provides interrupt-vector numbers to the CPU. What alternative would there be if it did not do this?

**5.17** Identify as many reasons as you can why the PC architects may have chosen to decode only 10 I/O address lines.

**5.18** The clock cycle of the IBM PC is about 210 ns, almost as fast as that of the VAX 11/780 at 200 ns. Yet the PC is much slower than the VAX 11/780. Explain. (*Hint:* Consider differences that might result from 32-bit buses versus 8-bit or 16-bit buses.)

# Chapter Index

8086 microprocessor 233
8087 coprocessor 269
8088 microprocessor 233
80286 microprocessor 234
80386 microprocessor 235
80386SX microprocessor 235
80486 microprocessor 235
addressing-mode byte 242
asynchronous transmission 266
basic input-output system (BIOS) 236
basic I/O mode of PPI 262
baud rate 265
bidirectional bus mode of PPI 262
bidirectional pins 245
bit time 265

card 237
chip set 237
code segment 244
Color Graphics Adapter (CGA) 235
conventional memory 275
coprocessor 238
CPU address 242
daisy chaining 254
data bit 265
data segment 244
data set 266
data terminal 266
daughter board 237
displacement byte 242
DMA autoinitialization 253
DMA base address 253

DMA base count 253
DMA block mode 254
DMA cascade mode 254
DMA command register 254
DMA current address 253
DMA current count 253
DMA demand mode 254
DMA mask register 254
DMA mode register 253
DMA request register 254
DMA single mode 253
DMA status register 254
DMA temporary address register 254
DMA temporary count register 254
DMA temporary register 254

Enhanced Expanded Memory Specification (EEMS) 278
Enhanced Graphics Adapter (EGA) 235
Expanded Memory Specification (EMS) 277
Extended Graphics Array (XGA) 236
Extended Industry Standard Architecture (EISA) bus 236
extra segment 244
framing error 266
handshaking 262
idle 265
IBM PC 232
Industry Standard Architecture (ISA) bus 237
initial-count register 268
interrupt-acknowledge sequence 249
interrupt-initiation sequence 250
interrupt-vector address 250
interval timer 268
latch 239
LIM 3.2 EMS 277
LIM 4.0 EMS 278
mainframe computer 232
mark bit 265
Monochrome Display Adapter (MDA) 235
Micro Channel Architecture (MCA) 235
microcomputer 237
microprocessor 233
minicomputer 232
modem 266
mod field 243
mode register (8253 timer) 268
mother board 237
op-code byte 242
overrun error 266
parallel I/O 260
parity error 266
PC AT 234
PC AT Bus 234
PC AT I/O Channel Bus 234
PC Bus 234
PC clone 236
PC I/O Channel Bus 234
personal computer 232
programmable parallel interface (PPI) 255
PS/2 235
Real Address mode 234
receiver clock 266
reg field 243
r/m field 243
ROM BIOS (basic input-output system) 273
segment-override-prefix byte 242
serial I/O 260
slot 237
stack segment 244
stop bit 265
strobed mode of PPI 262
supercomputer 232
system board 237
system initialization 273
terminal count 268
time-division-multiplexed (TDM) pin 245
transmitter clock 266
universal asynchronous receiver transmitter (UART) 255
Video Graphics Array (VGA) 235
wait state 247

# 6
## Pipelining and RISCs

**6.1 Pipelining** 286
    6.1.1 Arithmetic-unit Pipelining 289
    6.1.2 Instruction-unit Pipelining 294
    6.1.3 Scheduling Functional Units 298
**6.2 Pipelined Vector Processors** 304
**6.3 Reduced-instruction-set Computers** 306
    6.3.1 Historical Perspective 308
    6.3.2 RISC-CISC Controversy 309
    6.3.3 RISC Implementation Techniques 312

*In this chapter we focus on pipelining, the first of two major techniques for speeding up a computer. (Chapter 7 will discuss the second technique — parallel processing.) We discuss both arithmetic and instruction-decoding pipelines (Sections 6.1.1 and 6.1.2), and show how an instruction-set architecture (ISA) can limit the effectiveness of pipelining (Section 6.1.2). Then we illustrate how instruction-decoding pipelines schedule functional units (Section 6.1.3). In Section 6.2 we describe how vector-processing machines use pipelining, and we conclude in Section 6.3 with a detailed discussion of RISCs, computers with ISAs designed specifically to allow for efficient pipelined implementations.*

> **Key Terms**
>
> **Branch penalty** The delay that occurs in a pipelined instruction unit when a conditional branch succeeds and the hardware must purge nonbranch instructions that are already in the pipeline.
>
> **Delayed branch** Some reduced-instruction-set computers (RISCs) use delayed branch instructions to avoid the branch penalty. The compiler moves an independent instruction (or a NO OP instruction) into the position following a branch instruction. The CPU always executes the instruction following a branch instruction, whether or not the branch occurs.
>
> **Flowthrough time** The time it takes the first result to emerge from a pipeline once the CPU has placed the operands in it.
>
> **Instruction issue** The last process performed by an instruction-decoding pipeline. Instruction issue typically consists of reserving a functional unit, sending an operation code to it, and reserving the result register.
>
> **Pipeline (pipe)** A pipelined computer unit, such as an instruction decoder or arithmetic unit.
>
> **Pipelining** A hardware technique that allows many operations to execute concurrently, in assembly-line fashion, by dividing the operations into stages and providing special hardware for each stage.
>
> **Unifunction pipe** A pipelined functional unit that can perform only a single operation or a group of closely allied ones, such as add and subtract, or divide and square root.

The use of parallelism has been a major design objective since computer architects proposed the first digital computers in the late 1940s. Parallelism can take many forms:

1. concurrent processing of I/O using independent processors;
2. concurrent memory accesses using multiported storage systems and interleaved memory;
3. concurrent execution of instructions using pipelined functional units;
4. concurrent decoding of instructions using pipelined control units;

5. concurrent execution of instructions using multiple functional units;
6. concurrent transmission of data between devices using multiple buses.

In earlier chapters we briefly examined items 1 and 2, and in Chapter 7 we will take a look at item 6. Items 3 to 5 are the subject of this chapter.

## 6.1 ■ Pipelining

**serial processing**

A designer can decompose almost any process into stages. **Serial processing** is the execution of all stages of one process before starting the first stage of the next process. Thus one process completely finishes before the next is begun. A computer often executes the same staged process many times in succession. Rather than simply execute each staged process serially, a processor can speed up the processing through **pipelining**, in which it overlaps the stages of the repeating process. Figure 6.1 illustrates the basic principle of pipelining for a process with three stages.

**pipelining**

A pipelined unit, like a factor assembly line, consists of several processing stations, each of which performs a different stage in the total process. When this unit carries out a sequence of computations, each station repeatedly performs the same step, only on different elements in the sequence. As a result, the processor carries out many different computations concurrently, but at any given time each computation is in a different stage of execution.

As an analogy, consider how a teacher might use a class of students to collate an uncollated report. The teacher begins by handing the stack of first pages to the first student, who takes one and passes the remainder to the second student. Each student in turn takes one page and hands the remainder of the stack to the next student. As soon as the first student hands the page-1 stack to the second student, the teacher hands the first student the stack of second pages. If there are 15 pages in all, the teacher repeats the process 15 times, as does each student in the class. After handing the stack of last pages to the second student, the first student hands the collated report to the second student, who adds her or his collated report to the stack and passes it on. Finally, the last student hands the entire stack of collated reports back to the teacher. In the analogy, each student represents one processing stage in a pipeline and the class represents the pipeline itself. The pipeline processes numerous data (the pages) and produces a single result (the stack of collated reports). A corresponding arithmetic pipeline might process numerous data, say the elements in two matrices, and produce a single result, a product matrix.

Now let us analyze how effective the pipeline is. A teacher who does not have the students to help with the reports might begin by creating 40 stacks consisting of the first page of the report, with pages placed face down. The second step would be to add the second page to each stack, face down. After placing the 15th page on each stack, the teacher would pick up the collated reports. Suppose it takes 2 seconds for the teacher or students to perform a single step in the process. If the teacher works alone, processing each page takes 2 seconds for each of 40 reports plus an additional 80 seconds to pick up

**FIGURE 6.1** *Decomposition of a process into stages and the serial and pipelined execution of the same process. Time runs horizontally to the right. $T_s$, serial processing time; $T_g$, processing time for one stage; $T_p$, total staged processing time.*

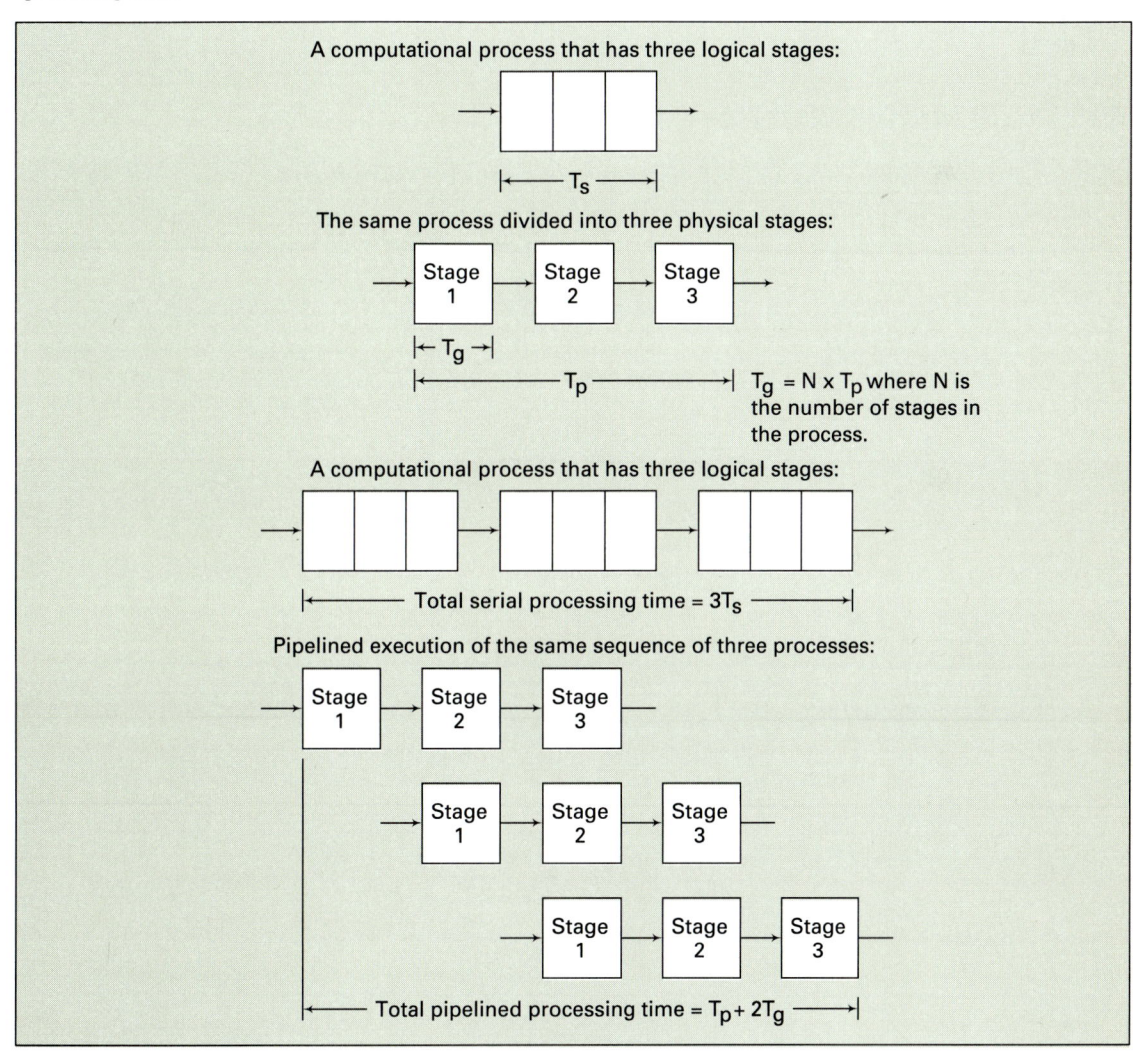

A computational process that has three logical stages:

The same process divided into three physical stages:

$T_g = N \times T_p$ where N is the number of stages in the process.

A computational process that has three logical stages:

Total serial processing time = $3T_s$

Pipelined execution of the same sequence of three processes:

Total pipelined processing time = $T_p + 2T_g$

the collated reports. The total is 1280 seconds. If the teacher works with the students, the teacher is done after 30 seconds (2 seconds/page × 15 pages). If there are 40 students in the class, the entire process takes 30 + 2 × 40 = 110 seconds, which is 11.6 times faster.

In a computer, circuitry replaces the students in our analogy. The computer designers divide critical processes, such as instruction processing, into stages, and develop special circuitry to process each stage. Latches (fast registers) hold the operands for each stage and hence the results of the previous stage. A clock synchronizes all stages in the pipeline by telling the latches when to read the results of the current stage and make them available to the next stage. The **pipeline** (also called the **pipe**) consists of all the circuits for the individual stages together with the latches that separate them (see Figure 6.2).

**pipeline**
**pipe**

**FIGURE 6.2**  *Components of a simple pipeline.*

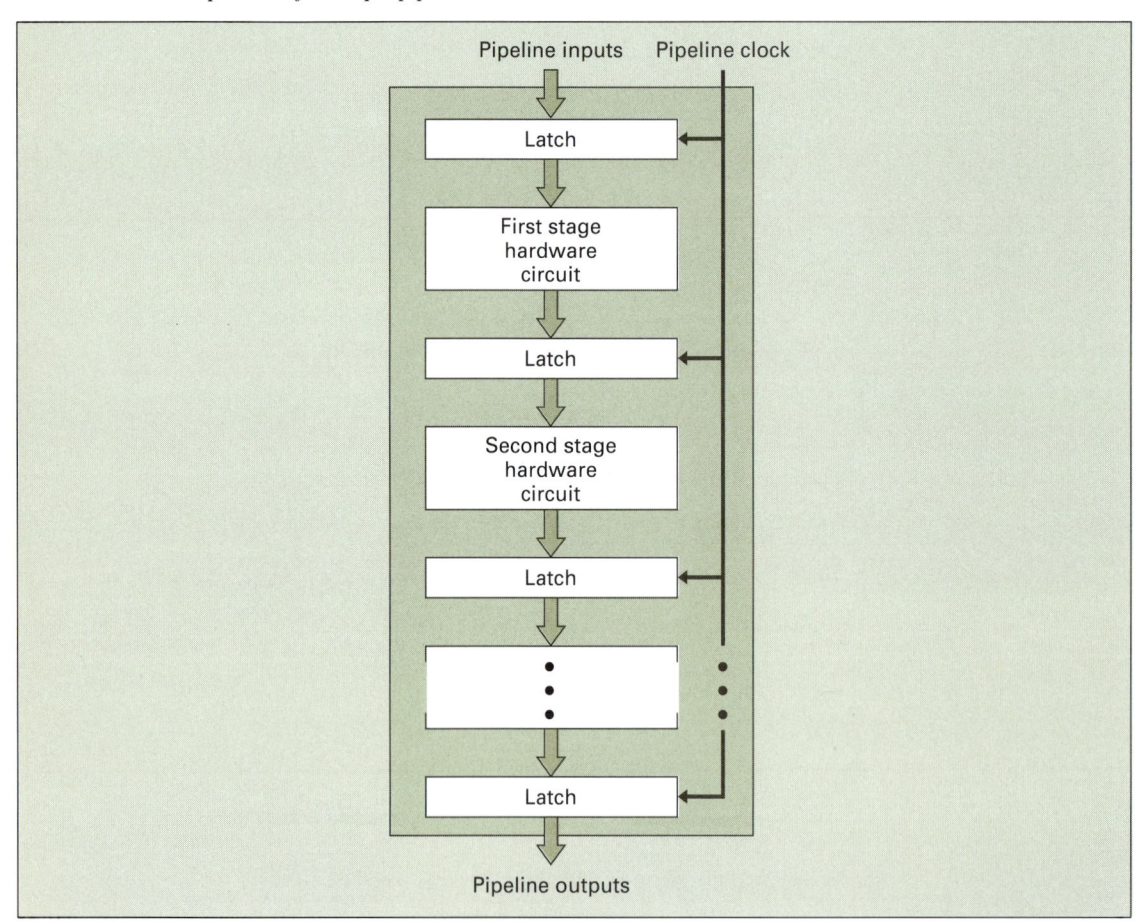

For a given pipeline, the time it takes the pipe to produce its first result is the **flowthrough time;** the time it takes the pipe to produce subsequent results is its **clock-cycle time.** In our teacher analogy, the clock-cycle time is 2 seconds while the flowthrough time is 110 seconds.

Computer designers have used various types of pipelines for a variety of different computational processes. **Unifunction pipes** implement a single function, such as multiplication or instruction decoding, whereas **multifunction pipes** are more general: A control unit can configure them for a variety of operations.

Pipelines generally fall into one of two broad categories: **arithmetic-unit pipelines** and **instruction-unit pipelines,** and the design principles for these two categories are quite different. For example, arithmetic-unit pipelines tend to be most useful for vector operations, while instruction-unit pipelines tend to be most useful for computers with simplified instruction sets—RISCs. We shall explore the differences and some of the design alternatives in the following sections.

*flowthrough time*
*clock-cycle time*

*unifunction pipes*
*multifunction pipes*

*arithmetic-unit pipelines*
*instruction-unit pipelines*

## 6.1.1 ■ Arithmetic-unit Pipelining

We shall illustrate the development of an arithmetic pipeline by considering unsigned binary multiplication. (Note, however, that this is but one of many alternate decompositions for the same operation.) First consider an example of binary multiplication as one might carry it out using pencil and paper:

```
        10111011      multiplicand
    ×    1101001      multiplier
        10111011
        00000000
        00000000
        10111011
        00000000
        10111011
    +   10111011
    ─────────────
    100110010110011   product                              (1)
```

To see how this comes about, notice that the multiplier can be written as $1 + 1000 + 100000 + 1000000$ and that $(1 + 1000 + 100000 + 1000000) \times 10111011$ becomes $10111011 + 10111011000 + 10111011 00000 + 10111011 000000$. These summands are the nonzero rows that are added in Eq. (1), where the colored zeros are unwritten in Eq. (1).

We can now separate Eq. (1) into a series of shifts and additions, as follows:

```
        10111011           multiplicand
      × 1101001            multiplier
        10111011           (1 × 2⁰ × 10111011)
      + 00000000           (0 × 2¹ × 00000000)
       010111011           intermediate result 1
      + 00000000           (0 × 2² × 10111011)
       0010111011          intermediate result 2
      +   10111011         (1 × 2³ × 10111011)
       11010010011         intermediate result 3
      +   00000000         (0 × 2⁴ × 10111011)
       011010010011        intermediate result 4
      +     10111011       (1 × 2⁵ × 10111011)
       1110111110011       intermediate result 5
      +      10111011      (1 × 2⁶ × 10111011)
       100110010110011     final product                (2)
```

The values printed in color are those that appear in the final product because only the value 0 is added to them. Finally the shifts and additions become the processing stages in a pipelined multiplier. (Notice that multiplying a binary number by $2^n$ is equivalent to shifting it to the left by $n$ bits and inserting zeros on the right.)

Figures 6.3 and 6.4 (on page 292) show binary multipliers, which are direct implementations of this computation. Figure 6.3 shows the flowthrough (nonpipelined) version; and Fig. 6.4 the final pipelined version. The adders add two 8-bit binary values to produce 8-bit results (with carry), and the bus gates either output all 0s (if the control input is a $0_2$), or they output their inputs (if the control input is a $1_2$). Figure 6.4 shows the latches that appear between the pipeline stages, but it does not show the clock signals. Notice that the latches hold all temporary values that the following stage needs.

**pipeline granularity**
**pipeline variability**

There are any number of different ways to decompose a given operation. **Pipeline granularity** refers to the coarseness of the decomposition, and **pipeline variability** refers to the number of ways the control unit of a multifunction pipeline can configure it for different operations. Figure 6.5 illustrates two different ways to pipeline a floating-point multiplication and illustrates that tradeoffs exist between the flowthrough time of a pipeline and the clock rate. The clock rate is the reciprocal of the time it takes the slowest stage to complete its work, but to decrease the stage time implies a finer decomposition and therefore more stages. Because of the latches, the flowthrough time increases as the number of stages increases. Figure 6.6 illustrates the dynamically reconfigurable pipeline used by the Texas Instruments Advanced Scientific Computer (TI ASC). The TI ASC control unit programs the pipe based on the operation the pipeline is to perform.

see Case Study 8

Figure 6.5 shows that to multiply two floating-point numbers the pipelines add exponents and multiply mantissas. This is because

$$M_1 R^{E_1} \times M_2 R^{E_2} = M_1 M_2 \times R^{E_1} R^{E_2} = M_1 M_2 R^{E_1+E_2},$$

where $M$, $R$, and $E$ refer to the mantissas, the radix, and the exponents, respectively. Finally, the resulting products may need normalization. The left

---

**FIGURE 6.3** *Flowthrough design of an unsigned-binary multiplier showing the first four stages. $I_1$ through $I_4$ represent the intermediate results in Eq. (2).*

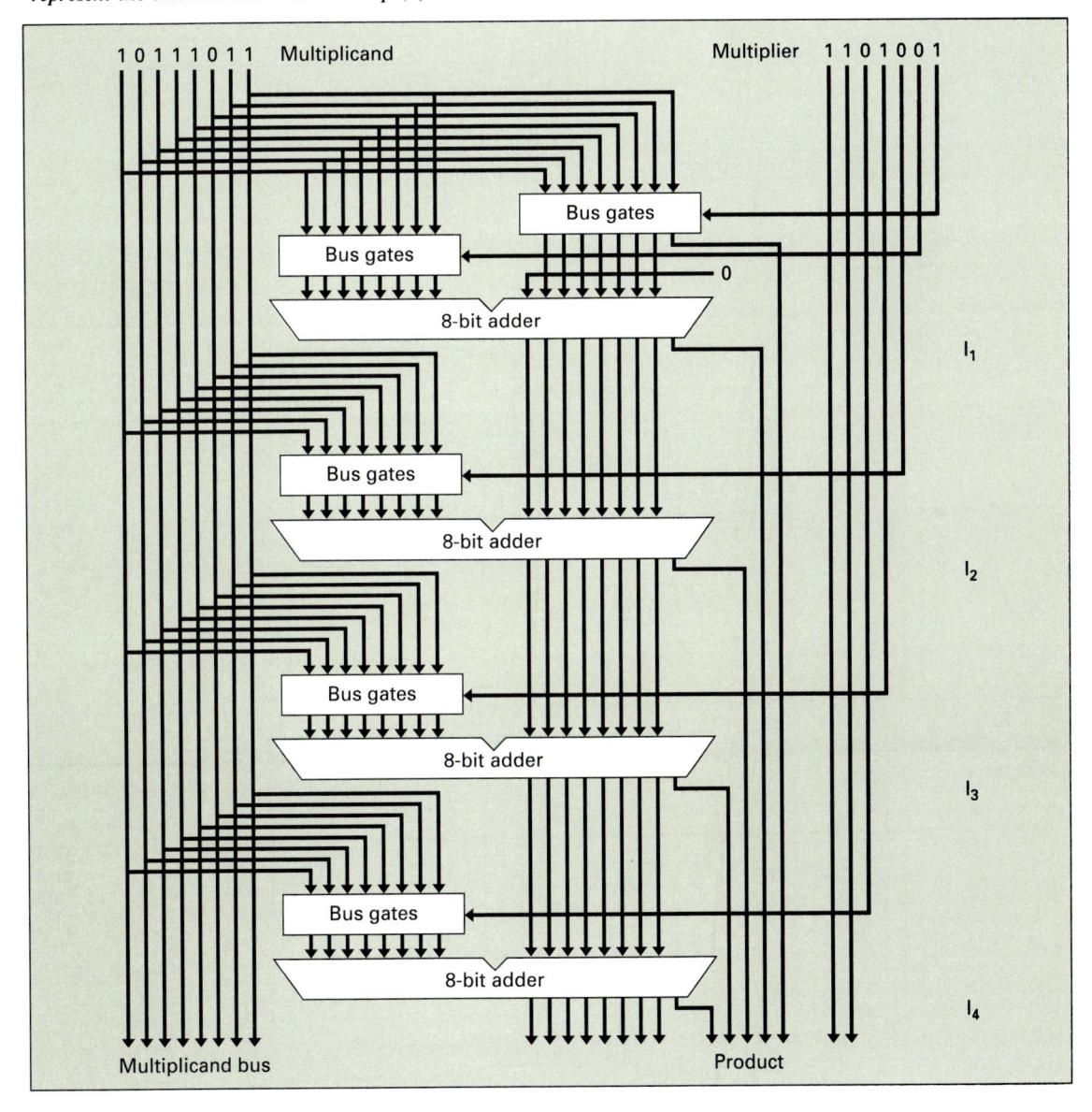

Stages 1

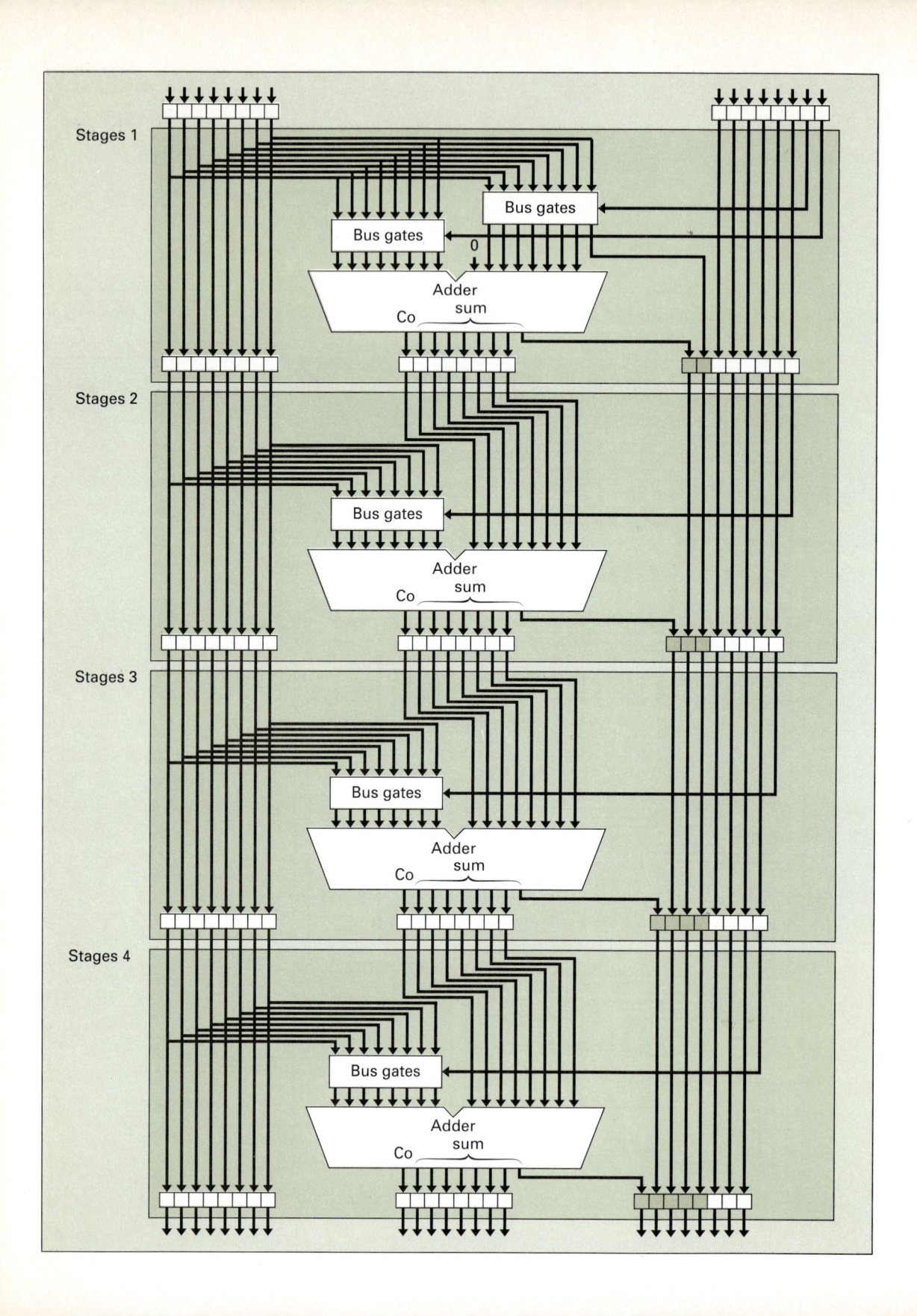

Stages 2

Stages 3

Stages 4

pipeline in Fig. 6.5 has a coarse granularity; the pipeline at the right has a finer granularity because the multiplication circuit has been divided into stages. The resulting pipeline is faster but has a longer flowthrough time.

When a CPU can keep an arithmetic pipeline full, the pipeline can produce a result with every clock cycle. Thus a designer would like to speed up the clock as much as possible while at the same time keep the pipeline full.

FIGURE 6.4 *(On page 292).* *First four stages of a pipelined, unsigned-binary multiplier. The latches are represented by the three groups of eight boxes at the bottom of each stage. The shaded latches at the right of each stage hold the bits of the final product. These bits correspond to the values printed in color in Eq. (2). Co, carry out.*

FIGURE 6.5 *Two floating-point pipelines for reciprocal floating-point multiplication. The highly pipelined unit on the right produces vector results at a higher rate but takes more time to do a single multiplication.*

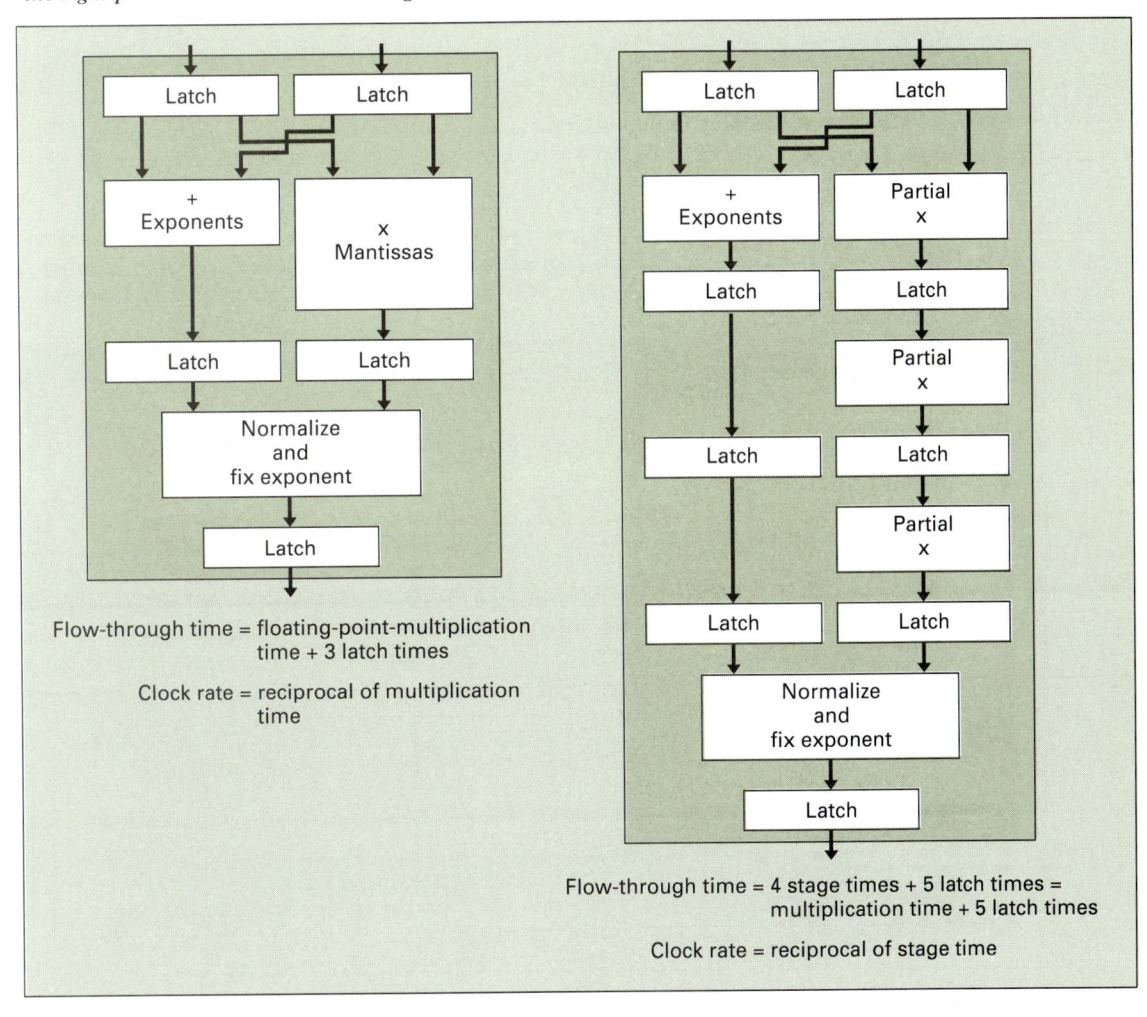

However, these competing goals are difficult to achieve simultaneously. Keeping a pipeline full requires code with sequences of identical computations (vector code), but vector code is the exception rather than the rule, and compilers are usually unable to produce code sequences that utilize fast pipelines. Pipelines that are very fast generally have many stages, and therefore the flowthrough time is long, but the flowthrough time determines how quickly a pipeline can perform an unrepeated computation (a scalar operation). Yet most compilers produce scalar code (sequences of scalar operations) rather than vector code.

In addition, there is a high cost associated with keeping a very fast pipeline supplied with operands: The instruction unit must be able to fetch and decode instructions at the same speed, and the storage system must have sufficient bandwidth to supply both the pipeline with operands and to accept the corresponding results for storage. Section 6.1.2 will focus on the responsibility of the instruction-processing unit and techniques for speeding up instruction processing, and Section 6.2 will briefly discuss pipelined vector processors.

### 6.1.2 ■ Instruction-unit Pipelining

For a conventional computer with a program in main memory, executing an instruction has several logical parts. First, the CPU must determine the address

FIGURE 6.6  *The TI ASC pipeline showing routing topologies for floating-point addition (left) and fixed multiplication (right). The figure does not show the interstage latches. The stage preceding the output stage is an accumulator and is used for computations such as scalar product.*

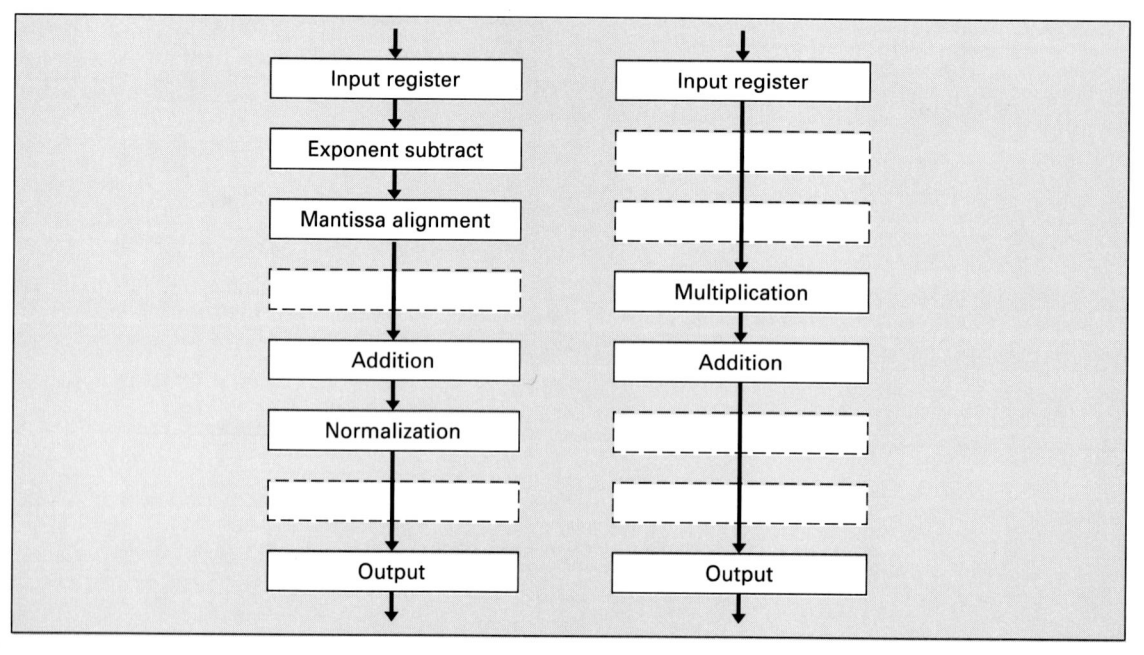

of the instruction and fetch it from memory (or from a cache). Next, the control unit must analyze the op code. For operate instructions, it must determine the address of each operand, the operation to be performed, and the address of the result. Each address determination may take many steps depending on the complexity of the addressing mode. For memory-indirect addressing modes, address generation may require several memory accesses and take an unpredictable amount of time. Fetching the operands also may take an unpredictable amount of time due to memory contention, which occurs when several different processors attempt simultaneous accesses to the same bank of memory. For branch instructions, the control unit must determine whether the branch test succeeds; if it does, the control unit must then replace the content of the program counter (PC) with the branch-target address and then fetch the branch-target instruction. To speed up the process some control units prefetch the branch-target instruction; that is, fetch it before performing the branch test. Figure 6.7 illustrates some of the times involved during the fetch and execution of a typical operate instruction for a simple machine.

Figure 6.8 illustrates the times it would take a pipeline to process five instructions, $I_1$ to $I_5$, assuming that the pipeline can compute the instruction address with a one-stage process and that other stages can operate at the same speed.

A number of events may decrease the rate at which instructions can flow through a pipeline. First, the functional units must be able to keep up with

**FIGURE 6.7** *Stages of fetching and executing a single memory-resident operate instruction. If the memory-cycle time is very long, there may be a delay between the time the operand address is ready and the time the storage system can start to fetch the operand.*

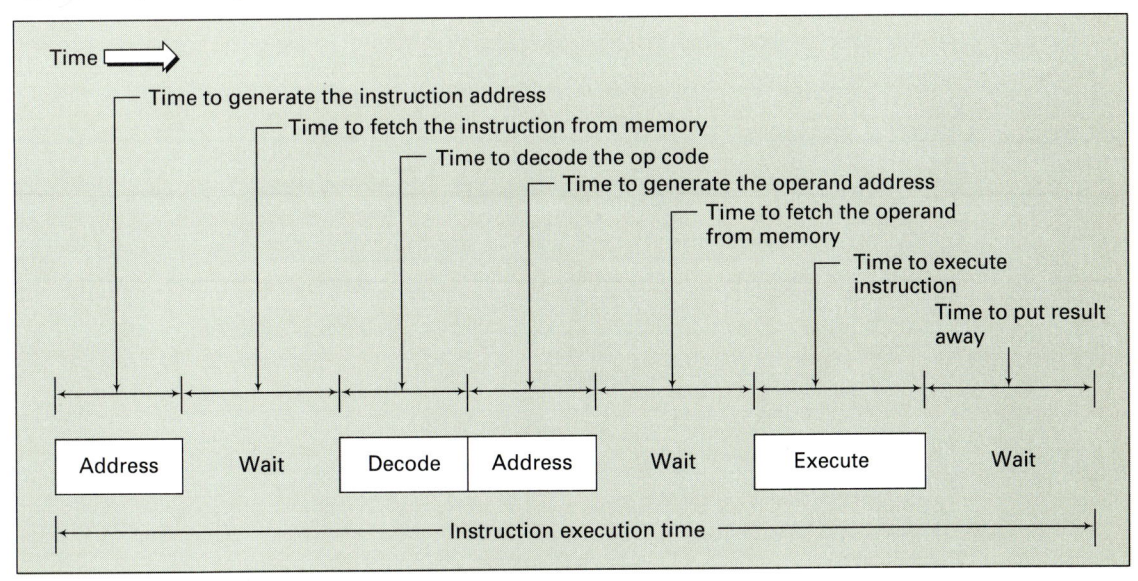

the instruction unit. Some operations, particularly floating-point operations, take more than 1 clock cycle to complete. Second, **interinstruction dependencies** can prevent parallelism. Two examples of interinstruction dependency are where one instruction must write a value to a register that holds the current source for another instruction, and where two or more instructions must write values to the same result register. Third, the storage system must be able to supply instructions to the instruction unit at the same rate the instruction unit can process them (i.e., the memory bandwidth must be sufficiently high).

Another limiting factor is that the instruction unit must logically execute some instructions sequentially, such as conditional branches. When the control unit processes a conditional branch instruction, it may need to hold up the execution of successive instructions until it can determine the outcome of the branch test.[1] If the branch test succeeds, the control unit must **flush the pipeline,** that is, purge all instructions that followed the conditional branch instruction into the pipeline. It must then refill the pipeline beginning with the instruction at the branch-target address. The time required to refill the pipeline after a conditional branch succeeds is called the **branch penalty.** The

---

1. Some computers allow successive instructions to execute but not to store their results. If the branch follows the expected path, the control unit then allows the instructions to store their results; otherwise it purges the results from the execution unit.

---

FIGURE 6.8  *Parallelism possible when a pipelined instruction unit can process one address after another without hesitation. Notice that, with the illustrated timing, about eight instructions would be executing at the same time. Thus, under ideal conditions, instruction throughput could increase by a factor of 8. $I_1$–$I_5$, instructions; Address, time to decode an instruction or operand address; Dec, time to decode the op code; Execute, time to execute the instruction.*

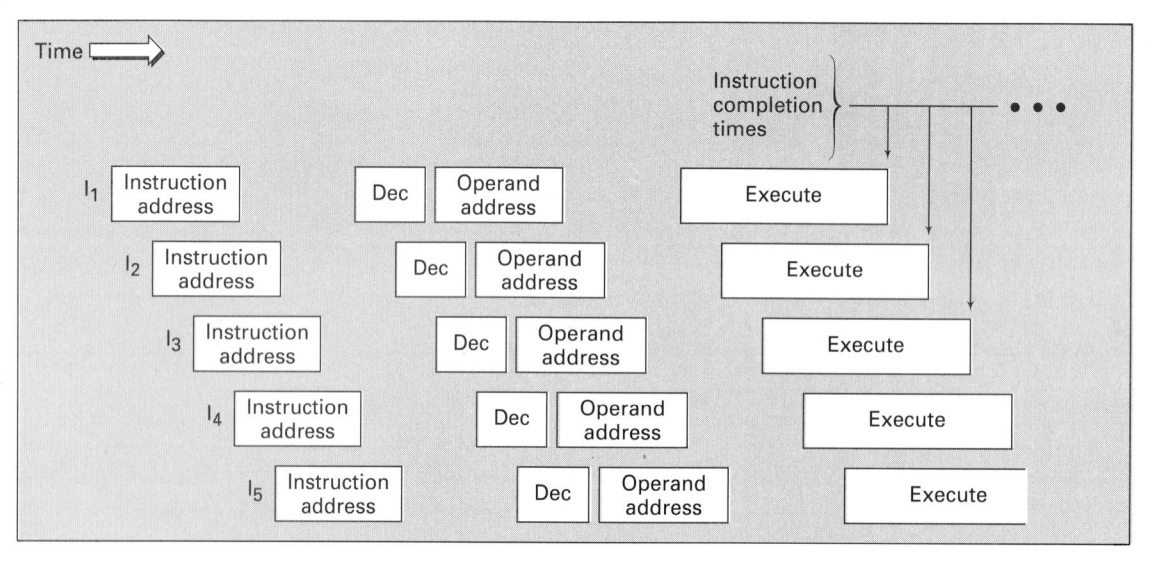

branch penalty is equal in clock cycles to the number of stages in the pipe. The tradeoff between the number of stages in the pipeline (hence the branch penalty) and the clock-cycle time is an important design consideration.

In general, a pipeline with more stages requires more circuitry to handle architectural and machine-organization interlocks. For example, suppose a STORE instruction writes to the address of an instruction that is already in the pipeline. Without adequate hardware tests, the CPU might modify the instruction in memory but not the copy that is already in the pipeline. If the ISA allows for program self-modification, the control unit must be able to detect this type of dependency and recover from it, either by updating the instruction in the pipeline or by flushing and refilling the pipeline. Both the complexity of the circuitry for detecting this type of dependency, and the time it takes to recover from one, depend on the number of stages in the pipeline.

To illustrate the tradeoffs, the instruction-decoding pipeline of the CDC 6600 is particularly simple. (Refer to the *Case Studies* for details.) First of all, all CDC 6600 operate instructions are register-to-register instructions. Thus the instruction unit does not need to resolve operand addresses, nor does it need to fetch operands. Second, instructions are either 15 or 30 bits long and have only two formats. Thus the instruction-decoding pipeline can easily decode them. Because the CDC 6600 does not support program self-modification, the instruction unit does not need to detect write operations to addresses of instructions that are already in the pipeline. Finally, conditional branch instructions test the contents of operational registers, not a condition-code register, so the pipeline can determine when to perform the branch test by checking the specified result register.

see Case Study 2

For complex-instruction-set computers (CISCs), like members of the IBM System/370, VAX, Burroughs, Motorola 68000, and Intel $80x86$ families, pipelining the control unit is much more difficult, for several reasons. For instructions with operands in memory, the control unit must resolve the addresses, a process that often takes many clock cycles depending on the complexity of the addressing modes. For conditional branch instructions that test a condition-code register, the control unit must wait for the completion of all condition-code-setting instructions. Furthermore, it must not issue other instructions until it evaluates the outcome of the branch. If the ISA allows a program to modify itself, the instruction unit must have appropriate hardware interlocks to detect interinstruction dependencies. These and other considerations limit the usefulness of instruction pipelining on CISCs.

A recent trend, which we shall investigate in detail in Section 6.1.3, is to develop instruction sets that allow high-speed pipelined implementations. For these computers the ultimate goal is to provide instructions that are efficient yet allow circuit designers to pipeline the instruction and execution units. The crucial factor for these machines is not the complexity of the individual instructions but the choice of instructions that lend themselves to pipelined execution.

### 6.1.3 ■ Scheduling Functional Units

The goal of an instruction pipeline is to maximize the rate of instruction issues. When a computer has multiple functional units, the control unit issues instructions to them as quickly as possible, and they carry out the operations specified by the instructions. An **instruction issue** usually consists of reserving a functional unit, sending an op code to it, and reserving the result register. However, before the control unit can issue an instruction, it must determine that the appropriate functional unit is free and that no data dependencies exist between the current instruction and those that are still executing. For example, if the control unit issues two instructions that have the same result register, then a data dependency exists and the first instruction must store its result first. If the second instruction stores its result before the first instruction does, the first instruction will overwrite the logically newer value produced by the second instruction.

*instruction issue*

To illustrate these ideas, we will describe in detail how the CDC 6600 issues instructions and schedules its functional units. The same principles apply equally well to other machines.

**CDC 6600 Instruction Issue**

The CDC 6600 has a load-and-store instruction set, and all operate instructions specify a functional unit, an operation mode (Fm), two operand registers (Fj and Fk), and a result register (Fi). The operation mode tells the functional unit what operation to perform.

The CDC 6600 register set includes 24 operational registers and several control registers, including the PC. The control registers are not important for this discussion. The operational registers form three groups of eight registers each: eight address registers (A0 through A7), eight index registers (B0 through B7) and eight accumulators (X0 through X7). The operational registers are sometimes called **XBA registers.**

*XBA registers*

The CDC 6600 has 10 functional units that operate independently. The functional units consist of an adder (18 bits), a long adder (60 bits), two increment units, two multiply units (60 bits), a divide unit (60 bits), a branch unit, a boolean unit (60 bits), and a shift unit (60 bits).

Each functional unit has two operand registers, a result register, a **mode register** (which holds the operation mode), and a **busy flag** (which indicates whether the functional unit is busy or available). These five registers, although not part of the CDC 6600's ISA, are crucial for instruction scheduling.

*mode register*
*busy flag*

The control unit, called the **scoreboard** in 6600 parlance, consists of a number of control registers that schedule the functional units, registers, and buses (Fig. 6.9). The scoreboard registers are also not part of the 6600's ISA. One set of scoreboard registers is the **XBA result-register designators** (where X, B, and A refer to the accumulator, index, and address registers, respectively). There is one result-register designator for each XBA operational regis-

*scoreboard*

*XBA result-register designators*

ter, and it specifies which functional unit is to supply that register with a value. One set of scoreboard registers are **entry-operand-register designators** (Fj and Fk). There is one entry-operand-register designator for each functional-unit operand register, and it indicates which XBA register will supply a value to the operand register. Each entry-operand-register designator has an associated **read flag** (RFj and RFk). When set, a read flag indicates that the corresponding register holds a valid operand (hence can be read). Each entry-operand-register designator has an associated **function-unit designator** (Qj and Qk). A

entry-operand-register designators

read flag

function-unit designator

FIGURE 6.9 *XBA registers, selected functional units, and selected control registers of the CDC 6600. The figure shows the situation where functional units F1 and F2 are both waiting for operands. F1 is waiting for F2 to complete its result. F2 will place its result in register X4, which is to supply F1 with its second operand. The first operand for F1 is register X1, which holds the correct value. F2 is waiting for F5 to complete its result and place it in register X6; X6 will then supply F2 with operand 2. F2 gets operand 1 from register X5, which holds the correct value.*

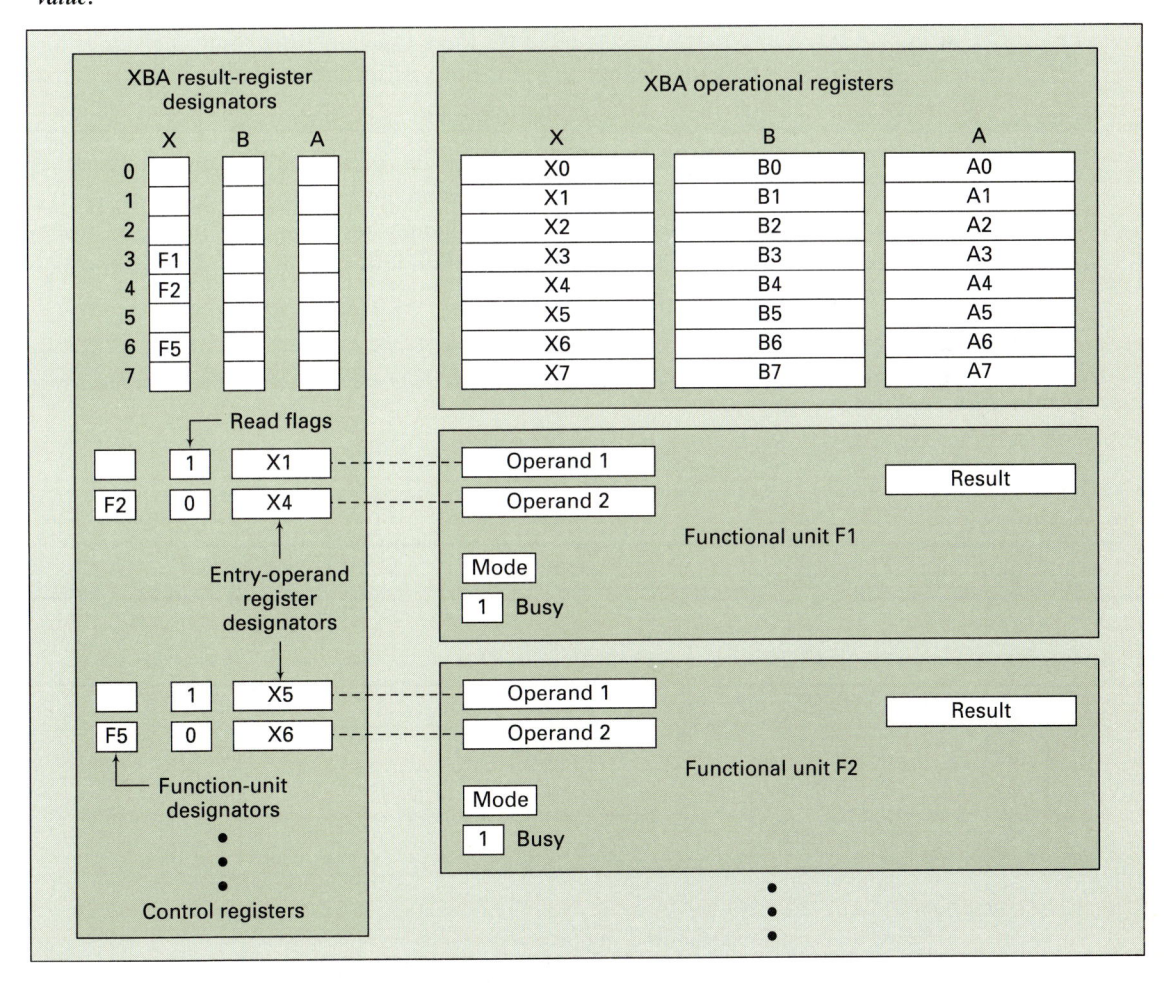

function-unit designator indicates, by function-unit number, which functional unit will produce the operand if it is not yet valid (and hence the corresponding read flag is not yet set). The scoreboard sets and clears these control registers. Figure 6.10 shows the control registers in tabular form.

The CDC 6600 uses a two-stage instruction-decoding pipeline that extracts instructions from the instruction stream and issues them as soon as possible. The first stage of the pipeline extracts individual instructions from instruction words and determines which functional unit and result register are required by the instruction. The second stage of the pipeline determines whether the required functional unit and result register are free and if so issues the instruction. If instruction issue is not possible, the pipeline freezes (i.e., stops issuing instructions) until the conditions for instruction issue become satisfied.

To issue an instruction, the instruction-decoding pipeline first verifies that

1. the register designated for the result is not the result register of another instruction that has not yet finished executing, and
2. that the required functional unit is available.

If both conditions are satisfied, the pipeline issues the instruction. If not, it freezes until they are satisfied. To issue an instruction the pipeline sets the functional unit's busy flag to "busy" (thereby reserving the functional unit), and it stores the value of Fm in the function unit's mode register. It also stores the Fj and Fk values in the entry-operand-register designators, and it reserves

**FIGURE 6.10** *Control registers used for scheduling. The 10 functional units are listed across the top of the array; the condition flags are listed down the side.*

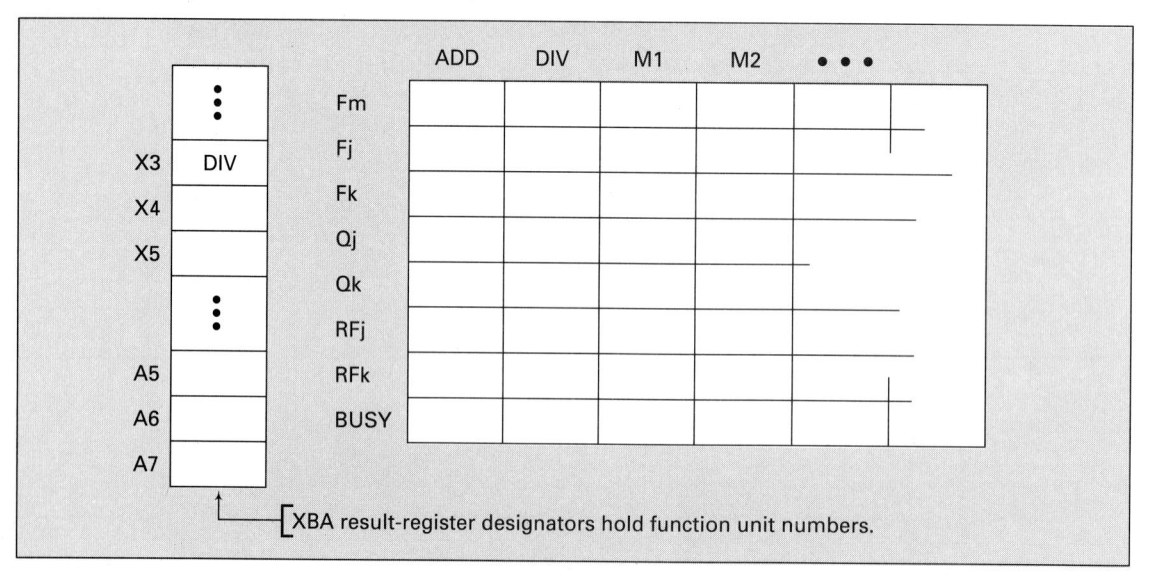

XBA result-register designators hold function unit numbers.

the result register by storing the Fi number in the correct result-register designator. Once the instruction-decoding pipeline issues an instruction, it will not issue another instruction that uses the same functional unit or result register until the current instruction finishes executing. After the pipeline issues an instruction, the scoreboard controls its execution.

The instruction-decoding pipeline guarantees that conditions 1 and 2 are satisfied because there is only one set of control registers for each functional unit and one result-register designator for each register. Issuing an instruction that violates either of rules 1 and 2 would destroy scheduling information needed by the scoreboard or functional unit.

**Releasing the Results**

After performing an operation, a function unit holds its result until the scoreboard gives it permission to release the result. Once given permission, the function unit releases the result, which the scoreboard sends to the designated result register. The XBA result-register designators control the data transfer.

**Instruction Execution**

After the instruction-decoding pipeline issues an instruction, the scoreboard controls the transfer of operands to the functional units and results to the result registers. The functional units perform their operations independently and often concurrently. To assure program correctness, the scoreboard does the following things:

1. Although the pipeline issued an instruction, the instruction's operands might not yet be available. That can happen if other functional units are still evaluating them. Thus the scoreboard must assure that each functional unit gets the correct operands.
2. Instructions may finish executing out of sequence. The scoreboard must assure that a newer result does not destroy a value still needed as an operand by another functional unit. It also must assure that a result produced by one functional unit does not destroy a logically newer result that was produced first (out of sequence) by another functional unit.

As a result of these requirements, the instruction-decoding pipeline and scoreboard must detect and prevent errors that would result if the various data dependencies just mentioned went undetected.

*Operand Availability*

Functional units must wait for their operands. Consider these two instructions:

$$X6 \leftarrow X1 \times X2$$
$$X5 \leftarrow X6 + X4$$

Because these instructions use different result registers and different functional units, the instruction-decoding pipeline can issue both of them without delay. Note that the second instruction must wait for the first one to finish executing, because the first one produces an operand for the second. If the addition unit were to start before the multiplication unit produces X6, the result would be wrong. The scoreboard detects these data dependencies by checking the read flags and assuring that all operands are available before sending any of them to the functional unit.

### Result-register Dependencies

Data dependencies occur if a functional unit has not yet used a value held by a result register. Consider the following sequence of instructions:

$$X3 \leftarrow X1/X2$$
$$X5 \leftarrow X4 \times X3$$
$$X4 \leftarrow X0 + X6$$

As in the previous example, the instruction-decoding pipeline can issue all three without delay. Note that the division unit now produces an operand for the multiplication unit. Hence the multiplication unit must wait for the division unit to finish before it can begin. Consequently, the scoreboard will not transfer either operand (X4 or X3) to the multiplication unit until the division unit has released its result. Note also that the addition unit can begin executing as soon as the instruction-decoding pipeline issues it, because both of its operands are already available. However, if it places its result in register X4 before the multiplication unit starts executing, the new value of X4 will overwrite the old value, which the multiplication unit still requires. Hence the result would be incorrect.

The scoreboard deals with result-register dependencies by preventing functional units from releasing their results until the result register is no longer the operand register for prior unstarted instructions. The scoreboard uses the Qj and Qk register designators and the RFj and RFk read flags for this test. Figure 6.11 shows the sequence of steps that take place during instruction issue and execution for this example.

To summarize, when a computer has several functional units that can operate concurrently, the instruction unit must detect data dependencies and prevent instructions from issuing if dependencies occur. A data dependency clearly exists when two instructions specify the same result register. Hence, an ISA with many operational registers has an advantage over one that has few. A functional-unit dependency exists if two instructions require the same functional unit. One way to eliminate this dependency is to pipeline the functional units, and current RISC machines do exactly that. The following section explores these issues in greater depth.

---

**FIGURE 6.11** *(On page 303). State of the control registers used during the execution of the example instruction sequence. (a) After the pipeline issues the first instruction. (b) After the pipeline issues the second instruction; note that the division unit is producing the k-operand for the multiplication unit. (c) After the pipeline issues the third instruction.*

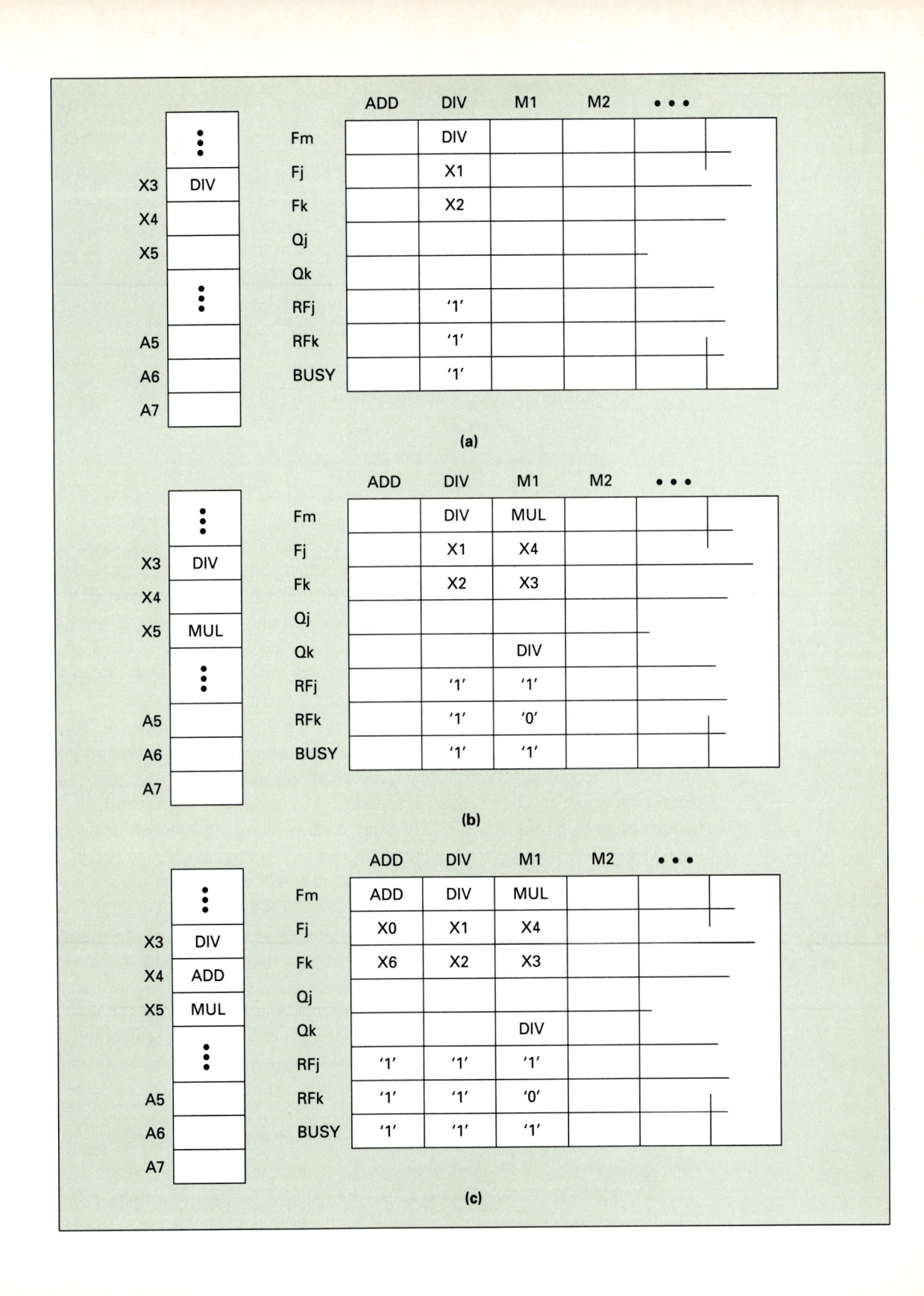

**(a)**

| | ADD | DIV | M1 | M2 | ••• |
|---|---|---|---|---|---|
| Fm | | DIV | | | |
| Fj | | X1 | | | |
| Fk | | X2 | | | |
| Qj | | | | | |
| Qk | | | | | |
| RFj | | '1' | | | |
| RFk | | '1' | | | |
| BUSY | | '1' | | | |

X3: DIV
X4:
X5:
A5:
A6:
A7:

**(b)**

| | ADD | DIV | M1 | M2 | ••• |
|---|---|---|---|---|---|
| Fm | | DIV | MUL | | |
| Fj | | X1 | X4 | | |
| Fk | | X2 | X3 | | |
| Qj | | | | | |
| Qk | | | DIV | | |
| RFj | | '1' | '1' | | |
| RFk | | '1' | '0' | | |
| BUSY | | '1' | '1' | | |

X3: DIV
X4:
X5: MUL
A5:
A6:
A7:

**(c)**

| | ADD | DIV | M1 | M2 | ••• |
|---|---|---|---|---|---|
| Fm | ADD | DIV | MUL | | |
| Fj | X0 | X1 | X4 | | |
| Fk | X6 | X2 | X3 | | |
| Qj | | | | | |
| Qk | | | DIV | | |
| RFj | '1' | '1' | '1' | | |
| RFk | '1' | '1' | '0' | | |
| BUSY | '1' | '1' | '1' | | |

X3: DIV
X4: ADD
X5: MUL
A5:
A6:
A7:

## 6.2 ■ Pipelined Vector Processors

Computer architects have capitalized on the repetitive nature of vector operations by building pipelined vector processors, such as the CRAY-1 supercomputer and its descendants, the TI ASC, the Star-100, and more recently the NEC SX family, the Siemans VPx and Fujitsu VP$x$-EX families, and a number of conventional architectures with vector facilities. The principal techniques used in designing both supercomputers and RISCs include the following:

- pipelined instruction-decoding;
- multiple pipelined functional units that operate concurrently;
- asynchronous banks of interleaved memory;
- independent instruction and data caches;
- numerous buses to transfer data, addresses, and control signals.

There are two reasons that vector operations lend themselves so well to pipelined processing. First, relatively simple and inexpensive hardware can greatly speed up vector operations. Second, compilers can detect sequences of code that can take advantage of vector operations with little more difficulty than they have with normal code optimization. But the instruction set needs to include vector instructions in order for compilers to take advantage of them. In Chapter 2 we described most of the important types of vector operations. When a computer has vector instructions, a single instruction can control the entire sequence of operations implicitly specified by the instruction.

At the simplest level the vector instruction may be nothing more than microprograms that execute multiple operations instead of a single operation. This facility provides the instructions, and some architects have used it to add vector processing to conventional computers. The result is a reduction in the number of instructions that the CPU must fetch from memory, which tends to improve performance because of reduced memory contention. Also, the microcode branch used to loop in the microprogram will generally be faster than the branch it replaces in the ordinary code loop, resulting in further program speedup. From our discussion of pipelining, it should be apparent that these microprogrammed vector operations are very inexpensive to add to a microprogrammed computer design.

For vector instruction, the computational circuitry performs the same operation on each element (usually a pair of values) of a sequence of operands. A pipelined execution unit can therefore produce a result every clock period, and by decomposing arithmetic operations into suitably short stages, a designer can build an arithmetic pipeline with a significantly decreased clock period. Two ways of viewing the speedup offered by vector processing are as follows:

- The instruction fetching is greatly reduced, to the point that essentially all memory bandwidth is available for data.

- There is essentially no overhead for branching, which is now implicit in the vector operation.

Suppose the CPU is fully pipelined and can produce one result with every clock cycle. Also suppose the control unit can fetch and store operands at the same rate. Then the time it takes to perform a vector operation is $LR + K - R$, where $L$ is the vector length, $R$ is the **result rate,** and $K$ is the **startup time.** The startup time is the time it takes to do one operation (the time to fetch the first operand from memory plus the time to fill the arithmetic pipeline plus the time to store a result). In general, computer architects characterize vector operations by their result rate and startup time.

Some of the tradeoffs that a computer designer must consider—whether for CISCs or RISCs—are those between clock rate and startup time. As the number of stages in a pipeline increases, the time to do a single operation also increases. There are two performance parameters for a vector computer that an architect must minimize for maximum vector operation usefulness:

result rate
startup time

$N_{crossover}$    The vector length where vector speed equals scalar speed.

$N_{1/2}$    The vector length where vector speed equals half of the asymptotic or maximum vector speed.

$N_{crossover}$

$N_{1/2}$

If $N_{crossover}$ or $N_{1/2}$ is too large, then vector processing is only useful for long vectors, and compilers need to make special efforts to lengthen vectors so that vectorization improves performance.

Generally the storage system must have sufficient bandwidth to process read and write requests at the pipeline rate. In a memory-to-memory architecture (one whose operands and results for arithmetic, logical, and shift instructions are in memory), the memory bandwidth will have to be about three times the pipeline rate. As an aside, the memory bandwidth ordinarily contributes a major part of the cost of a computer system. Architects use various techniques to ensure adequate memory bandwidth, such as multiword data paths and low-order memory interleaving.

There is one additional reason that vector processing increases performance. Because each vector instruction generates a large number of similar operations, the computer can prepare for the operations. This means that vector pipelines can operate faster than pipelines for less regular operations. This is especially important for operations with long delays, such as large memory accesses.

Recapping, vector processing is faster than scalar processing due to

- reduced memory contention from fewer instruction accesses;
- reduced instruction decoding;
- predictable behavior, which is especially important for
  - implicit indexing and memory accesses,
  - implicit branching.

> see Case
> Studies 7 and 8

In the *Case Studies* we describe two pipelined vector processors, the CRAY-1 and the TI ASC. These machines reflect considerably different design philosophies and architectural heritages, as well as different ways for increasing the execution speed of the CPU. The CRAY-1 is a descendent of the CDC 6600 family and the parent of a family of about six machines as of 1990. The TI ASC, which resembles the IBM System/360 family architecture in some respects, was a supercomputer of the early 1970s. Texas Instruments built only a few of them, and none are in use today (as far as we know). We have included the TI ASC as a point of direct contrast with the CRAY-1.

Most commercial high-performance vector processors are pipelined. Many are multiprocessors as well, having two to eight CPUs that usually share the same main memory using a high-speed crossbar or the equivalent. Many current architectural families have one or more high-end models with vector coprocessors, many with several CPUs, and many machines are available in a variety of CPU speeds. All of these are pipelined. Table 6.1 compares a few prominent computers, both single processor and multiprocessor. We include the DEC VAX and IBM PC models to show the wide range of performance that exists in the machines of the 1990s.

## 6.3 ■ Reduced-instruction-set Computers

> see Case
> Study 5

In the early 1980s, largely because of the complexity of the VAX instruction set (see the *Case Studies*), a "back to basics" movement started. Several architects started investigating computers with simple ISAs, similar to that of the CDC 6600. Computer scientists coined the term RISC, for reduced-instruction-set computer, to describe these machines, and the term has stuck. The term is applied to a number of machines, but no definition is universally accepted. We shall define a RISC as a computer that has *most* of the following properties:

1. Instructions are conceptually simple.
2. Instructions are of a uniform length.
3. Instructions use one (or very few) instruction formats.
4. The instruction set is orthogonal (i.e., there is little overlapping of instruction functionality).
5. Instructions use one (or very few) addressing modes.
6. The architecture is a load-and-store architecture: (Only LOAD and STORE instructions reference memory; all operate instructions are register-to-register instructions).
7. The ISA supports two (or a few more) datatypes (typically integer and floating point).

Some architects have added other attributes to the definition of a RISC; our reasons for not including these in our definition are given in parentheses:

**Table 6.1** Several LINPACK benchmarks for a variety of computers, ranging from PCs to high-performance multiprocessors.

| Computer | Number of Processors | LINPACK Benchmark (Clock-cycle Time) |
|---|---|---|
| Cray Y-MP/832 | 8 | 275 |
| Cray Y-MP/832 | 4 | 226 |
| Cray Y-MP/832 | 2 | 144 |
| Cray Y-MP/832 | 1 | 90 |
| Cray-1S | 1 | 27 |
| Alliant FX/2800 | 14 | 26 |
| Alliant FX/2800 | 8 | 22 |
| Alliant FX/2800 | 4 | 16 |
| Alliant FX/2800 | 2 | 9.9 |
| Alliant FX/2800 | 1 | 6.4 |
| IBM RISC System/6000-550 | 1 | 27 |
| IBM RISC System/6000-320 | 1 | 9 |
| IBM 370/195 | 1 | 2.5 |
| IBM 370/165 | 1 | 0.77 |
| CDC 7600 | 1 | 2.0 |
| CDC 6600 | 1 | 0.48 |
| Sun SPARCstation 1 | 1 | 1.6 |
| DEC VAX 11/780 | 1 | 0.14 |
| DEC VAX 11/750 | 1 | 0.057 |
| IBM PC AT w/80287 | 1 | 0.012 |
| IBM PC XT w/8087 | 1 | 0.012 |

*Source:* From Dongarra, 1991.

8. Almost all instructions execute in 1 clock cycle. (This is an implementation detail, not an architectural characteristic.)

9. The architecture takes advantage of the strengths of software. (All reasonable architectures do this.)

10. The architecture should have many registers. (This is not part of RISC but very useful for speeding up the CPU.)

The CDC 6600 satisfies all criteria except the second (it has two instruction lengths), so it is a RISC. The other extreme is the VAX, which satisfies none of them. It is clearly a CISC. The CDC 6600 has about 75 instructions, including all addressing choices; the VAX has several hundred, each with several addressing modes for each operand or result. Table 6.2 shows where a number of computers fall on the continuum between RISC and CISC.

The *Case Studies* discuss three current RISCs: the MIPS R2000, the Sun SPARC, and the IBM System/R6000. The R2000 is an early RISC system.

see Case Studies 9–11

**Table 6.2**  Some machines and the complexity of their instruction sets.

| RISC | CISC |
|---|---|
| CDC 6600* | IBM System/360*   B6700* |
| B-1700    PDP-8* | PDP-11*   VAX-11* |
| Motorola 88000 | Motorola 68020*   Intel 80386* |
| CRAY-1* | TI ASC* |
| MIPS R2000* | Star-100 |
| Sun SPARC*   IBM System/R6000* | |

*Described in the *Case Studies*.

It satisfies all RISC criteria except number 7. Although the Sun SPARC and the IBM System/R6000 are considered to be RISCs they satisfy fewer of the RISCs criteria. However, their architects developed them based on the general principles that have emerged from the RISC philosophy of design, so we have grouped them together. We discuss the RISC design philosophy in detail next.

### 6.3.1 ■ Historical Perspective

Designers of the earliest computers used conventional control units because they had not yet developed the technology of microprogrammed control. Wilkes and Stringer (1953) first described the concepts of microprogramming, and in the late 1950s, IBM (and others) developed the technology for it. IBM introduced microprogrammed control in 1964 with its System/360 computer family. Since then, microprogrammed control units have seen widespread use, for several reasons:

- Instruction-set designers can easily implement complex instructions using them.
- The cost of microprogramming is far less than the cost of implementing a conventional hardwired control unit.
- It is easy to add new instructions or modify existing ones (to improve performance or correct an error) when instructions are microprogrammed.
- Complex operations, such as those required for bootstrap loading, error recovery, and system reconfiguration after a failure, generally require microprograms, so microprogram-type memory is present in most computer systems for reasons other than for complex instructions.

Because microprogramming facilitates large instruction sets and makes complex instructions feasible, designers have used microprogrammed control units on most machines. For example, without microprogramming, the breadth of the System/370 and VAX families would be diminished: It would not be possible to make the low-cost members of the families. There are only two real exceptions to the use of microprogrammed control units: top-of-the-line models of large architectural families (i.e., those designed for the highest performance) and RISCs.

Microprogrammed control units generally use small, high-speed memories for the control store to hold microprograms. Consequently the control unit can access the control code faster than it can access main memory. It seems logical, therefore, to assume that complex instructions implemented in microcode would execute faster than an equivalent sequence of simpler instructions implemented in machine code, and that may indeed be true. As a simple example, consider the autoincrement-addressing mode of the VAX-11. The single instruction

$$\text{ADD INCREMENT} \quad (R2) \leftarrow (R2) + R5; R2 \leftarrow R2 + 1$$

adds the content of register R5 to the content of the memory location whose address is held in register R2 and then increments the content of R2. This CISC instruction generally executes faster than the equivalent sequence of four RISC instructions:

$$\begin{array}{lll} \text{LOAD} & R3 & \leftarrow (R2) \\ \text{ADD} & R3 & \leftarrow R3 + R5 \\ \text{STORE} & (R2) & \leftarrow R3 \\ \text{INCREMENT} & R2 & \leftarrow R2 + 1 \end{array}$$

In this RISC sequence the second instruction adds the content of register R5 to the content of R3, which the first instruction loaded from the memory location whose address is held in register R2. The third instruction stores the result back in memory, and the fourth instruction increments index register R2. In the CISC case, the hardware fetches and executes a single instruction. In the RISC case, the hardware fetches and executes four instructions, which requires three extra memory accesses.

## 6.3.2 ■ RISC-CISC Controversy

At present there are two schools of thought on instruction-set design: one favors complex instruction sets, the other favors reduced instruction sets. Proponents of CISC architectures give many arguments in their favor, including the following:

- Richer (more complex) instruction sets improve the merit of the architecture, since operations implemented in microcode execute faster than operations implemented in software.
- Richer instruction sets do not increase the cost of implementation (in dollars) over that of simpler instruction sets.

- The need for upward compatibility within a family results in an increase in the instruction-set size, and upward compatibility is easier to implement in microcode.
- Richer instruction sets simplify compiler design.
- Complex instructions sets make cloning of a computer more difficult, thus protecting proprietary designs.

Changes in technology and software are diminishing many of these CISC advantages. In 1964, when IBM first announced the System/360, designers used magnetic-core main memories and a variety of ROM technologies for their control stores. Because of the slow switching times of the magnetic cores, however, the control stores tended to be about 10 times faster than core memory (albeit costlier to manufacture). Consequently, complex instructions executed more quickly than the equivalent sequences of simple machine instructions, and this favored CISCs. Since then, a number of changes in memory technology and software have diminished this speed differential between memory and control stores. Semiconductor memories, which are faster than magnetic-core memories, have replaced them. As the instruction sets became more complex, they required larger control stores, which are consequently slower. Also, the use of cache memory has further increased the effective speed of main memory, eroding some of the speed advantages of a special control store and hence of microprogramming.

Designers must consider issues other than speed. Compilers tend to take advantage of few of the available instructions, particularly the complex ones on CISCs, and programmers can code infrequently used complex instructions using simpler ones. The instructions and addressing modes compilers use most frequently are also the simplest ones (loads from memory and stores to memory, register-to-register transfers, branches, and simple operate instructions) and the ones that satisfy the RISC criteria. With demand-paged memory the control unit must be able to restart any instruction that can be interrupted by a page or segment fault. The more complicated the instruction, the more difficult it is to build in the necessary hardware interlocks to interrupt and restart instructions.[2] In addition, it becomes increasingly difficult to introduce parallelism into the control unit. For computers with writable control stores, which designers sometimes use so they can optimize instruction sets for particular audiences, it may take a considerable amount of time to reload the control store.

In essence, the architects of CISC machines freeze into microcode the sequences of operations that programmers find useful, such as the sequences

---

2. There are actually two restart strategies to choose from: restart at the point of interruption, or go back to the beginning and reissue the instruction if possible. Both are difficult to implement for complex instructions.

that implement procedure-linkage instructions. They therefore optimize code sequences during the design of the ISA. RISC proponents correctly argue that compilers can generate the same sequences of operations and that with a suitable cache memory the instructions for a RISC machine would all appear in the cache when needed. RISC instructions would therefore be as quick to execute as CISC microinstructions, and the cache *dynamically* optimizes the code sequences.

Taking these and other factors into consideration, several researchers and manufacturers concluded that RISCs could in many cases outperform CISCs. They began to advocate the use of computers with simple instruction sets (as described earlier), caches, and hard-wired control units.

Some of the reasons proponents give in favor of RISC architectures are these:

- The basic hardware is simpler, so it can be cheaper and faster, more than compensating for the increased number of instructions required to perform some operations.
- Instruction caches easily compensate for the large number of bits in the instructions required by a RISC.
- It is easier to compile for a RISC than for a CISC architecture.
- Design effort, and hence development cost, for a RISC is less than for a CISC.
- It is easier to introduce parallelism into the control unit of a RISC than a CISC.

All of these arguments have merit, although some of the supporting arguments are not very convincing. It is probably true that a machine with fewer gates can have a faster clock cycle than one with many gates, but the apparent higher speed of the RISC chips may well be due to the fact that their simple design was optimized for high clock speed rather than high system speed. The streamlined RISC instruction set can simplify code generation, but code generation is a minor part of compilation. The RISC benchmarks show that the portable compilers used on RISC systems are better suited to RISC architectures, rather than showing that RISC architectures are superior. Given fewer gates and a larger percentage of gates in registers, it is almost certainly true that RISC machines are easier to design. However, it is inappropriate to compare the development of a single RISC chip to that of a complete system represented by a commercial microprocessor chip set (such as the Intel family) or to that of a commercial minicomputer.

From the standpoint of designing a computer-family, the major tradeoffs an architect must consider when deciding between a RISC or a CISC architecture are complex. They include such factors as the following:

1. If the ISA is successful and too simple, it invites plug-compatible competition (cloning).

2. If the ISA is too complex, supercomputer and microcomputer implementations may be impossible.
3. If the instruction encoding is too inefficient, large programs will use excessive memory and memory bandwidth.
4. The memory system and its connection to the CPU is an expensive component of computers. The increased memory bandwidth of a RISC may well make it more expensive, negating a major RISC advantage.

The first issue above is outside the scope of this book, but points 2 to 4 illustrate the need for a rather delicate tradeoff analysis to select an appropriate level of complexity. There is no way to avoid the influence of current hardware and software technology on the choice of an ISA, but the architect must give careful consideration to the long-term implications of the choice.

Designers of CISCs introduced many instructions simply because it was easy to do so or because competitors did so. The unnecessary or unusable instructions introduced for these reasons increase costs in several ways:

- Manufacturing cost is increased because of the need to test all operations and combinations of operations during system checkout.
- Design cost is increased for future systems because of the need to retain upward or forward compatibility.

It is our opinion that designers of ISAs should err on the side of simplicity when there is an unclear choice, and leave out instructions whenever their need for or usefulness of those instructions has not been demonstrated or is not known.

### 6.3.3 ■ RISC Implementation Techniques

We shall conclude this section by listing the major techniques architects use to increase the performance of RISC computers. (We assume the basic RISC properties 1 to 7 itemized at the beginning of Section 6.3.)

1. RISCs use pipelining to speed up instruction decoding and execution.
2. RISCs do not allow program self-modification, which eliminates the need for hardware interlocks to detect possible modifications to the program.
3. RISCs use Harvard architectures; separate instruction and data streams reduces the von Neumann bottleneck, and the lack of program self-modification makes the implementation straightforward.
4. RISCs use large register sets to reduce the CPU-to-memory bandwidth and the result-register dependencies that occur with small register sets. Some RISCs use independent registers for floating-point operands and results.

5. All RISCs have separate functional units for instruction processing and instruction execution, and most have independent floating-point functional units (or support for a floating-point coprocessor).

6. RISCs use **delayed branches** to avoid the branch penalty. The instruction position following a branch instruction is called the **branch-delay slot.** The CPU always executes the instruction in the branch-delay slot, even for conditional branches; execution of the branch is therefore delayed for one instruction. For conditional branches some RISCs allow the program to flag the instruction in the branch-delay slot as conditional: If an **annul bit** is set and the branch succeeds, the CPU annuls the instruction. This use of the annul bit makes it unnecessary for the compiler to fill the branch-delay slot with a NO OP instruction if it cannot move another (usually earlier) instruction into the branch slot.

*delayed branches*

*branch-delay slot*

*annul bit*

7. Use of **delayed loads** avoids the operand-fetch delay. The instruction position following a LOAD instruction is the **load-delay slot.** The CPU always executes the instruction in the load-delay slot.

*delayed loads*

*load-delay slot*

8. RISCs prefetch branch-target instructions to reduce the branch delay.

9. RISCs use specialized cache memories to decrease the memory-to-CPU delay. They also use separate instruction and data caches optimized by the architects for the corresponding pattern of memory accesses; the programs control the caches.

10. RISCs use optimizing compilers. Optimizing compilers rearrange the code sequences to take maximum advantage of the CPU parallelism. Here are some examples of what optimizing compilers do.
    a. fill the load-delay and branch-delay slots with independent instructions (not NO OPS) whenever possible;
    b. allocate registers to reduce result-register dependencies;
    c. move LOAD instructions as early as possible in the instruction stream to reduce the load-delay penalty;
    d. move instructions that evaluate branch addresses as early as possible in the instruction stream to reduce the branch-delay penalty;
    e. move instructions that are necessary for evaluating the branch test (e.g., condition-code-setting instructions) as early as possible (for the same reason as item d).

11. Some RISCs use overlapping register sets to speed up parameter passage during subroutine calls and returns.

12. Some RISCs support string operations by loading and storing multiple registers and using them as string operands.

13. Some RISCs support vector operations by treating multiple registers as vector registers.

Many companies have introduced RISC architectures, and a few of these RISCs are beginning to dominate the market (as of 1991): the MIPS

R2000, the Motorola 88000, the Sun SPARC, the IBM System/R6000, Intel's i860, and Hewlett-Packard's Spectrum. Whether RISC architectures will predominate in the future is still not clear. The end of the current CISC families is nowhere in sight, but equally clear is the fact that the RISCs have made giant strides in performance and now outperform their CISC competitors in many current applications areas, such as workstations and high-performance, low-cost laboratory machines.

# Summary

Many computers use concurrent processing, one form of which is pipelining. Two of the earliest computers to incorporate pipelining were the CDC 6600 and the IBM System/360 Model 91. Current RISC machines use virtually all of the techniques these early pipelined machines did, and others.

Architects must address many issues when designing a pipelined processor. For concurrent instruction execution, the maintenance of program correctness is essential, so the architect must include appropriate hardware interlocks (or tools so the software can provide the interlocks) to assure that the outcome of a program execution is the same on a pipelined processor as on an equivalent von Neumann machine. In other words, the hardware must preserve precedence among individual instructions. When the cost of maintaining precedence is too high, the architect may alternatively include a mechanism to disable the concurrency. The hardware hazard detection, arithmetic pipeline disabling mechanism, and fork and join control mechanisms of the TI ASC are examples.

There are a number of problem areas that tend to reduce or eliminate potential concurrency. The instruction that follows a conditional branch depends on the outcome of the branch test. Hence any instructions whose outcome influences the result of the branch test must be complete before the CPU can perform it. Nonetheless, prefetching the branch target instruction, as well as prefetching the next instruction, can improve system performance.

Although parallelism gives some increase in processor speed for ordinary architectures, the greatest benefit occurs for vector operations. For them, all operations are the same on elements of the vectors, which benefits the design in three ways: (1) computation of vector-element addresses is systematic and hence can be delegated to a special memory-interface unit (increasing the parallelism), (2) the pipeline rate can be increased by increasing the number of pipeline stages, and (3) one instruction can specify many ALU operations. Reducing the number of instruction accesses decreases memory contention for operand accesses. Although the startup time may increase if the number of pipeline stages increases, the throughput of the pipeline also increases with a potential net gain in performance. However, unless the software uses vector instructions efficiently, the potential gain in performance may never be realized.

In general, when using a pipeline, the storage system must be able to provide operands and accept results at the maximum pipeline rate. For vector processors, architects have solved this problem by increasing the CPU-to-memory bandwidth by fetching blocks of words (octets, for example) and buffering them, or by providing vector registers and supporting only register-to-register vector instructions. For RISC processors, architects have solved the memory-bandwidth problem by using specialized caches, Harvard architectures, and wide data paths.

The RISC-CISC tradeoff equation is not simple, and architects continue to improve the performance of CISCs as well. High-performance caches, pipelined instruction units, pipelined ALUs, and pipelined floating-point coprocessors are among the techniques now in use. Although it may be more difficult for architects to apply pipelining techniques to CISCs than to RISCs, they continue to do so in increasingly ingenious ways. In so doing, they insure the life of the current CISC families.

# Exercises

*6.1* Find a general formula for the time it takes a teacher to collate reports using the method described in the text. Let $T_p$ be the time it takes teacher and students to process a single page, let $N$ be the number of students in the class, and let $P$ be the number of pages in the report. Assume there are more students than reports to be collated.

*6.2* Identify two advantages and two disadvantages of a fine-grained pipeline. Name two advantages and two disadvantages of a multifunction pipeline.

*6.3* Show the final three stages of the multiplication pipeline given in Fig. 6.4. Then show the values held by each of the latches for the seven clocks required to produce the result of 10111011 × 1101001.

*6.4* Refer to Fig. 6.4 and assume that the values 11000011 (multiplicand) and 10011 (multiplier) follow the previous values (10111011 and 1101001) into the pipe. Show the values that appear in the latches during the computations of both products. Copy the figure below and fill in the blanks for each step, or at least for representative ones.

*6.5* Assume the pipeline clock in Fig. 6.4 operates at 5 MHz. How long does it take the pipe to produce 10 products?

*6.6* Show how to decompose a floating-point multiplication into stages for pipelining. Consider a coarse decomposition, staging only the operations of exponent alignment, mantissa multiplication, normalization, and roundoff.

**6.7** Show how to decompose floating-point addition into stages for pipelining. Show how to combine floating-point addition and floating-point multiplication into a single multifunction pipeline.

**6.8** Under what circumstances is a $k$-stage pipeline $k$ times faster than a serial machine?

**6.9** One of the characteristics of a pipelined unit for decoding and issuing instructions is that branch instructions normally stop the pipeline, which has the apparent affect of causing branch instructions to take as many clock cycles as there are stages in the pipe. This is called the branch penalty. Igor's Better Machines is building a "hot box," a computer with very high CPU performance, and is planning to use branch-prediction logic to reduce the branch penalty. If the instruction pipeline is 6 cycles long and a crude branch prediction ("assume each branch does what it did the last time") is correct 80% of the time, how much better could very complicated branch-prediction strategies be? Assume the following: When branches are correctly predicted, there is no extra delay; when branches are predicted incorrectly, they cause an extra 10-cycle delay; and branches comprise 15% of the instructions.

**6.10** A typical RISC machine requires 4 cycles (fetch instruction, compute address, load, put result away) for LOAD and STORE instructions, and 3 cycles (fetch instruction, execute, put result away) for each of the other instructions. Consider the following program:

```
LOAD       R1 ← X
SUBTRACT   R1 ← R1 − R2
STORE      X  ← R1
ADD        R2 ← R1 + R2
```

Draw a timing diagram showing the execution of these four instructions, and calculate how long it takes the processor to execute them. Assume maximum instruction overlap.

**6.11** Identify two advantages and two disadvantages for a supercomputer to control branching by testing condition codes instead of registers.

**6.12** Show how to program the dot product of two vectors of complex data. Assume the data are stored in memory as $real_1$, $imaginary_1$, $real_2$, $imaginary_2$, $real_3$, $imaginary_3$, ....

**6.13** In 1989 Digital introduced vector processing for the VAX computers. Before vectorizing loops, version 1.0 of their vectorizing compiler checks the loop-iteration count: It will not vectorize loops with loop-iteration counts of 7 or less. What do they assume their vector startup time to be?

**6.14** As vice president of R&D for the Kludge Komputer Kompany, you want to demonstrate to the head of sales that peak speeds are not very important. You do this by computing the speed of the SAXPY kernel (given below) for various vector-unit speeds while keeping scalar speeds constant. Show your graphs, and detail your assumptions.

SAXPY   **do** I = 1, 1000
            X(I) = A × X(I) + Y(I)
        **end do**

**6.15** Suppose an $n$-element-vector operation takes $I + pn$ cycles, where $I$ is the initialization time and $p$ is the pipeline stage time in clock cycles. Also suppose a scalar loop for the same operation takes $Sn$ cycles. For what values of $n$ is the vector coding faster than the scalar coding? Answer this both for the general case, and for the CRAY-1 where $I = 5$, $p = 1$, and $S = 2$.

**6.16** Consider a family of computers that implements both scalar and vector operations. Plot the speed ratios of two computers with vector accelerators as a function of the percent of vectorization. One vector accelerator performs vector operations 4 times faster than scalar operations; the other 20 times faster.

**6.17** Ivanova's computer has an old vector accelerator that is to be replaced by a faster one. (Refer to Problem 6.32.) As a function of the old vector accelerator's speedup, plot the percentage of speed increase required of a new vector accelerator to achieve double the performance. Assume 75% code vectorization.

**6.18** Suppose that adding a cache to a scalar computer increases its general performance by 50% and doubles its performance on vectorizable code. Adding a vector accelerator instead of a cache to the same computer increases its performance on vectorizable code by a factor $N$. The value of $N$ is the vector-accelerator speedup. As a function of the percent vectorization, plot the vector-accelerator speedup required to double the performance of the uncached system. Do the same for the cached system. (Normally, $4 < N < 14$.)

**6.19** A pipelined vector processor uses a five-stage pipeline to perform vector addition. Each pipeline stage requires 10 ns, and the vectors have 48 elements each. How long does it take to compute the result vector?

**6.20** If a vector computer runs 10 times faster on vectorized code than on scalar code, what percentage of vectorization is required to achieve vectorization speedups by factors of 2, 4, 6, and 8? Calculate the vectorization percentages for the same speedup factors if the vector computer is 100 times faster.

**6.21** Suppose a program is $v\%$ vectorizable (i.e., $v\%$ of the code will use vector hardware). On a vector machine with vector operations 10 times faster than scalar code, for what value of $v$ will the machine have to be twice as fast on the program as a similar scalar machine? If the vector machine's scalar operations are only half as fast as those of the scalar machine, how big does $v$ have to be for the vector machine to be twice as fast? Generalize your results for various values of $v$ as a function of the required speedup and increased speed of vectorization.

**6.22** The Cray-1S supercomputer uses 22-bit addressing with an address granularity of 64 bits. How many bytes is its logical address space?

**6.23** The CDC 6600 has two floating-point multipliers. The CRAY-1 has only one, but it is fully pipelined. Identify two advantages of each design approach.

## Reference-needed Exercises

**6.24** What are some techniques for vectorizing loops that include branches? (In other words, what special array operations are included or might be included on vector computers to allow parallel execution of conditional operations?)

**6.25** Review the discussion of RISC versus CISC in Section 6.3.2. Which advantages and disadvantages seem to apply to the 80x86 and 68000 families, and why?

**6.26** Compare the virtual-memory policy of the R2000 with that used by the PDP-11. Why might the division of the virtual-address space into kernel- and user-address spaces facilitate the development of operating-system functions?

**6.27** Referring to the R2000 virtual addresses, what possible advantages are there to having two logical segments map to the same physical addresses?

**6.28** Referring to the virtual addresses of the R2000, what does the segmentation hardware imply about the permissible boundaries for aligning segments in memory?

## Exercises for Electrical Engineers

**6.29** Like most other parts of a computer, a designer can pipeline a cache to increase the performance. This will not decrease the access time to the cache, but it will increase the rate at which the cache can accept and return data. Show how to pipeline a cache.

**6.30** Show how to pipeline binary multiplication using word adders with no carry propagation at each stage of the process. (*Hint:* Consider full adders. The result may be a fine-grained pipeline.)

**6.31** Design a pipelined load-from-memory system for a machine that has the following:
1. 3 cycles for address generation and transmission to memory;
2. 4 cycles to get a value from a 16-way low-order interleaved memory;
3. 4 cycles for parity checking, data correction, and return data transmission.

That is, show what takes place in each stage of the pipeline, and show the address and data paths. (*Note:* Instead of having the CPU check for conflicts, you can have the storage system use queues to hold requests when it detects conflicts.)

# Problems

**6.32** Ivanova's Best Machine Company has decided that a loop (or repeat) instruction is the way to get the best performance. This instruction tells the machine to execute the next $N$ instructions as a loop (to repeat them) until some specified condition is true. What are three advantages of Ivanova's approach as compared to Igor's in Exercise 6.9?

**6.33** Most vectors (as high as 90% to 95%) have a stride of 1. If a cache has a refill block of $N$ words and a vector has a stride greater than 1, then the cache refill may well slow the vector access when there is a cache miss. For example, if $N = 8$, a typical value, than a vector access with a stride of 8 or more will generally only be able to access its data during every eighth cycle. Estimate the significance of this effect.

*6.34* Describe three restrictions you would like to put on a vector processor so that it can have simple demand-paged memory. Specifically, consider what happens when there are one or more page faults during the execution of an instruction or a sequence of chained instructions.

*6.35* Many scientific and engineering computations compute $AX + Y$. Suppose that you could build a functional unit to do that operation for only 10% more than the cost of the adder alone.
   a. Is it worth it? That is, justify the cost, if you can.
   b. Present two disadvantages to providing such instructions on a register-to-register vector processor.

*6.36* Most computers with complex instruction sets actually use a simple, RISC computational element and an instruction decoder, which translates machine instructions into RISC instructions. What are the relative sizes of the code spaces for a given program for the RISC, CISC, and expanded microcode for the CISC? Be as quantitative as you can.

*6.37* Consider the instruction mix given in Problem 2.81. How do you expect it to vary with the architecture of the computer? Specifically, consider the differences between RISC and CISC and between scalar and vector computers.

*6.38* What techniques can a compiler use for determining when an instruction can be moved in the instruction stream to fill a delay slot?

## Challenging Problems

*6.39* In designing a pipelined computer, you might think that increasing the pipelining always speeds up the machine. To its horror, the Zeno Computer Company (named for Zeno's paradox, which it intended to exploit) has found this not true. Every time the number of stages in a pipeline is increased, an additional delay is introduced because an additional set of latches must be added to the pipe to hold the intermediate data for the extra stage. Quantify how the amount of logic in a computer increases as the pipeline delay approaches the delay of a single latch. Quantify how the speed changes in the same situation. What if 10% of the instructions are branch instructions that must wait for the pipeline to drain before they can execute?

*6.40* Whether by software or hardware, evaluating most functions, even such basic ones as trigonometric, logarithmic, and exponential functions, is done by expanding a polynomial or a piecewise polynomial. (In a piecewise polynomial the coefficients vary somewhat depending on the argument.) How do computers with lots of registers or a deep stack compare in evaluating such functions? For each architecture consider at least two cases: when the arguments are passed in memory, and when they are passed in registers or on the stack.

*6.41* Branches, especially conditional branches, are a nuisance for computer designers because they alter the simple pipeline flow of control, making high-speed operation more difficult. Two reasons that vector instructions enhance performance are that they implicitly include a large number of branches and they can include a large number of memory references. The implicit branches in the control of the vector instructions themselves do not present a comparable control difficulty—why? Why does the predictability of memory referencing improve performance? Answer this last question for a paged memory system.

*6.42* Discuss the general characteristics of ISAs as they relate to pipelining. Discuss those features that are easily pipelined and those that are difficult to pipeline. What can you conclude about the current trend in RISC instruction-set design?

*6.43* Branch instructions in supercomputers tend to be relatively slow. Some machines use branch-prediction logic to speed up these operations, and correct prediction rates of over 80% are seen. Evaluate some of the other techniques that have been used or proposed:

   a. adding special instructions for loops so the computer can assume that these branches will be taken;
   b. adding special instructions to allow the compiler or programmer to tell the machine the expected direction (forward or backward in the code stream) of the next branch;
   c. adding instructions to allow the compiler or programmer to eliminate branch instructions by replacing them with "logical" operations, such as R1 ← MAX(R2, R3);
   d. adding vector instructions, which include an implicit branch operation.

## Discussion/Team Problems

**6.44** What advantages do various types of pipelining provide for highly sequential (or scalar) computation (i.e., a large fraction of the operations in a computation depend on other recent computations.)

**6.45** Architects use pipelined instruction decoding to decrease the effect of the von Neumann bottleneck. An alternative is to decode multiple instructions at each cycle. The Hugely Powerful Computer Company has hired you as chief architect for a new family of supercomputers. If you want to leave as many options as possible available for increasing the speed of the machines, what choices of instruction format will you make?

**6.46** Levesque's law states that it is always possible to make one computer run slower than another. If you were trying to make a Cray look slower than a PC, what type of benchmark would you select?

**6.47** Vector registers add hardware to a computer. They also increase the software complexity because, among other things, the software must "stripmine" (segment) the loops. How real are these concerns? What are some of the reasons for using vector registers instead of memory-to-memory vector operations? (*Hint:* What are the reasons for having scalar registers instead of providing only memory-to-memory scalar operations?)

**6.48** The CDC 6600 has two floating-point adders and two increment units (for accessing memory). Few recent computers have multiple units like the CDC 6600; instead they use pipelined units. What are the advantages or disadvantages of each approach? (*Hint:* The answer depends on technology.)

**6.49** Describe three techniques a compiler can use to optimize code for a RISC processor. How does optimized RISC code differ from optimized CISC code?

**6.50** Suggest ways the operating system can use the translation lookaside buffer (TLB) to speed up memory accesses. Why might a software-controlled TLB be more effective than a hardware-controlled TLB?

**6.51** Why should software want to access random TLB entries?

**6.52** Make a general comparison of the instruction sets and instruction execution policies of the R2000 and the CDC 6600 computers. Consider such factors as the execution speed of the operate instructions (e.g., arithmetic, logical, and shift) and the speed of the memory accesses.

**6.53** Superspeed Corporation proposed to build a superfast computer by dividing every operation into 1000 stages and pipelining all operations. The pipeline clock could then operate at 50 ps (1 psec = 0.001 ns). Critique Superspeed's proposal.

**6.54** Most of the original vector computers and the highest-performance vector supercomputers use no data cache, only an instruction cache. Give three reasons for this design.

# Chapter Index

annul bit 313
arithmetic-unit pipeline 289
branch-delay slot 313
branch penalty 296
busy flag 298
clock-cycle time 289
delayed branch 313
delayed load 313
entry-operand-register designator 299
flowthrough time 289
flushing a pipeline 296
function-unit designator 299
instruction issue 298
instruction-unit pipelines 289
interinstruction dependency 296
load-delay slot 313
mode register 298
multifunction pipe 289
$N_{1/2}$ 305
$N_{crossover}$ 305
pipe 288
pipeline 288
pipeline granularity 290
pipeline variability 290
pipelining 286
read flag 299
result rate 305
scoreboard 298
serial processing 286
startup time 305
unifunction pipe 289
XBA registers 298
XBA result-register designator 298

# 7
# Parallel Processors

**7.1 Interconnection Networks** *323*
- 7.1.1 Taxonomy *324*
- 7.1.2 Interconnection Topologies *327*
- 7.1.3 Application of Interconnection Networks for Parallel Processors *338*

**7.2 SIMD Machines** *341*
- 7.2.1 Types of SIMD Architectures *341*
- 7.2.2. SIMD Operations *344*

**7.3 MIMD Machines** *364*
- 7.3.1 Running Processes on an MIMD Processor *365*
- 7.3.2 Requirements for Multiprocessor Systems *365*
- 7.3.3 Cache Coherence *367*
- 7.3.4 Loosely Coupled Multiprocessors *370*
- 7.3.5 Fault-tolerant Computers *377*

**7.4 Alternate Architectures** *383*
- 7.4.1 Dataflow Architectures *384*
- 7.4.2 Neural Networks *389*

*In this, our final chapter, we focus on the second of two major techniques for speeding up a computer: parallel processing. Parallel processors come in three major varieties: SIMD machines, multiple-instruction-stream, multiple-data-stream (MIMD) machines, and alternate architectures. Because parallel processors use interconnection networks to link the processors together, we begin with a discussion of interconnection networks and their properties (Section 7.1). Next we look at SIMD machines, which include processor arrays, associative processors, and hypercube machines (Section 7.2). In Section 7.3 we discuss multiprocessors, or MIMD machines, where our focus is on their use in fault-tolerant architectures*

> **Key Terms**
>
> **Connection machine** An SIMD computer that uses an interconnection network with hypercube topology to connect its processors and memories together.
>
> **Dataflow model of computation** A formal computational model that uses a dataflow graph, rather than a program, to specify a computation.
>
> **Fault-tolerant computer** A computer with the capability to continue operation even when a component fails.
>
> **Hardware-intensive architecture** An architecture whose potential speedup is proportional to the amount of available hardware. Examples are associative processors and processor arrays.
>
> **Interconnection network** A network for connecting processors and memories together. Options on the characteristics of interconnection networks include centralized or distributed control; circuit switching or packet switching; and variations in expandability, redundancy, bandwidth, and topology.
>
> **Processor array** A single-instruction-stream, multiple-data-stream (SIMD) machine in which the interconnection network has the topology of an array with nearest-neighbor interconnections.
>
> **Tightly synchronized multiprocessors** Multiprocessors of a fault-tolerant system that operate in lock-step, with each processor duplicating in real time the computation of the other.

*and on the problem of cache coherence. We conclude in Section 7.4 with a brief discussion of two alternate parallel architectures: dataflow machines and neural networks.*

Parallel processors are computers with more than one CPU, and in Chapter 1 we loosely divided them into three major groups: SIMD machines, MIMD machines (also called multiprocessors), and alternative architectures. The SIMD category includes associative processors, processor arrays, and hypercube machines. The MIMD category is composed of GM-MIMD and LM-MIMD machines (where GM refers to global memory and LM to local memory). The GM-MIMD category includes the tightly coupled commercial multiprocessors; machines in the LM-MIMD category include the loosely coupled multiprocessors and are also called multiple processors. The alternative architectures include dataflow machines and neural networks.

MIMD and SIMD machines have been around for a long time. A single CPU with an independent I/O channel is a tightly coupled multiprocessor, and manufacturers introduced commercial machines of this type in the early 1960s. Companies have also produced dual-processor computers since the 1960s; dual processors require little more than two CPUs and a small amount of control hardware (and, of course, an appropriate operating system). Multiprocessors with four or more CPUs have been around nearly as long, and various research groups and computer manufacturers have produced processor arrays and loosely coupled multiprocessors since the 1970s. In the *Case Studies* we present examples of historically important parallel processors.

**see Case Studies 14–18**

Although parallel processors have been with us for several decades, the massive parallelism available in the newest SIMD processors—up to 65,536 processing elements (PEs) in 1991—is a relatively recent development. Several technological changes have led to the feasibility of these highly parallel machines:

- the evolution in logic technology to very large scale integration (VLSI);
- a dramatic reduction in power requirements;
- decreased cost;
- increased speed;
- increased reliability.

The demand for increasing amounts of computing power is probably the biggest driving force in the computer industry. Von Neumann architectures are limited by component and signal speeds, which are in turn limited by the speed of light. Yet specialized applications continue to make increased demands on computers. Simulations of complex physical systems, seismic data processing, weather forecasting, molecular modeling, electronic design, large database systems, and image processing are typical applications requiring vast amounts of computation. Hence there is a real need for computer architectures that are not limited by the von Neumann CPU-to-memory bottleneck. (Recall that this bottleneck results from the disparity between high CPU speeds and much lower memory speeds.)

Many of the applications that require massive amounts of computation have one feature in common: data analysis requires the same calculation on large amounts of data. In Chapter 6 we showed how pipelined processors, particularly the vector processors, take advantage of this computational repetition. Commercial, tightly coupled multiprocessors are usually dual-processor or four-processor versions of the same single-processor systems, and most of them are also pipelined. Some commercial multiprocessors have a dozen or so CPUs.

Pipelined processors and commercial multiprocessors take advantage of computational repetition. The SIMD machines do so also but in a very different way. They distribute a given computation over many identical PEs; later in the chapter we shall describe several algorithms that illustrate how they do so.

Although by far the greatest percentage of commercial processors today fall within the categories of SISD (von Neumann machines), SIMD, and MIMD, a great deal of recent research has focused on alternative architectures, including dataflow processors, reduction machines, and neural networks. Chapter 7 concludes with a brief introduction to these classes of machines.

## 7.1 ■ Interconnection Networks

In multiprocessor systems, multiprocessor-multimemory systems, and processor arrays, one key design issue is the **interconnection network,** which is the network for connecting processors and memories together. Researchers have done a tremendous amount of theoretical work in this field, but there has been almost no transfer of this to practice. Because the largest problems require large multiprocessors, any complete family of machines will have to allow systems with many processors.

*interconnection network*

Interconnection networks come in a variety of types and topologies. The suitability of a particular type depends on the use to which it will be put. Let us consider some typical uses; the examples given in parentheses are discussed later in the chapter:

1. to pass control signals among processors;
2. for connecting the CPU and I/O processors to different banks of memory (e.g., the high-speed multistage crossbar switch in most large modern computers);
3. for passing messages between processors (e.g., the hypercube interconnection network of the Connection Machine);
4. for reorganizing data for transfer (e.g., permutation networks);
5. for relatively long term interconnections (e.g., crossbars used by some computers to connect processors to I/O devices).

In this section we present a general overview of interconnection networks. Section 7.1.1 begins by considering different ways to categorize them according to several important design and performance factors. We then describe a number of common interconnection topologies (Section 7.1.2), and conclude by discussing their applicability to both multiprocessors and processor arrays (Section 7.1.3).

### 7.1.1 ■ Taxonomy

**Terminology**

Before considering the number of ways to classify interconnection networks, some terminology will be useful to know. **Nodes** are the junction points of an interconnection network. Here the word will be used generically to designate a processor, a memory module, an interconnection link, or other component in a group of interconnected components. For a parallel-processor system, each processor may connect to one node of an interconnection network, but several processors may also connect to a single node.

When one processor communicates with another processor across a network, the node that initiates the communication is the **master node,** and the one that responds to the communication is the **slave node.** When viewed in this way, a processor making a memory request on a system bus is a master node and the memory it accesses is a slave node during the bus cycle.

It is generally useful to distinguish two types of networks: circuit-switched and packet-switched. Designers use **circuit-switched networks** primarily when the system repeatedly requires a particular routing pattern. Circuit-switched networks set up a connection between the communicating nodes for the duration of a communication, much as a phone system appears to its users. **Packet-switched networks** are those where each **packet** of information finds its own way through the network. A packet is a group of bits and is also called a **message.** The nodes of packet-switched networks have buffers for holding the packets. Sometimes called **seeing-eye packets,** each packet of information includes the routing information for the communication (i.e., the address of the slave node), the datum being communicated, and a specification of what the slave node is to do with the datum.

Some networks require many switches between nodes while others require a single switch. Although in most applications the exact number of switches is an implementation detail, multiple switches tend to imply longer communications time but simpler switching elements. Interconnection networks with many stages of simple switches are called **multistage interconnection networks (MINs)** and are generally the only type found in systems with a large number of nodes.

Interconnection networks may also be categorized by their control systems. Some networks, notably the circuit-switched networks, use **centralized control.** Processors request service from a single network controller, which arbitrates among requests, establishes priorities, and sets up the necessary routing. See Fig. 7.1. Buses are generally of this type, as are some staged networks. (The bus and staged-network topologies will be discussed in Section 7.1.2.) Processor arrays generally use centralized control with control coming from the central control unit. Some networks, such as packet-switched networks, use **distributed control.** For them each node in the network independently handles requests for its use and the network lacks the centralized network control unit that appears in Fig. 7.1. A routing tag, which is part of each packet, specifies the address of the destination node for the packet. Most commercial systems with interconnection networks are of this type.

One may categorize interconnection networks by their timing control. A **synchronous network** uses a centralized clock to regulate its activity, while an **asynchronous network** makes connections or transfers messages on demand. Message-passing networks with distributed-control are usually asynchronous.

*synchronous network*
*asynchronous network*

**Design Factors**

The following factors also influence the appropriateness of a particular interconnection strategy to an application.

*Communication Diameter*

Also called **communication distance,** the **communication diameter** is the number of nodes through which a message must travel to reach its destination. If the diameter is large, messages will take longer to travel. For long distances the time may also increase because of network contention.

*communication distance*
*communication diameter*

*Expandability*

A designer expands a network by adding nodes to it. The cost of adding a node depends largely on the number of components and connections required for adding the node. For some networks the cost of adding a node is fixed. For

**FIGURE 7.1** *Structure of an interconnection network with centralized control.*

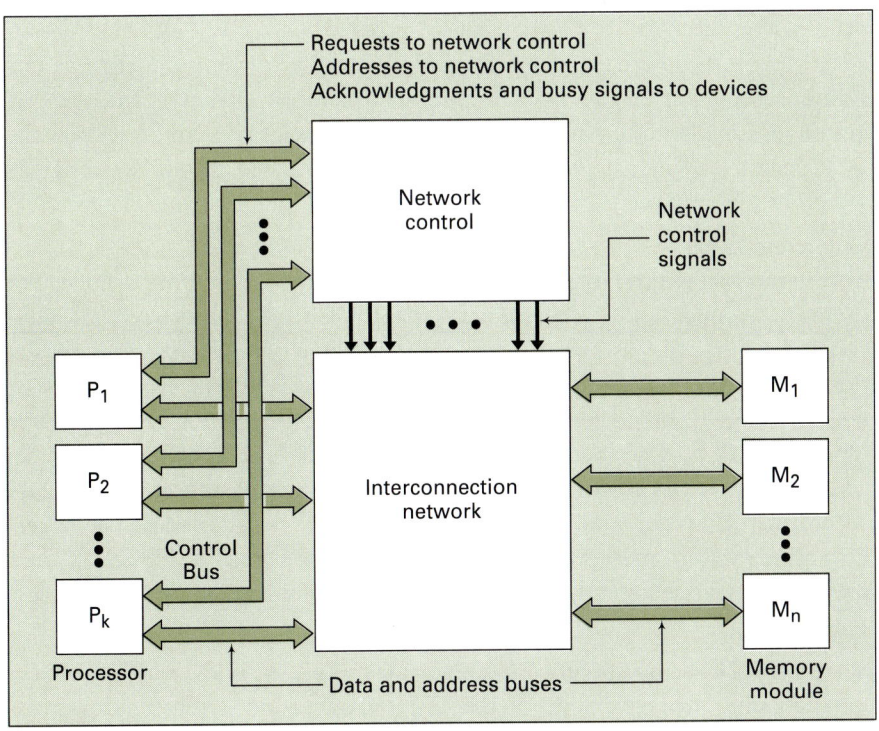

others the cost increases linearly or quadratically as a function of network size. For still others the cost is a logarithmic function of network size. Cost is often the limiting factor for expanding a given network topology, as we will show shortly.

### Redundancy

**Redundancy** refers to the number of different paths a message may travel from its source to its destination. If there is no redundancy, a defective node will prevent all messages needing to pass through that node from reaching their destinations. A redundant network may not only be better able to tolerate faulty components; it may also enable alternate routings and thereby alleviate traffic congestion.

### Routing

A message-passing network should be able to route information easily from source to destination. The routing difficulty depends on the network uniformity and may be influenced by faulty nodes, local traffic patterns, and other factors. For staged, circuit-switched interconnection networks, the complexity of setting up the switches is also an important consideration. The network control unit, whether a single control unit or a distributed control mechanism, must be able to keep up with the demands for services.

### Bandwidth and Network Latency

The **bandwidth** of a network is the amount of data that can be sent over it per unit of time. For computer networks this is usually measured in millions of bytes per second (MBS) or billions of bytes per second (GBS) and does not include the overhead part of the information actually transmitted, such as bits giving information on parity or control. The **network latency** is the time required for a message to pass through it. When messages do not all require the same length of time, as is common in packet-switched networks, designers sometimes specify the average, minimum, and maximum network latencies.

### Connection Degree

The **connection degree** refers to the number of pathways leaving a node. For example, the nodes of a processor array that implement nearest-neighbor interconnections (north, east, west, south) have a degree of 4, whereas the connection degree for the nodes of the CM-1 hypercube is 12 since each network node contacts 12 other network nodes. Both nearest-neighbor and hypercube topologies will be described later in Section 7.1. The higher the connection degree, the higher the cost. However, the communication distance may decrease accordingly. Consider a multiprocessor with 4096 ($2^{12}$ or $64^2$) nodes: The largest distance a message must travel is 12 for a hypercube of degree 12 but 126 for a processor array having only nearest-neighbor interconnections.

### Tap Structure

Some networks bring all network connections into the nodes. The 12 connections coming into each node of the CM-2 Connection Machine are an example. An alternative is to use a **network tap** of some type, so that each node has only a single connection to the network. The star network, illustrated later in Fig. 7.4, is of this type. We shall refer to these as having distributed or centralized switches, respectively.

## 7.1.2 ■ Interconnection Topologies

Architects have proposed and implemented numerous interconnection topologies. Following is a brief description with illustrations of some of them.

### Networks with Constant-degree Communications

In the absence of contention, the following communications networks allow any two nodes to communicate in the same amount of time.

### *Bus*

The **single-bus architecture,** illustrated in Fig. 7.2, is generally used by minicomputer and microcomputer systems today. It is useful when the maximum number of processors is small (i.e., the maximum bus traffic is low compared to the bus bandwidth). It is inexpensive and hence suitable for small multiprocessor systems. It can also be useful on a local basis in a tree-structured system. (Tree-structured networks are discussed later in Section 7.1.2.) However, it does limit communications to one connection per bus cycle.

   **Multibus architectures,** those with several buses, are useful for higher-performance systems, since they enable several devices to communicate with several other devices simultaneously. However, scheduling parallel buses is more complex, as is maintaining cache coherence for such systems. Figure 7.3 illustrates a system with two buses.

FIGURE 7.2 *Single-bus architecture.*

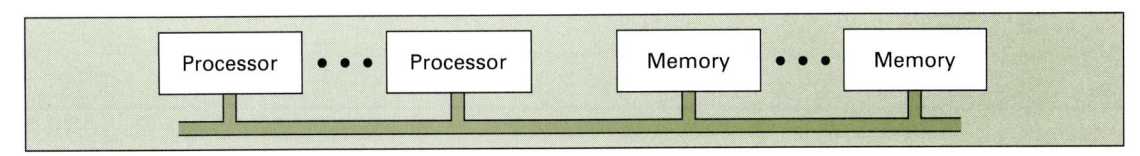

FIGURE 7.3 *Two-bus architecture.*

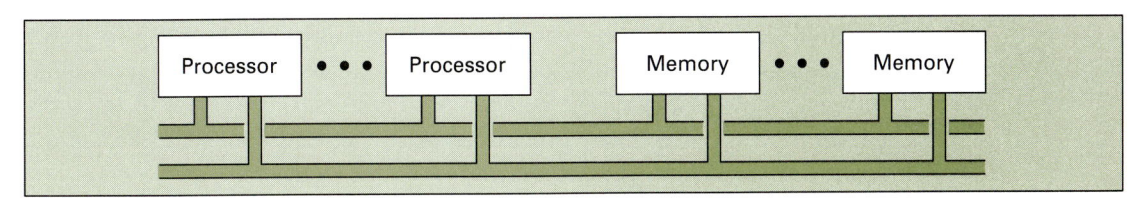

### Star

The **star topology** consists of any number of degree-1 nodes contacting a special designated node called the **hub**. In practical terms this topology is limited to a few dozen processors because of contention for use of the hub. See Fig. 7.4.

### Full Crossbar

This network and the next one allow communication in constant time, even if the network is busy, provided only that there is no contention at the slave node itself.

A $p \times m$ **crossbar** is a switch that can connect $p$ processors to $m$ memory banks (or other devices) with a concurrency equal to $\min(p, m)$. When $m$ equals the number of memory banks, the crossbar is a **full crossbar,** also called a **nonblocking crossbar.** See Fig. 7.5. Virtually all multiprocessors use a crossbar or the equivalent that is programmer-invisible and hence outside the scope of this chapter. A full crossbar is too expensive for a very large number of processors because the number of switching elements grows as the product of the number of processors and the number of memories. It is very useful, however, on a local basis, for example, among a small cluster of processors and memories at the lowest level of a tree-structured system.

### Complete Processor-to-Processor Interconnections

The complete processor-to-processor interconnection topology is similar to a full-crossbar but with the switches distributed to the nodes. However, the cost of adding nodes becomes prohibitive even for a modest number, because the connection degree increases with number of nodes. See Fig. 7.6. In a practical sense the size is severely limited because the nodes have a fixed number of possible connections.

### Networks Whose Communication Time Depends on the Number of Nodes

The following networks pass information between the nodes and are suitable for packet switching.

### Linear or Ring

The **linear topology** is one of the simplest available. All nodes are degree 2, so the cost of adding a node is fixed. However, communication time depends on the distance between the nodes, and a faulty node may disrupt communications between all processors separated by the faulty node. In practice, designers build the nodes to be **fault-tolerant nodes.** Fault-tolerant nodes remove themselves from the network when faulty and allow the message to pass by.

The **ring topology** is a linear network with ends connected, as illustrated in Fig. 7.7. Messages can now bypass a faulty node by going the other way around, and the cost of adding a node is still fixed. Because the communication time increases with the number of processors, this topology is impractical for a system with many processors. Also, network contention becomes a significant problem as the number of processors increases.

**FIGURE 7.4** *Star topology.*

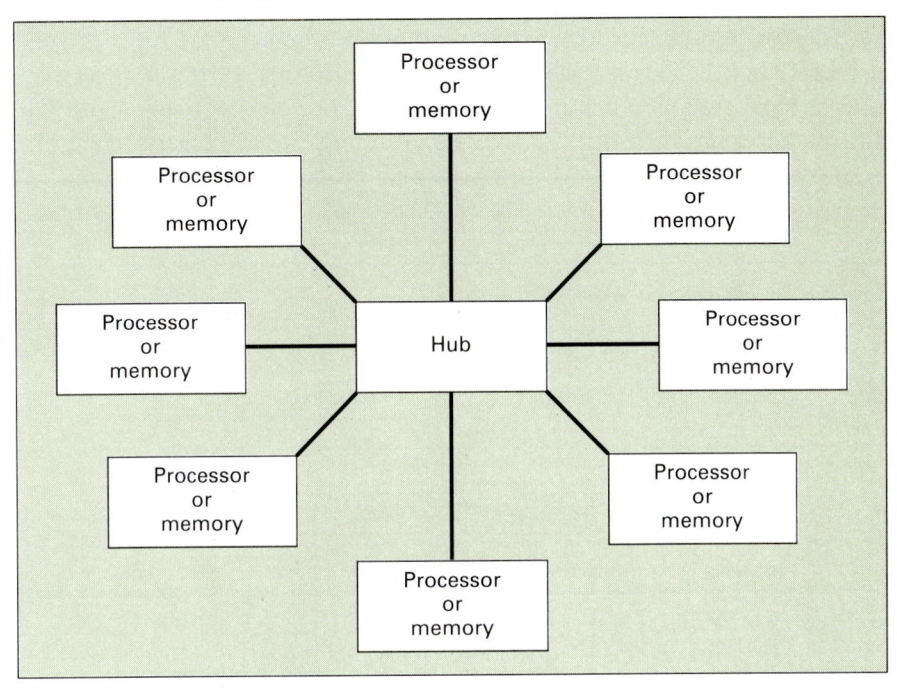

**FIGURE 7.5** *Crossbar topology. Notice that the crossbar can simultaneously connect any number of processors to different memory modules.*

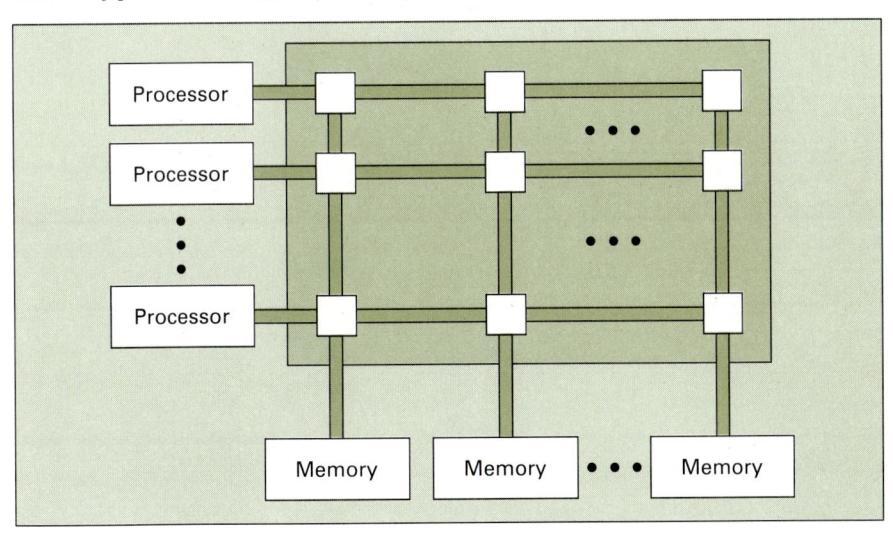

330    Computer Architecture

*Tree*

**tree-structured networks**

A number of recent research machines have used tree-structured or hierarchical interconnection networks. **Tree-structured networks** appear to be promising for all but the lowest levels of large multiprocessors, where the processors in each local group are tightly coupled to a single memory through a crossbar switch, for example. Figure 7.8 shows two examples, both binary trees. The Sum-OR tree of Goodyear's Massively Parallel Processor (MPP) is also an example of a tree-structured interconnection network. (Refer to the *Case Studies*.)

**see Case Study 17**

**FIGURE 7.6**   *Complete interconnection topology.*

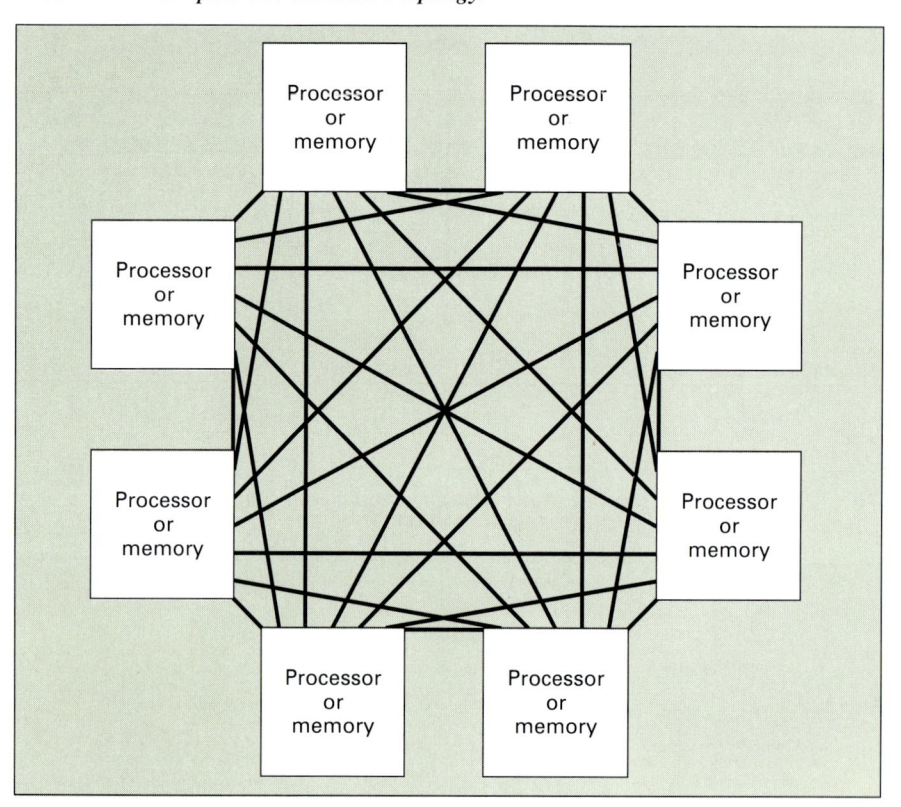

**FIGURE 7.7**   *Ring topology.*

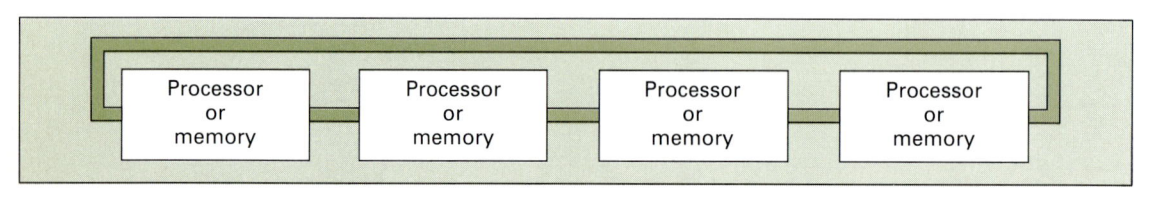

## Nearest Neighbor

The **nearest-neighbor topology,** used by the ILLIAC IV, MPP, and CM-1, is suitable for processor arrays but is too difficult to use in a general-purpose multiprocessor system. In this topology, processors occupy the intersections of a two-dimensional grid, and two processors are connected if they are adjacent (neighbors) on the grid, either left-right or up-down. **Edge connections** are those where the right-most processors of each row connect to the left-most processors of the same or next row, and similarly for the processors of the top

nearest-neighbor topology

edge connections

**FIGURE 7.8** *Two tree-structured interconnection networks. (a) Uses degree-2 nodes and localized system buses; (b) uses degree-3 nodes.*

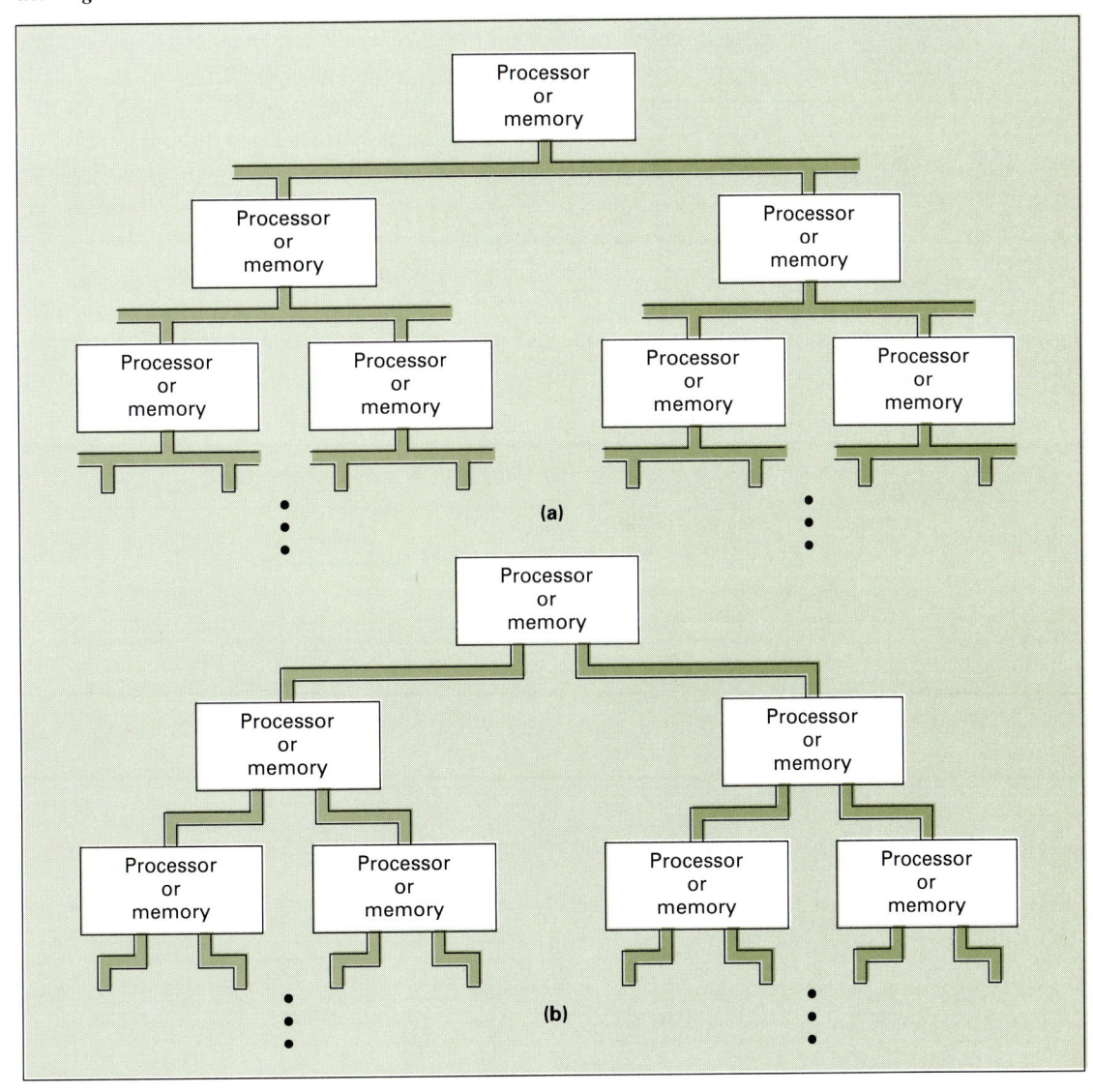

and bottom rows of the array. Edge connections yield cylindrical, toroidal, spiral, and spiral-toroidal topologies, depending on whether the connections are to the same row or column or the next row or column.

### Staged Networks

**staged interconnection networks**

Researchers have studied many types of **staged interconnection networks,** which are interconnection networks that use multiple switching elements between inputs and outputs. Staged interconnection networks can either be circuit-switched or packet-switched. For packet-switched networks, some of the stages have latches for holding the packets while forwarding or preparing to forward them to the next stage. Networks of this type are particularly useful for pipelined processors.

Staged interconnection networks generally use small crossbar switches (from $2 \times 2$ to $8 \times 8$ crossbars). Figure 7.9 illustrates the two states of a $2 \times 2$ crossbar and also shows a crossbar with latches for a packet-switched network.

**broadcast**

Some crossbar switches provide a **broadcast** capability in addition to their switched states. Using broadcast states, the switch can broadcast the value arriving at one input to various subsets of outputs. Figure 7.10 shows the two broadcast states of a $2 \times 2$ switch.

One reason for considering staged networks is their cost. An $N \times N$ crossbar requires on the order of $N^2$ components; a staged network for connecting $N$ devices to $N$ other devices requires on the order of $N \log N$ components. However, while a full crossbar can simultaneously make any set of

FIGURE 7.9 *2 × 2 Crossbar. (a) States and (b) with latched outputs.*

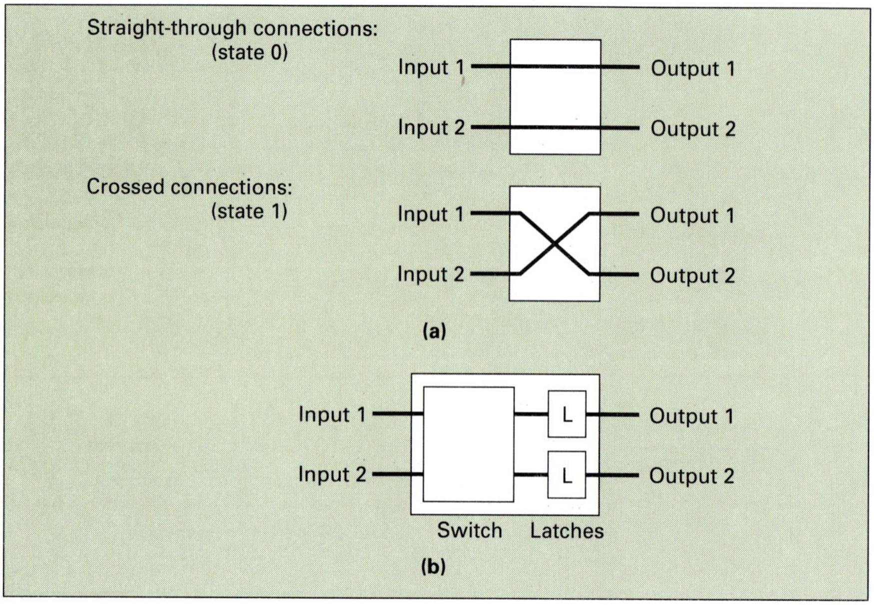

connections (if there are no duplicate output requests), the staged networks cannot generally do this.

Among the many types of staged networks are **Banyan networks,** in which there is exactly one path between any input-output pair. Hence there is no redundancy. There are many varieties of Banyan networks, which differ in their interconnection patterns and in the way in which they are controlled. Most of them do not appear to be particularly promising for connecting large numbers of processors in multiprocessor systems, but they may be useful for interconnecting clusters of processors in place of a tree interconnection. We shall illustrate these ideas with two interconnection networks.

*Banyan networks*

## Hypercube

The **hypercube topology** can be defined geometrically as having $N$ nodes on the corners of a "cube" in $n$-space where $n = \log_2 N$. A **0-cube** is a point ($2^0$ for 1 PE), a **1-cube** is a line segment ($2^1$ for two PEs), a **2-cube** is a square ($2^2$ for four PEs), a **3-cube** is a cube ($2^3$ for eight PEs), and so on.

*hypercube topology*
*0-cube*
*1-cube*
*2-cube*
*3-cube*

A hypercube interconnection topology can also be defined iteratively as follows. One node alone needs no connections. A single path directly connects two 0-cubes (nodes) to form a 1-cube, or hypercube of dimension 1. Two paths directly connect the corresponding nodes of two 1-cubes to form a 2-cube, a square or hypercube of dimension 2. Figure 7.11 shows cubes of dimensions 0, 1, and 2. Suppose the goal is to connect $2^n$ elements. We form a hypercube of dimension $n$ by taking two hypercubes of dimension $n - 1$ and directly connecting corresponding nodes. Figures 7.12 shows a 3-cube, which is a hypercube having eight nodes, and Fig. 7.13 shows a **4-cube,** which is a hypercube having 16 nodes. A 3-cube is a simple cube with edge connections, and a 4-cube consists of two cubes with directly connected corresponding corners. Notice that the number of connections from each node increases by 1 as the dimension of the hypercube increases by 1, but the total number of connec-

*4-cube*

**FIGURE 7.10** *Upper and lower broadcast states of a 2 × 2 switch. For a lower broadcast the switch ignores the upper input (Input 1), and for an upper broadcast the switch ignores the lower input (Input 2).*

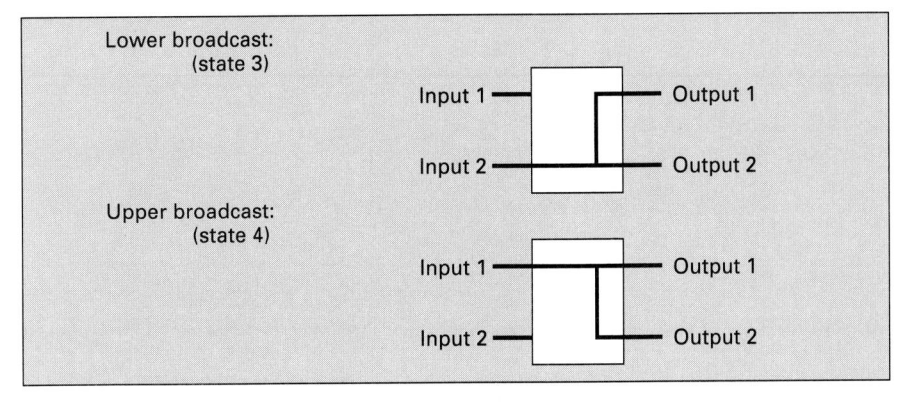

**334** *Computer Architecture*

tions increases by $2^n$ when the dimensionality of the hypercube increases from $n$ to $n + 1$ (i.e., from $2^n$ PEs to $2^{n+1}$ PEs).

**node addresses**

Let us assign binary numbers, called **node addresses,** to the nodes. One way to form a hypercube is to connect nodes whose binary addresses differ in exactly one bit position. For example, for a hypercube having $2^{12}$ PEs, a bus would directly connect the two PEs having addresses 0000 0101 1100 and 0000 1101 1100. The figures show how the connection topologies relate to the node addresses.

Figure 7.14 illustrates a Banyan network, which implements a hypercube topology. It also performs shuffle and exchange operations and is called

**FIGURE 7.11** *Simple Hypercubes. (a) A 0-cube has one processor; (b) a 1-cube has two processors; and (c) a 2-cube has four processors.*

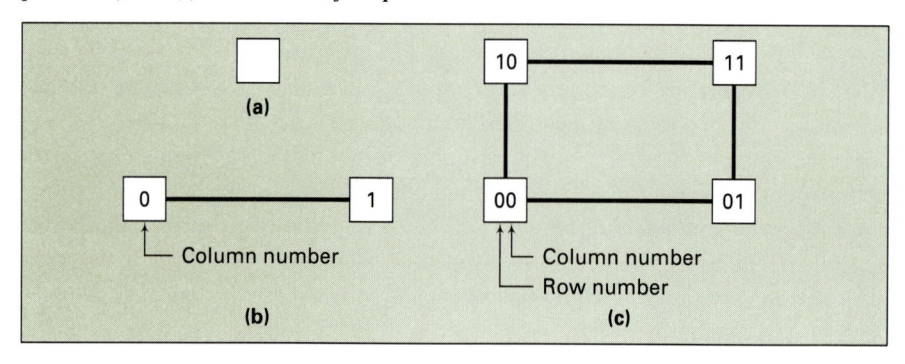

**FIGURE 7.12** *3-cube. Note that this is a three-dimensional cube with edge connections and eight processors.*

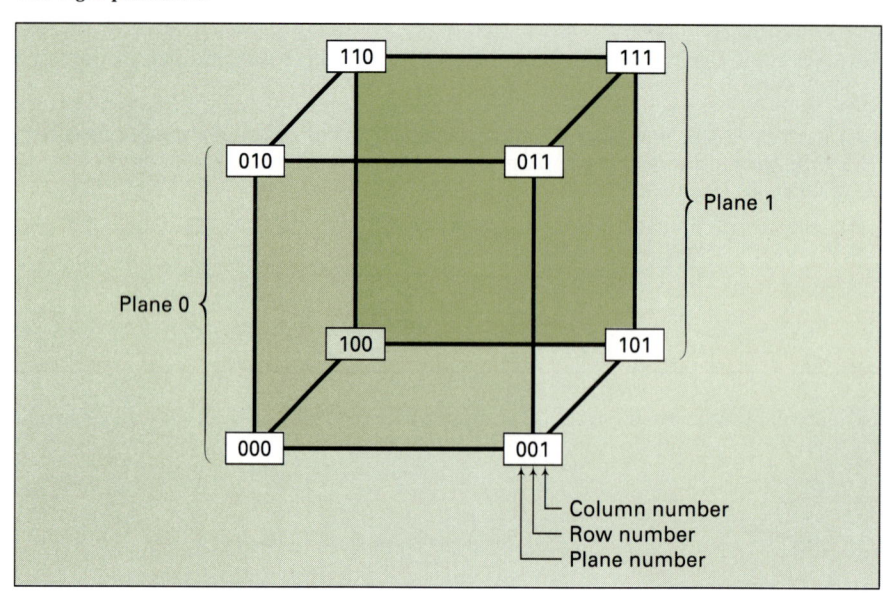

*Parallel Processors* 335

**FIGURE 7.13** *4-cube. A 4-cube has 16 processors placed at the nodes of two 3-cubes.*

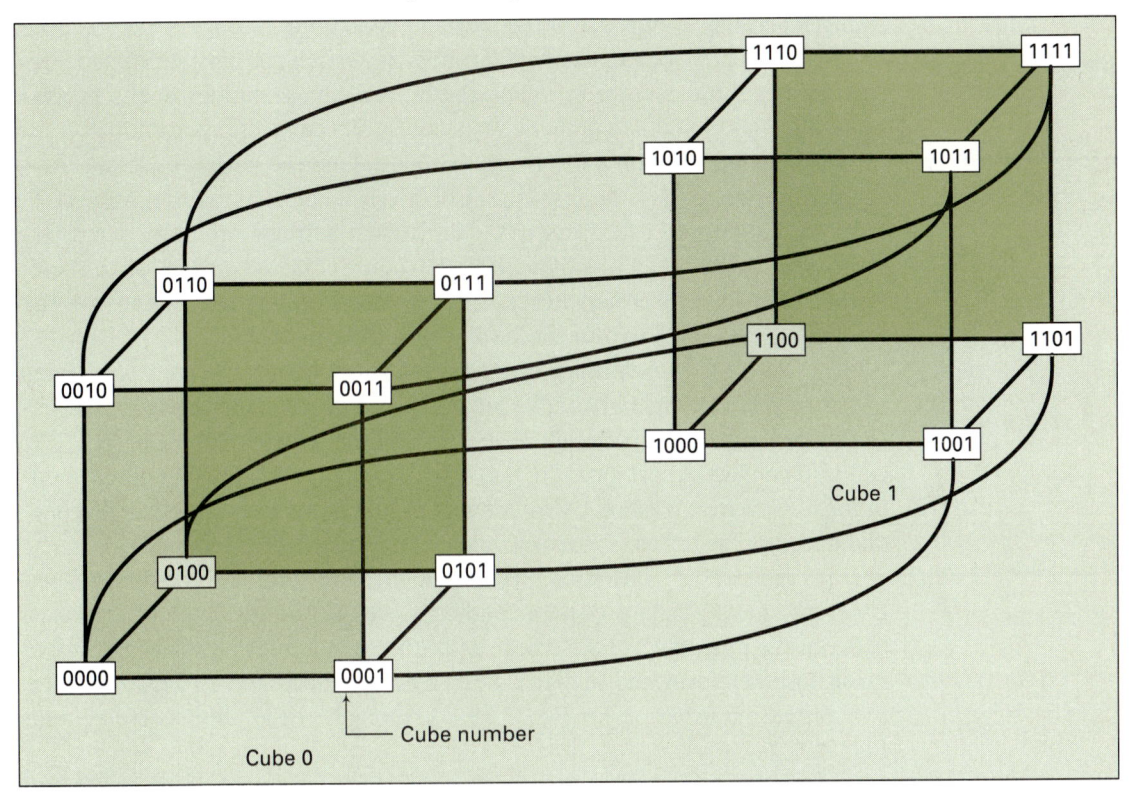

**FIGURE 7.14** *Generalized-cube network. P, processor numbers; M, memory-module numbers.*

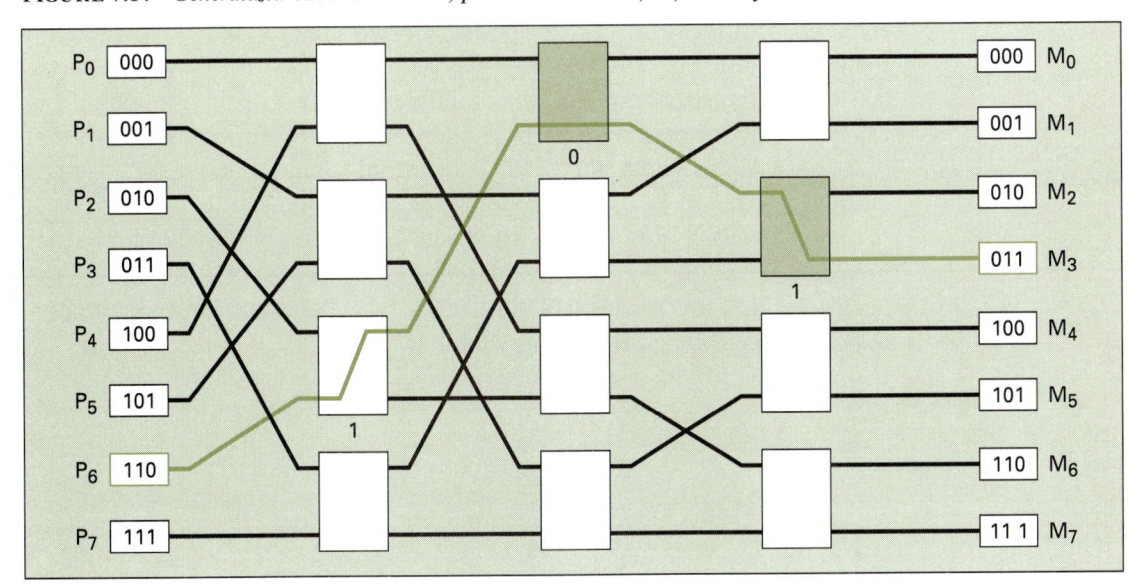

**Omega network**

**shuffle operation**
**exchange operation**

an **Omega network.** (For $2N$ inputs, $I_0$ to $I_{2N-1}$, and $2N$ outputs, $O_0$ to $O_{2N-1}$, a **shuffle operation** connects $I_j$ to $O_{2j \bmod N}$, where $0 \leq j \leq 2N - 1$, and an **exchange operation** connects $I_j$ to $O_{j+1}$ when $j$ is odd and $I_j$ to $I_{j-1}$ when $j$ is even or zero.) A controller can easily determine the switch settings for a particular routing. Let $b_2 b_1 b_0$ and $m_2 m_1 m_0$ be the binary representations of the processor and memory-module numbers, respectively. To connect processor $b_2 b_1 b_0$ to memory module $m_2 m_1 m_0$, the three switches along the pathway are set to $b_2$ XOR $m_2$, $b_1$ XOR $m_1$ and $b_0$ XOR $m_0$, respectively.[1] For example, to connect $P_6$ (address $110_2$) to M3 (address $011_2$) the switch settings are 1-0-1 (crossed–uncrossed–crossed), as highlighted in the figure. One advantage of this network is that for a packet-switched network, the control circuits can use the routing tag contained within the packet to set the switches.

Note that a controller can simultaneously connect several processors to several different memory banks provided there are no conflicting switch settings along any of the pathways. For example, the network shown in Fig. 7.14 can also connect processor $P_0$ to $M_4$, $P_1$ to $M_1$, or $P_5$ to $M_5$ (among other possibilities). However, it cannot also connect $P_0$ to $M_2$, for instance, since the second and third switches (shaded) would require conflicting settings.

Figure 7.15 illustrates one way of implementing a three-dimensional hypercube having eight processors and eight memory banks. Each of the boxes between the processors and memory banks is a $2 \times 1$ multiplexor of which two taken together form one of the $2 \times 2$ crossbars illustrated in Fig. 7.14. The two shaded multiplexors in Fig. 7.15 correspond to the colored crossbar in Fig. 7.14.

We now describe how to connect the processor at node 000 in Fig. 7.15 to the memory bank at node 011. First, notice that all multiplexors at the same level of every node select the same inputs, either left or right; these correspond to the straight-through and crossed connections, respectively, in the crossbars of Fig. 7.14. Because the source and destination addresses are 000 and 011 respectively, the top multiplexors select their left inputs (no change in the leftmost address bits) and the bottom two multiplexors select their right inputs (both the second and third address bits differ). Consequently, the top multiplexor at node 000 selects its input from processor 000, the middle multiplexor of node 010 selects its input from the top multiplexor of node 000, and the bottom multiplexor at node 011 selects its input from the middle multiplexor of node 010. The result is a connection between the processor at node 000 and the memory bank at node 011.

Designers have used the hypercube topology to add message-passing

---

1. If you recall, the addresses of two adjacent nodes in a hypercube differ in exactly one bit position. To send a packet from node $n_i \ldots n_1 n_0$ to node $n_i' \ldots n_1' n_0'$, the switching network operates as follows. Let $n_i \ldots n_1 n_0$ differ from $n_i' \ldots n_1' n_0'$ in $k$ positions, say $j_1, j_2, \ldots, j_k$. Then at step $p$ ($1 \leq p \leq k$) the network sends the packet across link $j_p$.

facilities to processor arrays (e.g., the CM-1 and CM-2), and for some local-memory multiple-processor computers, such as the iPSC/2.

*Delta Network*

A **delta network** is a staged interconnection network with the following properties:

- It has $k$ stages.
- Each stage consists of crossbars having $m$ inputs and $n$ outputs ($m \times n$ crossbars).

*delta network*

**FIGURE 7.15** *Three-dimensional hypercube illustrating the origin of the connection pattern of Fig. 7.14.*

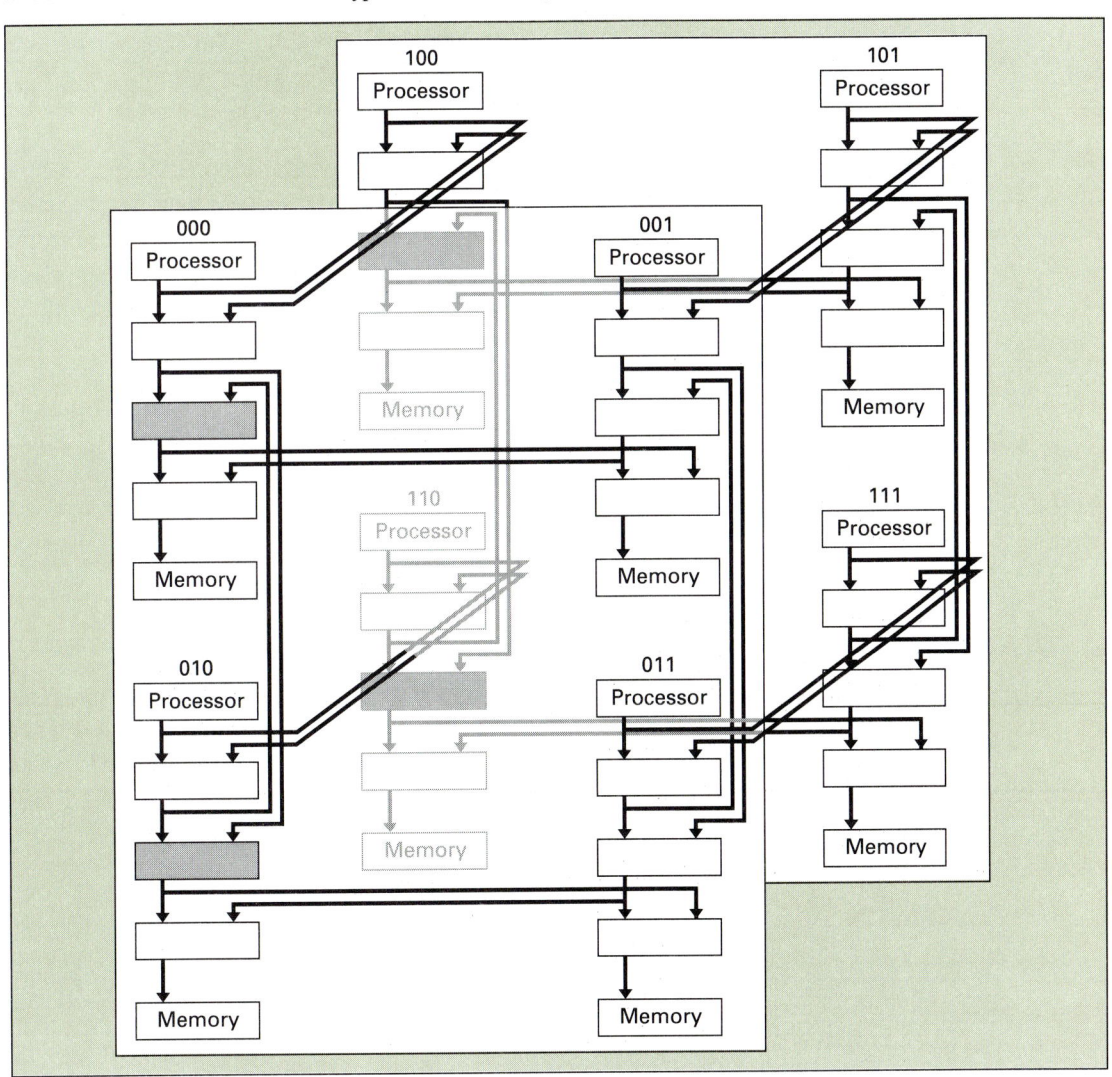

- The entire network has $m^k$ inputs and $n^k$ outputs, and hence is an $m^k \times n^k$ switching network.
- The connections allow for exactly one path from any input to any output.
- If $A$ is the destination address, expressed in base $n$, of a desired connection, then the digits of $A$ specify the crossbar settings to establish the desired connection.

Figure 7.16 shows a three stage $2^3 \times 2^3$ delta network that uses $2 \times 2$ crossbars with broadcast capabilities. The figure shows the connection pattern for allowing memory M0 to broadcast its value to processors P1, P4, P5, and P6.

### 7.1.3 ■ Application of Interconnection Networks for Parallel Processors

The following two sections discuss the requirements on interconnection networks imposed by processor arrays and multiprocessors.

#### Networks for Processor Arrays

Communications networks for processor arrays pose special problems, and the movement of data is generally a major architectural feature. On the one hand, all of the processing elements do the same thing (or nothing at all), so the communications are **globally synchronized.** On the other hand, the communication pathways fix the array size and topology and directly affect the algorithms that the machines can perform efficiently.

*globally synchronized network*

There are two application areas where processor arrays hold sufficient promise to be worthy of special investigation: scientific and engineering com-

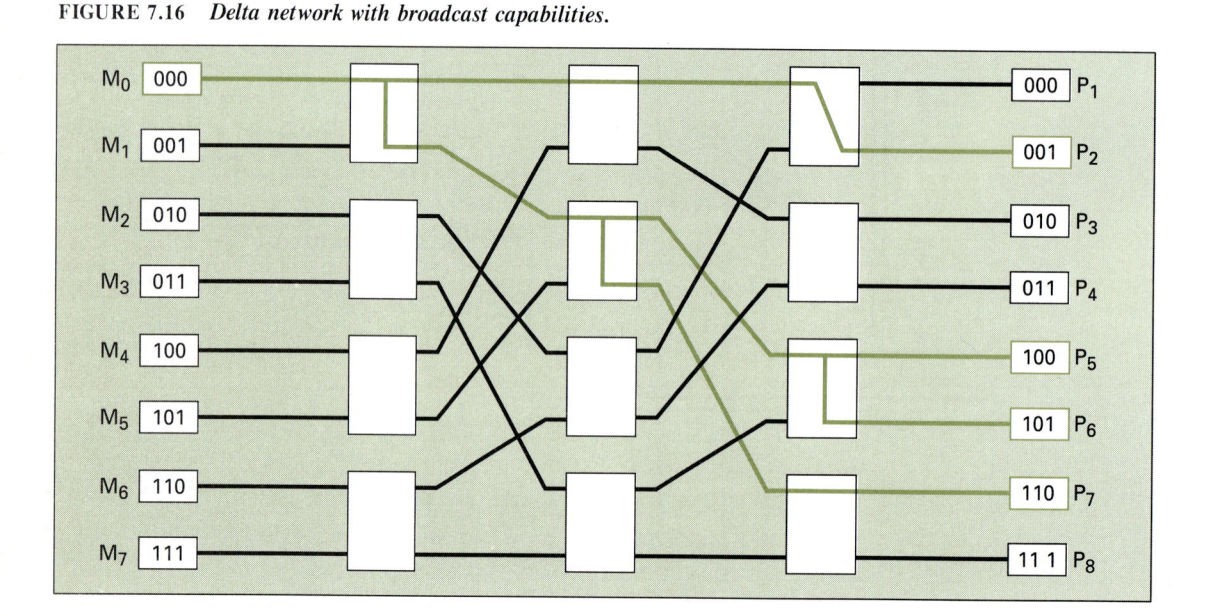

**FIGURE 7.16** *Delta network with broadcast capabilities.*

putation, and image processing. In the former case, users have treated processor arrays as vector processors, even when the designers had other intentions. Since most of the existing processor-array systems support both linear and nearest-neighbor communications, this has not been a problem. Processors with hypercube interconnection networks, such as the CM-2 or the iPSC/2, show even greater promise for these applications than do processor arrays, as the *Case Studies* show.

*see Case Studies 15 and 18*

For image-processing applications, users programmed processor arrays to operate on the two-dimensional arrays of pixels in an image. Perhaps the biggest obstacle to using them has been that instructions tend to be specific to the size of the processor array. Thus here as in other situations, it has been important for programmers to write code that depends on the actual number of processors in the array and on its logical shape (square or rectangular, for example). Digitized images tend to be at least $100 \times 100$ pixels and are often thousands of pixels on a side, while the largest processor array as of 1991 was limited to $128 \times 128$ PEs, and most are much smaller. The CM-2, an LM-SIMD hypercube processor, has 65,536 PEs and can operate as a $256 \times 256$ processor array. It is the largest machine to date. It appears that image-processing applications have and will continue to have an unlimited appetite (by current standards) for processors in an array. In contrast, a modest processor array may comprise only $8 \times 8$ processors.

Thus the major problem is that programs tend to be very specific to the size of the processor array. No local-memory processor array has hidden the size of its processor array from the programmer. Indeed, with the exception of memory-to-memory vector machines, no pre-1985 vector systems have masked their vector sizes. The CM-2, by way of contrast, can operate on arrays of any size even for a configuration with a small number of PEs. Both the hardware and the software of this family have successfully hidden the number of PEs from the user.

For processor arrays, which have their PEs arranged on two-dimensional grids with nearest-neighbor connections, each PE represents a node of degree 4—it has exactly four connections. Sending information from one PE to another can take as many as $2(\sqrt{N} - 1)$ steps for a machine with $N$ PEs. With a hypercube topology, an $N$ PE–machine requires at most, $\log_2 N$ steps to route information from one PE to another. Thus the diameter decreases, but the complexity and cost of the interconnection network can sharply increase.

**Networks for Multiprocessors**

An architect must consider many problems when selecting an addressing mechanism for a large multiprocessor architecture. Addressing is not particularly difficult for small programs, because they will generally be able to execute within the local-address space of one processor. However, researchers have done little work to characterize global or any nonlocal characteristics of large programs. Nonetheless, there are good reasons to believe that processors in a large multiprocessor system should be grouped in small clusters with the clusters connected together in assembly-line fashion using a tree or hypercube topology. Some tendencies of the large programs that require large multiprocessors and support this belief are as follows:

1. They are readily decomposed into small blocks of code, each of which has many instructions.
2. Compilers can sufficiently determine how these blocks interact to verify that they may be correctly processed in parallel.
3. The number of statements within these blocks that a compiler can make parallel with verified correctness is small.
4. The data flows through a program in an assembly-line fashion, each "processing station" being a large collection of routines mostly disjoint from the routines in other processing stations.

Factors 1 through 3 indicate the need for small clusters of tightly coupled processors, while factor 4 indicates the usefulness of many of these clusters. Item 4 also indicates that loose coupling among them is acceptable. The locality measures of programs, and the utility of overlay and segment loaders, give heuristic support to this high-level dataflow view of large programs claimed in item 4.

With these observations in mind, having linear addressing of all memory throughout the entire multiprocessor system is reasonable. Such a system is certainly uniform in its appearance and simple in design. An architect can further reduce the complexity by segmenting the address, with a specific portion of the address referring to the cluster, that is, to a specific memory, and the rest of the address, whether used or not, referring to the local address within the cluster.[2] This makes the addressing linear even though it may have "holes" (i.e., some addresses may not have actual memory).

We note that in a multiprocessing system, each processor can use local memory almost all of the time. That implies that local addresses are restricted to a small fraction of the total system memory. It follows, therefore, that a processor does not require frequent-access to data scattered at addresses with widely varying, high-order address bits. This susggests that special hardware could be used to optimize local-memory accesses. Any tightly coupled multiprocessor with caches at each processor or cluster does this.

Perhaps the most important facet in the design of an interconnection network is that it remains relatively invisible to the programmers. Once the network has been made invisible, a computer architect can design almost any-

---

2. An alternative is to put memory-mapping tables at each switch, thus allowing the addressing to be arbitrarily divided between memory modules, clusters of modules, etc.

thing else in the architecture as he or she desires. It appears that multiprocessor interconnections should be hierarchical and uniform at every level. Note, however, that this assumes certain behavior and capabilities of the compilers and operating systems that use these systems.

## 7.2 ■ SIMD Machines

An SIMD machine has a single systemwide control unit and many PEs. The systemwide control unit executes a single instruction stream, like any other von Neumann machine, and generates all of the control signals for the PEs, which it broadcasts (simultaneously sends) to all PEs. The PEs operate in lockstep fashion, each performing the same operation (or perhaps none at all) on their own data. Clearly the control unit together with one active PE *is* a von Neumann Machine (see Fig. 7.17).

SIMD machines have **hardware-intensive architectures:** their potential speedup is proportional to the amount of available hardware. The resulting parallelism enables SIMD machines to achieve tremendous speeds, sometimes exceeding several thousand MFLOPS (millions of floating-point operations per second).

*hardware-intensive architectures*

### 7.2.1 ■ Types of SIMD Architectures

As mentioned earlier, there are three basic kinds of SIMD machines: associative processors, processor arrays, and hypercube machines. **Associative processors** implement **associative-memory operations,** which depend on the *values* of the data stored in memory, rather than on the addresses or locations of those data. The earliest associative processors operated on **bit-slices** rather than words of memory, and their PEs performed bit-serial operations on the data. (Recall from Chapter 4 that bit-slices consist of all the bits from the same position from a large number of words in memory.) Thus they were **bit-slice processors** as well as associative processors. One may view the PEs of an associative processor as consisting of a large number of 1-bit ALUs.

*associative processors*

*associative-memory operations*

*bit-slices*

*bit-slice processors*

FIGURE 7.17 *An SIMD machine. When only one PE is active, an SIMD machine is a von Neumann machine (shaded part).*

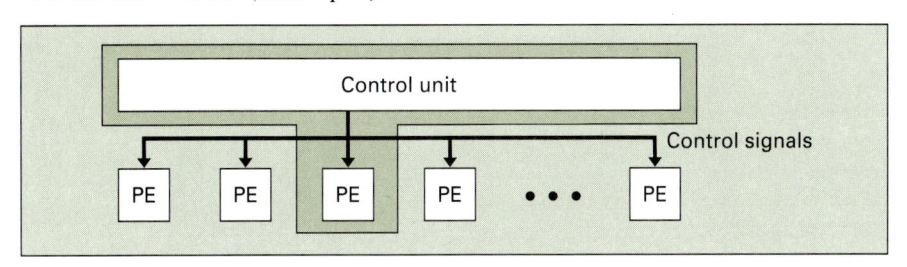

342   Computer Architecture

processor arrays

**Processor arrays** operate on two-dimensional arrays of data and come in two types: those that perform bit-serial operations (e.g., the MPP and CM-1), and those that perform word-parallel operations (e.g., the ILLIAC IV). The bit-serial processor arrays, descendants of bit-slice processors, operate on bit planes. **Bit planes** are the two-dimensional analogs of bit-slices: the PEs communicate using a two-dimensional interconnection network with nearest-neighbor interconnections.

bit planes

Figure 7.18 compares the architectures of an associative processor and a processor array.

Processor arrays differ among themselves in a number of ways, including their (1) PE structure, (2) control structure, (3) memory structure, (4) interconnection topology, and (5) I/O structure. Figure 7.19 illustrates three PE-to-memory structures, but there are many more. Goodyear's MPP resembles Fig. 7.19(a), Goodyear's STARAN resembles Fig. 7.19(b), and the ILLIAC IV resembles Fig. 7.19(c).

hypercube processor

A **hypercube processor** resembles a processor array but has its PEs connected using a hypercube interconnection network. For a hypercube processor with $2^N$ nodes, each node has a connection degree of $N$, and two PEs are

**FIGURE 7.18**  *Two types of SIMD architectures. (a) associative and (b) processor array.*

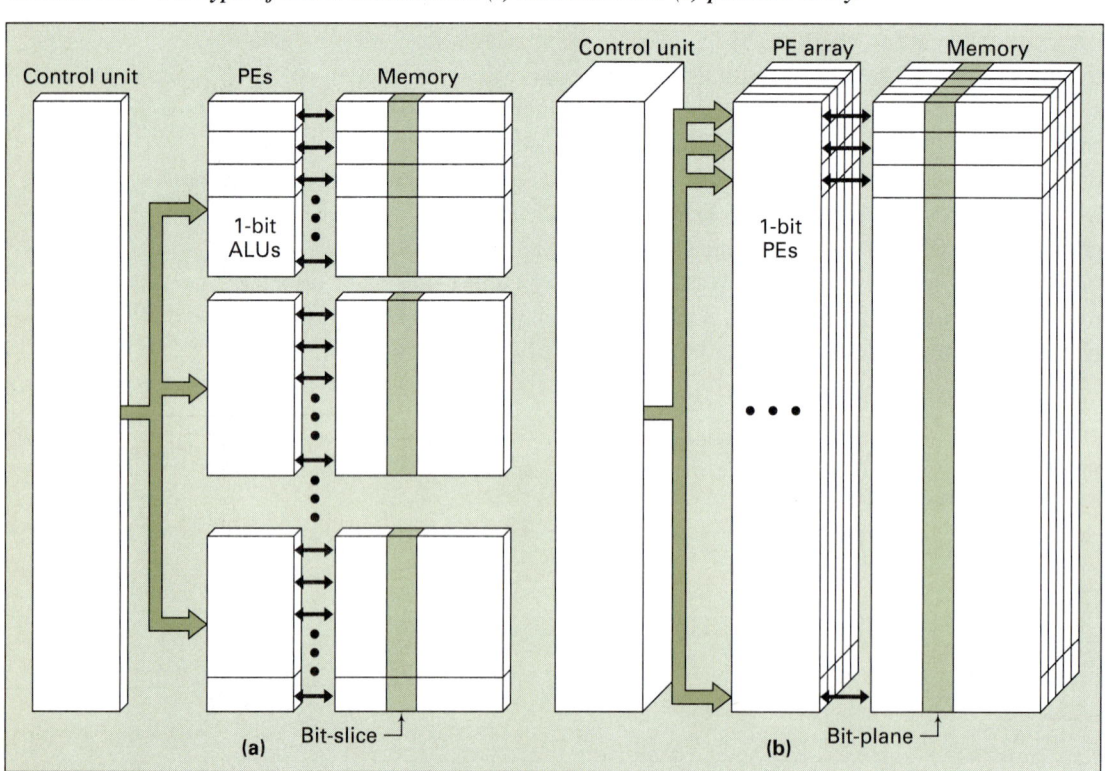

**FIGURE 7.19** *Three processor-array architectures. (a) The control unit has its own memory, and each PE has a private memory. (b) The control unit has its own memory, and several (perhaps all) PEs share memory. (c) The control unit shares memory with the PEs, but each PE can only access its own part of the total memory. In each case, the PE interconnection network (shaded) determines the topology of the processor.*

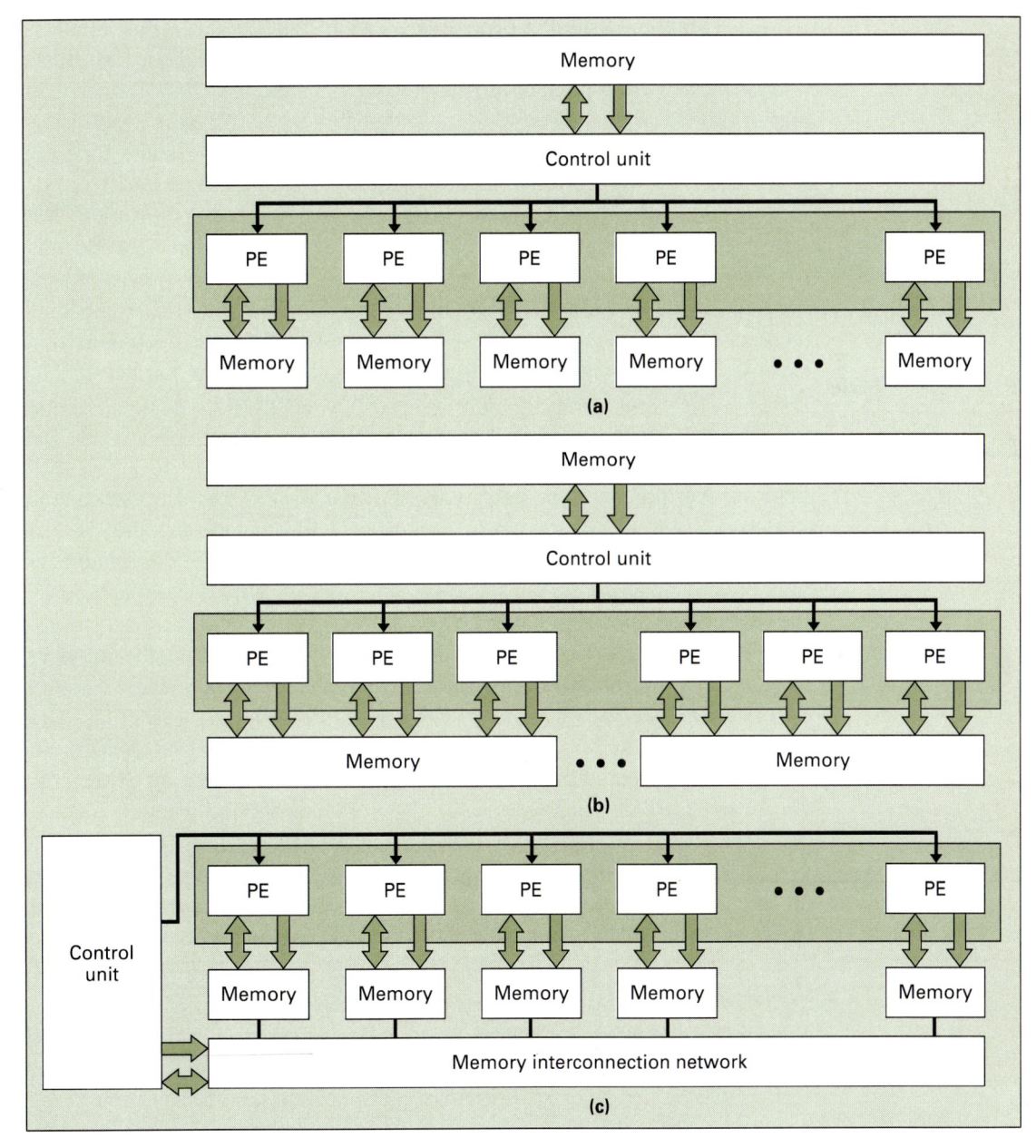

adjacent if their binary addresses differ in exactly one bit position. Hypercube processors have a much richer PE-interconnection structure than do their processor-array counterparts, but they are also restricted to a small number of PEs because of the cost of their interconnection networks.

Thinking Machine Corporation's CM-2 Connection Machine family is a practical alternative to the hypercube processor. It is a family of LM-SIMD processors where the number of PEs ranges from 8192 to 65,536. Rather than placing individual PEs at the nodes of a hypercube, a CM-2 has a 16-PE module at each node of the hypercube. Thus a CM-2 with a 12-cube topology would have 65,536 PEs, which is the largest configuration as of 1991.

As a rule, the PEs of an SIMD processor can only access their own local memory. They share data using the PE interconnection network, and thus the control unit determines how the PEs will share data. For most processor arrays, specific PE registers communicate directly with the corresponding registers of neighboring PEs. These connections form the PE interconnection network, and the control unit initiates data transmissions on the network by broadcasting a SHIFT instruction to the PEs. For example, if the interconnection topology is linear, a shift right operation would have each PE send data to the neighbor on its right. If the PE interconnection topology is an array, then there are four possible shift operations, shift north, shift east, shift south, and shift west. If the PE interconnection topology is a hypercube and all PEs shift data in the same direction, there would be one shift operation for each dimension. Finally, if each PE has an address register that specifies the destination PE, then a send operation would initiate an arbitrary pattern of data transmissions.

For an SIMD processor, all PEs use the same addressing for their local memory. For the entire processor, we can extend the notion of a memory address to include the PE number. If the PEs have $N$-bit addresses and there are $2^M$ PEs, then an $(M + N)$-bit address suffices to specify any location in memory. With a suitable interconnection network, the PEs of an SIMD machine can access any memory location by specifying the full memory address, consisting of the PE number plus the local address.

Having given a general overview of SIMD machines with an emphasis on processor arrays, we now turn to a detailed discussion of algorithms for all three types: associative, processor-array, and hypercube machines.

### 7.2.2 ■ SIMD Operations

This section describes five operations that illustrate the use of the three types of SIMD implementations. The operations we describe are associative search, vector addition, image blurring, matrix multiplication, and peak search.

#### Associative Search

*associative search*

**Associative search,** which is an associative-memory operation implemented on associative processors (as well as other SIMD machines), is the process of locating a datum based on its value. Consider, for example, the task of searching a database for all records describing females who have been employed since 1980 and who earn over $40,000. Assume that the database consists of two parts: (1) an index, and (2) a file of detailed information. The index, the only part of the database we shall consider, consists of records with the fixed fields *name, sex, position, salary, starting date,* and *file location*. Each index entry points to one or more records in the file of detailed information. Figure 7.20 illustrates a small part of the index of the database.

Assuming there is only one unordered index into the database, a von Neumann–machine program to search the index would read each record and check whether it meets the search criteria. The time it would take to search the entire index would therefore be proportional to the number of entries in the index. Using an associative memory, a program to search the index would first search for females (one step), then for salaries that exceed 40,000 (a second step), and finally for dates greater than 800000 (a third step). Thus, for a machine with associative-memory operations, the search time would depend on the type of search but not on the size of the database.

Figure 7.21 illustrates the use of an associative memory to perform the search just described. The algorithm initially assumes that all records match and therefore sets all match bits (Fig. 7.21a). The match for females leaves three match bits set (Fig. 7.21b). The algorithm now prepares for the salary match (also Fig. 7.21b). The match for salary leaves two remaining match bits set (Fig. 7.21c), and the algorithm prepares to match for the date. One match bit remains set after the match for the date (Fig. 7.21d). An associative algo-

FIGURE 7.20 *Part of the index of an employee database. The starting date is encoded as year-month-day.*

| Name | Sex | Position | Salary | Starting Date | File Location |
|---|---|---|---|---|---|
| ⋮ | ⋮ | ⋮ | ⋮ | ⋮ | ⋮ |
| Adams, John | M | Supervisor | 23,000.00 | 810416 | A1234 |
| Adams, Mary | F | Secretary | 16,295.00 | 860720 | A3551 |
| Adams, Sydney | M | Locksmith | 22,900.00 | 800201 | A7751 |
| Akers, Steve | M | Cook | 18,500.00 | 820815 | X7889 |
| Ashby, Monique | F | Supervisor | 41,200.00 | 801115 | M3342 |
| Bacon, June | F | Vice-president | 55,560.00 | 750101 | A0998 |
| ⋮ | ⋮ | ⋮ | ⋮ | ⋮ | ⋮ |

rithm for this search is listed below. The execution time of the algorithm does not depend on the size of the database.

Set all bits of the match register (MA) (to ready it for the initial search) (Fig. 7.21a).

Load the argument register (AR) with the argument "F" (to search for females).

Load the mask register (MR) with a mask that specifies the sex field (select the sex field).

Search for equality (clear any bits of MA where the records do not match) (Fig. 7.21b).

Load AR with the argument 40,000.00 (to search for the salary).

Load MR with a mask that specifies the salary field (select the salary field).

Search for ≥ (clear any match bits where the salary does not exceed the specified amount) (Fig. 7.21c).

Load AR with the argument 800000 (to search for the date).

FIGURE 7.21  *Steps in the associative search of a simple database. Each step of the search compares a different field within the database (illustrated in color). See text for additional explanation. AR, argument register; MR, mask register; MA, match register; MBR, memory-buffer register; AM, any match. See text for explanation. AM indicates when any match bits in MA are set.*

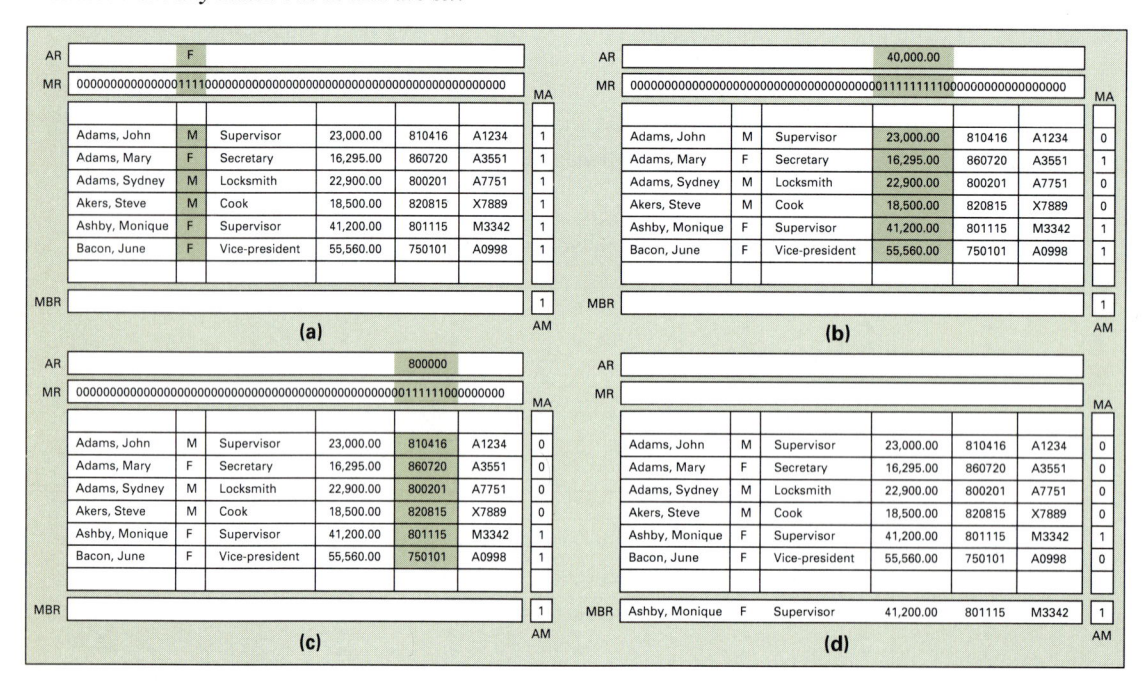

Load MR with a mask that specifies the starting-date field (select the starting-date field).

Search for ≥ (turn off any match bits where the starting data is before 1980) (Fig. 7.21d).

The cost of a large associative memory, and hence a truly associative processor, is currently prohibitive, so computer manufacturers have not yet built any commercial machines that use them. However, architects have designed and built a number of SIMD machines that implement associative-memory operations, and these are called associative processors.

In the early 1970s, Goodyear's architects undertook an ambitious project and built an associative processor called STARAN. However, rather than implementing it as an associative memory, they implemented it using a bit-slice processor. In many respects, bit-slice processors are similar to von Neumann machines. They load information from memory, operate on it, and store the result back in memory. However, the number of words on which they can operate simultaneously depends only on the amount of available hardware.

STARAN was an unusual SIMD machine because each PE's local memory was an orthogonal memory. Hence each PE could operate either on bit-slices or on words. Figure 7.22 illustrates the organization of STARAN's PEs and shows that during a bit-slice operation, each PE operates an a small part of the bit slice. For word operations, each PE operates like a conventional processor.

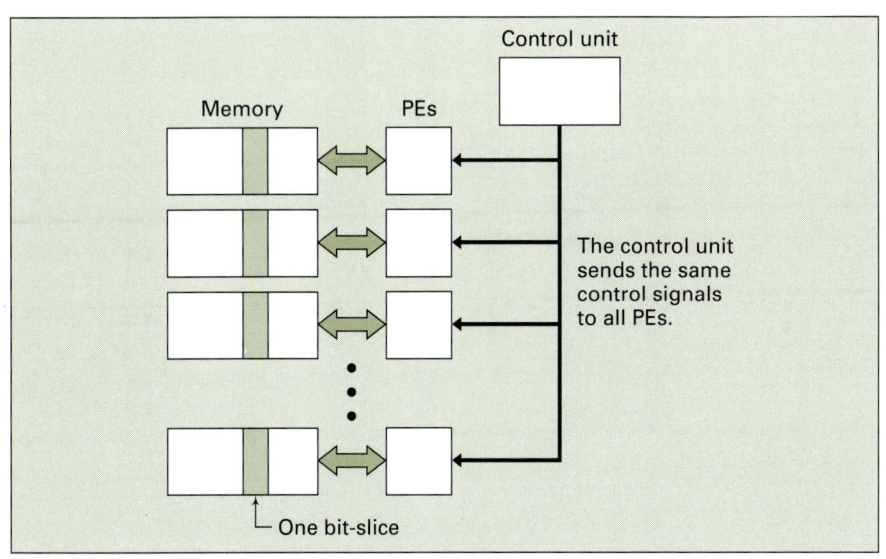

**FIGURE 7.22** *Architecture of a bit-slice PE.*

To carry out bit-slice operations, bit-slice processors first fetch a bit-slice from memory and send it to an array of 1-bit ALUs for processing. Depending on the architecture, many ALUs may be housed in a single PE. For example, one could logically view each of STARAN's PEs as consisting of 256 1-bit ALUs. Figure 7.22 illustrates such an architecture. After the ALUs process a bit-slice, the processor stores the resulting bit-slice back in memory. Figure 7.23 shows the details of a PE that consists of a number of 1-bit ALUs. From the view point of any given ALU in such a PE, the memory is global.

Following is a more detailed description of the associative-search algorithm using bit-slice operation. Assume that each PE has a word register R1 in addition to the bit-slice registers R2 through R$k$. The algorithm searches all words in memory for those having the $k$-bit pattern held in register R1, the argument register. It then sets the bits of R3 corresponding to the words in memory that match the pattern, and it sets the bits of R4 corresponding to those whose binary value exceeds the binary value initially held in register R1. Table 7.1 defines the notation used in the algorithm, and Figure 7.24 illustrates the starting configuration and the results of the first two iterations.

**FIGURE 7.23** *Enlargement of part of Fig. 7.22 showing one bit-slice PE and its attached local memory.*

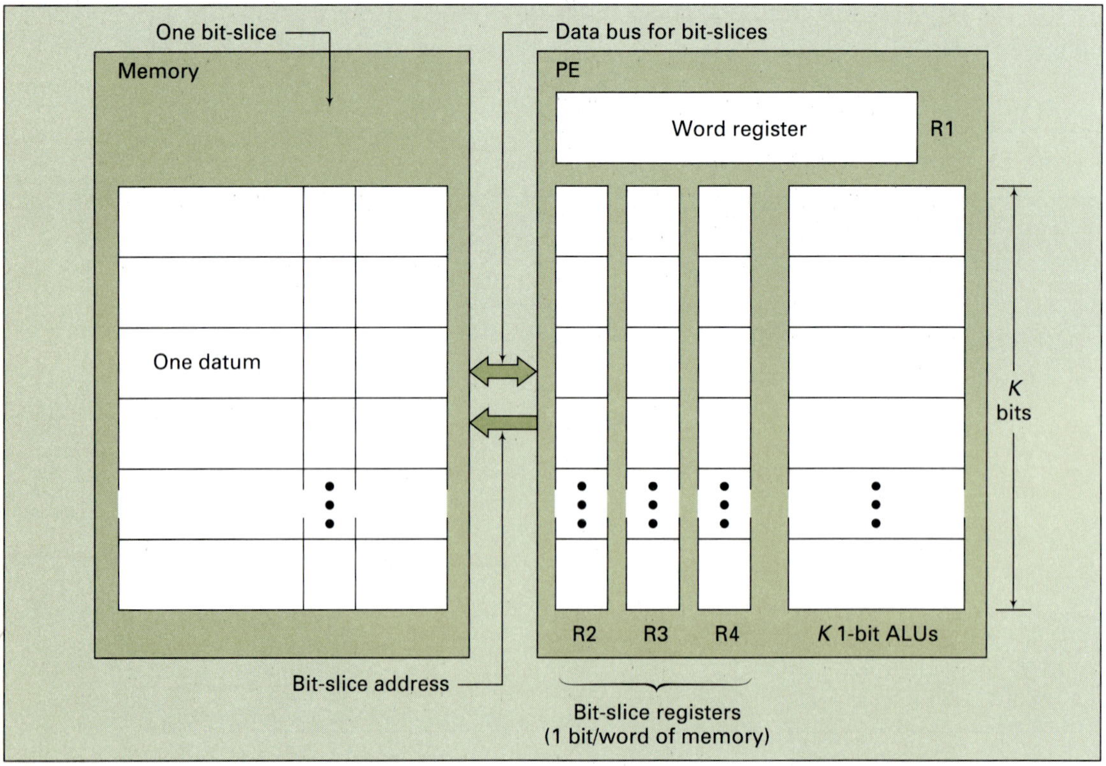

**FIGURE 7.24** *Associative search. Values to be compared are shown in color. (a) Initial register and memory contents. R4 is zeroed, and R3 is set to all 1s. The algorithm will check bit-slice 1 for the value 0. (b) Situation after the first iteration. R4 shows that the second and last data already exceed the comperand. R3 shows that the first and third through fifth data match the comperand as far as the algorithm can tell so far. (c) Situation after the second iteration. Now R3 contains 1s where the first two bits match.*

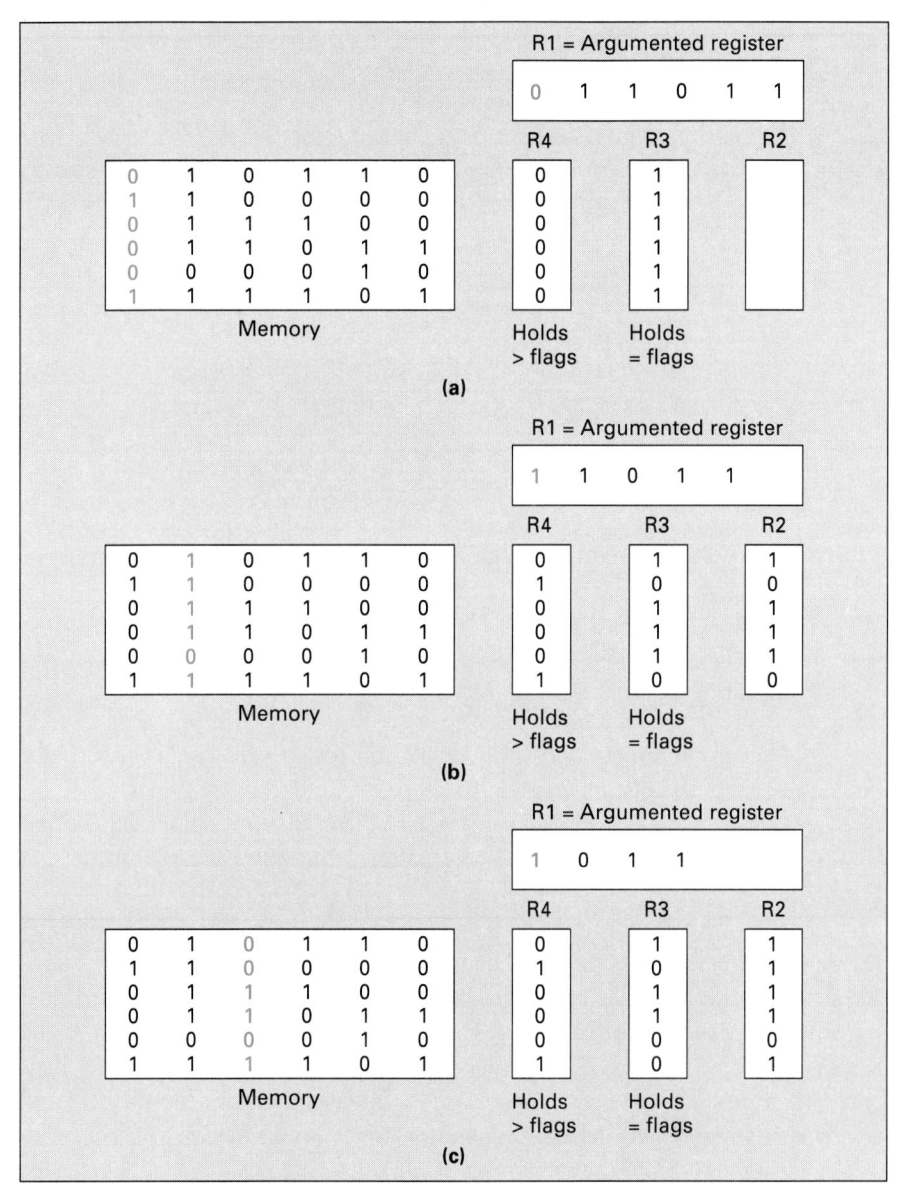

**Table 7.1** Notation for the bit-slice associative-search algorithm.

| Notation | What it Designates |
| --- | --- |
| R$i$ | Register $i$ |
| $\leftarrow$ | Conventional (word) STORE or LOAD to R1 |
| $\Leftarrow$ | Column (bit-slice) STORE or LOAD using R2 to R$k$. |
| X[I] | Address X indexed by I |
| LEFTBIT(R1) | Left-most bit of register R1 |
| SHIFT LEFT(R1) | A 1-bit left shift of the bits of R1 |
| NORMALIZE(R1) | A function that returns the number of leading zeros in R1 (say $N$) and shifts the content of R1 to the left $N$ times to eliminate them. |

| | |
| --- | --- |
| R1 $\leftarrow$ search argument | |
| R3 $\Leftarrow$ 1111$\cdots$11111 | Initialize "=" register. |
| R4 $\Leftarrow$ 0000$\cdots$00000 | Initialize ">" register. |
| **do** (I = 0, K $-$ 1) | |
|   R2 $\Leftarrow$ X[I] | Load R2 with bit-slice I. |
|   **if** (LEFTBIT(R1) = 0) | Words in memory can be larger. |
|     R4 $\Leftarrow$ R4 OR (R3 AND R2) | Set ">" mask for larger words. |
|     R2 $\Leftarrow$ NOT(R2) | Invert bits of R2 for equality test. |
|   **endif** | |
|   R3 $\Leftarrow$ R3 AND R2 | Test next bit of words for equality. |
|   R1 $\Leftarrow$ SHIFT LEFT(R1) | Prepare for next iteration. |
| **repeat** | |

During the execution of the algorithm, register R2 holds the bit-slice being processed, the bits of register R3 keep track of words that match the pattern, and the bits of register R4 keep track of those that are numerically larger than the pattern. Register R1 holds the pattern. Initially the algorithm clears R4 and sets the bits of R3 to $1_2$.

The algorithm processes words in memory one bit-slice at a time. During the first iteration, it loads the first column (called column 0 or bit-slice 0) into register R2. It then compares the bits of that bit-slice with the leftmost bit of the pattern, which R1 holds. R1 has been placed horizontally above the associative array in Fig. 7.24 to make this correspondence clear. The algorithm then performs the tests for = and $\geq$, updates registers R3 and R2, and finally shifts register R1 left in preparation for the next iteration.

Although STARAN was not a commercial success, it was the ancestor of Goodyear's MPP, a processor array of the 1980s. The current SIMD processors, such as MPP and CM-2, can easily implement associative-memory operations, and these machines provide special hardware to help identify the set of PEs that entertain a successful associative match.

**Vector Addition**

Next we present an algorithm that shows how a bit-slice processor might perform vector addition. For a processor array or hypercube processor, the same algorithm would add corresponding elements of two arrays to produce the sum array. We assume the programmer has logically divided the words in memory into $N$-bit fields, and that each $N$-bit field holds an $N$-bit integer. The variables $A$, $B$, and $C$ hold the bit numbers of the leftmost bits of the vectors. Figure 7.25 shows this arrangement. One may then think of the columns in memory as holding vectors of values, one element per word for each of the vectors. The following algorithm adds two such vectors to produce a third:

| | |
|---|---|
| $R4 \Leftarrow 0000\cdots00000$ | Initialize the carry register. |
| **do** ($I = N - 1$ **down to** $0$) | |
| $\quad R2 \Leftarrow A[I]$ | R2 gets column I of A. |
| $\quad R3 \Leftarrow B[I]$ | R3 gets column I of B. |
| $\quad C[I] \Leftarrow \overline{R4}(R3 \oplus R2) \vee R4\overline{(R3 \oplus R2)}$ | Column I of C gets the sum bits of adding A[I] to B[I] and the previous carry flags. |
| $\quad R4 \Leftarrow \overline{R4}(R3 \cdot R2) \vee R4\overline{(R3 \oplus R2)}$ | R4 gets the carry flags after adding A[I] to B[I] and the previous carry flags. |
| **repeat** | |

This algorithm, like the previous one, uses registers R2, R3, and R4 to hold intermediate values. The algorithm performs bit-serial addition on the $N$-bit values of A and B and places the $N$-bit results in C. It uses R4 to hold the intermediate carry bits. After the vector addition, R4 contains the final carry bits.

**FIGURE 7.25** *Organization of three 8-bit vectors in memory.*

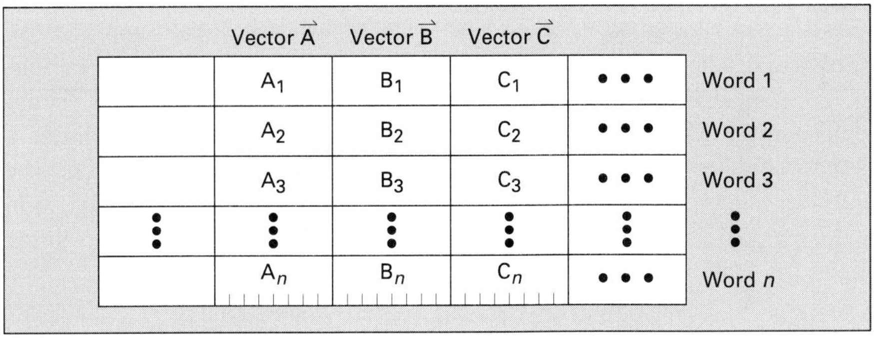

| | Vector $\vec{A}$ | Vector $\vec{B}$ | Vector $\vec{C}$ | | |
|---|---|---|---|---|---|
| | $A_1$ | $B_1$ | $C_1$ | $\bullet\bullet\bullet$ | Word 1 |
| | $A_2$ | $B_2$ | $C_2$ | $\bullet\bullet\bullet$ | Word 2 |
| | $A_3$ | $B_3$ | $C_3$ | $\bullet\bullet\bullet$ | Word 3 |
| $\vdots$ | $\vdots$ | $\vdots$ | $\vdots$ | $\vdots$ | $\vdots$ |
| | $A_n$ | $B_n$ | $C_n$ | $\bullet\bullet\bullet$ | Word $n$ |

### Blurring an Image

Consider the task of analyzing a real-time sequence of digitized images. A standard television camera creates 30 images per second, and one goal might be to design a computer that can analyze them in real time. An image with moderate resolution will have, perhaps, 525 × 600 pixels. (The term *pixel* stands for one picture element and usually requires 1 byte of storage for monochrome or several bytes for color.) A full-color digitized television image may require several megabytes of storage for each image or frame.

Conventional architectures, even pipelined processors, as we have shown earlier, are limited by the memory-to-CPU bandwidth. They are also limited because the time it takes them to produce results is proportional to the amount of data they must process. Although the time it takes a bit-slice processor to produce results does not depend on the amount of data it must process, bit-slice processors do not appear to be a good choice for image processing. However, processor arrays are well suited for image processing. And like the bit-slice processors, the time it takes them to produce results does not depend on the amount of data they must process.

There are many ways to process images, but a common strategy is to decompose them in stages. The first stages apply various low-level transformations to the image, which do not depend on what the image represents. Low-level transformations are analogous to adjusting the brightness and contrast on a television set. After low-level processing, image-analysis programs apply various medium-level and high-level transformations to the resulting images. Examples of medium-level processes are the detection and location of object boundaries and regions defining object surfaces; examples of high-level processes are locating and identifying objects in images and determining spatial relationships between the objects.

**blurring**

**image mask**

We shall discuss the low-level transformation of **blurring** to illustrate how an array computation works. Blurring eliminates bad pixels, as might be caused by an error in picture transmission. Blurring transforms an input image by cross-correlating it with a second image, called an **image mask** (see Fig. 7.26). The mask often represents a Gaussian distribution. The details of a Gaussian distribution are unimportant except to note that we can approximate a Gaussian distribution with a mask of a limited size—for example, 9 × 9 pixels.

Imagine that the mask is aligned with the upper-left corner of the input image. We have indicated the alignment in the figure by highlighting a 9 × 9 subimage of the input image. This alignment imposes a correspondence between pixels of the input image $I$ and the mask $M$. The blurring algorithm calculates the upper-left value of the blurred image $B$, also highlighted in the figure, as follows:

$$B_{11} = \sum_{ij=0}^{8} M_{ij} I_{ij}$$

We have numbered the pixels for *I*, *M*, and *B* with row-column subscripts. Notice that the image and mask begin with row 0 and column 0 but we have placed the first result of the blurred image ($B_{11}$) in row 1 and column 1.

The algorithm repeats this process after shifting the mask right by 1 pixel, and the new result becomes the second element of the blurred image. The algorithm computes all elements of the blurred image exactly the same way. Because the mask can only be aligned in $K - 8$ row positions and in $L - 8$ column positions, where the image is $K \times L$ pixels in size, the resulting blurred image has a size of $(K - 8) \times (L - 8)$. Here are the essential loops in a procedure that blurs an image with a $9 \times 9$ mask:[3]

---

3. If the edge of the frame is important, obvious modifications to this algorithm will allow it to extend all the way to the edge of the image.

---

**FIGURE 7.26** *Formation of a blurred image. Each element in the blurred image is the sum of products of the elements in the mask and corresponding elements in a mask-sized subimage of the input image. Shown here is the formation of the upper-left pixel in the blurred image.*

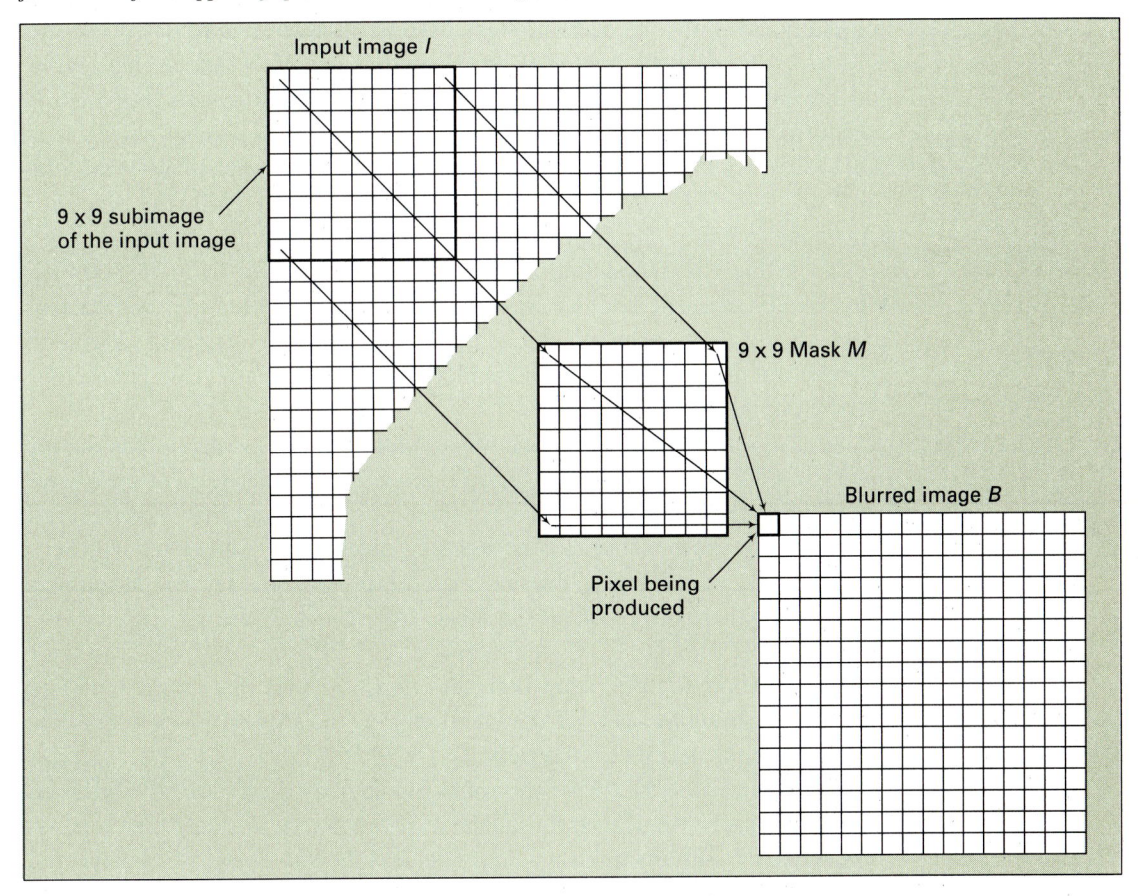

```
      do (K1 = 1, K − 8)
        do (L1 = 1, L − 8)
          S = 0
          do (K2 = 0, 8)
            do (L2 = 0, 8)
              S = S + I(K1 + K2 − 1, L1 + L2 − 1) × M(K2, L2)
          repeat
        repeat
        B(K1, L1) = S
      repeat
    repeat
```

We shall now analyze the computational demands of the process. The blurring algorithm requires 81 products and 80 sums to produce 1 pixel in the blurred image. If there are 480 columns and 525 rows in the input image, the algorithm requires about 472 × 517 × (80 + 81) or about 40-M operations. To keep up with television input, the processor must transform 30 images per second or produce about 600-M additions and 600-M multiplications per second. Such computational demands are beyond the capabilities of most machines, and blurring is only one of many steps used to analyze images.

Looking at the computation somewhat differently, notice that the algorithm performs 472 × 517 = 244,024 identical operations to produce the transformed image. Suppose we could build a processor array having, say, 480 × 525 = 252,000 PEs. Each PE could then hold 1 input-image pixel. Because all of the PEs in a processor array operate concurrently, the processor array could produce the entire transformation in roughly 81 steps.

In the past it was impractical to build a processor with 252,000 PEs. With 64 PEs, the ILLIAC IV was a first step in that direction, and current commercial systems, such as the CM-2, have 65,536 PEs. Companies will soon manufacture processors with 250,000 PEs, but it will be many years before they become commonplace.

We shall now describe one way to blur an image using a processor array. Figure 7.27 shows an 8 × 8 image $I$ and a 3 × 3 mask $M$. (For brevity we have chosen a smaller image and mask than those shown in Fig. 7.26 and used in our general introduction to the blurring algorithm.) The result will be a 6 × 6 blurred image $B$. We assume that the processor-array has at least as many PEs as there are pixels in the image to be blurred. We also assume that each PE already holds 1 pixel of the image. The PEs can send values to their nearest neighbors (above, below, left, and right), and all PEs always send and receive data simultaneously; if they send data to the PEs on the left, they receive data from the PEs on the right.

Because the PEs have the same topology as the image, they may be numbered with row and column indices like the pixels. We may therefore assume that PE $ij$ initially holds pixel $I_{ij}$. That is, PE 00 holds $I_{00}$, PE 01 holds $I_{01}$, and so forth. We shall assume, for this algorithm, that memory location 10 of each PE holds $I_{ij}$. Finally, we assume that PE 11 gets the first element of the result—the blurred image.

The control unit begins the blurring process by broadcasting the mask pixels to all PEs. With each mask pixel the control unit instructs the PEs to multiply the mask pixel by the image pixel they hold in location 10 and store the value in a specified memory location, say 11 for the first element, 12 for the second element, 13 for the third element, and so on. For example, during the first step PE $ij$ will compute $M_{00} \times I_{ij}$ and store the result in location 11. (The $ij$ subscripts indicate that all PEs compute and store similar products at the same time, and they all store them in the same local address.) The control unit then broadcasts the next mask pixel and instructs the PEs to compute the next product and store it in location 12. The control unit repeats this process

**FIGURE 7.27**  *First step in the formation of a blurred image.*

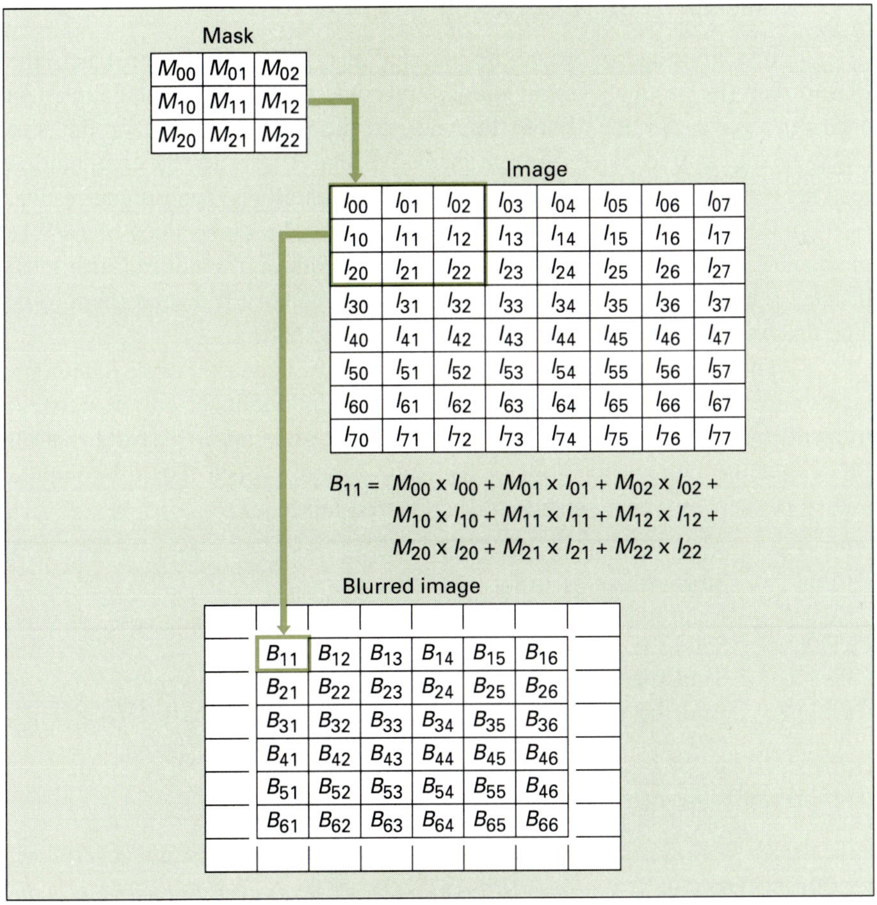

until it has broadcast all mask pixels and the PEs have stored the corresponding products. Figure 7.28 shows the appearance of the upper-left corner of the PEs' memory after they have computed and stored all nine products. We have divided the algorithm into two parts for ease of explanation. The first part of the algorithm appears here; all operations are PE operations unless the algorithm specifically mentions the control unit (CU):

> CU broadcasts $M_{00}$ to the PEs.
> 
> CU instructs the PEs to multiply $M_{00} \times$ the content of location 10 and store the results in location 11.
> 
> CU broadcasts $M_{01}$ to the PEs.
> 
> CU instructs the PEs to multiply $M_{01} \times$ the content of location 10 and store the results in location 12.
> 
> $\vdots$
> 
> CU broadcasts $M_{33}$ to the PEs.
> 
> CU instructs the PEs to multiply $M_{33} \times$ the content of location 10 and store the results in location 19.

In the second phase of the blurring algorithm, the CU instructs the PEs to read the products from memory and route them to their neighbors. As each PE receives a value, it adds the value to the running sum of products to compute the desired blurred-image pixel. We shall illustrate the computation for PE 11, but all PEs will at the same time compute their own unique results.

Refer again to Fig. 7.28, which highlights the nine values that PE 11 must add to produce $B_{11}$. For PE 11 to get these values, the control unit must instruct the neighboring PEs to load them from memory and send them to it. The arrows show one possible routing of the information.

The second part of the blurring algorithm appears below. The comments delimited by /* */ brackets indicate what PE 11 and its neighbors must do to form $B_{11}$. PE 11 places $B_{11}$ in its local memory, at location 20. Note that all PEs simultaneously perform all of the same actions; hence they all compute and store their own components of the blurred image.

| | |
|---|---|
| /*PE 11*/ | Read memory location 15. |
| /*PE 11*/ | Store the value in location 20. |
| /*PE 00*/ | Read memory location 11 /*$M_{00} \times I_{00}$*/. |
| /*PE 00*/ | Send the value right. |
| /*PE 01*/ | Send the received value down. |
| /*PE 11*/ | Add the received value to the value in location 20 /*$M_{11} \times I_{11}$*/, and store the result in location 20. |
| /*PE 01*/ | Read memory location 12 /*$M_{01} \times I_{01}$*/. |
| /*PE 01*/ | Send the value down. |

**FIGURE 7.28** *(On page 357). Upper-left corner of the PE array after the completion of the first part of the blurring algorithm. The highlighted values are those needed by PE11 to produce $B_{11}$.*

*Parallel Processors* 357

| | |
|---|---|
| /*PE 11*/ | Add the received value to the value in location 20, and store the result in location 20. |
| /*PE 02*/ | Read memory location 13 /*$M_{02} \times I_{02}$*/. |
| /*PE 02*/ | Send the value left. |
| /*PE 12*/ | Send the received value down. |
| /*PE 11*/ | Add the received value to the value in location 20, and store the result in location 20. |
| /*PE 10*/ | Read memory location 14 /*$M_{10} \times I_{10}$*/. |
| /*PE 10*/ | Send the value right. |
| /*PE 11*/ | Add the received value to the value in location 20, and store the result in location 20. |
| /*PE 12*/ | Read memory location 16 /*$M_{12} \times I_{12}$*/. |
| /*PE 12*/ | Send the value left. |
| /*PE 11*/ | Add the received value to the value in location 20, and store the result in location 20. |
| /*PE 20*/ | Read memory location 17 /*$M_{20} \times I_{20}$*/. |
| /*PE 20*/ | Send the value right. |
| /*PE 21*/ | Send the received value up. |
| /*PE 11*/ | Add the received value to the value in location 20, and store the result in location 20. |
| /*PE 21*/ | Read memory location 18 /*$M_{21} \times I_{21}$*/. |
| /*PE 21*/ | Send the value up. |
| /*PE 11*/ | Add the received value to the value in location 20, and store the result in location 20. |
| /*PE 22*/ | Read memory location 19 /*$M_{22} \times I_{22}$*/. |
| /*PE 22*/ | Send the value left. |
| /*PE 21*/ | Send the received value up. |
| /*PE 11*/ | Add the received value to the value in location 20, and store the result in location 20. |

Although the bracketed numbers indicate the PEs that produce values for PE 11, a single execution of the algorithm produces the entire blurred image. Figure 7.29 shows how the algorithm operates from PE 23's point of view. When the algorithm finishes, each PE will hold its unique blurred-image value in its own memory location 20. Thus a processor array can produce a blurred image in time that is proportional to the size of the mask but independent of the size of the image. The only requirements are that the processor array have one PE for each image pixel, and that the PEs be able to communicate with their nearest neighbors.

### Matrix Multiplication

Processor arrays can perform many other operations besides image processing. We shall show one way to use a linear processor array (one in which the PEs form a single chain) to multiply matrices of up to $N \times N$ elements, where $N$

---

**FIGURE 7.29** *(On page 359).* *Values assembled by PE 23 during the second part of the blurring algorithm.*

Parallel Processors  359

| | PE 00 | | PE 01 | | PE 02 | | PE 03 | | PE 04 |
|---|---|---|---|---|---|---|---|---|---|
|11|$M_{00} \times I_{00}$|  |$M_{00} \times I_{01}$|  |$M_{00} \times I_{02}$|  |$M_{00} \times I_{03}$|  |$M_{00} \times I_{00}$|
|12|$M_{01} \times I_{00}$|  |$M_{01} \times I_{01}$|  |$M_{01} \times I_{02}$|  |$M_{01} \times I_{03}$|  |$M_{01} \times I_{04}$|
|13|$M_{02} \times I_{00}$|  |$M_{02} \times I_{01}$|  |$M_{02} \times I_{02}$|  |$M_{02} \times I_{03}$|  |$M_{02} \times I_{04}$|
|14|$M_{10} \times I_{00}$|  |$M_{10} \times I_{01}$|  |$M_{10} \times I_{02}$|  |$M_{10} \times I_{03}$|  |$M_{10} \times I_{04}$|
|15|$M_{11} \times I_{00}$|  |$M_{11} \times I_{01}$|  |$M_{11} \times I_{02}$|  |$M_{11} \times I_{03}$|  |$M_{11} \times I_{04}$|
|16|$M_{12} \times I_{00}$|  |$M_{12} \times I_{01}$|  |$M_{12} \times I_{02}$|  |$M_{12} \times I_{03}$|  |$M_{12} \times I_{04}$|
|17|$M_{20} \times I_{00}$|  |$M_{20} \times I_{01}$|  |$M_{20} \times I_{02}$|  |$M_{20} \times I_{03}$|  |$M_{20} \times I_{04}$|
|18|$M_{21} \times I_{00}$|  |$M_{21} \times I_{01}$|  |$M_{21} \times I_{02}$|  |$M_{21} \times I_{03}$|  |$M_{21} \times I_{04}$|
|19|$M_{22} \times I_{00}$|  |$M_{22} \times I_{01}$|  |$M_{22} \times I_{02}$|  |$M_{22} \times I_{03}$|  |$M_{22} \times I_{04}$|
|20| | | | | | | | | |
|21| | | | | | | | | |

| | PE 10 | | PE 11 | | PE 12 | | PE 13 | | PE 14 |
|---|---|---|---|---|---|---|---|---|---|
|11|$M_{00} \times I_{10}$|  |$M_{00} \times I_{11}$|  |$M_{00} \times I_{12}$|  |$M_{00} \times I_{13}$|  |$M_{00} \times I_{14}$|
|12|$M_{01} \times I_{10}$|  |$M_{01} \times I_{11}$|  |$M_{01} \times I_{12}$|  |$M_{01} \times I_{13}$|  |$M_{01} \times I_{14}$|
|13|$M_{02} \times I_{10}$|  |$M_{02} \times I_{11}$|  |$M_{02} \times I_{12}$|  |$M_{02} \times I_{13}$|  |$M_{02} \times I_{14}$|
|14|$M_{10} \times I_{10}$|  |$M_{10} \times I_{11}$|  |$M_{10} \times I_{12}$|  |$M_{10} \times I_{13}$|  |$M_{10} \times I_{14}$|
|15|$M_{11} \times I_{10}$|  |$M_{11} \times I_{11}$|  |$M_{11} \times I_{12}$|  |$M_{11} \times I_{13}$|  |$M_{11} \times I_{14}$|
|16|$M_{12} \times I_{10}$|  |$M_{12} \times I_{11}$|  |$M_{12} \times I_{12}$|  |$M_{12} \times I_{13}$|  |$M_{12} \times I_{14}$|
|17|$M_{20} \times I_{10}$|  |$M_{20} \times I_{11}$|  |$M_{20} \times I_{12}$|  |$M_{20} \times I_{13}$|  |$M_{20} \times I_{14}$|
|18|$M_{21} \times I_{10}$|  |$M_{21} \times I_{11}$|  |$M_{21} \times I_{12}$|  |$M_{21} \times I_{13}$|  |$M_{21} \times I_{14}$|
|19|$M_{22} \times I_{10}$|  |$M_{22} \times I_{11}$|  |$M_{22} \times I_{12}$|  |$M_{22} \times I_{13}$|  |$M_{22} \times I_{14}$|
|20| | | | | | | | | |
|21| | | | | | | | | |

| | PE 20 | | PE 21 | | PE 22 | | PE 23 | | PE 24 |
|---|---|---|---|---|---|---|---|---|---|
|11|$M_{00} \times I_{20}$|  |$M_{00} \times I_{21}$|  |$M_{00} \times I_{22}$|  |$M_{00} \times I_{23}$|  |$M_{00} \times I_{24}$|
|12|$M_{01} \times I_{20}$|  |$M_{01} \times I_{21}$|  |$M_{01} \times I_{22}$|  |$M_{01} \times I_{23}$|  |$M_{01} \times I_{24}$|
|13|$M_{02} \times I_{20}$|  |$M_{02} \times I_{21}$|  |$M_{02} \times I_{22}$|  |$M_{02} \times I_{23}$|  |$M_{02} \times I_{24}$|
|14|$M_{10} \times I_{20}$|  |$M_{10} \times I_{21}$|  |$M_{10} \times I_{22}$|  |$M_{10} \times I_{23}$|  |$M_{10} \times I_{24}$|
|15|$M_{11} \times I_{20}$|  |$M_{11} \times I_{21}$|  |$M_{11} \times I_{22}$|  |$M_{11} \times I_{23}$|  |$M_{11} \times I_{24}$|
|16|$M_{12} \times I_{20}$|  |$M_{12} \times I_{21}$|  |$M_{12} \times I_{22}$|  |$M_{12} \times I_{23}$|  |$M_{12} \times I_{24}$|
|17|$M_{20} \times I_{20}$|  |$M_{20} \times I_{21}$|  |$M_{20} \times I_{22}$|  |$M_{20} \times I_{23}$|  |$M_{20} \times I_{24}$|
|18|$M_{21} \times I_{20}$|  |$M_{21} \times I_{21}$|  |$M_{21} \times I_{22}$|  |$M_{21} \times I_{23}$|  |$M_{21} \times I_{24}$|
|19|$M_{22} \times I_{20}$|  |$M_{22} \times I_{21}$|  |$M_{22} \times I_{22}$|  |$M_{22} \times I_{23}$|  |$M_{22} \times I_{24}$|
|20| | | | | | | | | |
|21| | | | | | | | | |

| | PE 30 | | PE 31 | | PE 32 | | PE 33 | | PE 34 |
|---|---|---|---|---|---|---|---|---|---|
|11|$M_{00} \times I_{30}$|  |$M_{00} \times I_{31}$|  |$M_{00} \times I_{32}$|  |$M_{00} \times I_{33}$|  |$M_{00} \times I_{34}$|
|12|$M_{01} \times I_{30}$|  |$M_{01} \times I_{31}$|  |$M_{01} \times I_{32}$|  |$M_{01} \times I_{33}$|  |$M_{01} \times I_{34}$|
|13|$M_{02} \times I_{30}$|  |$M_{02} \times I_{31}$|  |$M_{02} \times I_{32}$|  |$M_{02} \times I_{33}$|  |$M_{02} \times I_{34}$|
|14|$M_{10} \times I_{30}$|  |$M_{10} \times I_{31}$|  |$M_{10} \times I_{32}$|  |$M_{10} \times I_{33}$|  |$M_{10} \times I_{34}$|
|15|$M_{11} \times I_{30}$|  |$M_{11} \times I_{31}$|  |$M_{11} \times I_{32}$|  |$M_{11} \times I_{33}$|  |$M_{11} \times I_{34}$|
|16|$M_{12} \times I_{30}$|  |$M_{12} \times I_{31}$|  |$M_{12} \times I_{32}$|  |$M_{12} \times I_{33}$|  |$M_{12} \times I_{34}$|
|17|$M_{20} \times I_{30}$|  |$M_{20} \times I_{31}$|  |$M_{20} \times I_{32}$|  |$M_{20} \times I_{33}$|  |$M_{20} \times I_{34}$|
|18|$M_{21} \times I_{30}$|  |$M_{21} \times I_{31}$|  |$M_{21} \times I_{32}$|  |$M_{21} \times I_{33}$|  |$M_{21} \times I_{34}$|
|19|$M_{22} \times I_{30}$|  |$M_{22} \times I_{31}$|  |$M_{22} \times I_{32}$|  |$M_{22} \times I_{33}$|  |$M_{22} \times I_{34}$|
|20| | | | | | | | | |
|21| | | | | | | | | |

is the number of PEs in the chain. We shall illustrate matrix multiplication for 3 × 3 matrices. Recall that the formula for matrix multiplication is $xy = z$, where

$$\begin{bmatrix} X_{11} & X_{12} & X_{13} \\ X_{21} & X_{22} & X_{23} \\ X_{31} & X_{32} & X_{33} \end{bmatrix} \begin{bmatrix} Y_{11} & Y_{12} & Y_{13} \\ Y_{21} & Y_{22} & Y_{23} \\ Y_{31} & Y_{32} & Y_{33} \end{bmatrix} = \begin{bmatrix} Z_{11} & Z_{12} & Z_{13} \\ Z_{21} & Z_{22} & Z_{23} \\ Z_{31} & Z_{32} & Z_{33} \end{bmatrix},$$

$$Z_{ij} = \sum_{k=1}^{3} X_{ik} Y_{kj}.$$

Figure 7.30 shows the storage representation assumed by the algorithm; we assume that the control unit (CU) can read the PE's memory. Here is the first part of the algorithm:

CU reads memory location 10 of PE 0 (the value of $X_{11}$).

CU broadcasts the read value ($X_{11}$) to all PEs.

FIGURE 7.30 *Storage representation of three matrices in a linear processor array.*

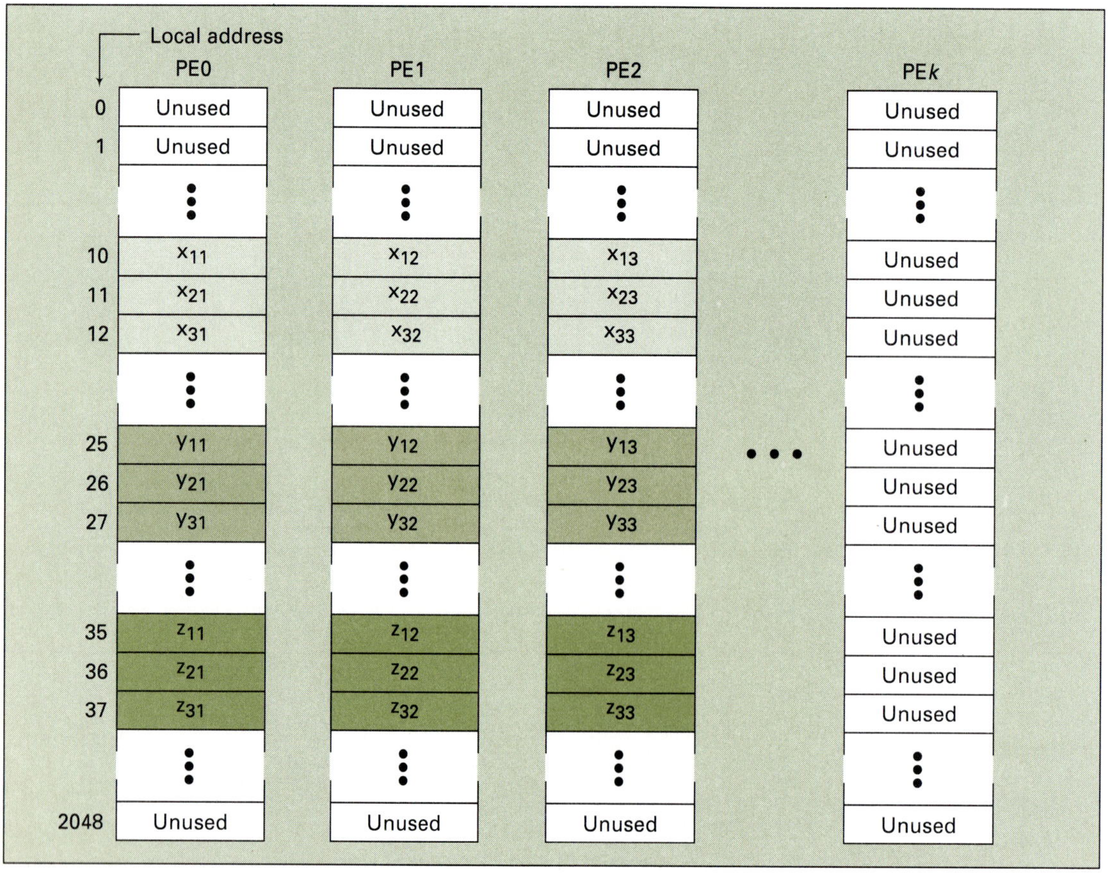

| Local address | PE0 | PE1 | PE2 | PEk |
|---|---|---|---|---|
| 0 | Unused | Unused | Unused | Unused |
| 1 | Unused | Unused | Unused | Unused |
| ⋮ | ⋮ | ⋮ | ⋮ | ⋮ |
| 10 | $x_{11}$ | $x_{12}$ | $x_{13}$ | Unused |
| 11 | $x_{21}$ | $x_{22}$ | $x_{23}$ | Unused |
| 12 | $x_{31}$ | $x_{32}$ | $x_{33}$ | Unused |
| ⋮ | ⋮ | ⋮ | ⋮ | ⋮ |
| 25 | $y_{11}$ | $y_{12}$ | $y_{13}$ | Unused |
| 26 | $y_{21}$ | $y_{22}$ | $y_{23}$ | Unused |
| 27 | $y_{31}$ | $y_{32}$ | $y_{33}$ | Unused |
| ⋮ | ⋮ | ⋮ | ⋮ | ⋮ |
| 35 | $z_{11}$ | $z_{12}$ | $z_{13}$ | Unused |
| 36 | $z_{21}$ | $z_{22}$ | $z_{23}$ | Unused |
| 37 | $z_{31}$ | $z_{32}$ | $z_{33}$ | Unused |
| ⋮ | ⋮ | ⋮ | ⋮ | ⋮ |
| 2048 | Unused | Unused | Unused | Unused |

PEs multiply the received value × the value in memory location 25 and store the result in memory location 35.

CU reads memory location 10 of PE 1 (the value of $X_{12}$).

CU broadcasts the read value ($X_{12}$) to all PEs.

PEs multiply the received value × the value in memory location 26.

PEs add the result to the value in memory location 35 and store the result in memory location 35.

CU reads memory location 10 of PE 2 (the value of $X_{13}$).

CU broadcasts the read value ($X_{13}$) to all PEs.

PEs multiply the received value × the value in memory location 27.

PEs add the result to the value in memory location 35 and store the result in memory location 35.

(This finishes the computation of $Z_{11}$ by PE 0, $Z_{12}$ by PE 1, and $Z_{13}$ by PE 2).

CU reads memory location 11 of PE 0 (the value of $X_{21}$).

CU broadcasts the read value ($X_{21}$) to all PEs.

PEs multiply the received value × the value in memory location 25 and store the result in memory location 36.

...

Notice that the time it takes a processor-array to multiply two matrices is proportional to the number of elements in the first matrix (there are four steps in the above algorithm for each element of matrix $X$) instead of the product of the number of elements of the first matrix and the number of rows in the second matrix. Thus the speedup is proportional to the number of rows in the second matrix. For small matrices, vector processors can easily achieve equal speed increases, which reduces the utility of the processor arrays for matrix applications.

**Peak Search**

Our final algorithm, suitable for hypercube processors, shows how to find the maximum value in an array of $N$ values and how to get the address of the PE that holds it. Searching for the minimum value is similar. The algorithm operates in $\log_2(N)$ time. For example, if the PEs evaluate correlation coefficients in an image-processing application, the algorithm will locate the maximum correlation coefficient and identify the PE that holds it. If each PE has a flag indicating the outcome of a binary comparison (*true* or *false*), the algorithm can locate the first PE whose flag is set to *true*.

Our illustration uses a hypercube of dimension 4. Figure 7.31 shows a 4-cube. Each node (vertex) contains a PE address (i.e., PE number), as follows: The left-most bit indicates which 3-cube (or simply cube) contains the node; the second bit indicates which 2-cube (square face) contains the node (0 for the front-left vertical face and 1 for the back-right vertical face of each

362  Computer Architecture

cube); the third bit tells which 1-cube (horizontal line) contains the node (line 0 for the top and line 1 for the bottom of each face) and the rightmost bit indicates which end of the line contains the node (0 for the left end, 1 for the right end). For example, the address of the highest node in the figure, 0100, indicates that it is at the left end of the top line on the rear face of the left cube.

*N*-buddies

It is helpful in search operations to diagram the nodes of a hypercube as the leaf nodes of a binary tree (see Fig. 7.32). Nodes are ***N*-buddies** if their node numbers differ only in bit position *N*. For example, nodes 0100 and 0101 are 1-buddies, nodes 1101 and 1111 are 2-buddies, nodes 0110 and 0010 are 3-buddies, and nodes 0000 and 1000 are 4-buddies.

In the first step of the peak-search algorithm all nodes whose node number ends in 1 send their values to their 1-buddies. The thinnest arrows in

**FIGURE 7.31** *A 4-cube. The arrows indicate the direction of movement of information that takes place during the search algorithm.*

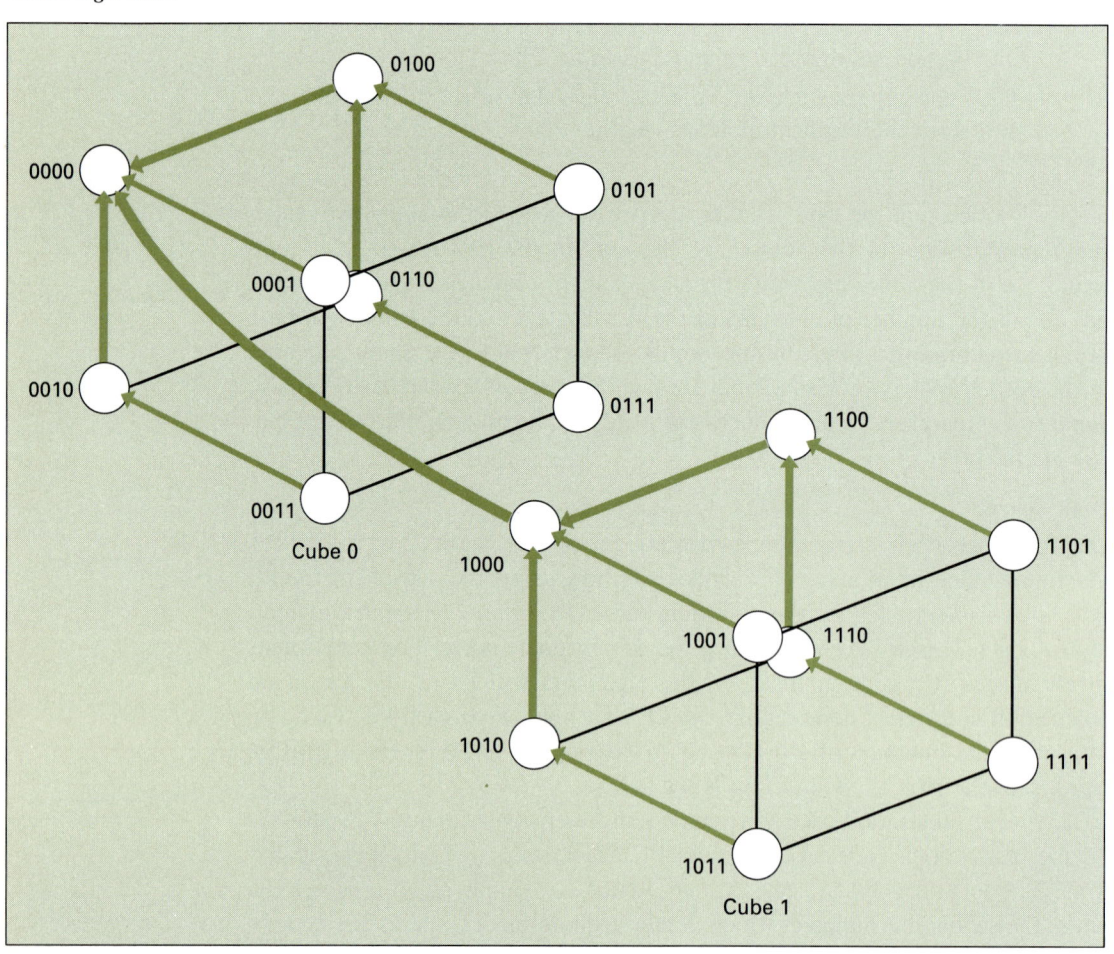

Figs. 7.31 and 7.32 indicate this movement. The nodes receiving the values compare them with their own values to determine a winning value (the maximum value during peak-value search, the minimum value during minimum-value search, and so on). The receiving nodes then sends to their 2-buddies both the address of the winner (either their own address or the address of their 1-buddy) and the winning value. When there is no winner (i.e., both buddies have the same value), then the node doing the comparison sends its buddy's node number to its 2-buddy.

During the second step, nodes whose addresses end in 00 compare the values they just received with their own values, and send both the address of the winner and the winning value to their 3-buddies. The third step is similar, except that the only nodes making comparisons are those whose addresses end in 000 (i.e., nodes 0000 and 1000). Node 0000 receives the results of these comparisons and in step 4 performs the final test. Thus after four steps node 0000 will hold both the maximum value and the node address of the node having that value.

In the following algorithm, buddy (N, A) denotes the $N$th buddy of the PE whose address is A and mod($I, J$) denotes the remainder after dividing $I$ by $J$. Also, each pair of braces specifies both a send operation and a matching receive operation. The PEs in one set send values to the PEs in the other set and the receiving PEs store the values in local registers.

    Let N be the loop count;
    Let V denote the value of interest;
    Let A denote the address of the PE;
    Let VB denote the value of buddy (N, A);
    Let AB denote the address of buddy (N, A);
    Let VW denote the winning value;
    Let AW denote the address of the winner;
    N ← 1;

**FIGURE 7.32** *Nodes of a 4-cube as the leaf nodes of a binary tree.*

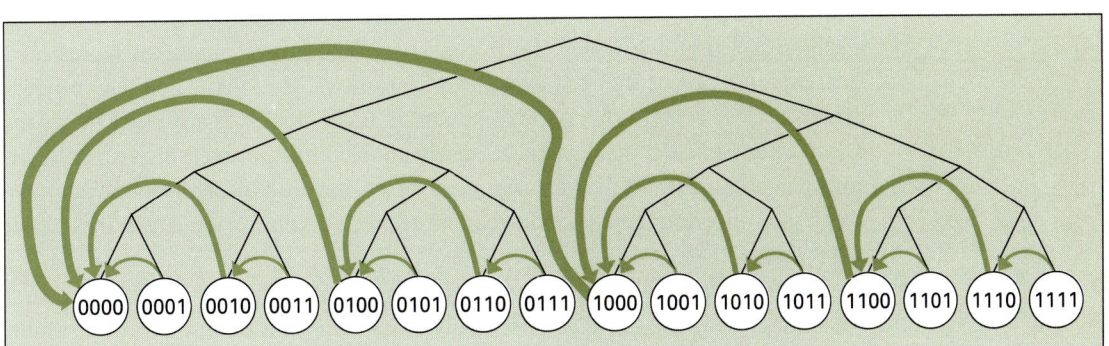

Activate all PEs;
   {    **For all** PEs **such that** $\mod(A, 2) = 1$ **do**;
        Send V to buddy(N, A);
     **For all** PEs **such that** $\mod(A, 2) = 0$ **do**;
        Place value from buddy(N, A) in VB;  }
   { **For all** PEs **such that** $\mod(A, 2) = 1$ **do**;
        Send A to buddy(N, A);
     **For all** PEs **such that** $\mod(A, 2) = 0$ **do**;
        Place value from buddy(N, A) in AB;  }
**Do while** N < dimensionality of hypercube
   Activate all PEs **such that** $0 = \mod(A, 2^N)$;
   **if** V > VB **then** VW ← V **else** VW ← VB;
   **if** V > VB **then** AW ← A **else** AW ← AB;
   N ← N + 1;
   { **For all** PEs **such that** $\mod(A, 2^N) = 2^{N-1}$ **do**;
        Send VW to buddy(N, A);
     **For all** PEs **such that** $\mod(A, 2^N) = 0$ **do**;
        Place value from buddy(N, A) in VB;  }
   { **For all** PEs **such that** $\mod(A, 2^N) = 2^{N-1}$ **do**;
        Send AW to buddy(N, A);
     **For all** PEs **such that** $\mod(A, 2^N) = 0$ **do**;
        Place incoming value in AB;  }
   **end do**;
Activate PE 0000
   **if** V > VB **then** VW ← V **else** VW ← VB;
   **if** V > VB **then** AW ← A **else** AW ← AB;

Upon completion of the algorithm, the PE 0000 holds the maximum value and the address of the PE that generated it.

## 7.3 ∎ MIMD Machines

An MIMD machine is a multiprocessor where each individual processor has its own control unit and executes its own program, but the processors share the same memory system. When the processors share a single global memory (GM-MIMD) using a high-speed circuit-switched interconnection network the machine is a tightly coupled multiprocessor. When each processor has is own local memory out of which it executes programs (LM-MIMD), but the processors can access each other's local memories using a packet-switched interconnection network, the machine is a loosely coupled multiprocessor, also called a multiple processor. Multiple processors often have additional global memory which the individual processors can access, and they often have their own I/O systems.

    We begin this section by discussing tightly coupled multiprocessors. We show that to use them requires only a multiprogramming operating system with appropriate hardware for loading processes and interrupting active processes (Section 7.3.1). We then discuss requirements for multiprocessor systems (Section 7.3.2). Next we discuss the problem of cache coherence in multiprocessor systems (Section 7.3.3) and the architecture of an early experimental loosely coupled multiprocessor (Section 7.3.4). We conclude in Section 7.3.5 with an introduction to fault-tolerant computing, a major application area for commercial, loosely coupled multiprocessors.

### 7.3.1 ■ Running Processes on an MIMD Processor

Tightly coupled multiprocessors have independent processors that share one memory system, usually through a crossbar switch or the equivalent. Most commercial multiprocessors are of this type, and users (not the operating system) can use them as though they are single-processor systems. However, if user programs spawn several tasks, the operating system may allocate them to different processors. In that case the system must provide the user program with appropriate facilities for process synchronization.

For processes that do not generate subprocesses, a multiprogramming operating system can regard the CPUs of a multiprocessor as a simple set of computational resources. After loading several programs in main memory, the operating system starts each one on an available CPU. If there are no available CPUs, a process simply waits, just as it might on a single-processor system.

Figure 7.33 illustrates a multiprocessor with two processors. The figure shows the situation where three programs reside in main memory. CPUs 1 and 2 are executing programs 1 and 2, respectively. Program 3 is not executing but resides in memory and its processor context is stored in the appropriate save area, also in memory. To execute program 3, the operating system would interrupt one of the other programs, say program 2, and save its processor context to a save area. The operating system would then load program 3's processor context into the available CPU and start executing it. (We assume that the operating system saves the processor context of each memory-resident program in a save area in preparation for assigning a processor to it.)

Notice that the operating system can load a program's processor context into any available CPU because all CPUs share the same address space. If the processors use virtual memory, then the operating system must regard a program's page and segment maps as part of the processor context. If there are $N$ CPUs, the operating system can load a program into any one of them. Similarly, any set of $N$ programs can simultaneously operate on an $N$-processor system of this type.

### 7.3.2 ■ Requirements for Multiprocessor Systems

All multiprocessor systems must provide support facilities for five task-management capabilities:

1. ***Initiation.*** A process must be able to spawn (i.e., generate and activate) other processes.

*process initiation*

process synchronization
    2. *Synchronization.* A process must be able to suspend itself or another process until some "external" event occurs. This event may be that other, slower processes "catch up" to it.

process exclusion
    3. *Exclusion.* A process must be able to monopolize a resource, such as some code or data, so that no other process can access the monopolized resource.

process communication
    4. *Communication.* A process must be able to send messages to other processes and receive messages from them. For efficiency, sending with and without awaiting a reply, accepting or deferring acceptance of messages, and broadcasting messages are all useful facilities.

process termination
    5. *Termination.* A process must be able to terminate itself or another process and free any resources being used.

These facilities are required whether the system supports many or few independent tasks. Moreover, the need for efficient support grows with the number of processors.

We illustrate these capabilities by supposing that one main process is executing and wants to perform a sum reduction or a column addition (see Section 2.4.5); the numbers in parentheses refer to the capabilities listed above:

FIGURE 7.33 *A dual-processor multiprogramming system. Shown here are programs in main memory, of which two are executing. The shading in the two CPUs matches the respective programs in memory that each CPU is currently processing.*

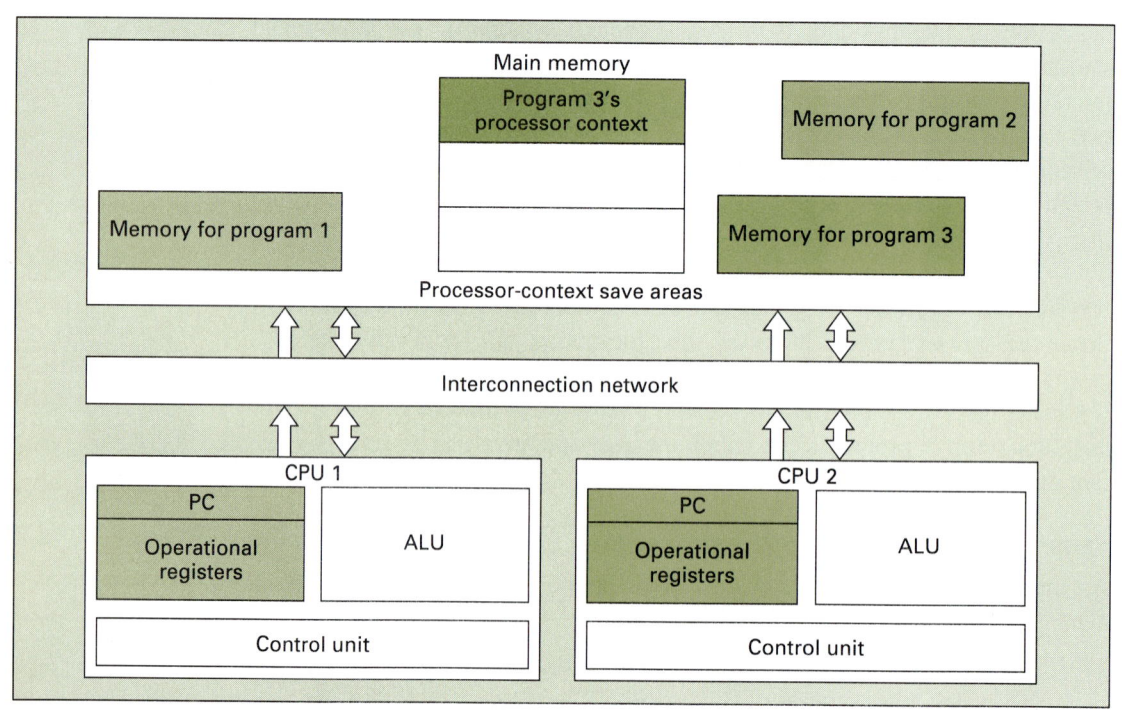

a. The main process spawns a number of subprocesses (1).

b. Each spawned subprocess performs part of the summation. The main process communicates with the subprocesses to parcel out subsets of addends (4).

c. When each subprocess finishes its addition, it adds its partial result to the total, which requires exclusion to prevent overlapping updates of the total (3).

d. Subprocesses terminate, and the main process continues execution when the summation is completed. Awaiting completion of all subprocesses requires synchronization (5, 2).

There are certainly single mechanisms that can provide all of the required facilities for spawning, synchronizing, and terminating processes. For example, programmers have used Hoare's message-passing mechanisms and Concurrent Pascal's monitors to provide all or most of these functionalities with one mechanism. But a key problem is to develop these or comparable mechanisms in forms suitable for systems with thousands of processors. To date architects have not done this.

Although hardware support is not strictly necessary for process synchronization, most commercial multiprocessors provide some form of hardware support. We showed in Chapter 2 that a test-and-set operation with a binary semaphore and shared register would provide support for mutual exclusion and process synchronization, but what kind of hardware would be appropriate for a high-performance multiprocessor? Architects of the Cray X-MP, a tightly coupled four-processor system, chose to supply a set of shared CPU registers for that purpose. They included 32 binary semaphores plus eight data registers and several sets of eight address registers. Having these resources within the processor would provide hardware support for fine-grained multiprocessing (at the loop level). The architects concluded that conventional memory-based synchronization instructions would significantly degrade system performance, particularly because the memory delay is 12 to 14 clock cycles.

## 7.3.3 ■ Cache Coherence

We showed in Chapter 4 that architectures could increase the apparent speed of a storage system by placing a cache memory between the memory system and the CPU. However, use of cache storage brings with it the potential problem of maintaining **cache coherence** (also called **data consistency**) between values in memory and those in cache. **Stale data** are outdated (and thus incorrect) values in either the cache or main memory, and can result whenever a computer system holds two or more copies of any datum. The computer system must use some mechanism to maintain cache coherence. In this section we focus on some of the architectural solutions for maintaining cache coherence.

When only one device accesses memory, the cache always reflects the latest values in memory, and thus cache coherence is maintained. Figure 7.34

cache coherence
data consistency
stale data

illustrates a storage system with a single write-through cache in main memory. In this system words in cache will always contain the same values as their assigned words in main memory, thus maintaining cache coherence. Whenever the storage system updates main memory, it automatically updates the cache. In this way the CPU avoids getting stale values from either memory or cache.

When more than one device (whether CPU or I/O) can access a storage system, maintaining cache coherence is no longer automatic. For example, consider the two-processor system illustrated in Fig. 7.35 whose CPUs include write-through caches. For one CPU, words in cache may not contain the same values as their assigned words in main memory if the other CPU or an I/O device modifies the main-memory values. Without a mechanism to prevent it, the CPU would then read such stale values if it accessed them from its own cache.

Before describing the techniques that different multiprocessor systems use for maintaining cache coherence, it is worthwhile to note that coherence need not be maintained except when several devices simultaneously access some memory location and that memory location is also mapped into a cache. For a cache that resides in the CPU, one common cause of cache incoherence is loading a program into main memory from an I/O device. When a program relinquishes control, it leaves its own cache entries behind. Another cause is the delay between the CPU posting a write and a write-back cache sending it to main memory.

Whenever two separate devices want to share a datum that one of them is modifying, they must synchronize their operations. Sometimes this is done intrinsically with other operations, such as a CPU writing a block of data to

**FIGURE 7.34** *A von Neumann machine with a write-through cache embedded in storage. All memory accesses go through the cache, so neither the memory nor the cache ever has stale data.*

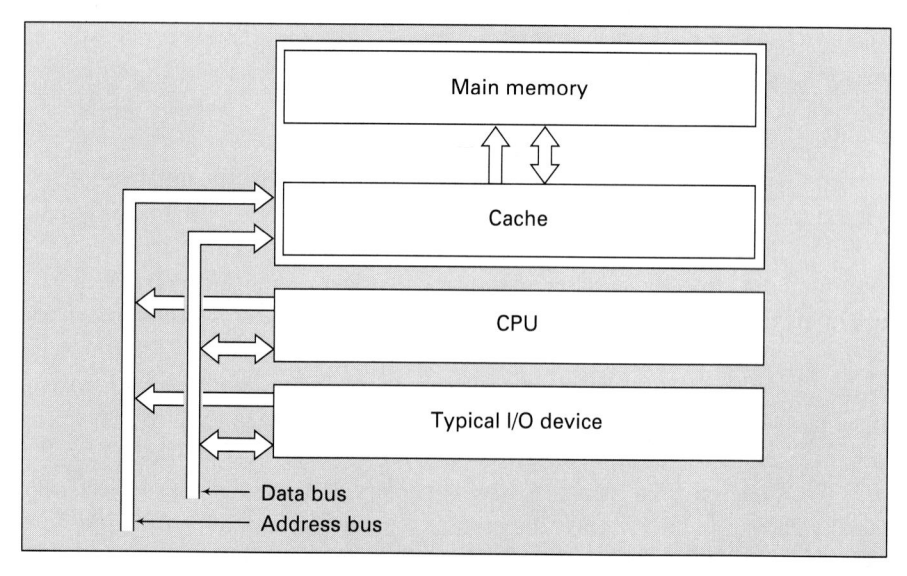

memory before telling an I/O device to start its output. Sometimes it is done explicitly, with synchronization instructions.

Without synchronization there is no way to guarantee that different devices will access the intended values. To see this, consider a single CPU with a cache and an independent I/O channel. Refer to Fig. 7.36. Every CPU write operation is cached. Assume the CPU is setting up block B of data to be written out to a peripheral device. The CPU writes the values to cache, but for a cache with posted write, B may not yet be in main memory. After writing B to the cache the CPU creates a pointer P in memory to tell the channel where B

**FIGURE 7.35** *A two-processor system where each processor has its own cache. Here there can be three copies of a datum (shaded) for a single main-memory address, one in memory and one in each cache. One or two of these copies could be stale values.*

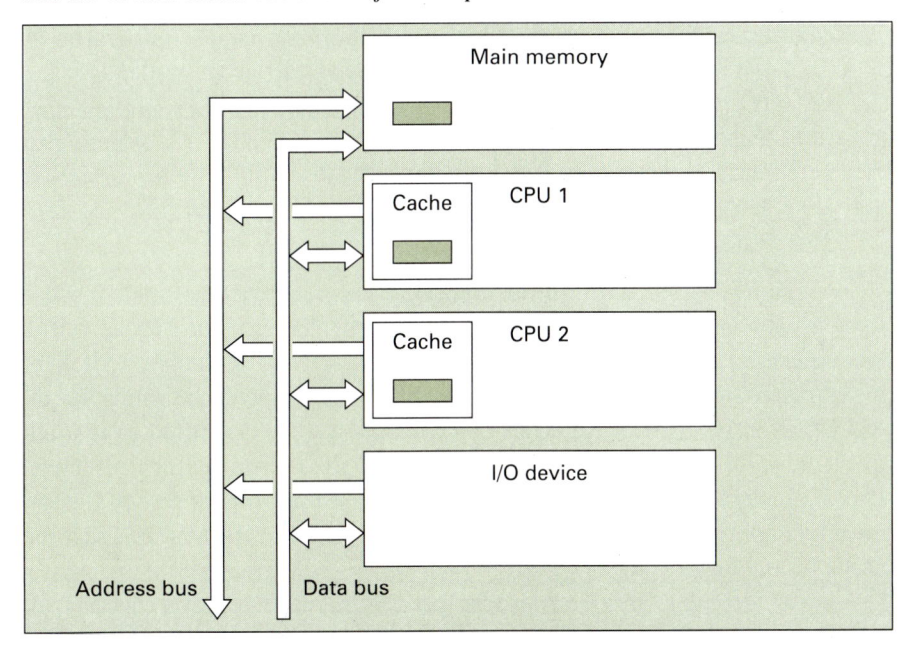

**FIGURE 7.36** *Sequencing of output operations.*

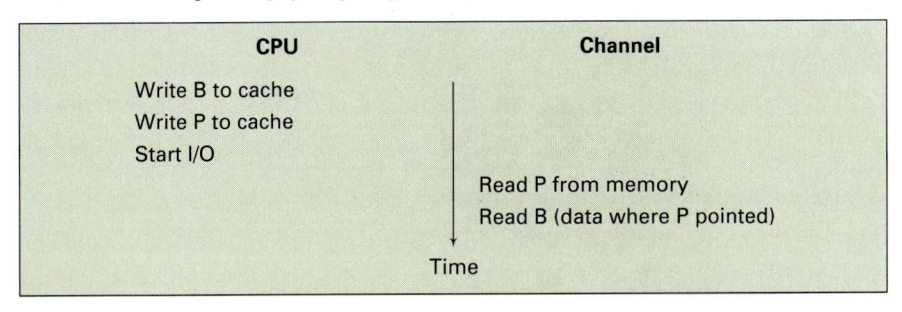

is. (The CPU writes P to the cache, however.) If P is only in cache but not yet in memory, the channel gets a stale pointer and accesses the wrong block of data. If P is in memory but B is only in cache, the cache reads the block of data at the correct address, but the data are stale. Notice that this will not happen if the cache is a write-through cache.

Software, hardware, or both can maintain cache coherence. Here are some of the mechanisms that computers use to maintain cache coherence:

- The system writes values to all caches and to main memory at the same time whenever any write operation occurs. This guarantees coherence between main memory and all caches.

- The system invalidates cache entries that hold potentially corrupted or stale data. For example, software may **flush the cache** whenever the operating system moves or deactivates a process or when another processor such as an I/O device completes an operation. As another example, the hardware also may "snoop" on (watch) all traffic on the bus to memory to know which cache entries to invalidate.

- If more than one device can simultaneously use the same memory locations, mark these locations as noncacheable. (A system that marks memory locations as noncacheable still requires processor synchronization.)

- Variation among these options.

*flushing a cache*

*snoopy caches*
*bus watcher*

Hardware solutions for maintaining cache coherence on single-bus systems usually include **snoopy caches.** The designer provides each cache with a **bus watcher,** a special circuit for monitoring bus activity. If the bus address of a write operation matches an address the cache holds, the cache simply invalidates that entry. If the local processor attempts a write operation to that address during the invalidation cycle, the cache stalls the processor for 1 cycle. If it attempts a read access, the cache indicates a miss, which forces a main-memory read. This technique requires that all units go to the bus (i.e., that the cache be write-through).

*invalidation bus*

A technique that can also be used with set-associative caches is to provide an **invalidation bus,** which broadcasts to all caches in the system the set number for each memory-write operation. Each cache then invalidates the corresponding set without checking whether any specific datum within the set is valid. The tradeoff between a snoopy cache and an invalidation bus is the higher cost of bus watchers for the former versus the decreased performance resulting from invalidating so many cache entries in use of the latter. The effect on performance depends on the ratio of cache invalidations to memory accesses: a small ratio implies little effect.

### 7.3.4 ■ Loosely Coupled Multiprocessors

Loosely coupled multiprocessors, also called multiple-processor computers, consist of a number of interconnected processors, where each processor has its own local memory and generally executes programs out of it. The feature that distinguishes a multiple-processor computer from a network of interconnected computers is that the processors of the former share the same logical-address space.[4] Thus each processor can access the local memory of another processor as if it were its own, although an access to nonlocal memory may take much longer than an access to local memory.

Two examples of interconnected systems that are *not* multiprocessors are **local-area networks (LANs)** and **wide-area networks (WANs).** In neither case do the processors share the same logical-address spaces. Yet both LANs and WANs are collections of computers that use an interconnection network to share resources, such as files and electronic mail. A LAN typically uses high-performance cables to let the computers within a limited area share disk storage and printers; a WAN covers a greater distance by using long-distance communications networks, such as satellites or microwave channels, to interconnect the computers. Each computer of a LAN or WAN connects to one node of an interconnection network.

**local-area networks (LANs)**
**wide-area networks (WANs)**

Architects must address several issues when designing multiple-processor computers, including interconnection-network structure and topology, memory structure, addressing structure, and techniques of processor control and synchronization. The researchers at Carnegie-Mellon University confronted these issues when they built the Cm* (circa 1975), an experimental loosely coupled multiprocessor. To give some insight into these general problems, we shall briefly describe their solutions to the problems of structuring memory and controlling the processors. Then we shall look at more recent examples of multiple-processor computers, those in Intel's iPSC/2 family.

**Carnegie-Mellon's Cm***

*Address Hierarchies*
When designing a multiple-processor computer, each individual processor should have access to the entire logical address space of the system. One may view the address space as consisting of blocks of addresses, where some blocks correspond to the addresses of the processors' local memories, some correspond to the port addresses of I/O devices, and some correspond to the control-port addresses of special hardware devices, such as page and segment maps. Figure 7.37 illustrates this idea.

Addressing is not uniform within a multiple-processor computer, although it should appear to be uniform from each individual processor's point of view. For example, the system generally uses less hardware when a processor accesses its own local memory than when it accesses the local memory of another processor. Likewise, the system uses less hardware when a processor ref-

---

4. Some authors use the term *tightly-coupled* to refer to multiprocessors whose processes operate in a single address space and *loosely-coupled* to refer to systems of interconnected processors in which the processes have independent address spaces.

erences the memory of another processor that is within a group of localized processors than when it passes information between different groups.

The Cm* has a three-level hierarchical structure (see Fig. 7.38). The lowest level consists of an arbitrary number of **computer modules.** Each module contains (1) an LSI-11 microprocessor, (2) a bus-interface processor called a Local Switch, (3) a local bus, (4) local memory, and (5) local devices as needed. The LSI-11 is essentially a PDP-11 microprocessor; see the *Case Studies* for a description of the PDP-11 architecture. A **Local Switch** resembles a page map and is a relatively simple device; it is one of two types of address maps designed for the Cm* (the second to be described shortly).

The second level of the hierarchy consists of a number of **clusters** of computer modules. Via a Map Bus, a processor within a cluster can access the local memory of another processor within the same cluster, but now the memory access takes slightly longer than if it were accessing its own local memory.

**computer modules**

**see Case Study 4**
**local switch**

**clusters**

FIGURE 7.37 *A memory map of the address space of a multiple-processor computer. Shaded areas represent assigned addresses belonging to processors and devices; unshaded areas are unused.*

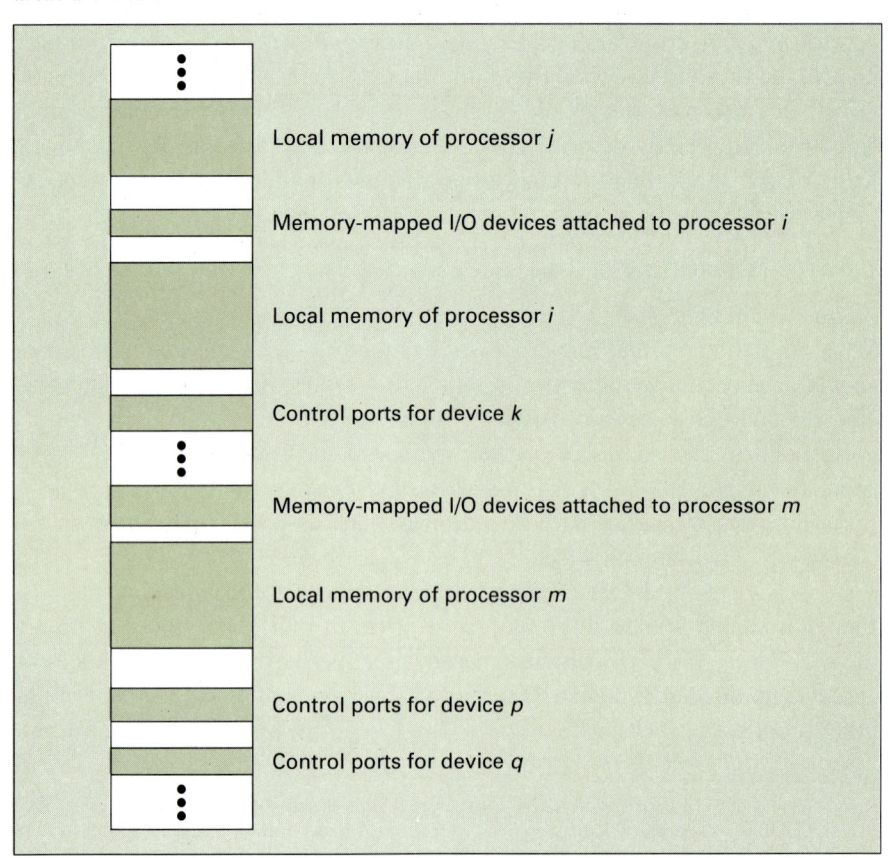

- Local memory of processor *j*
- Memory-mapped I/O devices attached to processor *i*
- Local memory of processor *i*
- Control ports for device *k*
- Memory-mapped I/O devices attached to processor *m*
- Local memory of processor *m*
- Control ports for device *p*
- Control ports for device *q*

Map buses are controlled by **Kmaps**, the second type of address map designed for the Cm*. A *K*map is an intelligent controller; it can arbitrate interprocessor-memory accesses and intertask communications, check privileges, raise exceptions, and so forth.

*Kmaps*

    The third and highest level of the hierarchy consists of a group of clusters connected by Inter-Cluster Buses. A processor can access memory across clusters, but now accesses are considerably slower. Like Map Buses, the Inter-Cluster Buses are controlled by *K*maps. Both the intra- and intercluster networks are packet-switched, and the intercluster messages may pass through several stages of control. The entire system forms a tree structure with computer modules as the leaf nodes.

### *Addressing*

The address space of a multiprocessor may be larger than the address spaces of the individual processors, as is the case for the Cm*, and the architects must therefore provide memory-mapping hardware to map an individual processor's effective addresses into systemwide physical addresses. In the Cm* the Local Switches perform the address mapping within the computer modules while the *K*maps perform the address mapping for intra- and intercluster memory accesses.

**FIGURE 7.38** *Structure of a Cm\* cluster. The Kmap controls the cluster's Map Bus. It also sends messages to other Kmaps across the Inter-Cluster Buses.*

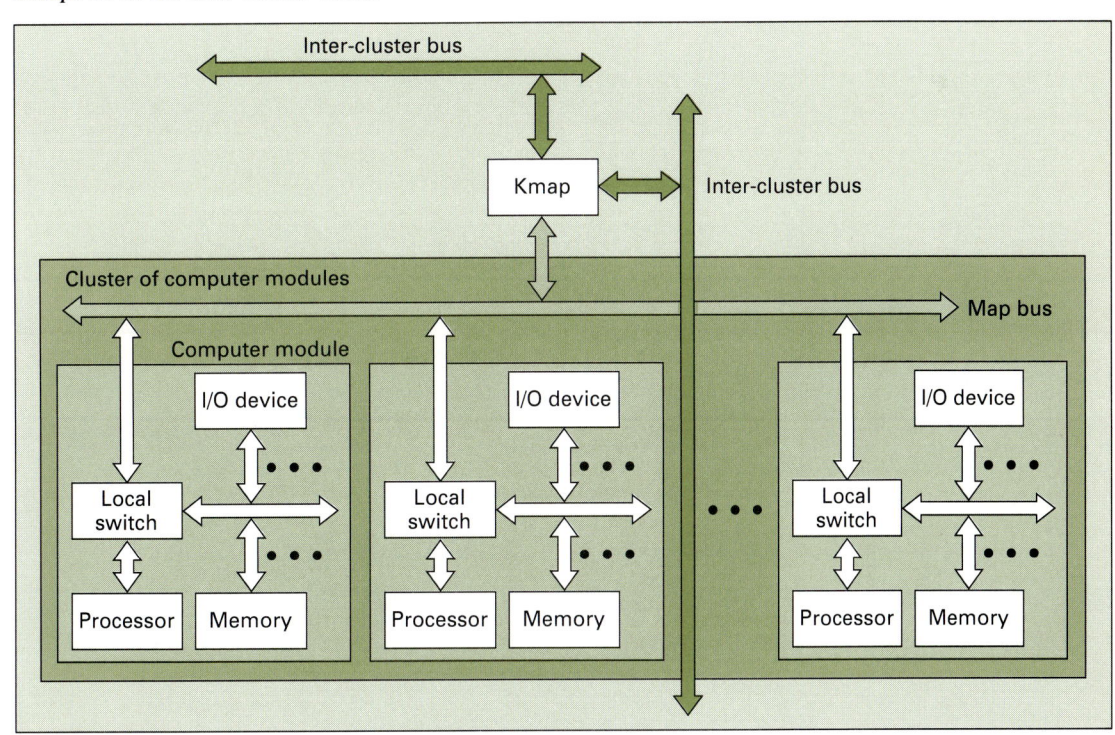

374    Computer Architecture

Cm*'s logical-address space has 64-K segments of up to 4 KB each. On the other hand, each processor generates 16-bit effective addresses, which the Cm* treats as logical addresses. To perform the local-address translation, each Local Switch contains 32 relocation registers. See Figure 7.39. The relocation registers supply the local-memory segment numbers for each local-memory

**FIGURE 7.39** *Address mapping done by Cm*'s Local Switches and Kmaps. The Local Switches process local-memory requests. For nonlocal accesses, the Local Switches send service requests to the Kmaps. The Kmaps process the service requests and generate either 23-bit Map-Bus addresses or 31-bit Inter-Cluster Bus addresses, depending on the type of memory reference.*

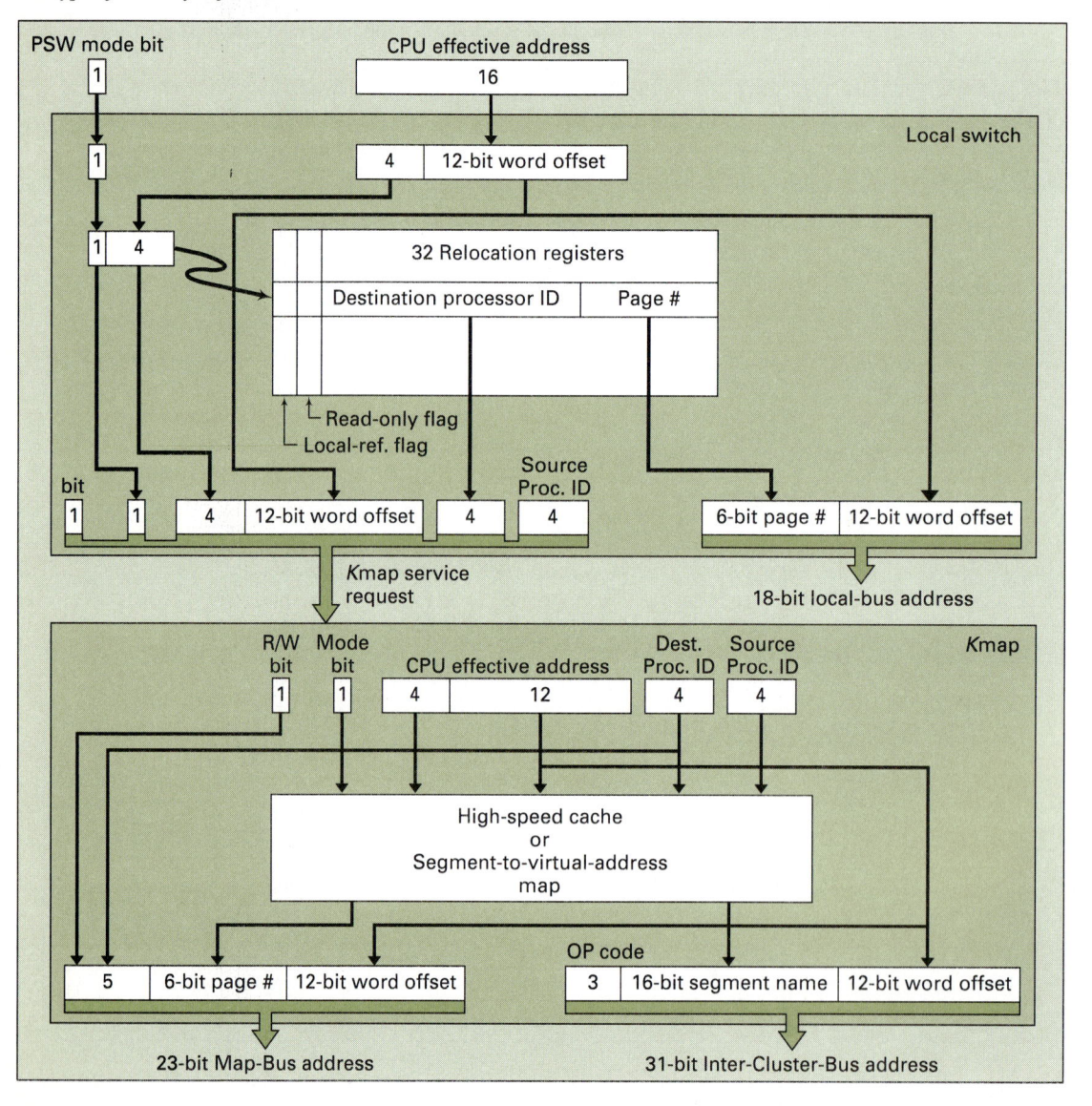

access. When a processor sends a 16-bit effective address to its Local Switch, the Local Switch uses the 4 high-order address bits plus the processor's mode bit from its processor status word, or PSW, to form a 5-bit selector for one of 32 relocation registers. The relocation register indicates whether the reference is local or nonlocal. For a local access, the relocation register provides a 6-bit page number, which the Local Switch concatenates with the 12 low-order bits from the processor's effective address to form an 18-bit physical address. Using this mechanism, each user process can locally address up to 64 segments, but only 16 segments at a time without modifying the relocation registers.[5]

Nonlocal accesses are either intracluster or intercluster references. In either case, the Local Switch issues a **service request** to the *K*map, which requests it to perform the address translation. To issue a service request, the Local Switch sends five items of information to the *K*map: the CPU's 16-bit effective address, the identification numbers of the source and destination processors (4 bits each), the CPU mode (1 bit), and the type of access (read or write). The Local Switch sends these values by writing them to the *K*map's control registers, which have assigned addresses within Cm*'s physical-address space.

*service request*

To process a service request, the *K*map uses the 4 high-order bits of the CPU's effective address, the CPU's mode bit, and the source and destination processor IDs to reference its segment tables. The segment-table entry indicates whether the requesting processor has permission to make the desired memory access. If not, the *K*map raises an exception. Otherwise it generates the proper Map-Bus address (for intracluster references) or Inter-Cluster-Bus address (for intercluster references), creates a message packet, and sends it along the appropriate bus.

The *K*maps perform the address translations, but they do not participate in data transfers. Once the *K*maps determine the address and type of transfer, the Local Switches transfer the data directly, without *K*map intervention.

*Processor Control*

The Cm* uses **memory-mapped control,** which resembles memory-mapped I/O. The Cm* reserves special control-port addresses through which any processor, with suitable privileges, can control any other processor or function of the system. There are special addresses to control all processor functions. By writing to these addresses, a processor can start, stop, or restart other processors; transmit requests for service to the *K*maps; alter privileges; and so forth. For example, each Local Switch has several registers that respond to reserved addresses within the local-address space. One of them holds the Map-Bus address for a nonlocal access. The *K*map fetches the address from that register when the Local Switch requests *K*map service.

*memory-mapped control*

---

5. The LSI-11 processors execute in either user mode or kernel mode, and the PSW has a bit that indicates the current mode. Because the Local Switch uses the mode bit as part of the relocation-register selector, a user process can access only 16 of the 32 relocation registers; the kernel process can access the other 16 relocation registers.

The Cm* also reserves a portion of each processor's address space for **window registers.** Window registers describe all segments the processor may access. Unless it has suitable privileges, a processor can select segments but not change the segment lists. Given suitable privileges, a processor can access all of Cm*'s memory.

*Packet-switched Network*

The Cm* implements nonlocal communications with packet switching. All buses except the local buses are packet-switched. The packets contain addresses, control information, and data. The control information specifies the operation (read or write, for example). Once a *K*map creates a packet, it sends it via other *K*maps to its destination. The *K*map at the destination cluster transfers the packet to the Map Bus, where the Local Switch steals memory cycles and places the address, data, and control functions on the local bus. Because the Cm* maps all control functions into memory accesses, this mechanism allows each processor to control every system function, provided it is given permission to do so.

The techniques that Cm*'s architects devised for extending the address spaces of the processors, distributing the control functions through the physical-address space, and organizing the processors into clusters are general techniques. The hierarchical organization gave all processors rapid access to their own local memory and only slightly reduced performance for extramodule, intracluster references. It provided a general and extendable architecture and control regimen, and provided adequate facilities for process synchronization.

### iPSC/2

As a second illustration of the trend in loosely coupled multiprocessors, we shall briefly describe the iPSC/2 family, which Intel introduced in 1988. The iPSC/2 family uses Intel's 80386 microprocessors at its CPU modules and a packet-switched, hypercube interconnection network to connect them together. Each multiprocessor has 16 to 128 CPU modules. In addition to the 80386, each CPU module has up to 16 MB of memory, a 64-KB cache, dedicated I/O channels, and a special direct-connect router for the hypercube network. A user can augment the CPU modules with 80387 floating-point coprocessors and special tightly coupled, piplelined, vector coprocessors.

The maximum amount of memory per module depends on the total number of processors in the system and on the processor configuration. The maximum amount of memory for each CPU module of a 128-processor nonvector configuration is 4 MB. A vector system also can have up to 4 MB of memory per CPU module but a maximum of only 64 CPU modules. For the vector system, each vector processor has 1 MB of memory, which occupies part of the address space of the CPU. Hence the CPU has direct access to the vector processor's memory.

Although it is too early to know how successful and widespread the iPSC/2 family will become, the trend toward multiprocessor architectures has clearly been set. The *Case Studies* describes in more detail the iPSC/2 and its successor, the iPSC/860.

see Case Study 15

## 7.3.5 ◼ Fault-tolerant Computers

One area in which multiprocessors have gained some prominence is fault-tolerant computing. Applications areas include computer-controlled telephone switching, system and process control (air traffic control and monitoring of power and chemical plants), and online transaction-processing systems (OLTPs: airline reservation systems, automated tellers, automatic funds transfer, and lottery and betting terminals). These systems often have a large number of terminals that share the same database, so consistency, integrity, and system availability are critical issues.

### Kinds of Malfunction

We shall use the term **fault** to indicate a component error or malfunction and **failure** to indicate the nonperformance of a system. An **error** is any incorrect response of a component or system. This terminology is thus hierarchical in nature and depends on the context. A fault at one level in a system may result in a failure at the next higher level. As an analogy, consider that tennis players who foot fault do not necessarily fail (lose the game), although they may. A **fault-tolerant computer,** is a system that does not fail in the face of (some) faults. Being completely fault-tolerant means that no single fault will cause failure (i.e., there is no single point of failure).

fault
failure
error

fault-tolerant computer

There are three categories of malfunction that a system designer must consider: component faults, software failure, and operator errors. **Component faults** are of two types: hard and soft or transient. **Hard faults** are permanent and may result from a momentary condition, such as shock, high humidity, power transients, insufficient cooling, or various sorts of gremlins (such as radioactive disruption ($\alpha$-particles), static electricity, and vibration, among others). They may also be due to old age or manufacturing defects, and they are particularly critical in harsh environments such as factories and automobiles. **Soft faults** are momentary faults; the are not persistent. Examples are altered bits in a memory due to radiation. They usually do not recur. **Software failures** include a program's improper response to a hardware condition, such as a faulty component, an incorrect data structure or data set, or an erroneous program state, such as a system deadlock. Systems are particularly prone to failures when novice users interact with fragile software. **Operator errors** include incorrect operating procedure such as improper tape mounting or turning off a device at the wrong time. We shall focus on fault-tolerant multiprocessor architectures but mention some related software issues as well.

component faults
hard faults

soft faults
software failures

operator errors

Ordinary systems have many components whose failure will cause the entire system to fail. Such critical components include integrated circuits, power supplies, I/O controllers, and bus switches. In contrast, architects design fault-tolerant computers to withstand these and other hardware failures.

**depth of faults**
**coverage of faults**
**reliability**
**maintainability**
**availability**

With reference to fault tolerance, **depth of faults** refers to the number of faults a particular kind a system can tolerate, while **coverage of faults** refers to the range of faults a system can anticipate. The **reliability** of a system is inversely proportional to its failure rate, **maintainability** refers to the range of techniques needed to repair or upgrade a system, and **availability** is the probability of a system being operational at any given time.

**mean time between failures (MTBF)**

Reliability and availability are related, as follows. One measure of a system's reliability is its **mean time between failures (MTBF),** which is the average operating time between the start of a system's normal operation and its first electronic or mechanical failure. Scientists measure MTBF in millions of hours for individual components and in hours, months, or years for most computers. (For most computers, failure of any component will cause the system to fail as well.) If only one failure is possible, as with individual components, it is common to speak of the **mean time to failure (MTTF).** For computers that are repaired, the concern is the **mean time to repair (MTTR),** which is the average amount of time it takes a technician to repair a system from the time of its failure. The availability is given by the formula

**mean time to failure (MTTF)**
**mean time to repair (MTTR)**

$$\text{Availability} = \frac{\text{MTBF}}{\text{MTBF} + \text{MTTR}}.$$

However, be aware that this concept is ill-defined. For the X-31 airplane a 10-ms failure of its control computer can result in the loss of the aircraft's wings; thus a 10-ms outage is a catastrophic failure. On the other hand, for most systems used by people, a 10-ms outage is irrelevant. Thus, careful definition of what constitutes "being in service" is important. A claim of 99.995% availability for time-sharing computer may mean that the system was never out-of-service for more than 1 s except for 0.005% (about 26 min/year). Many faults can be found and corrected in a second. On the other hand, 99.995% availability for the X-31 computer might mean that less than once in 20,000 one-hour flights would the computer be out of service for 1 ms.

**Fault-tolerance Techniques**

Designers and users employ a number of techniques to provide fault tolerance. One is **fault avoidance:** The manufacturer avoids faults by using highly reliable components and proven design and manufacturing techniques, such as component burn-in, careful signal-line routing, shielding, circuit isolation, power-line surge protection, and filtering. Another is **data recovery:** A system may include facilities for restoring damaged data, such as the periodic saving of critical data, audit trails, record locking, and duplicate data sets. A third is to provide facilities for **error detection and correction:** For example, many storage systems include parity bits and hardware for detecting double errors and correcting single errors (**double-error detection and single-error correction [DEDSEC] memory**). Other techniques include data check-sums and I/O retry.

**fault avoidance**

**data recovery**

**error detection and correction**

**double-error detection and single-error correction (DEDSEC) memory**

Essentially all modern fault-tolerant systems achieve fault tolerance by using redundant components in one form or another. Many systems run duplicate components concurrently, with one acting as a spare for the other. Some systems that run duplicate components simply compare their outputs to check the validity of the computations.

We shall examine many fault-tolerance techniques in the remainder of Section 7.3.5, including the use of backup processors, dual-ported peripherals, and closely coupled or tightly coupled dual processors. These techniques often provide the capacity to detect the presence of faults and also the ability to reconfigure by replacing a faulty component with an operational one.

*Backup Computers*

The earliest form of fault tolerance was for the computing center to provide a complete **backup** or **spare system,** including memory, CPU, and I/O processors. In case of a computer failure, personnel transferred all work to the backup system, which then took over until repair personnel could fix the main system. This form of redundancy was the standard for critical operations, such as military defense systems and space exploration systems.

*backup spare system*

*Processor Reassignment*

Recall from Section 7.3.4 that a multiprocessor is loosely coupled if each of its processors has its own local storage. The processors frequently communicate by sending messages to one another. Since the storage is not a single component, the system can achieve fault tolerance by reassigning tasks from faulty components to operational components.

In contrast, in a tightly coupled multiprocessor the processors share the same memory. Here the processors form a pool of specialized devices, and a process recruits processors to accomplish its goals; for example, a process requiring an I/O operation recruits an I/O processor to perform it. The system achieves fault tolerance by maintaining multiple copies of all data.

In both kinds of multiprocessors the software plays an essential role in achieving fault tolerance.

*Checkpointing*

Systems that use backup components use checkpointing to recover from a failure by going back to a recent (almost up-to-date) data set and restarting from there. Conceptually, the main system and backup system operate concurrently. The main system is always up to date. The backup system is almost up to date. The main system periodically (perhaps every few seconds) communicates with the spare to bring its data up to date and provide it with the necessary information, called **checkpoint information.** Message-oriented systems use **checkpoint messages.** If the main system fails, the backup system takes over. Where possible the current transactions are then brought up to date; if the main computer failed in the middle of a transaction, the steps of processing the transaction up to that point must be negated (undone) and the aborted transaction restarted.

*checkpoint information checkpoint messages*

### Reconfigurable Duplication

**Reconfigurable duplication,** similar to the technique of using a backup computer except that it occurs at the component level, is the ability of a system with redundant components to reconfigure itself dynamically. The designers pair components and supply them with circuitry for comparing their results. The operating system selects one of the components to be the main component and the other to be the spare. When the results do not match, the comparator generates an error signal. The operating system then determines which component failed and uses the other. See Fig. 7.40. Notice that the comparison unit and switch are critical components in the illustrated configuration.

### Watchdog Timers and Heartbeats

When two or more systems operate concurrently, each one needs some way of notifying the others that everything is okay. One mechanism is for each process to periodically notify the others that it is operational; such notification is called an **I'm alive notice** or a **heartbeat**. If a processor does not receive a heartbeat from another processor when it expects to, the first assumes the second has died and operates accordingly. For example, if two processes are designated main process and backup and the backup does not receive a heartbeat from the main process, the backup then takes control and operates as the main process.

A related mechanism is for the main processor and the spare processor to run different timer processes. The main program must periodically reset the spare's timer process. A timeout fault occurs if it doesn't, and the spare takes over as the main process.

### Pair-and-spare

The **pair-and-spare strategy** uses redundancy both for error detection and reconfigurable duplication and is essentially reconfigurable duplication at the system level. At the component level the designer uses a pair of identical components to build a unit that detects its own errors. The two components receive exactly the same inputs and simultaneously perform the same operation on those inputs. The components are highly synchronized. Comparison circuitry checks the outputs and generates an error signal if a mismatch occurs. The signal indicates that the paired unit has failed or, more precisely, that one of its components has failed. Computers using the pair-and-spare strategy are **tightly synchronized multiprocessors.**

At the system level of organization, the designer builds a computer using a *pair* of the error-detecting units just described. One pair operates as the main unit and the other as a spare unit. Thus there are four copies of the system components. See Fig. 7.41. In general, each main unit and spare unit operate in a tightly synchronized mode. If either the main unit or its spare generates an error signal, a control unit disables it and reports the failure to the operator. The control unit automatically switches operation to the spare if the main unit fails, so the computer continues to operate using the functional unit as the main unit. After the repair personnel fix or replace the faulty unit, the system brings both units into synchronous operation again.

## N-modular Redundancy with Voting

Pair-and-spare logic pairs two identical components as a way of detecting faults. **N-modular redundancy** is similar, but with $N$ components ($N \geq 3$). Now, however, special **voting logic** compares the outputs and accepts the majority output as correct. Thus the system not only detects an error but **masks** (corrects) it. Units of this type are particularly useful in systems that cannot

N-modular redundancy
voting logic
masking errors

**FIGURE 7.40** *Hardware for reconfigurable duplication.*

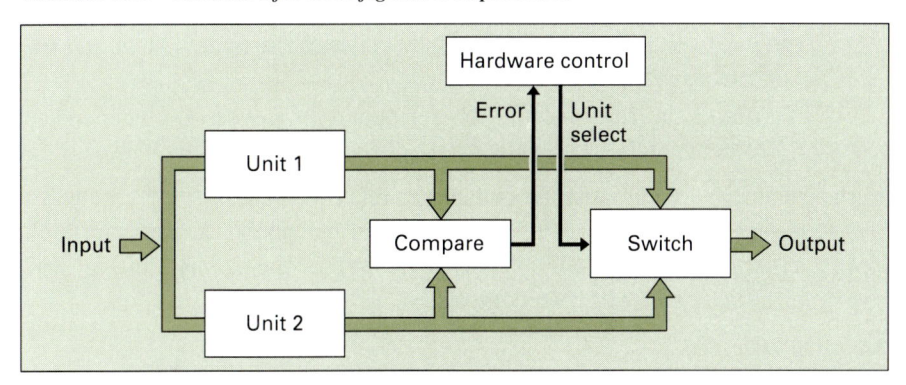

**FIGURE 7.41** *Organization of a pair-and-spare unit. E, error signal.*

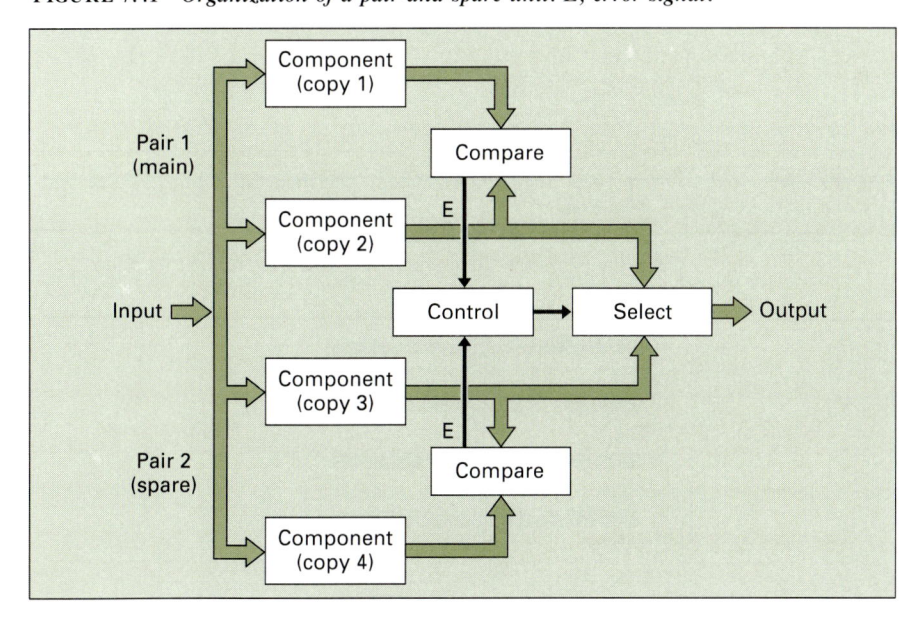

be repaired, such as on-board computers for guidance control, but architects also use them within other computers that can be repaired.

Designers can apply voting logic as just described to the hardware, and they can also use voting logic at the software level. When used at the software level, several processors execute the same program and then compare their own results with the results produced by other processors. A computer that disagrees with the majority disables itself. Alternatively, software systems may use different programs to mask software errors.

### Dual-ported Peripheral Devices

OLTP system designers have taken two evolutionary steps toward dynamic redundancy:

1. adding switches to the peripheral devices so that operators or operating systems could switch easily between the main system and the backup system;
2. adding **multiple ports** to the peripheral devices so that independent systems could access them.

*multiported peripherals*

In the event that a CPU fails, the switches enable the operator or operating system to quickly change devices or control. When peripheral devices have multiple ports, more than one CPU can access them, as the example in Fig. 7.42 shows for a disk drive with two controllers.

### Mirrored Data Sets

When there is only one copy of a data set, a device failure, (e.g., a crashed disk), a faulty device controller, or an inoperative port may result in temporary or permanent data loss. One technique to reduce the risk of data loss is for the system to maintain **mirrored data sets:** Two or more independent physical devices operate concurrently and maintain identical copies of the data. If one

*mirrored data sets*

**FIGURE 7.42** *A dual-ported disk has two controllers. The illustrated unit has four platters and two sets of read-write heads.*

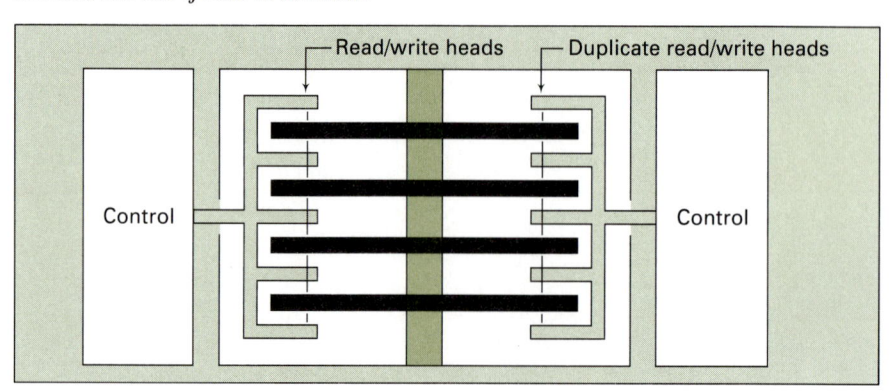

device fails, either the operator reconfigures the system or the system reconfigures itself to exclude the faulty device and include the operational one. Since the data set maintained by the second device is up to date, the system can continue to run using it.

One advantage of this technique is the system can read whichever disk it easier to use (i.e., is faster, or involves less contention). Because read operations are more common than write operations, the resulting improvement in performance can be substantial. One difficulty arises from software failure, which may corrupt the data on both data sets. Thus systems with mirrored data sets generally use checkpointing as described earlier.

One pioneer manufacturer of fault-tolerant systems is Tandem, and we describe the Tandem/16, a historically prominent machine, in the *Case Studies*.

see Case Study 14

## 7.4 ■ Alternate Architectures

Many applications place severe computational demands on computers, and architects have responded by designing specialized processors to satisfy these demands. Most of the specialized processors are flow-control architectures and thus use a program counter. They differ from general-purpose computers in the specialized hardware they bring to bear on the target application. Examples are image-processing machines, artificial intelligence (AI) machines, and database machines. Architects design image-processing machines with special I/O devices that can handle the high I/O bandwidths required for processing and displaying images, and they often employ pipelined arithmetic units specifically tuned for operations like blurring and image correlation. Architects design AI machines with special processors designed to meet the needs of symbolic computations, often using one processor for allocating memory and a second for reclaiming unused memory (garbage collection). They design database machines to support large external high-speed storage devices with special facilities for database operations.

In general, the special-purpose architectures use many of the techniques we have described throughout this volume. The following sections, which conclude this book, briefly discuss two alternatives to conventional flow-control architectures. One of these is dataflow processors. Unlike in von Neumann machines, in which the programs determine when they will perform operations, it is the availability of data that determines when a dataflow processor will perform operations.

Another class of recently introduced alternate architectures is neural networks. These are loosely based on biological systems and consist of large numbers of very simple computational elements that operate in parallel. Although not intended to be general-purpose computers, neural networks are beginning to show promise in signal-processing and pattern-recognition applications.

### 7.4.1 ■ Dataflow Architectures

Algorithms, like directions and menus, are sequences of steps that define a process. Most programming consists of developing sequential algorithms expressed in a procedural programming language. When there is a break in the sequence (a branch), the program itself specifies what instruction the computer must execute next. Architects design von Neumann machines to execute sequences of instructions, which is why they are so well suited for executing programs written in procedural languages.

There are several alternatives to using sequential algorithms to express computations, and in this section we will discuss two of them: the dataflow model and the reduction machine.

**Dataflow Model**

*dataflow model of computation*
*dataflow graph*

The **dataflow model of computation** is nonprocedural: a programmer specifies a computation by giving its **dataflow graph,** not by writing a program for it. A dataflow graph defines the operations and their data dependencies, not the order of the operations' execution. It is the availability of data and of computational resources that determines the order of execution of the operations.

*nodes*
*arcs*

*argument slots*

Each dataflow graph represents a computation. A graph consists of **nodes** that indicate the operations and **arcs** indicating where the nodes send their results. For convenience the nodes may be labeled. Either the arcs terminate at the **argument slots** of other nodes, or they leave the graph. Argument slots hold the inputs for the nodes. Some dataflow models restrict nodes to two argument slots, which correspond to the arguments for binary arithmetic operations. We shall not make that restriction here. Arcs leaving the graph are **output arcs,** and arcs entering the graph from outside are **input arcs** (see Fig. 7.43).

*output arcs*
*input arcs*

*empty slot*
*full slot*
*token*

Argument slots hold operands for the operations. An argument slot may be either empty or full. An **empty slot** does not yet hold a value, while a **full slot** holds a value, or a **token**. We shall use square brackets to denote tokens. As an example, the second argument of the minus operation holds a token having the value 4. Some arguments are constant and appear as numbers in the graphs. An example is the second argument to the plus operation, which always holds the value 3. Conceptually, each node knows where to send its result (or results), but it does not know where its operands come from. Finally, **input tokens** are external values brought into a dataflow graph, and **output tokens** carry results away from the graph.

*input tokens*
*output tokens*

*firable node*

A **firable node** is a node that can begin its operation. All argument slots must be full before a node becomes firable, but some dataflow models impose additional restrictions as well. After becoming firable, a node may fire. It then consumes its argument tokens, performs its assigned operation, and produces one or more result tokens, which it sends along the proper outgoing arcs to the receiving or **destination nodes.** (Showing an outgoing arc is equivalent to specifying the destination node, and when a graph is shown we often do not

*destination nodes*

explicitly give the destination node or nodes). With reference to an actual implementation, a node fires when the computer issues an instruction (or a block of instructions) that implements the node.

## Control Nodes and Control Tokens

Subgraphs, which correspond to subroutines and functions in programs, represent computations. Using only the node types presented so far, the dataflow model is limited. What it lacks are capabilities for conditional execution of subgraphs, and hence for iteration (loops). One way to expand the model is to add control tokens and control nodes.

**Control tokens** represent the boolean values *true* and *false*, and nodes that produce control tokens are **test nodes** or **predicates** (see Fig. 7.44). For example, node B1, illustrated in the figure, produces *true* tokens when $A < B$ and *false* tokens when $A \geq B$; node B2 produces *false* tokens when $A \neq B$ and *true* tokens when $A = B$.

There are many possible types of **control nodes,** but two useful types are switch nodes and merge nodes. A **switch node** consumes a control token and routes a data token along one of two outgoing arcs depending on the value of the control token. A **merge node** also consumes a control token. It selects a data token from one of two incoming arcs (depending on the control token's value) and sends it along its outgoing arc. A merge node can fire when it receives a control token along its control input and a data token on the input pathway selected by the control token. See Fig. 7.45.

control tokens

test nodes
predicates

control nodes
switch node

merge node

**FIGURE 7.43** *Simple dataflow graph for the computation* $(A + 3) \times (B - C)$. *The value [4] has entered the graph for the token C. The boxes represent nodes, the arrows are arcs, parentheses indicate argument lots, and brackets hold tokens.*

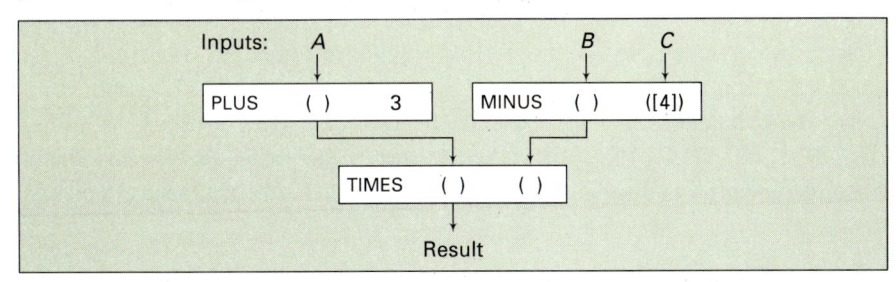

**FIGURE 7.44** *Test nodes produce control tokens.*

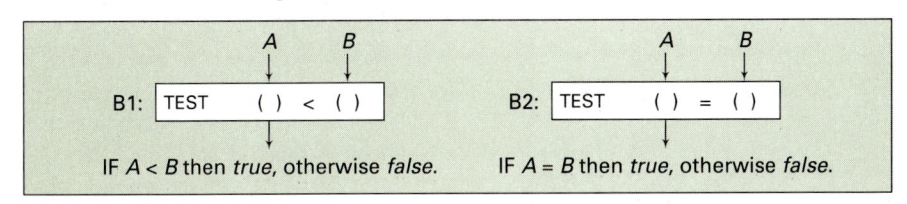

### Computational Threads

One of the chief ways to gain parallelism in the dataflow model is to use well-behaved subgraphs as code blocks and invoke them from other subgraphs. One vital property of a well-behaved subgraph is that its output depends *not* on its history of inputs but only on the current inputs. Such a subgraph is **reentrant.**

So far all the nodes we have been discussing produce a single result token and send it to one specified place. (Note that this includes the switch node in Fig. 7.45b: although two output arcs are shown, only one will fire for a given implementation of the node.) In contrast, **fork nodes** produce multiple tokens. However, fork nodes do not alter the tokens they receive but simply copy them and send the copies to two or more places. Therefore they generate multiple **computational threads,** also called **threads of control.** A dataflow graph with one input arc and no fork nodes has a single thread of control. Such a graph corresponds to a single process in a von Neumann machine.

Since each computational thread corresponds to an independent process, multiprocessor architectures are well suited to execute dataflow programs. Multiple threads may be rejoined into a single thread by nodes with two or more argument slots. For programs with multiple threads of control, different dataflow models may place restrictions on the operands of nodes that join them. As an example, a model may require that all tokens that cause a node to fire come from the same initial thread of control.

### A Number Generator

Figure 7.46, which shows the dataflow graph for a number generator, illustrates many of the basic dataflow concepts we have introduced. The graph realizes a single loop that increments the value of a data token $i$. The path shown in color on the right carries data tokens, while the path shown on the left carries control tokens. The number generator works as follows. To start it the operating system injects (loads) the token $[-1]$ into test node T1. In response, T1 generates a control token, $[true]$, and sends it to merge node M. When M receives $[true]$ it selects its *true* operand, the constant $-1$, and uses it to initialize $i$. M then sends $i$, the token $[-1]$, to the increment node. The increment node increments $i$ and sends $[0]$ to fork node F1. F1, in turn, sends copies to

FIGURE 7.45  *Control nodes: (a) a MERGE node and (b) a SWITCH node.*

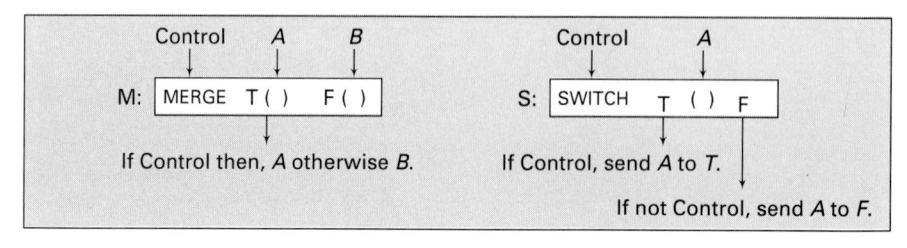

test node T2 and switch node S. T2 generates [*false*] for S. In response, S sends [0] to fork node F2. The generator now outputs the first value, [0]. Notice that copies of [0] also go to test node T1 and merge node M for the next iteration of the loop.

Now consider the pathway shown in color, which carries tokens holding the values being generated. Notice that M selects input *i* if it receives [*false*] from T1. Because T1 has just now received a copy of the first output token, [0], from F2, it generates the required token [*false*]. Thus M sends [0] to the increment node, which adds 1 to it. The incremented value, 1, becomes the current value for *i*. The process then continues exactly as just described.

To see how the generator stops, look at test node T2. If the value it receives exceeds [100], it generates [*true*], which it sends to S. S then attempts to send the final data value, which is [101], along its [*true*] arc. Since that arc terminates without a destination node, no new tokens enter the generator, and it halts.

*A Prototypical Dataflow Architecture*

We can divide dataflow graphs into two different models depending on the number of tokens at a time allowed on a given arc. Those that restrict arcs to one token at a time are **static dataflow models;** those that treat the arcs as potentially infinite queues are **dynamic dataflow models.** Architectures that im-

static dataflow models

dynamic dataflow models

FIGURE 7.46 *A generator for the integer values between 0 and 100. Notice that when S gets a [true] control token it does not send its input data token anywhere. The arcs for data tokens are in color, while those for control tokens are in black.*

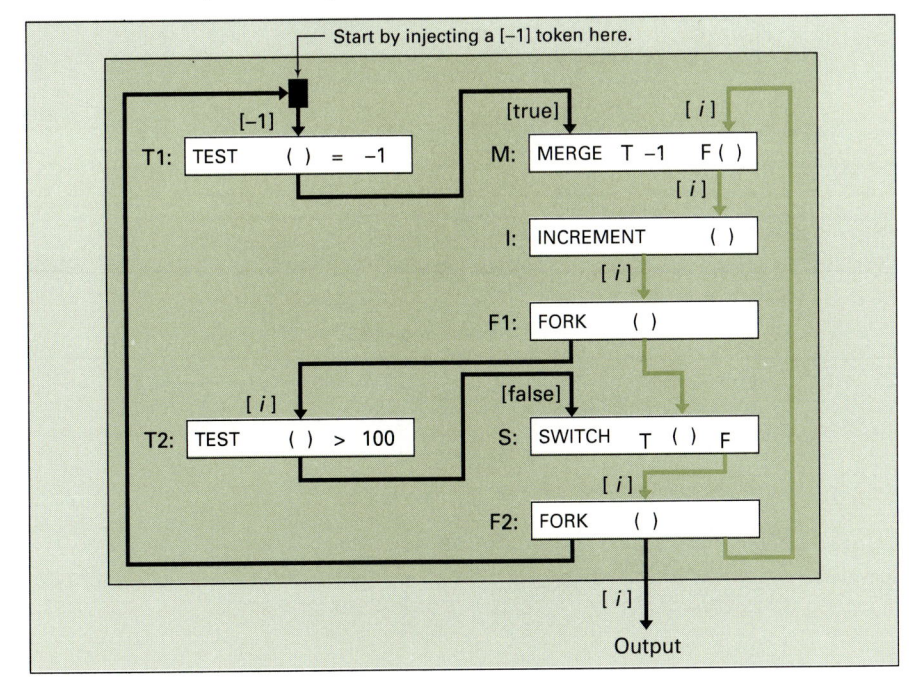

**static dataflow architectures**
**dynamic dataflow architectures**

plement these two models are **static dataflow architectures** and **dynamic dataflow architectures,** respectively. The differences in parallelism can be quite significant.

**tagged token**

Because dynamic dataflow models allow more than one token at a time on an arc, they generally tag the tokens to make them distinguishable. A **tagged token** carries information in addition to the data it represents, and often indicates how and when the token originated. As an example, when a program spawns multiple threads of control, it is sometimes useful to view the resulting tokens as being tagged. The execution of a fork node, then, may produce a set of tokens having the same tag. When a nonfork node processes a tagged token, it produces a tagged token with the same tag. Because each incoming arc may have several tokens, the nodes that combine tokens must apply specific rules for combining tags and producing new tags. If the tags represent separate data sets, then one combination rule might be that computational nodes must combine tokens with similar tags.

The architectures of dataflow processors differ from those of von Neumann machines. Fig. 7.47 illustrates a prototypical dynamic dataflow architecture. Dynamic dataflow architectures include two subsystems not found in static dataflow architectures: token matching and token processing.

**node data structure**

Logically we may view each node of a dataflow graph as a **node data structure** in memory. The dataflow processor has a pool of processing elements

**FIGURE 7.47** *Architecture of a prototypical dynamic dataflow machine.*

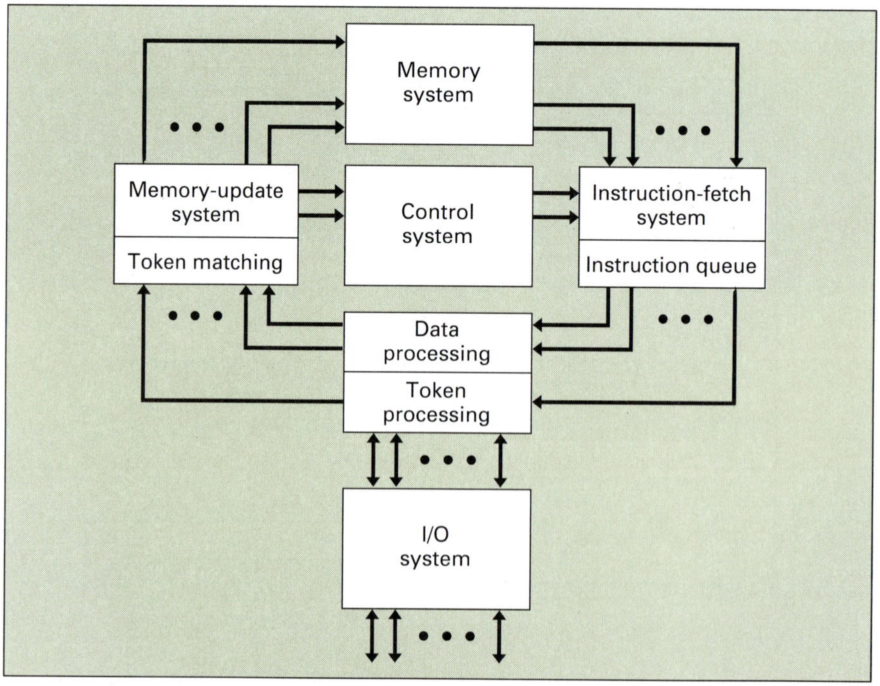

that process **instruction packets.** Each instruction packet represents a specific instance of a firable node—the operation, its arguments, and its destination addresses. The processor builds instruction packets in the node data structures.

  The memory system is the same as in conventional von Neumann machines. The fetch system consists of a number of fetch units that operate in parallel and check to see whether any node data structures represent firable nodes. When a fetch unit finds a firable node, it generates an instruction packet and transfers it to the instruction queue, where it waits for an available processing element (PE). When a PE becomes available, the instruction queue issues an instruction packet and passes the packet to the PE for execution. Note that a dynamic dataflow processor may have separate PEs for processing data and tags. When a PE has finished executing an instruction packet, it generates a **result packet,** which includes the result token, its destination address, as well as any tags. The PE sends the result packet to the memory-update system. The memory-update system consists of an arbitrary number of memory-update units, which also operate in parallel. The memory-update system sends the result packet to the appropriate unit for processing. The memory-update unit stores the result tokens in the destination locations and then checks to see whether the token corresponds to an argument slot in a node data structure. If so, the memory-update unit notifies the fetch system of that fact and tells the fetch system the address of the node data structure. The entire process continues either indefinitely or until there are no firable instruction packets.

  There are no commercial dataflow processors at present, although some processors, such as the CDC 6600 and current RISC machines, use dataflow techniques to control instruction execution. Many laboratories are studying dataflow techniques and building dataflow processors, but their future remains an open question. (For recent surveys of current research, see Arvind and Culler, 1986; Veen, 1986.)

**Reduction Machines**

An alternative method of exploiting the parallelism implicit in a dataflow computation is to have the computer evaluate the expressions on a demand-for-data basis, rather than a data-availability basis. Recall that in the dataflow model, nodes fire when their arguments become available. Consequently, nodes at the top of a dataflow graph fire first while those at the bottom fire last. This is top-down processing. An alternative way of processing a dataflow graph is to evaluate nodes from the bottom of the graph to the top by allowing a node to fire only when a successor demands its result. A computer that operates in this bottom-up fashion is a **reduction machine,** and several laboratories are experimenting with reduction-machine design (Arvind and Culler 1986).

## 7.4.2 ■ Neural Networks

Architects, in their continuing desire to use the parallelism inherent in natural systems, have designed computer architectures that are loosely based on biological neural networks. Although artificial neural networks, like their biological counterparts, require a large number of computational elements, four facts have made them feasible:

1. The underlying components, the simulated neurons, have a modest computational complexity and hence a small (a few dozen or so) gate count.
2. Their interconnections are reasonably simple, and they tend to be repetitive.
3. The need to communicate only with neighbors within a fixed radius.
4. Components for very large scale integration (VLSI) have become inexpensive, so the cost of building systems with a large number of processors is not prohibitive.

**neurons**

Biological neural networks consist of a large number of independent computational elements called **neurons**. A neuron consists of a cell body, a single long extension called an axon for sending output electrical signals, and many smaller extensions, called dendrites, for receiving input signals. These neurons are generally arranged in parallel layers, or lamina, and the layers form computational networks called nuclei. Within these nuclei, neurons of one layer generally receive their inputs from those of another layer and send their outputs to the neurons of another layer; some neurons receive inputs from and send outputs to neurons in the same layer. In any case, the connections between neurons are unidirectional; that is, a given axon sends signals in one direction only.

Biological neurons are in a constantly changing state of biochemical activity. One can think of the state of a neuron at any given time as representing a value. The values held by the neurons of a particular layer thus form a two-dimensional pattern, much like the values of the pixels in a digitized image. These patterns are the brain's representations of the world. The connections between neurons are weighted. The connection between two neurons that do not contact each other logically is said to have a **coupling weight** of 0; when not 0, the coupling weight from one neuron to the next specifies the influence that the activity of the first neuron has on the activity of the second.

**coupling weight**

The operation of a biological neural network is conceptually quite simple. Each neuron sends its current value to all other neurons that it contacts, and the effective values received by the other neurons are the products of the transmitted values times the coupling weights. Each neuron sums the effective values that is receives, and the sum becomes its new value.

### Formal Neurons

**formal neuron**
**mathematical neuron**

Based on this simplified conceptual model, researchers have mathematically modeled the computations performed by biological neural networks. The earliest neural-network models used very simple thresholding elements to simulate biological neurons. A **formal neuron,** also called a **mathematical neuron,** say $q$, is either *on* (its state equals 1) or *off* (state equals 0) and is characterized by a state function $f_q(t)$ and a **threshold function** $\theta_q(t)$. A **neural network** thus consists of a collection of formal neurons that are connected together. If neuron $p$ contacts neuron $q$, a single coupling weight $w_{pq}(t)$ characterizes the influence neuron $p$ has on $q$. If neuron $p$ is *on* at time $t_k$, it would contribute an amount $w_{pq}(t_k)$ toward neuron $q$'s state. If the sum of contributions to $q$ exceeds its threshold $\theta_q(t)$, neuron $q$ will turn *on*. That is,

threshold of firing neural networks

$$f_q(t) = \begin{cases} 1 & \text{if } \Sigma f_p(t)w_{pq}(t) \geq \theta_q(t) \\ 0 & \text{if } \Sigma f_p(t)w_{pq}(t) < \theta_q(t) \end{cases} \qquad (1)$$

where summation is over $p$ (i.e., all contributing neurons).

In Eq. (1) the coupling parameters (threshold values and coupling weights) depend on time because they are adaptive. A user can modify the coupling weights to change how a network responds to its inputs, and the rules that the user applies are called **training rules.** Frank Rosenblatt (1962) showed that various networks can be taught to recognize simple patterns or sets of patterns. Moreover, he showed that if a set of coupling weights existed that would make a network respond correctly to a universe of patterns, then his training rule would find such a set of weights and teach the network to respond that way. Rosenblatt devised one of the earliest adaptive networks called a perceptron, which we shall look at next.

training rules

## Perceptrons

The **perceptron** consists of three layers of mathematical neurons: a retina, an association layer, and a response layer. The **retina** is the input layer; it holds the input pattern. Neurons of the retina randomly contact neurons of the **association layer,** which in turn randomly contact neurons of the **response layer.** See Fig. 7.48(a).

perceptron<br>retina<br>association layer<br>response layer

The user turns on the neurons of the input layer to represent visual patterns, such as alphanumeric characters. Figure 7.48(b) shows how a lowercase "a" might appear. The user assigns desired responses to neurons of the response layer. For example, he or she might assign one cell to respond when an "a" is present, another to respond when a "b" is present, and so forth. These cells indicate how similar the input pattern is to a stored pattern. The perceptron responds correctly if it produces the correct (desired) response for every input pattern.

The perceptron training rule is this. Trainers present the first input pattern to the perceptron. If it responds correctly, they proceed to the next pattern. Otherwise, they modify the coupling weights as follows: If a response neuron $r$ is *on* but should be *off*, and if neuron $q$ in the association layer contacts cell $r$ and is *on*, then reduce the coupling weight $w_{qr}(t)$ by a constant amount $\Delta$. If $r$ is *off* but should be *on*, and if $q$ in the association layer contacts $r$ and is *on*, then increase the coupling weight $w_{qr}(t)$ by $\Delta$. The trainers modify all appropriate weights simultaneously. This adaptation step is repeated until the perceptron responds correctly to the current pattern. The trainers then present the next pattern to the perceptron and repeat the adaptation step until it responds correctly. Then they retry the previous pattern (or patterns) and repeat the adaptation process. Ultimately the perceptron will respond correctly for all patterns if there is a set of coupling weights that will make it do so. If the perceptron fails to learn the correct responses, then for that perceptron and for that universe of patterns there is no set of coupling weights that will make it respond correctly. This model allows coupling weights to grow arbitrarily large. There are other adaptive rules that constrain the coupling weights, but the differences are not important to this presentation.

More recent adaptive networks use feedback signals to mask unwanted features in the retina. If, for example, a trainer teaches a neuron in the response layer to respond to an "a," then the network uses feedback signals from that response neuron to facilitate activity of other neurons on the pathways that lead to its response and inhibit activity of neurons on other pathways.

**Neural-network Hardware**

Architects implement neural networks using several different approaches. One approach is to simulate them using digital computers. Another approach is to use stochastic components to simulate neurons. Several researchers studied this approach in the early 1970s but found stochastic components to be limited by the fan-in and fan-out ratios of the components. (Fan-in is the number of different input sources a circuit can process, while fan-out is the number of different circuits a component can send signals to directly.) Perhaps a reevaluation of this approach would be fruitful in light of the newer VLSI technologies. A third approach is to use either optical or electrooptical technology to imple-

FIGURE 7.48  *(a) A simple perceptron. (b) Input pattern for a perceptron.*

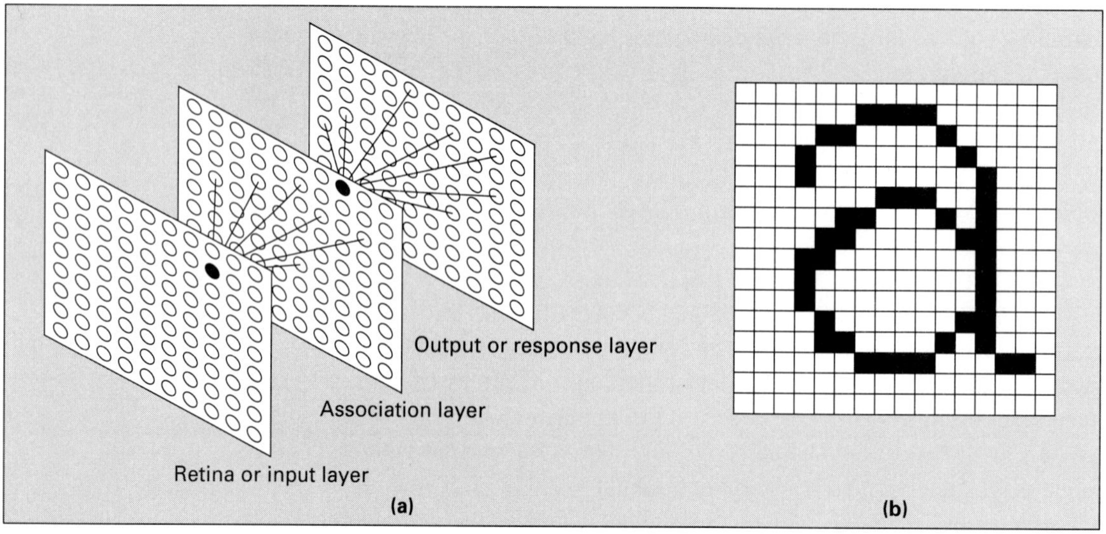

ment the neural networks. These approaches are beyond the scope of this text. We shall focus on a fourth approach, which is to build networks using electronic neurons with components that are analog rather than digital. Here both the patterns of coupling and the coupling weights are programmable. Recent VLSI technology supports this approach.

Analog components work as follows. At the lowest level, amplifiers simulate the integrative activity of the cell body. When an amplifier is active, the neuron is *on* or firing. (This approach treats a neuron as being either *on* or *off*; it does not simulate a neuron as firing at a particular rate.) An active amplifier (neuron) generates a current, which flows through a collection of resistive elements to other amplifiers (neurons). The resistive elements represent the dendritic inputs from other neurons and are programmable; that is, they can be turned *on* or *off*, thus simulating the presence or absence of connections with the axons of other neurons. See Fig. 7.49. The designers use inverters (devices that negate their input signals) to generate inhibitory signals. Using current technology, manufacturers have produced several thousand elements on a single chip.

Many laboratories are investigating the utility of neural networks, and several companies produce neural-network hardware. It is still too early to know how successful the new neural-network technologies will be. At present the neural networks are quite simple and do not begin to model either the complexity or specialization of biological neural networks. In the future perhaps they will rival biological networks in complexity and power.

FIGURE 7.49  *Schematic of an implemented neural network. The user sets the values of the resistive elements at the junctions to program the coupling parameters.*

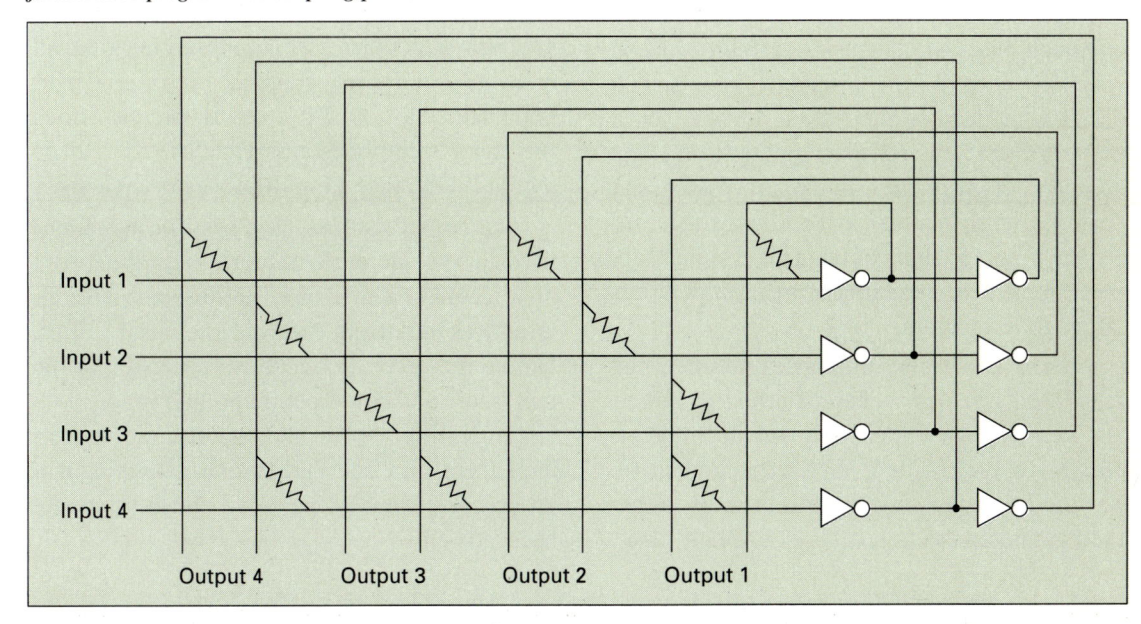

# Summary

The focus in this and the previous chapter was on the use of parallelism to speed up a computer. The previous chapter focused on pipelining; this chapter focused on processor parallelism.

To achieve processor parallelism, architects use many computational components, such as specialized functional units or identical PEs, which they then interconnect using an interconnection network. We therefore started our discussion by describing and classifying various interconnection networks, their control characteristics, and their topologies.

Architects have introduced processor parallelism in a number of different ways, and the remainder of the chapter focused on those ways. SIMD machines have a single control unit and execute a single instruction stream, but they duplicate the computation on a number of different data streams. MIMD machines have a number of independent processors, each with its own control unit and therefore executing its own instruction stream. Additionally, each processor operates on its own data stream. Dataflow and demand-driven architectures achieve parallelism by using a number of different computational components, but rather than executing a control-flow program they execute dataflow models of computation. Finally, neural networks achieve parallelism by employing large numbers of identical, simple processors that perform multiplications and additions to evaluate the weighted sums of their input values, and they implement neural-network computations rather than programs.

There are many differences between current SIMD machines. They differ in the number and complexity of their PEs, in the interconnection topologies they implement, and in the way the PEs communicate with memory. When the PE interconnection network logically places the PEs at the intersections of a rectangular grid and allows only the nearest neighbors to communicate, the machine is a processor array. When the machine's instruction set implements associative-memory operations, the machine is an associative processor; when the PEs can access and operate on bit-slices of memory rather than words of memory, the machine is a bit-slice processor. Architects implemented early associative processors using bit-slice architectures. An SIMD machine is a hypercube processor when its PEs communicate using an interconnection network with a hypercube topology. Finally, as a general rule, SIMD machines with bit-serial PEs have more of them and achieve greater parallelism than those with word-parallel PEs.

MIMD machines, also called multiprocessors, either share memory using a circuit-switched interconnection network and are tightly coupled, or they share memory using a packet-switched interconnection network and are loosely coupled. Loosely coupled multiprocessors are often called multiple-processor architectures. Most commercial high-performance machines, including pipelined vector machines, are tightly coupled, while most fault-tolerant machines are loosely coupled. Because of their importance for OLTP systems, we described the major techniques architects use for achieving fault tolerance in multiprocessor systems.

Our final sections gave brief introductions to dataflow architectures and neural-network architectures, which show promise as viable alternatives to current control-flow architectures. Unlike the other architectures discussed in the text, these machines require programming models that differ from the algorithmic models implemented by conventional programming languages, and their commercial viability has not been proven.

# Exercises

**7.1** Describe how to implement vector addition on a bit-slice processor. Describe two operations that are easy to perform on a vector processor but difficult to perform on a bit-slice processor.

**7.2** How many steps can be required for routing a single datum on an $64 \times 64$ processor array? How many for a 4096-node hypercube? As usual, state your assumptions carefully.

**7.3** For a centrally controlled $n \times n$ crossbar, give an algorithm for setting the switches. Assume there are $n$ processors and $n$ banks of memory, and the $n$ processors request different banks of memory. You may assume $n$ is a power of 2.

**7.4** For a packet-controlled $n \times n$ crossbar, give an algorithm for setting the switches. Assume there are $n$ processors and $n$ banks of memory, and the $n$ processors request different banks of memory. You may assume $n$ is a power of 2.

**7.5** Show how to set the switches of the delta network (Fig. 7.16) to connect processor $P$ (address $p_2 p_1 p_0$) to memory module $M$ (address $m_2 m_1 m_0$).

**7.6** Rent's rule says that circuits with $N$ gates need a number of signal connections proportional to $N^{0.5}$. One of the academic arguments against full crossbars is that the number of gates required to implement them grows as the square of the number of nodes. If the circuits for switching follow Rent's rule for the ratio of inputs and outputs to gates, what does that say about using full crossbars?

**7.7** E. Arjomandi, M. J. Fischer, and N. A. Lynch effectively showed that without fast broadcasting, an interconnection network is not suitable for a large SIMD computer. For the networks described in this chapter, how long does it take each one to broadcast one datum to all processors?

**7.8** Typical interconnection networks delay the signals passing through them by a time that is proportional to the number of stages. What are the delays (number of stages) of the interconnection networks described in this chapter?

**7.9** Design a bit-slice algorithm for adding a constant held in a register, say R1, to all words in memory.

**7.10** Refer to the blurring algorithm, and trace through the computations for $PE\,35_8$. Also show the value $PE\,35_8$ holds at the final step in the computation. Do the same for $PE\,00_8$.

**7.11** Write an algorithm for a bit-serial processor array to adjust the contrast of an image so that the output image has a gray scale ranging from 12 to 52 and centered at the value 32. Use an $n \times n$ window for computing the average, maximal, and minimal gray to be displayed in each new window, and use linear scaling to adjust the pixel intensity. For the purposes of algorithm design, assume that $n$ will typically be about 10.

**7.12** Most microprocessors that would be used in database machines have a 32-bit word length. How does one provide addressing for the $2^{40}$ sectors of the database? (A disk sector typically holds about 1 KB.)

**7.13** Suppose that when a program is run on a multiprocessor system, synchronization and communication overhead requires $20N$ instruction-execution times for an $N$-processor system. Plot the speedup of this system if synchronization or communication is required every 50, 500, and 5000 instructions as a function of the number of processors in the system.

**7.14** Two important methods for improving the speed of a processor are (1) using a large number of general-purpose registers and (2) using a cache memory. Consider a shared-memory multiprocessor where the processors have either

    a. 1024 registers, or
    b. an equivalent amount of cache.

Compare these organizations relative to the following issues:

    1. context-switching overhead;
    2. instruction format and size;
    3. coherence.

**7.15** Refer to Problem 7.41. If an airline will tolerate a frequency of paired simultaneous seat assignments as high as 1 in 50 flights, and each flight is assigning 250 seats in 20 min before flight time, how many users (ticket agents) can access the system for seat assignments? Assume each seat assignment takes 30 seconds.

**7.16** Current estimates are that the transaction-processing computing and I/O loads are increasing at a rate of over 50% per year. Much of this additional load is a response to the need for friendlier user interfaces, such as better menus. Assuming this description is accurate, will computing systems tend to become more centralized or more distributed? Why?

*7.17* If a disk has an average access time of 20 ms, what is the average access time with mirrored copies of this disk?

*7.18* Assuming 64-bit data paths, how many connections are needed to provide full interconnection of an array of $2N$ nodes? How many are required for connecting $N$ nodes to $N$ nodes via a full crossbar? How many are required for connecting $2N$ nodes to a bus? Assuming that connections fail at a rate of once in a billion hours, what are the approximate failure rates of these interconnections? (The data given here are about correct for a 32-bit system because typically at least 64 signal lines are required for 32-bit data transfers.)

*7.19* If an engineer's PC is broken for a day, what does it cost in lost time? If a mainframe being used by 500 engineers is down for 1 hour, how much does it cost in lost time? Quantify your lost-time in dollars. (The actual cost of an engineer is about $10,000 per month.)

*7.20* Determine the relative degrees of fault tolerance and the effect on performance of I/O with the following:
   a. daisy-chained devices versus separate connections to each device;
   b. polled I/O devices versus interrupting I/O devices;
   c. mirrored disks, where data are written to two disks whenever they are written to one. (i.e., each disk has a mirror of its data).

*7.21* Many systems are available for estimating the reliability or failure rates of electronic equipment. They are all based on the extreme reliability of the components, which implies that one can ignore the joint probabilities of several components failing at the same time. This means that, to a better approximation than the failure-rate data, the failure rate of a computer (or any electronic equipment) is the sum of the failure rates of its components. The MTTF, then, is the reciprocal of the failure rate. Because the most common failures have generally been in the I/O pins of devices, a relatively good way to determine the device's failure rate is simply to multiply the number of individual chip pins by their failure rate of about 1 failure in $10^9$ hours (referred to as 1 FIT, for "failure in time").

The Humongous Parallel Machine Company (HPMC) is going to build a super parallel computer consisting of thousands of microprocessor-based PEs. Suppose each of the PEs includes a 150-pin microprocessor, 36 memory chips with 18 pins each, and 15 support chips with an average of 24 pins each.
   a. How many PEs can HPMC use if the MTTF must be at least 5 days (100 hours)?
   b. How many PEs can HPMC use if the MTTF must be at least 45 days (1000 hours)?
   c. If fault tolerance allows any one of each group of 64 PEs to fail without the system failing, what is the failure rate of a 1024-PE system?

*7.22* One approach designers have used in systems where extremely high data integrity is required is triple modular redundancy (TMR). A TMR computer system has three CPUs whose outputs are routed to a "voter". The voter accepts the majority output of the three CPUs as the correct output.
   a. What is the MTBF (mean time between failures) of a TMR computer compared to the MTBF of one of its three component CPUs?
   b. What is the MTBF (mean time between crashes, i.e., when two CPUs have failed) if no repair is made of a faulty CPU? Notice that data integrity is still very high with only two CPUs, as long as they do not disagree. It is just that there is no way to tell which output to select if the two remaining CPUs are in conflict.

*7.23* See Problem 7.22. If a TMR computer system has a CPU fault rate of $10^{-4}$ per hour and is repaired within 1 month (500 hours, say), what is its expected MTBF? That is, how soon do you expect to get a second CPU fault while one CPU is awaiting repair?

*7.24* In a dataflow system based on a multiprocessor with SEND and RECEIVE, where receiving from an empty cell suspends a process, what should a "node" (instruction packet for a processor) do to the input memory cells it occupied after its processing is finished?

*7.25* What is the data rate of the human eye? What is its processing rate? For the sake of simplicity, assume that the eye has $10^8$ photodetectors, each of which can resolve about 30 levels of intensity in three different colors. The photodetectors send their data through two principal layers of neurons, the second having $10^7$ neurons and the third and final layer having $10^6$ neurons. The output therefore has $10^6$ components. Assume that the neurons in each layer linearly combine the inputs from about 20 neurons of the previous layer and that the system can resolve 10 images per second.

### Exercises for Electrical Engineers

*7.26* Draw a graph showing where the generalized $n$-cube uses fewer gates than an $n \times n$ crossbar. If a designer uses two side-by-side generalized cubes for redundancy and to reduce congestion, where does this fall on the graph? If the designer uses an $n$-dimensional cube, where does this fall on the graph? (*Hint:* Assume an $n \times n$ crossbar uses $n^2$ gates.)

*7.27* Show how to build an $n \times n$ crossbar using $n \times 1$ multiplexors and $1 \times n$ demultiplexors.

*7.28* Present the design for a 32-word by 32-bits-per-word orthogonal storage system.

*7.29* When designing a fault-tolerant computer, the designer should take into account how often various types of failures are expected to occur. Completely Dependable Computer's management has just heard about *interactive memory failures,* where a failure on one chip interacts with others and causes bad data from a single fault. For example, if an address pin on a memory chip suddenly starts sending 1s, then all the memory chips that are ganged with it may receive 1s for that address bit, no matter what address the CPU sends. Design a memory system that will tolerate such interactive failures. (They are presumed to be extremely rare, perhaps 1% of all hard DRAM failures.)

# Problems

*7.30* For circuit-switched networks, it is often important that they be *nonblocking*, which means that establishing one circuit will not prevent another from being made betweeen a pair of idle nodes. Which of the interconnection networks discussed in the text are nonblocking?

*7.31* Program a $3 \times 3$ matrix multiplication on a one-dimensional, linear array of PEs using nine PEs.

*7.32* The algorithm for associative search in Section 7.2.2, page 350, contains these statements:

(1) R4 ⇐ R4 OR (R3 AND R2)
(2) R2 ⇐ NOT (R2)
(3) R3 ⇐ R3 AND R2

Explain how statements (1) to (3) perform the tests for = and > in the search algorithm.

*7.33* Write an algorithm for a processor array to evaluate the determinant of a matrix and the dot product using the formulas given below. You may abbreviate the assembly syntax in any convenient way. Equation (a) is for a $2 \times 2$ matrix and Eqs. (b) and (c) are for $3 \times 3$ matrices.

a. $\det(\mathcal{A}) = a_{11}a_{22} - a_{12}a_{21}$.
b. $\det(\mathcal{A}) = a_{11}a_{22}a_{33} + a_{12}a_{23}a_{31} + a_{13}a_{21}a_{32} - a_{11}a_{23}a_{32} - a_{12}a_{21}a_{33} - a_{13}a_{22}a_{31}$.
c. $\mathcal{A} \cdot \mathcal{A} = a_{11}a_{11} + a_{12}a_{12} + a_{13}a_{13} + a_{21}a_{21} + a_{22}a_{22} + a_{23}a_{23} + a_{31}a_{31} + a_{32}a_{32} + a_{33}a_{33}$.

*7.34* Compare the blurring algorithm given in this chapter with one you might write for a pipelined vector computer. Discuss how the software must change to increase the image size on the two architectures. What is it about the SIMD architecture that makes the programming so much more complex?

*7.35* Show that a 4-cube has the same topology as a $4 \times 4$ array with toroidal edge connections. (*Hint:* Show that the PE addresses can be arranged in a $4 \times 4$ array whose adjacent elements differ in exactly one bit position. Also show that the right and left addresses on each row differ in exactly one bit position and likewise for the top and bottom addresses in each column.)

*7.36* Vectorizing compilers generally detect loops that can be executed on a pipelined vector computer. Are the vectorization algorithms used by vectorizing compilers suitable for MIMD machine parallelization? Justify your answer.

*7.37* What types of conflicts must a compiler detect for MIMD parallelization, SIMD parallelization, and vectorization?

*7.38* When are snoopy caches appropriate for achieving cache coherence on a multiprocessor computer system?

*7.39* Sometimes caches are designed to "check out" data from main memory when they update it. This technique allows many processors to read a datum without conflict, but it protects the processors from simultaneously updating the same location in memory. Designers often use this technique when the processors use write-back or write-around caches. Describe in detail how such a scheme can work.

**7.40** As head of marketing for the Nefarious Electronics Company, you want to show that multiprocessing is a flop. Design a benchmark program for this purpose. Your benchmark should document the machine's slowdown as more and more processors are added to solve the benchmark test. In other words, for $n > 2$ the solution time for $n$ processors is greater than for $n - 1$ processors.

**7.41** Consider a large distributed transaction-processing system such as that used by tellers in a bank or gate agents in an airline. The users need to access some shared resource, such as the disk file, where a bank's account-number verification file or an airliner's seat reservations are kept. In a multiprocessor system, each lock that controls access to any shared resource must be kept in a commonly accessible location. If the system uses locks that take 1 $\mu$s to lock and 0.1 ms in use, how many connected users accessing the lock each minute can the lock support? If the maximum delay must be less than 100 ms 95% of the time, how many users can use the system?

**7.42** Show how to use a multiprocessor with send and receive operations to build a dataflow system in a very natural way. Do you need to use send and receive for instructions *and* data? If not, what are the advantages in doing it anyway?

**7.43** How does the control system shown in Fig. 7.47 correspond to the control system required to implement SEND and RECEIVE on a conventional multiprocessor? What functions does each perform? What are their similarities and differences?

## Challenging Problems

**7.44** For the generalized cube shown in Fig. 7.14, find an algorithm that determines whether a set of connections given by $(P_{i1} - M_{j1}, P_{i2} - M_{j2}, P_{i3} - M_{j3}, P_{i4} - M_{j4}, \ldots)$ has a conflict.

**7.45** It is easy to pipeline the flow of data through a circuit-switched network, as long as the connections being used are not changing. The Circuit-switching Dataflow Company has hired you to design a circuit-switching network that allows pipelining the flow of data when the network is switching during the transmission. Is it possible? If so, sketch the design for one.

**7.46** If a network is blocking (see Problem 7.30), it may still be possible to establish a new connection pair by rearranging one or more of the existing connections. Which of the networks discussed in the text are nonblocking with rearranging?

**7.47** Sketch an algorithm for floating-point addition suitable for use on a bit-slice or bit-plane architecture. Assume the IEEE 32-bit floating-point format.

**7.48** A *sparse matrix* is one whose elements are mostly zeros. Assume the value of each matrix element of a sparse matrix is stored with its row number and column number in one word of an associative processor. Write a bit-slice algorithm for multiplying two sparse matrices together. (See below).

**7.49** Consider the blurring algorithm described in this chapter. Show how to implement an algorithm for arbitrary-sized images and arbitrary-sized masks using an 8 × 8 array of PEs. Using your algorithm, estimate the speedup in using a processor array as

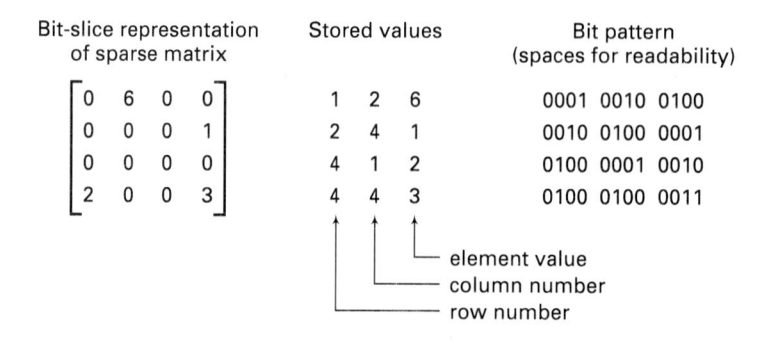

| Bit-slice representation of sparse matrix | Stored values | Bit pattern (spaces for readability) |
|---|---|---|
| $\begin{bmatrix} 0 & 6 & 0 & 0 \\ 0 & 0 & 0 & 1 \\ 0 & 0 & 0 & 0 \\ 2 & 0 & 0 & 3 \end{bmatrix}$ | 1 2 6<br>2 4 1<br>4 1 2<br>4 4 3 | 0001 0010 0100<br>0010 0100 0001<br>0100 0001 0010<br>0100 0100 0011 |

- element value
- column number
- row number

compared to a single-processor computer having similar circuit speeds.

**7.50** Show how to implement matrix multiplication on a linear array of PEs for arbitrarily large arrays (having more than $N$ elements, where $N$ is the number of PEs).

**7.51** Describe a suitable storage representation for sparse matrices (see Problem 7.48) on a processor array. Write an algorithm for multiplying two sparse matrices together on a processor array.

**7.52** A common operation in digital-signal processing is

$$y_i = S \sum_{j=-n}^{m} a_j x_{i+j} + S \sum_{j=1}^{n} b_j y_{i-j}.$$

This operation is used for filtering data in many applications and is the digital version of ordinary, analog RC filters. The input data are $\{x_i\}$ and the filter outputs are $\{y_i\}$; assume data or outputs with negative subscripts are zero. Terms $a_i$ and $b_i$ are characteristics of the filter, and typical values for $m$ and $n$ are 1 to 10.

    a. Using any or all of the architectures that we have described or any multiprocessor of your own design, how rapidly can you compute the outputs? Assume that multiplication and addition each take unit time?

    b. If synchronization operations take $s$ units of time, how fast does the system run? Can you make the system or systems synchronous (so $S = 0$)?

**7.53** The figure shown here illustrates a simple computer system using DMA I/O controllers and memory-mapped I/O. Parts (b) and (c) illustrate two alternate multiprocessor organizations that could be made with components from the uniprocessor and a $2 \times 2$ crossbar switch.

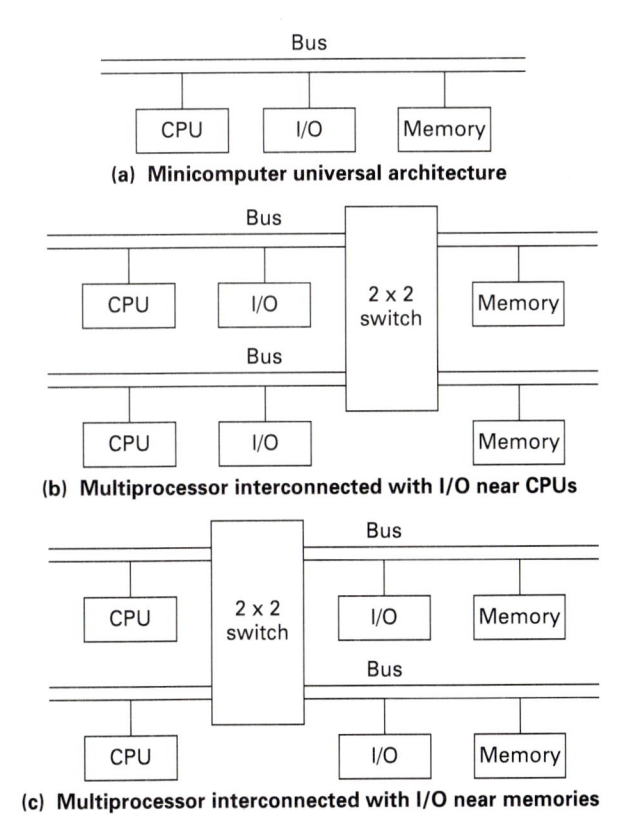

**(a)** Minicomputer universal architecture

**(b)** Multiprocessor interconnected with I/O near CPUs

**(c)** Multiprocessor interconnected with I/O near memories

For each of the two multiprocessor alternatives, what problems would an operating system engineer have to confront in designing the I/O handling component of the operating system? What are the advantages and disadvantages of each organization? Which organization would most successfully isolate the user from the problems related to I/O access?

*7.54* One way to achieve cache coherence on a multiprocessor computer is as follows. The main memory can have a directory of all the caches that are connected to it and the data they contain. Whenever a processor writes a datum to a memory cell, the memory sends update messages to all caches that have copies of the datum. These update messages are like cache refills in many respects. Discuss the validity of this technique. What are its areas of applicability? (*Hint:* consider the number of processors and the average number of cycles between memory accesses, for example.)

*7.55* Fly-by-Might Airlines (FMA) has developed a database management system (DBMS) for its airline reservations, which did not have to maintain perfect data integrity. (FMA's customers are hardly angels; some are no shows, for example. Thus FMA tolerates some lost reservations.) FMA developed the system for use on a large group of loosely coupled processors that access data on shared disks. FMA has decided to sell its DBMS for other uses, where errors caused by simultaneous updates could be catastrophic. Devise a set of database-integrity support operations so that FMA can safely sell its system.

## Discussion/Team Problems

*7.56* What advantages do various types of special-purpose architectures provide for highly sequential (or scalar) computation? (By *highly sequential* and *highly scalar* we mean that a large fraction of the operations in the computation depend on other recent computations.)

*7.57* Pipeline computers are sometimes characterized as multiple instruction stream, single data stream (MISD). How is this characterization applicable, and how is it misleading? What is a good example of an MISD system? (*Hint:* Consider systems with multiple computers.)

*7.58* In Section 1.2.2 we outlined Flynn's (1966) taxonomy of computers. Consider that when a pipelined vector computer executes a vector instruction, it is logically operating as an SIMD machine. Find two other examples where his taxonomy is not very useful.

*7.59* Make a 16-entry table of the various types of networks and their control, and suggest applications or uses for each type, or indicate why they are not very useful. (*Hint:* Consider circuit versus packet, single stage versus multistage, centralized versus distributed, and synchronous versus asynchronous.)

*7.60* Three types of networks are sometimes distinguished: WANs, LANs, and interconnection networks. WANs are characterized by long and unpredetermined transmission time and multiple routing possibilities. Usually LANs are conceptually a single cable linking a number of nodes. Interconnection networks are those described here for interconnecting the units of a multiprocessor computer system, for example.

Listed below are some alternatives that are used for communication protocols on networks. Which are appropriate for each type of network? The answers depend on the environment you assume, so justify your choices.

   a. circuit switching or packet switching;
   b. packets of a fixed size, a few fixed sizes, or variable in size;
   c. message header defines sender and destination or defines destination only;
   d. messages are acknowledged by receiver (except acknowledge messages).

*7.61* An alternative to Flynn's (1966) taxonomy is to classify computers in terms of their instructions and operations: The *instruction set* can be (1) scalar, (2) scalar/vector, or (3) scalar/vector/array (vectors are the subset of arrays that are one-dimensional). The *hardware operations* can be (1) scalar, (2) multifunction scalar, (3) pipeline vector, (4) parallel vector, (5) pipeline array and/or (6) parallel array. The *memory* can be (1) local or (2) global. There are other possibilities and refinements, but this covers most of the spectrum of control-flow computers. Give examples (hypothetical or actual) of as many of the 36 possibilities created by this classification as you can.

*7.62* Define high-level programming-language statements that will simplify the use of an associative processor. These statements should enable a programmer to write programs easily based on associative operations.

**7.63** Although conventional memory is now rather inexpensive, associative memory is still costly. Discuss ways to use a large conventional memory to back up the contents of an associative memory in order to make a large associative processor practical.

**7.64** Suppose 32 processors share 1 GB of RAM that is divided into 32 equal-capacity modules. Answer the following questions about the interconnection network between the processors and the memories.

  a. What advantages and disadvantages would a multilevel network, such as an Omega network or a generalized cube network, have over a full 32 × 32 crossbar switch?
  b. What system software techniques can be used to reduce network contention and memory-module contention?

**7.65** Consider the design of a shared-memory multiprocessor with a 32-MB primary memory and 64 high-performance 32-bit microprocessors. The processor-memory interconnection network should have a manageable complexity, and memory contention should be reduced as much as possible. Discuss advantages and disadvantages of each of the following interconnection schemes:

  a. a bus (time-shared);
  b. a multistage interconnection network;
  c. a crossbar switch.

**7.66** What are the relative merits of the following approaches for the operating system of a multiprocessor? Under what situations is each or are any best?

  a. Designate a single processor as the master. The master is the only processor that can perform critical operations, such as resource allocation and I/O.
  b. Allow any one processor to be the master, but the designation can go to any of the CPUs (if none is already master).
  c. Partition critical resources among the CPUs, so that each CPU controls a subset of the critical resources.
  d. Use a monitor process for controlling the resources, and let any processor grab the monitor process and do its own resource allocation.
  e. Use a separate monitor for controlling each individual resource, and let any processor grab whatever monitor or monitors it requires.

**7.67** Consider a shared-memory multiprocessor in which the processors are RISC architectures. You are given the task of designing and implementing an operating system for such a machine. Discuss the instructions that you would insist the RISC machines have in order to make your implementation of the operating system easier. Describe whether there are any difficulties in implementing these instructions under the RISC philosophy. (*Hint:* Begin by listing the important areas in which architecture and operating system interact. Make sure you address each of these areas in your answer.)

**7.68** *Deadlock* (or *deadly embrace*) is a concern in any system where multiple processes can be active at the same time. Listed below are some techniques that designers have used to avoid deadly embrace in resource allocation. Are there any hardware implications of using one or another of these techniques? What are the advantages of each? Show how they prevent deadlock.

  a. *Alphabetical allocation.* Whenever a process needs additional resources, it first releases all resources it has and then acquires all the resources it needs in some specific order.
  b. *Greedy allocation.* Whenever a process needs resources, it grabs all it needs. If it fails to get them all, it release all of them and tries again later.
  c. *Two-phase commit.* This is the same as the greedy allocation, but the process first requests and then grabs them if all resources are available. The reason for using two-phase commit instead of greedy is that resources are frequently held during periods when they are not needed, unless another request is made for them, which reduces release and re-request handling.
  d. *Centralized allocation.* A single resource allocation process apportions the resources among all requestors.

**7.69** What are three key differences between multiprocessors and networks of computers?

**7.70** Give some examples of situations where multiprocessors require more memory than scalar processors if they are to run faster than a scalar machine. (*Hint*: You may need to make some assumptions about the memory characteristics.)

**7.71** Give the advantages (and disadvantages) of microprogrammed (as opposed to hard-wired) control for a machine that must have a high degree of the following:

  a. fault tolerance;
  b. fault detection;
  c. fault recovery.

*7.72* One can make interesting philosophical discussions about the possibility of a completely fault-tolerant system. In the movie *Dr. Strangelove* the Russians built a doomsday machine, one that would destroy the world if they were attacked. How can its designer test such a system? Describe how to make a switch that is completely fault-tolerant.

*7.73* Software fault tolerance is sometimes implemented by using multiple programs all executing the same physical task. This method is unlikely to produce identical answers for voting (see Problem 7.22). What additional fault tolerance does this provide? (*Hint:* Consider the use of both analog and digital techniques.)

*7.74* You are buying a personal computer and have a choice between two models. One claims a MTBF of 10,000 hour and the other claims a MTBF of 100,000 hours. Is it worth paying extra for the second model? If you are recommending personal computers for a company that is buying 1000 PCs, is the difference worth considering? Justify your choices.

*7.75* There are two basic approaches to providing fault tolerance: hardware-intensive, sometimes called HIFT, and software-intensive, called SIFT. Multiple computers with voting is the prototypical HIFT approach (see Problem 7.22, for example), whereas stopping at checkpoints and comparing results, especially for outputs, is prototypical SIFT. What are the advantages of each approach? What application areas seem more appropriate for each?

# Chapter Index

0-cube, 333
1-cube, 333
2-cube, 333
3-cube, 333
4-cube, 333
arc, 384
argument slot, 384
association layer, 391
associative-memory operation, 341
associative processor, 341
associative search, 344
asynchronous network, 325
availability, 378
backup system, 379
bandwidth network, 326
Banyan network, 332
bit plane, 342
bit slice, 341
bit-slice processor, 341
blurring, 352
broadcast, 332
bus watcher, 370
cache coherence, 367
centralized control, 324
checkpoint information, 379
checkpoint message, 379

circuit-switched network, 324
cluster, 372
communication diameter, 325
communication distance, 325
component fault, 377
computational thread, 386
computer module, 372
connection degree, 326
control node, 385
control token, 385
coupling weight, 390
coverage of faults, 378
data consistency, 367
dataflow graph, 384
dataflow model of computation, 384
data recovery, 378
delta network, 337
depth of faults, 378
destination node, 384
distributed control, 324
double-error detection and single-error correction (DEDSEC) memory, 378
dynamic dataflow architecture, 388
dynamic dataflow model, 387
edge connections, 331

empty slot, 384
error, 377
error detection and correction, 378
exchange operation, 336
failure, 377
fault, 377
fault avoidance, 378
fault-tolerant computer, 377
fault-tolerant node, 328
firable node, 384
flushing a cache, 370
fork node, 386
formal neuron, 390
full crossbar, 328
full slot, 384
globally synchronized network, 338
hard fault, 377
hardware-intensive architecture, 341
heartbeat, 380
hub, 328
hypercube processor, 342
hypercube topology, 333
image mask, 352
I'm alive notice, 380

input arc, 384
input token, 384
instruction packet, 389
interconnection network, 323
invalidation bus, 370
*K*map, 373
linear topology, 328
local-area network (LAN), 371
Local Switch, 372
maintainability, 378
masking errors, 381
master node, 324
mathematical neuron, 390
mean time between failures (MTBF), 378
mean time to failure (MTTF), 378
mean time to repair (MTTR), 378
memory-mapped control, 375
merge node, 385
message, 324
mirrored data sets, 382
multibus architecture, 327
multiported peripheral, 382
multistage interconnection network (MIN), 324
*N*-buddies, 362
*N*-modular redundancy, 381
nearest-neighbor topology, 331
network latency, 326
network tap, 327
neural network, 391

neuron, 390
node, 324, 384
node address, 334
node data structure, 388
node (of a dataflow graph), 384
node (of an interconnection network), 324
nonblocking crossbar, 328
Omega network, 336
operator error, 377
output arc, 384
output token, 384
packet, 324
packet-switched network, 324
pair-and-spare strategy, 380
$p \times m$ crossbar, 328
perceptron, 391
predicate, 385
process communication, 366
process exclusion, 366
process initiation, 366
processor array, 342
process synchronization, 366
process termination, 366
reconfigurable duplication, 380
reduction machine, 389
redundancy, 326
reentrant graph, 386
reliability, 378
response layer, 391
result packet, 389
retina, 391

ring topology, 328
seeing-eye packet, 324
service request, 375
shuffle operation, 336
single-bus architecture, 327
slave node, 324
snoopy cache, 370
soft fault, 377
software failure, 377
spare system, 379
staged interconnection network, 332
stale data, 367
star topology, 328
static dataflow architecture, 388
static dataflow model, 387
switch node, 385
synchronous network, 325
tagged token, 388
test node, 385
thread of control, 386
threshold of firing, 391
tightly synchronized multiprocessors, 380
token, 384
training rule, 391
tree-structured network, 330
voting logic, 381
wide-area network (WAN), 371
window register, 376

# APPENDIX A
# Some Notational Conventions

As in any field, computer science has a number of conventions for ways of expressing numbers, units, and components in algorithms. Some of these are borrowed from mathematics and physics, while others are particular to the field of computer science. We present a few of these here, along with some conventions adopted especially for this text, such as the arrow conventions used in the figures.

## A.1 ■ Octal and Hexadecimal Notation

Binary numbers are usually expressed in binary notation. (See Section 2.1.2). For large numbers, however, it is often convenient to use octal (base 8) or hexadecimal (base 16) notation. An octal digit represents 3 binary bits, and a hexadecimal digit represents 4 binary bits. Table A.1 lists the values of the numbers between 0 and 20 in these three notations.

To avoid ambiguity we use subscripts after numbers to denote the number's base, when the latter is not decimal. For example, 100 (in decimal) = $144_8 = 64_{16} = 1100100_2$. We have made an effort to distinguish decimal from nondecimal, even in cases where the distinction is somewhat pedantic. For example, we generally subscript a binary 0 or 1 as $0_2$ or $1_2$. We ignore the fact that computers virtually all work in binary, however, and present most of our examples in decimal notation to make them easier to follow.

To convert from octal or hexadecimal notation to binary, simply replace each digit by its binary equivalent. Be sure to include leading zeros where needed. To convert between octal and hexadecimal notations, simply use the table to write each octal or hexadecimal digit in binary, group the bits into threes (for octal) or fours (for hexadecimal), and use the table to find the digit values in the desired notation. For example, $A3F2_{16}$ becomes $1010\,0011\,1111\,0010_2$, which is the same as $1\,010\,001\,111\,110\,010_2$, which becomes $121762_8$. Similarly, $7310_8$ becomes $111\,011\,001\,000_2$, which is the same as $1110\,1100\,1000_2$, which becomes $EC8_{16}$.

405

**Table A.1** Numbers 0 to 20 in decimal, binary, octal, and hexadecimal notation.

| Decimal | Binary | Octal | Hexadecimal |
|---|---|---|---|
| 0 | 000 | 0 | 0 |
| 1 | 001 | 1 | 1 |
| 2 | 010 | 2 | 2 |
| 3 | 011 | 3 | 3 |
| 4 | 100 | 4 | 4 |
| 5 | 101 | 5 | 5 |
| 6 | 110 | 6 | 6 |
| 7 | 111 | 7 | 7 |
| 8 | 1000 | 10 | 8 |
| 9 | 1001 | 11 | 9 |
| 10 | 1010 | 12 | A |
| 11 | 1011 | 13 | B |
| 12 | 1100 | 14 | C |
| 13 | 1101 | 15 | D |
| 14 | 1110 | 16 | E |
| 15 | 1111 | 17 | F |
| 16 | 10000 | 20 | 10 |
| 17 | 10001 | 21 | 11 |
| 18 | 10010 | 22 | 12 |
| 19 | 10011 | 23 | 13 |
| 20 | 10100 | 24 | 14 |

## A.2 ■ Units of Time

For readers unfamiliar with the common units of time that computer scientists use to describe events in computers, we present a brief review here. The most common units are as follows:

1 millisecond (ms) = one-thousandth second = $10^{-3}$ second
1 microsecond ($\mu$s) = one-millionth second = $10^{-6}$ second
1 nanosecond (ns) = one-billionth second = $10^{-9}$ second
1 picosecond (ps) = one-trillionth second = $10^{-12}$ second

To illustrate these units, let us look at some examples of computer events. Peripheral storage devices, such as disks, can access one character in roughly 10 ms. Once they access one character, they can transfer consecutive characters at a rate of about 1 to 10 characters/$\mu$s, or 1 million to 10 million characters per second. In contrast, the CPUs of the fastest machines can transfer characters from one register to another in about one-billionth of a sec-

**Table A.2** Standard numeric prefixes and their abbreviations.

| Prefix | Number | Factor Base 10[a] | Factor Base 2[a] | Abbreviation |
|---|---|---|---|---|
| atto | quintillionth | $10^{-18}$ | | a |
| femto | quadrillionth | $10^{-15}$ | | f |
| pico | trillionth | $10^{-12}$ | | p |
| nano | billionth | $10^{-9}$ | | n |
| micro | millionth | $10^{-6}$ | | $\mu$ |
| milli | thousandth | $10^{-3}$ | | m |
| kilo | thousand | $10^{3}$ | $2^{10}$ | K |
| mega | million | $10^{6}$ | $2^{20}$ | M |
| giga | billion | $10^{9}$ | $2^{30}$ | G |
| tera | trillion | $10^{12}$ | $2^{40}$ | T |
| peta | quadrillion | $10^{15}$ | $2^{50}$ | P |
| exa | quintillion | $10^{18}$ | $2^{60}$ | E |

[a]The exact value for any prefix is generally apparent from the context. The slight differences between base-2 or base-10 values are inconsequential in most cases. For example, 1 MB stands for 1 megabyte or $2^{20}$ bytes, but 1 MHz stands for 1 megahertz or $10^6$ hertz.

ond, which is $10^{-9}$ second or 1 ns. Thus, the times for individual character operations range from tens of milliseconds down to about 1 ns, a difference of seven orders of magnitude just for these common devices.

Computers operate at different speeds. Current PCs execute at speeds ranging from less than 1 instruction/$\mu$s to perhaps 30 times that fast, or about one instruction every 50 ns. Switching times for the fastest computer components are less than 0.1 ns. For comparison, electrical signals travel about 20 cm/ns and are limited absolutely to the speed of light.

An internal clock synchronizes the various systems in most computers. The speed of the clock regulates the computer's speed, which is limited by the switching speed of the circuitry. If a computer's clock ticks once every microsecond, or 1 million times per second, its clock rate is one **megahertz (MHz)**. Today's PCs have clock rates of about 1 to 30 MHz. The fastest 1988 computers had clock rates close to 250 MHz, or one tick every 4 ns.

*megahertx (MHz)*

When describing time, clock rates, and memory sizes, we use prefixes to indicate millions, billions, and trillions of units. Table A.2 shows the prefixes that are in use today.

As a general rule, because of the way address-decoding circuits operate, memories come in sizes that are powers of 2. A 1-KB memory holds $2^{10}$ or 1024 bytes, a 64-KB memory holds $2^{16}$ or 65,536 bytes, and a 1-MB memory holds $2^{20}$ or 1,048,576 bytes.

## A.3 ■ Algorithmic Notation

For our machine-language or assembly-language code examples, we use a combination of mnemonic symbols and algebraic language. We have chosen this style because it is generally obvious where we mean individual machine instructions, and because it avoids the ambiguity of which operand gets the result of the operation. We also indicate instruction names in small capitals: ADD indicates the addition instruction and MULTIPLY indicates the multiplication instruction. For computers that have complex instructions, we write the component parts of all operations on a single line. The following are examples of our special notation.

| | | |
|---|---|---|
| ADD | X ← R1 + R2 | Add the contents of registers R1 and R2, and store the result in the memory location whose address is X. |
| ADD-INCR | X ← R1 + R2, R1 ← R1 + 1 | Same as the previous line, but the CPU "automatically" increments register R1 after storing R1 + R2. |
| MULTIPLY | A ← A × (ADDRESS) | Multiply the content of the accumulator and the content of the memory location whose address is ADDRESS, and put the result in the accumulator. |

We use a single letter and sometimes a number to designate registers in a manner that should be obvious. For example, A designates the accumulator, R1 designates general-purpose register 1, V1 designates vector register 1, I1 designates index register 1, and so on.

## A.4 ■ Figure Conventions

We have used a number of different types of arrows within the figures. Some arrows indicate data paths, some indicate pointers, and some are parts of the labels and point to a component in the figure that the label references. Figure A.1 illustrates these conventions.

**FIGURE A.1** *Figure conventions. (a) Arrows with triangular heads denote data paths. Heavy arrows denote buses. Light arrows may denote either single wires, such as control lines, or buses. The arrow shafts are always straight with sharp angles. (b) Curved arrows with nontriangular heads denote address pointers and register selectors. For example, the B field of the instructions selects a base register. The content of the selected base register is added to the displacement D to get the address of (a pointer to) the operand in memory. (c) Arrows with sharp bends and nontriangular heads either label components in the figure, as here, or show the dimension or extent of an item in the figure, as in (b) where the width of the base registers is shown.*

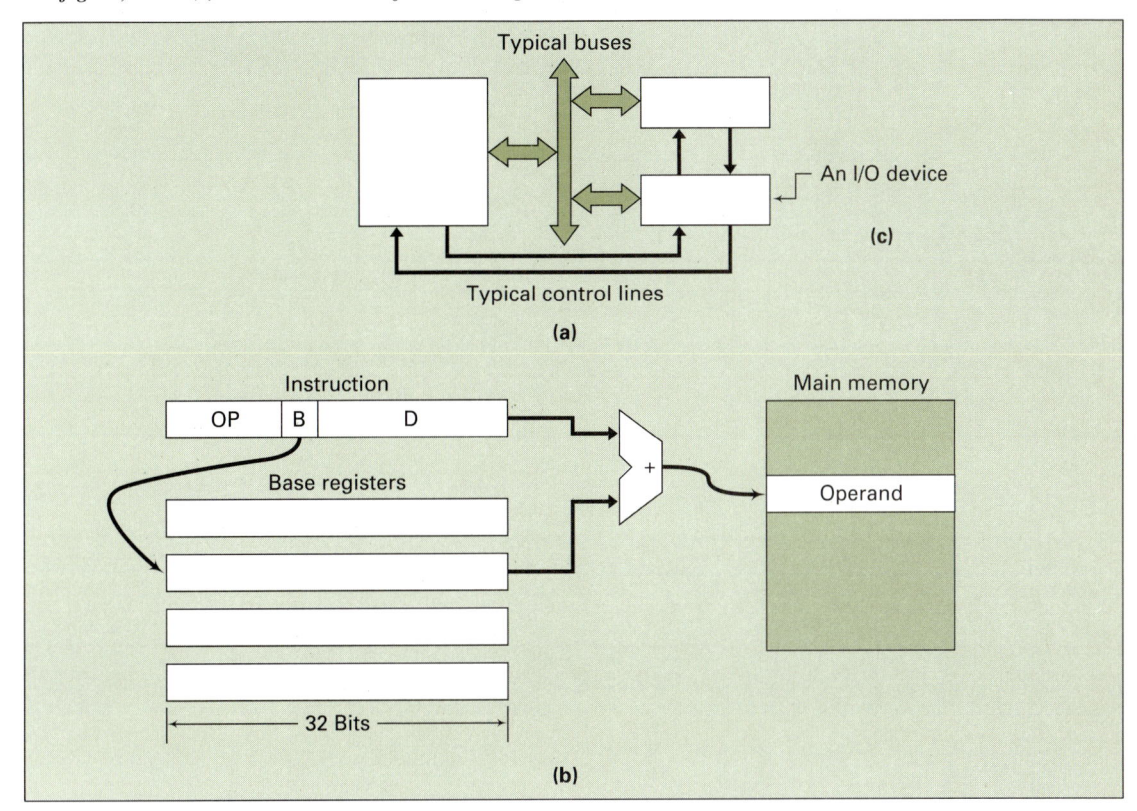

# Appendix B
# Digital Components

In this appendix we shall present a brief review of digital logic, focusing on the primary building blocks of computers. Students unfamiliar with these components, or whose background in this area is weak, should consult one of the many excellent textbooks on digital logic design. We shall begin with a brief discussion of component technology. We then discuss combinatorial circuits (Section B.2) and sequential circuits (Section B.3), and we end with a look at devices that combine combinational and sequential logic (Section B.4).

## B.1 ■ Circuit Components

Computers are composed of huge collections of switches connected by wires. The wires are the signal pathways. Before the advent of the transistor, the basic switching component was the vacuum tube. Each one was quite large, as a quick glance into an antique radio will show, and each one furnished one or two switches. With the advent of the solid-state transistor, tubes were virtually eliminated from computers. Manufacturing techniques and technology advanced rapidly, and now manufacturers can produce many switches, currently in the millions, in digital components called **integrated circuits (ICs)**. ICs are also called **chips**, which refers to the small (generally less than $\frac{1}{2}''$ square) piece of silicon on which the circuit components are integrated.

During the late 1960s and throughout the 1970s and 1980s, techniques for fabricating solid-state switching circuits changed radically. Companies were soon able to manufacture many devices on a single chip. Devices with a few components use **small-scale integration (SSI),** and devices with a few hundred components use **medium-scale integration (MSI).** Manufacturers can now produce entire processors comprising over a million transistors on a single chip. Chips having in excess of a thousand switches use **large-scale integration (LSI),** and those with hundreds of thousands of switches use **very large scale integration (VLSI).** Current predictions suggest that chips having over 4 million switches will be available in the mid-1990s.

integrated circuits (ICs)
chips

small-scale integration (SSI)
medium-scale integration (MSI)
large-scale integration (LSI)
very large scale integration (VLSI)

**pins**

**dual inline package (DIP)**

**pin grid arrays (PGAs)**

**plastic quad flat pack (PQFP)**

One common way of packaging chips is to encapsulate them in a plastic package having external connections called **pins**. The pins conduct the electrical signals to and from the chip's components. See Fig. B.1. One type of package is the **dual inline package (DIP).** The name comes from the fact that each chip has two sets (dual) of parallel pins (inline) that project from opposite edges of the package. A single DIP can have from a few to about 80 pins. Some chips, such as **pin grid arrays (PGAs),** have their pins in concentric squares on the bottom, and some, such as **plastic quad flat pack (PQFP),** have their pins lining all four edges. Both PGAs and PQFPs may have well over 100 pins on them. A small computer, such as an IBM PC or Apple Macintosh, contains dozens of chips, but with the rapidly changing technology, capabilities of individual chips have markedly increased, so the chip count has actually decreased.

Manufacturers build circuits mainly out of wires, switches, resistors, capacitors, diodes, and chips. When manufacturers produce the wires by etching metallic foils that they laminated on thin, nonconductive circuit boards, the wires are called **lines** or **traces**. The boards themselves are called **printed circuit boards (PCBs)** or simply **cards**. Cards can have as few as two independent conductive layers of traces to as many as dozens of them, and the components are either soldered directly to the traces or they are plugged into sockets

**lines**
**traces**
**printed circuit boards (PCBs)**
**cards**

FIGURE B.1  *Connection patterns for several different packaging technologies. (a) Dual in-line package (DIP). (b) Pin grid array (PGA). (c) Plastic quad flat pack (PQFP).*

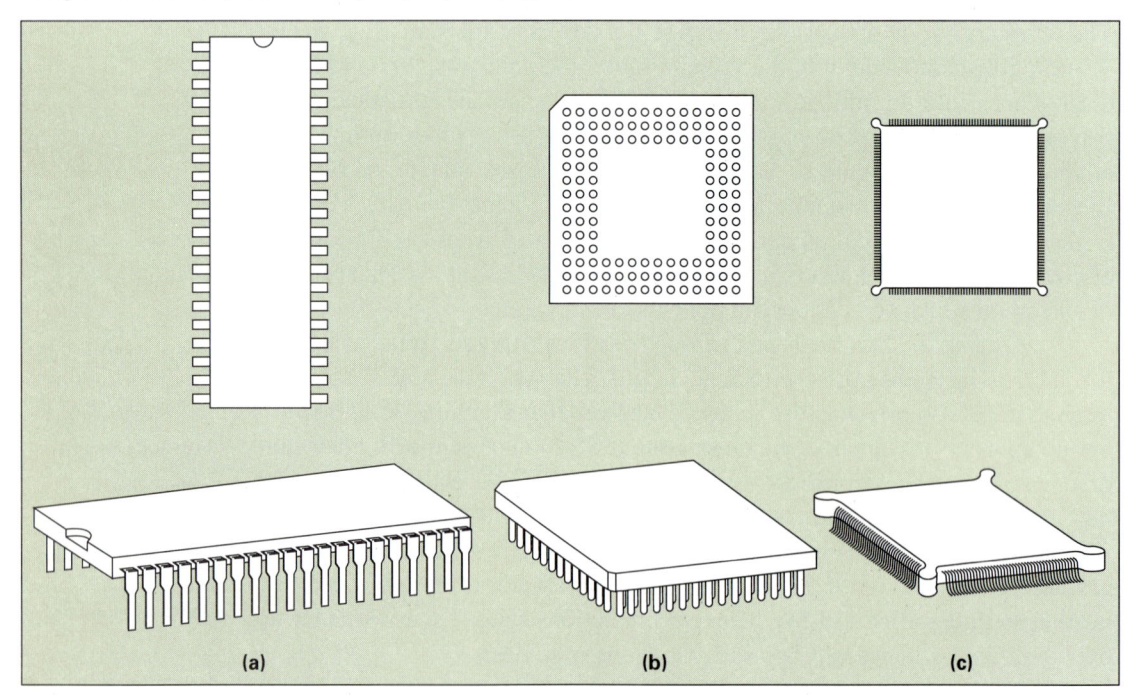

that are soldered to the traces. The large circuit board within a personal computer that holds many of its components if often called a **mother board,** and the smaller cards that a user may plug into the sockets on the mother board are often called **daughter boards.**

Within a given technology a specific voltage represents the logic value *true* and a second voltage represents the logic value *false*. (Sometimes these values are represented by specific currents rather than voltages.) For example, **transistor–transistor logic (TTL)** technology uses voltages between 2.4 and 5 V to represent *true* (also called **high** or **logic level 1**) and voltages between 0 and 0.7 V to represent *false* (also called **low** or **logic level 0**). *True* and *false* (1 and 0 or high and low) are the only values that the circuits can represent. All information processed by the computer must be encoded in terms of these two values. We shall use "1," "*true*," and "*high*" to mean the logic level *true* and "0," "*false*," and "*low*" to mean the logic level *false*.

Designers represent chips schematically by diagrams that show and label the pins. In addition to power and ground pins, chips have signal pins for inputs and outputs; sometimes signal pins are used for both input and output. Figure B.2 illustrates the relationship between a physical circuit and a logic diagram for the circuit. The lines, which represent wires or traces, conduct the signals. A given line can only be at one logic level at a time. If one device outputs or asserts *high* on an output pin, then any devices whose input pins are connected to that pin are said to receive, be driven to, or be held at logic level 1. Engineers use the phrases *pull a signal down, assert low,* or *deassert* to describe sending a *false* signal, and *raise a signal, assert high,* or simply *assert* to describe sending a *true* signal.

Chip manufacturers use standard conventions to label the pins on their devices. If they label an input pin with a bar above it, then an input must assert *false* to activate the function. For example $\overline{\text{RES}}$ (reset) is an input pin on many chips that resets the circuit. To reset the circuit, then, an external device must assert *false* at $\overline{\text{RES}}$. Moreover, there is an implicit assumption that the external device will assert *true* during normal operation of the circuit. As a second example, R/W (read/write) is a common pin label (often denoted R/$\overline{\text{W}}$), where 1 implies R and 0 implies W. *True* implies that a read operation will take place, while *false* implies that a write operation will take place.

It is usually the case that within a given computer's circuitry, all devices use similar or compatible technology. This means that designers can connect them together without using special interface circuits, or **buffers.** Said another way, the designers can connect the output pins from one device directly to the input pins of other devices, and the devices can share the same power supply. Figure B.2 illustrates this idea.

In addition to the two logic states, certain gates called **tristate logic gates** can enter a **high impedance state,** which is logically equivalent to being disconnected. Unless an external device asserts 1 at the **enable input** to the

mother board

daughter boards

transistor–transistor logic (TTL)
high (logic level 1)
low (logic level 0)

buffers

tristate logic gates
high impedance state
enable input

**FIGURE B.2** Relationship between the physical implementation of a circuit and the logic diagram of the circuit. (a) Logic diagrams of a 7400 chip (quad 2-input NAND gates) and a 7486 chip (quad 2-input XOR gates). (b) Logic diagram of a simple logic circuit. (c) Implementation of the circuit using two logic chips and a power supply. In (a) and (b) the cup- and arrow-shaped symbols are gates (see Section B.1.2); in (b), A, B, and C are input signals and D is an output signal.

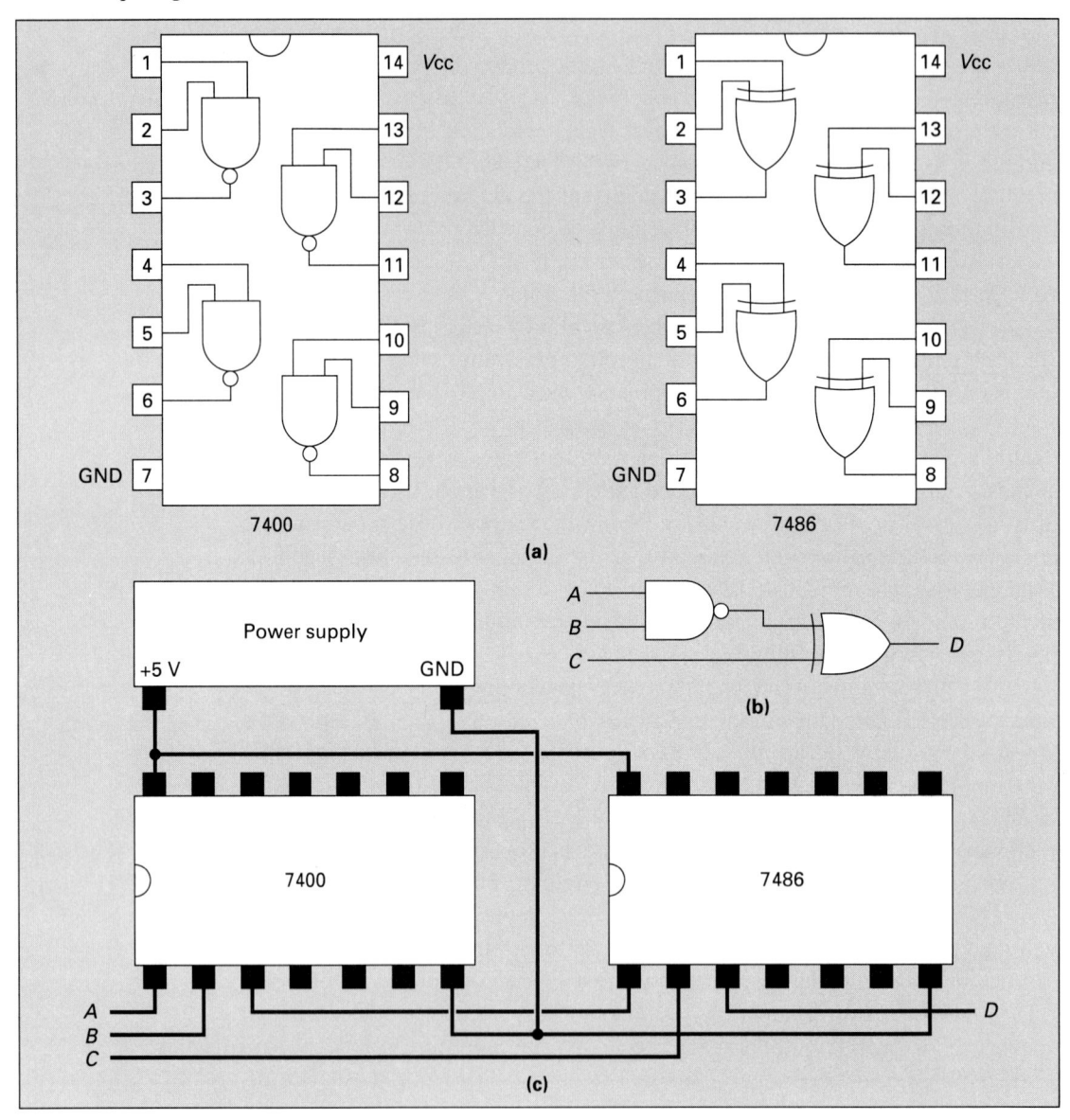

gate, the outputs of the gate remain in their high-impedance or disconnected state and are said to **float**. (Sometimes a tristate logic gate has a **disable input** rather than an enable input. A user must then deassert the disable input to enable the gate to output a signal.)

*float*
*disable input*

Many devices use tristate logic gates to control their outputs. For these devices, a single input generally controls all of the outputs from the chip. Control inputs that allow the device to output its values are commonly labeled **CS** for **chip select** and **EN** for **enable**, and control inputs that disable the device are labeled $\overline{\text{CS}}$, $\overline{\text{EN}}$, or **DS** (for **disable**). Sometimes manufacturers provide several chip selects, such as **CS1**, **CS2**, and $\overline{\text{CS3}}$, to decrease the cost of using the chips.

*chip select (CS)*
*enable (EN)*
*disable (DS)*

## B.1.1 ■ Buses

Designers frequently connect the outputs of several components directly to a common set of wires, called a **bus**. If two connected components were to assert logic levels on the same wire, the result could be a short circuit and a burned-out device.[1] Devices connected to a common bus therefore must be able to disconnect themselves, and that is one reason for the tristate logic and the chip-select inputs described earlier. When the designers connect several components directly to a bus, they also design the circuit so it will select (enable) only one device at a time. The selected device **drives the bus,** that is, it asserts its logic values on the bus, while the other (disabled) devices float their outputs.

*bus*

*drives the bus*

Special devices, **bus controllers,** control the activity on a bus. Chapter 3 describes the principal types of buses. Figure B.3 illustrates two ways of representing a simple bus with two attached devices. The wiring diagram shows a higher level of detail than the schematic, but often this level of detail is unnecessary; indeed, most of the circuit diagrams in this text use the system-level schematic.

*bus controllers*

## B.1.2 ■ Gates

While transistors are the basic physical component of virtually all computers, gates are the basic logical element. Gates use from zero to six or more transistors, depending on the technology.

There are only a few different basic types of gates. Figure B.4 shows the six most common gates with their symbolic diagrams and truth-table values. Complex gates include gates with complementary outputs, such as AND/NAND and

---

1. In some technologies it is not a problem if two devices assert the same logic levels on a bus, and various manufacturers use this fact in their designs. As an example, EISA devices and EISA bus controllers momentarily assert the same values on the bus while the bus controller takes control of the bus from the device. Some technologies, under some conditions, allow multiple devices to assert different values on the same wire. In such cases, the wire implicitly uses some logic function to resolve the conflict.

**FIGURE B.3** *Two common ways of illustrating bus connections. (a) Detailed wiring diagram. (b) System-level schematic.*

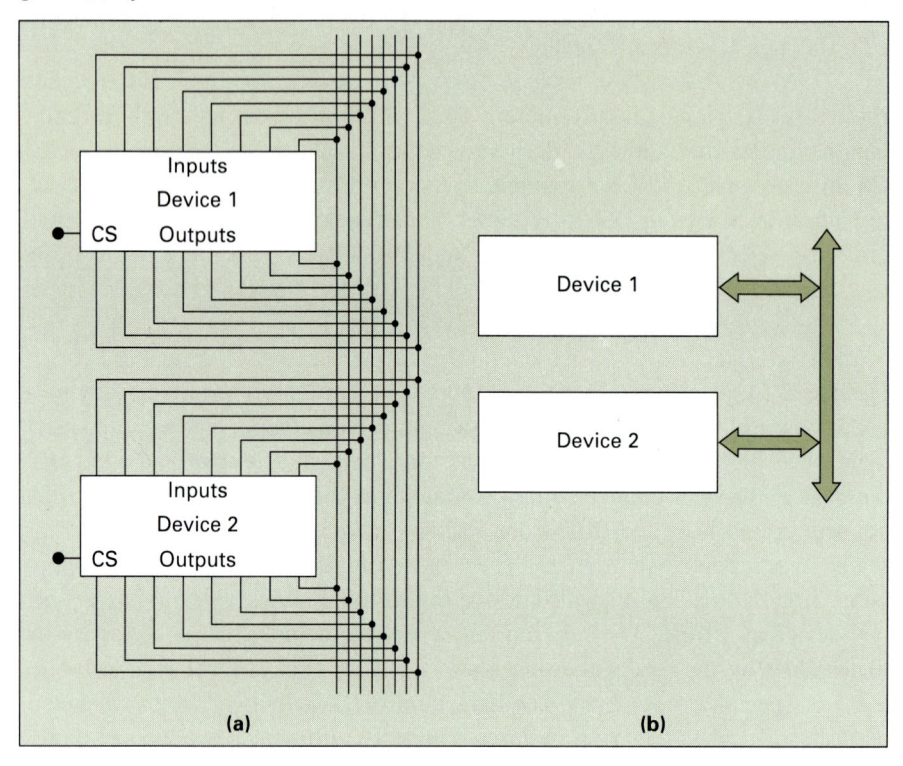

**FIGURE B.4** *Symbols and truth tables for six common gates.*

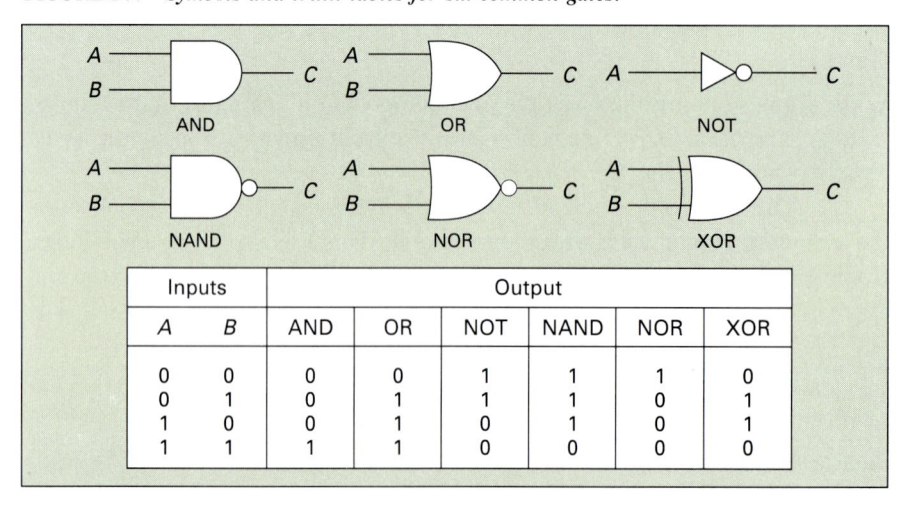

| Inputs | | Output | | | | | |
|---|---|---|---|---|---|---|---|
| A | B | AND | OR | NOT | NAND | NOR | XOR |
| 0 | 0 | 0 | 0 | 1 | 1 | 1 | 0 |
| 0 | 1 | 0 | 1 | 1 | 1 | 0 | 1 |
| 1 | 0 | 0 | 1 | 0 | 1 | 0 | 1 |
| 1 | 1 | 1 | 1 | 0 | 0 | 0 | 0 |

OR/NOR, or gates that require several transistors, such as EQV gates. (An EQV gate generates a 1 if both inputs are 0 or both inputs are 1 and a 0 otherwise. Thus EQV is $\overline{\text{EOR}}$.) Whether a gate is complex or basic is determined by the number of transistors needed, in a given technology, to make the gate.

The basic gates shown in Fig. B.4 each have one or more inputs and generate a single output. (Complex gates sometimes have two.) This means that it has one or more input signals (*true* or *false*) and it has a single output signal, which will be either *true* or *false*. The gate will not work correctly with other input signals, and *in theory* it will never generate an output signal other than *true* or *false*. We say "in theory" because, although mathematical gates behave as described here, physical ones may violate the rules. Note that a gate also has input lines that deliver power to it—the gate must be plugged in just like a lamp or radio—but other than providing power, these wires do not alter the computational logic of the circuit. (See Fig. B.2.) If the circuit is a tristate device, an additional enable or disable input will also be present.

The next two sections describe a few of the building blocks of computers, which can be divided into two categories: combinatorial or memory-free circuits, and sequential circuits.

## B.2 ■ Combinatorial Logic

**Combinatorial logic circuits** are loop-free circuits. **Loop-free** means that the output of a gate in the circuit is not an input to the gate or to any other device that makes an input to the gate. This must be understood recursively. The essential property of a combinatorial circuit is that its output does not depend on the history of inputs; it has no memory. In this section we shall describe the most common combinatorial circuits.

combinatorial logic circuits
loop-free

### B.2.1 ■ Encoders and Decoders

A **complete binary decoder** is a device that has $n$ inputs, $I_0, I_1, \ldots, I_{n-1}$, and $2^n$ outputs, $O_0, O_1, \ldots, O_{2^n-1}$. The decoder generates the unary representation of the input: line $O_k$ is active (*true*) when the input is the binary encoding of the value $k$, and all other output lines are inactive (*false*). For example, if the device in Fig. B.5 receives the binary input $101_2$ (5 decimal), it will generate a signal only on output line $O_5$. Similarly, it will raise output $O_0$ when it receives $000_2$, and it will raise output $O_7$ when it receives $111_2$.

complete binary decoder

A computer can use a decoder for converting a register number into the signal that selects the specified register. Figure B.6 illustrates the idea. Memory systems use decoders to convert addresses into control signals for selecting the specified memory location.

**Encoders** do exactly the opposite of decoders. A unary-to-binary encoder, for example, generates a binary value when an external device activates

encoders

**FIGURE B.5** *A complete 3-bit binary decoder. (a) Wiring diagram. (b) Symbolic diagram. The active lines (with logic level 1) for the input value 6 ($110_2$) are shown in color.*

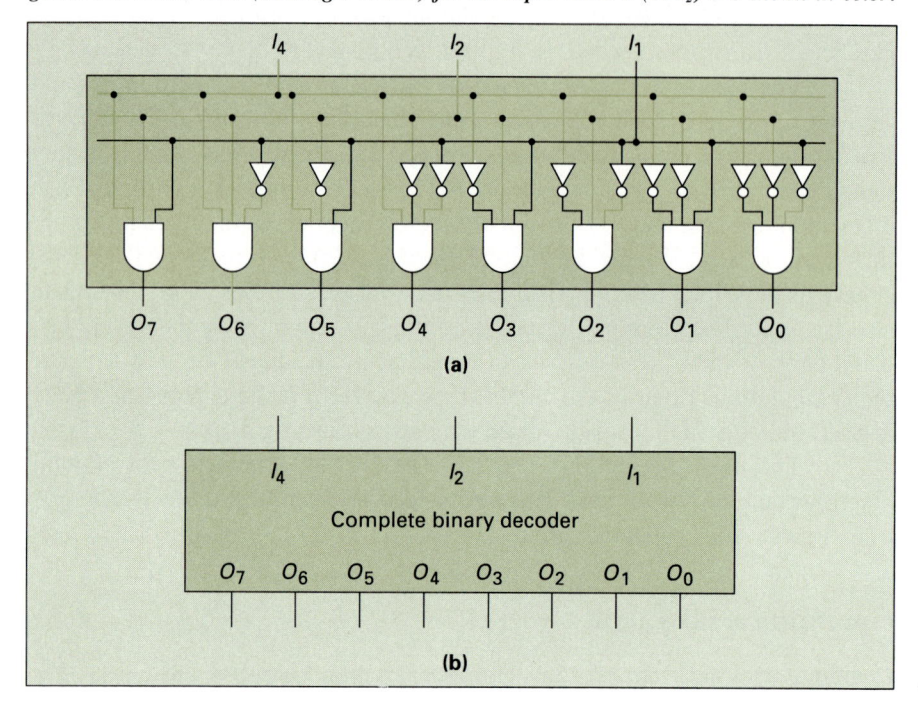

**FIGURE B.6** *Use of a decoder for selecting a register. The enabled register places its content on the data bus.*

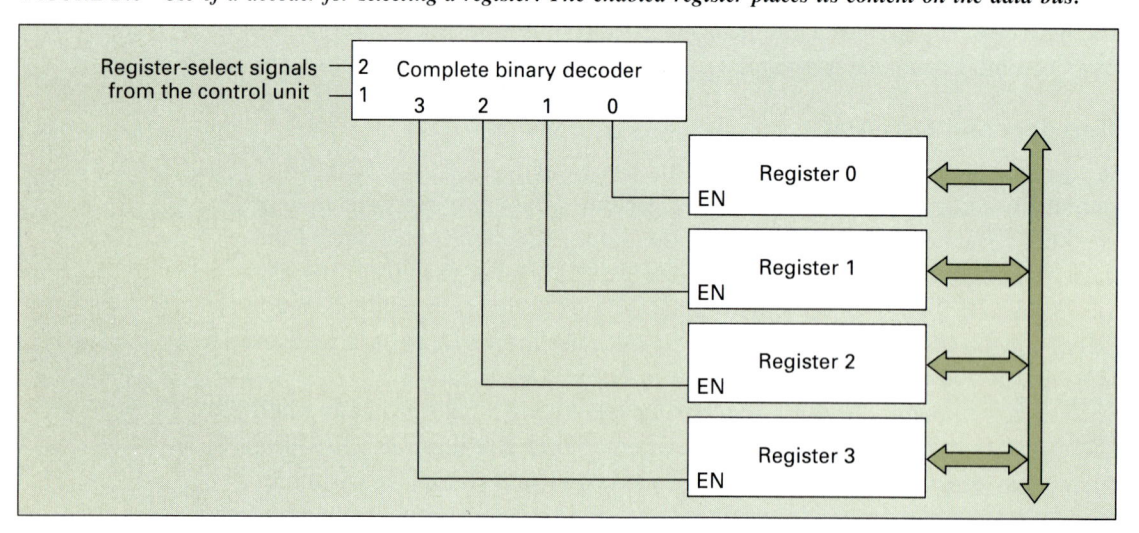

a single input. Figure B.7 illustrates how a unary-to-binary encoder generates the binary value $101_2$ when an external device asserts 1 on input line $I_5$. Note that only one input line should be active at a time.

A computer can use a unary-to-binary encoder to convert an interrupt signal into the device number of the device requesting the interrupt. If more than one device can generate simultaneous interrupt signals, however, the designer can use a **priority network,** which is another type of encoder, to ensure that only one signal reaches the unary-to-binary encoder at a time. A priority network has $N$ inputs, $I_1$ to $I_N$ and $N$ outputs, $O_1$ to $O_N$. It generates a single output, $O_i$, where $I_j$ is 0 for $j < i$, and $I_i = 1$. Figure B.8 shows a four-input priority network.

priority network

## B.2.2 ■ Multiplexors and Demultiplexors

Computer designers use **multiplexors** to connect several input devices to a common output device. The multiplexor therefore acts as a switch to establish

multiplexors

**FIGURE B.7**  *A unary-to-binary encoder.*

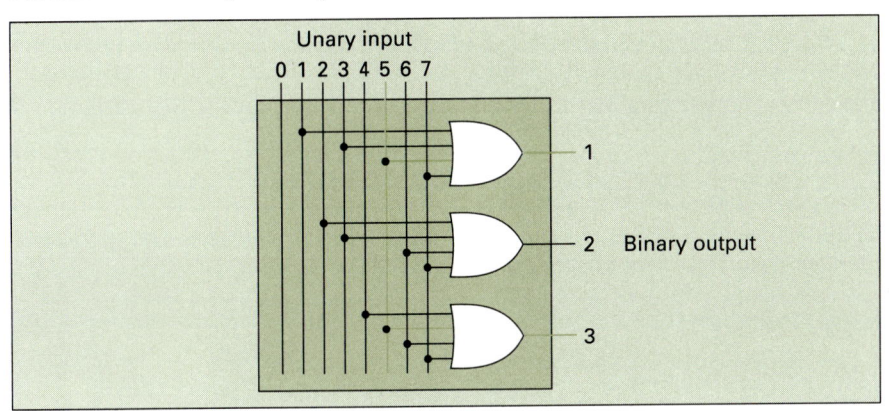

**FIGURE B.8**  *Four-input priority encoder. Only $O_2$ is high when $I_2$ and $I_4$ are both high.*

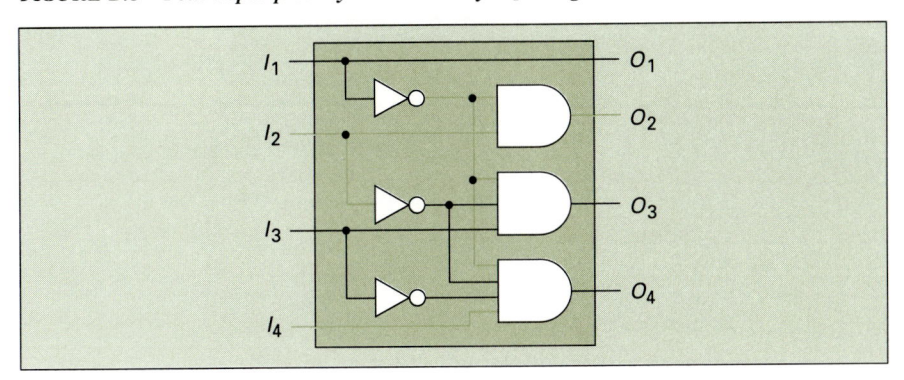

**demultiplexors**

a connection between one selected input and the common output. If a multiplexor can switch $2^k$ inputs to one output, it will have $k$ control inputs, called select-inputs, that determine which input line the multiplexor will select, where $k$ is generally a small number. Figure B.9(a) gives the logic diagram of a 1-bit 4:1 multiplexor.

**Demultiplexors** are devices for taking a single input signal and distributing it to one of a fixed number of places. In essence, a demultiplexor performs the opposite function of a multiplexor. The selected output is the one whose binary value is presented to the select inputs. Designers frequently gang demultiplexors so they will distribute a selected set of inputs to a common set of outputs, and they frequently use them for data bus switching. Note that a demultiplexor is essentially a decoder whose outputs are gated by an input bit. Figure B.9(b) gives the logic diagram of a 1-bit 1:4 demultiplexor.

Figure B.10 illustrates a circuit that uses a multiplexor and demultiplexor for routing information over a common data bus. The circuit consists of four source devices, a multiplexor (MUX), a common data bus, a demultiplexor (DEMUX), and four destination devices. Suppose the multiplexor-select inputs ($C_0$ and $C_1$) convey the value $10_2$ to the multiplexor and the demultiplexor-select inputs convey the value $00_2$ to the demultiplexor. If the control unit (not shown) sends enable signals to both the multiplexor and the demultiplexor, then the common data bus will temporarily connect source 2 to destination 0

**FIGURE B.9** *Logic diagrams of a multiplexor and a demultiplexor. (a) A 1-bit 4:1 multiplexor. (b) A 1-bit 1:4 demultiplexor. Figure B.10 shows typical schematic symbols for multiplexors and demultiplexors.*

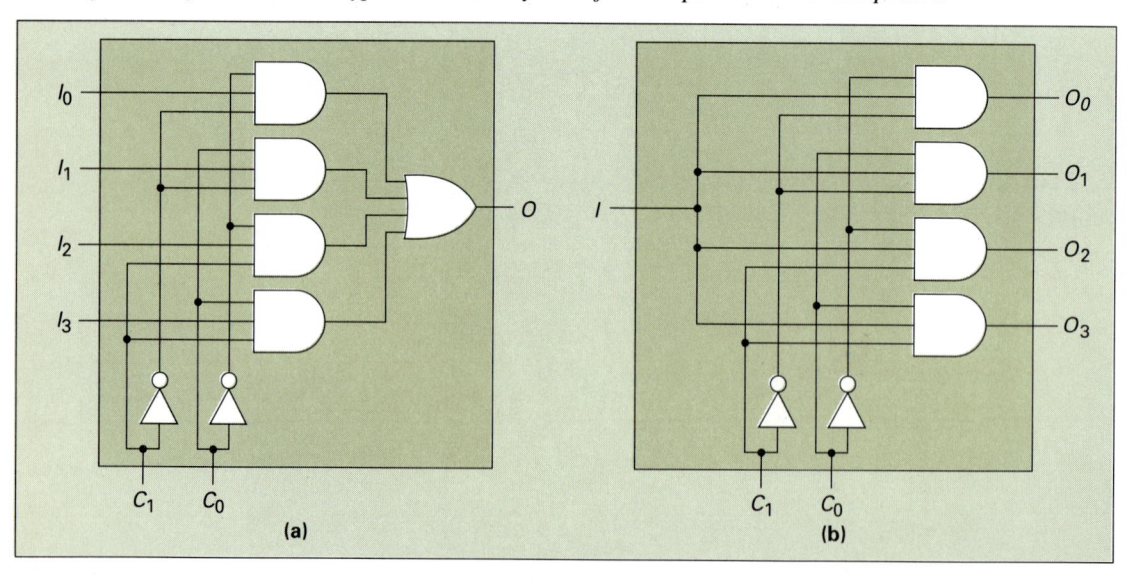

(highlighted in color in the figure). A telephone system is a common example of a system that uses multiplexors and demultiplexors in this way.

## B.2.3 ■ Shifters

Shifters shift their inputs to the left or right, perhaps circularly. An $n$-bit $q$-shifter, for example, shifts its $n$-bit input $q$ bits left or right. Figure B.11 illustrates an 8-bit 4-shifter.

A designer can implement an arbitrary $k$-bit shift operation as a sequence of $m$-bit shift operations, where $m$ varies over the powers of 2. For example, an 11-bit shift would become an 8-bit shift followed by a 2-bit shift

**FIGURE B.10** *A multiplexor (MUX), demultiplexor (DEMUX), common data bus, and eight devices. The multiplexor control inputs $C_0$ and $C_1$ select one of the four source devices, and the demultiplexor control inputs $C_0$ and $C_1$ select one of the four destination devices. The enable (EN) inputs control the outputs of the multiplexor and demultiplexor. The control inputs therefore affect a temporary connection between a selected source and a selected destination device.*

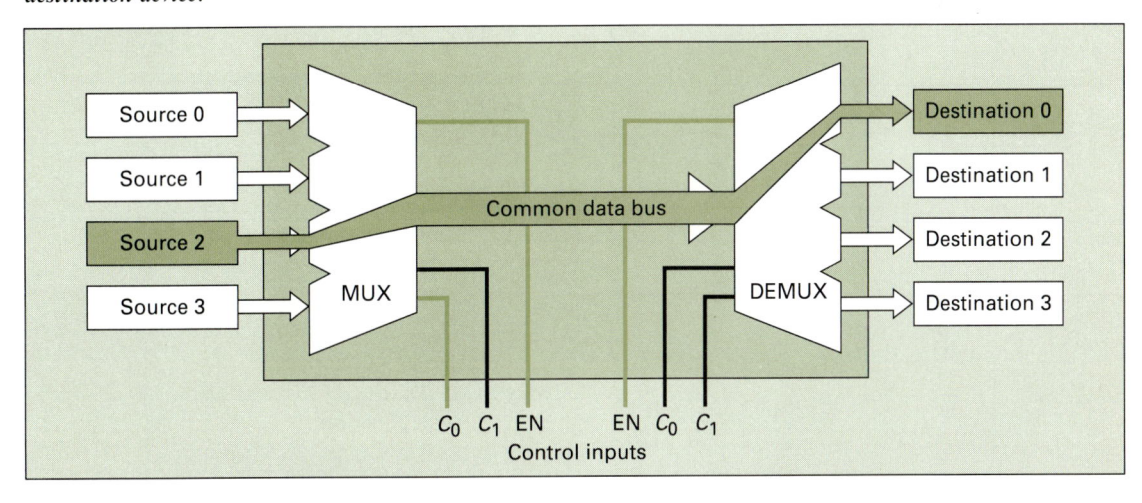

**FIGURE B.11** *An 8-bit 4-shifter. If $C = 0$, there is no shift. If $C = 1$, the input is shifted 4 bits to the left.*

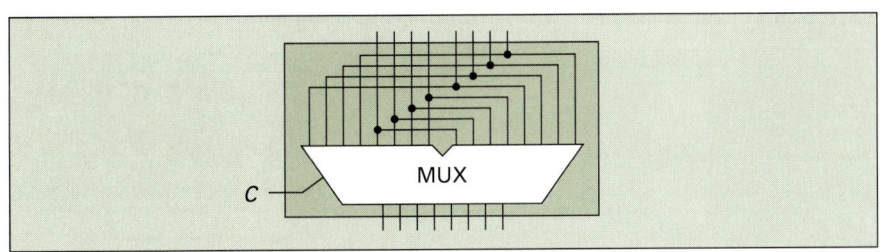

barrel shifter    followed by a 1-bit shift. A **barrel shifter** implements this idea, as Figure B.12 illustrates.

### B.2.4 ■ Adders

half-adder    A **half-adder** is a circuit that accepts two binary inputs, $A$ and $B$, and computes their sum (modulo 2), $S$, and their carry-out $C_o$. See Fig. B.13.

full adder    A **full adder** is a circuit that adds two binary inputs plus a carry-in and

**FIGURE B.12** *A barrel shifter. The shift-count register holds the binary representation of the shift count. If $C_i = 0$, then stage i does not shift its input; otherwise it shifts its input by $2^i$ bits. To shift the input by N bits, the barrel shifter uses the kth bit of the binary representation of N to control the kth shift unit.*

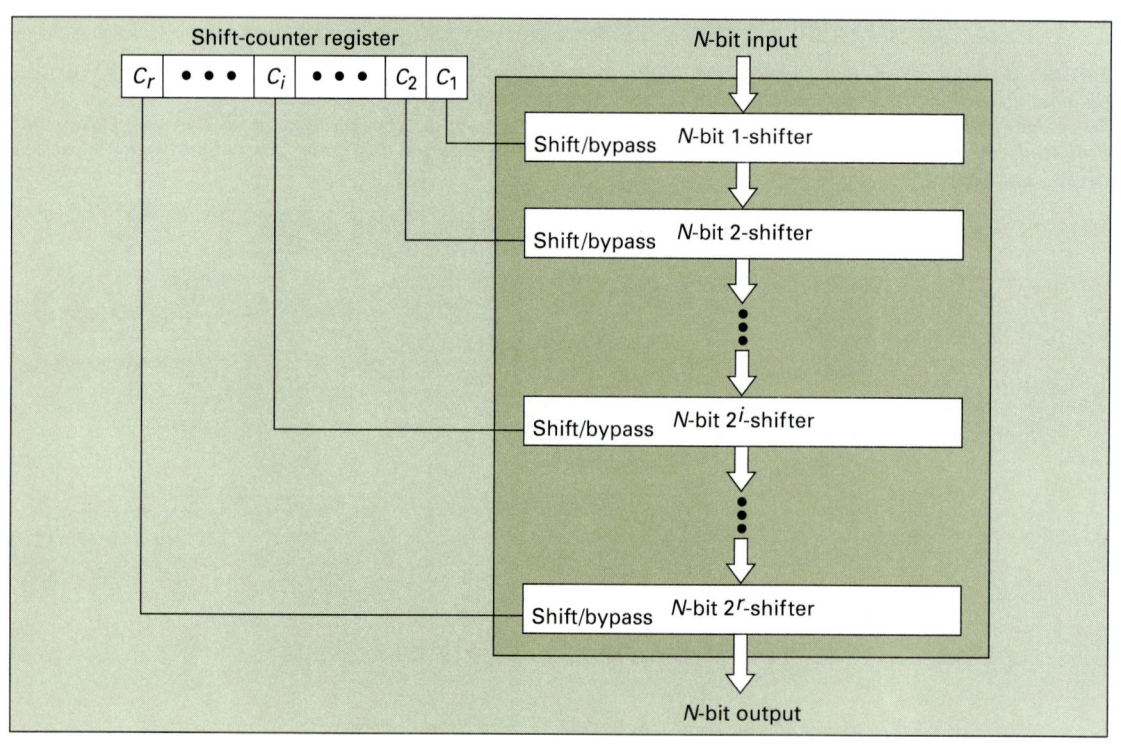

**FIGURE B.13** *Half-adder. (a) Logic circuit. (b) Symbolic diagram. (c) Truth table.*

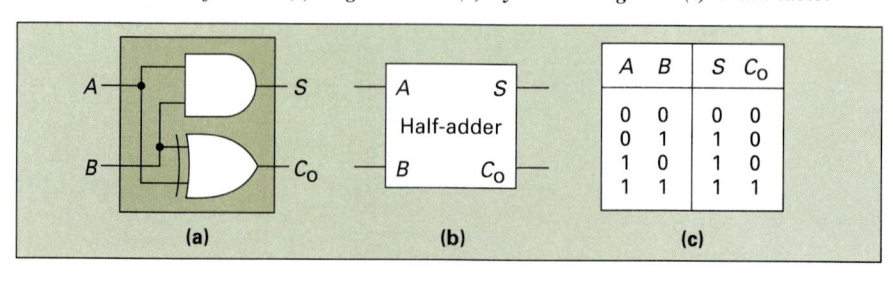

| A | B | S | $C_o$ |
|---|---|---|---|
| 0 | 0 | 0 | 0 |
| 0 | 1 | 1 | 0 |
| 1 | 0 | 1 | 0 |
| 1 | 1 | 1 | 1 |

produces the binary sum and a carry-out. Figure B.14 shows an implementation and the truth table. The inputs for each circuit are $A$, $B$, and $C_i$, and each circuit generates two outputs, $S$ and $C_o$. $C_i$ designates carry-in, and $C_o$ designates carry-out.

An ***n*-bit binary adder** is a combinatorial device that adds two *n*-bit binary numbers. An *n*-bit binary adder receives $2n + 1$ inputs: $A_n, A_{n-1}, \ldots, A_3, A_2, A_1$ and $B_n, B_{n-1}, \ldots, B_3, B_2, B_1$, and $C_i$. It generates $n + 1$ outputs: $\Sigma_n, \Sigma_{n-1}, \Sigma_3, \Sigma_2, \Sigma_1$, and $C_o$. If $A_n, \ldots, A_2, A_1$ and $B_n, \ldots, B_2, B_1$ designate *n*-bit binary integers and $C_i$ designates a carry-in, then this circuit computes their binary sum $\Sigma_n, \cdots, \Sigma_2 \Sigma_1$ and carry-out $C_o$. As an example, if $n$ is 4 and $A_4 A_3 A_2 A_1$ has the value $1001_2$ (9), $B_4 B_3 B_2 B_1$ has the value $0111_2$ (7), and $C_i = 1_2$, then the output $\Sigma_4 \Sigma_3 \Sigma_2 \Sigma_1$ is $0001_2$ (1) and $C_o = 1_2$ (indicating a carry). Figure B.15 shows the circuit for a 4-bit binary adder using full adders. Because the carry

*n*-bit binary adder

**FIGURE B.14** *A full adder. (a) Logic circuit. (b) Symbolic diagram. (c) Truth table.*

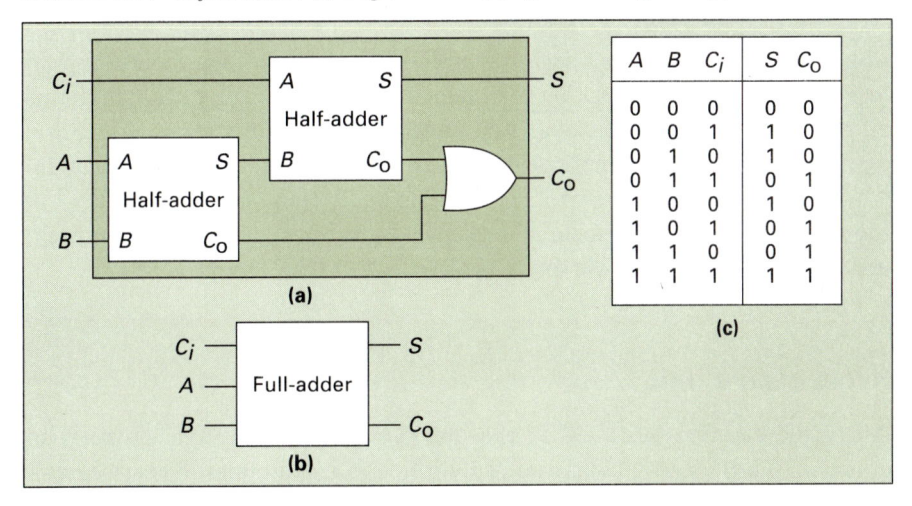

| A | B | $C_i$ | S | $C_o$ |
|---|---|---|---|---|
| 0 | 0 | 0 | 0 | 0 |
| 0 | 0 | 1 | 1 | 0 |
| 0 | 1 | 0 | 1 | 0 |
| 0 | 1 | 1 | 0 | 1 |
| 1 | 0 | 0 | 1 | 0 |
| 1 | 0 | 1 | 0 | 1 |
| 1 | 1 | 0 | 0 | 1 |
| 1 | 1 | 1 | 1 | 1 |

**FIGURE B.15** *4-bit binary adder. (a) Logic circuit. (b) Symbolic diagram.*

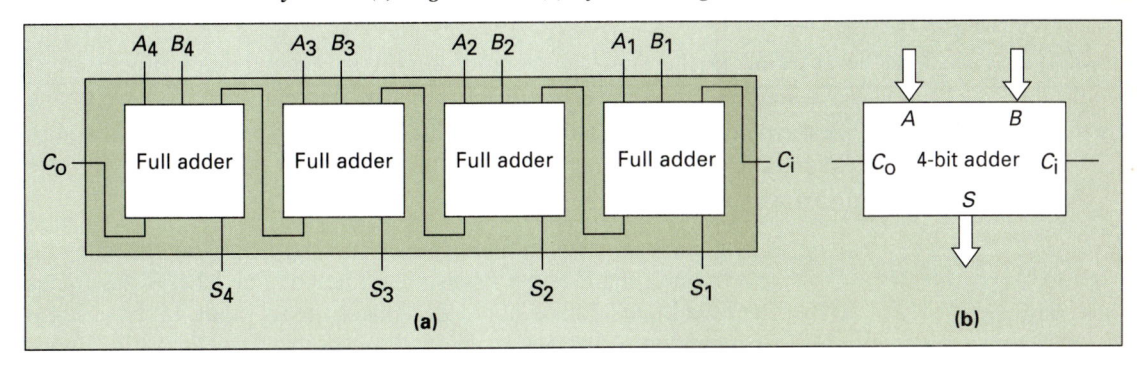

from each addition stage ripples to the stage on the left, this type of adder is called a ripple-carry adder.

There are many types of adders. Binary adders (Fig. B.15) operate on unsigned binary operands to produce unsigned binary results. Some adders operate on specific numeric representations to produce results of the same type. For example, a two's-complement adder operates on two's-complement integers to produce a two's-complement result (and an overflow indication when overflow results). As another example, a floating-point adder operates on floating-point operands to produce floating-point results, and a given adder will operate on a specific floating-point representation.

For high-performance processors, designers often use special circuits to speed up the adder's operation. The use of a **carry look-ahead circuit** is an example. An adder that uses a carry look-ahead circuit is faster than one that propagates the carries, because the carry look-ahead circuits can produce the carries faster that the sum generators can produce and propagate them.

### B.2.5 ■ Arithmetic and Logic Units (ALUs)

Logic units are circuits that perform logical operations on their inputs. Typical logic operations include AND, OR, NOT, and XOR. Often a single circuit performs all types of logical operations as well as addition and subtraction. For such a logic circuit, an external input device raises the enable input and selects an operation by asserting a value on its control inputs. Because an adder has most of the gates necessary to perform all basic logic functions, most adders are packaged as **arithmetic and logic units (ALUs).**

## B.3 ■ Sequential Logic

All of the circuits illustrated in the previous sections have one property in common: They are combinatorial or loop-free. Once a circuit has a feedback path, its output may depend on prior inputs. When this is the case, the circuit has memory, is called **sequential**, and is decidedly more complex to analyze.

### B.3.1 ■ Flip-flops

The **flip-flop** is the simplest memory circuit in a computer's processor. It stores a single logic value—*true* or *false*. A flip-flop can only hold 1 bit. The simplest type of flip-flop, called an **SR flip-flop** (for set-reset), is illustrated in Fig. B.16. Digital logic books describe SR flip-flops in detail, so we will only summarize their behavior here.

- There are a variety of input labels for flip-flops, but for the one shown here, the $R$ and $S$ labels are common. The label $R$ designates the **reset input** and the label $S$ designates the **set input.** In the absence of inputs on $R$ and $S$ (i.e., both $R$ and $S$ are 0, or *low*), the circuit will remain stable in one of two configurations, either *reset* (where the output $Q = 0$ and the output $\overline{Q} = 1$) or *set* (where $Q = 1$ and $\overline{Q} = 0$). The bar signifies a logical complement: Whatever value $Q$ has (0 or 1), $\overline{Q}$ will have the opposite (1 or 0).

- A 1 (high) input on $R$ (and 0 input on $S$) will cause the circuit to go to the *reset* state. Once the circuit is reset, it is no longer necessary to hold the R input high.
- A high input on $S$ (and a low input on $R$) will cause the circuit to flip to the *set* state. Once the flip-flop is set, it is no longer necessary to hold the $S$ input high.
- Except during the transient condition where the flip-flop is actually changing states, the two outputs $Q$ and $\overline{Q}$ always have opposite values.
- If both inputs $R$ and $S$ are high at the same time, the subsequent behavior of the flip-flop is unpredictable.
- The time it takes for a flip-flop to switch states is its **switching time**.

One characteristic of an SR flip-flop is that if both of its inputs are high at the same time, its outputs oscillate and its final state (after the inputs are turned off) is indeterminate and may even remain in a state of oscillation. However, because it has few components, it is also very fast. The switching time of its components determines its speed, which for very fast circuitry may be on the order of nanoseconds.

An SR flip-flop does not use clock signals to govern its switching times; it switches the moment an $R$ or $S$ input arrives. It is therefore **asynchronous**. In contrast, flip-flops that use clocks to govern their switching times are **synchronous**.

Another common type of flip-flop is the **JK master-slave,** which is a synchronous flip-flop. A master-slave flip-flop really consists of two flip-flops, a **master** and a **slave**. Figure B.17 illustrates the flip-flop and its circuit diagram. The JK master-slave flip-flop does not change state when the clock input ($C$) is low regardless of what the $J$ and $K$ inputs do. However, when the clock is high, the master "watches" the inputs and changes state to the opposite of the current state of the slave if either (1) both $J$ and $K$ go high, or (2) $J$

**FIGURE B.16** *Logic diagram of an SR flip-flop.*

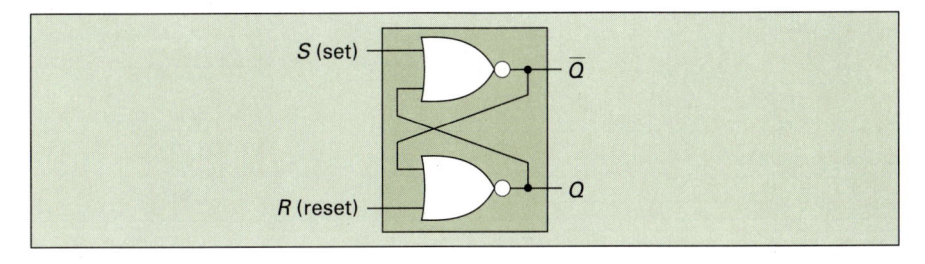

goes high when the flip-flop is clear or *K* goes high when the flip-flop is set. In either case, the slave changes state only when the clock goes low, and because the slave controls the output of the flip-flop, the outputs change when the clock goes low. Thus the clock controls the switching time, which is why it is called synchronous.

synchronous D flip-flop

The **synchronous D flip-flop** is another common flip-flop. It requires only one input, labeled *D*. A D flip-flop that is clocked when *D* is high becomes set; one that is clocked when *D* is low becomes reset.

There are many other types of flip-flops, but it is not necessary to understand them for purposes of using this text. The interested reader should consult a logic design textbook.

### B.3.2 ■ Clock Generators

multiphase clock

A clock generator is a device for generating a sequence of signals having a uniform size and duration. Hence most computers use them to regulate their timing. A **multiphase clock** is a clock that generates several different sequences of signals. For example, a two-phase clock generates two different sequences of pulses. The signals tend to be very specific for a given computer, but knowing their timing characteristics is not important for understanding computer architecture. We will not describe clock circuits here, except to mention that they use devices other than gates, and they generate signals like those illustrated in Fig. B.18.

### B.3.3 ■ Registers and Counters

registers

In contrast with flip-flops, which store a single bit of information, **registers** are devices that store many bits of information. An *n*-bit register is composed

**FIGURE B.17**  *A clocked JK master-slave flip-flop. (a) Logic diagram. (b) Symbolic diagram.*

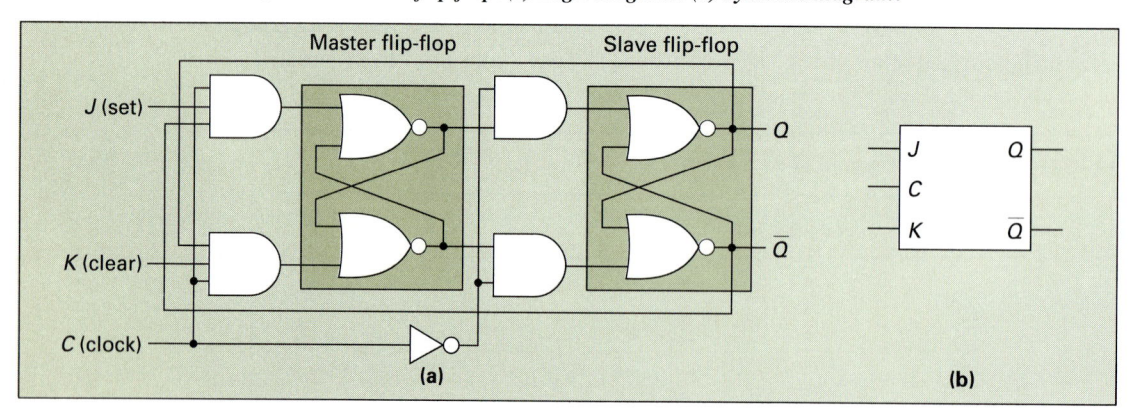

of *n* flip-flops and can store *n* bits of data. A 32-bit register, as its name implies, is a device that stores 32 bits of information. The information may be a 32-bit integer, a sequence of four 8-bit characters, a 32-bit floating-point number, or some other 32-bit value.

Registers are of different types. Figure B.19 illustrates an **8-bit D register,** which is composed of eight D flip-flops. As the figure shows, the clock and enable inputs, which control the flip-flops and their outputs, go to all of the flip-flops, so they all switch at the same time, synchronously. The *I* inputs and the *O* outputs of each flip-flop are independent; each flip-flop stores its own bit of information. Because the clock inputs are common, however, all flip-flops of this register accept the input data concurrently. That is the essence of a register. It is not possible, for example, to enter data in the third flip-flop without entering data in the other flip-flops at the same time.

8-bit D register

**FIGURE B.18** *Outputs from two clocks. (a) Single-phase clock. (b) Two-phase clock.*

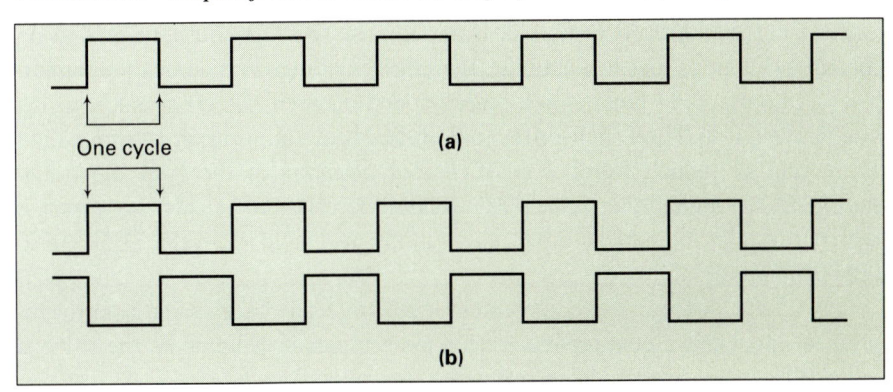

**FIGURE B.19** *8-bit D register. The components illustrated as triangles on the output lines are tristate buffers. When the enable input is low, the register floats its outputs (i.e., its outputs are effectively disconnected).*

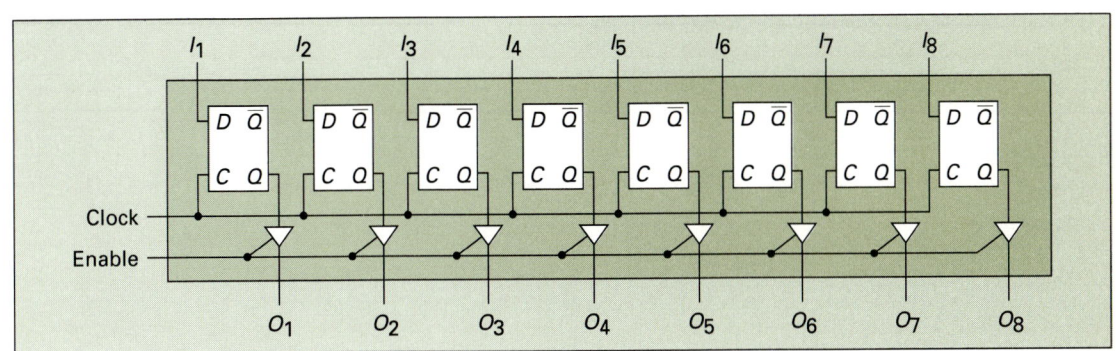

**428** Computer Architecture

Some registers use a single set of input and output lines. Internally the circuitry uses tristate buffers to control the movement of data. Figure B.20 illustrates such a circuit, where the basic flip-flops are of type D. (A D flip-flop is a synchronous flip-flop that has a single data input, $D$. If $D$ is high, the clock sets the flip-flop; if $D$ is low, the clock clears the flip-flop.)

Registers store data and make them available for other circuits. Some registers have additional computational circuitry and can perform logical operations on the data they hold. The most common special "registers" are counters and shift registers.

**counters**

**Counters** are registers that can increment or decrement their contents. In addition to the data, clock, and enable inputs, a counter has an increment input. When an external device raises the increment signal, the counter increments the value it holds. If an 8-bit binary counter holds the binary value $0000\,1010_2$, for example, and an external devices raises its increment input, the counter will modify its content to become $0000\,1011_2$. A counter may have a carry output and generate a carry signal when it increments its maximum. For an $n$-bit binary counter, when the counter increments the value $2^n - 1$, the counter generates a carry and resets to 0. A designer can use the carry output signal as an increment input to another counter, thereby extending the size of the counter.

Figure B.21 illustrates a binary-coded decimal (BCD) counter, which counts from 0 to 9 and then resets to 0 on the 10th count input. If a four-digit BCD counter (which would consist of four counters of the type illustrated in Fig. B.21) holds the value 0349 ($0000\,0011\,0100\,1001_2$) and an external device raises its increment input, the counter will hold the value 0350 ($0000\,0011\,0101\,0000_2$).

Some counters have decrement inputs instead of (or in addition to) increment inputs. If a counter has a decrement input, it decrements the value it holds when an external device raises the decrement input.

**shift register**

A **shift register** is a register that can shift the bits it holds to the left or the right. For a shift-right register, the binary value $0101\,1110_2$ becomes

**FIGURE B.20** *D register with bidirectional I/O lines.*

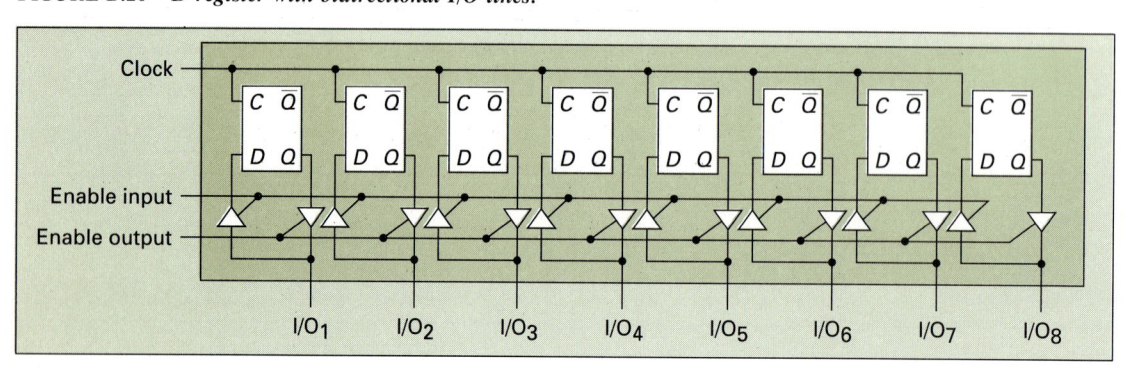

$X$ 010 1111$_2$ when shifted right, where $X$ is an input to the register. The input labeled $S_i$ in Fig. B.22 delivers the value the register enters into the leftmost bit position, and the output labeled $S_o$ delivers the value from the rightmost bit position, which the register loses.

Some shift registers can shift their values right or left, depending on a control input, and some can shift their values by more than one bit position at a time.

## B.4 ■ Devices That Combine Combinatorial and Sequential Logic

Many devices combine the components we have described into complex computational subsystems. We shall illustrate a few of the more common circuits of this type in this section.

**FIGURE B.21** *A single-digit synchronous BCD counter.*

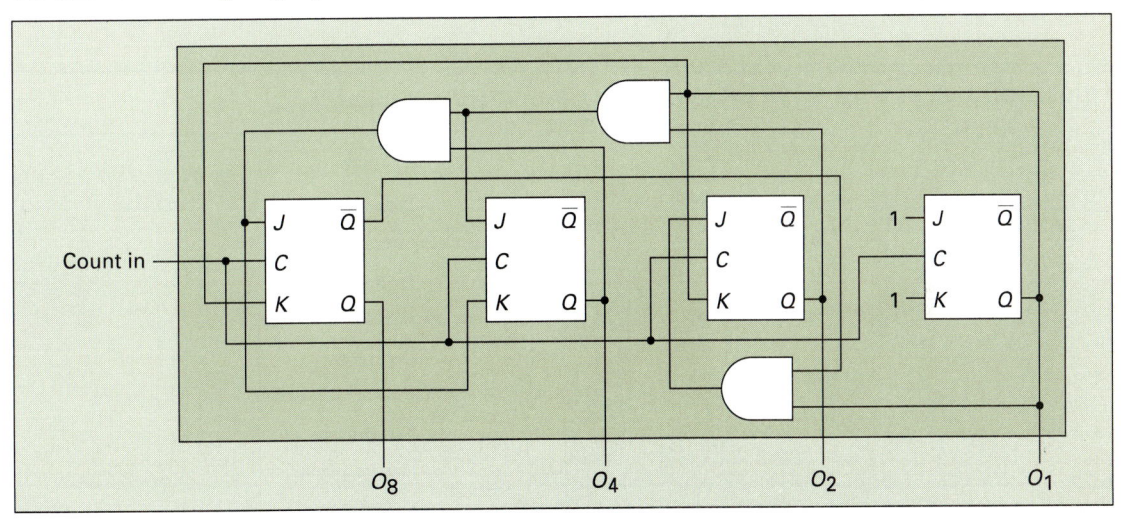

**FIGURE B.22** *Symbolic diagram of a shift-right register.*

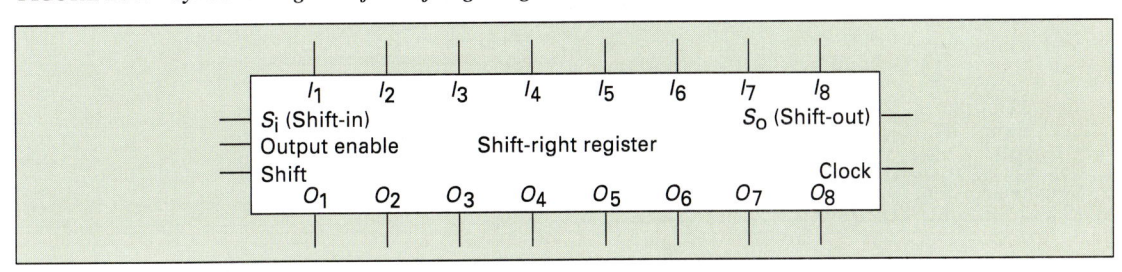

### B.4.1 ■ Register Files

Designers often organize registers into files. Figure B.23 illustrates a file of eight D registers that use a common bus. The control unit selects one of the registers by sending a register number to the decoder. To recall the value in the selected register, the control unit sends the enable signal to the register file. To store a new value in the selected register, the control unit sends a clock signal to the register file.

Figure B.24 illustrates a register file that can deliver two operands to an ALU and accept one result from the ALU simultaneously, which it can place in any register. Some high-performance processors have circuitry that can deliver as many as eight operands simultaneously.

### B.4.2 ■ Hardware Stack

stack   A **stack** is a storage device that uses the last-in-first-out (LIFO) storage policy. Figure B.25 illustrates how to use a register file and counter to build an eight-element register stack. To push a value into the stack, the control unit issues an increment signal followed by a clock signal. To pop a value from the stack,

**FIGURE B.23**  *An eight-register file composed of D registers. Register 5 is selected.*

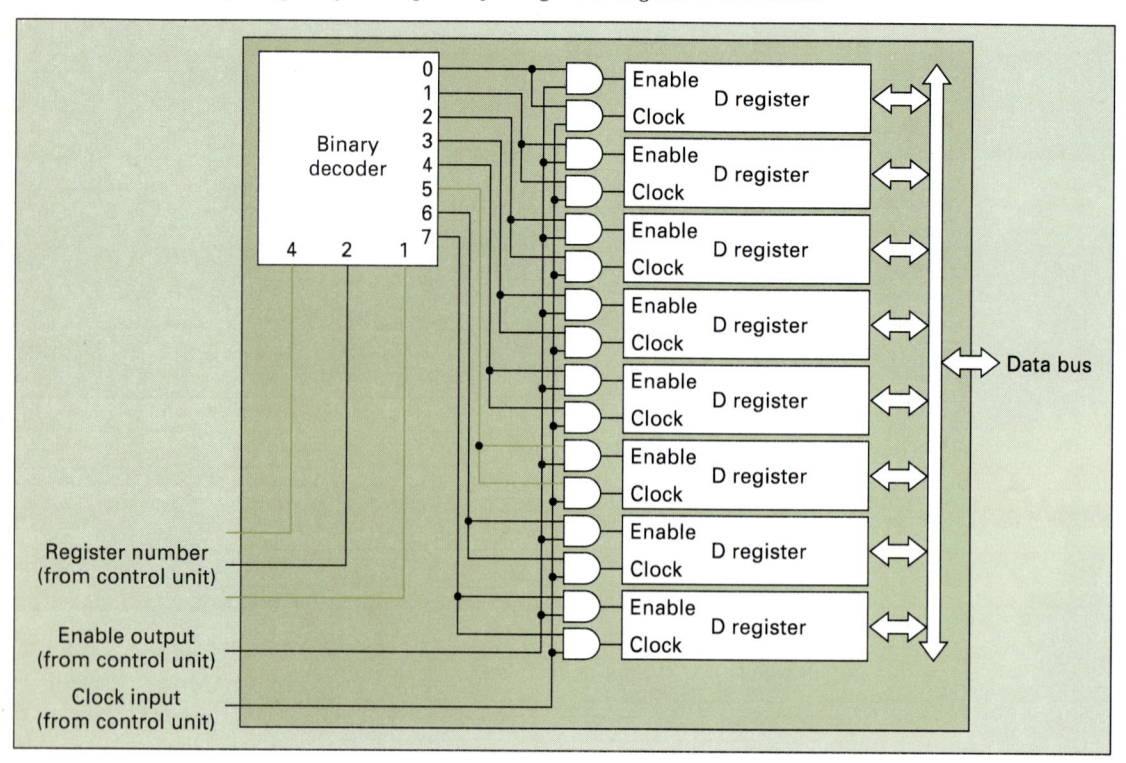

the control unit issues an output-enable signal followed by a decrement signal. To read the stack top, the control unit simply issues an output-enable signal. The counter holds the address (register number) of the current stack top.

### B.4.3 ■ Multiplication Circuits

Although designers can build multipliers without using sequential logic, many incorporate sequential logic. Figure B.26 illustrates such a device: a binary multiplier. To multiply two numbers, the external control first loads them into the multiplication unit and then issues the multiply signal. The external control loads the multiplier by sending the load-multiplier signal to the multiplica-

**FIGURE B.24** *Another implementation of a register file. This file uses multiplexors for selecting the source registers and a demultiplexor for selecting the destination register.*

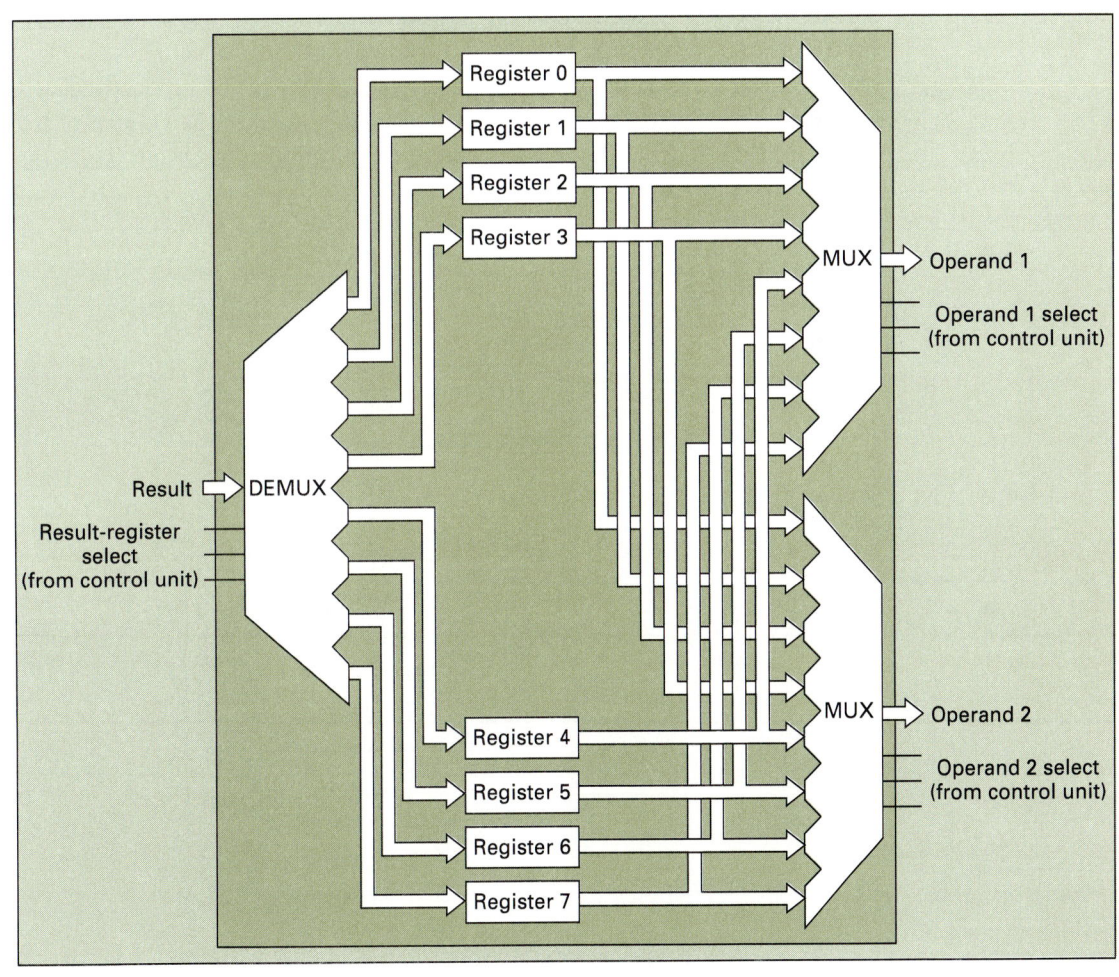

tion unit while placing the multiplier on the data bus. It loads the multiplicand by asserting the load-multiplicand signal while placing the multiplicand on the data bus. In response to these control signals, the multiplication control unit sends $C_2 = 1$ (to load the multiplier) and then $C_{10} = 1$ and $C_{11} = 1$ (to load the multiplicand). While loading the multiplicand, the multiplication control unit also sends $C_5 = 1$ to the product register, which clears it. (Control signal $C_5$ loads the product register with the value from the adder. However, the adder output is disabled ($C_7 = 0$), so the multiplicand gets the value 0.)

When the external device issues the multiply signal, the multiplication control unit performs the multiplication through a sequence of $N$ additions and $N$ shift operations, where $N$ is the number of bits in the registers. First, notice that the least-significant bit (LSB) of the multiplier goes to the enable input (EN) of the multiplicand register. If the LSB of the multiplier register is 0, the adder adds 0 to the value in the product register (which is always available to the adder). If the LSB of the multiplier register is 1, the adder adds the content of the multiplicand register to the content of the product register. Control $C_7$ enables the output from the adder, which goes to the product register. Simultaneously, the carry output $C_o$ from the adder goes to the $D$ input of the carry flip-flop. During the addition, the multiplication control unit issues the

**FIGURE B.25** *An eight-element hardware stack. INC, increment; DEC, decrement.*

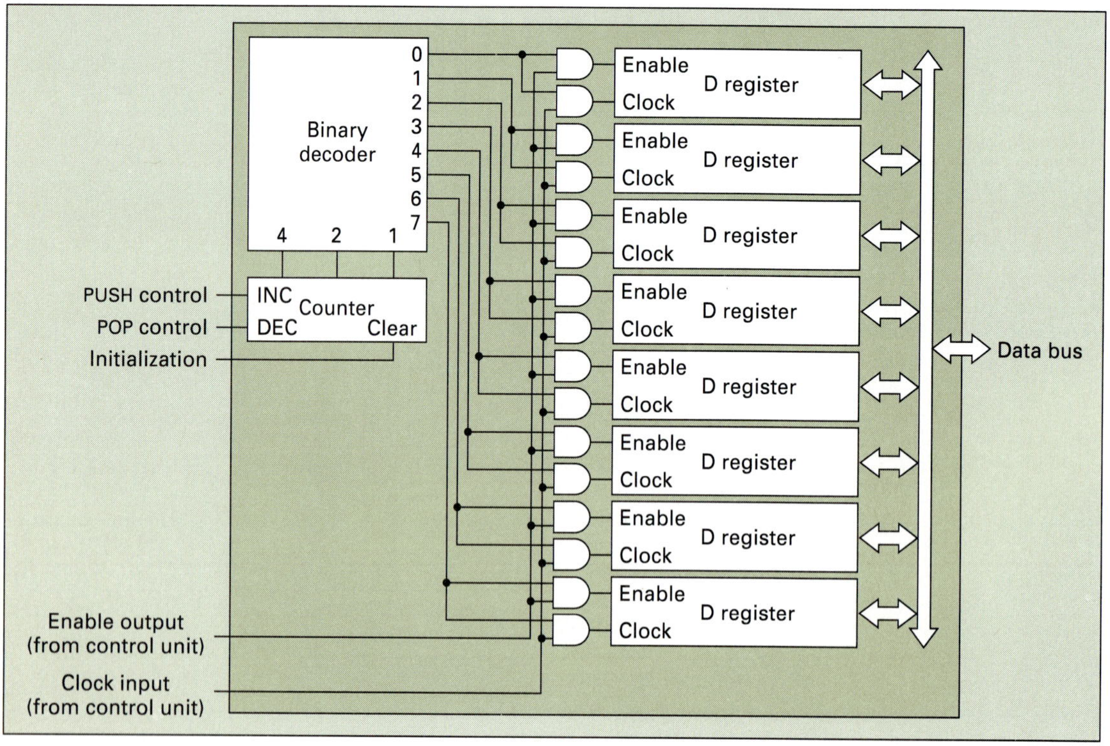

clock signals to the carry flip-flop ($C_9$) and to the product register ($C_5$). Consequently the sum from the adder replaces the previous value in the product register, and the carry flip-flop captures the carry from the addition.

Next, the multiplication control unit shifts the contents of the product and multiplier registers to the right by 1 bit; the LSB of the product is lost, and the carry becomes the most-significant bit of the product. To perform the shift, the multiplication control unit issues $C_4$, $C_5$, $C_1$, $C_2$, and $C_8$.

After repeating the addition and shift operation $N$ times, where $N$ is the number of bits in the three registers, the product register holds the $N$ high-order bits of the product, and the multiplier holds the $N$ low-order bits of the product. The multiplication control unit now generates the done signal to inform the external control that the product is available.

The final step is for the external control to transfer the result from the multiplication unit. The external control issues the send multiplier signal, and the multiplication control unit responds by sending $C_3$ to multiplier register, which sends its content to the data bus. The external control now issues

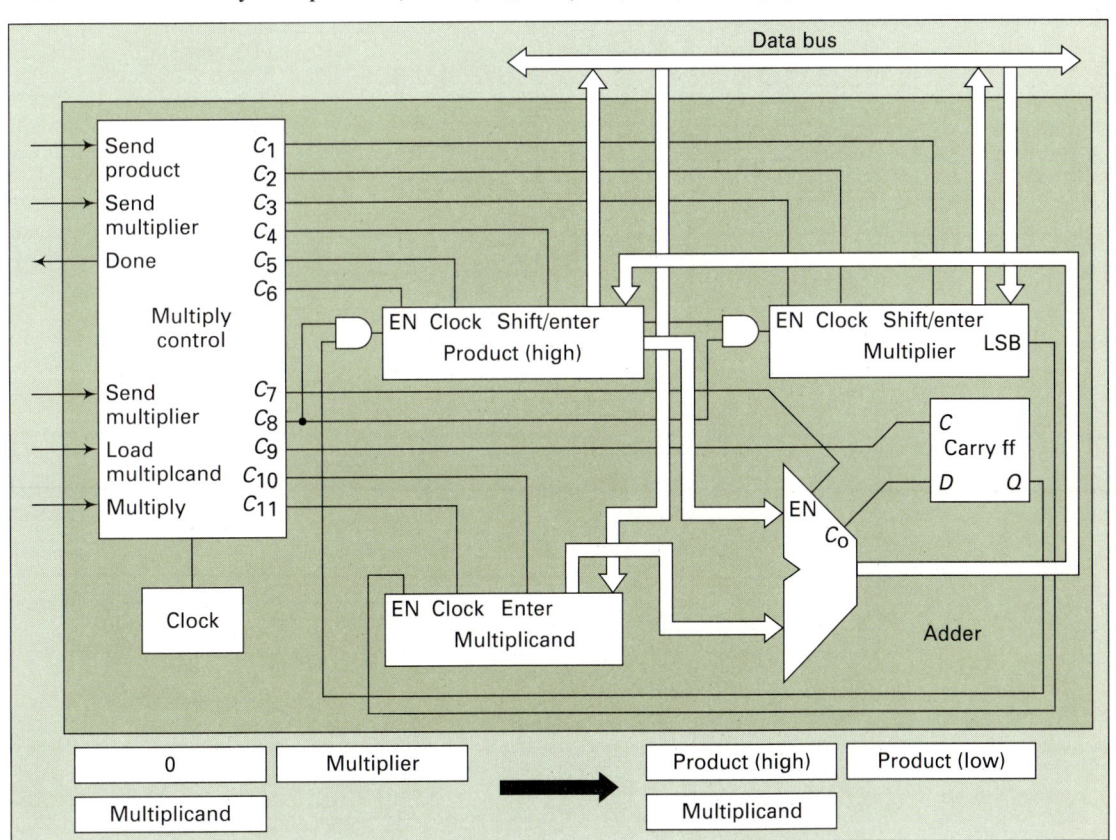

**FIGURE B.26** *A binary multiplier. EN, enable; $C_o$, carry-out; LSB, least-significant bit.*

the send-product signal, and the multiplication control unit responds by sending $C_6$ to the product register, which sends its content to the data bus.

Figures B.27 and B.28 summarize the steps of a multiplication. Figure B.27 shows the sequence of values in the three registers after the addition step, for a 6-bit multiplication, and Fig. B.28 shows the control signals issued by the multiplication control unit during the same process.

---

**FIGURE B.27**  $25 \times 19 = 475$. $11001_2 \times 10011_2 = 111\,011\,011_2$. Colored bits in the pro-duct (high) and multiplicand registers in the left column are added giving the colored value in the product (high) register in the right column. Colored bits in the product (low) registers are bits that appear in the result.

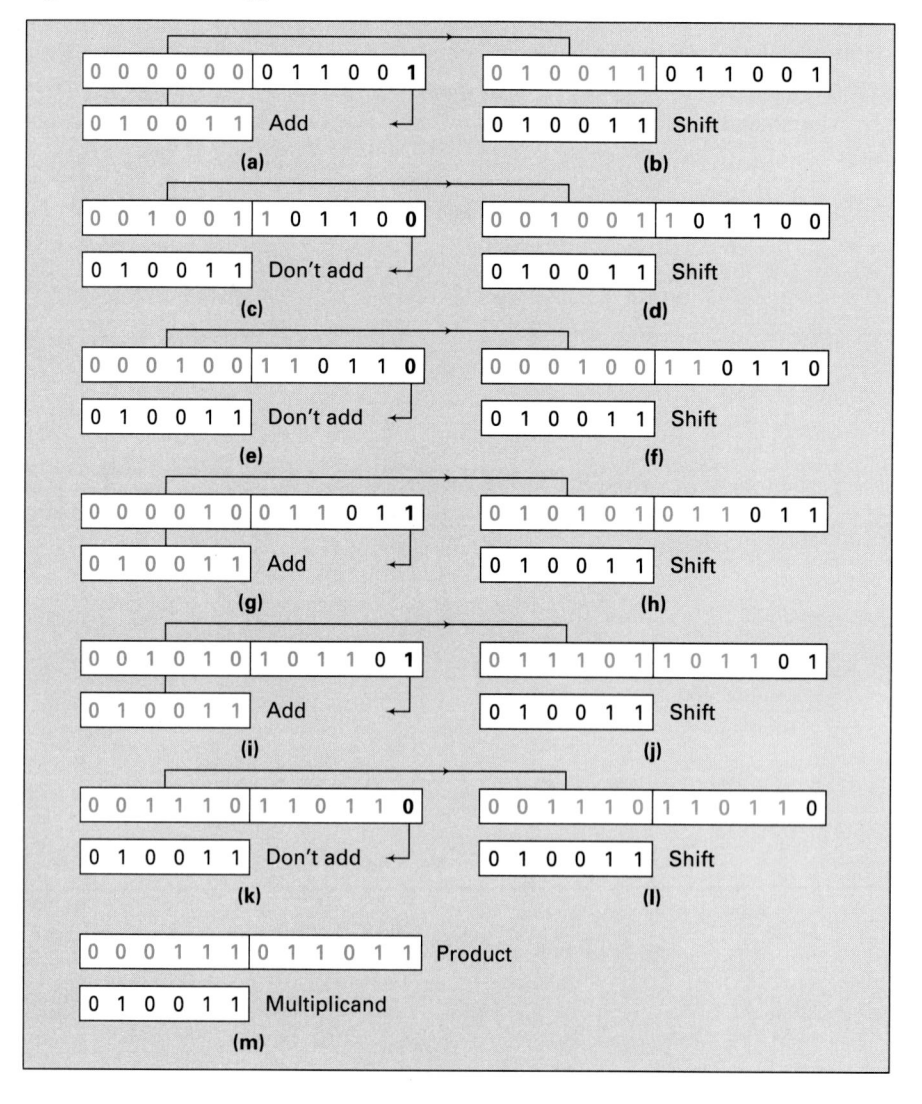

| (a) 0 0 0 0 0 0 \| 0 1 1 0 0 1 ; 0 1 0 0 1 1 Add | (b) 0 1 0 0 1 1 \| 0 1 1 0 0 1 ; 0 1 0 0 1 1 Shift |
| --- | --- |
| (c) 0 0 1 0 0 1 \| 1 0 1 1 0 0 ; 0 1 0 0 1 1 Don't add | (d) 0 0 1 0 0 1 \| 1 0 1 1 0 0 ; 0 1 0 0 1 1 Shift |
| (e) 0 0 0 1 0 0 \| 1 1 0 1 1 0 ; 0 1 0 0 1 1 Don't add | (f) 0 0 0 1 0 0 \| 1 1 0 1 1 0 ; 0 1 0 0 1 1 Shift |
| (g) 0 0 0 0 1 0 \| 0 1 1 0 1 1 ; 0 1 0 0 1 1 Add | (h) 0 1 0 1 0 1 \| 0 1 1 0 1 1 ; 0 1 0 0 1 1 Shift |
| (i) 0 0 1 0 1 0 \| 1 0 1 1 0 1 ; 0 1 0 0 1 1 Add | (j) 0 1 1 1 0 1 \| 1 0 1 1 0 1 ; 0 1 0 0 1 1 Shift |
| (k) 0 0 1 1 1 0 \| 1 1 0 1 1 0 ; 0 1 0 0 1 1 Don't add | (l) 0 0 1 1 1 0 \| 1 1 0 1 1 0 ; 0 1 0 0 1 1 Shift |

(m) 0 0 0 1 1 1 \| 0 1 1 0 1 1  Product
    0 1 0 0 1 1  Multiplicand

**FIGURE B.28** *Control signals for a 6-bit multiplication, using the multiplier in Fig. B.26.*

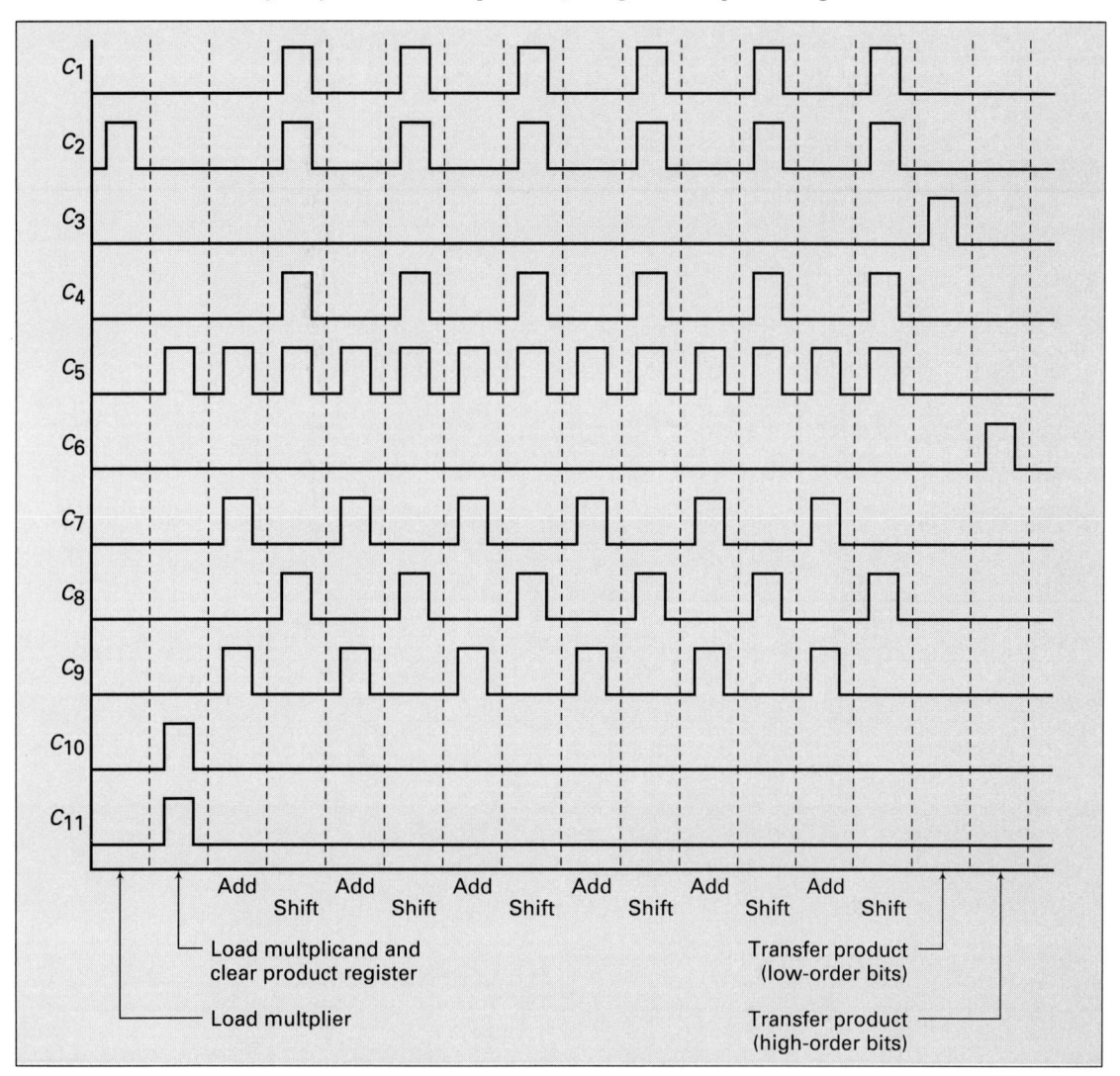

# Suggested Answers to Selected Exercises and Problems

## Chapter 1

*1.5* Table of improvements:

| Year | 1 | 2 | 3 | 4 | 5 | 6 | 7 | 8 |
|---|---|---|---|---|---|---|---|---|
| Cache | 2 | 2 | 2 | 2 | 2 | 2 | 2 | 2 |
| Compiler | 1.1 | 1.2 | 1.3 | 1.5 | 1.6 | 1.8 | 1.9 | 2.1 |

Therefore the compiler performance overtakes the cache improvement in 8 years.

*1.10* Average speed = $0.2 \times A1 + 0.8 \times A2$.

## Chapter 2

*2.5* The natural order is to put the most significant part first and the least significant part last. This means that the number would be divided into (from left to right) sign, exponent, and then mantissa. This is natural in the sense that integer representations are like this, assuming the high-order (leftmost) bit is the sign bit. With this obvious choice, one can make comparisons independent of the datatype (but *not* across datatypes).

*2.10* To get an exponent range of $10^{\pm 25}$ requires $N$ chosen so that $2^N \geq 10^{25}$ or $N \log_{10} 2 \geq 25$, so $N \geq 84$. To get this exponent range requires 7 bits. Therefore suggest an IEEE-like representation with 24 bits of mantissa, 7 bits of exponent, and 1 exponent sign bit. With 24-bit mantissa precision (1 bit is for the sign, but 1 bit is elided), the precision is about $\log_{10} 2^{24}$, or about 7.2 digits. We have assumed that the exponent range is more important than the mantissa precision. This design is 10% below the marketing department's requirement.

*2.15* One solution: Pick the values 1 to $n$ for the $n$ keys, except for Shift and Shift Lock. Assign 62 to Shift and 63 to Shift Lock. Code 62 is an escape which in effect tells the computer to use the alternate alphabet (capitals if lowercase before and vice versa) for the next character. Code 63 tells the computer to switch to the alternate alphabet until a 62 is encountered.

*2.20* Note that $N$ is an immediate operand of the AND and OR instructions. If we know which bits are to be set or cleared at compile time, we can use OR to set the desired bits and AND to clear the desired bits without changing any other bits, as follows: Let bit number 0 be the rightmost bit of a word, and let $i_1 i_2, \ldots, i_k$ be the numbers of the bits to be set or cleared. Then R ← R OR #$N$ clears the desired bits, where $N = 2^{i_1} + 2^{i_2} + \cdots + 2^{i_k}$, and R ← R AND #M to clear the same bits, where $M$ is the complement of $N$. For example, if R has 8 bits, we can clear bits 1, 2, and 6 by performing R ← R OR #$01000110_2$, and we can set the same bits by performing R ← R AND #$10111001_2$.

If we do not know which bits are to be set or cleared at compile time, there are two solutions. First, we can build the desired instructions in memory (as just described) and then use EXECUTE to execute them. However, if EXECUTE is unavailable, we can call a subroutine that will set or clear the desired bits. The subroutine accepts $N$ as an argument, tests the individual bits of $N$, and then invokes precompiled AND and OR instructions to set or clear desired bits.

*2.25* Because MATCH AND REPLACE suffices for synchronization, it is enough to show how to make a MATCH AND REPLACE using COMPARE AND SWAP. Except for exclusion, COMPARE AND SWAP is the same as MATCH AND REPLACE.

Thus, it further suffices to show how to achieve exclusion with COMPARE AND SWAP.

> MATCH AND REPLACE: COMPARE AND SWAP
> **If** swap was successful,
> **then done**
> **Else goto** MATCH AND REPLACE

*2.30* Autoincrement and autodecrement addressing modes can be used to implement push and pop operations. To push an element onto the stack, use either (1) an INCREMENT AND STORE instruction or (2) a STORE AND INCREMENT instruction. To pop an element from the stack, use (1) a LOAD AND DECREMENT instruction or (2) a DECREMENT AND LOAD instruction. For the first solution the stack pointer points to the top of the stack; for the second solution it points to the next available stack position.

*2.45* 1. In the event of a program error, the actual code that caused the problem may have been destroyed, increasing the difficulty of debugging.
2. Neither reentrant procedures (procedures that may be entered before a previous activation of the same procedure finishes) nor recursive procedures are possible if the code modifies itself.
3. It is generally more difficult to understand exactly what a self-modifying program is actually doing. Comments are far more important than with most programs.
4. It may be impossible for programs to retry to recover from (hardware) errors.

*2.50* The utility of the MAX instruction depends on the ability of compilers to detect the places where it can be used. Some common functions, of course, can use it directly. These include, in addition to MAX and MIN, the absolute value and signum ($-1$ for negative, 0 for zero, $+1$ for positive), all of which use branches in the obvious way of programming them. On highly pipelined machines, branches are expensive (slow), so architects look for tricks like the use of MAX and MIN to reduce their incidence.

*2.55* (See figure below.)

| LOAD | R ← A | Load word A into R. |
| LOGICAL SHIFT LEFT | R left 3 byte positions | Put the first character, B1, of string left justified into R and put zeros into 3 low-order bytes of R. |
| LOAD | R1 ← A + 1 | Load word A + 1 into another register, R1. |
| LOGICAL SHIFT RIGHT | R1 right 1 byte position | Put characters B2 to B4 of string into R1 and put zero into high-order byte of R1. |
| OR | R ← R OR R1 | Bingo! |

*2.60* Op code $0000_{16}$ should be an operating system call because an inadvertent attempt to execute integer data will then generate a call to the operating system so the error will be detected quickly. ("Execute integer data" here means to attempt to execute a data-set as though it were code; This can occur when data is inadvertently written over code or when the target of a branch instruction is (incorrectly) the data.) Note that the number of $0_2$ bits in $0000_{16}$ depends on the instruction layout—the number of bits in the opcode.

*2.65* Assume here that the overflow checking is done dynamically, not in advance as in Exercise 2.38.

**Answer 2.55**

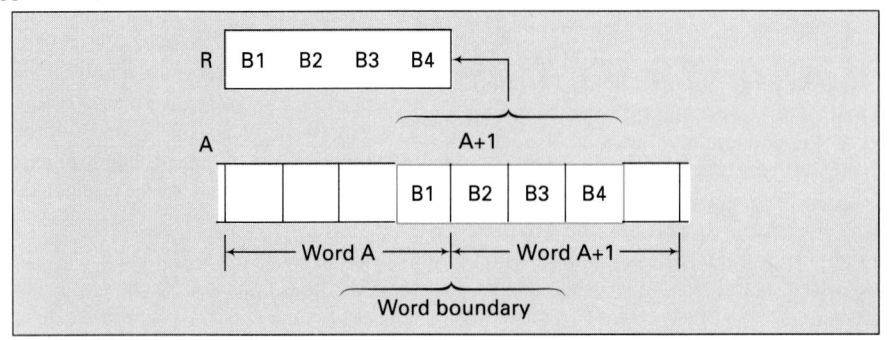

factorial: **If** R1 < 1, call the error handler.
**If** there is no space on the stack, call the error handler.
**If** R1 < 3, **return** R1.
**Else**
Push R1 onto the stack
R1 ← top-of-stack × factorial (R1 − 1)
On overflow, **goto** error handler.
**Endif**

Notice here and in 2.38 that the usual definition of 0! = 1 is ignored.

*2.70* Following is one solution: Assume that all memory accesses use indexed addressing using index register N. We will clear N and use what amounts to absolute addressing. The following three instructions clear N (as well as A and CCR):

| LOAD A ← 0(N) | Load A with the arbitrary value found at address 0 indexed by the value that is initially in N. |
| SUBTRACT A ← A − 0(N) | Subtract the same arbitrary value from A to clear it. |
| COPY N ← A | Copy A to N, clearing N and CCR. |

Let *EP* be the entry-point address of the called procedure. When the calling procedure wishes to jump to the called procedure, it executes a JUMP *EP* instruction (after clearing CCR as above). However, it must first place the return address, which is the address of the statement following the JUMP *EP* instruction, in a place where the called procedure can use it to return with. Assume that there is a JUMP instruction immediately preceding the entry point of the called procedure, that the address of this JUMP instruction is *RET*, that the address of the second word of the JUMP instruction is *BTA*, and that *BTA* holds the branch-target address of the JUMP instruction itself. We let the calling procedure store the return address there. (Note that this is self-modifying code.) The called procedure can then return to the calling procedure by branching to the instruction at *RET*, which then branches to the return address just placed there by the calling procedure.

We may assume that the compiler has loaded some memory location, say *RAL* in the calling procedure, with the required return address. Then the following code sequence within the calling procedure sets up the return code and branches to the called procedure:

| LOAD A ← *RAL*(N) | Put the return address in A. |
| STORE *BTA*(N) ← A | Modify the JUMP instruction at *RET* so it will branch to the return address. |
| JUMP *EP* | Jump to the called procedure. |

The called procedure can return to the calling procedure by executing the following code:

| JUMP *RET* | Jump to the instruction at *RET*, which then jumps to the return address placed there by the calling procedure. |

The calling procedure may pass arguments to the called procedure by storing them in some preassigned addresses within the called procedure, say just before the instruction that returns control to the calling procedure.

*2.75* As a general rule, when passing parameters by value, the calling procedure passes copies of the arguments to the called procedure, and when passing parameters by reference, the called procedure passes the addresses of the arguments to the called procedure. The choice of mechanism, then, depends on the type of procedure (e.g., nonrecursive, recursive, coroutine) and the types of arguments (simple variables, arrays, or structures).

1. Passing the arguments in a stack supports call by value and works for nonrecursive and recursive procedures. However, coroutines require a more flexible save mechanism. The use of a stack works for simple variables, but it is not suited for structures, and large arrays may use up the stack.
2. The use of registers for arguments is fast, supports call by value only, and limits the types of arguments to a few simple values. It does not work for recursive procedures or coroutines (without an additional save mechanism).
3. Passing parameter addresses in a stack precludes call by value, because the called procedure can alter the actual parameters. It is also slower than the previous techniques because of the extra level of indirection. However, it works for nonrecursive and recursive procedures as well as for coroutines, and it is suitable for simple variables, arrays, and structures.

4. The use of a parameter list supports call by value. With a suitable mechanism for allocating memory for the parameter list (e.g., heap allocation), it will support coroutines as well as recursive and nonrecursive procedures. For recursive procedures and coroutines the called procedure will additionally need to save the address of the parameter list.
5. This is similar to method 4 but supports parameter passage by reference. Resolving the arguments is slightly slower because of the extra level of indirection involved, but the called procedure does not need to copy the arguments, which saves both time and memory.

*2.80* Accessing arrays of data is naturally done with index registers and is difficult without them.

## Chapter 3

*3.5* The delay can be as long as it takes the CPU to execute the entire instruction if the instruction is non-interruptible and the interrupt comes at the very beginning of the instruction. By assumption, the MOVE STRING instruction can move (copy) a 16-KB string from one memory location to another; we will further assume that each move operation takes two memory cycles, one for fetching and one for storing the characters.
   a. Each fetch-and-store operation moves 16 bytes and takes 40 ns. Thus the maximum time is about (40ns)(16K)2/16, or a little more than 80 $\mu$s.
   b. Each fetch-and-store operation moves 2 bytes and takes 125 ns. Thus the timing is about (125ns)(2)(16K)/2, or a little more than 2 ms.

*3.10* If a low-priority interrupt is pending following a RETURN FROM EXCEPTION, then the CPU will immediately respond to that interrupt, unless it is masked or below the minimum priority allowed (assuming maskable or prioritized interrupts).

*3.15* The memory-port controller controls a single memory unit on a bus. It receives requests from the system bus but must request access to the system bus from the bus controller. The bus controller effectively controls all the devices connected to the bus. Most of these devices have local control, for cycling the memory unit, for example, but the bus controller determines what data or requests are allowed to use the bus and when.

*3.20* The instructions use 2 MBS, so 3 MBS are available for DMA I/O. If each I/O operation requires two instructions and if the I/O is done with a load operation and a store operation, it is reasonable to assume that half of the bandwidth is for data and half for I/O. In this case only 0.5 MBS of bandwidth are used by the I/O.

*3.30* When an interrupt occurs, the processor stores its program context at a specific memory location and masks all interrupts. It then moves its program context to a convenient memory location (probably on a stack used for this purpose), clears the interrupt mask, and continues handling the interrupt. When another interrupt occurs, the specific memory location is available again.

*3.35* If the addresses indicate that the requests are for the two separate banks, which involves comparing only a single bit of the address, then both requests are sent to the memory units at the same time. These memory requests use different data paths. If they are to the same bank, then requestor 0 gets priority and requestor 1 must try again. The grant lines tell the requestors when they have connections to memory. (See figure on pg. 441.)

*3.40* Programs used in scientific and engineering applications tend to require complicated arithmetic operations. As a result they are CPU-intensive programs, which use much less than 1 byte of I/O per instruction. In contrast, I/O-intensive applications are typically those used in business data processing such as payroll and inventory, which involve very simple arithmetic and large amounts of data. If a computer has a small memory, more of its data will have to be kept on disks (for paging, for example). Thus small-memory computers are more likely to need this much I/O.

## Chapter 4

*4.4* Low-order interleaving guarantees that array elements are stored in many banks of memory so array access can be faster. Instruction access can be faster, if pipelined, because successive instructions are in different memory banks. Low-order interleaving does a good job of randomizing memory locations so

## Answer 3.35

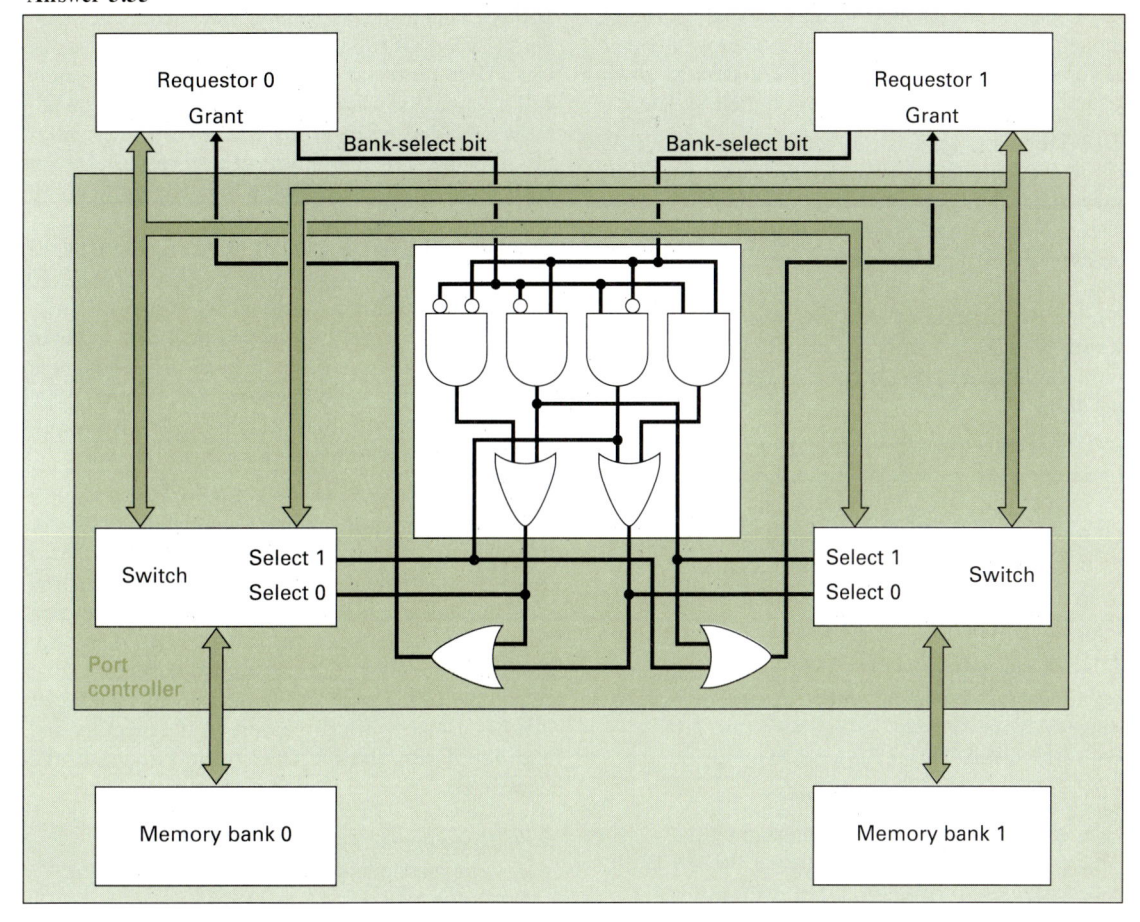

that simultaneous access to different memory locations is likely to be to different memory banks.

If there is a hard (persistent) memory failure, high-order interleave allows relatively simple use of the remaining memory. High-order interleave allows the program to determine which bank of memory is used for a given purpose and to put instructions and data, say, in different banks. Arrays can be put in different memory banks so that multiple arrays can be accessed simultaneously.

**4.5** Because the MAR is within the physical memory unit, the CPU can send the address to the memory unit ahead of the data, and the memory unit can store the address in the MAR. With the MAR loaded, the CPU can later send the data to the MDR using the same bus. For read operations, the CPU sends the address to the MAR and at some later time the memory unit sends that data from the MDR to the CPU. In both of these cases the address and data are in transit at different times so it is economic to multiplex the same bus lines for addresses and data. (For very high speed computers, the multiplexing slows operation, so multiplexing is not usually used for them.)

**4.10** $\log_f(B/b \times W/w)$ devices are in each path from the CPU to the memory chips themselves. Each of these decoders will have, say, two gate delays. Thus there are $2 \times \log_f(B/b \times W/w)$ gate delays for the memory described. As the number of devices in the memory increases, the time required to create all the copies of the address increases. Note that even though the memory devices continue to grow, another factor also causes the number of decoders to grow: Users want ever-larger memories on their systems.

*4.14* Direct-mapped cache requires only a single cache access followed by a check of the tag and address fields. Fully associative cache requires an associative memory table look-up followed by the cache access and, then perhaps, a tag check. Fully associative cache allows the maximum flexibility in determining the location of an entry. Any situation that causes a miss in a fully associative cache causes a miss in any other type of cache, but the converse is not true.

*4.19* The effective access time $A$ of a memory system with a two-level cache is given by
$$A = c_1 h_1 + c_2(h_2 - h_1) + m(1 - h_2).$$
Using the values suggested in Exercises 4.18 and 4.19,
$$A = 1.7 + 1.56 + 0.8 = 4.06.$$
Thus this memory system is about 10 times faster than one without the two caches.

*4.24* The performance of computers with cache will equal that of computers without cache in $n$ years, where $n$ is the smallest integer such that $1.15^n \geq 2$. For $n$ the ceiling is $(\log 2)/(\log 1.15) = 5$.

*4.28* \$32 + \$5/MB of main memory.

*4.34*
1. In a memory that is addressed by the look-up key: Here the size of the key is limited to the size of the table.
2. In a memory that is addressed by part of the key, the low-order bits, say: The high-order bits are then in the table along with the value, and the high-order key bits are checked against the overflow bits to be sure that the correct table entry is found. Overflow, entries that fall on the same key value, is kept in memory and accessed by a special mechanism.
3. Do the same as in method 2, but allow each key to address several table values. Then the high-order bit comparison selects the one that matches, if one does. If there is no match, the special mechanism determines which entry to discard when making room for the new one.
4. Use a table that is accessed not by the key as an address but as the content of part of the memory. In other words, use an associative or content-addressable memory.

*4.38* One additional assumption is needed that was not articulated in the exercise statement: The number of disks that can be simultaneously written at one time. Here we make the assumption that the system will have one disk controller and that the system administrator has reserved space for writing the power-fail state in contiguous blocks of disk space. Thus we need to determine how long it will take to write all 16 GB.

The write rate is 100 KB in 10 ms, or $10^7$ bytes/second. Thus 16 GB requires $16 \times 10^3$ MB/10 MBS = 1600 seconds, or about 27 minutes. It may be worth noting that the hypothetical disk is about 5 times faster than most mainframe disks. Thus the actual write time would be more like $2\frac{1}{2}$ hours. Also, the CPU time and initial delay is irrelevant because it takes so long to transfer the data to the disks.

*4.44* When a device other than the CPU accesses a bank of memory, that memory bank will be busy for one memory cycle. Under the assumption that a memory cycle is longer than a CPU clock cycle, the CPU may not access the same bank of memory during the memory cycle. Thus the memory has been "stolen" for some CPU cycles. Even if the memory cycle equals the CPU cycle, an I/O device will steal cycles if it has a higher-priority access to the memory and both the device and the CPU request access to the same bank.

*4.48*
1. soldered connections;
2. capacitors on a punch card (IBM 360);
3. diodes;
4. permanently charged magnetic cores;
5. permanently charged magnetic rods;
6. gates in ICs;
7. ICs with mask-programmed memory;
8. ICs with fuses for connections;
9. permanent horseshoe magnets in a magnetic-core structure;
10. toggle switches.

*4.53* With 25- to 50-ms disk access time, spending 1 ms in software to decide what to do (which would be slow for most current computers) does not affect access time much. On the other hand, adding even one entire microsecond on accessing main memory from cache would be very noticeable. Also, because of the relative sizes, the hit rates in cache are nearly always low compared with those in the main, paged memory. Furthermore, because the disk access time is so slow, most computers will try to find some other task to execute while waiting for the data from disk. However, starting another task requires that the operating system be called to start it. Thus some of the software overhead for the disk access is also used to decide what else to do while the access is being performed.

*4.58*  1. If code and data are mingled, corruption of the code is much more likely when a program has an error in it. This makes determining what actually caused the error more difficult.
2. Code usually goes to the instruction decoder of the CPU, while data generally goes to the execution units or registers.
3. The optimal caching algorithms are very different for code than for data. Thus separating the code from data facilitates choosing "optimal" algorithms for each.
4. If separate caches are used for code and for data, as point 3 suggests, then separation of the code and data spaces keeps the data cache from being "polluted" by instructions and vice versa.

Obviously any type of program that changes data to code, like loaders and compilers, must have some special mechanisms to do this. Following are some of the ways that loaders and compilers can operate on code as if it were data:
1. Have a special class of I/O that transfers code images from disk to the code area of memory. This then requires that linking or compiling be done to files on a disk and that the actual loading be done from a disk. Most systems use disk files like this for executable codes.
2. Allow the code-space and data-space definitions to be under program control. Then the problem becomes how to securely change the mode of memory access, not how the different uses can access the same memory location. Many computers use this approach.
3. Obviously there could be a special type of operation to allow what is normally a data store to go to code space.

*4.68*  Some partial solutions:
1. Add a cache to the memory system.
2. Increase the size of main memory so that fewer accesses go to the disk, which, relative to memory, is extremely slow. This will suffice by itself only if the apparent access time to main memory is much less than 200 ns, which requires a cache.
3. Increase the I/O transfer rate. (This method requires others techniques too.)
4. Add a cache to the disk to reduce average disk access time (needs others techniques too).
5. Increase the size of I/O accesses so that, for example, entire jobs are paged in when the first page fault occurs, which reduces the number of disk accesses.
6. Increase the intelligence of the paging system to reduce the number of accesses to the disk.

*4.73*  a. The cache is simplified because it deals mostly with alignment requests. The CPU can use its microcode to do the segmentation to aligned blocks.
b. This method reduces the complexity of the CPU microcode, putting some of it in the cache, in effect. It also allows the cache to optimize its operation depending on the characteristics of the cache and memory.
c. This one avoids thrashing the contents of the cache with a single instruction that references very large data sets. It avoids any problems of not having cache space for the data of a single instruction.

It is unlikely that any of these methods is superior for most architectures or even for most implementations.

*4.78*  The multiplexing of data and the fan-out of the address both require $\log_2 N$ gate delays for $N$ memory cells. Therefore the access time is at least $2 \log_2 N$ gate delays.

Because memories continue to grow exponentially, the number of gate delays to access memory will continue to increase indefinitely. CPU speeds should increase slightly faster than gate speeds because of increasing parallelism in CPUs.

## Chapter 5

*5.5*  In 30 ms the PC can execute 30,000 instructions. In 1/3600th of a minute, it can execute 16,666 instructions, and on the average the rotational latency is $\frac{1}{2}$ revolution. Thus the CPU can execute 8333 instructions.

*5.9*  Having separate control lines allows for expansion to more complex bus functions such as DMA,

444    Computer Architecture

which can simultaneously issue a I/O-read and memory-write operation or an I/O-write and memory-read-operation.

## Chapter 6

**6.5** The time it takes the pipe to produce 10 products is

$$N \text{ operations} = (\text{number of stages} + N - 1) \times \text{cycle time}$$
$$= (4 + N - 1) \times 200 \text{ ns}$$
$$= (N + 3) \times 200 \text{ ns}$$
$$= 2.6 \text{ } \mu\text{s}.$$

**6.10** The no-overlap and maximum-overlap cases are illustrated below. In the maximum-parallelism case, it is assumed that the result can be put away and delivered as an operand to another unit in the same cycle.

**6.15** Vector speed is greater when $I + pn < Sn$ or $I < (S - p)n$. For reasonable machines $S > p$, so $S - p > 0$. Thus the vector speed exceeds scalar speed when $n > I/(S - p)$. For the CRAY-1 this is true when $n > 5$.

**6.20** Instead of dealing with speed, it is easier to deal with time. The total time for a job, where $v$ is the fraction of vectorized code, $R$ is the scalar speed, and $S$ is the vector speedup, is

$$\text{Time} = \frac{1 - v}{R} + \frac{v}{RS} = \frac{S(1 - v) + v}{RS}.$$

The table for this function is as follows:

| Percent Vectorization | Job Time 10 × scalar | Speedup of Job | Job Time 100 × scalar | Speedup of Job |
|---|---|---|---|---|
| 0.400 | 0.640 | 1.563 | 0.604 | 1.656 |
| 0.500 | 0.550 | 1.818 | 0.505 | 1.980 |
| 0.600 | 0.460 | 2.174 | 0.406 | 2.463 |
| 0.700 | 0.370 | 2.703 | 0.307 | 3.257 |
| 0.750 | 0.325 | 3.077 | 0.258 | 3.883 |
| 0.800 | 0.280 | 3.571 | 0.208 | 4.808 |
| 0.850 | 0.235 | 4.255 | 0.159 | 6.309 |
| 0.900 | 0.190 | 5.263 | 0.109 | 9.174 |
| 0.950 | 0.145 | 6.897 | 0.060 | 16.807 |
| 1.000 | 0.100 | 10.000 | 0.010 | 100.000 |

From the table it is easy to see that the following approximate vectorizations, estimated by interpolation, are required for the requested speedups:

| Speedup requested | 2 | 4 | 6 | 8 |
|---|---|---|---|---|
| Vectorization at 10× | 56 | 84 | 91 | 97 |
| Vectorization at 100× | 51 | 76 | 84 | 87 |

**6.25** Following are the issues in the RISC/CISC discussion that apply to the 80x86 and 68000 families of processors:

The richer instruction set of CISC probably does improve the execution speed of these processors.

The richer instruction sets clearly cost something because so many instructions were added from one generation to the next.

**Answer 6.10**

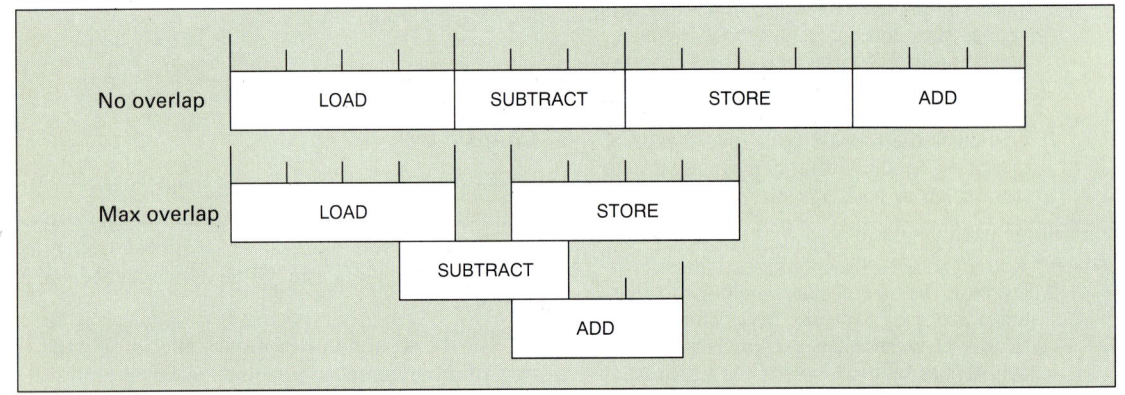

The larger instruction sets actually complicate rather than simplify compiler designs, as CISC advocates claim, because the code generator has more options.

The legal battle between AMD and Intel indicates that AMD put a lot of value on its clone. To our knowledge, no other companies have cloned either of these chips because of both difficulty and legal barriers. (Although some designs have been duplicated under license from Intel or Motorola.)

Because of the expense of I/O pins on chips, the arguments that cache reduces the importance of the reduction of the instruction-stream bandwidth is not as valid for single-chip microprocessors.

Until 1990 the overlap of instructions in microprocessors was not much of a concern. This is probably about to change. The movement toward RISC microprocessors is partially fueled by the fact that they can use multiple instruction-issue designs, which increase their virtual clock speed.

Which of RISC or CISC architectures are faster has not been determined.

Instruction caches have been available on most 68000s and on the newer 80x86s, so CISCs can use them also.

RISCs are simpler to design than CISCs, but this advantage may well be offset by the fact they are also much easier to clone.

*6.30* An array of adders can clearly be used to do the multiplication by reproducing the pencil-and-paper multiplication method. Without carry propagation, it is merely necessary to have (many) more stages to add in the carry bits. Thus this sort of technique naturally leads to very fine grained pipelining by putting latches between each pair of adders.

*6.35* Justification of adding a SAXPY (AX plus y)-instruction: Its use is relatively easy to detect, but it is only widely useful in scientific and engineering computations. Thus its justification certainly depends on the market for the machines.

Disadvantages: (1) A SAXPY functional unit is almost certainly only for a single type of operand: floating point. Decimal SAXPY, for example, is probably not useful. Thus SAXPY is probably worthless for commercial-application machines. (2) Trying to use a SAXPY certainly complicates a compiler's code generators.

*6.40* The usual way to evaluate a polynomial is to compute $(\cdots(((a_n x + a_{n-1})x + a_{n-2})x + a_{n-3})x \cdots)$.

For the stack, $x$ is pushed onto the stack, the coefficient $a_n$ are pushed onto it, and the operations are performed. It is not easy to take advantage of the much shorter time it takes to execute the operations than to fetch the operands from memory. In other words, operations operate at the memory (cache) cycle rate, not the faster CPU cycle rate. Whether the $a$ and $x$ values are passed in the stack or pointers to them are passed, the discussion is the same.

For a register machine, instructions to load the $a$- and $x$-values can precede the arithmetic instructions, so many instructions are issued between the time a LOAD instruction is issued and the time the loaded value is required. Thus the register machine can approach operating at the CPU clock rate.

*6.45* Issues to consider in this tradeoff analysis are those that may facilitate or make difficult either of the alternatives. In general, it is desirable to leave open all possibilities for future implementations.

Allowing branch destinations to be only multiples of 4 or 8 words, for example, simplifies jumping to an instruction block that is to be decoded simultaneously, called a superinstruction or a superword of instructions.

Also, allowing branches to occur only at similarly infrequent intervals similarly eases multiple-instruction decoding.

Having all the instructions be the same length simplifies decoding them, whether they are going through a pipelined decoder or a simultaneous-instruction decoder.

If all instructions have the same layout or the same format, then fast instruction decoding is facilitated for either a pipelined or a multidecoding system.

Providing vector or array instructions is useful for scientific supercomputing. Again, to facilitate both highly pipelined and simultaneous decoding of instructions, the quantity of some operations in a superinstruction may need to be limited. Vector operations allow the reduction of branch penalties.

LOOP or REPEAT, MAX and MIN instructions allow the elimination of some branch instructions, one of the nemeses of superspeed computing in all situations.

Instructions for multiprocessing must either be provided or provided for. Possibilities that appear powerful and scalable to many processors include SEND, RECEIVE, FETCH AND ADD, and MATCH AND REPLACE. Again, restrictions on the number and mix of these instructions in a superword of instructions may help in the future.

*6.50* Software control of the TLB, in the sense of dictating that some values are to be locked into the TLB, allows for faster and more predictable operation of instructions. For example, during time sharing the operating system might lock into the TLB some values that it uses frequently. During batch operation it might then unlock them, under the assumption that the time interval between operating system calls is much greater.

## Chapter 7

*7.5* For each value of $k$, set switch $k$ to "straight through" if $p_k = m_k$, and set to "crossed" otherwise. (Here the switches have been numbered in the order signals go through them from the memory modules to the processors; i.e., switch $k$ is the one in the $k$th column, starting from 0 on the left of Fig. 7.16.)

*7.10* PE35$_8$ multiplies the value in its memory location 10 by the 9 $M_{ij}$ values and stores them in its locations 11 to 19. It then reads location 15 into its accumulator. It loads location 14 from its left neighbor and adds it to its accumulator. It repeats this for its other three neighbors. It then reads location 11 from its left neighbor and stores it in its own location 20. Next it reads location 20 from its upper neighbor, which now has the diagonal element it needs. This is then added to the partial sum in its accumulator. This is repeated for the other three diagonal elements. At that point the blurred value is in the accumulator. The data layout is shown here, where each box is a blurring coefficient and the number in the box is the memory location where it is stored.

| 11 | 12 | 13 |
|----|----|----|
| 14 | 15 | 16 |
| 17 | 18 | 19 |

For PE00$_8$ the data are all the same but the loads from neighbors outside the picture must specify that they do not wrap around the PE array (to PEs that are processing pixels from the middle of the picture). If there is no such load (LOAD/NOWRAP), then each load must be masked where the mask zeros elements that are loaded from edge-around wrapping.

*7.20* Daisy chaining peripheral devices makes the operation of all of the devices in the string dependant to some extent on the correct working of the others. Some types of faults will cause all devices on the chain to be inaccessible, some will disconnect all those further from the CPU than the faulty one, and some will only affect the faulty device. Therefore daisy chaining is not a very reliable interconnection strategy. Daisy chaining also means that only one device in the string is accessible at one time. Thus daisy chaining, though it allows connecting the CPU to many devices, does not produce very high performance.

Polling peripheral devices theoretically allows a more reliable operating system design. However, most operating systems are interrupt-driven, and experience leads to reliability. Thus, interrupt-driven systems are probably actually more reliable. There is likely little effect on performance of this choice.

Mirroring disks is normally done with two separate controllers for the two disks where the two copies of the data are stored. Thus a failure in either disk or its controller does not prevent access to the data. Furthermore, in every read operation, data can be read from the disk that is closer to being in the correct rotational position. Thus, read operations will occur in about 4 ms less time on the average. However, mirroring takes twice as much disk space. It also complicates some system functions and slows write operations because two writes of each data block are required. Reads normally outnumber writes by anywhere from 10 to 1, to 5 to 1, so this performance penalty is small in comparison with the read performance enhancement.

*7.25* The idea of data rates is not really appropriate in this case. However, this nicety can be ignored by treating the data as though they are all digital. Then the input data rate is $10^8 \times 15$ bits/(0.1 sec) $\approx 10^{10}$ bits/second. The output data rate is about $10^8$ bits/second. The processing rate is approximately

$$\frac{10^7 \times 20 + 10^6 \times 20}{0.1 \text{ second}}$$

$$= 2.2 \times 10^9 \text{ operations/second}.$$

Note that this processing occurs in the eye—before signals get near the brain.

*7.35* Assign binary numbers to the PEs in a 4 × 4 array as follows:

```
0000  0100  1100  1000
0001  0101  1101  1001
0011  0111  1111  1011
0010  0110  1110  1010
```

Notice that this numbering assigns all values between 0 and 15 to the PEs and uses a gray code. Now notice that each PE number differs from the numbers of its adjacent neighbors in exactly 1 bit and that the PE number of the first element of each row or column differs in exactly 1 bit from the PE number of the last element of the same row or column. Thus toroidally adjacent PEs in the above mapping correspond to adjacent PEs within a 4-cube; the two geometries are topologically equivalent. As a final observation, the four $2 \times 2$ subsquares in the above mapping correspond to four parallel subsquares in a 4-cube.

**7.40** An obvious choice is any code that is essentially a nonlinear recursion computation such as $x_i \leftarrow f(x_{i-1})g(y_{i-1}) + h(x_{i-1})$, where $f$, $g$, and $h$ are functions that depend on the values of $x$, $y$, and $i$. The key requirement of the functions is that there be no way to compute $x_{i+1}$ until $x_i$ is computed. Then extra processors will not speed up the computation and the extra synchronization time may actually slow the program somewhat.

**7.45** It is probably not possible to come up with a complete solution. Here are a few of the things to try as you solve the design problem:
1. Whenever a changed connection is made, all data in transit are aborted and retried. This obviously works but does not provide the desired performance.
2. Stop all connections when switching is done. Try to complete sending the data after the reconfiguration is complete. Resend any data that do not get to their destinations.
3. Pipeline the reconfiguration so it "follows" the last data through the switch.

**7.50** Let us suppose we wish to perform the matrix product $\mathcal{A} = \mathcal{B}C$, where $\mathcal{B}$ is a $J \times I$ matrix, $C$ is an $I \times K$ matrix, and $\mathcal{A}$ will be a $J \times K$ matrix. Suppose we have $N$ PEs, numbered 1 to $N$, where $N < J$. Let $F = \text{CEIL}(J/N)$, where $\text{CEIL}(X)$ is the smallest integer greater than $X$. We will store the first $F$ rows of $\mathcal{B}$ in PE 1, the next $F$ rows of $\mathcal{B}$ in PE 2, and so forth. The last PE, PE $N$, may hold less than $F$ rows of $\mathcal{B}$. The figure below shows the computation of $\mathcal{A} = \mathcal{B}C$ using a linear chain of $N$ PEs. The shading shows which PEs hold the row elements of $\mathcal{B}$ and compute the row elements of $C$. The value of $F$ is 2.

For each column of $C$, each PE will produce $F$ results. For column 1, PE 1 will produce elements $a_{11}$, $a_{21}, a_{31}, \ldots, a_{F1}$. For column 2, PE 0 will produce $a_{12}$, $a_{22}, a_{32}, \ldots, a_{F2}$. When finished, PE 1 will have produced all entries in the first $F$ rows of $\mathcal{A}$, PE 2 will have produced all entries of rows $F + 1$ to $2F$ of $\mathcal{A}$, and PE $M$ will have produced all product entries of rows $(M - 1)F + 1$ to $MF$ of $\mathcal{A}$.

To perform the computation, the control unit broadcasts all entries of $C$ to the PEs in column order. The PEs simultaneously produce the dot products of the columns of $C$ and the rows they hold of $\mathcal{B}$. Thus for each element of $C$ that the control unit broadcasts, the PEs perform $F$ multiplications and $F$

**Answer 7.50**

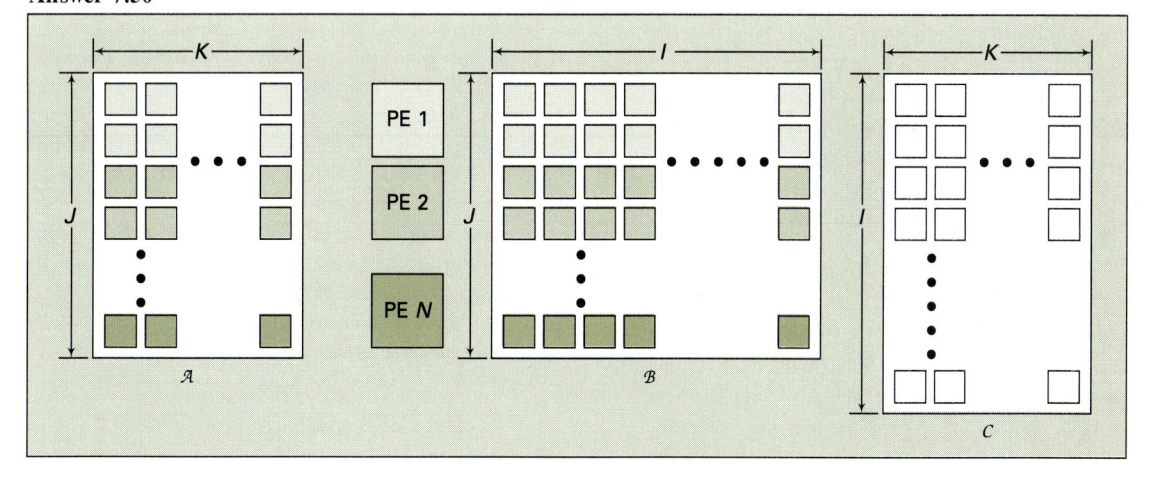

additions, producing $F$ partial results. After the control unit finishes broadcasting column 1 of $C$, the PEs will have produced the first column of $\mathcal{A}$.

Note that the speedup equals $N$ if $N$ evenly divides $J$, the number of rows in the product matrix, and is almost equal to $N$ otherwise.

**7.55** The specific operation that must be protected is the updating of records. The hazard that must be guarded against is illustrated when two processes fetch a single record, update it, and then store their updated values. Because the updates are occurring at the same time, only the one to store its result last will have been performed. (As an analogy, visualize the situation where both you and a friend withdraw $200 from your account using two different ATMs, and at the same time. If the hazard described above were allowed, you would only be charged for one of the two withdrawals.) To do this, some type of exclusion operation must be available. There are probably two main ways that this is done: by a semaphore in one of the processors, or on the disk. In either case, all updates must be protected by this semaphore and allowed by it.

The other problem that can occur is illustrated by the following situation. Suppose a single logical record is spread across several disks. After the computer starts to update the record, it finds that part of the record is on another disk that is locked. (If the computer tries to lock all disks in advance, it may end up in a deadly embrace, a deadlock caused by, e.g., two processes each waiting for a disk the other has reserved). The way record update is usually done is with a two-phase commit: In the first phase all the disks that hold parts of the record are checked to be sure that they can be accessed. They are then reserved. If there is a problem with reservation, then all of the disks are released and this first phase is restarted at a later time. In the second phase all the updates are done and the disks are then released. Two-phase commit does not require any special functionality beyond that normally available in a multiprocessor.

**7.60** a. Both LANs and WANs generally use packet switching rather than circuit switching, which is reserved for some interconnection networks. The reason for this is that circuit switching is usually centrally controlled.

b. Interconnection networks will generally use only one or a few packet sizes. LANs and WANs will generally need a variety of packet sizes for efficient use. Acknowledge packets are very small, message packets are of intermediate sizes, and data packets are generally large. There is one notable exception. In the case of telephone messages, where the data is almost continuous, the packets can all be of a single size.

c. The choice of whether the source of a packet is included is related more to the need for fault tolerance. If messages must be acknowledged, then the source is needed for the reply. If occasional missing packets can be tolerated, as in a telephone network, then there is little need for the source of the packet to be included.

d. As above, acknowledgment is primarily a matter of fault tolerance. If the sender has to be sure that a message (packet) has been received, then acknowledgment is needed. For interconnection networks, this can be guaranteed in simpler ways, so they will not normally use acknowledgment packets, even if fault tolerance is required.

**7.65** a. A bus is not generally suitable, because of contention. This follows from the number of processors and the fact that they are high-performance processors.

b. A multistage interconnection network is the most likely choice. A single stage network is somewhat less likely because of its greater cost.

c. A full crossbar switch is unlikely, again because of cost. However, every network provides crossbar functionality. In practice, a $64 \times 64$ crossbar is most likely to be implemented in several stages because of the complexity of a $64 \times 64$ full crossbar.

**7.70** One of Amdahl's rules of thumb is that memory is proportional to processing power. Because multiprocessors have higher computing power they will thus have more memory. In addition, the higher processing power requires a wider memory bandwidth. This tends to imply more memory banks so there will be more memory.

Some multiprocessing algorithms are different from scalar algorithms; more memory is required to implement many of these.

Synchronization burdens a multiprocessor with a slightly larger amount of program space. This factor is probably lost in the noise of the two items above.

**7.75** Typical HIFT advantages are as follows: Little or no software development is required, which tends to imply more reliable software. The fault detection is very frequent, so the time to recover is short. When a fault has occurred, the fault-tolerance hardware will generally isolate the error so repair is simple.

Typical HIFT applications include simple programs like those used in control applications (machinery, plants, aircraft); situations where fast repair is required; and situations where hardware faults are more likely than software faults.

Typical SIFT advantages are as follows: SIFT can readily support $n$-version programming where multiple teams program the same application to reduce the probability of software errors affecting the system. It can also catch some types of software errors, as well as hardware errors. Moreover, it uses less hardware.

Typical SIFT applications include complex programs such as those used in commercial applications; situations where minutes to repair is OK (because when rolling back to a checkpoint a restarting may take minutes); and commercial transaction processing.

# References and Suggested Readings

**Periodicals**

Students who wish to deepen their understanding of computer architecture should become familiar with the vast literature available in almost every university library. We strongly recommend the following journals:

- *Computer*, published monthly by the IEEE (Institute of Electrical and Electronics Engineers) Computer Society, contains excellent articles, technical summaries, and book reviews, among other topics of current interest. It is a must for any serious student of computer architecture.
- *Communications of the ACM* is published monthly by the Association for Computing Machinery (ACM). Like *Computer*, it does not focus on computer architecture, but it often has good articles of interest.
- *ACM Computing Surveys,* which appears bimonthly, presents excellent surveys and tutorial articles on all aspects of computer science. Topics relevant to computer architecture often appear and have included interconnection networks, microprogramming, virtual memory, fault tolerance, multiprocessors, and system deadlock avoidance.
- *IEEE Transactions on Computers* is probably the leading resource for articles on computer architecture and hardware. Its papers describe current research on many aspects of computer architecture and design.

The following journals contain articles that focus on more specific areas than those just listed. The articles describe specific computers or systems, research studies, new products and systems, and systems under development.

- *Advances in Computers*
- *Byte*
- *Computer Architecture News*
- *Computer Design*
- *Future Generations Computer Systems*
- *IBM Journal of Research and Development*

- *IBM Systems Journal*
- *IEEE Micro*
- *International Journal of Computer and Information Sciences*
- *Microcomputing*
- *Microprocessing and Microprogramming*
- *Microprocessors and Microsystems*
- *Microsystems*
- *Micro Systems Journal*
- *Mini-micro Systems*
- *Oxford Surveys in Information Technology*
- *Systems and Computers in Japan*

In addition to the wide variety of journals, the ACM, IEEE, and AFIPS (American Federation of Information Processing Societies) publish a large number of conference proceedings, workshops, standards, tutorials, videotapes, and monographs. Primary among them are (1) the Annual International Symposia on Computer Architecture, sponsored jointly by the IEEE, the IEEE Computer Society, and the ACM Special Interest Group on Computer Architecture (SIGARCH); and (2) the International Conference on Architectural Support for Programming Languages and Operating Systems (ASPLOS), sponsored jointly by the ACM SIGARCH, the ACM Special Interest Group on Programming Languages (SIGPLAN), and the IEEE Computer Society. ASPLOS focuses on issues that relate programming languages and compilers to architectural support features. The importance of the software support in the definitions of an architecture and in its operation becomes increasingly important for RISC architectures, whose operation depend on correct and optimized software. These sources present the most up-to-date descriptions available on a wide variety of research topics.

### References and Readings

We have organized the following reference material according to the general topics in the chapters. The references are intended as a starting point for further reading rather than as a complete or comprehensive bibliography on the topics. The references are divided according to the following topics:

- Associative and Bit-slice Processors..........................
- Cache Coherence in Multiprocessors..........................
- Cache Memory ...............................................
- Computer Architecture ......................................
- Computer Organization .....................................
- Dataflow and Demand-driven Architectures ..................
- Digital System Design .....................................

- Early Computers and Computer History
- Fault Tolerance
- IBM PC and Intel Microprocessors
- Instruction-set Issues
- Interconnection Networks
- Memory and Memory Technology
- Microprocessors
- Microprogramming and Mircoprogrammed Control
- Multiple-processor Systems
- Neural Computing
- Operating Systems
- Parallel Processors and Supercomputers
- Performance Benchmarks
- Pipelining
- RISC and CISC
- SIMD Processors and Processor Arrays
- System Deadlocks
- Taxonomy
- Vector Processors

## Associative and Bit-slice Processors

Foster, C. C. (1976) *Content-addressable Parallel Processors.* New York: Van Nostrand Reinhold.

Thurber, K. J. (1976) *Large Scale Computer Architecture: Parallel and Associative Processors.* Rochelle Park, N. J.: Hayden Book Company.

Thurber, K. J., and Wald, L. D. (1975) Associative and parallel processors. *ACM Computing Surveys, 7(4),* 215–255.

Weems, C., Lawton, D., Levitan, S., Riseman, E., Hanson, A., and Callahan, M. (1985) Iconic and symbolic processing using a content addressable array parallel processor. *Proceedings of the 1985 IEEE Computer Society Conference on Computer Vision and Pattern Recognition.* Los Angeles: IEEE Computer Society Press, pp. 598–607.

Yau, S. S., and Fung, H. S. (1977) Associative processor architecture—a survey. *ACM Computing Surveys, 9(1),* 3–27.

## Cache Coherence in Multiprocessors

Censier, L. M., and Feautrier, P. (1978) A new solution to coherence problems in multicache systems. *IEEE Transactions on Computers, C-27(12),* 1112–1118.

Chaiken, D., Fields, C., Kurihara, K., and Agarwal, A. (1990) Directory-based cache coherence in large-scale multiprocessors. *Computer, 23(6),* 49–58.

Cheong, H., and Veidenbaum, A.V. (1988) A cache coherence scheme with fast selective invalidation. *Proceedings of the 15th Annual International Symposium on Computer Architecture.* Washington, D.C.: IEEE Computer Society Press, pp. 299–307.

Cheong, H., and Veidenbaum, A.V. (1990) Compiler-directed cache management in multiprocessors. *Computer, 23(6),* 39–47.

Dubois, M., and Briggs, F. A. (1982) Effects of cache coherency in multiprocessors. *IEEE Transactions on Computers, C-31(11),* 1083–1099.

Dubois, M., and Thakkar, S. (1990) Guest editors' introduction: Cache architectures in tightly coupled multiprocessors. *Computer, 23(6),* 9–11.

Hill, M. D., and Larus, J. R. (1990) Cache considerations for multiprocessor programmers. *Communications of the ACM, 33(8),* 97–102.

Patel, J. H. (1982) Analysis of multiprocessors with private cache memories. *IEEE Transactions on Computers, C-31(4),* 296–304.

Rudolph, L., and Segall, Z. (1984) Dynamic decentralized cache schemes for MIMD parallel processors. *Proceedings of the 11th Annual International Symposium on Computer Architecture.* Los Angeles: IEEE Computer Society Press, pp. 340–347.

Stenström, P. (1990) A survey of cache coherence schemes for multiprocessors. *Computer, 23(6),* 12–24.

Sweazey, P., and Smith, A. J. (1986) A class of compatible cache consistency protocols and their support by the IEEE Futurebus. *Proceedings of the 13th Annual International Symposium on Computer Architecture.* Washington, D.C.: IEEE Computer Society Press, pp. 414–423.

Tang, C. K. (1976) Cache system design in the tightly coupled multiprocessor system. *AFIPS Conference Proceedings NCC, 45,* 749–753.

### *Cache Memory*

Archibald, J., and Baer, J.-L. (1986) Cache coherence protocols: Evaluation using a multiprocessor simulation model. *ACM Transactions on Computer Systems, 4(4),* 273–298.

Bell, J., Casasent, D., and Bell, C. G. (1974) An investigation of alternative cache organizations. *IEEE Transactions on Computers, C-23(4),* 346–351.

Briggs, F. A., and Dubois, M. (1983) Effectiveness of private caches in multiprocessor systems with parallel-pipelined memories. *IEEE Transactions on Computers, C-32(1),* 48–59.

Glass, B. (1989) Caching in on memory systems. *Byte, 14(3),* 281–285.

Goodman, J. R. (1983) Using cache memory to reduce processor-memory traffic. *Proceedings of the 10th Annual International Symposium on Computer Architecture.* Washington, D.C.: IEEE Computer Society Press, pp. 124–131.

Higbie, L. (1990) Quick and easy cache performance analysis. *Computer Architecture News, 15(2),* 33–44.

Hill, M. D. (1988) A case for direct mapped caches. *Computer, 21(12),* 25–40.

Jouppi, N. P. (1990) Improving direct-mapped cache performance by the addition of a small fully-associative cache and prefetch buffers. *Proceedings of the 17th Annual International Symposium on Computer Architecture.* Los Angeles: IEEE Computer Society Press, pp. 364–373.

Meade, R. M. (1971) Design approaches for cache memory control. *Computer Design, 10(1),* 87–93.

Patterson, D. A., Garrison, P., Hill, M., Lioupis, D., Nyberg, C., Sippel, T., and Van Dyke, K. (1983) Architecture of a VLSI instruction cache for a RISC. *Proceedings of the 10th Annual International Symposium on Computer Architecture.* Los Angeles: IEEE Computer Society Press, pp. 108–116.

Przybylski, S. A. (1990) *Cache and Memory Hierarchy Design: A Performance-Directed Approach.* San Mateo, Calif.: Morgan Kauffman Publishers.

Przybylski, S. A., Horowitz, M., and Hennessy, J. L. (1988) Performance trade-offs in cache design. *Proceedings of the 15th Annual International Symposium on Computer Architecture.* Washington, D.C.: IEEE Computer Society Press, pp. 290–298.

Smith, A. J. (1982) Cache memories. *ACM Computing Surveys, 14(3),* 473–530.

Smith, A. J. (1985) Disk cache—miss ratio analysis and design considerations. *ACM Transactions on Computer Systems, 3(3),* 161–203.

Smith, A. J. (1986) Bibliography and readings on CPU cache memories and related topics. *Computer Architecture News, 14(1),* 22–42.

Smith, A. J. (1987) Line (block) size choice for CPU cache memories. *IEEE Transactions of Computers, C-36(9),* 1063–1075.

Smith, J. E. (1981) A study of branch prediction strategies. *Proceedings of the 8th Annual International Symposium on Computer Architecture.* Los Angeles: IEEE Computer Society Press, pp. 135–148.

Smith, J. E., and Goodman, J. R. (1985) Instruction cache replacement policies and organizations. *IEEE Transactions on Computers, C-34(3),* 234–241.

## Computer Architecture

Baer, J.-L. (1980) *Computer Systems Architecture.* Rockville, Md.: Computer Science Press.

Baer, J.-L. (1984) Computer architecture. *Computer, 17(10),* 77–87.

Bell, C. G., and Newell, A. (1971) *Computer Structures: Readings and Examples.* New York: McGraw-Hill Book Company.

Dasgupta, S. (1984) *The Design and Description of Computer Architectures.* New York: John Wiley & Sons.

Dasgupta, S. (1989) *Computer Architecture. A Modern Synthesis.* Volume 1: *Foundations.* New York: John Wiley & Sons.

Dasgupta, S. (1989) *Computer Architecture. A Modern Synthesis.* Volume 2: *Advanced Topics.* New York: John Wiley & Sons.

De Blasi, M. (1990) **Computer Architecture.** Reading, Mass.: Addison-Wesley Publishing Company.

Doran, R. W. (1979) *Computer Architecture: A Structured Approach.* New York: Academic Press.

Flores, I. (1969) *Computer Organization.* Englewood Cliffs, N. J.: Prentice-Hall.

Foster, C. C., and Iberall, T. (1985) *Computer Architecture.* Third edition. New York: Van Nostrand Reinhold Company.

Hennessy, J. L., and Patterson, D. A. (1990) *Computer Architecture: A Quantitative Approach.* San Mateo, Calif.: Morgan Kaufmann Publishers.

Huck, J. C., and Flynn, M. J. (1989) *Analyzing Computer Architectures.* Washington, D.C.: IEEE Computer Society Press.

Kain, R. Y. (1989) *Computer Architecture: Software and Hardware.* Englewood Cliffs, N.J.: Prentice-Hall.

Keller, R. M. (1975) Look-ahead processors. *ACM Computing Surveys, 7(4),* 177–195.

Klingman, E. E. (1977) *Microprocessor Systems Design.* Englewood Cliffs, N.J.: Prentice-Hall.

Kuck, D. J. (1978) *The Structure of Computers and Computations.* Volume I. New York: John Wiley & Sons.

Kuck, D. J., Lawrie, D. H., and Sameh, A. H. (1977) *High Speed Computer and Algorithm Organization.* New York: Academic Press.

Lavington, S. H. (1976) *Processor Architecture.* Manchester, England: NCC Publications.

Maytal, B., Iacobovici, S., Alpert, D., Biran, D., Levy, J., and Tov, S.Y. (1989) Design considerations for a general-purpose microprocessor. *Computer, 22(1),* 66–76.

Myers, G. J. (1982) *Advances in Computer Architecture.* Second edition. New York: John Wiley & Sons.

Shiva, S. G. (1985) *Computer Design and Architecture.* Boston, Mass.: Little, Brown, & Company.

Siewiorek, D. P., Bell, C. G., and Newell, A. (1982) *Computer Structures: Principles and Examples.* New York: McGraw-Hill Book Company.

Stallings, W. (1990) *Computer Organization and Architecture.* Second edition. New York: Macmillan Publishing Company.

Stone, H. S. (1990) **High-Performance Computer Architecture.** Second edition. Reading, Mass.: Addison-Wesley Publishing Company.

Stone, H. S., editor (1980) *Introduction to Computer Architecture.* Second edition. Chicago: Science Research Associates.

Van de Goor, A. J. (1989) **Computer Architecture and Design.** Reading, Mass.: Addison-Wesley Publishing Company.

Ward, S. A., and Halstead, R. H., Jr. (1990) *Computation Structures.* Cambridge, Mass.: MIT Press.

**Computer Organization**

Gear, C. W. (1969) *Computer Organization and Programming.* New York: McGraw-Hill Book Company.

Gorsline, G. W. (1986) *Computer Organization: Hardware/Software.* Second edition. Englewood Cliffs, N.J.: Prentice-Hall.

Hamacher, V. C., Vranesic, Z. G., and Zaky, S. G. (1984) *Computer Organization.* Second edition. New York: McGraw-Hill Book Company.

Hayes, J. P. (1978) *Computer Architecture and Organization.* New York: McGraw-Hill Book Company.

Hellerman, H. (1973) *Digital Computer System Principles.* Second edition. New York: McGraw-Hill Book Company.

Hill, F. J., and Peterson, G. R. (1973) *Digital Systems: Hardware Organization and Design.* New York: John Wiley & Sons.

Sloan, M. E. (1972) *Computer Hardware and Organization: An Introduction.* Chicago: Science Research Associates.

Stone, H. S. (1972) *Introduction to Computer Organization and Data Structures.* New York: McGraw-Hill Book Company.

Tanenbaum, A. S. (1976) *Structured Computer Organization.* Englewood Cliffs, N.J.: Prentice-Hall.

**Dataflow and Demand-driven Architectures**

Ackerman, W. B. (1982) Data flow languages. *Computer, 15(2),* 15–25.

Agerwala, T., and Arvind (1982) Data flow systems: Guest editors' introduction. *Computer, 15(2),* 10–13.

Arvind, and Culler, D. E. (1986) Dataflow architectures. *Annual Review of Computer Science, 1,* 225–253.

Carlson, W. W., and Hwang, K. (1985) Algorithmic performance of dataflow multiprocessors. *Computer, 18(12),* 30–40.

Davis, A. L., and Keller, R. M. (1982) Data flow program graphs. *Computer, 15(2),* 26–41.

Gajski, D. D., Padua, D. A., Kuck, D. J., and Kuhn, R. H. (1982) A second opinion on dataflow machines and languages. *Computer, 15(2),* 58–69.

Gurd, J. R., Kirkham, C. C., and Watson, I. (1985) The Manchester prototype dataflow computer. *Communications of the ACM, 28(1),* 34–52.

Treleaven, P. C., Brownbridge, D. R., and Hopkins, R. P. (1982) Data-driven and demand-driven computer architecture. *ACM Computing Surveys, 14(1),* 93–143.

Veen, A. H. (1986) Dataflow machine architecture. *ACM Computing Surveys, 18(1),* 365–396.

Watson, I., and Gurd, J. (1982) A practical data flow computer. *Computer, 15(2)*, 51–57.

**Digital System Design**

Bartee, T. C. (1985) *Digital Computer Fundamentals.* Sixth edition. New York: McGraw-Hill Book Company.

Breeding, K. J. (1989) *Digital Design Fundamentals.* Englewood Cliffs, N.J.: Prentice-Hall.

Gosling, J. B. (1980) *Design of Arithmetic Units for Digital Computers.* New York: Springer-Verlag New York.

Hayes, J. P. (1984) *Digital System Design and Microprocessors.* New York: McGraw-Hill Book Company.

Hwang, K. (1979) *Computer Arithmetic: Principles, Architecture, and Design.* New York: John Wiley & Sons.

IEEE (1985) IEEE standard for binary floating-point arithmetic, ANSI/IEEE Standard 754-1985, © 1985 by IEEE. Reprinted in *SIGPLAN Notices, 22(2)*, 9–25.

Langdon, G. G., Jr. (1982) *Computer Design.* San Jose, Calif.: Computeach Press.

Lewin, D. (1972) *Theory and Design of Digital Computers.* New York: John Wiley & Sons.

Lewin, M. H. (1983) **Logic Design and Computer Organization.** Reading, Mass.: Addison-Wesley Publishing Company.

Mano, M. M. (1984) *Digital Design.* Englewood Cliffs, N.J.: Prentice-Hall.

Mano, M. M. (1988) *Computer Engineering: Hardware Design.* Englewood Cliffs, N.J.: Prentice-Hall.

Marino, L. R. (1986) *Principles of Computer Design.* Rockville, Md.: Computer Science Press.

Scott, N. R. (1985) *Computer Number Systems and Arithmetic.* Englewood Cliffs, N.J.: Prentice-Hall.

Seidensticker, R. B. (1986) **The Well-Tempered Digital Design.** Reading, Mass.: Addison-Wesley Publishing Company.

Taub, H. (1982) *Digital Circuits and Microprocessors.* New York: McGraw-Hill Book Company.

Wakerly, J. F. (1990) *Digital Design Principles and Practices.* Englewood Cliffs, N.J.: Prentice-Hall.

Waser, S., and Flynn, M. T. (1982) *Introduction to Arithmetic for Digital Systems Designers.* New York: Holt, Rinehart, & Winston.

Wells, M. (1976) *Computing Systems Hardware.* Cambridge: Cambridge University Press.

Wilkinson, B. (1987) *Digital System Design.* Englewood Cliffs, N.J.: Prentice-Hall International.

## Early Computers and Computer History

Bell, C. G., and Newell, A. (1971) *Computer Structures: Readings and Examples.* New York: McGraw-Hill Book Company.

Burks, A. R., and Burks, A. W. (1988) *The First Electronic Computer: The Atanasoff Story.* Ann Arbor, Mich.: University of Michigan Press.

Burks, A. W., and Burks, A. R. (1981) The ENIAC: first general-purpose electronic computer. *Annals of the History of Computing, 3(4),* 310–399.

Burks, A. W., Goldstine, H. H., and von Neumann, J. (1946) Preliminary discussion of the logical design of an electronic computing instrument. In W. Aspry and A. W. Burks, editors, *Papers of John von Neumann on Computing and Computer Theory.* Cambridge, Mass.: MIT Press, pp. 97–146.

Eckert, J. P., Jr., Weiner, J. R., Welsh, H. F., and Mitchell, H. F. (1951) The UNIVAC system. *Joint AIEE-IRE Computer Conference,* pp. 6–16.

Goldstine, H. H. (1972) *The Computer from Pascal to von Neumann.* Princeton, N.J.: Princeton University Press.

Leeds, M. B., Bucci, W., Scrupski, S., Chang, J., Aiken, E., and Moskowitz, C. (1968) The transistor: Two decades of progress. *Electronics,* 41 (Special Report), 77–130.

Mackintosh, A. R. (1988) Dr. Atanasoff's computer. *Scientific American, 259(2),* 90–96.

Mollenhoff, C. R. (1988) *Atanasoff: Forgotten Father of the Computer.* Ames, Iowa: Iowa State University Press.

Rosen, S. (1969) Electronic computers: A historical survey. *ACM Computing Surveys, 1(1),* 7–36.

Runyan, L. (1991) 40 Years on the Frontier. *Datamation, 7(6),* 34–58.

Samuel, A. L. (1957) Computers with European accents. *Proc. WJCC,* pp. 14–17.

Shurkin, J. (1984) *Engines of the Mind: A History of the Computer.* New York: W. W. Norton & Company.

Siewiorek, D. P., Bell, C. G., and Newell, A. (1982) *Computer Structures: Principles and Examples.* New York: McGraw-Hill Book Company.

Taub, A. H. ed. (1963) *The Collected Works of John von Neumann.* Vol. 5. New York: The Macmillan Company.

von Neumann, J. (1951) The general and logical theory of automata. In L. A. Jeffress, editor, *Cerebral Mechanisms in Behavior. The Hixon Symposium.* New York: John Wiley & Sons, pp. 1–41.

Wilkes, M. V. (1985) *Memoirs of a Computer Pioneer.* Cambridge, Mass.: MIT Press.

Wilkes, M. V., Wheeler, D. J., & Gill, S. (1951) *The Preparation of Programs for an Electronic Digital Computer.* Reading, Mass.: Addison-Wesley Press.

## Fault Tolerance

Adams, G. B., III., Agrawal, D. P., and Seigel, H. J. (1987) A survey and comparison of fault-tolerant multistage interconnection networks. *Computer, 20(6),* 14–27.

Avižienis, A., and Kelly, J. P. J. (1984) Fault tolerance by design diversity: Concepts and experiments. *Computer, 17(8),* 67–80.

Chean, M., and Fortes, J. A. B. (1990) A taxonomy of reconfiguration techniques for fault-tolerant processor arrays. *Computer, 23(1),* 55–69.

Cristian, F. (1991) Understanding fault-tolerant distributed systems. *Communications of the ACM, 34(2),* 56–78.

Denning, P. J. (1976) Fault-tolerant operating systems. *ACM Computing Surveys, 8(4),* 359–389.

Johnson, B.W. (1989) ***Design and Analysis of Fault-tolerant Digital Systems.*** Reading, Mass.: Addison-Wesley Publishing Company.

Laprie, J.-C., Arlat, J, Béounes, C., and Kanoun, K. (1990) Definition and analysis of hardware- and software-fault-tolerant architectures. *Computer, 23(7),* 39–51.

Maxion, R. A., Siewiorek, D. P., and Elkind, S. A. (1987) Techniques and architectures for fault-tolerant computing. *Annual Review of Computer Science, 2,* 469–520.

Nelson, V. P. (1990) Fault-tolerant computing: Fundamental concepts. *Computer, 23(7),* 19–25.

Sarrazin, D. B., and Malek, M. (1984) Fault-tolerant semiconductor memories. *Computer, 17(8),* 49–56.

Serlin, O. (1984) Fault-tolerant systems in commercial applications. *Computer, 17(8),* 19–30.

Siewiorek, D. P. (1984) Architecture of fault-tolerant computers. *Computer, 17(8),* 9–18.

Siewiorek, D. P. (1990) Fault tolerance in commercial computers. *Computer, 23(7),* 26–37.

Siewiorek, D. P., and Swarz, R. S. (1982) *The Theory and Practice of Reliable System Design.* Bedford, Mass.: Digital Press.

Siewiorek, D. P., Hsiao, M.Y., Rennels, D., Gray, J., and Williams, T. (1990) Ultra-dependable architectures. *Annual Review of Computer Science, 4,* 503–515.

Singh, A. D., and Murugesan, S. (1990) Guest editors' introduction: Fault-tolerant systems. *Computer, 23(7),* 15–17.

Toy, W. N., and Morganti, M. (1984) Guest editors' introduction: Fault-tolerant computing. *Computer, 17(8),* 6–7.

## IBM PC and Intel Microprocessors

Cornejo, C., and Lee, R. (1987) Comparing IBM's Micro Channel and Apple's NuBus. *Byte, 12(12),* 83–92.

Crosswy, C., and Perez, M. (1987) Upward to the 80386. *PC Tech Journal, 5(2),* 51–66.

Cushman, R. H. (1987) EDN's 14th annual μP/μC chip directory. *EDN, 32(24),* 101–187.

DeVoney, C., and Summe, R. (1982) *IBM's Personal Computer.* Indianapolis: Que Corporation.

Henry, G. G. (1986) IBM small-system architecture and design—past, present, and future. *IBM Systems Journal, 25(3/4),* 321–333.

Intel (1991) *Microprocessors.* Volumes 1 and 2. Santa Clara, Calif.: Intel Corporation.

Norton, P. (1985) *The Peter Norton Programmer's Guide to the IBM PC.* Redmond, Wash.: Microsoft Press.

Rector, R., and Alexy, G. (1980) *The 8086 Book.* Berkeley, Calif.: Osborne/McGraw-Hill.

Sargent, M., III, and Shoemaker, R. L. (1986) **The IBM Personal Computer from the Inside Out.** Reading, Mass.: Addison-Wesley Publishing Company.

Shiell, J. (1987) The 32-bit Micro Channel. *Byte, 12(12),* 59–64.

White, R. (1990) The EISA Bus. *PC Computing, 3(4),* 204–205.

### *Instruction-set Issues*

Flynn, M. J., Johnson, J. D., and Wakefield, S. P. (1985) On instruction sets and their formats. *IEEE Transactions on Computers, C-34(3),* 242–254.

Lunde, Å. (1977) Empirical evaluation of some features of instruction set processor architectures. *Communications of the ACM, 20(3),* 143–153.

### *Interconnection Networks*

Arjomandi, E., Fischer, M. J., and Lynch, N. A. (1983) Efficiency of synchronous versus asynchronous distributed systems. *Journal of the ACM, 30(3),* 449–456.

Barnes, G. H., and Lundstrom, S. F. (1981) Design and validation of a connection network for many-processor multiprocessor systems. *Computer, 14(12),* 31–41.

Bhuyan, L. N., and Agrawal, D. P. (1983) Design and performance of generalized interconnection networks. *IEEE Transactions on Computers, C-32(12),* 1081–1090.

Bhuyan, L. N., and Agrawal, D. P. (1984) Generalized hypercube and hyperbus structures for a computer network. *IEEE Transactions on Computers, C-33(4),* 323–333.

Bhuyan, L. N. (1987) Guest editor's introduction: Interconnection networks for parallel and distributed processing. *Computer, 20(6),* 9–12.

Bhuyan, L. N., Yang, Q., and Agrawal, D. P. (1989) Performance of multiprocessor interconnection networks. *Computer, 22(2),* 25–37.

Chen, P.-Y., Lawrie, D. H., Padua, D. A., and Yew, P.-C. (1981) Interconnection networks using shuffles. *Computer, 14(12),* 55–64.

Dias, D. M., and Jump, J. R. (1981) Packet switching interconnection networks for modular systems. *Computer, 14(12),* 43–53.

Feng, T.-Y. (1981) A survey of interconnection networks. *Computer, 14(12),* 12–27.

Kruskal, C. P., and Snir, M. (1983) The performance of multistage interconnection networks for multiprocessors. *IEEE Transactions on Computers, C-32(12),* 1091–1098.

Kumar, V. P., and Reddy, S. M. (1987) Augmented shuffle-exchange multistage interconnection networks. *Computer, 20(6),* 30–40.

Marcus, M. J. (1977) The theory of connecting networks and their complexity: A review. *Proceedings of the IEEE, 65(9),* 1263–1271.

Mudge, T. N., Hayes, J. P., and Winsor, D. C. (1987) Multiple bus architectures. *Computer, 20(6),* 42–48.

Patel, J. H. (1981) Performance of processor–memory interconnections for multiprocessors. *IEEE Transactions on Computers, C-30(10),* 771–780.

Reed, D. A., and Grunwald, D. C. (1987) The performance of multicomputer interconnection networks. *Computer, 20(6),* 63–73.

Siegel, H. J. (1979) Interconnection networks for SIMD machines. *Computer, 12(6),* 57–65.

Siegel, H. J. (1980) The theory underlying the partitioning of permutation networks. *IEEE Transactions on Computers, C-29(9),* 791–801.

Siegel, H. J., and McMillen, R. J. (1981) The multistage cube: A versatile interconnection network. *Computer, 14(12),* 65–76.

Spragins, J. D. (1991) **Telecommunications, Protocols, and Design.** Reading, Mass.: Addison-Wesley Publishing Company.

Tanenbaum, A. S. (1981) *Computer Networks.* Englewood Cliffs, N.J.: Prentice-Hall.

Thompson, C. D. (1978) Generalized connection networks for parallel processor intercommunication. *IEEE Transactions on Computers, C-27(12),* 1119–1125.

Wilson, A. W., Jr. (1987) Hierarchical cache/bus architecture for shared memory multiprocessors. *Proceedings of the 14th Annual International Symposium on Computer Architecture.* Washington, D.C.: IEEE Computer Society Press, pp. 244–252.

*Memory and Memory Technology*

Beausoleil, W. F., Brown, D. T., and Phelps, B. E. (1972) Magnetic bubble memory organization. *IBM Journal of Research and Development, 16(11),* 587–591.

Bosch, L. J., Downing, R. A., Keefe, G. E., Rosier, L. L., and Terlep, K. D. (1973) 1024 bit bubble memory chip. *IEEE Transactions on Magnetics, MAG-9(3),* 481–484.

Briggs, F. A., and Davidson, E. S. (1977) Organization of semiconductor memories for parallel-pipelined processors. *IEEE Transactions on Computers, C-26(2),* 162–169.

Burnett, G. J., and Coffman, E. G. (1970) A study of interleaved memory systems. *AFIPS Conference Proceedings SJCC, 36,* 467–474.

Byers, T. J. (1983) *Microprocessor Support Chips: Theory, Design, and Applications.* New York: McGraw-Hill Book Company.

Chang, H. (1972) Bubble domain memory chips. *IEEE Transactions on Magnetics, MAG-8(3),* 564–569.

Crouch, H. R., Cornett, J. B., Jr., and Eward, R. S. (1976) CCDs in memory systems move into sight. *Computer Design, 15(9),* 75–80.

Denning, P. J. (1970) Virtual memory. *ACM Computing Surveys, 2(3),* 153–189.

Hanlon, A. G. (1966) Content-addressable and associative memory systems. *IEEE Transactions on Electronic Computers, EC-15(4),* 509–521.

Hodges, D. A. (1977) Microelectronic memories. *Scientific American, 237(3),* 130–145.

Matick, R. E. (1977) *Computer Storage Systems and Technology.* New York: John Wiley & Sons.

Sarrazin, D. B., and Malek, M. (1984) Fault-tolerant semiconductor memories. *Computer, 17(8),* 49–56.

White, R. M. (1980) Disk storage technology. *Scientific American, 243(2),* 138–148.

## *Microprocessors*

Anceau, F. (1986) **The Architecture of Microprocessors.** Reading, Mass.: Addison-Wesley Publishing Company.

Holt, C. E. (1985) *Microcomputer Organization: Hardware and Software.* New York: Macmillan Publishing Company.

Tocci, R. J., and Laskowski, L. P. (1982) *Microprocessors and Microcomputers: Hardware and Software.* Second edition. Englewood Cliffs, N.J.: Prentice-Hall.

Toong, H.-M. D. (1977) Microprocessors. *Scientific Amercian, 237(3),* 146–161.

Zaks, R. (1977) *Microprocessors.* Berkeley, Calif.: Sybex Inc.

## *Microprogramming and Microprogrammed Control*

Agrawala, A. K., and Rauscher, T. G. (1976) *Foundations of Microprogramming.* New York: Academic Press.

Banerji, D. K., and Raymond, J. (1982) *Elements of Microprogramming.* Englewood Cliffs, N.J.: Prentice-Hall.

Chu, Y. (1972) *Computer Organization and Microprogramming.* Englewood Cliffs, N.J.: Prentice-Hall.

Damm, W., and Döhmen, G. (1985) Verification of microprogrammed computer architectures in the S*-system. *Proceedings of the 18th Annual Workshop* on *Microprogramming.* Washington, D.C.: IEEE Computer Society Press, pp. 61–73.

Dasgupta, S. (1979) Some aspects of high level microprogramming. *ACM Computing Surveys, 12(3),* 295–324.

Dasgupta, S. (1979) The organization of microprogram stores. *ACM Computing Surveys, 11(1),* 39–66.

Davidson, S., and Shriver, B. (1978) An overview of firmware engineering. *Computer, 11(5),* 21–33.

Davies, P. M. (1972) Readings in microprogramming. *IBM Systems Journal, 11(1),* 16–40.

Ercegovac, M. D., and Lang, T. (1985) *Digital Systems and Hardware/Firmware Algorithms.* New York: John Wiley & Sons.

Flynn, M. J., and Rosin, R. F. (1971) Microprogramming: An introduction and a viewpoint. *IEEE Transactions of Computers, C-20(7),* 727–731.

Husson, S. S. (1970) *Microprogramming: Principles and Practices.* Englewood Cliffs, N.J.: Prentice-Hall.

Koopman, P. Jr. (1987) The WISC concept. A proposal for a writable instruction set computer. *Byte, 12(4),* 187–194.

Kraft, G. D., and Toy, W. N. (1981) *Microprogrammed Control and Reliable Design of Small Computers.* Englewood Cliffs, N.J.: Prentice-Hall.

Patterson, D. A. (1983) Microprogramming. *Scientific American, 248(3),* 50–57.

Rauscher, T. G., and Adams, P. N. (1980) Microprogramming: A tutorial and survey of recent developments. *IEEE Transactions on Computers, C-29(1),* 2–20.

Rosin, R. F. (1969) Contemporary concepts of microprogramming and emulation. *ACM Computing Surveys, 1(4),* 197–212.

Salisbury, A. B. (1976) *Microprogrammable Computer Architectures.* New York: American Elsevier Publishing Company.

Schultz, G.W. (1974) Designing optimized microprogrammed control sections for microprocessors. *Computer Design, 13(4),* 119–124.

Wilkes, M.V., and Stringer, J. B. (1953) Microprogramming and the design of the control circuits in an electronic digital computer. *Proceedings of the Cambridge Philosophical Society, 49(pt. 2),* 230–238.

*Multiple-processor Systems*

Athas, W. C., and Seitz, C. L. (1988) Multicomputers: Message-passing concurrent computers. *Computer, 21(8),* 9–24.

Das, C. R., Kreulen, J.T., Thazhuthaveetil, M. J., and Bhuyan, L. N. (1990) Dependability modeling for multiprocessors. *Computer, 23(10),* 7–19.

Enslow, P. H., Jr. (1977) Multiprocessor organizations—a survey. *ACM Computing Surveys, 9(1),* 103–129.

Feitelson, D. G., and Rudolph, L. (1990) Distributed hierarchical control for parallel processing. *Computer, 23(5),* 65–77.

Frieder, O. (1990) Multiprocessor algorithms for relational-database operators on hypercube systems. *Computer, 23(11),* 13–28.

Gajski, D. D., and Peir, J.-K. (1985) Essential issues in multiprocessor systems. *Computer, 18(6),* 9–27.

Gehringer, E. F., Siewiorek, D. P., and Segall, Z. (1987) *Parallel Processing: The Cm\* Experience.* Bedford, Mass.: Digital Press.

Hwang, K. (1985) Multiprocessor supercomputers for scientific/engineering applications. *Computer, 18(6),* 57–73.

Murakami, K., Kakuta, T., Onai, R., and Ito, N. (1985) Research on parallel machine architecture for fifth-generation computer systems. *Computer, 18(6),* 76–92.

Patton, P. C. (1985) Multiprocessors: Architecture and applications. *Computer, 18(6),* 29–40.

Rettberg, R., and Thomas, R. (1986) Contention is no obstacle to shared-memory multiprocessing. *Communications of the ACM, 29(12),* 1202–1212.

Satyanarayanan, M. (1980) *Multiprocessors: A Comparative Study.* Englewood Cliffs, N.J.: Prentice-Hall.

Stenström, P. (1988) Reducing contention in shared-memory multiprocessors. *Computer, 21(11),* 26–37.

Swan, R. J., Bechtolsheim, A., Lai, K.-W., and Ousterhout, J. K. (1977) The implementation of the Cm\* multi-microprocessor. *AFIPS Conference Proceedings NCC, 46,* 645–655.

Swan, R. J., Fuller, S. H., and Siewiorek, D. P. (1977) Cm\*—a modular, multi-microprocessor. *AFIPS Conference Proceedings NCC, 46,* 637–644.

**Neural Computing**

Aleksander, I., editor (1989) *Neural Computing Architectures: The Design of Brain-like Machines.* London: North Oxford Academic Publishing Company.

DARPA (1988) *DARPA Neural Network Study. October 1987–February 1988.* Fairfax, Va.: AFCEA International Press.

Graf, H. P., Jackel, L. D., Hubbard, W. E. (1988) VLSI implementation of a neural network model. *Computer, 21(3),* 41–49.

Hecht-Nielsen, R. (1990) **Neurocomputing.** Reading, Mass.: Addison-Wesley Publishing Company.

Khanna, T. (1990) **Foundations of Neural Networks.** Reading, Mass.: Addison-Wesley Publishing Company.

Kohonen, T. (1988) An introduction to neural computing. *Neural Networks 1(1),* 3–16.

Rosenblatt, F. (1962) *Principles of Neurodynamics.* Washington, D.C.: Spartan Books.

Wasserman, P. D. (1989) *Neural Computing: Theory and Practice.* New York: Van Nostrand Reinhold Company.

## Operating Systems

Deitel, H. M. (1990) *An Introduction to Operating Systems.* Second edition. Reading, Mass.: Addison-Wesley Publishing Company.

Organick, E. I. (1973) *Computer System Organization. The B5700/B6700 Series.* New York: Academic Press.

Padua, D. A., and Wolfe, M. J. (1986) Advanced compiler optimizations for supercomputers. *Communications of the ACM, 29(12),* 1184–1201.

## Parallel Processors and Supercomputers

Buzbee, B. L., and Sharp, D. H. (1985) Perspectives on supercomputers. *Science, 227(4687),* 591–597.

Christ, N. H., and Terrano, A. E. (1984) A very fast parallel processor. *IEEE Transactions on Computers, C-33(4),* 344–350.

Cohler, E. U., and Storer, J. E. (1981) Functionally parallel architecture for array processors. *Computer, 14(9),* 28–36.

Dongarra, J. J., editor (1987) *Experimental parallel computing architectures.* New York: North-Holland.

Duncan, R. (1990) A survey of parallel computer architectures. *Computer, 23(2),* 5–16.

Fox, G. C., and Messina, P. C. (1987) Advanced computer architectures. *Scientific American, 257(4),* 66–77.

Higbie, L. C. (1973) Supercomputer architecture. *Computer, 6(12),* 48–58.

Hockney, R.W. (1987) Classification and evaluation of parallel computer systems. *Springer-Verlag Lecture Notes in Computer Science,* no. 295, pp. 13–25.

Hoshino, T. (1989) *PAX Computer: High-speed Parallel Processing and Scientific Computing.* Reading, Mass.: Addison-Wesley Publishing Company.

Hwang, K., and Briggs, F. A. (1984) *Computer Architecture and Parallel Processing.* New York: McGraw-Hill Book Company.

Kuck, D. J. (1977) A survey of parallel machine organization and programming. *ACM Computing Surveys, 9(1),* 29–59.

Levine, R. D. (1982) Supercomputers. *Scientific American, 246(1),* 118–134.

Lipovski, G. J., and Malek, M. (1987) *Parallel Computing. Theory and Comparisons.* New York: John Wiley & Sons.

Mokhoff, N. (1984) Parallelism makes strong bid for next generation computers. *Computer Design, 23(9),* 104–131.

Ranka, S. & Sahni, S. (1990) *Hypercube Algorithms.* New York: Springer-Verlag.

Schneck, P. B. (1987) *Supercomputer Architecture.* Norwell, Mass.: Kluwer Academic Publishers.

Schneck, P. B. (1990) Supercomputers. *Annual Review of Computer Science, 4,* 13–36.

## Performance Benchmarks

Berry, M., Chen, D., Koss, P., and Kuck, D. (1988) *The Perfect Club Benchmarks: Effective Performance Evaluation of Supercomputers.* CSRD report 827, Center for Supercomputing Research and Development, University of Illinois at Urbana-Champaign.

Conte, T. M., and Hwu, W.W. (1991) Benchmark characterization. *Computer, 24(1),* 48–56.

Cybenko, G., et al. (1990) Supercomputer performance evaluation and the Perfect Club. *Proceedings of the International Conference on Supercomputing.* Los Angeles: IEEE Computer Society Press.

Dongarra, J. J. (1984) *Performance of Various Computers Using Standard Linear Equations Software in a Fortran Environment.* Technical memorandum 23, Argonne National Laboratory, Chicago, Ill.

Dongarra, J. J. (1991) *Performance of Various Computers Using Standard Linear Equations Software.* Technical report CS-89-85, Computer Science Department, University of Tennessee, Knoxville.

Dongarra, J. J., Bunch, J. R., Moler, C. B., and Stewart, G.W. (1979) *LINPACK User's Guide.* Philadelphia, Penn.: SIAM Publications.

Kahaner, D. K. (1988) Benchmarks for "real" programs. *SIAM News,* 21(6), 16–17.

McMahon, F. M. (1986) *The Livermore FORTRAN Kernels: A Computer Test of Numerical Performance Range.* Technical report UCRL-55745, Lawrence Livermore National Laboratory, University of California, Livermore.

Weicker, R. P. (1984) Dhrystone: A synthetic systems programming benchmark. *Communications of the ACM, 27(10),* 1013–1030.

Weicker, R. P. (1990) An overview of common benchmarks. *Computer, 23(12),* 65–75.

## Pipelining

Chen, T. C. (1971) Parallelism, pipelining, and computer efficiency. *Computer Design, 10(1),* 69–74.

Cotten, L.W. (1965) Circuit implementation of high-speed pipeline systems. *AFIPS Conference Proceedings FJCC, 27(pt. 1),* 489–504.

Cotten, L.W. (1969) Maximum-rate pipeline systems. *AFIPS Conference Proceedings SJCC, 34,* 581–586.

Hallin, T. G., and Flynn, M. J. (1972) Pipelining of arithmetic functions. *IEEE Transactions on Computers, C-21(8),* 880–886.

Kogge, P. M. (1981) *The Architecture of Pipelined Computers.* New York: McGraw–Hill Book Company.

Kunkel, S. R., and Smith, J. E. (1986) Optimal pipelining in supercomputers. *Proceedings of the 13th Annual International Symposium on*

*Computer Architecture.* Washington, D.C.: IEEE Computer Society Press, pp. 404–414.

Lilja, D. J. (1988) Reducing the branch penalty in pipelined processors. *Computer, 21(7),* 47–55.

McFarling, S., and Hennessy, J. (1986) Reducing the cost of branches. *Proceedings of the 13th Annual International Symposium on Computer Architecture.* Washington, D.C.: IEEE Computer Society Press, pp. 396–403.

Ramamoorthy, C.V., and Kim, K.H. (1974) Pipelining—the generalized concept and sequencing strategies. *AFIPS Conference Proceedings NCC, 43,* 289–297.

Ramamoorthy, C.V., and Li, H.F. (1977) Pipeline architecture. *ACM Computing Surveys, 9(1),* 61–102.

Smith, A.J., and Lee, J. (1984) Branch prediction strategies and branch target buffer design. *Computer, 17(1),* 6–22.

Thornton, J.E. (1970) *Design of a Computer—The Control Data 6600.* Glenview, Ill.: Scott, Foresman & Company.

Weiss, S., and Smith, J.E. (1984) Instruction issue logic in pipelined supercomputers. *IEEE Transactions on Computers, C-33(11),* 1013–1022.

## *RISC and CISC*

Clark, D.W., and Strecker, W.D. (1980) Comments on "the case for the reduced instruction set computer." *Computer Architecture News, 8(6),* 34–38.

Colwell, R.P., Hitchcock, C.Y., III, Jensen, E.D., Sprunt, H.M.B., and Kollar, C.P. (1985) Computers, complexity, and controversy. *Computer, 18(9),* 8–19.

Flynn, M.J., Mitchell, C.L., and Mulder, J.M. (1987) And now a case for more complex instruction sets. *Computer, 20(9),* 71–83.

Gimarc, C.E., and Milutinović, V.M. (1987) A survey of RISC processors and computers of the mid-1980s. *Computer, 20(9),* 59–69.

Goering, R. (1990) RISC processors. *High Performance Systems, 11(3),* 55–57.

Gunn, L. (1989) The problems of RISC-based designs. *Electronic Design, 37(24),* 69–74.

Huang, V.K.L. (1989) High-performance microprocessors: The RISC dilemma. *IEEE Micro, 9(4),* 13–14.

Johnson, T.L. (1987) The RISC/CISC melting pot. Classic design methods converge in the MC68030 microprocessor. *Byte, 12(4),* 153–160.

Katevenis, M.G.H. (1985) *Reduced Instruction Set Computer Architectures for VLSI.* Cambridge, Mass.: MIT Press.

Marcus, N. (1990) *i860 Microprocessor Architecture.* Berkeley, CA: Osborne/McGraw-Hill.

Marshall, T. (1988) Real-world RISCs. *Byte, 13(5),* 263–268.

Marshall, T., and Tazelaar, J. M. (1989) Worth the RISC. *Byte, 14(2),* 245–249.

Patterson, D. A. (1985) Reduced instruction set computers. *Communications of the ACM, 28(1),* 8–21.

Patterson, D. A., and Ditzel, D. R. (1980) The case for the reduced instruction set computer. *Computer Architecture News, 8(6),* 25–33.

Piepho, R., and Wu, W. S. (1989) A comparison of RISC architectures. *IEEE Micro, 9(4),* 51–62.

Robinson, P. (1987) How much of a RISC? The past, present, and future of reduced instruction set computers. *Byte, 12(4),* 143–150.

Stallings, W. (1990) *Reduced Instruction Set Computers (RISC).* Second edition. Washington, D.C.: IEEE Computer Society Press.

Wallich, P. (1985) Toward simpler, faster computers. *IEEE Spectrum, 22(8),* 38–45.

## SIMD Processors and Processor Arrays

Almasi, G. S., and Gottlieb, A. (1989) *Highly Parallel Computers.* Menlo Park, Calif.: Benjamin/Cummings Publishing Company.

Frenkel, K. A. (1986) Evaluating two massively parallel machines. *Communications of the ACM, 29(8),* 752–758.

Goodyear Aerospace Corporation (1983) *General Description of the MPP.* Akron, Ohio: Goodyear Aerospace Corporation.

Gottlieb, A., and Schwartz, J. T. (1982) Networks and algorithms for very-large-scale parallel computation. *Computer, 15(1),* 27–36.

Haynes, L. S. (1982) Highly parallel computing: Guest editors' introduction. *Computer, 15(1),* 7–8.

Haynes, L. S., Lau, R. L., Siewiorek, D. P., and Mizell, D. W. (1982) A survey of highly parallel computing. *Computer, 15(1),* 9–24.

Hillis, W. D. (1985) *The Connection Machine.* Cambridge, Mass.: MIT Press.

Hillis, W. D. (1987) The connection machine. *Scientific American, 256(6),* 108–115.

Hillis, W. D., and Steele, G. L., Jr. (1986) Data parallel algorithms. *Communications of the ACM, 29(12),* 1170–1183.

Karplus, W. J., and Cohen, D. (1981) Architectural and software issues in the design and application of peripheral array processors. *Computer, 14(9),* 11–17.

Louie, T. (1981) Array processors: A selected bibliography. *Computer, 14(9),* 53–57.

Maron, N., and Brengle, T. A. (1981) Integrating an array processor into a scientific computing system. *Computer, 14(9),* 41–44.

Rushton, A. (1989) *Reconfigurable Processor-Array: A Bit-sliced Parallel Computer,* Cambridge, Mass.: MIT Press.

Theis, D. J. (1981) Array processor architecture: Guest editor's introduction. *Computer, 14(9),* 8–9.

Thinking Machines Corporation (1990) *Connection Machine Model CM-2 Technical Summary, Version 6.0, November 1990.* Cambridge, Mass.: Thinking Machines Corporation.

Tucker, L.W., and Robertson, G.G. (1988) Architecture and applications of the connection machine. *Computer, 21(8),* 26–38.

## *System Deadlocks*

Coffman, E.G., Jr., Elphick, M.J., and Shoshani, A. (1971) System deadlocks. *ACM Computing Surveys, 3(2),* 67–78.

Dijkstra, E.W. (1965) Solution of a problem in concurrent programming. *Communications of the ACM, 8(9),* 569.

Dijkstra, E.W. (1968) Cooperating sequential processes. In F. Genuys, editor, *Programming Languages.* New York: Academic Press, pp. 43–112.

Dubois, M., Scheurich, C., and Briggs, F.A. (1988) Synchronization, coherence, and event ordering in multiprocessors. *Computer, 21(2),* 9–21.

Holt, R.C. (1972) Some deadlock properties of computer systems. *ACM Computing Surveys, 4(3),* 179–196.

Isloor, S.S., and Marsland, T.A. (1980) The deadlock problem: An overview. *Computer, 13(9),* 58–78.

Newton, G. (1979) Deadlock prevention, detection and resolution: An annotated bibliography. *Operating Systems Review (ACM), 13(2),* 33–44.

## *Taxonomy*

Anderson, G.A., and Jensen, E.D. (1975) Computer interconnection structures: Taxonomy, characteristics, and examples. *ACM Computing Surveys, 7(4),* 197–213.

Baer, J.-L. (1983) Wither a taxonomy of computer architecture. *Proceedings of the IEEE International Workshop of Computer System Organization.* Silver Spring, Md.: IEEE Computer Society Press, pp. 3–9.

Dasgupta, S. (1990) A hierarchical taxonomic system for computer architectures. *Computer, 23(3),* 64–74.

Flynn, M.J. (1966) Very high-speed computing systems. *Proceedings of the IEEE, 54(12),* 1901–1904.

Flynn, M.J. (1972) Some computer organizations and their effectiveness. *IEEE Transactions on Computers, C-21(9),* 948–960.

Hockney, R.W. (1981) A structural taxonomy of computers. In Blaauw, G.A., and Händler, W., editors. *Workshop on Taxonomy in Computer Architecture.* Nuremberg: Friedrich Alexander Universität Erlangen-Nurnberg, pp. 77–92.

Kavi, K.M., and Cragon, H.G. (1983) A conceptual framework for the description and classification of computer architecture. *Proceedings of the IEEE International Workshop on Computer Systems Organization.* Los Angeles: IEEE Computer Society Press, pp. 10–19.

Reddi, S. S., and Feustel, E. A. (1976) A conceptual framework for computer architecture. *ACM Computing Surveys, 8(2),* 277–300.

Skillicorn, D. B. (1988) A taxonomy for computer architectures. *Computer 21(11),* 46–57.

### *Vector Processors*

Hack, J. J. (1986) Peak vs. sustained performance in highly concurrent vector machines. *Computer, 19(9),* 11–19.

Hwang, K., Su, S.-P., and Ni, L. M. (1981) Vector computer architecture and processing techniques. In M. C. Yovits, editor, *Advances in Computers.* Volume 20. New York: Academic Press, pp. 115–197.

Ibbett, R. N. (1982) *The Architecture of High Performance Computers.* New York: Springer-Verlag.

Johnson, P. M. (1978) An introduction to vector processing. *Computer Design, 17(2),* 89–97.

Patt, Y. N. (1989) Guest editor's introduction. Real machines: Design choices/engineering trade-offs. *Computer, 22(1),* 8–10.

# Glossary/Index

*Boldface entries and numbers refer to marginal terms in the text and where they are defined.*

**0-address instruction** 1. A stack instruction, which has no operand address because the operands come from a stack and the result goes to the stack. 2. An instruction that has only implicit operands; e.g., CLEAR CARRY: *55, 56*
 *See also* stack instruction

0-cube  A hypercube of dimension 0 consisting of a single processor: *334*

0WS  *See* zero-wait-state line

**1-address instruction**  An instruction that uses an accumulator and specifies a single memory operand: *55, 57*

**1-cube**  A hypercube of dimension 1 consisting of two nodes with one connection between them; the topology of a line: *333, 334*

**2-cube**  A hypercube of dimension 2 consisting of two 1-cubes with connections between corresponding nodes (no diagonals); the topology of a square: *333, 334*

**3-cube**  A hypercube of dimension 3 consisting of two 2-cubes with connections between corresponding nodes; the topology of a cube: *333, 334, 337*

**4-cube**  A hypercube of dimension 4: *333, 335*

4004  An early 4-bit microprocessor (circa 1971) by Intel: *9, 233*

68020  A 32-bit microprocessor by Motorola (circa 1984); used in the original Apple Macintosh: *308*

7400 chip  A integrated-circuit chip having four two-input NAND gates: *414*

7486 chip  An integrated-circuit chip having four two-input exclusive-or (XOR) gates: *414*

754  *See* IEEE Floating-point standard

**8-bit D register:**  *427, 428*

80x86 family  *See* Intel 80x86 family

**80286**  A 16-bit microprocessor (circa 1983) by Intel that has the same CPU as the 8086 microprocessor, includes hardware support for segmentation, and has a 24-bit physical-address space; used in the IBM PC AT and many clones:  *9, 234, 238, 239, 257, 277*

80287  An Intel arithmetic coprocessor for the 80286 microprocessor: *238*

**80386**  A 32-bit microprocessor (circa 1986) by Intel that has a 32-bit physical-address space, hardware support for paging and segmentation, and when operating in Real Address Mode emulates the 8086 instruction-set architecture; used in the IBM PS/2 Model 80 and many IBM PC clones:  *9, 235, 236, 238, 277, 279, 308, 376*

**80386SX**  A 32-bit microprocessor (circa 1988) by Intel with the same instruction-set architecture as the 80386 microprocessor, a 16-bit (rather than 32-bit) data bus, and a 24-bit (rather than 32-bit) physical-address space; used in several IBM PS/2 models and in many IBM PC clones: *235, 238*

80387  An Intel floating-point coprocessor for the 80386: *238, 376*

**80486**  A 32-bit microprocessor (circa 1989) by Intel with an internal cache, support for floating-point arithmetic, and an instruction-set architecture similar to that of the 80386; used in many IBM PC clones: *9, 198, 235, 238, 279*

80586  The projected successor to the 80486 microprocessor: *9*

8080  An early 8-bit microprocessor (circa 1974) by Intel, and predecessor of the Intel 80x86 family; used in the Altair 8800 personal computer: *9, 233*

**8086**  An early 16-bit microprocessor (circa 1978) by Intel and first member of the 80x86 family of microprocessors; uses segment-register addressing to support both a 20-bit logical-address space and a 20-bit physical address; used in the

473

IBM PS/2 Model 25 and some PC clones: *9, 233, 236, 238*
**8087** An Intel floating-point coprocessor for the 8086 and 8088 microprocessors: *269–272, 238, 239*
   bus control: *271–272*
   datatypes of: *269–270*
   register set: *270–272*
   operation of: *271–272*
   synchronization: *271*
**8088** An Intel microprocessor with the same instruction-set architecture as that of the 8086 but with a limited, 8-bit data bus; used in the original IBM PC and in many clones: ***233**, 234, 239, 247, 249, 269, 277*
   instruction format: *242*
   instruction-set architecture of: *239–245*
8235S  An Intel bus master interface controller: *258*
8235T  An Intel integrated system peripheral: *258*
8237A  An Intel direct-memory-access (DMA) controller: *239, 253–257*
   IBM PC port-address assignment: *274*
   register set: *253–254*
   transfer modes in: *253–254*
8250  A universal asynchronous receiver-transmitter (UART) by Intel: *260, 265*
   control signals of: *266–267*
   IBM PC port-address assignment: *274*
8253  A programmable interval timer by Intel: *251*
   IBM PC port-address assignment: *274*
   registers: *268*
8255A  A programmable parallel interface (PPI) by Intel: *260–265*
   control register in: *261*
   data register in: *261*
   IBM PC port-address assignment: *262, 274*
   modes of: *261*
   operation: *262*
   registers: *261*
8259A  An interrupt controller by Intel: *250, 251*
   IBM PC port-address assignment: *274*
   interrupt processing: *251*
8288  A bus controller by Intel: *256, 259*
88000  A 32-bit RISC microprocessor (circa 1989) by Motorola: *308*

ABC computer   Atanasoff-Berry Computer; first special-purpose electronic digital computer, built by John Atanasoff and Clifford Berry at Iowa State University in 1942: *5*

**absolute address**   *See* absolute-binary address
**absolute-binary address**   A binary address that designates the physical address of the reference; also called absolute address: *86, 87, **107***
   in branch instructions: *68*
   in exception handling: *148*
**absolute-binary number**   A base-2 number representation in which an $n$-bit value can represent any integer from 0 to $2^n - 1$; the $k$th bit from the right, starting with 0, represents the value $2^k$. Also called unsigned-binary number: *37*
   in the 8088 microprocessor: *239*
ABSOLUTE VALUE, in the 8087 coprocessor: *270*
**accept signal**   A handshake signal (e.g., a bus-grant signal) sent by a controller to a requesting device indicating that the controller has granted the device permission for the intended activity: ***122***
**access key**   A memory-protection key used on IBM System/360 and System/370 computers: ***192**, 193*
**access time**   *See* disk access time
**accumulator**   The main operational register on an accumulator machine, which generally holds one operand and gets the result of each operate instruction: *54, **56**, 128*
   in the 8088 microprocessor: *240, 241*
   in the CDC 6600: *298*
**accumulator machine**   A computer that has a single accumulator and uses it as an implied operand for all operate instructions. Hence most accumulator-machine instructions are 1-address instructions: ***56**, 83, 138*
ACK   Acknowledge. A control signal used by the 8255A programmable parallel interface during input and output: *256, 262, 263*
**active process**   In a multiprogramming system, the process that currently controls the CPU: ***64***
   For contrast, *see also* inactive process
active storage   A type of storage device, such as associative store, that operates on the data it holds: *187–188*
ADD   An instruction that specifies addition: *57, 137, 309*
   in the 8087 coprocessor: *270*
   microprogram for: *142–143*
   stack instruction: *56*
ADD3: *56*
adder   A device for addition
   in pipelined multiplication: *290*
   in segmentation hardware: *211*
**address buffer**   A buffer used for holding addresses: *237*

**address bus** A special-purpose bus that carries only addresses: *120, 156, 176*

**address-computation circuitry** Special-purpose circuitry that computes the effective address of a memory reference (e.g., by adding the base, index, and displacements together): *129, 130, 134, 139, 141, 220, 260*

address decoder In the IBM PC (and in other processors), a decoder for generating an enable signal when a specified address is present on an address bus: *251, 260, 261*

address-decoding circuitry *See* address decoder

**addressed memory** Memory that uses an address to select a storage cell during a read or write operation: *176, 184,* **185,** *186*

For contrast, *see also* associative memory

**addressed operand** An operand whose location is specified by its address, usually in a register or in main memory: **59**

For contrast, *see also* immediate operand

address enable line (AEN) A bus control line that carries an address-enable signal: *124*

**address-enable signal** A signal that a bus master asserts on an address-enable line when it places an address on an address bus: *124*

addressing The set of techniques a processor uses for specifying addresses

in the 8088 microprocessor: *242–245*

in the Cm* computer: *373–375*

design tradeoffs: *101–102*

**addressing efficiency** The ease with which the addressing modes of a given instruction-set architecture can designate variables in memory: *98,* **101**–*102*

**addressing homogeneity** The degree to which an instruction-set architecture has no preferred addresses. Thus the hardware treats all addresses in an equivalent way: *98,* **99**–*101*

addressing inhomogeneity The degree to which there are preferred addresses; i.e., many microprocessors prefer page-0 addresses to other addresses, and many microprocessors prefer intrasegment addresses to intersegment addresses: *220*

**addressing-mode byte** In the instruction format for the 8088 microprocessor, the byte in the address specification that indicates the addressing mode: *242–243*

addressing modes: *82–98*

in CISCs: *102*

addressing range: *98*

addressing techniques The techniques used by a CPU to specify the addresses of an operand: *82–102*

address latch A high-speed register for holding an address while placing it on a bus: *238, 239, 245, 247, 256*

in the IBM PC: *249, 251*

address map *See* Kmap; memory map; page map; segment map

address pins Pins that carry only addresses: *245*

address register A register that holds an address or address offset: *344, 267*

address relocation The mapping of addresses from one address space to another by the addition of a constant offset: *99*

**address resolution** The hardware translation of an instruction's address specification into an effective address: **59**

address space The set of addresses available to a process or processor: *85, 365*

of the IBM PC: *275*

*See also* I/O-address space; logical-address space; memory-address space; physical-address space

address-space size The number of bytes (usually) in an address space; $\log_2 n$ of the number of bits in an address: *220*

**address specification** The way an instruction specifies the address of an operand, e.g., absolute binary, register indirect, indexed, or base displacement: **59,** *60*

**address tag** In a cache memory, the address information maintained about each refill line; used to determine whether a cache hit occurs when given a main-memory address. The number of bits in an address tag depends on the type of cache: *196,* **197,** *198, 203*

address translation Any technique for translating (mapping) addresses from one address space to another: *191*

*See also* address relocation; address resolution

AD*i* The time-division-multiplexed data and address lines of the 8088 microprocessor, where $i = 0, 1, \ldots, 7$: *245–247*

ADJUST, in the 8088 microprocessor An instruction for adjusting the result of adding two ASCII characters: *240*

Advanced Scientific Computer *See* TI ASC

AEN *See* address-enable line

A*i* Address line *i* of the 8088 microprocessor, where $i = 0, 1, \ldots, 7$: *245–247*

Aiken, H.: *6, 12*

AL The low byte in the A register of the 8088 microprocessor: *245, 252, 262*

algorithm A problem solution given as a set of instructions that can be followed in a step-by-step fashion, in a finite number of steps: *106*

**algorithmic notation**  A formal notation for specifying algorithms: *408*

**aligned words**  *See* boundary alignment

ALL  *See* AND reduction

Alliant FX, LINPACK benchmark of: *307*

**alphabet**  A finite set of symbols; the letters and symbols (including punctuation marks and numerals) of a language: *50, 51*

Altair 8800  One of the first personal computers, introduced in kit form in 1974 by Micro Instrumentation and Technology Systems (MITS); used an Intel 8080 microprocessor: *233*

ALU  *See* arithmetic and logic unit

**American Standard Code for Information Interchange (ASCII)**  A 7-bit code that maps binary values into characters and control codes: *37, 50, 51, 163, 168*

A*n*  index register *n* in the CDC 6600, where *n* ranges from 0 to 7: *298, 303*

AND  A two-operand instruction that specifies a bitwise boolean and (∧) operation: *60, 137, 150*
  of the 8088: *240*

AND reduction  A vector-reduction operation that performs a boolean AND on all of the elements of a vector to produce one result; also called ALL: *73*

**annul bit**  A bit within the instructions of some RISC machines that allow the hardware to cancel the execution of the instruction in the delay slot of a delayed-branch instruction if the branch succeeds: *313*

ANSI  American National Standards Institute: *44*

ANY  *See* OR reduction

**any-match bit**  The boolean OR of all bits in the match register of an associative memory: *187*

Apollo: *27*

Apple II  An early (circa 1977) 8-bit microcomputer by Apple Corporation based on MOS Technology 6502 microprocessor: *233*

Apple Corporation: *215, 233, 234*

Apple Macintosh  *See* Macintosh

Apple NuBus  The system bus of the Apple Macintosh: *120*

**applicability**  The range of applications for which a particular architecture is suitable: *21–23*
  of the IBM PC: *279*

AR  *See* argument register

**arbiter**  *See* arbitration network

**arbitration network**  A network that controls the use of a resource by checking all requests for its use, prioritizing them, and granting permission to one requesting device for its use; generally operates on a cycle-by-cycle basis. Also called an arbiter
  within a bus control network: *120, 121, 156, 157*
  within a port controller: *157*

**arc**  A line in a dataflow graph that shows where a node will send its result: *384*

**architectural merit**  An assessment of the quality of an architecture, based primarily on its applicability, malleability, expandability, and compatibility: *23–24*
  of the IBM PC: *279–280*

architecture  *See* computer architecture

**archival memory**  Memory used for long-term storage of data, generally offline; characterized by a low cost per bit and a high data-retention life: *177, 189*

ARCTAN, in the 8087 coprocessor  An instruction for evaluating the arctangent of an operand: *270*

Argonne National Laboratories: *27*

**argument**  A parameter used to pass information from a calling procedure to a called procedure: *48*
  *See also* parameter

**argument register (AR)**  Within an associative memory, the register that holds the argument for an associative search: *187, 346, 347*

**argument slot**  Within a node of a dataflow graph, the receptacle for holding an incoming token until the node can fire: *384, 386*

**arithmetic and logic unit (ALU)**  The component of a computer that carries out the operations specified by the operate instructions: *12, 55, 124–126, 146, 424*
  *See also* arithmetic-unit pipeline; pipelining

arithmetic exception  An exception triggered by the ALU to signal an error condition, e.g., division by zero or exponent overflow: *150*

arithmetic instruction  An operate instruction, such as ADD or MULTIPLY, that specifies an arithmetic operation for the arithmetic and logic unit to carry out: *13, 60–61*

**arithmetic mean**  The average of two or more measurements (i.e., the sum of measurements divided by the number of measurements); often simply referred to as "the mean": *28*
  For contrast, *see also* geometric mean; harmonic mean; weighted arithmetic mean

arithmetic operation  An operation on numeric quantities; examples are addition, subtraction, division, and multiplication: *36*

arithmetic overflow  Overflow resulting from an arithmetic operation: *53*

arithmetic overflow flag  *See* overflow flag

ARITHMETIC SHIFT RIGHT   A shift-right instruction that, in addition to shifting all bits (including the sign bit) to the right, lets the value remain in the sign-bit position: *60, 61, 137, 139*

**arithmetic-unit pipeline**   A pipeline for arithmetic operations: ***289***

For contrast, *see also* instruction-unit pipeline

Arjomandi, E.: *395*

**array**   A data structure whose data elements are referenced by the array name followed by a subscript list for selecting one of the data elements. The dimensionality of the array is given by the number of subscript positions in the subscript list, and the size of the array is the total number of elements: *16, **45**, **47**, 52, 88, 89*

array address   The address of the first element of the array: *89*

**array element**   A single variable within an array: *47*

artificial intelligence machine   A computer designed specifically for artificial intelligence applications (e.g., a computer optimized for the LISP programming language): *20, 383*

artificial intelligence programming language   A programming language (e.g., LISP) intended for symbolic computations: *20*

Arvind: *389*

ASC   *See* TI ASC

ASCII   *See* American Standard Code for Information Interchange

Ashton-Tate Corporation: *232, 278*

assert high   Place a $1_2$ signal (*true*) on, e.g., a bus: *413*

assert low   Place a $0_2$ signal (*false*) on, e.g., a bus; also called deassert: *413*

**association layer**   In a perceptron, the middle layer of cells, which has adaptive thresholds whose values affect learning within the perceptron: ***391***

**associative cache**   A cache that can map any refill line to any line in memory; also called a fully associative cache: *184, **199**, 200–203*

**associative memory**   A storage system that locates data by searching its memory cells for a specific bit pattern. The user supplies the bit pattern by giving two values: an argument and a mask; the argument holds the value being sought, and the mask specifies which argument bits to use when comparing the argument to the value in each cell. Also called content-addressable memory: *187, 188, 201, 345–347*

For contrast, *see also* addressed memory

associative-memory operation   An operation that depends on the values of the data stored in memory, rather than on the addresses or locations of these data: *341*

associative processor   A processor that implements associative-memory operations: *321, 341*

**associative search**   A search by content: ***344–351***

*See also* associative memory

associative store   *See* associative memory

AST Research: *236, 278*

asynchronous banks of memory   Banks of memory whose access cycles are not synchronized: *304*

**asynchronous flip-flop**   A flip-flop that is not clocked; it can be set or reset at any time: ***425***

asynchronous interrupt   *See* interrupt

**asynchronous network**   A network whose activity is not synchronized by a central clock: ***325***

**asynchronous transmission**   Transmission in which sender and receiver use different clocks: ***266***

AT   Advanced Technology; refers to the IBM PC AT and its clones.

Atanasoff, J.: *5*

Atari   A low-cost 6502-based personal computer: *215*

**atomic instruction**   An instruction for an operation that the CPU performs on a specified word of memory while blocking all other processors from accessing that word until it finishes the operation; also called indivisible instruction: ***65–67***.

*See also* process synchronization primitive

**autodecrement addressing**   An addressing mode in which an instruction selects a register that holds an address; the CPU automatically decrements that address before using it to access the operand: ***96***

**autoincrement addressing**   An addressing mode in which the instruction selects a register that holds an address; the CPU automatically increments that address after using it to access the operand: ***96**, 309*

autoinitialization   *See* DMA autoinitialization

**availability**   The percentage time of a fault-tolerant computer is running and working (e.g., 100% availability implies a processor that never fails): ***378***

AX   Accumulator register of the 8088 microprocessor: *245*

axon   1. In a biological neuron, the filament that carries signals away from the cell body: *390*. 2. In a formal neuron, the signal line that carries the output signal: *393*

B-1700   A 24-bit minicomputer by Burroughs Corporation (circa 1976) with a writable control store: *96, 308*

**B-5500** An early execution-stack architecture (circa 1965) by Burroughs Corporation; predecessor of the B6700: *41*

**B6700** A Burroughs Corporation execution-stack machine (circa 1970) that had a tagged architecture and provided multiprogramming, segmentation, and direct hardware support for Algol and other block-structured programming languages: *56, 308*

BACKSPACE BLOCK A channel command for a magnetic tape device: *160*

**backup system** In a fault-tolerant computer, an off-line processor that can replace a faulty processor (i.e., a spare processor): ***379***

**bandwidth** The rate of transmission of data (excluding parity, framing, and other nondata bits)
   of a disk drive: ***166***, *168*
   in the I/O system: *29*
   in an interconnection network: ***326***
   *See also* baud rate; memory bandwidth

banked memory   *See* memory banking

banking hardware   *See* memory banking

**bank-select register** In memory-banking hardware, the register that selects a memory bank: ***216***, *217, 218*

**Banyan network** A staged interconnection network that has only one path (and hence no redundancy) between each input and output device: ***332***, *334*

Bardeen, J.: *7*

**barrel shifter** An *n*-staged sequential circuit that provides stages for shifting data by $2^n$ bits (or not shifting the data). The circuit can shift its input by any amount from 0 to $2^n - 1$ bits by controlling the stages that perform a shift operation: ***422***

base 16   *See* hexadecimal notation

base 8   *See* octal notation

**base address** An address that specifies the start of a block in memory. Thus the base address of an array is the address of its first (or zero) element: ***92***

**base-address register** A register of the 8237 direct-memory-access controller: *253*

**base-count register** A register of the 8237 direct-memory-access controller: *253*

**base-displacement addressing** An addressing mode in which the CPU adds the contents of a base register to the displacement found within the instruction to form the effective address of the operand: *88*, ***92–94***, *97, 99, 192, 220*
   with and without indexing: *93*

**base pointer (BP)** A base register in the 8088 microprocessor: *241, 243, 244*

**base register** A register that holds a base address: *92, 94, 98, 193, 220*
   BX, in the 8088 microprocessor: *240, 241, 243, 244*
   in program relocation: *192*

**base-relative addressing** An addressing mode of the 8088 microprocessor: *243*

**base-relative direct addressing** An addressing mode of the 8088 microprocessor: *243*

**base relative direct indexed addressing** An addressing mode of the 8088 microprocessor: *243*

**base relative direct indexed stack addressing** An addressing mode of the 8088 microprocessor: *243*

**base relative direct stack addressing** An addressing mode of the 8088 microprocessor: *243*

**base relative indexed addressing** An addressing mode of the 8088 microprocessor: *243*

**base relative indexed stack addressing** An addressing mode of the 8088 microprocessor: *243*

**BASIC** A programming language that is part of the IBM PC: *278*

**basic input-output system (BIOS)** That part of the I/O system on a PC or similar processor that directly controls the hardware interface devices (e.g., PPIs and UARTs); usually found in ROM: ***236***, *238, 273*

**basic I/O mode,** a peripheral processing unit (PPI) A processing mode of the 8255A PPI in which the PPI latches the output but not the input and does not use handshake signals: *262*

**batch-processing operating system** An operating system that automatically loads and executes programs, which relieves the operator of this function and speeds up program execution: *7, 8*

**baud rate** In serial transmission, the number of bits (including parity and framing bits) the device sends per second; the reciprocal of the bit time: ***265***
   in serial I/O: *266*

BCD   *See* binary-coded decimal

Bell Telephone Laboratories: *7*

**benchmark** A standardized battery of programs run on a computer to determine its absolute speed and its speed relative to other computers: *25–30, 307*
   of RISCs: *311*
   of vector and scalar processors: *307*

B*i* An index register of the CDC 6600 processor, where i ranges from 0 to 7: *298–299*

**bias** The value *n* in an excess-*n* integer; subtracting *n* from the representation gives the value being represented (e.g., 8 represents 4 in an excess-4 representation): *39*

**biased integer**   *See* excess-*n* integer

biased-integer exponent, of the CDC CYBER 170 floating-point representation: *41*

**bidirectional bus mode, of peripheral processing unit (PPI)**   A processing mode of the 8255A PPI in which port A functions as an input and output port and port B can operate as either an input port or an output port: *262*

**bidirectional pin**   *See* time-division-multiplexed pin

**billions of floating-point operations per second (GFLOPS or gigaflops)**   A unit for reporting the performance of a CPU: *26*

**binary-coded decimal (BCD)**   A number representation in which 4 bits encode a single decimal digit and the 4-bit unit is the smallest allowed piece of information: *37, 60, 268, 428*

   in the 8088 microprocessor: *240*

binary-coded decimal counter   A counter that counts from 0 to 9 and then resets (goes to 0): *428, 429*

binary decoder   *See* complete binary decoder

binary fraction   A fraction in which the leftmost bit represents 1/2, the next bit represents 1/4, and so forth: *39*

binary multiplication   The multiplication of two absolute-binary numbers to produce an absolute-binary result

   a flowthrough implementation: *293*

   a pipelined implementation: *289–293*

   a sequential circuit for: *431–435*

binary notation   The representation of numbers using base-2 notation: *405*

**binary point**   In binary fractions, the point that separates the bits representing integers on the left from bits representing fractions on the right (e.g., 110.1011 represents $4 + 2 + 0 + \frac{1}{2} + \frac{0}{4} + \frac{1}{8} + \frac{1}{16} = 6.6875_{10}$): *40, 52*

binary tree   A tree in which each node has one or two successor nodes: *330, 362*

BIOS   *See* basic input-output system

**bit plane**   A unit of information consisting of 1 bit from each processing element (PE) in a bit-serial processor array, such as the MPP or the CM-2; all bits in a bit plane have the same local (PE) address: *342*

bit-serial operation   An operation (e.g., addition) that processes the operands 1 bit at a time; used by some early computers and by some massively parallel SIMD machines: *341, 342*

   multiplication: *433*

   For contrast, *see also* word-parallel operation

bit-serial transmission   *See* serial data transmission

**bit-slice**   The set of bits from the same bit position in a group of words (e.g., bit-slice 3 from a group of *i* words would consist of the set of third bits from each word, the number *i* of words thus determining the number of bits in the bit-slice): *187, 341*

bit-slice operation   An operation on bit-slices rather than words; used by some parallel and associative processors: *347, 348*

**bit-slice processor**   A processor (e.g., STARAN) that performs bit-slice operations (possibly in addition to word operations): *341*

bit string   A string whose data are bits: *76*

   in serial I/O: *266*

**bit time**   The time it takes a universal asynchronous receiver-transmitter (UART) to transfer 1 bit of information; is the reciprocal of the baud rate: *265*

**block**   1. A page frame in a paged virtual-memory system: *206, 212.* 2. A group of data to be transferred by a direct-memory-access controller during a block-mode transfer: *167*

   *See also* DMA block mode

**block floating-point**   A floating-point representation in which a block of values share a single exponent field, thus providing additional bits for increasing the precision of the mantissas: *52*

   For contrast, *see also* floating floating-point

**block-oriented memory**   *See* block-oriented random-access device

**block-oriented random-access device**   A random-access device (e.g., a disk drive) that accesses blocks of data rather than single words; also called block-oriented memory: *167, 168*

blurring   *See* image blurring

boolean instruction   *See* logical instruction

boolean vector   *See* logical vector

Borland International: *232*

bottom-up processing   In a dataflow graph, the evaluation of the nodes on a demand-for-output basis: *389*

   For contrast, *see also* top-down processing

boundary alignment   The alignment of information within a memory so that the beginning of each unit of information falls on a boundary of the same size as the unit (e.g., the alignment of a word on a word boundary or a page on a page boundary): *82–84*

BP   *See* base pointer

**branch**   An alternation in the normal sequential flow of control from one instruction to the next: *71*

   hardware-initiated   *See* exception; trap; interrupt

**branch address** The address of a branch-target instruction; also called a branch-target address or simply target address: *68, 70, 90, 133*

in pipelining: *295*

**branch-delay slot** For RISC processors, the instruction position in a program following a branch instruction: *313*

**branching microinstruction** A microinstruction that holds branch addresses and microorders for the address-computation circuitry, and perhaps some microorders for the rest of the computer: *133, 139*

**branch instruction** An instruction that causes a break in the sequential execution of instructions in a program by altering the content of the program counter, either conditionally or unconditionally: *58, 67–69, 89*

See also conditional branch instruction; JUMP

**branch microinstruction** A microinstruction that causes a branch in the microcode: *134*

BRANCH ON CONDITION A conditional branch instruction: *56*

BRANCH ON NEGATIVE A conditional branch instruction that branches if its operand is negative: *68, 133, 134*

**branch penalty** The delay that occurs in a pipelined instruction unit when a conditional branch succeeds; results from the hardware having to purge instructions already in the pipeline and replace them with the branch-target instructions: *296, 297*

branch-target address *See* branch address

**branch-target instruction** For an unconditional branch, the next instruction to be executed; for a conditional branch, the instruction the CPU will execute when the branch test succeeds. Also called target instruction: *68, 90, 94*

**branch test** The test that determines whether a conditional branch instruction will succeed or fall through; the operand for a conditional branch instruction: *67, 68, 69*

in pipelining: *296*

Brattain, W.: *7*

**broadcast** The act of simultaneously sending the same value to a number of processors (e.g., the control unit of a processor array broadcasts control signals and constants to the processing elements in the array): *332*

**broadcast capability** A property of some crossbars and other switches enabling them to send one input to several outputs: *338*

**broadcast state** The setting of a switch with broadcast capabilities that enables it to broadcast a selected input to two or more outputs: *332, 333*

BSP Burroughs Scientific Processor: *19*

**buffer** A high-speed memory interposed between two devices to match the speed of one device with the other: *14, 413*

in a disk: *252*

Burks, A. R.: *5*

Burks, A. W.: *5, 6, 13*

**burning a PROM** The one-time process of storing values in a ROM, often by driving large currents through a set of resistive elements that are to be destroyed; the pattern of surviving resistive elements determines the values of the stored bits: *184*

Burroughs Corporation: *8, 41*

See also B-1700, B-5500, B6700, BSP

**burst-mode transfer** A mode of operation in which a DMA controller relinquishes control of the bus only after it completes an entire block transfer; called DMA block mode in the 8237A controller: *158*

in the EISA bus: *258*

For contrast, see also DMA single mode

**bus** A collection of wires for conducting information between system components: *120–124, 324, 415*

illustration conventions: *416*

**bus arbiter** *See* arbitration network

**bus controller** The control circuits for a system bus; includes a bus arbiter, which may be distributed among the devices, and flags for holding bus requests: *120, 121, 156, 234, 237, 238, 415*

of the PC Bus: *248*

bus-control lines, types of: *124*

**bus-control signals** Control signals used by buses (e.g., bus-request and bus-grant signals): *124*

**bus cycle** A fixed sequence of bus states through which a bus passes during a given type of bus transfer; types of bus cycles include memory read cycles, memory write cycles, I/O read cycles, and I/O write cycles: *122, 124, 157, 234, 247*

EISA bus: *259*

PC Bus: *248*

types of: *124*

**bus gate** A circuit that either sends all input signals to their respective output lines or places zeros on all the output lines: *290*

**bus-grant line** A dedicated bus line that the bus controller uses to inform an attached device when it will be the bus master: *121, 122, 124*

in the 8088 microprocessor: *248*

**bus interconnection topology** The interconnection topology of a system that uses a single system bus: *327*

bus-interface processor, in the Cm* See Local Switch

**bus master** The device that controls a bus during a bus cycle: **122**
   8237 during I/O: *253*
   of the EISA bus: *258*
   *See also* slave device

**bus protocol** The algorithm for requesting and granting permission to use a bus: **122**
   of the 8087 coprocessor: *271–272*

**bus-request line** A dedicated control line used by a device to send a bus request signal to the bus controller: *121*, **122**, *124*

**bus-request signal** A signal sent over a bus-request line to the bus controller by a device wishing to use the bus: **122**
   in the 8088 microprocessor: *248*

**bus state** The condition of a bus with respect to a given type of bus transfer (e.g., a bus may go through three states during a memory read operation: address transfer, data transmission, and idle in preparation for the next bus cycle): **122**
   in the 8088 microprocessor: *246*

**bus transfer** The transmission of one or more data over a bus in one (logical) bus operation: **122–124**

**bus watcher** A device that decodes all addresses or bus control signals and notifies an attached device when specified signals occur (e.g., a snoopy cache has a bus watcher): **370**

**BUSY** Designates a busy flag in the CDC 6600: *300, 303*

**busy bit** *See* busy flag

**busy flag** A control bit within each CDC 6600 functional unit to indicate when that unit is busy; also called a busy bit: **298**

**BX** *See* base register, BX

**byte** An 8-bit unit of information: *36, 37, 85*

**byte address** The address of an item expressed in bytes; the byte number of the start of the item regardless of its size or datatype (e.g., for 32-bit words, the byte address of word 0 is 0, of word 1 is 4, of word 2 is 8, and so on): *83*

**byte boundary** A point in memory that falls between bytes; corresponds in a byte-addressed memory system, to any address boundary and in a bit-addressed memory to any address divisible by 8: *84*

**byte offset**, in segment address A part of the logical address in a segmentation system which gets added to the base address to get the physical address of the reference: *211*

C *See* carry flag

**cache** A high-speed buffer that holds copies of the most frequently accessed values in memory; placed between a memory system and its user to reduce the effective access time of the memory system. Also called cache memory: *184, 188*, **191**, *196–204, 214, 219, 235*
   design alternatives: *201–204*
   in multiprocessor systems: *367–370*
   in pipelining: *304*
   specialized caches: *313*

**cache coherence** The state in a system in which all copies of any common datum within all caches and main memory are the same: *367–370*

**cache entry** An item in a cache memory: *197*

**cache-entry invalidation** The process of marking a cache entry invalid to force the cache to reread the item from memory; used to maintain cache coherence: *197, 370*

**cache hit** The situation that results when a device requests a memory access to a word that is present in cache memory; the cache quickly returns the requested item: *197, 198*

**cache memory** *See* cache

**cache miss** The situation that results when a device requests access to a datum not present in cache; the cache fetches the item from memory, which takes longer than a cache hit: *197, 215*

**cache organization** The way a cache maps memory addresses into its own local cache addresses: *199–203*

**cache performance** A measure of the effectiveness of a cache, usually expressed as the percentage of cache accesses that result in cache hits: *204*

**cache refill line** The smallest groups of data in memory that a cache can process; i.e., the group a cache loads when the CPU references any element of the group: *199, 200, 202, 215*

**cache refill-line address** The address of a cache refill line: *203*

**cache sector** A block of data that the hardware treats as a unit; also called a row: **201**

CALL A subroutine-linkage instruction that saves the content of the program counter (the return address) prior to branching: *240*

**called procedure** The procedure to which control is transferred when a program (the calling program) executes a CALL instruction, and one which returns control to the calling program by executing a RETURN instruction: *48, 70, 104*
   in the CDC 6600: *103*

**calling procedure** A procedure that calls another, the called procedure: *48, 96, 104*
   in the CDC: *6600 103*
   *See also* called procedure

CAM   Content-addressable memory. *See* associative memory

capacitor   An electronic component that stores a charge of electricity; a component in a charge-coupled-device memory (among other uses): *184*

card   A physical circuit board that contains devices or memory; users can add PC cards to their PCs by plugging them into any vacant slot. Also called daughter board: *237, 413*

card punch   An archaic output device for punching IBM punched cards: *154*

card reader   An archaic input device for reading punched cards: *155*

Carnegie-Mellon Cm*   *See* Cm*

carry flag (C)   A status bit in many computers that holds the carry-in to the adder and gets the carry-out of the adder (among other uses): *53, 59–61, 125, 126*

**carry look-ahead circuit**   A type of arithmetic circuit that computes the carry of an addition; used in carry look-ahead adders to reduce the delay caused by carry propagation: ***424***

For contrast, *see* ripple-carry adder

carry-in   An input to a full adder; receives the carry-out of the previous stage of addition: *422, 423*

carry-out   An output from a full adder; gives the overflow that results when adding two numbers whose sum exceeds the number of bits in the adder: *423*

cascade mode   *See* DMA cascade mode

CC   *See* condition code

CCD   *See* charge-coupled device

CDC   *See* Control Data Corporation

CDC 6600   The first of Control Data Corporation's pipelined supercomputers (circa 1965). This machine has 60-bit words, a load-and-store instruction set, and 10 independent functional units: *4, 19, 42, 57, 104, 126, 145, 179, 192, 193, 219, 304, 308, 389*

  floating-point number of: *103*
  instruction execution in: *298–303*
  LINPACK benchmark of: *307*
  peripheral processing units of: *163, 164*
  program relocation and protection in: *193*

CDC 7600   A successor to the CDC 6600 by Control Data Corporation having a similar (but not completely compatible) instruction-set architecture: *219*

  LINPACK benchmark of: *307*

CDC CYBER 170   A successor to the CDC 6600 by Control Data Corporation: *5*

  floating-point numbers of: *41–43*

CDC STAR   An pipelined vector processor of the mid-1970s by Control Data Corporation: *179*

centralized clock   A clock used for regulating the speed of an entire system: *9*

**centralized control**   Any (logically) localized control system: ***324***

  for an interconnection network: *325*

  For contrast, *see also* distributed control

central memory   *See* primary memory

**central processing unit (CPU)**   That part of a von Neumann machine consisting of the control unit, arithmetic and logic unit, and register file but excluding the main memory and I/O systems: *3, 11, **124–152***

  single chip: *233*

CGA   *See* Color Graphics Adapter

CHANGE SIGN   An 8087 coprocessor instruction: *270*

**channel**   1. A simple DMA I/O processor that can assemble data (e.g., from bytes into words), disassemble data, control attached I/O devices, and interrupt the CPU: ***158–164***, *181*; input-output processing with: *158–163*. 2. Any independent path for the transfer of data, such as a channel within an 8237 DMA controller: *253*

**channel command**   An instruction for a channel: ***160***

**channel program**   The program, consisting of channel commands, that a channel executes: *158, 160–162*

channel-program address   The entry-point address for a channel program: *162*

**channel protocol**   The standard way a CPU and channel communicate: *158, 161, 162*

channel status information   Information that describes the current state of a channel and its operation: *163*

**character**   A datatype for which the only operate instructions are movements and comparison tests (e.g., lexical equality); usually requires 1 byte of storage in memory: *37, 50, 51*

character data   Data composed entirely of characters (i.e., nonnumeric data, such as text): *51*

**character instruction**   An operate instruction that manipulates characters: *58, 61*

**character string**   A sequence of zero or more characters. Computers generally reference strings by giving both the address of the first character and the length of the string: *45, 96, 100, 101*

**character-string instruction**   An instruction for processing character strings, such as MOVE STRING and COMPARE STRING: *13, 58, 61, 209*

charge packet   The quantity of charge used to represent a $1_2$-bit in a charge-coupled device: *186*

**charge-coupled device (CCD)** A type of dynamic storage element in which a packet of charge represents a $1_2$ bit and its absence a $0_2$ bit; the storage cells (capacitors) form a shift register and move the charge packets from one cell to the next: *186*

**checkpoint information** The data and state information necessary to restore a process to a checkpoint, which is a state known to be correct: *379*

**checkpoint message** A message used to update checkpoint information: *379*

**chip** A physical circuit component manufactured on a single chip of material: *8, 411*

**chip select** An input to a circuit that enables the chip's operation; often labeled CS: *415, 416*

**chip set** A set of chips (e.g., CPU, bus controller, interrupt controller, DMA controller, programmable interval timer, and I/O interfaces), that operate at the same logic levels and use common timing and control signals. Thus manufacturers create the chips so designers can easily interconnect them for building computers: *237*

circuit board  *See* printed circuit board

**circuit-switched interconnection network** A network that allows two devices to communicate by physically connecting them together for the duration of a transmission: *324, 326, 332*

For contrast, *see also* packet-switched interconnection network

CISC  *See* complex-instruction-set computer

CLEAR  An instruction for clearing a register or memory location: *64, 65, 67*

CLEAR CARRY  An instruction for clearing the carry flag: *56, 59, 127*

CLEAR IF, in the 8088 microprocessor  An instruction for clearing the interrupt flag: *240*

clear to send (CTS)  One of the handshake signals on a universal asynchronous receiver-transmitter; generated by the receiving device to tell the sending device that the receiving device is ready to receive the data: *266*

**clock** A device that produces a continuous sequence of timing signals of specified duration and frequency: *237, 239, 256*

in a pipeline: *288*

in the IBM PC: *249, 251*

**clock cycle** A primitive unit of computation equal to one tick of the centralized clock, which synchronizes the events occurring inside a computer; also called a computation cycle: *9*

**clock-cycle time** The speed of a clock; the reciprocal of its frequency (e.g., the clock-cycle time of a 20 MHz clock is $0.5 \times 10^{-7}$ seconds or 50 ns: *289*

clock frequency  The reciprocal of clock-cycle time in serial I/O: *266*

**clock ticks per instruction (TPI)** For a given computer, the average number of clock cycles between consecutive instruction issues: *29*

clone  A computer designed to have the same instruction-set architecture as the one being cloned: *236, 310, 311*

**closed architecture** An architecture whose specification is proprietary (not published) by its manufacturer: *24*

For contrast, *see also* open architecture

**cluster** A group of processors within a multiprocessor that are interconnected with a single local bus: *340, 372*

in the Cm*: *376*

Cm*  An experimental multiprocessor computer developed at Carnegie-Mellon University (circa 1975), in which the designers grouped processors into local clusters and organized clusters into a tree structure: *19, 371–376*

CM-1 Connection Machine  The first connection machine manufactured by Thinking Machines (circa 1987): *19, 326, 331, 337, 342*

CM-2 Connection Machine  The second connection machine manufactured by Thinking Machines (circa 1989): *326, 339, 342, 344, 354*

code  Program instructions generated by an assembler or a compiler (or by hand) that implement an algorithm

generation: *311*

private: *194*

shared: *194*

**code segment** 1. A segment of memory composed entirely of executable code: *96, 210*. 2. One of four 64-KB segments of memory that the 8088 microprocessor can access directly; the only segment that holds code for the current instruction: *244*

*See also* data segment; extra segment; stack segment

code-segment register (CS)  A register in the 8088 microprocessor that holds the base address of the code segment: *241, 244*

use during interrupt initiation: *250*

use during system initialization: *273*

coefficient  *See* mantissa

**Color Graphics Adapter (CGA)** A color video display standard introduced by IBM for its first PC, with a resolution of $320 \times 200$ pixels and four colors: *235*

in the IBM PC: *277*

IBM PC port-address assignment: *274*

column, in direct-mapped cache: *199*

column number, in a set-associative cache: *201*

column order  *See* row-minor order

COM1, IBM PC port-address assignment: *274*

COM2, IBM PC port-address assignment: *274*

**combinatorial logic circuit**  A logic circuit whose output does not depend on the history of inputs to the circuit; hence a circuit without any memory components: **417**

command-address register, in a channel: *160*

command-code register, in a channel: *160*

command register  *See* DMA command register

Commodore Business Machines: *233*

**communication**  Transmission of data from one device to another: *63, 365*

**communication diameter**  The number of intervening nodes between a source and a destination node in a communications network; also called communication distance: **325**

communication distance  *See* communication diameter

communications protocol  *See* input protocol, output protocol

Compaq Computer Corporation: *236*

COMPARE  In the 8088 microprocessor, any of a set of instructions for comparing two values; whether immediate, held in a register, or held in memory: *240*

COMPARE AND SWAP  A synchronization instruction for the IBM System/360-370. The arguments specify a memory location and two registers. The instruction compares the value at the specified memory location with the value in a register and sets the condition code; if the two values are equal, the instruction swaps the content of the memory location with that in the second register: *66*

COMPARE CHARACTERS  An operate instruction that compares two characters: *61*

COMPARE DOUBLE AND SWAP  Similar to COMPARE AND SWAP, but the comparands are double-precision quantities: *66*

COMPARE STRINGS  An operate instruction that compares the corresponding characters of two strings: *56, 61*

**compatibility**  A measure of how well one computer can run the programs intended for another computer: *5, 23, 104–105*

 *See also* downward compatibility; forward compatibility; upward compatibility

**compilation**  The process of converting a program written in a high-level language into machine instructions: *85, 106, 311*

**compiler**  A program that compiles high-level language programs for a target computer: *27, 55, 85, 98–104, 310, 340, 341*

 optimizing: *313*

COMPLEMENT  An instruction that complements each bit of its operand: *139*

 microprogram for: *141–142*

 vector instruction: *73*

**complementing the bits**  *See* ones' complement integer

**complete binary decoder**  A device that has $n$ inputs and $2^n$ outputs and generates a signal on output line $i$ when the input is the binary representation for the number $i$; also called a binary decoder: *417, 430*

**complete instruction set**  An instruction set that does not lack any functionality for the intended group of users: *102*

complete interconnection topology  An interconnection topology in which every processor has a direct connection to every other processor: *330*

completeness  A property of instruction sets that measures how easily they can implement all desired operations: *104*

**complex-instruction-set computer (CISC)**  In essence, a description for any computer that lacks the properties of being a reduced-instruction-set computer; generally, a computer with the following properties: complex addressing modes, instructions with many sizes, instructions that have memory-to-memory or memory-to-register operations, and a microprogrammed control unit: *10, 19, 21, 64, 65, 67, 101, 108, 305, 307, 309, 310*

**component fault**  A transient error in a component (e.g., a parity error in a storage cell); a device with an intermittent problem: *377*

COMPRESS  A vector instruction that initiates a vector-compression operation: *78*

compression  *See* vector compression

**computational thread**  Within the dataflow model of computation, the parallel sequences of nodes through which dataflow tokens move as a consequence of fork-node operations: *386*

**computation cycle**  *See* clock cycle

**computation-intensive application**  An application that requires a large amount of computation on a high-speed processor (e.g., image processing, weather forecasting, seismic analysis, animation, and simulation): *21*

**computer**  An information-processing machine that accepts input data and executes prescribed programs, expressed as machine instructions, to produce results: *3*

**computer-aided design(CAD)** The use of computers in the design process: *20*

**computer-aided manufacture (CAM)** The use of computers in the manufacturing process: *20*

**computer architecture** The design of computers and the study of their organization, including instruction-set architecture and hardware-system architecture: *3*

   classification of: *11–20*

   table of categories: *19*

**computer family** A set of computers with the same instruction-set architecture: *4*

**computer-family architecture** The architecture of a set of similar computers without regard to implementation details such as memory size, control-unit design, speed, and technology; in effect the instruction-set architecture of a computer: *4, 24*

**computer module** A unit comprised of a CPU, some local memory, and a set of local I/O devices for a processor node in a multiprocessor such as the Cm* computer: *372*

computer startup *See* machine startup

CONCAT An instruction that produces the concatenation of two strings: *45, 46*

**concatenation** The formation of a new string by combining two source strings end to end. If $S1 = c_1c_2\ldots c_n$ and $S2 = d_1d_2\ldots d_k$, then the concatenation of S1 with S2 denoted $S1 \parallel S2$, is $c_1c_2\ldots c_nd_1d_2\ldots d_k$: *45, **46***

**conditional branch** A branch that depends on the outcome of a branch test (e.g., whether the value in a register is zero): *76, 103, 313*

   in a channel: *160*

   in pipelining: *296*

**conditional branch instruction** An instruction that specifies a conditional branch operation and the branch test for its determination: *58, 69, 102*

**condition code (CC)** A bit pattern that indicates the general outcome of a computation (e.g., whether the result is zero, positive, negative, or caused overflow): ***53–54**, 159, 163*

   in pipelining: *297*

   in the 8087 coprocessor: *271*

**condition-code register** A register that holds the condition code: *54, 60, **66**, **68***

   *See also* flags register; program status word

**condition-code-setting instruction** An instruction that sets, e.g., the processor-status bits in the condition-code register: ***68**, **69**, 313*

**configuration switch** In the IBM PC, a switch that the user sets to indicate the presence of an attached device, such as a coprocessor or a color graphics adapter: *264*

**conflict resolution** In an associative memory, the algorithm for determining which memory location to access when more than one location indicates a match: *187*

**connection degree** In an interconnection network, the number of other nodes that a given node contacts without intervening nodes: *326*

connection machine An SIMD computer whose processing elements occupy the vertices of a hypercube interconnection network: *323, 344*

   *See also* CM-1; CM-2; Intel iPSC/2

console *See* terminal

console interrupt An interrupt triggered by a computer operator from a terminal: *143, 150*

content-addressable memory (CAM) *See* associative memory

context The state of the CPU and memory during execution of a program: *144–145, 365*

   *See also* memory context; processor context

context restoration The restoration of a program's context; occurs, e.g., when an exception handler returns control to the interrupted program: *145*

**continuation point** The place where a procedure returns control when it finishes executing. For block-structured programs, this is usually the instruction following the CALL instruction; for coroutines, the continuation point is generally the instruction following the previously executed resume operation: *69*

**continuation-point address** *See* return address

control bus A bus that carries only control information: *120*

   *See also* address bus; data bus; system bus

Control Data Corporation (CDC): *4, 5, 8, 39, 163*

   *See also* CDC 6600; CDC 7600; CDC CYBER 170; CDC STAR

control-flow model A control paradigm in which each instruction specifies its own successor instruction, either implicitly using a program counter, or explicitly by executing a branch instruction: *102–103*

   For contrast, *see also* dataflow model

control instructions Instructions that alter the sequential flow of execution of a program (e.g., branch instructions, state-swapping instructions, procedure-linkage instructions): *67–70*

control lines Lines that make up a control bus and carry control information rather than data or addresses: *127*

   in a bus: *124*

   in the PC AT Bus: *257*

**control node** A node in a dataflow graph used to regulate the movement of tokens: *385* control pins   Pins that send and receive control information rather than data or addresses: *245*

**control port**   A port used to deliver control signals to a device: *164, 262*

control register   A register that controls the operation of a device; hence sending a value to a control register initiates a device operation

   in the 8087 coprocessor: *271*

   in the 8250: *267, 268*

   in the CDC 6600: *300, 302*

   in DMA I/O: *158*

   *See also* 8255A, control register in

control ROM   A ROM that holds control information (e.g., microprograms): *136*

control-signal bus   A bus that transmits control signals rather than data or addresses: *122*

   within a control unit: *133*

   within a CPU: *137*

   *See also* 8250, control signals of

**control store**   The memory store, frequently read-only, that holds the control words (microinstructions) of a computer using microprogrammed control: *129, 130, **139**, 310*

**control token**   In a dataflow graph, a logical token used for control, not data: *385, 386*

**control unit (CU)**   The part of a computer that generates the signals controlling the computer's operation: *12, 14, 16, 17, 124, 126–143, 146, 149*

   conventional: *143, 308, 311*

   microprogrammed: *129–137*

**conventional control unit:**   A control unit that uses conventional logic to generate the control signals, as opposed to one that reads and executes microprograms to generate control signals; also called hard-wired control unit: *128*

**conventional memory**   For the IBM PC family, the first megabyte of main memory: *275, 277, 278*

conventions   *See* figure conventions

CONVERT   An instruction in the 8088 microprocessor for converting a word operand to a byte value or vice versa: *240*

**coprocessor**   A support chip manufactured to operate in parallel with a CPU, usually a microprocessor, and add functionality to it: *238*

   *See also* 8087; 80287; 80387; floating-point coprocessor

COPY   The monadic vector instruction that copies the elements of one vector into another or a single scalar into all elements of a vector: *73*

**core**   The basic storage element in a magnetic-core memory: *7, **176***

core memory   A nonvolatile storage device, prominent in the 1960s, that stored bits of information in magnetic cores: *176*

   *See also* primary memory

**core plane**   A group of magnetic cores within a core-memory system that share the same control circuitry: *176*

coroutine   A procedure within a set of procedures that have equal status. Coroutines can transfer control back and forth arbitrarily, rather than obeying the call and return conventions of ordinary subroutines: *48*

cost   *See* system cost

count register (CX)   A register in the 8088 microprocessor that serves as a counter for certain instructions: *240, 241, 244*

**counter**   A device that increments or decrements the value it holds: ***428***

**coupling weight**   In a neural network, a measure of the influence that one neuron has on another: *390, 391*

**coverage of faults**   Within a fault-tolerant computer, the range of faults the system can tolerate without failure: *378*

CPU   *See* central processing unit

**CPU address**   In Intel's segment-register addressing, the address the CPU computes during program execution before it converts it into an effective address by adding the content of a segment register to it: *96, **242***

CPU bus   *See* local bus

CPU-controlled I/O   A type of I/O where the CPU transfers data directly to and from the I/O devices and controls them using I/O instructions: *154, 165*

   *See also* direct-memory-access (DMA) I/O; memory-mapped I/O

CPU cycle time   The clock-cycle time of the CPU: *181*

CPU performance evaluation   The use of various benchmark programs for determining the absolute speed of a computer (e.g., instruction executions per second, millions of floating-point instructions per second) or its speed relative to another processor (e.g., the VAX 11/780): *26–30*

CPU-to-memory bandwidth   The speed at which a computer can transfer data to and from memory, usually stated in megabytes per second (MBS): *312*

CRAY-1   The first pipelined vector processor by Cray Research (circa 1975): *219, 304, 308*

CRAY 1A: *179*

CRAY 1S:  *179*
   LINPACK benchmark of:  *307*
Cray-2:  *219*
Cray 2A:  *179*
Cray Research:  *42*
Cray X-MP:  *19, 179, 219, 367*
Cray Y-MP, LINPACK benchmark of:  *307*
critical data set   A data set shared by more than one process:  *67*
**critical section**   A section of code that can access a shared variable:  ***64, 67***
crossbar   A switch that can simultaneously connect a number of processors to a number of memory banks (or other devices):  *181, 323, 330, 338*
   multistage:  *323*
crossbar topology   The topology of a crossbar; hence, having complete processor-to-memory connections:  *329*
crosscorrelation   A mathematical operation that measures how similar two functions are; used in, e.g., image processing for blurring images:  *352*
CS   *See* chip select; code-segment register
CTS   *See* clear to send
CU   *See* control unit
Culler, D. E.:  *389*
Curnow, H. J.:  *27*
current address register   A register within the 8237A DMA controller:  *253*
current count   A count of the number of bytes transferred; kept by an 8237A DMA controller:  *255*
current count register   A register within the 8237A DMA controller for holding the current count:  *253*
CX   *See* count register
CYBER 170   *See* CDC CYBER 170
**cycle stealing**   Any situation in which an I/O device (e.g., DMA controller or channel) causes the CPU to wait because the device has exclusive access to a shared resource (e.g., a system bus or a storage system); the device is said to steal cycles from the CPU:  *157, 158, 163*
**cycle time**   The time required for a device (e.g., bus or storage system) to complete an operation due to the physical characteristics of the device
   for magnetic-core memory:  ***176***
   *See also* memory cycle
**cylinder**   On a disk storage device, the set of tracks that the read-write heads can access without moving; i.e., the set of tracks at a given distance from the spindle:  *165,* ***166***
cylinder number   The ordinal number of a cylinder on a disk; i.e., its cylinder address:  *165*

cylindrical topology   The topology of a cylinder; an interconnection topology formed from a two-dimensional grid by connecting the opposite ends of each row together:  *332*

DACK*n*   DMA acknowledge line *n*:  *256*
DADD2   An instruction that performs double-precision addition with two operands:  *56*
**daisy chaining**   A way of connecting more than one device to a single control line (e.g., interrupt line). Only one device contacts the control line directly; the next device contacts the first device, and so on, with all devices forming a single chain. If a device has a request, it blocks any requests from attached devices but sends its own request; otherwise, it passes the request it receives to the device it contacts, or to the control line if it is the first device in the chain:  ***254***
data-address register   A channel register that holds the address in main memory of the next item to be stored:  *160*
database machine   A special-purpose computer designed to efficiently implement the operations required for constructing and maintaining databases; (often has large, high-performance disks, and having a high transactions-per-second rate):  *383*
**data bits**   For a serial data transmission, the bits conveying the data. There may also be framing bits (start and stop bits), synchronization bits, parity bits, and address bits:  *265*
**data buffer**   A buffer for holding data during input or while placing data on a bus:  *237, 238, 256*
   in the IBM PC 251
**data bus**   A bus that transfers only data:  *120, 156*
**data consistency**   In a system where a single datum can appear in several places (e.g., cache, buffer, and main memory), the condition occurring when all copies are the same:  *367*
   *See also* cache coherence
data dependencies   The situation that arises when, e.g., two operations store values in the same location and the final value depends on the order of evaluation and the specific data:  *298, 384*
   in the CDC 6600 301, 302
data-enable line   A bus control line that carries a data-enable signal, which informs the attached devices that a bus master is placing a datum on the bus:  *124*
**dataflow architecture**   A computer architecture in which the primary control derives from the availability of the data rather than from the execution of a program. Architects design dataflow

computers for executing dataflow graphs; thus they are an alternative to von Neumann computers: *11, 19, 384–389*

**dataflow graph**   A graph whose nodes specify operations and whose arcs indicate where the nodes should send their results; hence the arcs specify data dependencies, not the order for evaluating the operations: *384, 389*

For contrast, *see also* program

**dataflow model**   A formal computational model that uses a dataflow graph, rather than a program, to specify a computation: *19, 384, 385*

parallelism in: *386*

For contrast, *see also* control-flow model

dataflow processor   A processor designed for evaluating dataflow graphs: *323, 383*

For contrast, *see also* von Neumann machine

**dataflow program**   A formal way of specifying a dataflow graph: *386*

**data pins**   Pins on an integrated circuit chip that carry only data: *245*

**data pointer**   A register in the 8087 coprocessor: *271*

**data precision**   The accuracy of a representation, often expressed in the number of digits it can encode: *48–52*

**data recovery**   In a fault-tolerant system, the use of techniques to restore damaged data: *378*

*See also* error detection and correction; fault avoidance

data register (DX), of the 8088 microprocessor: *240, 241*

*See also* 8255A, data register

data representation   The way the fields of a value appear in memory and the techniques used by the hardware and software to encode values in those fields: *36–48*

**data segment**   1. An area in memory containing only data: *96, 98*. 2. One of four 64-KB segments of memory that the 8088 microprocessor can access directly: *210, 244*

*See also* code segment; extra segment; stack segment

data segment register (DS)   A segment register in the 8088 microprocessor that holds the base address of the data segment: *241, 244*

**data set**   A place in memory for holding data, e.g., data received during a serial transmission: *266*

data set ready (DSR)   A control signal sent by, e.g., a modem to a universal asynchronous receiver-transmitter (UART) that tells the UART the modem is ready to send data: *266*

**data stream**   The sequence of data items transferred between the CPU and memory: *13, 15*

For contrast, *see also* instruction stream

data structure   A structure whose elements are items of data and whose organization is determined by the relationships between the data items and the access functions that the software or hardware uses to store and retrieve them. Examples are arrays and stacks: *45–48, 92, 100*

**data terminal**   A device for sending and receiving data, such as an 8250 universal asynchronous receiver-transmitter : *266*

data terminal ready (DTR)   A control signal sent by a universal asynchronous receiver-transmitter (8250 UART) to, e.g., a modem that tells the modem the UART is ready to receive data: *266*

data token   *See* token

data transceiver   A buffer for placing data on a data bus and for receiving data from the bus.

in the IBM PC: *247, 249*

**datatype**   A set of values together with a set of operations on them. For example, integers are a datatype. Integer values typically range from $-2^{N-1}$ to $2^{N-1} - 1$ on a computer having $N$-bit words, and integer operations typically include addition, subtraction, multiplication, division, and various comparison tests: *36, 41, 58*

*See also* 8087, datatypes of

**daughter board**   *See* card

deassert a signal   *See* assert low

**debit/credit benchmark**   A test for determining the performance of a computer system for transaction processing; based on a model of supporting typical teller operations of a bank: *29*

DEC   *See* Digital Equipment Corporation

decimal   A number expressed in base 10: *38, 51*

decimal arithmetic   Arithmetic performed on decimal numbers: *175*

for contrast, *see also* floating-point arithmetic

decimal digit   A single digit in a decimal representation: *20, 37*

decoder   A device for converting signals expressed in one representation to another (e.g., $n$-bit binary values to signals on one of $n$ lines): *418*

within a microinstruction unit: *135, 136*

DEC PDP-11   *See* PDP-11

DEC PDP-8   *See* PDP-8

DECREMENT STACK POINTER   An 8087 coprocessor instruction: *270*

DEC VAX   *See* VAX

DEDSEC   *See* double-error detection single-error correction

default segment register, in the 8088 microprocessor: *244*

**delayed branch**   A type of branch instruction in which the CPU always executes the instruction following it; used by some RISC machines to avoid the branch penalty: *313*

**delayed load**   A load operation in which the CPU concurrently executes the instruction following the LOAD instruction; used by some RISC machines to avoid the penalty that would otherwise occur while waiting for the address computation and associated read latency of the LOAD instruction: *313*

**delayed page fault**   In a paging system, a page fault that occurs during the execution of a complex instruction, e.g., MOVE STRING: *209*

**delta network**   A staged interconnection network that has a unique connection between each pair of inputs and outputs, and in which the address bits of the source and destination processors (or memory banks) control the pattern of connections: *337, 338*

**demand-driven architecture**   An architecture that resembles a dataflow architecture but that fires the nodes only when there is demand for a result; the first nodes to fire are those that produce the outputs: *11*

See also dataflow architecture; reduction machine

**demanded page**   The page of memory in a demand-paged system that holds the word the CPU requires: *208*

**demanded segment**   The segment of memory in a demand-segmented system that holds the word the CPU requires: *211*

demand-mode transfer   See DMA block mode

**demand-paged virtual memory**   A paged virtual-memory system that automatically loads into memory the demanded page whenever that page is not in memory: *196, 205*

demand paging   See demand-paged virtual memory

**demand-segmented virtual memory**   A segmented virtual-memory system that automatically loads into memory the demanded segment whenever that segment is not in memory: *205*

**demultiplexor (DEMUX)**   A device that has one input and many outputs and sends the input to exactly one of the outputs as specified by an external control: *138, 420, 421*

within microinstruction decoder: *135, 136, 137*

DEMUX   See demultiplexor

dendrite   1. The input filaments of a biological neuron: *390*. 2. The adaptive electrical inputs of a formal (electronic) neuron: *393*

**depth of faults**   The number of simultaneous faults of a given type that a system can detect (e.g., a DEDSEC storage system has a depth of 2): *378*

**destination address**   The address specified by an instruction that stores a value in memory: *61*

for a MOVE STRING instruction: *62*

destination index (DI)   A value maintained by the 8088 microprocessor: *241*

destination index register (DI)   A register in the 8088 microprocessor: *240, 241, 244*

**destination node**   In a dataflow graph, the node receiving the value when a token-producing node fires: *384*

destination register   A general term designating the register that gets the result of an operation; same as result or target register: *107*

See also Fi; result register; source register

destructive read   The process in a memory technology, such as DRAM, where the physical act of reading a value destroys the stored copy of the value. The storage system must therefore rewrite the value after reading it: *184, 185*

**destructive-read memory**   A storage system that uses a destructive-read technology (e.g., magnetic-core memory): *184, 185*

DF   See direction flag

DI   See destination index register

Digital Equipment Corporation (DEC):  *5, 19, 45*

See also PDP-8; PDP-11; UNIBUS; VAX; VAX-11; VAX 11/780; VAX 8600; VAX 8700

digitized image   The representation of an image used by a computer: *339, 352, 390*

DIP   See dual inline package

direct address   An addressing mode in the 8088 microprocessor: *243*

direct-connect router   A node in the hypercube interconnection network of the iPSC/2: *376*

direct indexed addressing   An addressing mode in the 8088 microprocessor: *243*

direction flag (DF)   A status bit in the 8088 microprocessor: *240*

**direct-mapped cache**   A cache that can map a given memory refill line to a single line in its own RAM: *199, 200–203*

direct mapping   See direct-mapped cache

**direct-memory-access (DMA) controller**   A device that executes the computer's side of the protocol for a direct-memory-access I/O operation: *157*

in the IBM PC: *234, 252–258*

operation of: *252–257*

direct-memory-access (DMA) I/O   A type of I/O in which a special DMA controller, rather than the CPU, transfers data between main memory and the I/O devices: *154, 157–164, 238*

For contrast, see also channel; CPU-controlled I/O; memory-mapped I/O

**dirty bit** A bit used to indicate that a device (e.g., the CPU) has modified the page, segment, cache refill line, or other block of memory: *99, 206, 207*

in paging: *209*

in segmentation: *211*

**dirty cell** A cell in a write-back cache holding a posted but uncompleted write to main memory; the dirty bit indicates that the mapped value in main memory is stale: *198*

**disable** An input to a tristate logic device or integrated-circuit chip that disables the device (i.e., places its outputs in the disconnected or high-impedance state): *415*

For contrast, *see also* enable

DISABLE INTERRUPTS An 8087 coprocessor instruction: *270*

**disconnected state** The state in which a tristate logic device floats its outputs, effectively disconnecting itself from the circuit: *415*

**disk access time** The time it takes a disk drive to access a single word: *167*

**disk drive** A device that holds and processes magnetic storage disks, such as floppy disks or a hard disk: *158, 165, 166, 167*

in paging: *208*

diskette controller, IBM PC test of, during system initialization: *275*

**disk sector** The smallest addressable unit on a disk drive; holds the smallest block of data that the disk controller can transfer. For an IBM PC, a sector usually consists of 512 bytes: *158, 165, 166*

floppy disk: *252*

**displacement** In an instruction, an address field that specifies an offset relative to a base value; the displacement is usually too small to address all of main memory: *92*

size of, in relation to instruction-set architecture: *101*

**displacement byte** One of two bytes in the address specification of instructions for the 8088 microprocessor that access memory: *242–243*

See also address-mode byte

**distributed control** A control paradigm in which the hardware distributes the control logic among a number of different processing elements (e.g., the nodes in an interconnection network with distributed control each have some control responsibility): *324*

in an interconnection network: *325, 326*

For contrast, *see also* centralized control

DIVIDE An operate instruction that specifies a division operation: *60,*

in the 8087 coprocessor: *270*

DMA *See* direct-memory-access I/O

**DMA acknowledge line** A dedicated control line used by a DMA controller to inform a requesting device that the request has been granted

in the PC AT Bus: *257*

in the PC Bus: *255*

**DMA autoinitialization** A mode of operation of the 8237A DMA controller in which a DMA channel automatically initializes itself to a specified state as soon as it completes its assigned operation: *253*

**DMA base address** The beginning address of a block of data to be transferred: *253*

**DMA base count** The total number of bytes to transfer: *253*

**DMA block mode** A type of transfer in which the 8237A DMA controller does not relinquish the bus until it finishes transferring the entire block of data, such as a disk sector; same as burst-mode transfer: *254, 255*

**DMA cascade mode** A technique for daisy chaining two or more 8237A DMA controllers to a PC. When two DMA controllers operate in cascade mode, the CPU controls one of them, which in turn sends control signals directly to the other (cascaded) DMA controller: *254*

DMA channel An independent unit within a DMA controller for controlling an I/O device: *155, 159, 163*

**DMA command register** A control register within the 8237A DMA controller that holds the operation code for the controller in additional to other control bits: *254*

DMA-controlled I/O *See* direct-memory-access I/O

DMA controller *See* direct-memory-access controller

**DMA current address** The main-memory address of the current byte or word being transferred: *253*

**DMA current count** The offset of the current byte or word being transferred; a count of the number of bytes or words already transferred for the current request: *253*

**DMA demand mode** A type of transfer by the 8237A DMA controller where the attached device tells the controller when to relinquish the bus. This mode is useful for buffered transfers and disk accesses, where the device can transfer an entire block of data at high speed: *254, 255*

**DMA mask register** A control register within the 8237A DMA controller that masks interrupt requests that it would otherwise request: *254*

**DMA mode register**  A control register within the 8237A DMA controller that determines the mode of a DMA transfer: *253*

DMA port-address assignment, in the IBM PC: *274*

DMA programming, during system initialization: *274*

DMA request line
  in PC AT Bus 257
  in PC Bus 248, 255

**DMA request register**  The 8237A DMA control register that initiates a DMA transfer: *254*

**DMA single mode**  An operation mode of the 8237A DMA controller in which it requests use of the bus for each item it wants to transfer; also called single-cycle DMA: *253–255*

  For contrast, *see also* burst mode transfer

**DMA status register**  The control register within the 8237A DMA controller that holds the status of the current transfer: *254*

**DMA temporary address register**  One of three temporary registers within the 8237A DMA controller that it uses during an I/O transfer: *254*

**DMA temporary count register**  One of three temporary registers within the 8237A DMA controller that it uses during an I/O transfer: *254*

**DMA temporary register**  One of three temporary registers within the 8237A DMA controller that it uses during an I/O transfer: *254*

Dongarra, J.: *27, 307*

**dot product**  A vector-reduction operation, also called scalar product, that produces the inner product of two vectors. If $\vec{V1} = (v_1, v_2, \ldots, v_k)$ and $\vec{V2} = (w_1, w_2, \ldots, w_k)$, then $\vec{V1} \cdot \vec{V2} = v_1 w_1 + v_2 w_2 + \cdots + v_k w_k$, where "$\cdot$" denotes dot product: *75, 82, 83*

**double-error detection single-error correction (DEDSEC) memory**  A storage system that uses parity bits to correct single errors (i.e., a $0_2$ bit has erroneously become a $1_2$ bit or vice versa) and can detect (but not correct) double errors (two errors in one word): *378*

**double precision**  A datatype specification, most often used for floating-point numbers, that uses a two-word representation: *37*
  arithmetic: *84*,
  IEEE floating-point format: *44–46*
  *See also* single precision

**doubleword**  A unit of memory consisting of two words: *37, 84, 85*

**downward compatibility**  The characteristic allowing an earlier, low-performance member of a computer family to run programs originally intended to run on later, high-performance machines in the same family: *5*
  of the EISA bus: *258*

**DRAM**  *See* dynamic random-access memory

**driving a bus**  Placing a value on a bus: *415*

**DRQ***i*  DMA request line *i*: *256*

**DS**  *See* data segment register

**DSR**  *See* data set ready

**DTR**  *See* data terminal ready

**dual-inline package (DIP)**  A packaging technology for integrated circuits where the pins are aligned in two parallel rows: *270, 412*

**dual-processor computer**  A multiprocessor having two CPUs: *322*

**dump**  A listing of all the values in memory: *196*

**DX**  *See* data register

**dynamic dataflow architecture**  An architecture based on the dynamic dataflow model of computation: *387, 388, 389*

**dynamic dataflow model**  A dataflow model that does not restrict the number of tokens on an arc: *387*

  For contrast, *see also* static dataflow model

**dynamic program relocation**  The movement of a program from one place to another in main memory after the program has started executing: *192, 193*

  For contrast, *see also* initial program relocation

**dynamic random-access memory (DRAM)**  Memory that requires refreshing to keep the data active. A cell in DRAM generally consists of a capacitor and transistor. The capacitor's charge decays, due to leakage, so the system must periodically refresh the charge to maintain the value: *178, 184, 185, 198, 237*
  refreshing: *257, 258, 268, 269*
  physical characteristics of: *186*

  For contrast, *see also* static random-access memory

dynamic relocation  *See* dynamic program relocation

**ease of repair**  A measurement of the quality of a computer architecture that focuses on how easily a technician can repair a faulty computer: *30*

**ease of use**  A measurement of the quality of a computer architecture that focuses on how easily a systems programmer can use the instruction set to implement the operating system's functions: *22*
  of the IBM PC: *280*
  of the CDC 6600: *103*

**EBCDIC**  *See* Extended Binary Coded Decimal Interchange Code

Eckert, J. P. Jr.: *5, 6, 13*

**edge connections**  Connections in a nearest-neighbor interconnection topology in which the rightmost processors of each row connect to the leftmost processors of the same or next row, and similarly for the top and bottom rows: *331*

EDSAC  Electronic Delay Storage Automatic Calculator. An early stored-program computer and one of the first to use binary numbers; designed by Maurice Wilkes in 1949 at Cambridge University: *5, 6*

EDVAC  Electronic Discrete Variable Computer. An early stored-program computer built at the Moore School of the University of Pennsylvania (circa 1945) and designed in part by John von Neumann: *5, 6*

EEMS  *See* Enhanced Expanded Memory Specification

**effective address**  The address the CPU generates to reference an instruction or variable in memory using the instruction-provided addressing modes such as base displacement and indexing but not using the address-translation mechanisms of virtual memory; usually the same as the compiler's logical address but not the same as the computer's physical address: *86, 89, 92, 97, 191, 205, 211, 213*

  in the 8088 microprocessor: *243, 244*

  in the Cm*: *374, 375*

**efficiency**  A measure of the quality of a computer architecture that focuses on how much of a system's hardware normally remains in use during its normal operation: *21–22, 29*

EGA  *See* Enhanced Graphics Adapter

EGA ROM, IBM PC address assignment for: *278*

EISA  *See* Extended Industry Standard Architecture bus

EISA card:  A card designed to be plugged into a slot that uses the EISA bus: *258*

**electrically alterable ROM (EAROM)**  Electrically alterable read-only memory; differs from other types of ROM in that a user can program it without special laboratory equipment and without removing it from the computer: *184*

  physical properties of: *186*

electrooptical technology  A technology that combines electrical and optical signal processing: *392*

elementary function  A mathematical function in the class that includes power, exponentiation, the trigonometric functions and their inverses, and combinations of these: *44*

elided normal bit  For binary fractions, the leftmost bit, called the normal bit, represents the value $\frac{1}{2}$. For nonzero normalized binary fractions, the leftmost bit is always $1_2$. Some computers that use normalized binary fractions omit (elide) the normal bit and increase the precision by 1 bit. After eliding the normal bit, the leftmost bit represents the value $\frac{1}{4}$: *44–46*

  of the DEC PDP-11 and VAX floating-point representations: *44*

**elision**  The omission of the normal bit in a normalized, binary fraction: *40*

**embedded control**  Describes a device in which the control processor is an integral part of the device (e.g., a laser printer): *20*

*empty*  In computers that use the SEND and RECEIVE synchronization instructions, the state of a memory cell that has been read by a RECEIVE instruction and not yet been refilled by a SEND instruction; hence a cell that is *empty* is not *full*: *65*

EMPTY  The instruction that performs an empty operation on a stack; hence returns *true* if the stack is empty and *false* otherwise: *47*

**empty operation**  The operation that tests whether a stack is empty or not empty: *47*

**empty slot**  In a dataflow graph, an argument slot that has not received an input token: *384*

empty stack  A stack having no values in it: *62*

empty-stack error  The error that results when a POP or TOP instruction attempts to read an empty stack: *47*

EMS  *See* Expanded Memory Specification

EMS card  An add-in card for the IBM PC that contains expanded memory: *277*

**enable**  An input to a device that enables its operation; the same as chip select: *415*

**enable input**  An input to a tristate logic device that, if not asserted high, places the device in its high-impedance or disconnected state: *413, 421*

ENABLE INTERRUPTS  A control instruction for the 8087 coprocessor: *270*

**encoder**  A device that converts signals from one representation to another (e.g., from unary to binary): *417*

END I/O  The last channel command in typical channel programs for I/O transfers: *161*

end-of-process line (EOP)  A line activated by an 8237A DMA controller when it finishes transferring an entire block of data (i.e., it reaches terminal count): *255*

**Enhanced Expanded Memory Specification (EEMS)**  An extension of the EMS standard for expanding memory that allows the CPU to execute programs directly out of the memory; adopted in 1987 by Lotus, Intel, and Microsoft, hence also called LIM 4.0 EMS: *277, 278, 279*

**Enhanced Graphics Adapter (EGA)** A color video display standard with a resolution of 640 × 350 pixels and 16 colors; introduced by IBM for the PC AT: *235*

enhanced memory  *See* Enhanced Expanded Memory Specification

enhanced VGA  A nonstandard video display mode that is upward-compatible with the VGA standard but which supports up to 256 colors at a resolution of 1024 × 768 pixels: *235*

ENIAC  Electronic Numerical Integrator and Calculator. One of the first operational electronic digital computers; built in 1946 by John Eckert and John Mauchly at the University of Pennsylvania: *5, 6*

Enterprise System Architecture/370  *See* IBM Enterprise System Architecture/370

**entry-operand-register designators**  Control registers in the CDC 6600 that specify which of the XBA operational registers hold the operands for currently executing instructions: *299*

**entry-point address (EPA)**  The address of the first instruction to be executed in a called procedure: *69, 70, 132*

   in the CDC 6600: *103*

   of a microprogram: *139*

EPA  *See* entry-point address

EPROM  *See* erasable PROM

Epson America: *236*

EQUAL  An operate instruction that tests the equality of two strings: *45, 46*

**erasable PROM (EPROM)**  Programmable read-only memory; a ROM that a technician can program using special laboratory equipment and later reprogram by first erasing its contents using strong ultraviolet light: *184*

   physical characteristics: *186*

   *See also* electrically alterable ROM

**error**  Any abnormal condition that occurs during a computer's operation: *377*

   empty stack: *47*

   in serial I/O transmission: *265–268*

**error detection and correction**  One of several approaches to building fault tolerance into a computer system, where error detection refers to the use of special hardware (such as parity bits or redundant circuitry) to detect the presence of errors in a system, and error correction refers to the restoration of damaged data resulting from faulty software or hardware: *378–383*

error recovery  The restoration of the normal operation of a computer after the hardware or software has detected an error condition: *194*

ES  See extra segment register

<ESC>  See escape character

ESCAPE  An instruction used by the 8088 microprocessor to control the operation of an 8087 coprocessor: *240, 271–272*

escape character  A special character that an application or system reserves for the purpose of flagging an escape sequence; the value of the escape character in the ASCII character set, denoted <ESC>, is $27_{10}$: *51*

**escape sequence**  A sequence of characters whose first value is an escape character; the escape character indicates that subsequent characters represent values other than the standard values for the character set: *51*

   For contrast, *see also* op-code encoding

**evaluation-stack architecture**  An architecture that has an evaluation stack, which it uses as an implied source for operands and an implied destination for results; hence all the operate instructions are 0-address instructions: *55*

**exception**  A hardware-initiated branch that transfers control from the executing program to an exception handler; exceptions triggered by events external to the program are interrupts, while those triggered by program events are traps: *70, 71, 143, 144, 150*

   in the Cm*: *375*

   prioritized: *152*

**exception and state-swapping instructions**  Special instructions, such as SUPERVISOR CALL or INTERRUPT, that initiate exceptions under software control, and special instructions, such as RETURN FROM INTERRUPT, that help the software return from an exception: *70-72, 143–152*

exception flag (IF), in the 8087 coprocessor: *271*

**exception handler**  A program that assumes control after an exception and processes the exception; may correct or log an error and abort the offending program or return control to it: *92, 144–148*

exception hardware  Any hardware specifically designed to support interrupt or trap processing: *148*

exception initiation  The actions taken by the CPU to switch execution from the current program to the exception handler; usually consists of saving the values in critical CPU registers, (e.g., the program counter and processor status bits) and replacing them with values appropriate for the exception handler, including the new PC value that causes the branch to the exception handler: *149–150*

exception masking  The disabling of exceptions of selected priorities: *150–152*

**exception number**  A number associated with each type of exception and used by the hardware to transfer control to the proper exception handler: *148*

*See also* interrupt-vector number

**exception processing**  All of the events that take place from the time an event triggers an exception until the exception handler returns control of the CPU to the interrupted program (or operating system); includes exception initiation as well as returning from the exception: *145*

*See also* interrupt processing

**exception-processing hardware**  Special hardware that receives request signals from the devices that can trigger exceptions, prioritizes and masks the requests, and initiates the exceptions: *143–152*

**exception vector**  The address of an exception handler: *146–148*

**exception-vector table**  A table containing exception vectors. During exception initiation the exception-processing hardware uses the exception number as an offset into the exception-vector table and then uses the resulting exception vector to transfer control to the exception handler: *148, 149*

**exception-vector-table address register**  A register that points to the beginning of the exception-vector table in memory: *148, 149*

**excess-1023 integer exponent**, of the IEEE floating-point representation: *45*

**excess-1024 inter exponent**, of the CDC CYBER 170 floating-point representation: *42*

  of the IEEE floating-point representation: *45*

**excess-127 integer exponent**, of the IEEE floating-point representation: *45*

**excess-128 integer exponent**, of the DEC PDP-11 and VAX floating-point representations: *44*

**excess-3**: *38*

**excess-64 integer exponent**, of the System/370 floating-point representation: *43*

**excess-$n$ integer**  An integer representation in which the binary value $n + K$ represents the integer $K$; $n$ is the bias; also called a bias-$n$ integer: *39–40*

EXCHANGE JUMP  A CDC 6600 instruction that swaps the processor context of one program with that of another program: *145*

**exchange operation**  An operation that permutes pairs of adjacent bits; input bit $I_i$ becomes output bit $I_{i+1}$ for even values of $i$, and $I_{i-1}$ for odd values of $i$: *334, 336*

exclusion  *See* mutual exclusion; process exclusion

EXECUTE  A special instruction that causes the computer to execute a single instruction at a specified memory address: *103, 104*

**execute cycle**  The cycle during which a von Neumann machine performs the operation specified by an instruction: *126*

For contrast, *see also* fetch cycle

**execute-only page**  A page in a virtual memory system that is marked as containing code that may be read and executed but not modified; i.e., a read-only code page: *209*

**execution-stack architecture**  An architecture in which a stack is an integral part of the central processing unit. Operate instructions use the stack as an implied source for operands and an implied destination for results; hence all operate instructions are 0-address instructions. Also called stack architecture: *8*

**executive mode**  A privileged mode of operation of a CPU in the DEC PDP-11 and VAX families: *71*

EXPAND  A vector instruction that initiates a vector expansion operation: *78*

**expandability**  A measure of the quality of a computer architecture that focuses on the ease with which an architect can extend capabilities of the architecture by adding, e.g., memory or I/O devices to it: *23*

  of the IBM PC: *280*

**expanded local bus**  A local bus with special extensions for use outside the CPU that provides standard control signals as well as address and data pathways: *121–123, 238*

**expanded memory**  A type of physical memory that may be added to a PC to provide it with additional high-speed RAM: *191, 217–218, 277–279*

  in the IBM PC: *277–279*

*See also* Expanded Memory Specification

**expanded-memory manager**  The software system that manages the expanded-memory hardware on an IBM PC: *218*

**Expanded Memory Specification (EMS)**  A specification for expanded memory introduced by Lotus, Intel, and Microsoft (LIM); also called LIM 3.2 EMS. The EMS controller maps the addresses within a window (an unused block of memory addresses) into addresses in its own (EMS) address space. Using memory banking, the EMS card can map the same block of physical addresses into different blocks of EMS memory: *277*

expansion  *See* vector expansion

**explicit operand**  An operand of an instruction specified by a field or fields other than the opcode field: *59, 87*

**exponent** The part of a floating-point representation that holds the power to which the radix must be raised when computing the value of the floating-point number. The value is $(-1)^S M \times R^E$, where $M$ is the coefficient, $R$ is the implicit radix, $E$ is the exponent, and $S$ is the sign (0 implies positive and 1 implies negative): *37, 40, 41, 52*

   in NaN: *44*

**exponent base** *See* radix

**exponent bits** The bits in a floating-point representation that hold the exponent: *41*

**Extended Binary Coded Decimal Interchange Code (EBCDIC)** A character representation used in IBM mainframes: *37*

**Extended Graphics Array (XGA)** A color video standard introduced by IBM in 1991 that supports 1024 × 768 pixels with 256 colors or 640 × 480 pixels with 65,536 colors: *236*

**Extended Industry Standard Architecture (EISA) bus** A bus standard that extends the IBM PC and PC AT buses to 32 bits: *236, 237, 258–259*

   bus cycle of: *258*

**external storage** Memory (e.g., disk memory) that is not part of the main storage system of a computer: *165, 191*

**extra segment** One of four 64-KB segments of memory directly addressed by the 8088 microprocessor; holds data for string operations: *234, 244*

   *See also* code segment; data segment; stack segment

**extra-segment register (ES)** A register of the 8088 microprocessor that holds the base address of the extra segment: *241, 244*

**extremal reduction** An operation that finds the maximum or minimum value (or sometimes its address) in a vector: *75*

**failure** The incorrect operation of a computer component (either hardware or software) that results in an operational error in the system: *377*

   *See also* hard fault, soft fault; software failure

**fault** The failure of a system component: *205, 215, 377*

**fault avoidance** A technique for providing fault tolerance in a system by using highly reliable components and proven design and manufacturing techniques: *378*

   *See also* data recovery; error detection and correction

**fault-tolerant computer** A computer that can tolerate faults by applying fault-tolerance techniques: *377–383*

**fault-tolerant multiprocessor** A fault-tolerant computer having more than one processor: *377*

**fault-tolerant node** In an interconnection network, a node that removes itself from operation when faulty, so that messages can pass by: *328*

FETCH AND ADD A synchronization instruction that fetches a value from memory, adds a second value to it, and stores the result back in memory in one indivisible operation: *64, 65*

FETCH AND INCREMENT A FETCH AND ADD instruction that always adds the value 1 to the datum in a memory: *64, 65*

**fetch cycle** The cycle of a von Neumann machine during which the CPU fetches an instruction from memory and increments the program counter: *126*

**fetch-execute cycle** The principle mode of operation of a von Neumann computer; consists of an unending sequence of fetch and execute cycles: *14*

**fetch microcode** The microprogram that controls the fetch cycle of a computer: *149*

**fetch system, in a dataflow architecture** The system that inspects memory for firable nodes, retrieves the corresponding instruction packets, and readies them for execution by a processing element: *389*

**F-floating point representation, of the VAX:** *45*

**Fi** Designates a destination register in a CDC 6600 instruction: *298, 303*

**field, in an instruction** *See* instruction field

**field extraction** The operation of extracting a field from a datum: *61*

**field length (FL)** With reference to the CDC 6600, the number of words the operating system permits a program to access. The memory-protection hardware generates an exception on any attempt by a program to read or write to an address that exceeds the field-length bounds: *193*

**field-length register (FL)** A special register within the CDC 6600 memory-protection hardware that holds the field length of the memory partition that the currently executing program may access: *193, 194*

**FIFO** *See* first-in first-out storage policy

**figure conventions:** *408–409*

**firable node** In a dataflow graph, a node that has one token in every argument slot: *384, 389*

**first-generation computer** Any of the computers built between about 1949 and 1960 that used vacuum-tube technology and either a batch-operating system or no operating system; one-of-a-kind experimental machines: *5*

*See also* ABC; EDSAC; EDVAC; ENIAC; Mark-I to Mark-IV

**first in, first out (FIFO) storage policy** A policy for certain memory-accessing operations that retrieves the item stored for the longest time; the storage policy of a queue: *208*

*See also* instruction queue

Fischer, M. J.: *393*

fixed disk *See* hard disk

Fj Designates an operand register in a CDC 6600 instruction: *298, 299, 303*

Fk Designates an operand register in a CDC 6600 instruction: *298, 299, 303*

FL *See* field-length register

FL *See* field length

**flag** A 1-bit register that holds processor-status information: *13, 127, 130, 149*

*See also* carry flag; condition-code register; negative flag; positive flag: overflow flag; zero-result flag

**flags register** A register, often in the arithmetic and logic unit of a computer, comprising the computer's status flags: *125*

in the 8088 microprocessor: *240, 241*

in the IBM PC during system initialization: *273*

*See also* carry flag; condition code; negative flag; positive flag; overflow flag; processor status bits; zero-result flag

**flip-flop** A storage device that holds a single bit of data: *184,* **424,** *428*

**floating floating-point** A number representation that uses two floating-point exponent fields to increase the range of exponent values (at the expense of reduced mantissa precision): *52*

For contrast, *see also* block floating-point

floating-point The representation of a floating-point number on a computer: *40–45, 51–52*

of the Burroughs B-5500: *41*

of the CDC CYBER 170: *41–42*

of the DEC PDP-11 and VAX families: *43–44*

of the IBM System/370: *43*

of the IEEE Floating-point Standard 754: *43*

floating-point adder: *424*

floating-point arithmetic Arithmetic whose operands and results are floating-point numbers: *20, 21, 235*

in the IBM PC: *279*

For contrast, *see also* decimal arithmetic

floating-point coprocessor A coprocessor that provides a CPU chip with floating-point hardware (and usually hardware for integer arithmetic as well): *104, 126, 313, 376*

*See also* 8087; 80287; 80387

floating-point functional unit A functional unit for performing floating-point arithmetic; available on most high-performance computers and RISCs: *313*

pipelined *See* floating-point pipeline

**floating-point number** A noninteger value represented in four parts: the sign, $S$ (0 for positive and 1 for negative), the exponent $E$ (an integer), the mantissa $M$ (either an integer or a fraction), and the radix (or exponent base) $R$ (an integer usually implied by the hardware). The value represented by the number $(S, E, M, R)$ is $(-1)^S M \times R^E$: **36,** *37,* **40–46,** *60, 163*

precision of: *50–52*

floating-point pipeline A pipelined functional unit for floating-point operations: *293*

**floppy disk** A disk storage device that uses a removable, flexible disk for the storage medium: *165, 166, 185, 252*

controller for: *255, 260*

**flowthrough time** Once the CPU places the operands in the pipeline, the time it takes the first result to emerge: *289, 293*

flowthrough binary multiplier A sequential circuit for binary multiplication: *293*

**flushing a cache** The process in which the CPU voids or clears all cache entries; done when, e.g., the values in cache become stale: *370*

**flushing a pipeline** The process of allowing all operations in a pipeline to run to completion without placing any new operands in the pipeline: *296*

Flynn, M. J.: *14*

Flynn's classification The classification of computer architectures, by M. J. Flynn, consisting chiefly of the following four classes: SISD, SIMD, MISD, MIMD: *14–16*

Fm A designation for the operation mode in a CDC 6600 instruction: *298, 303*

font A complete set of characters (including letters, numerals, punctuation marks, and special symbols) having a given face (e.g., Times Roman, Helvetica), weight (e.g., bold, light), and point size: *50, 51*

**fork node** A node in a dataflow graph that generates more than one output token; hence causes a fork in an operation and multiple threads of control: *386, 388*

**formal neuron** In a (mathematical) neural network, a computational unit that simulates the electrical behavior of a biological neuron; also called a mathematical neuron: *390*

Fortran FORmula TRANslator; a programming language introduced by IBM (circa 1960) for

## Glossary/Index

specifying programs in an English-like syntax: *76*

**forward compatibility** Program compatibility where a newer computer in an existing family or a descendent family will correctly run programs written for older machines in the family: *5, 106*

**fourth-generation computer** Computers beginning in the mid-1970s characterized by solid-state memory, very large scale integrated circuits, and multiprogramming operating systems: *8*

**fraction** A value represented by the quotient of two integers. In computers, binary fractions are common, where the leftmost bit represents $2^{-1}$, the next bit represents $2^{-2}$, and so forth: *37–39*

**framing error** During bit-serial data transmission, the error that results when the receiver samples the incoming data at the incorrect time: *266*

Fujitsu VPx-EX: *304*

*full* For computers that use SEND and RECEIVE synchronization instructions, said of a cell in memory that holds a value. A cell in memory that does not hold a value is *empty*: *65, 66*

**full adder** A sequential circuit that adds two binary operands and a carry and produces their sum (modulo 2) and carry-out: *422, 423*

**full crossbar** A crossbar switch that can concurrently connect each processor to an independent memory bank; also called a nonblocking crossbar: *328, 332*

**full slot** An argument slot in a dataflow graph that holds an input token: *384*

**fully associative cache** *See* associative cache

function In a programming language, a self-contained unit of code that can receive arguments from a calling program and return a value to it: *48*

**functional unit** An ALU or other device for performing, e.g., an arithmetic, shift, or logical operation: *125, 137, 138*

  microprogrammed control of: *137*

  scheduling of: *298–303*

**function-unit designator** A tag used by the CDC 6600 to designate a functional unit; designated by Fm: *299–300*

game I/O adapter, IBM PC port-address assignment: *274*

garbage collection In a memory-management system, the process of reclaiming unused memory: *383*

gate *See* logic gate

GATHER A vector instruction for performing a gather operation: *76, 79*

**gather operation** A vector operation that creates a new vector by using an index array to select elements from an existing vector; that is, $V_{new}(I) \leftarrow V_{old}(INDEX(I))$: *78*

Gaussian distribution A mathematical distribution often used in image-processing applications for blurring images: *352*

**general-purpose register** Registers that instructions can use for many different functions, e.g., as accumulators, index registers, address registers, and base registers: *53, 57, 92*

For contrast, *see also* special-purpose registers

**generality** A measure of the quality of a computer architecture that focuses on how applicable the instruction-set architecture is to a wide range of applications: *20–22*

generalized-cube *See* hypercube

**general-purpose register-set machine** A machine that mainly uses general-purpose registers rather than special-purpose registers: *57, 92*

*See also* special-purpose register-set machine

**geometric mean** The *n*th root of the product of *n* data: *28*

For contrast, *see also* arithmetic mean; harmonic mean; weighted arithmetic mean

**gigaflops** Billions of floating-point operations per second. A common measure of the performance of a scientific computer; also abbreviated GFLOPS: *25*

**globally synchronized network** An interconnection network whose operation is synchronized by a single systemwide clock: *338*

*See also* centralized control; distributed control

**global-memory (GM)** Memory in a multiprocessor system that is common to all processors: *16, 19*

*See also* local memory; GM-MIMD; GM-SIMD

**global-memory system architecture** An architecture with memory that is global to some or all of its processors: *16*

For contrast, *see also* local-memory system architecture

GM *See* global memory

GM-MIMD: *19, 321, 322, 364*

  *See also* global memory; multiple instruction stream, multiple data stream

GM-SIMD: *19*

  *See also* global memory; single instruction stream, multiple data stream

Goldstine, H. H.: *13*

Goodyear Aerospace Corporation: *187, 330, 342, 347*

  *See also* MPP

**granularity** *See* pipeline granularity

**half adder** A sequential circuit that adds two binary values and produces their sum (modulo 2) and carry-out: *422, 423*

half byte  Four bits; also called a nibble: *37*

halfword  A unit of storage equal to one-half of a word; used by computers having large words (e.g., 32 bits and 64 bits) for holding small values or values not requiring the full precision of a word: *84*

HALT  An instruction for halting an 8088 microprocessor: *240*

HALT I/O  An I/O channel instruction for terminating its activity: *70, 159*

handshake lines, in the 8250 UART: *266*

handshake signals, in the 8250 UART: *268*

**handshaking**  A general method of controlling the flow of information between two communicating processors or devices, in which permission to send is requested and granted before the data are sent, and often an acknowledgment of receipt of data is given after the transmission: *262–268*

in the 8250 UART: *265–268*

in the 8255A PPI: *262–265*

**hard disk**  A storage device that uses from one to many fixed (nonremovable) disks for holding the data: *165–167*

hard-disk controller, in the IBM PC: *274, 276, 277*

port-address assignment of: *274*

**hard fault**  The permanent failure of a component in a computer system (e.g., a crashed disk or an inoperative integrated circuit): *377*

For contrast, *see also* soft fault

**hardware-intensive architecture**  An architecture (e.g., SIMD) in which the computational potential is proportional to the amount of available hardware: *341*

hardware interlocks in pipelining  Circuits in a pipelined processor that detect data dependencies and control the scheduling of instructions to avoid incorrect results: *297*

hardware stack  A stack that stores the entries in registers rather than in memory: *430, 432*

**hardware-system architecture (HSA)**  The design of the hardware system of a computer, including its central processing unit, dataflow organization, bus structure, control organization, and input-output system: *3, 4, 119, 137, 230, 232*

of the IBM PC: *245–279*

hard-wired control unit  *See* conventional control unit

**harmonic mean**  The reciprocal of the average of the reciprocals of a set of data. This gives the average speed of a CPU when given individual speed measurements, while the arithmetic mean does not: *28*

For contrast, *see also* arithmetic mean; geometric mean; weighted arithmetic mean

**Harvard architecture**  A von Neumann architecture with independent data and instruction paths to memory (or cache): *11, 12, 204, 312*

Harvard University: *6*

head-positioning delay  *See* seek time

**heartbeat**  In a fault-tolerant computer, a message sent from one processor to another indicating that the sender is operational; also called watchdog timer or I'm alive notice: *380*

Hewlett-Packard Company (HP): *27, 236, 314*

HP Spectrum 314

hexadecimal notation  A notation in which values are expressed in base 16: *405–406*

hexadecimal point: *40*

**high impedance state**  The state of a tristate logic device in which the outputs are effectively disconnected from the circuit: *413, 415*

high-level-language machine  A machine designed primarily for executing programs expressed in a single high-level programming language, such as LISP or Algol: *20*

high-level programming language  A programming language that allows a user to express programs in a highly symbolic way; a single statement in a high-level programming language often compiles into hundreds of machine instructions: *8*

**high-order bit**  The leftmost bit in a binary representation of a number; the bit conveying the most significance: *37*

**high-order interleave**  A memory system where the high-order address bits select the bank of memory and the low-order bits select the word within the bank; consecutive addresses appear in the same or adjacent bank of memory: *179, 181, 182*

For contrast, *see also* low-order interleave

**high signal**  A signal that represents the value $1_2$, or true: *413*

HIO  *See* HALT I/O

Historical overview of computers: *5–11*

hit rate, of cache  The percentage of memory accesses that are satisfied by a cache; thus the ratio of cache hits to the total number of hits plus misses: *202, 204, 215*

HOLD request  Within the IBM PC, for example, a request by a device such as DMA controller or a floating-point coprocessor to use the bus: *250*

**homogeneous addressing** Addressing in which all addresses are preferred equally by the hardware: *99*

*See also* inhomogeneous addressing

**horizontal control** Control where each control bit regulates a single gate or machine operation: *134, 135–137*

For contrast, *see also* vertical control

**host computer** A general-purpose computer that controls the operation of a special-purpose computer. Many computers use host computers, including the ILLIAC IV, Goodyear's MPP, and Thinking Machine's CM-2 Connection Machine: *16*

**HSA** *See* hardware-system architecture

**hub** In a network having a star interconnection topology, the central node to which all other nodes are attached; used by some local-area networks: *328*

**hypercube** An interconnection network having the hypercube topology: *335, 340*

in the iPSC/2: *376*

**hypercube processor** An SIMD processor whose processing elements occur at the nodes of a hypercube: *321, 339, **342**, 344, 361*

**hypercube topology** An interconnection topology having $2^N$ nodes, such that each node has a unique binary address on the range 0 to $2^N - 1$ and there is a direct connection between every two nodes whose addresses differ in exactly 1 bit position; the degree of the hypercube is $N$: *326, **333**, 334, 339*

**I** *See* interrupt disable flip-flop

**i860** *See* Intel i860

**IAS** A first-generation computer designed by John von Neumann and his colleagues and built at the Institute for Advanced Studies at Princeton University: *6*

**IBF** *See* input buffer full

**IBM** *See* International Business Machines Corporation

**IBM 7090** An early IBM scientific computer (circa 1960) that used discrete-transistor technology: *179*

**IBM Enterprise System Architecture/370** A descendant of the IBM System/370 that has a similar instruction-set architecture, additional addressing facilities, better support for multiprocessors, and improved stack facilities for subroutine linkage: *5*

**IBM Micro Channel Architecture** IBM's expanded-local-bus architecture introduced in its PS/2 family of personal computers: *122*

**IBM MIPS** A measure of performance relative to an IBM computer: *26–28*

**IBM PC** A personal computer introduced in 1981 by IBM that uses the 8088 microprocessor: *4, 19, 24, 71, 84, 104, 164, 165, 215, 217, **232–280**, 304*

LINPACK benchmark of: *307*

port-address assignments of: *274*

*See also* PC I/O Channel Bus

**IBM PC AT** An IBM PC computer that uses the 80286 microprocessor and has a PC AT I/O Channel Bus: *22, 234, 236, 237, 257, 279*

LINPACK benchmark of: *307*

*See also* PC AT I/O Channel Bus

**IBM PC XT** An IBM PC with a hard disk. *See* IBM PC

**IBM PS/2** A family of computers (Personal System/2) introduced in 1987 to replace the IBM PC family; the highest-performance models have a bus with Micro Channel Architecture: *232, **235**, 236*

**IBM RISC System/6000** A family of superscalar (capable of issuing more than one instruction during each clock cycle) RISC machines introduced in 1990: *307, 314*

LINPACK benchmark of: *307*

**IBM RS/6000** *See* IBM RISC System/6000

**IBM System/360** Introduced by IBM in 1964, a family of 32-bit general-purpose register-set machines intended for both business and scientific applications: *4, 5, 24, 94, 106, 193, 209, 219, 220, 308*

interrupt structure of: *163*

memory protection in: *192–193*

program relocation in: *192–193*

**IBM System/370** A descendent family of the System/360 that supports a larger logical address space and virtual memory: *19, 24, 42, 57, 66, 152, 219, 309*

**IBM System/R6000** *See* IBM RISC System/6000

**ICR** *See* interrupt-code register

**IC** *See* integrated circuit

**idle** The state of a serial I/O interface that is not sending or receiving data: *265*

**IEEE** *See* Institute of Electrical and Electronics Engineers: *42*

**IEEE floating-point standard** Standard number 754, developed in 1985 by a committee of the Institute of Electrical and Electronics Engineers (IEEE), presents a comprehensive specification for the floating-point datatype, including formats, operations, roundoff, elementary functions, infinite and indefinite numbers, and unnormalized representations: *43, **44**, 45, 51, 107, 270*

IF  *See* interrupt flag

ILLIAC IV  A one-of-a-kind SIMD processor array (circa 1966) developed at the University of Illinois and consisting of 64 word-parallel processing elements (PEs), a PE control unit, and a Burroughs host computer:  *4, 8, 19, 331, 342, 354*

image  A digital representation of a picture consisting of a large number of values, called pixels (picture elements), which represent sampled image intensity and color values:  *352–356, 358*

**image blurring**  The process of reducing random noise in an image by cross-correlating the image with a mask to eliminate bad pixels (e.g., those resulting from errors in picture transmission):  *344, 352–354*

   processor-array algorithm for:  *352–358*

image digitizer  A device for scanning an image and producing a digitized image:  *154*

**image mask**  A small image used for various image-processing operations, such as blurring:  ***352, 353, 355***

image processing  The processing of an image by a computer, such as enhancing its quality or extracting information from it:  *339*

image-processing machine  A computer designed primarily for image processing:  *20*

**I'm alive notice**  *See* heartbeat

immediate-data byte  A byte in an 8088 instruction that holds an immediate operand:  *242*

**immediate operand**  An operand that appears within the instruction stream, generally within the instruction itself:  ***59, 82, 107***

   For contrast, *see also* addressed operand

implementation  The realization of a computer in hardware, including the choice of technology, speed, amount of memory, and so forth:  *4, 119*

implicit branching  Branching that takes place implicitly during, e.g., the execution of a vector instruction:  *304*

implicit indexing  Indexing that takes place implicitly during, e.g., the execution of a vector instruction:  *304*

**implicit operand**  An operand implied by the op code but not otherwise specified (e.g., an accumulator in a 1-address instruction):  ***59, 83, 87***

implied addressing  In the 8088 microprocessor, addressing that uses only the default segment register, because the instruction itself does not specify a displacement:  *243*

IMR  *See* interrupt-mask register

IN  The input instruction of the 8088 microprocessor:  *240, 245, 252, 258, 261*

   use during PPI input:  *264*

**inactive process**  A process (e.g., a suspended process) that does not have control of a processor:  ***64***

   For contrast, *see also* active process

incompleteness  One property of an instruction set that lacks some functionality:  *103*

increment  *See* vector stride

INCREMENT  An instruction for adding 1 to an operand:  *67, 309*

**increment node**  In a dataflow graph, a node that specifies an increment operation:  *387*

INCREMENT STACK POINTER  An 8087 coprocessor instruction:  *270*

indefinite number  The result of an indeterminate operation, such as division of 0 by 0; called NaN in the IEEE floating-point standard:  *44*

**index**  1. An address offset that the indexing hardware automatically adds to the instruction address when the instruction specifies indexed addressing:  ***53***.  2. The ordinal position of the first character of a substring within a string (e.g., the index of the substring 'CD' within the string 'ABCEDF' is 3:  ***46***

INDEX  An operate instruction that searches one character string for another as a substring and returns its index if found:  *45, 46*

index array  An array whose elements select the elements from a second structure, such as a vector:  *76*

**indexed addressing**  An addressing technique in which the instruction specifies an address and an index register; the hardware automatically adds the content of the index register (the index) to the instruction address to get the effective address of the operand:  ***53, 88–92***

**indexed-indirect addressing**  One of two addressing techniques that combines indexing with indirect referencing:  ***91–92***

   in exception handling:  *148*

   *See also* preindexed-indirect addressing, postindexed-indirect addressing

indexed-indirect jump  A branch instruction that uses an index to access a value in a table and then uses that value as the branch-target address; used by the 8088 microprocessor during interrupt processing:  *250*

**indexing**  The process of adding an index to an address to get an indexed address:  ***88***

   hardware:  *53, 89*

**index register**  A register that holds an index or address displacement:  ***53, 88, 89, 92, 101, 220***

   of the 8088 microprocessor:  *240*

   of the CDC 6600:  *298*

**index-register designator** The field in an instruction that designates an index register: *89*

**indirect address** An address that specifies a memory location whose content is the address of an operand, rather than the operand itself: *89, 90, 92, 96*

in branch instructions: *89*

**indirect addressing** Any addressing technique in which the instruction specifies the address of an indirect address rather than the address of the operand; the indirect address is then the address of the operand; also called indirection: *68*

**indirect branch** A branch instruction that uses indirect addressing to specify the branch-target instruction: *90*

*See also* indexed-indirect jump

**indirection** *See* indirect addressing

**indivisible instruction** *See* atomic instruction

**Industry Standard Architecture (ISA)** Another name for an IBM PC AT–compatible bus: *237*

**infinite loop** A program loop that does not terminate: *144*

**infinite number** A number too large for any finite representation (e.g., the result of division by 0 of a positive value): *44*

**inhomogeneous addressing** A property of the address space of some computers in which the hardware prefers some addresses to others (e.g., some microprocessors prefer page-0 addresses to other addresses because they require fewer instruction bits): *99*

For contrast, *see also* homogeneous addressing

**initial-count register** A register in an 8253 programmable interval timer that holds the number of clock ticks until an event: *268*

INITIALIZE PROCESSOR An 8087 coprocessor instruction: *270*

**initial program relocation** A relocation process that the operating system performs when it loads a program into main memory prior to that program's execution, which consists of loading the program at addresses that differ, often by a single relocation offset, from the program's logical addresses. Also called static program relocation: *94, 192*

For contrast, *see also* dynamic program relocation

INITIATE INTERRUPT An 8088 microprocessor instruction for initiating a trap: *240*

**inner product** *See* dot product

INPUT An input instruction: *70*

**input-acknowledge** A status signal sent by the 8255A PPI during input to acknowledge the receipt of data: *262*

**input arc** On a dataflow graph, an arc into which the operating system or control program injects input tokens: *384*

**input buffer full (IBF)** A status flag used by the 8255A PPI during input: *262–264*

**input-output** *See* I/O

**input-output system** *See* I/O system

**input pattern** In a neural network (e.g., a perceptron), the pattern of values being applied to the network as an input: *391–392*

**input port** An I/O port that is configured to accept data from an I/O device or I/O controller and send it to memory or the CPU: *164, 262*

**input protocol** The protocol used by an I/O device or interface during an input operation

for the 8255A PPI: *263*

for the 8250 UART: *267*

*See also* handshaking

**input strobe** An external input to an 8255A PPI which tells it that the input data are available: *262*

**input token** A data token that the operating system injects into a dataflow processor to start it going: *384*

Institute for Advanced Studies: *6*

Institute of Electrical and Electronics Engineers (IEEE): *42*

**instruction** A datatype that specifies a machine operation, the addresses of the operands, and the locations of the results; also called a machine instruction: *13, 131, 136, 143, 150*

types of: *57–81*

*See also* channel command; microinstruction

**instruction address** An address as specified by an instruction and given in terms of the particular addressing techniques supported by the computer's hardware: *85*

**instruction broadcast** In an SIMD processor, the simultaneous transmission of identical control signals to all processing elements: *344*

**instruction counter** *See* program counter

**instruction decoding** The analysis of an instruction by the control unit to determine what operation to perform, to resolve the operand addresses, and to fetch the operands: *14, 285*

in the CDC 6600: *300, 301*

parallelism in pipelining: *296, 304*

**instruction execution** That part of a machine cycle in which the CPU carries out the operation specified by an instruction: *13, 14*

in the CDC 6600: *301–303*

**instruction fetch** That part of a machine cycle during which the CPU fetches an instruction from memory and decodes it prior to execution: *13, 132*

microprogram for: *139–141*

in pipelining: *304*

instruction-fetch system  The system in dataflow architecture that determines when instructions are firable and retrieves them from memory: *388*

**instruction field**  A portion of an instruction that specifies a particular item of information; e.g., the op-code field specifies the operation, and a register-specification field gives the number of a register for the operation: *13, 104*

**instruction format**  The way the instruction fields are laid out in memory: ***13, 107***

**instruction issue**  The last process performed by an instruction-unit pipeline; typically consists of reserving a functional unit, sending an operation code to it, and reserving the result register: ***298***

in the CDC 6600: *301*

**instruction packet**  Within a dataflow machine, a data structure comprising an operation code, a set of operand tokens, and the address of where to send the result token; the equivalent of a machine instruction: *389*

instruction pipelining  The simultaneous decoding of several instructions by a pipelined instruction unit: *294–303*

instruction pointer  *See* program counter

instruction prefetch  The retrieval from memory of an instruction, such as a branch-target instruction, before it is needed by the control unit: *295*

instruction prefix  A byte in memory that precedes an instruction and alters the way the CPU executes the instruction; also called prefix. *See* REPEAT; segment-override prefix

instruction processing  *See* instruction execution

instruction queue  A queue that holds instructions prior to their execution; an instruction buffer: *248, 388, 389*

**instruction register (IR)**  A control-unit register that holds the instruction while the circuitry decodes and executes it; not generally part of the computer's instruction-set architecture: *53, 126, 127, 129, 130, 132, 137, 139, 141, 142, 160*

**instruction set**  The set of all valid instructions for a computer: ***13, 22, 54***

**instruction-set architecture (ISA)**  The appearance of a computer from a machine-language programmer's point of view, including its datatypes, register set, instruction set, and run-time operation (interrupt and I/O structure): ***3, 4, 10***, *22, 34–36, 58, 98, 101, 102, 107, 119, 137, 160, 233*

datatypes of: *36*

of the IBM PC: *239–245*

in relation to pipelining: *10*

instruction-set design  The process of selecting datatypes, operations, addressing modes, instructions, and instruction formats for a computer: *101–108*

**instruction size**  The number of units of memory (usually in bits or bytes) that an instruction uses: *13*

**instruction stream**  The sequence of instructions fetched by the CPU for execution: *15*

For contrast, *see also* data stream

**instruction-unit pipeline**  A pipeline that processes instructions in stages; used primarily in RISC machines and supercomputers: *289*

INT  An interrupt request signal: *256*

use during PPI input: *263, 264*

use during PPI output: *262*

**integer**  A binary datum representing an integer; any value from the infinite set {... −3, −2, −1, 0, 1, 2, 3, ...}: ***36–40, 60***

mantissa of the CDC CYBER 170 floating-point representation: *41*

range: *50*

**integrated circuit (IC)**  A single semiconductor component containing from two to millions of discrete components (e.g., transistors): ***411***

*See also* large-scale integration; medium-scale integration; small-scale integration; very large scale integration

Intel 80x86 family  The family comprising (as of 1990) the 8086, 8088, 80286, 80386, 80386SX, and 80486 microprocessors: *96*

Intel 4004  *See* 4004

Intel 80286  *See* 80286

Intel 80287  *See* 80287

Intel 80386  *See* 80386

Intel 80386SX  *See* 80386SX

Intel 80387  *See* 80387

Intel 80486  *See* 80486

Intel 80586  *See* 80586

Intel 8080  *See* 8080

Intel 8086  *See* 8086

Intel 8087  *See* 8087

Intel 8088  *See* 8088

Intel 82355  *See* 82355

Intel 82357  *See* 82357

Intel 8237A  *See* 8237A

Intel 8250  *See* 8250

Intel 8253  *See* 8253
Intel 8255A  *See* 8255A
Intel 8259A  *See* 8259A
Intel 8288  *See* 8288
Intel Corporation: *8, 9, 96, 217, 325, 238, 245, 270, 277–279, 311, 376*
Intel i860  A high-performance RISC processor by Intel: *314*
Intel iPSC/2  An MIMD hypercube processor by Intel, whose computer modules comprise 80386 microprocessors with optional vector coprocessors and floating-point coprocessors: *19, 337, 339, 371, 377–378*
**intelligent peripheral device**  A peripheral device with an embedded control (usually consisting of a microprocessor) that hides from the CPU the characteristics specific to that device; often buffers data also: **165**
Inter-Cluster Bus  A system bus in the Cm* computer; part of the packet-switched interconnection network: *373, 374*
intercluster reference  A reference initiated by a processor in one cluster of the Cm* to a device or memory module in a different cluster; hence a reference that uses an Inter-Cluster bus: *375*
   *See also* intracluster reference
**interconnection network**  A network for connecting devices together; the nodes of the network are the devices, and the arcs between nodes are the communications links: *18, 25, 323, 340*
   expandability of: *325–326*
   in MIMD machines: *18*
   taxonomy of: *324–327*
   topology of: *327–338, 342*
**interinstruction dependency**  A dependency that results, e.g., in a pipelined processor, when the execution of one instruction depends on the outcome of a previous instruction: **296**
interleaved memory  A memory system consisting of several independent banks of memory in which some address bits select the bank for a memory reference and the remaining address bits select a word within the bank: *180, 285*
   in pipelining: *304*
   *See also* high-order interleave; low-order interleave
International Business Machines Corporation (IBM): *4, 6, 8, 19, 26, 37, 71, 94, 158, 219, 220, 233, 308*
   *See also* IBM MIPS; IBM PC; IBM PC AT; IBM PS/2; IBM RISC System/6000; IBM System/360; IBM System/370; Micro Channel Architecture

**interrupt**  An asynchronous exception initiated by an external device, such as a timer or an I/O controller: **70, 143, 144, 149, 150, 194, 252**
   in the IBM PC: *250–251*
   in DMA I/O: *162*
   *See also* exception; trap
INTERRUPT  An instruction that triggers a trap: *71, 144*
**interrupt-acknowledge sequence**  An 8088-specific sequence of communications between a CPU and an interrupting device that lets the CPU determine the identity of the interrupting device: *249*
**interrupt-code flag**  A flag indicating that a device of that priority has requested an interrupt: **146**
**interrupt-code register (ICR)**  A register containing all the interrupt-code flags for the system: *147–152*
interrupt controller  A device (e.g., an 8259A) for providing interrupt support for a CPU; prioritizes interrupt requests, provides device numbers of interrupting devices, and communicates with the CPU using an interrupt-acknowledge sequence: *234, 237, 257*
   in the IBM PC: *268*
   test during system initialization: *275*
   *See also* 8259A
**interrupt cycle**  One type of bus cycle; used by the IBM PC during an interrupt-acknowledge sequence: **122**
**interrupt-disable flip-flop**  A flip-flop, often labeled I, that disables all nonmaskable interrupts: *147, 148, 149, 151*
interrupted program  The program that is executing when the system initiates an interrupt: *208*
interrupt flag (IF)  The interrupt-disable flip-flop of the 8088 microprocessor: *247, 250*
**interrupt handler**  A program that processes an interrupt: **144, 162, 163, 249**
   *See also* exception handler; trap handler
interrupt initiation  The process of saving the runtime context of a program, recording the interrupt information, and branching to the proper interrupt handler: *132*
   in the IBM PC: *250–252*
   *See also* exception initiation
**interrupt-initiation sequence**  The sequence of events that take place during interrupt initiation: **250**
interrupt line  A control line that carries interrupt requests
   for the EISA bus: *258*

**interrupt mask** On a system that masks interrupts, a bit pattern that disables certain types of interrupts (e.g., timer interrupts, I/O interrupts, and arithmetic-overflow interrupts): *149, 150*

**interrupt mask register (IMR)** The register that holds the interrupt mask: *149–152*

**interrupt-pending flip-flop** A flip-flop that is set by an interrupt-request signal to inform the control unit that an interrupt is pending. The control unit normally initiates the interrupt after completing the current instruction: *147, **148**, 149, 151, 152*

interrupt-pending signal The signal that informs the CPU that an interrupt is pending; often generated by an interrupt-pending flip-flop: *149*

**interrupt polling** The process of determining which device has requested an interrupt by interrogating the status registers of all devices that may have requested the interrupt (e.g., devices of a given priority): *148*

interrupt processing All the events that take place from the time a device requests an interrupt until the interrupt handler returns control of the CPU to the interrupted program (or operating system): *129*

   in the IBM PC: *249–252*

interrupt-request flag A flag that holds an interrupt request.

   in the 8087 coprocessor: *271*

**interrupt-request line** A dedicated control line that external devices use to request an interrupt: ***146***

   of the PC AT Bus: *257*

interrupt request signal: *147, 151*

   in the IBM PC: *239, 250*

interrupt system The system within a computer consisting of all interrupt-processing hardware and software, and generally entails all types of exceptions

   in the IBM PC: *238, 239, 248–252*

**interrupt-vector address** The address of an interrupt vector: *250*

   in the IBM PC during interrupt initiation: *250*

   in the IBM PC: *273*

interrupt-vector number An ordinal number, often the offset into an interrupt-vector table, of the specified type of interrupt: *251, 275*

interrupt-vector table A table containing all of the interrupt vectors of a system; the interrupt hardware often uses the interrupt number to compute an offset into the table, where it accesses the interrupt vector for the specified type of interrupt

   address assignment in the IBM PC: *278*

   in the IBM PC: *249, 276*

**interval timer** A timer in a computer that operates under software control to generate timing signals or interrupt the CPU after some specifiable time interval: *146, 239, **268***

INTR control Part of the interrupt system of the IBM PC: *239*

   in the IBM PC interrupt processing: *251*

intracluster reference A reference initiated by a processor in one cluster of the Cm* to a device or memory module in the same cluster; hence a reference that uses only a Map Bus: *375*

*See also* intercluster reference

**invalidation bus** A bus that broadcasts to all cache memories in a set-associative system the set number for each memory-write operation; each cache invalidates the corresponding set whether data in the set are valid or not: ***370***

invalidation of a cache entry The process of marking the cache entry as invalid: *197, 370*

I/O Input-output; any transfer of data between a computer and an external device

**I/O-address space** The set of all addresses available to the CPU while executing I/O instructions: ***164***

I/O buffer Any buffer used to hold information during an I/O operation; often managed by the operating system but sometimes provided in hardware by an I/O device or interface: *158*

I/O bus cycle The bus cycle initiated by a processor when executing an I/O instruction

   in the 8088 microprocessor: *245, 246, 253*

I/O channel *See* channel

I/O controller Any device for controlling an I/O operation (e.g., a channel, a DMA controller, a universal asynchronous receiver-transmitter, a peripheral processing unit, or a programmable parallel interface): *377*

I/O device Any device that performs input or output (e.g., card reader, tape drive, disk drive, mouse, modem, video display terminal, or printer): *16, 146, 157, 162, 164, 180, 220*

**I/O device address** The address an I/O device responds to during an I/O instruction: ***70***

**I/O instruction** An instruction (e.g., INPUT, OUTPUT, START I/O, HALT I/O, TEST I/O, or TEST CHANNEL) that send control signals to I/O devices: *58, 70, 159, 164*

   in the IBM PC: *259*

I/O interface *See* I/O interface adapter

I/O interface adapter A special I/O device (e.g., a programmable parallel interface or universal asynchronous receiver-transmitter) designed to

relay signals from a physical I/O device (e.g., terminal, modem, or printer) to the CPU or system bus, and vice versa: *122, 252, 154, 164, 265*
   in the IBM PC: *260–269*
   See also I/O processor
I/O interrupt  An interrupt initiated by an I/O device or interface: *21, 58, 143, 144, 150, 161, 164*
**I/O operations per second**  The number of distinct I/O operations that a system can perform in 1 second: **29**
   For contrast, see also bandwidth
I/O performance: *29*
**I/O port address**  An address, assigned by the system designers, that an I/O interface adapter responds to; usually during memory-mapped I/O and thus within the memory-address space: **164**
   in the IBM PC: *259, 260, 273*
**I/O processor**  Any of a large number of devices designed for I/O processing, including I/O interface devices, I/O channels, and peripheral processing units: *7, 8, 19,* **155, 156,** *323*
   See also I/O interface adapter
**I/O read cycle**  A bus cycle initiated by an I/O instruction during which the CPU gets (reads) data from an I/O device or I/O interface: **122**
   For contrast, see also memory read cycle
I/O request  A request by software to the operating system for an I/O operation: *155*
**I/O system**  The system a computer uses for getting data from or delivering data to the external world, by using various devices for that purpose: *3, 11, 12, 25,* **152–168,** *233, 388*
   in the Cm*: *371, 373*
   in fault-tolerant systems: *382–383*
   in the IBM PC: *236, 238, 239, 248–268, 272–278*
   performance of: *29*
   in relation to cache coherence: *367–370*
Iowa State University: *5*
**I/O write cycle**  A bus cycle initiated by an I/O instruction during which the CPU sends data to an I/O device or I/O interface: **122,** *265*
IP  The instruction pointer in the 8088 microprocessor: *241, 244*
   use during interrupt initiation: *250*
iPSC/2  See Intel iPSC/2
IR  See instruction register
ISA  See Industry Standard Architecture; instruction-set architecture
iteration count  See loop-iteration count

interactive algorithm  An algorithm that executes a program loop when computing a result: *50*
   For contrast, see also recursive procedure

**JK master-slave flip-flop**  A synchronous flip-flop that can be set, cleared, or toggled: **425, 426**
joystick  An input device used typically for interactive games: *154*
JSR  Jump and save register. A branch instruction that saves the content of the program counter before branching; primarily used in subroutine linkage: *69, 70*
JUMP  An unconditional branch instruction: *56*
   in the 8088 microprocessor: *240*

*k*-dimensional array  See array
kernel mode  One of the privileged modes of execution of various computers, such as the 80286 and later microprocessors and those of the DEC PDP and VAX families: *71*
key-controlled memory protection  A memory-protection technique in which the operating system associates a number (a protection key) with each bank of memory it assigns to the program. When the program executes, the CPU sends the key to the memory banks along with each address. The memory-protection hardware raises a protection-violation interrupt if a key mismatch occurs: *192, 209*
keyboard  An input device that resembles a typewriter keyboard but sends electrical signals (called scan codes) to the CPU when a user presses a key: *154, 233, 239, 255*
   in the IBM PC: *251, 264, 275*
**Kmap,** of the Cm*  In the Cm* computer, a special communications microprocessor; one of the nodes of the interconnection network: *373, 374, 376*
Kuck, D.: *27*

**large-scale integration (LSI)**  Characteristic of integrated circuits having thousands of transistors of them: *232,* **411**
   For contrast, see also medium-scale integration; small-scale integration; very large scale integration
laser printer  A high-resolution printer whose operation is based on xerography; a computer-controlled laser beam exposes the xerographic drum rather than a conventional light source: *154*

**last-in first-out (LIFO) storage** Stack storage, i.e., the last stored item is the first one that may be removed: *46, 430*
See also stack

**latch** A simple register that holds values and places them on a bus: *239, 245, 256, 257*
in the PC Bus: *258*
in a pipeline: *288, 290*

latched I/O A type of I/O in which the interface holds the datum during the transfer, rather than the CPU (for output) or the I/O device (during input): *262*

latched output, in a crossbar A crossbar that has internal latches for holding the data being transferred: *332*

latency See network latency; rotational latency

Lawrence Livermore National Laboratories: *27*

leakage The loss of charge by a dynamic RAM: *184*

**least recently used (LRU)** Refers to a replacement policy, e.g., in paging, where the system replaces the page of data the program referenced least recently: *208*

Leeds, M. B.: *7*

LEFTBIT An instruction that returns the value of the leftmost bit of a register: *350*

LENGTH A string instruction that returns the length of the argument string: *45, 46*

length of a string The number of characters in the string: *45*

**length of a vector** The number of elements in the vector: *47*

LIFO storage See last-in, first-out storage

LIM Refers to the consortium of three companies — Lotus, Intel, and Microsoft — that adopted standards for memory expansion in the 1980s

LIM 3.2 EMS See Expanded Memory Specification

LIM 4.0 EMS See Enhanced Expanded Memory Specification

LIM data area, IBM PC address assignment: *278*

linear addressing In a multiprocessor system, the policy of assigning nonoverlapping addresses from within a single linear address space to all processors and memories: *340*

linear communications Communications along a line; communications within a linear network: *339*

linear structure Any structure in which the elements are arranged (logically) in a row (e.g., list, string, or vector): *96*

**linear topology** The topology of a line; all nodes in the network have connection degree 2 and form a single chain: *328*

line printer An output device for printing data: *154, 158*

link A connection in an interconnection network: *324*

**linking** The process, performed by a loader, of altering a compiled program to make the address specifications in the instructions correctly refer to the physical locations of the program in memory: *58, 86*

**LINPACK benchmark** A test of CPU performance based on matrix operations: *27, 307*

LISP A high-level programming language (circa 1961) for artificial intelligence applications: *20*

list A data structure whose elements have a linear ordering: *96*
See also parameter address list; parameter list

**Livermore loops benchmark** A test of CPU performance based on a small number of Fortran code loops: *27*

LM See local memory

LM-MIMD Local memory, multiple instruction stream, multiple data stream: *19, 321, 322, 364*
See also multiple instruction stream, multiple data stream; multiple-processor; multiprocessor

LM-SIMD Local memory, single instruction stream, multiple data stream: *17, 19, 344*
See also hypercube processor; processor array; single instruction stream; multiple data stream

LOAD An instruction that loads a register with a value from memory: *54, 55, 58, 63, 67, 68, 87, 95, 306, 309*

vector: *72*

LOAD ADDRESS An instruction that loads a register with the effective address of its operand but does not otherwise access memory: *63, 94, 192*

**load-and-store instruction set** An instruction set in which all operate instructions are register-to-register instructions; special LOAD and STORE instructions allow the user to load the registers from memory and to store their contents into memory: *54*

LOAD CONTROL WORD An 8087 coprocessor instruction: *270*

**load-delay slot** For RISC processors, the instruction position in a program following a load instruction: *313*

LOAD ENVIRONMENT An 8087 coprocessor instruction: *270*

**loader** A part of the operating system that loads a compiled program into memory: *86, 192*

LOAD IMMEDIATE An instruction that loads a register with an immediate value: *62*

**load instruction** Any instruction for loading a register: *58*

**load module**  A program module ready to be loaded into memory and executed; consists of compiled and linked machine instructions: *106*

LOAD NEGATIVE  An instruction that, in addition to loading, sets the sign bit of the number to negative, regardless of its previous value: *63*

LOAD POSITIVE  An instruction that, in addition to loading, sets the sign bit of the number to positive, regardless of its previous value: *63*

**local address**  In a processor array, the address a processing element uses when referencing its own local memory: *344*

**local-address space**  In a multiprocessor system (e.g., the Cm*), the address space available to a processor without using the interconnection network: *375*

**local-area network (LAN)**  A network for linking computers together, typically PCs, for sharing files, printers, and electronic mail: *371*

**local bus**  A bus that remains within the CPU or one that the CPU controls: *120, 121*
  in the Cm*: *372*

**local memory**  In a multiprocessor system, memory a processor can access directly without using the interconnection network: *322, 344, 348*
  in the Cm*: *371, 372*
  See also global memory; LM-MIMD; LM-SIMD

**local-memory (LM) system architecture**  A parallel processor (with either SIMD or MIMD architecture) in which the individual processors have their own local memory, which they share with other processors: *16*
  processor array: *339*

**Local Switch**  A bus controller in the Cm*: *372–376*

LOCK  A control signal in the 8088 microprocessor used to maintain control of the bus while executing an instruction; used to implement synchronization operations: *240, 248, 250*

**lock-and-key protection**  See key-controlled memory protection

**locking a bus**  A control operation executed by a CPU to prevent other devices from using the bus: *248*
  See also LOCK

**locking a data set**  An operation executed by one process that makes the data in a data set inaccessible to all other processes: *65*

LOG2  An 8087 coprocessor instruction: *270*

LOGE  An 8087 coprocessor instruction: *270*

**logical address**  The address of an instruction or datum as seen by a program and independent of the hardware on which the program will execute. Logical addresses typically range between 0 and $2^N$, where $N$ is the number of address bits used by the program. Also called virtual address: *13, 85, 86, 190, 192, 212, 214, 215*
  For contrast, see also physical address

**logical-address space**  The set of all logical addresses available to a program; also called virtual-address space: *85, 189, 191, 195, 205, 206, 214, 371*
  in the Cm*: *374*
  For contrast, see also physical-address space

**logical instruction**  An instruction that performs a boolean operation (e.g., AND, OR, XOR, or NOT) on its operands: *13, 60–61*

LOGICAL SHIFT LEFT  An instruction that shifts a value to the left and inserts $0_2$ bits at the right: *60, 137*

LOGICAL SHIFT RIGHT  An instruction that shifts a value to the right and inserts $0_2$ bits at the left: *60*

**logical vector**  A vector whose elements are logical variables (i.e., the values are *true* and *false*): *76*

**logic gate**  A basic circuit component that implements a boolean operation using electrical signals, where one voltage (or current) represents *true* and a second voltage (or current) represents *false*: *415–417*
  Also see transistor-transistor logic

**long floating-point number**  A floating-point representation supported by the 8087 coprocessor: *269, 270*

**long integer**  An integer representation supported by the 8087 coprocessor: *269*

LOOP  An 8088 microprocessor instruction used to tell the CPU to execute the following instruction a number of times: *240*

**loop count**  See loop-iteration count

**loop-free circuit**  See combinational logic circuit

**loop-iteration count**  The number of times a loop has been entered (iterated) during execution; also called loop count: *50, 363*

**loop unrolling**  The process of duplicating the statements of a program loop as a way of eliminating the loop from the program: *220*

**loosely coupled multiprocessor**  A multiprocessor in which the individual processors have their own local memories and usually execute programs out of them but also share the memories of other processors; approximately equivalent to the category LM-MIMD: *18, 340, 364*

Lotus Development Corporation: *217, 232, 277, 278*

**low-order bit**  The rightmost bit in the binary representation of a number; the bit conveying the least amount of precision: *37*

**low-order interleave** A storage-system implementation in which the low-order address bits select a memory bank and the high-order address bits select a word within the bank; thus consecutive addresses are in different banks of memory: *179, 181, 182*

See also high-order interleave

**low signal** A signal that represents the logical value $0_2$ or *false*: *413*

LPT1, IBM PC port-address assignment: *274*

LPT2, IBM PC port-address assignment: *274*

LRU   See least recently used

LSI   See large-scale integration

LSI-11   A microprocessor having the instruction-set architecture of the PDP-11; used in the Cm*: *371, 375*

Lynch, N. A.: *393*

**(M + N)-address instruction** An instruction that specifies M operand addresses and N branch addresses: *55*

See also 0-address instruction; 1-address instruction; N-address instruction

MA   See mask register; match register

machine instruction   See instruction

machine startup   The first actions taken by the control unit of a computer after the power is turned on or after the system is reset to transfer control to an initialization and diagnostic procedure, usually in ROM: *129–132*

See also system initialization

Macintosh   A personal computer introduced by Apple Corporation in 1984 that uses a 32-bit Motorola 68000 microprocessor and a graphical interface: *22, 24, 234, 279*

magnetic bubble   A small domain of magnetism that represents the value $1_2$ in a magnetic-bubble memory: *186*

**magnetic bubble memory (MBM)** A memory technology in which the bits are stored in a film of magnetic material as magnetic bubbles: *176, 186*

magnetic core   An individual storage element, generally in the shape of a tiny toroid, that holds 1 bit in a magnetic-core memory: *176*

physical characteristics of: *186*

**magnetic-core memory** A memory technology that uses magnetic cores as the storage elements: *7, 8, 175*

magnetic disk   The storage medium of a disk drive; may be a floppy disk or a hard disk: *191*

magnetic tape   The storage medium in a magnetic-tape storage unit: *154, 165, 185, 189, 191*

See also tape cartridge; tape drive

**magnitude** Size, usually with reference to a numeric quantity; the value of a number without reference to its sign: *38*

**mainframe computer** A computer that nominally costs from $1 to $25 million; has a large main memory, many large external storage devices (e.g., tapes and disks) and a high-performance I/O system; and is targeted at large corporations and scientific data-processing centers: *37, 232*

main memory   See primary memory

**main-memory address**   See physical address

**maintainability** A property of computer systems that characterizes how easy it is for the support staff to maintain them: *378*

**malleability** A measure of the quality of a computer architecture that focuses on the ease with which an architect can implement a wide range of computers having the same instruction-set architecture but different sizes and performances: *22, 23*

of the IBM PC: *280*

**mantissa** That portion of a floating-point representation that holds the coefficient M, as follows: The value of a floating-point number is $(-1)^S M \times R^E$, where M is the coefficient, R is the implicit radix, E is the exponent, and S is the sign (0 implies positive and 1 implies negative) Also called the coefficient: *37, 40–44, 52*

of the DEC PDP-11 and VAX floating-point representations: *44*

of the Burroughs B-5500 floating-point representations: *41*

of the CDC CYBER 170 floating-point representations: *41*

of the IBM System/360 floating-point representations: *43*

of the IEEE floating-point standard: *44*

Map Bus   A packet-switched bus in the Cm* that connects together the computer modules of a single cluster: *373, 376*

See also Inter-Cluster Bus; Kmap; Local Switch

MAR   See memory address register

Mark-I, II, III, IV   Four early computers developed by Howard Aiken at Harvard University in the 1940s and having separate memories for programs and data; Mark-I and -II used electromechanical relays rather than vacuum tubes: *5, 6, 12*

mark bit   The first bit in a serial transmission, which coordinates the transmitter and receiver clocks for an asynchronous transmission: *265*

**mask** *See* image mask; interrupt mask

**maskable interrupt** An interrupt that the hardware can be configured to ignore (masked): *150*

*See also* interrupt mask; interrupt-mask register; priority interrupts

**masked exceptions** *See* exception masking; maskable interrupts

**masking of errors** The capacity of some fault-tolerant systems to hide the presence of errors from the system and its users, usually by using fault-tolerant techniques: *381*

**mask register (MR)** A register whose bits mask an operation (e.g., in an associative store the bits mask the fields that will not participate in a match; in an interrupt controller the bits mask interrupts; and in a DMA controller the bits mask incoming requests for service): *187*

MA: *346, 346*

*See also* 8237A register set; interrupt-mask register

**mask vector** A logical vector whose elements control the participation of another vector in a vector operation: *76, 77*

MASTER A control line in the IBM PC AT I/O Channel Bus that allows an alternative device to take control of the bus: *258*

**master flip-flop** Of the two flip-flops within a master-slave flip-flop, the one that controls the final state of the device: *425*

**master node** The node in an interconnection network that initiates a data transfer. The responding node is the slave node: *324*

MATCH AND REPLACE A synchronization instruction that compares a value in memory with a value in one register and, if the two values are the same, replaces the value in memory with a value in a second register: *64–67*

**match bit** *See* match register

**match register (MA)** The register in an associative memory that holds the results of an associative search. The match register has 1 match bit for each word in the memory. During an associative search, the hardware sets bit $i$ if word $i$ matched the argument: *187, 346, 347*

Mathematical Laboratory at the University of Cambridge: *6*

**mathematical neuron** *See* formal neuron

**matrix** A data structure comprising a two-dimensional array of values. If $M$ denotes a matrix, then $m_{ij}$ denotes the element of $M$ found in row $i$ and column $j$: *47*

**matrix element** An element $m_{ij}$ in a matrix, where the indices $i$ and $j$ indicate the element's row and column position, respectively, in the matrix: *47*

**matrix multiplication** *See* matrix product

**matrix operation** Any operation whose operands are matrices (e.g., matrix product): *72, 78–81*

**matrix product** Let $M$ be a matrix having $j$ rows and $k$ columns, and let $N$ be a matrix having $k$ rows and $l$ columns. If $O$ designates the product matrix, denoted $MN$, then $o_{rs}$ is $\Sigma m_{rt} n_{ts}$, where summation is over $t$: *78, 80–82, 344*

on a linear processor array: *358–361*

**matrix transpose** The matrix $(a_{ij}^t)$, derived from $(a_{ij})$ by the rule $a_{ij}^t = a_{ji}$ for all $i$ and $j$: *80, 81*

Mauchly, J. 5,: *13*

MBR *See* memory buffer register

MBS *See* megabytes per second

MCA *See* Micro Channel Architecture

MDA *See* Monochrome Display Adapter

mean *See* arithmetic mean

**mean time between failures (MTBF)** A measurement of system reliability for a fault-tolerant system; the average operating time between the start of normal operation and its first electronic or mechanical failure: *378*

**mean time to failure (MTTF)** A measurement of system reliability for a fault-tolerant system; used when only one failure is possible, such as a component failure: *378*

**mean time to repair (MTTR)** A measurement of the maintainability of a fault-tolerant system, when the concern is speed of repair: *378*

**medium-scale integration (MSI)** Characteristic of integrated circuits having hundreds of transistors on them: *8, 411*

For contrast, *see also* small-scale integration; very large scale integration

**megabytes per second (MBS)** A standard unit for reporting transfer rates: *29*

**megaflops (MFLOPS)** A measurement of the speed of a computer, usually applied to scientific computers rather than general-purpose computers, that focuses on floating-point operations, rather than instruction executions: *26*

memory *See* associative memory; cache memory; expanded memory; primary memory; virtual-memory system

types of: *183–189*

**memory-access instruction** A LOAD or STORE instruction; any instruction whose execution requires a memory access (aside from the access that fetches the instruction in the first place): *58, 63–67*

**memory access time** The average time the CPU requires to access memory, usually quoted in nanoseconds: *30*

memory address  *See* physical address

memory addressing  The way a computer system uses the bits in an instruction's address specification to determine the address of the operand: *85–98*

**memory address register (MAR)**  The programmer-invisible register in which the computer holds the address of a reference during a memory access; not part of the register set: **53**

  *See also* memory buffer register

**memory-address space**  The set of available addresses, either physical or logical, in a computer system. The number of address bits in an instruction, the size of the base and index registers, and the addressing techniques of the instruction-set architecture determine the logical-address space; the amount of physical memory present determines the physical-address space: ***164, 165, 219–221***

  *See also* I/O-address space

memory allocation  The assignment of memory to a program: *72, 86, 99, 193, 383*

  during exception handling: *146*

  in paging: *211*

**memory bandwidth**  The number of bytes per second that a memory system can send to the processor, usually measured in megabytes per second (MBS): *30, 219, 352*

  in pipelining: *296*

**memory bank**  An independent memory module within a larger memory system or within a system for banking memory: ***176, 180–182, 193, 323***

**memory banking**  A technique for expanding the amount of high-speed random-access memory available to a computer, usually a microcomputer, by replacing some physical memory with the banking hardware. The banking hardware consists of a number of banks of memory and a bank-select register. The banking system maps the addresses of the replaced physical memory into addresses within the selected bank: ***215, 216***

  *See also* Enhanced Expanded Memory Specification; expanded memory

**memory buffer register (MBR)**  A programmer-invisible buffer in which the computer holds data for a store operation and into which it receives data during a load operation; not part of the register set: **53**

  in an associative memory: *187–188*

  *See also* memory address register

memory bus cycle  A bus cycle that accesses memory: *245, 246, 253*

  *See also* interrupt cycle; I/O bus cycle

memory contention  The situation that results when more than one device attempts to access the same bank of memory at once

  in pipelining: *295, 304*

**memory context**  The state of a program's memory: *144–145*

  *See also* processor context

memory cycle  The time required between successive reads or writes to a memory due to the physical characteristics of the device: *163, 181*

memory data register (MDR)  *See* memory buffer register

memory deallocation  The reclaiming of memory assigned to a program: *146*

**memory hierarchy**  The set of all storage devices within a computer, including the register set, cache memory and other buffers, central memory, expanded memory, and any peripheral storage devices: ***191***

**memory map**  A device that converts addresses from one address space to another, such as from logical addresses into physical addresses: *100,* ***205***

  in the Cm* computer: *372–374*

  *See also* page map; segment map; translation-lookaside buffer; virtual-memory system

**memory-mapped control**  A control strategy that resembles memory-mapped I/O; one device controls another by writing control information to specific memory addresses, called control-port addresses, within the physical-address space: *375*

**memory-mapped I/O**  An I/O technique in which the CPU or DMA controller initiates I/O operations by writing control information and data to specific memory addresses, called I/O port addresses; special I/O interface devices, rather than storage devices, respond to these addresses and control the I/O operations: *154, 164–165*

  in the IBM PC: *259*

memory operand  An operand that comes from memory, as opposed to from a register or stack: *83*

memory-parity error  In a memory system that uses parity bits for error detection, the error that occurs when the hardware detects incorrect parity (i.e., the number of $1_2$ bits is even when it should be odd, or vice versa): *150*

**memory-port controller**  A device that accepts memory requests from several competing devices, prioritizes them, and connects to memory the device having the highest priority; also called port controller or memory traffic controller: ***156, 159, 163, 164, 181, 182***

**memory protection** The prevention of one program from accessing memory not assigned to that program by the operating system: *53, 72, 191, 192*

    hardware for: *146, 192–194*

    *See also* CDC 6600, program relocation and protection in; IBM System/360 memory protection; key-controlled memory protection; key-controlled protection

**memory-protection violation** The error that results when a program attempts to access memory not assigned to it: *144*

**memory read cycle** A bus cycle during which the CPU reads memory: *122, 124*

    For contrast, *see also* I/O read cycle

**memory-refresh circuits** *See* dynamic random-access memory

**memory-relocation hardware** Hardware that supports program relocation: *190–193*

    *See also* dynamic program relocation; initial program relocation

**memory size** The number of storage units, usually given in megabytes or number of words, in a memory system: *30*

**memory subsystem** The central memory system of a computer or the subsystem in a cache memory that holds the data: *199*

    *See also* primary memory; tag subsystem

**memory system** *See* primary memory; secondary memory

**memory technology** The technology of computer storage: *175–178, 186, 221*

    *See also* destructive read; magnetic bubble memory; magnetic-core memory; mercury-delay-line memory; nondestructive-read memory; nonremovable memory; read-only memory; vacuum tube

**memory-to-CPU bandwidth** *See* memory bandwidth

**memory-to-memory architecture** An architecture in which the operate instructions are memory-to-memory instructions: *304*

    vector processor: *339*

**memory-to-memory instruction** An instruction such as MOVE STRING that initiates a memory-to-memory operation: *54*

**memory-to-memory operation** An operation whose operands are in memory and that places its result in memory: *55*

**memory-to-register instruction** An instruction that gets one or more of its operands from memory: *54, 55*

**memory-traffic controller** *See* memory-port controller

**memory-update system** In a dataflow architecture, the subsystem that takes result tokens and stores them in their destination nodes in memory: *388–389*

**memory-update unit** A processing element in a memory-update system: *389*

**memory write bus cycle** *See* memory write cycle

**memory write cycle** A bus cycle during which the CPU writes to memory: *122, 124*

    *See also* I/O write cycle

**mercury-delay-line memory** An old memory technology in which $1_2$ bits were represented by electrical pulses in a column of mercury. The write circuits inserted the pulses at one end of the column, and the read circuits detected them a short time later at the other end: *175, 176*

MERGE *See* merge operation

**merge node** A special node in a dataflow graph that accepts input tokens from more than on source: *385, 386*

**merge operation** A vector operation that merges two vectors by inserting selected element of one vector into the other: *76, 78*

**merit** The quality of an architecture: *24*

**message** A group of bits that travel through a network as an information unit and often contains routing information in addition to data; also called a packet: *324*

    in the Cm*: *375*

**message-passing network** *See* packet-switched interconnection network

**MFLOPS** *See* megaflops

**Micro Channel Architecture (MCA)** IBM's expanded-local-bus architecture introduced in its PS/2 family of personal computers: *235, 237*

**microcomputer** A computer whose CPU is a microprocessor. Personal computers are usually microcomputers: *121, 237, 312*

**microinstruction** An instruction for a microprogrammed control unit that specifies the set of control signals the control unit must issue to cause a single action (e.g., a register-to-register transfer) to take place: *128–137, 311*

**microinstruction branch address** For a branching microinstruction, the address of the next microinstruction: *134*

**microinstruction buffer** Within a microprogrammed control unit, the register that holds the microinstruction while the control unit decodes and executes it: *129–131*

**microinstruction decoder** Within a microprogrammed control unit, a decoder that translates the fields of a microinstruction into microorders for issue: *129–133*

**microinstruction format** The arrangement in memory of the fields of a microinstruction: *139, 140*

**microorder** A single control signal issued by a control unit: *127–133, 137*
  within a microinstruction decoder: *134, 135, 136*
  *See also* microinstruction

**microprocessor** A single-chip CPU, such as a member of Intel's 80x86 family or Motorola's 68000 family: *8, 39, 84, 91, 96, 183, 191, 198, 233, 234*
  transistor count of: *9*
  *See also* 4004; 8008; 8080; 8086; 8088; 80286; 80386; 80386SX; 80486; 68020; 88000

**microprogram** The sequence of microinstructions issued by a microprogrammed control unit to implement one machine instruction: *128, 131–134, 139, 204, 218*
  for ADD: *142–143*
  for COMPLEMENT: *141–142*
  organization of, in a control store: *132*

**microprogrammed control unit** A control unit that generates control signals by reading and issuing microinstructions, rather than by using sequential logic: *128–143, 308*
  For contrast, *also see* conventional control unit

**microprogram counter (μPC)** The register within a microprogrammed control unit that points to the next microinstruction to be executed: *129–133*

**microprogramming** The art of writing microprograms for a microprogrammed control unit: *136–143, 310*

microsecond (1 μs) One millionth ($10^{-6}$) of a second: *406*

Microsoft Corporation: *217, 232, 277, 278*

**millions of floating-point operations per second** *See* megaflops

**millions of instructions per second** *See* MIPS

millisecond (1 ms) One thousandth ($10^{-3}$) of a second: *406, 407*

**MIMD** *See* multiple instruction stream, multiple data stream

**minicomputer** A computer that nominally costs between $100,000 and $1 million, has a multichip CPU and frequently a single-bus architecture, is suitable for a small company or laboratory, but does not have the performance or reliability of a mainframe computer: *232*
  memory size of: *178, 179*

**MIPS** Millions of instructions per second; a measure of the speed of a processor: *26–28*
  *See also* IBM MIPS; peak MIPS; VAX MIPS

**MIPS R2000** A 32-bit RISC machine (circa 1985) by MIPS Computer Systems: *19, 307, 308, 313, 314*

**mirrored data sets** Duplicate data sets maintained by some fault-tolerant computers to protect the user against hardware failure; the computer may use mirrored-pair disk volumes to hold them: *382*

**MISD** *See* multiple instruction stream, single data stream

**MITS** Micro Instrumentation and Technology: *233*

**mode** 1. The privilege state of execution of a processor (e.g., privileged, unprivileged, supervisor state, or problem state): *71*. 2. The mode of execution of an I/O interface device (e.g., strobed mode or bidirectional bus mode of a programmable parallel interface; block mode or demand mode of a DMA controller): *See* 8237A, transfer modes of; 8255A, modes of

**mod field** The field in the address-mode byte of an 8088 instruction that specifies the addressing mode for the instruction: *242, 243*
  *See also* reg field, r/m field

**modem** A term condensed from *modulator* and *demodulator*; refers to a device that converts serial data into sound signals for transmission over ordinary telephone lines, and converts the sounds it receives back into digital signals during data reception: *265, 266, 267*

**mode register** A control register that determines the mode of execution of a processor or device
  in the 8237A DMA controller: *253–254*
  in the 8253 programmable interval timer: *268*
  in the 8255A PPI: *262*
  in the CDC 6600: *298*

**module** *See* computer module

Mollenhoff, C. R.: *5*

**monadic vector operation** A vector operation that has one vector operand: *72–73*

**Monochrome Display Adapter (MDA)** The standard video display for the first IBM PC model, with one foreground color and one background color (e.g., green on black): *235*
  in the IBM PC: *274, 277*
  port-address assignment in the IBM PC: *274, 278*

Moore School of the University of Pennsylvania: *5*

**mother board** The main system board of a personal computer or workstation: *237, 413*
  in the IBM PC: *260, 264*

Motorola: *233*

**mouse** An input device, operated by movement and button presses, that converts the movements into the position of a cursor on the screen, and the button presses into control signals: *154*

MOVE A TO X   A load instruction that loads the accumulator with the value whose address is specified by X: *127, 128*

MOVE   In the 8088 microprocessor, a generalized move instruction that includes data transfers from memory to register, register to memory, and register to register: *240*

MOVE CHARACTER   An instruction that moves a single byte from one location in memory to another; in some computers, MOVE CHARACTER includes the operations of moving a string as well as a single character: *61*

MOVE STRING   An instruction that moves a string from one place in memory to another: *61, 62, 209*

MPP   Massively Parallel Processor. An SIMD processor built by Goodyear Aerospace Corporation in the early 1980s; had up to 16,384 1-bit processing elements: *19, 330, 331, 342, 350*

MR   *See* mask register

MS DOS   Microsoft Corporation's Disk Operating System; used in most IBM PC's and clones: *233*

MSI   *See* medium-scale integration

MTBF   *See* mean time between failures

MTTF   *See* mean time to failure

MTTR   *See* mean time to repair

**multibus architecture**   An architecture that has more than one bus to connect its components together; typical of fault-tolerant systems and some high-performance computers, but not of personal computers: *286, 327*

in pipelining: *304*

multidimensional array   *See* array

**multifunction pipe**   A pipelined functional unit that can perform many dissimilar operations (e.g., addition, subtraction, multiplication and division): *289*

For contrast, *see also* unifunction pipe

multilevel control   A technique in which the control system generates control signals in stages (e.g., some bits in a microinstruction may be used as an address into a second control store where further control bits are found): *136, 137*

**multilevel storage system**   A storage system with more than one kind of memory in the storage hierarchy, such as a main memory and a cache, or a peripheral storage device and main memory: *191*

For contrast, *see also* one-level storage system

**multiphase clock**   A clock that generates more than one sequences of timing pulses: **426**

**multiple instruction stream, multiple data stream (MIMD)**   In Flynn's classification, refers to computers that consist of several independent processors, each capable of executing a different program on its own set of data: *15–19, 321–323, 364–383*

**multiple instruction stream, single data stream (MISD)**   In Flynn's classification, refers to computers that have several processors, each capable of executing a different program but operating on the same sequence of data; no computers of this category exist: *15*

**multiple levels of indirection**   An indirect memory access that leads to a second indirect access (and perhaps from that to third, and so on) before locating the operand: *91*

**multiple processor**   A multiprocessor in which each processor has its own local memory, but the processors may also have some global memory; usually an LM-MIMD architecture: *4, 16, 19, 370*

*See also* multiple instruction stream, multiple data stream; multiprocessor

multiple program loading   *See* multiprogramming

**multiplexor (MUX)**   A circuit with several inputs and a single output that gates a selected input to the output: *125, 126, 138, 336,* **419–421**

multiplication circuit   A circuit that takes the representations of two numbers and produces the representation of their product: *431–435*

pipelined: *290–293*

*See also* binary multiplication

MULTIPLY   An instruction that initiates a multiplication operation: *60*

in the 8087 coprocessor: *270*

multiported memory   *See* multiported storage system

**multiported peripheral**   A peripheral device with two or more ports; used to provide redundancy in some fault-tolerant computers: *382*

**multiported storage system**   A storage system with more than one port to memory: *155, 156–157, 163*

**multiprocessor**   A parallel-processor architecture with two or more processors that share the same logical-address space; an LM-MIMD or GM-MIMD processor: *15, 16, 19, 304, 307, 323, 327, 330, 340, 364–382*

interconnection network for: *339*

two-processor 369

*See also* multiple processor

multiprogramming   A technique for increasing the utilization of the CPU by allowing several tasks to reside in memory at the same time. Although only one process controls the CPU at a time, whenever an I/O operation blocks one process, the operating system can quickly transfer control to another memory-resident process. Also called multiple program loading: *8*

**multiprogramming operating system** An operating system that supports multiprogramming. All modern operating systems, except for a few designed for personal computers, support multiprogramming: *7, 8, 144, 155–156, 189–194, 197, 364, 365*

multistage crossbar A crossbar that uses several stages of switching in its implementation: *323*

**multistage interconnection network (MIN)** An interconnection network that is composed of several stages; the data must traverse them in series: *324*

  *See also* Banyan network; delta network; hypercube; Omega network

multitasking The execution of more than one program at a time on a computer: *63*

multiuser operating system An operating system designed to allow more than one user at a time to share a computer by, e.g., allowing each user to control the CPU for a fixed percentage of time: *195*

**μPC** *See* microprogram counter

**mutual exclusion** In a multiprocessing environment, a control paradigm, often used for synchronization, in which only one process is allowed to access a shared resource (e.g., memory) at a time; when one process gains access to the resource, the system excludes all others from accessing it: *64*

MUX *See* multiplexor

N *See* negative flag

$n_{1/2}$ For a pipelined vector computer, the vector length where the vector speed is $\frac{1}{2}$ the asymptotic or maximum vector speed: *305*

**N-address instruction** An instruction that specifies N operand addresses and no branch addresses: *55*

NAND circuit A logic circuit for implementing the NAND operation: *414*

nanosecond (ns) One billionth of a second; $10^{-9}$ second: *406*

NaN Not a number. In the IEEE floating-point standard, refers to indefinite numbers (numbers that would result from dividing 0 by 0): *44, 46*

N-bit 1-shifter: *422*

**n-bit binary adder:** *423*

n-bit q-shifter: *421*

**N-buddies** Two nodes on a hypercube whose addresses differ only at bit position N: *362*

$n_{crossover}$ A performance measure for arithmetic pipelines, where n is the length of the smallest vector such that the computation rate (number of operations per second) exceeds the computation rate for scalar operations: *305*

nearest-neighbor communications *See* nearest-neighbor interconnection topology

**nearest-neighbor interconnection topology** An interconnection topology used by SIMD processors in which the processing elements (PEs) lie at the vertices of a two-dimensional Cartesian grid, and each PE communicates directly with its four nearest neighbors; in a three-dimensional topology, the PEs would lie at the vertices of a three-dimensional Cartesian grid with each PE contacting its six nearest neighbors: *326, 331, 339*

NEC SX A pipelined vector processor by NEC: *304*

NEC Technologies: *236, 304*

NEGATE 1. An instruction that negates the value on the top of a stack: *56*. 2. A monadic vector instruction that replaces the value of each vector element $V_i$ by $0 - V_i$: *72, 73*

negative flag (N) A processor status flag that indicates a negative result: *53, 68, 125, 126, 134*

negative-result flag *See* negative flag

network control The control circuits of an interconnection network, whether localized or distributed: *325*

**network latency** The time it takes a network to send a datum to the requested destination: *326*

**network tap** In an interconnection network, a single connection to the network: *327*

**neural network** A network whose computational elements are neurons, whether biological, mathematical, or electronic: *11, 19, 323, 383, 391, 389–393*

  biological: *389–390*

  electronic: *392–393*

  logical: *390–392*

**neuron** The basic processing element in a neural network: *390*

  electronic: *393*

NMI logic Nonmaskable interrupt logic; logic in the IBM PC for processing nonmaskable interrupts: *239, 251, 256*

  *See also* nonmaskable interrupt

NMI mask register, IBM PC port-address assignment: *274*

**N-modular redundancy** A fault-tolerance and fault-avoidance technique that uses $N$ parallel subunits with voting logic to decide the unit's output: *381*

**node** 1. A component, such as a processor or a memory unit, in an group of interconnected components: *324*. 2. A vertex that represents a computational unit in a dataflow graph: *384*

**node address** In a network, the designation of a node that the hardware uses, e.g., for routing information to it: *334*

**node data structure** The storage representation of a node in a dataflow machine; the structure of an instruction packet that implements a node: *388*

nonbinary floating-point number A floating-point number that uses an exponent base other than 2: *45*

**nonblocking crossbar** *See* full crossbar

**nonbranching microinstruction** A microinstruction that does not cause a branch in the microprogram: *133, 134, 139*

noncacheable memory locations When a cache is under software control, e.g., in some RISC processors, those memory locations that the software specifies should not be mapped into cache: *370*

**nondestructive-read memory** A memory-read operation that does not destroy the value stored in memory; used by some main-memory technologies (e.g., static RAM): *184, 185*

  For contrast, *see also* destructive read

nonmaskable interrupt An interrupt (e.g., a memory parity error interrupt) that the hardware cannot mask: *239*

  in the IBM PC: *250*

nonrecursive procedure A procedure that does not call itself either directly or indirectly: *70*

**nonremovable memory** A storage technology, other than main memory, where the storage medium cannot be easily removed from the storage device, such as the hard disk in a permanently sealed disk drive: *185*

**nonvolatile memory** A memory device that does not require power to hold its data (e.g., magnetic disk): *184, 185*

NO OP An instruction that has no associated operation; used, e.g., to control boundary alignment or to cause the CPU to pass time: *62, 313*

  in the 8087 coprocessor: *270*

  in the 8088 microprocessor: *240*

**normal bit** The high-order bit of the mantissa of a normalized floating-point (base-2) number; always set when the number is normalized: *40*

NORMALIZE An instruction that shifts its operand left until the high-order bit is a $1_2$, and then places the number of shifts it performed in a register: *350*

**normalized floating-point number** A floating-point number where the high-order digit of the mantissa is nonzero: *40*

  in the B-5500: *41*

  in the DEC PDP-11 and VAX floating-point representations: *44*

  in the System/370 floating-point representation: *43*

**normalized number** *See* normalized floating-point number

NOT An instruction whose operation is the single-operand boolean function that complements every bit of the operand: *137*

  in the 8088 microprocessor: *240*

notation *See* algorithmic; binary; hexadecimal; octal

nucleus A group of brain cells that function together as a computational subunit; hence a biological neural network: *390*

OBF *See* output buffer full

**object-code compatibility** Said of computers that can run the same object code (compiled and linked source code) without recompilation and linking, and provide the same results: *106*

octal notation A symbolic notation that uses only the numerals 0 to 7 to represent numbers, which are expressed in base 8: *44, 405–406*

octal point When expressing a fraction in octal notation, the point in the representation that separates the bits representing an integer on the left from the bits representing the fraction on the right (e.g., 135.47 represents $1 \times 8^2 + 3 \times 8^1 + 5 \times 8^0 + 4 \times 8^{-1} + 7 \times 8^{-2} = 64 + 24 + 5 + \frac{4}{8} + \frac{7}{64} = 93.609375_{10}$: *40*

**octet** A block of 8 words; a unit of data used by the storage systems of many high-performance computers, such as the CRAY-1, ILLIAC IV, and TI ASC: *37, 84*

**offset** The displacement of a word within a page, segment, or other data structure: *92*

Olivetti: *236*

OLTP *See* online transaction-processing system

**Omega network** A multistage interconnection network that has $N$ inputs, $N$ outputs, and uses $N/2$ switches at each of $\log_2 N$ identical stages. The switches are $2 \times 2$ crossbars with upper and lower broadcast, and the interconnection pattern between the stages performs a shuffle operation: *336*

**one-level storage system**  A storage system that uses a homogeneous, single-level of addressing and memory access:  *191*

For contrast, *see also* multilevel storage system

**ones'-complement integer**  An integer representation that uses absolute binary for positive values, and forms negative values by complementing the bits (converting zeros to ones and vice versa) of positive values (including all leading zeros). For example, the 10-bit representation of the number 14 is 00 0000 1110$_2$, and the 10-bit ones'-complement representation of $-14$ is 11 1111 0001$_2$:  *38, 39*

of the CDC CYBER 170 floating-point representation:  *42*

online transaction-processing system (OLTP):  *377*

**op code**  Operation code; the part of an instruction (usually the first field of the instruction) that specifies the operation:  *14, 56*

in pipelining:  *295*

**op-code byte**  The byte in every 8088 microprocessor instruction (and others) that gives the op code:  *242*

**op-code encoding**  A way of effectively increasing the size of the op code by letting a specific value in the op-code field indicate that the following byte or bytes will also contain part of the op code:  *107*

For contrast, *see also* escape sequence

**open architecture**  An architecture whose specifications are published:  *24, 234*

For contrast, *see also* closed architecture

**openness of an architecture**  The degree to which an architecture is open:  *24*

**operand**  One of the inputs to a function or instruction:  *13*

*See also* argument; parameter

operand address  The address of an operand:  *89*

operand availability  In a pipelined computer, e.g., the time when an operand that depends on the outcome of a previous instruction becomes available:  *301*

**operate instruction**  Any instruction that performs an arithmetic, logical, or shift operation on scalar or vector operands; translates or moves data; or manipulates a stack:  *58–62*

in pipelining:  *295*

vector:  *72*

**operating system**  The set of programs that controls the operation of a computer; includes, e.g., compilers, loaders, linkers, memory managers, interrupt handlers, and the basic input-output system (BIOS):  *72, 92, 99, 144, 155, 161–163, 189–196, 207, 208, 215, 341, 364, 365, 386*

in the IBM PC during system initialization:  *275*

in segmentation:  *212*

*See also* batch-processing operating system; multiprogramming operating system; multiuser operating system; time-sharing operating system

**operational register**  Any register that is visible to the program; hence, a register defined by the instruction-set architecture of the machine:  *36*

in exception processing:  *144*

in pipelining:  *297*

**operation code**  *See* op code

**operator error**  An error made by a computer operator (e.g., mounting the wrong tape on a tape drive, accidentally turning off the power, or specifying an incorrect value when entering a console command):  *377*

**optical disk**  A disk on which data are stored by thermally altering the reflective properties of tiny domains and are detected by measuring the amount of light reflected from the surface:  *189*

**optical technology**  Any technology that uses the physical properties of light and the reflective or transmissive properties of various films and solids to implement computations and storage:  *392*

OR  The instruction on two boolean operands A and B, such that A + B is *true* (1$_2$) if either A is *true* or B is *true*. When applied to binary operands, the boolean operation is performed bitwise:  *60, 137*

in the 8088 microprocessor:  *240*

OR reduction  A vector-reduction operation that performs the boolean OR on all elements of the vector to produce a single boolean result; also called ANY:  *73, 75*

**orthogonality**  The degree of independence among the instructions in an instruction set:  *105*

**orthogonal memory**  A storage system that can access memory both by words and by bit-slices:  *187*

OUT  An instruction of the 8088 microprocessor that initiates an I/O write cycle and sends the value in the AL (A, register, low byte) to the addressed I/O device:  *240, 245, 259, 261, 267*

use by a PPI during output:  *262*

OUTPUT  An output instruction:  *70*

**output arc**  In a dataflow graph, an arc that originates at a node and carries the output or result of that node:  *384*

**output buffer full (OBF)**  A flag that is set when the CPU loads the output buffer and which is cleared when the attached device reads the datum

for the 8255A PPI: *262*

**output port** An output connection of a computer or attached device (e.g., the port to which a printer is connected): ***164**, 262*

output protocol The protocol used by an I/O device or interface during an output operation

for the 8250 UART: *267*

for the 8255A PPI: *262*

*See also* handshaking

**output token** A token that delivers an output value from a dataflow graph: ***384***

**overflow** The state in which a number is too large for the intended representation (e.g., any value larger than 255 for an 8-bit binary representation): ***44***

overflow flag (V) The flag that the processor sets when an operation results in overflow: *53, 125, 126*

integer overflow: *51*

overlapping register sets Some RISC machines (e.g., the Sun SPARC) have register sets that the CPU accesses by window number $W$ and register number $N$, say $(W, N)$. The register sets overlap because some registers occur in more than one set; e.g., register $(1, 13)$ is the same as register $(0, 29)$; used to speed up parameter passage: *218, 313*

**overlay** A software technique that allows large programs to run on a computer with a small physical memory. The loader assigns the same addresses to two or more parts (overlays) of the program. The system then loads only the overlay it needs at the time: ***190***

For contrast, *see also* virtual memory

**overrun error** The error that occurs during serial data transmission when the receiving device loses data because it cannot keep up with the sending device: ***266***

P *See* positive flag

**p × m crossbar** A crossbar having $p$ inputs and $m$ outputs: ***328***

packed decimal In the 8088 microprocessor, a binary-coded decimal (BCD) representation in which two BCD digits are packed into each byte of storage: *240*

*See also* unpacked decimal

**packet** *See* message: *324*

**packet-switched interconnection network** A network that allows two devices to communicate by transmitting messages rather than by direct connection. The network routes these messages, which travel independently through the network, through intermediate communications nodes; also called message-passing network: ***324**, 325, 332, 336, 337, 367*

in the Cm* computer: *376*

For contrast, *see also* circuit-switched interconnection network

**page** A section of the logical-address space that the operating system, memory-mapping hardware, and memory-protection hardware treat as a unit. The high-order bits of a logical addresses specify the page number (or page address); the low-order bits specify the byte offset within the page. All pages of a given system are the same size, which is generally $2^K$ bytes long for some value of $K$: ***84***

in the CDC 6600: *193*

**page-0-indirect addressing** An addressing technique, used by some microprocessors, that specifies an operand address by giving only a page offset. The addressing hardware assumes the page number to be 0. The specified page-0 location holds the address of the operand: *88, **91***

**page-0-indirect instruction** An instruction that uses page-0-indirect addressing: ***91***

**page-0 instruction** An instruction, generally used by microprocessors, that uses page-0 direct or page-0-indirect addressing: ***88***

**page boundary** A point in the logical-address space (and in the physical-address space) where one page ends and another begins (i.e., addresses where the word offsets are 0): ***84**, 206*

paged memory management system *See* paging

paged-segmented virtual-memory system *See* segmentation with paging

**page fault** The exception (not an error condition) that occurs when a program references a page not present in main memory: ***208**, 209, 215*

**page frame** A physical block of memory that holds a page: ***206***

page-frame address: *214*

**page-frame number** The ordinal number of a page frame within the set of all page frames: ***207**, 208, 213*

**page map** In a paged, virtual-memory system, the relocation hardware that translates page numbers into page-frame numbers: ***206**, 208, 211*

in the Cm*: *371*

in paging: *209*

*See also* page table

**page number** In paging, the high-order bits in a logical address that specify which page holds the datum: *99, **206**, 208, 212, 213*

**page-replacement policy**  In paging, the protocol that determines which page the system will replace when all page frames are in use:  *208*

**page table**  In paging, the table that gives the association between the (logical) page numbers and the (physical) page-frame numbers:  *99, 206–208, 212, 213*

**page-table base register**  The register that points to the page table in main memory:  *207*

**page-table entry**  In a page table, the information concerning a single page; usually includes a validity bit, a dirty bit, protection bits, the address of the page in an external store, and the page-frame number (if the page is in memory):  *99, 206–208, 214*

**page thrashing**  A situation in which a program, because of how it is written, causes frequent page faults when executed:  *208*

**paging**  A virtual-memory addressing technique where the operating system divides the logical-address space into pages and the physical memory into page frames. Each page frame can hold one page. The operating system loads pages into page frames and keeps track of their locations using a page table or page map. The hardware translates a program's logical addresses into their proper physical address at execution time:  *99, 195, 205–214*

**pair-and-spare strategy**  A fault-tolerance technique that maintains a duplicate (spare) of each hardware device. If a hardware device fails, the system replaces it with its spare:  *379, 380*

**paper-tape punch**  An output device, no longer common, for punching paper tape:  *154*

**paper-tape reader**  An input device, no longer common, for reading punched paper tape:  *154*

**parallel I/O**  Said of devices (e.g., disk drives and printers) that transmit 1 or more bytes of data at a time:  *260*

For contrast, *see also* serial I/O

**parallel I/O device**  A physical I/O device that transfers bytes or words of data in parallel:  *255*

**parallel I/O interface**  An I/O interface adapter that controls a parallel I/O device:  *234*

in the IBM PC:  *260*

**parallelism**  Concurrent operation:  *285*

in pipelining:  *296*

**parallel processor**  A machine whose processors or processing elements can operate in parallel on more than one datum at a time; includes SIMD and MIMD:  *16, 321, 322*

*See also* multiple instruction stream, multiple data stream; multiprocessor; single instruction stream, multiple data stream

**parameter**  A value provided to a called procedure by a calling procedure; also called an argument:  *48, 96*

For contrast, *see also* argument; operand

**parameter-address list**  A list created by a calling procedure and sent to the called procedure that gives the addresses of the parameters the calling procedure wishes to pass to the called procedure:  *48, 49*

*See also* parameter list

**parameter list**  A list created by a calling procedure and sent to a called procedure that holds the actual parameters the calling procedure wishes to pass to the called procedure:  *48, 49*

*See also* parameter-address list

**parameter-list address**  The address of a parameter list:  *49*

**parameter passage**  The act of transferring data between subprograms:  *45, 47–48, 85, 96*

**parity**  A count of the number of $1_2$ bits in a data unit, such as a word or message. The parity is odd if there is an odd number of $1_2$ bits and even if there is an even number of $1_2$ bits (e.g., the parity of $101110_2$ is even):  *149*

in serial I/O:  *265, 266*

**parity bits**  Bits appended to a word so that error-detecting circuitry can use parity to detect errors:  *150, 265, 266, 378*

**parity error**  The errors that occur when a system that uses parity bits to detect errors receives a datum with even parity but expects a datum with odd parity, or vice versa:  *266*

**PC**  *See* IBM PC, IBM PC AT, personal computer

*See also* program counter

**PC AT**  *See* IBM PC AT

**PC AT Bus**  *See* PC AT I/O Channel Bus

**PC AT I/O Channel Bus**  The expanded local bus used by the original IBM PC AT. It has 98 lines (16 data lines, 24 address lines, and the rest power and control lines) and is an extension of the PC Bus. Also called PC AT Bus:  *234, 238, 257–258*

**PCB**  *See* printed circuit board

**PC Bus**  *See* PC I/O Channel Bus

**PC clone**  A non-IBM computer that has the same instruction-set architecture as a PC; a copy of an IBM PC:  *236, 259*

**PC I/O Bus**  *See* PC I/O Channel Bus

**PC I/O Channel Bus**  The expanded local bus used by the original IBM PC, which has 62 lines (8 data lines, 20 address lines, and the remainder power and control lines). Also called PC I/O Bus:  *122, 234, 237, 248–258, 264*

**PC-relative addressing** An addressing technique in which an address is specified relative to the content of the program counter; branch addresses are often PC-relative: *88*, **94**
   in branch instructions: *68*

PC slot *See* slot

PDP Programmed Data Processor. *See* PDP-11; PDP-8

**PDP-11** A 16-bit minicomputer introduced by Digital Equipment Corporation (circa 1970): *5, 44, 179, 308*

**PDP-8** An 8-bit minicomputer introduced by Digital Equipment Corporation (circa 1965): *5, 19, 308*

PE *See* processing element

**peak MIPS** The best MIPS performance attainable, as opposed to a sustained MIPS rating: *26*

peak search An operation for finding the maximum value in, e.g., a vector or array: *344*
   algorithm for a hypercube processor: *361–364*

**perceptron** An early (circa 1960) adaptive neural network: *391–392*

**Perfect Club Suite** Perfect stands for PERFormance Evaluation for Cost-effective Transformations. A suite of 13 scaled-down, real-world programs, taken from the sciences, for measuring the performances of computers: *27, 28*

performance A general measure of the speed of a computer: *25–30*
   *See also* cache performance; CPU performance evaluation

PERFormance Evaluation for Cost-effective Transformations *See* Perfect Club Suite

**performance metric** Results of running a benchmark test, given in relative or absolute terms: *25*

**peripheral processing unit (PPU)** An intelligent I/O processor; one that has sufficient local memory to hold I/O programs and buffer I/O operations, and has a relatively complex instruction set: *155, 158*
   *See also* channel

permanent support memory A nonremovable memory (e.g., main memory or hard disk): *184, 185*

**personal computer (PC)** A single-user computer with a base price of less than about $5000 (e.g., the IBM PC, the IBM PS/2, the Apple Macintosh): *4, 22, 37, 71, 88, 144, 154, 215, 232, 233, 413*
   *See also* Altair 8800; Apple II; PET; TRS-80

PET Personal Electronic Transactor computer; an early personal computer, introduced in 1977 by Commodore Business Machines: *233*

PGA *See* pin grid array

**physical address** The address in main memory of a memory reference, as opposed to the logical address of the reference; also called main-memory address: *13, 36, 86, 89, 124, 190–194, 197, 205, 211, 214, 215*
   in the Cm*: *375*

**physical-address space** The set of all possible physical addresses on a computer, limited by the number of bits in the computer's addressing hardware (i.e., for a computer with byte addressing, an n-bit address allows for a $2^n$-byte physical-address space): *86, 96, 99, 178, 191, 205, 214, 215, 234*
   of the 8088 microprocessor: *234*
   of the Cm*: *376*
   For contrast, *see also* logical-address space

**physical-addressing range** The range of physical addresses accessible to a program, as opposed to the physical-address space of the computer: *98, 99*
   For contrast, *see also* virtual-addressing range

physical I/O device A device (e.g., keyboard, printer, or mouse) that performs a physical I/O operation, as opposed to an I/O interface device (e.g., a programmable parallel interface or a universal asynchronous receiver transmitter): *152, 154, 158, 165–168*

physical memory A term used to refer to a physical storage device, as opposed to virtual memory: *100, 205, 206*

physical-memory address *See* physical address

picosecond One trillionth ($10^{-12}$) of a second: *406*

**pin** A physical connection to an integrated circuit; also called a signal pin: *245, 412, 413*

**pin grid array (PGA)** An integrated-circuit-packaging technology where the pins, which project from the bottom of the chip, are arranged in concentric squares: *412*

pipe *See* pipeline

**pipeline** A computer unit, such as an instruction decoder or an arithmetic unit, that uses pipelining. Also called pipe: *8, 10, 288*
   clock rate in: *293*
   multiplication pipeline: *290–293*

**pipelined functional unit** A functional unit that uses pipelining: *285*

**pipelined processor** A computer that uses pipelining in one or more of its systems; vector processors and RISCs are generally of this type: *10, 14, 219, 322, 332, 352*

pipelined vector processor, *See* vector machine, pipelined

**pipeline granularity** The coarseness of a pipeline, where a fine-grained pipeline has many stages and a coarse-grained one has fewer stages: *290, 293*

**pipeline variability** The range of operations that a pipeline can carry out: *290*

See also multifunction pipe; unifunction pipe

**pipelining** A hardware technique that allows many operations to execute concurrently, in an assembly-line fashion, by separating the operations into stages and providing special hardware for each processing stage; successive operations start, execute, and finish in sequence: *10, 126, 286–289, 312*

   arithmetic unit: *289–294*

**pixel** Picture element; one element in a digitized image or a video display: *339, 352–355*

**plastic quad flat pack (PQFP)** An integrated-circuit packaging technology in which the pins, which are soldered directly to the traces of a printed-circuit board, project from all four sides of a square integrated-circuit: *412*

**platter** One of the physical disks in a disk storage device (hard disk) that hold the stored information: *166*

POP An instruction that specifies a pop operation: *47, 55, 95*

   in the 8088 microprocessor: *240*

POP FLAGS An 8088 microprocessor instruction that pops the stack and uses the value to set the flags register: *240*

**pop operation** The operation on a stack that removes and delivers the top (logical) element from a stack: *47, 62*

**port** A connection point to a computer or memory for I/O: *163*

   of the 8255A PPI: *261*

See also control port; memory port; network tap

**portability** The quality of a storage device that measures how easy it is for a user to remove it and move the stored information (e.g., a floppy disk is highly portable while a hard disk is usually not): *106*

port address The address of a port: *164, 217*

   in the 8088 microprocessor: *245*

   assignments in the IBM PC: *274*

port controller See memory-port controller

positive flag (P) The processor-status flag that indicates a positive result: *53*

**postdecrementing** In autodecrement addressing, the decrementing of the address register after the CPU uses its content: *96*

**posted write** A write operation that a device (e.g., a cache) holds pending, e.g., memory availability: *198*

**postindexed-indirect addressing** Indirect addressing where the CPU uses the instruction address, without indexing, to locate the indirect address. The CPU then adds the index to the indirect address to get the address of the operand: *91*

power consumption The amount of power used by, e.g., a computer: *30*

power failure One possible situation that may give rise to an interrupt: *150*

power line A line on a system bus (e.g., PC I/O Channel Bus or PC AT I/O Channel Bus) that provides electricity to the attached devices: *257*

power pin A pin on an integrated-circuit chip that provides it with power: *245*

power supply A circuit that provides a computer or other device with power: *146, 233, 239, 256*

   in the IBM PC: *249, 251*

PPI See 8255A; programmable parallel interface

PPU See peripheral processing unit

PQFP See plastic quad flat pack

precision of basic datatypes: *49–50*

   of block floating-point numbers: *52*

   of floating-point numbers: *41*

**predicate** A function that returns a *true* or *false* value: *385*

prefetching a branch target instruction: *313*

prefix See instruction prefix

**preincrementing** In autoincrement addressing, the incrementing of the address register before the CPU uses its content: *96*

**preindexed-indirect addressing** Addressing in which indexing precedes indirect referencing: *91*

**primary memory** The part of the memory hierarchy that the CPU accesses directly; excluded are the peripheral storage devices. Also called main memory, central memory, core memory (archaic), or simply memory: *11, 177, 191, 233*

   in a dataflow architecture: *388, 389*

   design issues: *218–221*

   organization: *179–183*

   physical: *189, 190*

   See also associative memory; cache; expanded memory; virtual-memory system

Princeton University: *6*

**principle of locality of reference** The observation that the instructions and data used sequentially by a program tend to be clustered in memory: *197, 208*

**printed circuit board (PCB)** A thin, nonconductive board that holds the components of a circuit. The manufacturer laminates the board with conductive material and uses an etching process to remove unwanted material, leaving only the conductive wires (traces) that become the circuit; the integrated circuits and other components are then firmly attached to the board and the pins soldered to the traces: *412, 413*

printer  An output device that prints on paper: *155*

   status information: *168*

   *See also* laser printer

   IBM PC port-address assignment: *274*

prioritization algorithm  An algorithm, often implemented in hardware, that specifies how an arbiter will prioritize multiple requests for service: *157*

prioritized exceptions  Exceptions that the exception hardware prioritizes: *146–148*

priority address encoder  A network that accepts interrupt requests from several sources and generates the address of the interrupt handler (or interrupt-handler address) for the requestor having highest priority: *147, 151*

**priority network**  A device that accepts several input signals and generates an output signal indicating which input signal has the highest priority: ***419***

**privileged instruction**  Instructions that a CPU will execute only if it is operating in a privileged mode (e.g., supervisor state in the IBM System/360 or kernel mode in the DEC VAX family): *70,* ***71****, 72, 195*

   use in segmentation: *213*

**privileged mode**  The state or mode of a computer in which the CPU is allowed to execute privileged instructions; Also called priviledged state; and given different names in different systems (e.g., supervisor state in the IBM System/360 or kernel mode in the DEC VAX family): ***71****, 72, 191*

**privileged state**  *See* privileged mode

privilege level  The level of privilege corresponding to the current privilege state of the CPU: *70, 195, 196*

**problem mode**  The least-privileged execution mode of a processor, where the CPU disables privileged instructions; also called user mode or unprivileged mode: *53,* ***71***

   in segmentation: *212*

**procedure**  A self-contained program module (e.g., subroutine, function, or coroutine): *48, 58, 63, 69*

procedure linkage  The set of techniques used for allowing one procedure (the calling procedure) to call a second procedure (the called procedure) and pass parameters to it, and allowing the second procedure to return control to the calling procedure and pass results to it: *58*

procedure-linkage instructions  Instructions (e.g., CALL, RETURN, JSR) that help the programmer implement procedure linkage: *311*

process  An execution instance of a program or program thread; also called task: *63*

   *See also* active process, inactive process

**process communication**  The act of sending information from one process to another, often for synchronizing them: *366*

**process exclusion**  The ability of a process to monopolize a resource (e.g., some code or data) so that no other process can access it: *365,* ***366***

**processing element (PE)**  A processing node of a processor array, multiprocessor, or dataflow machine: ***10****, 17, 322, 338, 339, 344, 347, 354, 355, 363*

   in dataflow architecture: *389*

   interconnection network for: *343, 344*

**process initiation**  The commencement of executing a process; also called task initiation: *63,* ***366***

processor  A device (e.g., computer) that executes a process, as distinguished from the process itself: *63*

**processor array**  An SIMD machine whose processing elements communicate using an interconnection network having an array topology: *4, 10, 19, 321, 323, 331, 338–342, 343, 354*

**processor context**  The state of the CPU, including all operational-registers, the program counter, the processor status bits, and any other registers whose contents affect the execution of the program: *144–146, 365*

   *See also* memory context

processor state  The status of execution of a processor, including the status of the most recent operation (e.g., zero result, negative result, positive result, or overflow), the privilege mode of execution, and the status of any exceptions: *53*

**processor-status bits**  The set of bits a processor uses to report its state (e.g., the flags register of the 8088 microprocessor): *13,* ***53****, 54, 60, 68*

   use in exception processing: *144*

   in the IBM PC during system initialization: *274*

**process synchronization**  The operation performed by two or more processes to force them to enter specific points in their codes at particular times;

also called synchronization: *11, 23, 63, 365, 366, 367, 369*
  in MIMD machines: *18*
  in pipelining: *288*
  processor: *370*
**process synchronization instruction** An instruction, such as TEST AND SET, FETCH AND INCREMENT, or the pair of instructions SEND and RECEIVE, that helps one procedure prevent other procedures from accessing a shared memory location when it is doing so; also called a synchronization instruction or synchronization primitive: *58, 63–67*
**process termination** The ending or death of a process; the point in the execution of a program when it returns control to the operating system for the last time; also called task termination or termination: *67, 365, 366, 367*
**program** A complete sequence of instructions for a computer; used in control-flow architectures: *13, 63*
  For contrast, *see also* dataflow graph; dataflow model
**program context** The processor context plus memory context of a program: **144**, *145*
**program counter (PC)** The register in a CPU that points to the next instruction to be executed; also called an instruction pointer or instruction counter: *13, 14, 53, 94, 102, 103, 120, 126–128, 131, 134, 137, 138, 141, 148, 149, 152, 160, 161*
  in the 8087 coprocessor: *271*
  in the 8088 microprocessor: *241*
  during IBM PC initialization: *273*
  in exception processing: *144*
  in pipelining: *295*
  in subroutine linkage: *69, 70*
  *See also* IP
programmable interval timer *See* 8253; interval timer
**programmable parallel interface (PPI)** A programmable I/O interface that sends and receives all of the bits of a word at the same time, as opposed to one that operates in bit-serial fashion, i.e., sequentially on the bits of a word: *239, 255*
  For contrast, *see also* universal asynchronous receiver-transmitter
**programmable ROM (PROM)** A read-only memory that is programmable: *183*
  physical characteristics of: *186*
programming a port The process of configuring an input or output port in a programmable I/O device (e.g., in an 8250 UART or an 8255A PPI) by storing control information in its control registers: *262*
programming language A high-level language for specifying programs
  nonprocedural A programming language used to specify a nonprocedural computation (e.g., a dataflow graph): *384*
  procedural A programming language used to specify an algorithm: *384*
**program relocation** The positioning of a program and its data in memory: *86, 98,* **190**–***192***
  *See also* dynamic program relocation; initial program relocation
program self-modification The alteration of the image of a program in memory by the program itself: *297, 312*
  effect on pipelining: *297*
**program status word (PSW)** The word in a CPU that holds the processor-status bits and often additional information, such as protection key, interrupt-mask register, interrupt-code register, and program counter: **54**, *152, 153, 192*
  in the Cm*: *375*
  in interrupt processing: *153*
protection The isolation of one programs context from that of another program's context; the prevention of one program from accessing the memory allocated to another program: *196, 212*
**protection bits** In an entry in a table (e.g., a segment table or page table), the bits indicating which users may access the page or segment and for what kinds of operations (e.g., read only, or read and write): *99,* **207***, 211*
  in paging: *209*
  in segmentation: *211*
  *See also* memory protection
PS/2 *See* IBM PS/2
pseudo-random-access device A device that allows access to any word, but with slightly varying access times, or one that supports access to blocks of words (e.g., disks): *168, 189*
  *See also* sequential-access memory
**pseudo-random-access memory** Memory (e.g., magnetic-bubble memory or charge-coupled-device memory) that allows access to any word, but with slightly varying access times: **186**
PSW *See* program status word
pull a signal down Send a logical $0_2$ or *false* signal; deassert: *413*
PUSH An instruction that specifies a push operation: *47, 55, 95*
  in the 8088 microprocessor: *240*

PUSH FLAGS   A push operation of the 8088 microprocessor that pushes the content of the flags register into the stack: *240*

**push operation**   A stack operation that puts a new datum on the top of the stack: *47, 48, 55, 62, 95*

Qj   A function-unit designator in the CDC 6600: *299, 302, 303*

Qk   A function-unit designator in the CDC 6600: *299, 302, 303*

Quadram: *278*

**quadword**   A group of four contiguous words in memory: *37, 84, 85*

RA   *See* relocation-address register

Radio Shack: *233, 236*

**radix**   The exponent base of a floating-point number; usually a power of 2: *40, 41, 52*

  of the B-5500 floating-point representation: *41*

  of the CDC CYBER 170 floating-point representation: *42*

  of the System/370 floating-point representation: *43*

  *See also* exponent; floating-point number; mantissa

**radix point**   The point in the mantissa of a number that separates the integer part on the left from the fractional part on the right; generalization of the decimal point or binary point: *40*

raise a signal   Send a logical *true* or $1_2$ signal; assert: *413*

RAM   *See* random-access memory

RAM chip   An integrated circuit chip that implements a random-access memory: *177, 179, 180*

RAM technology   The technology of a random-access memory (e.g., vacuum tube, magnetic core, transistor): *221*

random-access device   Any addressed storage device (e.g., a disk with a suitable cache) that can access it data in essentially the same amount of time: *189*

**random-access memory (RAM)**   A memory that provides access to all of its data cells in essentially the same amount of time: *176, 177, 183, 185, 216, 217, 219, 237, 239*

READ   A channel command for reading a magnetic tape: *160*

**read-access time**   The time it takes to read a value from memory or a storage device: *185*

  *Also see* disk access time; network latency; rotational latency

READ A FROM DEVICE N   An input instruction for loading the accumulator (A) with a byte of data from device number *N*: *154*

read bus cycle   *See* read cycle, 2

**read cycle**   1. The physical memory cycle that occurs when a storage system reads a value from a memory cell: *185*. 2. A type of bus cycle that the CPU initiates when it wants to read a value from memory (or from a memory-mapped I/O interface): *123*

  bus 122

  in serial I/O: *265*

  *See also* bus cycle; interrupt cycle; I/O bus cycle; I/O read cycle; I/O write cycle; memory bus cycle

**read flag**   A flag within the CDC 6600 that indicates the availability of a register operand; denoted RFj or RFk: *299, 302, 303*

read head   An input head in a tape or disk device; senses the magnetic domains and generates the corresponding electrical signals: *178*

**read-only memory (ROM)**   A memory that can only be read: *129, 183, 185, 239*

  physical characteristics of: *186*

  technology: *310*

  test of, in the IBM PC test during system initialization: *274*

read-only page   A page in a demand-paged virtual memory system that is marked as read-only; any attempt to write to it will cause a memory-protection violation: *209*

read request   The signal a device sends to a port controller to request a memory access: *156*

**read-write head**   The physical mechanism within a disk or tape system that reads data from, or writes data to, the storage medium: *166*

  *See also* read head

**Real Address mode**   An execution mode of the 80286 microprocessor in which it emulates the instruction-set architecture of the 8088 microprocessor, i.e., it acts like a fast 8088: *234, 235, 257*

RECEIVE   A synchronization instruction that gives results similar to a memory-read operation, but also empties the memory location: *64–66*

receive-data register   The input buffer of the 8250 UART: *267*

received line signal detect (RLSD)   The input signal to the 8250 UART that indicates the presence of a carrier frequency on the transmission line: *267*

  *See also* ring indicator

**receiver clock** The clock that controls the rate of reception of serial data by a universal asynchronous receiver-transmitter: *266*
  See also transmitter clock
RECIPROCAL A monadic vector operation that replaces the value of each vector element $v_i$ by $1/v_i$: *72, 73*
**reconfigurable duplication** A technique of fault tolerance in which the system has duplicate components and can reconfigure itself by replacing a bad component with a good one in case a component malfunctions or fails: *380*
recursive code *See* recursive procedure
recursive procedure A programming technique in which a procedure can call itself; based on mathematical recursion, where a function is defined by giving its value at one or more fixed points, and then the remaining values are specified in terms of those already defined [e.g., $f(0) = 0; f(n) = n + f(n-1)$]: *70*
  in the CDC 6600: *103*
**reduced-instruction-set computer (RISC)** A computer with a relatively simple load-and-store instruction set and only register-to-register operate instructions. Typical RISC machines have large register sets, multiple functional units, and pipelined instruction and execution units: **10**, *19, 21, 54, 55, 60, 62, 72, 87, 92, 94, 101, 126, 129, 143, 197, 204, 302, 304, 305–314, 389*
  addressing modes: *102*
**reduction machine** An experimental dataflow machine that evaluates an expression by firing nodes whose outputs are demanded, as opposed to standard dataflow machines, which fire nodes when their operands are available: *323, 389*
**redundancy** A fault-tolerance technique where additional hardware or software, such as duplicate functional units, provides a means for checking results: *326*
reentrant code A program segment that can be executed by multiple processes at the same time; code whose execution does not depend on its history of activations: *103*
**reentrant graph** A dataflow graph whose execution does not depend on its history of operations: *386*
**refill line** *See* cache refill line
refill-line address *See* cache refill-line address
REFRESH A line in the IBM PC I/O Channel Bus that signals an in-progress dynamic random-access memory (DRAM) refresh operation: *257*
refresh circuitry, for dynamic random-access memory (DRAM) Circuitry for periodically refreshing DRAM: *184, 258, 269*

**reg field** One of three fields in the address-mode byte of an 8088 instruction; specifies what register the CPU will use when resolving the effective address: *242,* **243**
**register** A hardware device for holding a value. The size of the value is usually the word-size of the computer: **36,** *426*
  use in parameter passage: *48, 49*
  width for data precision: *48*
**register address** *See* register number
register addressing Addressing where the instruction specifies a register and that register holds the operand: *82–83*
register architecture A general classification of computers based on their register sets; includes evaluation-stack architectures, accumulator machines, general-purpose register-set machines, and special-purpose register-set machines: *55–57*
**register-deferred addressing** *See* register-indirect addressing
**register designator** *See* register number
register file: *126, 431*
**register-indirect addressing** Indirect addressing in which a register holds the indirect address; sometimes called register-deferred addressing: *87, 92, 96*
  in branch instructions: *68*
register number The number, usually given in absolute binary, that the CPU hardware uses to select a register; also called register address or register designator: *83*
**register operand** An operand that comes from a register, as opposed to from memory or a stack: *83*
**register set** The set of operational registers of a computer, hence those registers that a programmer can access using the machine's instruction set: *12, 53–57, 124, 158,* **153**
  of the 8088: *240–242*
  of the 8237A DMA controller: *253–254*
  of the 8253 programmable interval timer: *268*
  of the 8255A PPI: *261*
  of the 8087 floating-point coprocessor: *270–272*
  of a channel: *160–161*
  design of: *53–57*
  use of large, in RISCs: *312*
  use of multiple register sets: *218*
  *See also* register architecture
register stack A hardware stack within the 8087 coprocessor: *271*
**register-to-register instruction** An instruction whose operation is a register-to-register operation: **54,** *55, 62, 306*

**reliability** A measure of the dependability of a computer, often specified in terms of how long a computer is expected to run before failure, how long it is expected to run between failures, or how long it takes to repair: *30, 378*

relocation *See* program relocation

**relocation address (RA)** The starting address of a program in the computer's physical-address space. Hence, the value added to a logical address by the memory-relocation hardware to get the corresponding physical address of the reference, in the CDC 6600 memory protection: *190*

relocation address–field length protection The memory-protection technique used in the CDC 6600 computer: *190–195, 209*

**relocation-address register (RA):** *193–195*

in the Cm*: *374–375*

**relocation offset (*RO*)** An offset used for relocating a program in memory

in the CDC 6600: *190–192*

**removable support memory** Memory that can be physically removed from a computer, such as floppy disks and tapes, but not most hard disks or main memory: *184, 185*

REPEAT An instruction prefix for the 8088 microprocessor string-processing instructions; tells the CPU to execute the following instruction until the content of the count register (CX) goes to 0 or until a specified condition is met. After each execution of the instruction, the CPU decrements the content of CX: *240*

replacement algorithm An algorithm that specifies, e.g., which page or segment will be replaced during a page- or segment-replacement operation: *215*

request permission to send (RTS) One of the handshake signals generated by a universal asynchronous receiver-transmitter (UART) to inform the attached device that the UART has data it is ready to transmit: *266*

request register *See* DMA request register

reserved memory Memory in the address range from 640 K to 1 M in the IBM PC that the operating system has reserved for its own use: *278*

**reset input** An input to a flip-flop that resets the flip-flop, i.e., places it in the reset or 0 state: *424*

**reset state** One of the two states of a flip-flop; the 0 state: *425*

resetting a computer The act of forcing the computer to enter its startup routine and therefore begin processing at the address given by the reset vector. For the IBM PC, this act is triggered by pressing three keyboard keys simultaneously (Ctrl, Alt, and Delete); same as restarting a computer: *144*

**reset vector** The address of the program that starts a computer running; hence, the address that the hardware places in the program counter after a reset occurs: *131*

**reset-vector address** The address of the reset vector: *131*

resolving an address The process of converting an instruction address into an effective address (e.g., by adding the contents of an index register and a base register to the instruction-specified displacement): *86*

**response layer** The output layer of a perceptron: *391*

**restore cycle** For a destructive-read memory, the rewrite part of a read-write cycle: *185*

RESTORE STATE An 8087 coprocessor instruction: *270*

restoring a processor's context: *145*

**result** A value returned by a called procedure to the calling procedure: *48*

**result packet** In a dataflow architecture, the unit consisting of the result token, its destination address, and any tags; also called an output packet: *389*

**result rate** The rate at which a pipelined functional unit can produce results: *305*

result register An instruction-specified register into which the CPU will place the result of an operation; also called destination register: *54*

in the CDC 6600: *300*

result-register dependencies Data dependencies that exist in a pipelined processor when two instructions specify the same result register: *312–313*

in the CDC 6600: *302*

result-register designator *See* XBA result-register designator

result token In a dataflow processor, part of the result packet that a processing element generates when it executes an instruction; corresponds to the output token for the node that the instruction implements: *389*

**resuming a process** The act of transferring control back to a process that was previously suspended: *64*

RET *See* RETURN

**retina** The layer of receptive cells in a human or animal eye or analogously the input layer of a perceptron: *391*

RETURN The instruction a subprogram executes to return control to the calling program; takes the continuation-point address preserved by a CALL instruction and loads it in the program counter: *69, 71*

    in the 8088 microprocessor: *240*

**return address** The address of the instruction in a calling procedure where execution is to resume when the called procedure returns control to it (e.g., by executing a RETURN instruction); the program-counter address that the CPU saves when a program executes a CALL or JSR instruction. Also called continuation-point address: *69, **70***

    in the CDC 6600: *103*

    *See also* CALL, JSR

RETURN FROM INTERRUPT The instruction that returns control to the interrupted program and restores its state after an exception handler finishes processing the exception; similar to RETURN except that it also clears the interrupt flag: *71, 146, 152*

    in the 8088 microprocessor: *240*

RETURN FROM TRAP Similar to RETURN FROM INTERRUPT: *71*

RETURN JUMP TO A CDC 6600 instruction used for program linkage; executes an indirect jump operation through the location holding the return address: *103*

REWIND A channel command for a tape drive: *160*

RFj *See* read flag

RFk *See* read flag

RI *See* ring indicator

Ring indicator (RI) An input to the 8250 UART, generally from a modem, that becomes active when the telephone is ringing: *267*

    *See also* received line signal detect

**ring topology** An interconnection topology in which each node of the network is connected to two neighbors, and all nodes form a single closed loop: *328*

ripple-carry adder An $n$-bit binary adder composed of $n$ 1-bit full adders connected so that the carry-out from stage $i$ is the carry-in to stage $i + 1$: *424*

    For contrast, *see* carry look-ahead circuit

RISC *See* reduced-instruction-set computer

RISC-CISC controversy As of 1990, an ongoing discussion as to whether the principles of design for RISC processors will lead to better and faster computers than those in use for CISC processors: *309–312*

RLSD *See* received line signal detect

**r/m field** One of three fields in the address-mode byte of an 8088 microprocessor instruction; used to specify the addressing mode: *242, **243***

    *See also* mod field; reg field

RO *See* relocation offset

Rockwell International: *233*

**rollback** A technique for handling delayed page faults in which the hardware records enough information during instruction execution such that, if a page fault occurs, the system can restore the state existing before instruction execution: ***209***

**ROM** *See* read-only memory

**ROM BIOS** The basic I/O system of an IBM PC, which comes in a ROM chip on the mother board and provides direct control for the hardware devices: *252, **273**–277*

    address assignment of: *278*

Rosenblatt, F. Inventor of the perceptron: *391*

ROTATE An instruction that initiates a rotation operation: *68*

    in the 8088 microprocessor: *240*

ROTATE LEFT The instruction that causes an operand to be shifted left, with vacated bit positions on the right filled by the bits that overflow at the left: *60, 61*

ROTATE RIGHT Similar to rotate left, but the rotation is in the other direction: *60*

**rotational delay** *See* rotational latency

**rotational latency** The part of the latency of a disk read operation that is due to the time it takes the hardware to rotate the disk so the requested datum is under the read head; also called rotational delay: ***167**, 168*

ROUND An 8087 coprocessor instruction: *270*

round robin protocol A protocol in which each device is checked for having a service request pending before the first device is retested; thus all devices have equal priority for service: *157*

routing difficulty In an interconnection network, the complexity of setting the switches to implement the desired pattern of communication: *326*

row *See* cache sector

**row-major order** The organization of an array in memory such that the algorithm stores the elements of each row in contiguous memory locations; also called row order: *79, **81**, 208*

    in matrix multiplication: *81*

    *See also* row-minor order

**row-minor order** The organization of an array in memory in which the algorithm stores the elements of each column in contiguous memory locations; also called column order: *79, **81**, 208*

    in matrix multiplication: *81*

    *See also* row-major order

RTS *See* request permission to send:

**ruggedness** The quality of a computer that allows it to take a licking and keep on ticking: *30*

**run-time behavior** The activity of a program during its execution, which depends on its run-time state: *144*

**run-time state** The instantaneous state of an executing program, consisting of the values of all accessible words in memory together with the values in all operational registers in the CPU; thus the CPU context plus the memory context of a program: *144*

**S-100 bus** An early system bus (circa 1976) introduced by MITS, Inc., as part of the Altair computer: *120*

Sameh, A.: *27*

**sampling** A technique used in serial I/O to reduce framing errors in which a universal asynchronous receiver-transmitter uses a high-frequency clock to sample the input signal in the middle of a bit time to determine the value of the incoming bit: *266*

Samuel, A. L.: *5*

**save area** An area in memory used by a program (or the operating system) to save the run-time state of a program or procedure; used by programs to save their own states when calling subprograms so that they can resume executing when the subprograms return control to them, and by operating systems to save the run-time states of a program during exception processing: *145, 149, 365*

SAVE STATE An 8087 coprocessor operation: *270*

**scalar** A single value; a vector with only one element: *47*

**scalar code** Code intended for execution on a conventional processor, i.e., code not specifically written for execution on a vector processor: *77*

**scalar product** *See* dot product: *75, 83*

SCALE An 8087 coprocessor instruction: *270*

SCAN The 8088 microprocessor instruction for comparing characters; also used (e.g., with a REPEAT prefix) to implement string comparison: *240*

*See also* REPEAT

**scanner** An input device for converting pictures and printed material into digitized images; may be hand-held or full-page: *154*

SCATTER An instruction that initiates a scatter operation; the inverse of a gather operation: *76, 79*

**scatter operation** A vector store operation that stores selected elements of one vector into arbitrary element positions of a second vector; the elements of an index array specify the element positions (offsets) in the target vector: *78*

scheduling *See* function-unit scheduling

**scoreboard** That part of the control circuitry of the CDC 6600 that controls instruction execution: *298–302*

SDLC *See* synchronous data link control

search *See* associative memory; associative search; INDEX

**second-generation computer** A computer of the 1950s and 1960s that used discrete transistor technology and a batch-processing operating system: *7*

**secondary memory** The part of the memory hierarchy that resides on peripheral devices (e.g., tape storage, disk storage); memory that is not central to the CPU: *191*

in paging: *208, 209*

For contrast, *see also* primary memory

**sector** *See* cache sector; disk sector

**sector-mapped cache** A cache in which the tag system associatively maps sector addresses and then uses, in addition to the address tags, validity bits to keep track of which refill lines of the sector are present in cache RAM. A sector cache with one refill line per sector is fully associative: *201, 202*

**secure system** A system that can prevent access by unauthorized users as well as by authorized users who do not have permission to access particular data: *196*

**security** The precautions and techniques used to maintain a secure system: *193–196*

**seeing-eye packet** In a packet-switched interconnection network, a packet that contains routing bits so the hardware at each node can forward it to its intended destination; the name derives from the fact that during transmission the packet appears to find its own way through the network: *324*

**seek time** In a disk operation, the time it takes the hardware to move the read-write heads to the required cylinder; also called head-positioning delay: *167, 168*

**segment** In a segmented virtual-memory system or one that uses segment-register addressing, a block of logical addresses that the operating system, the memory mapping hardware, and the memory protection hardware treat as a unit. Segments may vary in size depending on usage: *92, 100, 210*

*See also* code segment; data segment; extra segment; stack segment

**segmentation** A virtual-memory addressing technique in which the operating system divides the logical-address space into segments of arbitrary size and references words by segment number and offset within segment. The virtual-memory hardware uses a segment table to convert effective addresses into physical addresses: *96, 210–215*

segmentation with paging A virtual-memory addressing technique that combines segmentation with paging. The operating system creates a page table for each segment and uses paging to load demanded parts of the segments: *212–215*

segmented addressing See segment-register addressing

**segment fault** The exception that results when a program makes a reference to a word whose segment is not present in main memory; not an error but a normal computer event: *211, 215*

segment loader The software component of a segmentation system that loads segments into memory: *340*

**segment map** In a segmentation system, the relocation hardware that translates the segment-number part of an effective address into the base address of that segment in memory: *211, 215*

   in the Cm* computer: *371, 375*

**segment number** The ordinal number of a segment; the segment address: *211, 213*

**segment-override prefix** An instruction prefix for an 8088 instruction; tells the CPU which segment register to use in lieu of the default segment register: *242*

**segment register** One of four registers in an 8088 microprocessor that holds a segment address; during address resolution the addressing hardware uses a default segment register, multiplies its content by 16, and adds the result to a displacement (and possibly an index) to form the effective address: *97, 98, 240, 242, 244, 247*

   during IBM PC initialization: *273*

**segment-register addressing** A modification of base-displacement addressing used by the Intel 80x86 family of microprocessors: *96–98, 240*

   in the 8088: *243*

**segment table** Part of the segment map in a segmentation system, the table used to map segment numbers into segment base addresses in memory and to hold protection and validity information about the segments: *212–214*

segment-table base address The beginning address in memory of a segment table: *213*

**segment-table base register** A register that holds a segment-table base address: *211, 212*

segment-table entry In a segment table, the information describing a single segment; usually includes a validity bit, a dirty bit, protection bits, the address of the segment in an external store, and, if the segment is in memory, its base address there: *212*

**segment-table length register** A register that holds the length of a segment table; used to prevent a user from performing an out-of-bounds segment-table access: *211, 212*

selection See vector selection

**semaphore** A flag that the CPU can access using the two synchronization instructions TEST AND SET and CLEAR; used by programs to enforce mutual exclusion: *65*

SEND A synchronization instruction that fills a memory location (i.e., marks it as *full*); complementary to the RECEIVE instruction (which marks a cell as *empty*): *64–67*

SENSE A channel instruction for a magnetic tape drive: *160*

**sequencer** The clock in a microprogrammed control unit: *130–133*

**sequential-access device** See sequential-access memory

sequential-access memory Memory that accesses data sequentially; thus the access times differ for different words or at different times: *176, 184, 186, 188–189*

   See also charge-coupled device; magnetic bubble memory; mercury-delay-line memory

**sequential-access device** A device (e.g., a tape drive) that must process successive bits of data serially, in contrast to pseudo-random-access devices and RAMs: *166*

**sequential circuit** A circuit with memory components and hence one whose output depends on its history of inputs (e.g., a circuit with flip-flops): *424*

serial communication line A transmission line (e.g., a telephone line) over which data are sent serially (1 bit at a time): *265*

serial data transmission The transmission of data in sequence (e.g., over a serial communication line); also called bit-serial transmission or telephone transmission: *255, 265–268*

**serial I/O** Refers to devices that transmit data 1 bit at a time over a single data line: *260*

   clock signals: *268*

   techniques of: *265–268*

   For contrast, see also parallel I/O

serial I/O interface See universal asynchronous receiver-transmitter

**serial port**  A port for serial I/O
  IBM PC port-address assignment: *274*
**serial processing**  A hardware technique in which all stages of one process execute before the first stage of the next process begins: *286*
**service-grant signal**  A signal that informs a requesting device that it has been granted service: *156, 157*
**service request**  In the Cm* computer, a memory-mapped control operation performed by a Local Switch that asks a *K*map to perform a service such as address translation: *375*
**service-request signal**  A signal that a device uses to request service from a second device (i.e., a bus request): *156*
SET IF  An 8088 microprocessor instruction that sets the interrupt flag (IF): *240*
**set input**  An input to a flip-flop that sets the flip-flop, i.e., places it in the set or $1_2$ state: *424*
**set state**  One of the two states of a flip-flop; the $1_2$ state: *425*
**set-associative cache**  A cache that partitions its RAM into *K* sets of *L* refill lines (*L* usually a small number) and main memory into *K* sets of *M* refill lines. The cache can map any refill line of set *I* in memory into any cache line of set *I*: *200, 202, 370*
  four-way: *202*
**shared address space**  An address space that more than one processor uses. In a loosely coupled multiprocessor system, each processor would ordinarily be assigned a nonoverlapping range of addresses within the shared address space; in a tightly coupled multiprocessor system, the processors use the same (overlapping) addresses: *195*
**shared data set**  A data set that several processes share: *64*
**shared resource**  Any resource that is shared by more than one device (e.g., an I/O processor): *158*
**shared variable**  A datum that several processes share: *64*
SHIFT  An instruction with two operands, a shift amount, and a datum to be shifted. The CPU shifts the bits of the datum by the specified amount: *68, 344*
  in the 8088 microprocessor: *240*
**shifter**  A sequential circuit for performing shift operations: *125, 126*
  *See also* barrel shifter
**shift instruction**  Any instruction, e.g., SHIFT LEFT or SHIFT RIGHT, that instructs the CPU to shift a datum: *13, 60–61*

SHIFT LEFT  An instruction that initiates a shift-left operation: *60, 61, 350*
**shift register**  A register that is designed for performing shift operations on its content: *428*
SHIFT RIGHT  An instruction that initiates a shift-right operation: *61*
**shift-right register**  A register designed for performing shift-right operations on its content: *429*
Shockley, W.: *7*
short floating-point number, of the 8087 coprocessor: *269, 270*
short integer, of the 8087 coprocessor: *269*
**shuffle operation**  An operation on $2N$ inputs and $2N$ outputs that connects input $I_j$ to output $O_{2j\,modulo\,N}$, where $0 \leq j \leq 2N - 1$: *334*
SI  *See* source-index register
Siemans VPx: *304*
**sign**  One of four parts of a floating-point number: *40, 41*
  *See also* sign bit
**sign bit**  The bit that distinguishes positive from negative numbers in signed-magnitude, one's-complement, and two's-complement notation; 1 for positive, 0 for negative: *38*
  in NaN: *44*
signal pin  *See* pin
**signed-magnitude integer**  An integer that is represented by a sign bit and a integral magnitude: *38–41*
SIMD  *See* single instruction stream, multiple data stream
**single-bus architecture**  An architecture that uses a single system bus to interconnect its components: *327*
**single-cycle DMA**  A type of DMA transfer in which the DMA controller requests permission to use the bus for each item it wants to transfer: *158*
**single instruction stream, multiple data stream (SIMD)**  In Flynn's classification, the architectural category that is composed of computers with a single control unit and many processing elements; applies to most processor arrays: *14, 15, 16, 321–323, 339, 341–363*
**single instruction stream, single data stream (SISD)**  In Flynn's classification, the architectural category composed of ordinary (von Neumann) computers; there is only one CPU, which executes one instruction at a time and fetches or stores just one datum at a time: *14, 15, 19, 323*
single-mode transfer  *See* DMA single mode
**single-phase clock**  A clock with a single output consisting of an unending sequence of pulses having a specified shape and frequency: *427*

**single precision** Refers to a number, usually floating point, that uses a single word for its representation: *37*

   floating-point format: *44*

   IEEE floating-point standard: *45, 46*

   *See also* double precision

SIO  Start I/O; an I/O channel command: *159*

**slave device** In a bus communication, any device or storage system that is responding to the bus master: *122*

**slave flip-flop** Of the two flip-flops within a master-slave flip-flop, the one that copies the state of the master flip-flop and produces the output of the device: *425*

**slave node** In an interconnection network, a node that responds to a request made by a master node: *324*

**slot** A plug in one circuit board designed to accept another circuit board; usually said of the plugs on the mother board of a personal computer into which a user can plug additional devices. The slots in IBM PCs are wired in parallel and connect to the IBM PC I/O Channel: *237, 257*

**small-scale integration (SSI)** Characteristic of integrated circuits having only a few transistors on each chip: *8, 411*

   For contrast, *see also* large-scale integration; medium-scale integration; very large scale integration

**snoopy cache** A cache that monitors (snoops on) the bus and automatically invalidates stale data; said to have snoopy coherency control: *370*

**soft fault** A momentary fault, one that cannot be duplicated (e.g., an erroneous bit in memory caused by cosmic rays): *377*

**soft sectoring** A form of disk organization in which the disk writes the sector numbers on each track at the start of each sector, and the software and hardware must search for the required sector: *166*

**software failure** A failure due to a software error: *377*

**software system interface quality** The user-friendliness of a software system: *30*

**software system, of the IBM PC:** *272–278*

**solid-state memory** A memory whose components are transistors or integrated circuits, as opposed to vacuum tubes, magnetic cores, or mercury delay lines: *7, 175*

**source address** The address of a source string in a string operation, e.g., in a MOVE STRING: *61, 62*

**source-code compatibility** Said of members of a family of computers if they can run programs after recompilation and linking: *106*

**source index** In the 8088 microprocessor, the index of a character in the source string of the operation; held by the source-index register: *241*

**source-index register (SI)** A register in the 8088 microprocessor that holds a source index during various string operations: *240*

**source register** Any register that holds an operand for an operation: *107*

   For contrast, *see also* destination register

SP  *See* stack pointer

**SPARC** A RISC architecture by Sun Microsystems: *19, 307, 308, 314*

**SPARCstation** A workstation by Sun Microsystems that uses the SPARC architecture: *307*

   LINPACK benchmark of: *307*

**spare system** *See* pair-and-spare strategy

**spawning a process** In a multitasking system, the operation of creating an independent process: *365*

**SPEC** System Performance and Evaluation Cooperative; group founded by Apollo, Hewlett Packard, MIPS, and Sun Microsystems to evaluate the performance of small computer systems: *27*

**SPEC Benchmark Suite** A group of 10 real-world applications taken from a variety of scientific and engineering applications and used to measure the performances of computers: *27, 28*

**special-purpose machine** A computer designed for a specific application area rather than for a broad segment of applications: *20*

**special-purpose registers** Registers with assigned functions, as opposed to general-purpose registers, which have many uses: *53*

   *See also* base register; DMA command register; condition-code register; control register; field-length register; flags register; index register; instruction register; interrupt-code register; interrupt- mask register; memory address register; memory buffer register; mode register; program counter; segment register; stack pointer; status register; vector register

**special-purpose register-set machine** A computer whose operational registers have specific assigned uses (e.g., index registers, base registers, or accumulators): *57*

   For contrast, *see also* general-purpose register-set machine

**SPECmarks** The unit for reporting the results of the tests in the SPEC Benchmark Suite; 1 SPECmark is roughly equivalent to 1 VUP, but the relationship between the two units is not linear: *27*

Spectrum A RISC processor by Hewlett-Packard: *314*

**spiral topology** For a processor array, the topology formed by connecting the processing element (PE) on the right edge of each row with the leftmost PE on the next row: *332*

**spiral-toroidal topology** For a processor array, the topology formed by connecting the processing element (PE) on the right edge of each row with the leftmost PE on the next row, and connecting each PE on the top row with the bottom PE on the same row: *332*

**splinter** An unused region in main memory that is too small to hold a segment. Splinters result from the allocation and deallocation of segments of arbitrary size in a virtual-memory system: *211*

SQUARE A monadic vector instruction that squares each element in a vector: *72*

SQUARE ROOT 1. An instruction in the 8087 coprocessor: *270*. 2. A monadic vector instruction for the square root of each element of a vector: *72*

**SRAM** *See* static random-access memory

**SR flip-flop** Set-reset flip-flop; an asynchronous flip-flop having two inputs, S and R. Asserting S sets the flip-flop, asserting R clears it, and asserting both S and R results in an unpredictable state: *424*

SS *See* stack-segment register

SSI *See* small-scale integration

**stack** A data structure or storage device in which the last item that was stored is the first one that can be removed, hence last in, first out (LIFO). Instructions for stacks include PUSH, POP, and TOP: *8, 45, 46–47, 55, 62, 94–96, 149,* ***430***

   in parameter passage: *48, 49*

   in subroutine linkage: *70*

stack addressing Addressing where a stack register holds the address of the operand. The hardware automatically decrements the stack register content after a write operation (hence implementing PUSH) and automatically increments it before a read operation (hence implementing POP): *96*

**stack architecture** *See* execution stack architecture

stack instruction An instruction for operating on a stack (e.g., PUSH, POP, TOP, and EMPTY): *61–62*

**stack pointer** A register that holds the address of the top element of a stack in memory; also called stack register: *54, 95, 120*

   in parameter passage: *49*

   SP, in the 8088 microprocessor: *241, 243*

stack register *See* stack pointer

**stack-register addressing** Addressing that helps to implement a stack in memory, typically by automatically incrementing or decrementing the content of a stack register: *96*

*See* autoincrement addressing; autodecrement addressing

**stack-register instruction** An instruction that facilitates the use of main memory to hold a stack, or an instruction that initiates a stack operation (e.g., the PUSH FLAGS instruction of the 8088 microprocessor pushes the contents of the flags register into the stack and automatically decrements the stack pointer): *94*

**stack segment** One of four 64KB segments of memory that the 8088 processor can access directly; the segment holding the current stack: *96, 98, 244*

*See also* code segment; data segment; extra segment

stack-segment register (SS) In the 8088 microprocessor, holds the base address of the stack segment: *241, 244*

stack-top pointer A stack pointer in the 8087 coprocessor: *271*

**staged interconnection network** An interconnection network that uses multiple switching elements between its inputs and outputs: *332, 233, 337*

stage time, of a pipeline The reciprocal of the clock rate for the pipeline: *293*

**stale data** Values in a cache whose images in memory have been updated: *367*

   in paging: *208*

stale pointer A pointer that is no longer correct (e.g., an address in an I/O channel that points to a page in memory that has been replaced): *370*

Star-100 An early supercomputer (circa 1970) by Control Data Corporation: *304, 308*

STARAN A bit-slice associative processor developed by Goodyear Aerospace (circa 1972) for associative-memory operations: *187, 342, 347, 350*

START I/O An I/O instruction that starts an I/O channel: *70, 159*

**star topology** A network topology in which all nodes connect to a single central node, or hub: *327, 328, 329*

startup *See* machine startup

**startup time** The time it takes a pipelined functional unit to produce its first result. Same as flowthrough time: *305*

state *See* mode

state function A mathematical function of time that specifies the state of a neuron in a neural network: *391*

**state-swapping instruction** An instruction that stores or restores the processor context of a program (e.g., initiates or returns from interrupts): *70–72*

*See* EXCHANGE JUMP

**static dataflow architecture** An architecture that implements the static dataflow model of computation: *387, 388*

**static dataflow model** A dataflow model in which the arcs can hold at most one data token at a time: *387*

For contrast, *see also* dynamic dataflow model

static memory *See* static random-access memory

static program relocation *See* initial program relocation

**static random-access memory (SRAM)** A RAM device that does not require refreshing to hold its data: *178, **184**–**186**, 197, 198*

physical characteristics of: *186*

For contrast, *see also* dynamic random-access memory

status bit *See* flag

status flag *See* flag

**status port** A port on an I/O device that the CPU can read to determine the current status of the device: ***164***

**status register** A register in the arithmetic and logic unit (ALU) that contains flags on the ALU status (e.g., carry, overflow, negative result, and zero result): ***126***

of the 8087 floating-point coprocessor register set: *272*

of the 8237A DMA controller register set: *254*

of the 8250 UART: *267*

**status signal** A signal that conveys status information: *122, 133, 134*

of a bus: *122*

during a PPI operation: *264*

STB *See* strobe input

**stop-bit I/O** Bits in a serial transmission that serve to synchronize the receiver with the transmitted bit stream; thus they help to e.g., frame characters of the data: *265, 266*

STORE An instruction that tells a processor to move a datum to the main memory: *54, 55, 58, 63, 67, 68, 87, 95, 306, 309*

vector: *72*

STORE CONTROL WORD An 8087 coprocessor instruction: *270*

STORE ENVIRONMENT An 8087 coprocessor instruction: *270*

**store instruction** Any instruction that stores a value in memory, e.g., STORE, or an operate instruction that places the result in memory: ***58***

STORE STATUS WORD An 8087 coprocessor instruction: *270*

**stride** *See* vector stride

**string** *See* character string

Stringer, J. B.: *308*

**string instruction** *See* character-string instruction

**string operation** An operation on strings, e.g., comparing the characters of two strings, searching a string for a specified substring, or concatenating two strings (appending the characters of the second onto the end of the first): *313*

in the CDC 6600: *103*

**string-processing instruction** *See* character-string instruction

string search *See* INDEX

**strobed mode,** of a programmable parallel interface (PPI) A mode of I/O in which the PPI uses handshake signals and latches values for input or output: ***262***

**Strobe input (STB)** A handshake signal used by the 8255 PPI: *263–264*

SUB *See* SUBTRACT

**subgraph** The counterpart of a subroutine in a dataflow graph: *385*

**subroutine** A subprogram that is not a function; does not return a result: *48, 96, 190*

**subroutine call** The transfer of control from a calling procedure to a called procedure: *48, 71, 196*

*See* CALL; RETURN

**subroutine-linkage instruction** An instruction, such as CALL and RETURN, for supporting procedure calls and returns: *48, **58**, 67–70*

in the CDC 6600: *103*

**subroutine-linkage register** A register that holds subroutine-linkage information (e.g., the return address, the address of a parameter list, the address of a parameter address list) during a subroutine call: *96*

**subscript** A value that appears in a subscript list and is used to designate an array element; e.g., in the statement B = A(3, 4, 5), the three values 3, 4, and 5 are all subscripts: ***89***

**subscript list** The list of subscripts that specify a particular array element; e.g., in the statement B = A(3, 4, 5), the subscript list is (3, 4, 5): ***47***

**subscript position** The ordinal number of a subscript in a subscript list; e.g., in the statement B = A(3, 4, 5), the subscript position of the "4" is 2: ***47***

**subscript value** The value of a subscript; e.g., in the statement B = A(3, 4, 5), the value of the second subscript is 4: ***47***

**substring** A string that is part of another string; possibly empty, possibly the entire string: *45, **46***

SUBSTRING An operate instruction that extracts a substring from a character string: *46*

SUBTRACT   Instruction that causes subtraction. Normally a computer provides several types of SUBTRACT instructions, one for each of its datatypes, such as integer subtraction, floating-point subtraction, and decimal subtraction; same as SUB: *60, 137*

  in the 8087 coprocessor: *270*

sum reduction   A vector operation that adds all the elements of a vector together to produce a single scalar result: *75*

Sun Microsystems: *27*

Sun SPARC   *See* SPARC

**supercomputer**   The fastest available computer for the current technology: *72, 177, 232, 312*

  memory size: *178, 179*

**super-VGA**   A nonstandard video display mode that is upward-compatible with the VGA standard but which supports up to 256 colors at a resolution of 800 × 600 pixels: *235*

SUPERVISOR CALL   An instruction that is similar to CALL but that transfers control to a supervisory program, usually by initiating a software exception (i.e., trap): *71, 144, 161*

**supervisor mode**   *See* supervisor state

**supervisor state**   A privileged mode of operation of the System/360 required for a computer to execute various privileged instructions, such as those for controlling the memory-protection hardware and the I/O instructions: *71*

**suspending a process**   The act of interrupting a process so that a resume operation can later reactivate it at the point of suspension; interrupts and exceptions both suspend processes, but the term suspension generally implies an interruption caused by a process synchronization instruction: *64*

**switch node**   A node in a dataflow graph used to control the flow of the data tokens: *385–387*

**switching time**   After changing the inputs to an electronic device, the time it takes the output of the device to stabilize at the correct (new) value: *425*

synchronization   *See* process synchronization

synchronization instruction   *See* process synchronization instruction

**synchronization primitive**   *See* process synchronization instruction

synchronous data link control (SDLC), IBM PC port-address assignment: *274*

**synchronous D flip-flop**   A clocked flip-flop having a single D input; the state of the flip-flop becomes 1 if D is 1 and 0 if D is 0 when the flip-flop is clocked: *426*

**synchronous flip-flop**   A clocked flip-flop, such as a JK master-slave flip-flop or a synchronous D flip-flop: *425, 426*

synchronous interrupt   *See* trap

**synchronous network**   A network whose timing is controlled by a single, centralized timing system, the clock: *325*

System/360   *See* IBM System/360

System/370   *See* IBM System/370

**system board**   The printed circuit board in a computer that includes the central processor and much of its control circuitry: *237*

**system bus**   A bus that has its own control circuitry and arbitrates among users, including the CPU, that wish to use it: *120, 121, 156, 158, 233*

system cost   The cost of a computer system: *30*

**system deadlock**   The situation that may result in a multiprocessing system in which all processes become suspended while waiting for a resource that one of the other processes has exclusive use of: *377*

**system initialization**   The initial operation of a computer from the time the power is first turned on until the operating system gains control of its operation; includes machine startup, programming of the DRAM refresh circuits, diagnostic tests of the hardware, programming of the I/O devices, and transferring control to the operating system: *72, 273*

  *See also* machine startup

**system performance**   Performance of the entire computer system, not just of the CPU: *25–30*

System Performance and Evaluation Cooperative   *See* SPEC

**system segment table**   In a segmentation system, the segment table that the hardware uses when the machine is in a privileged mode of operation: *212*

**system trap**   A trap that occurs when the operating system is executing in a privileged mode, as opposed to one that occurs when a user program is executing: *194*

**systolic arrays**   An alternative computer architecture consisting of a two-dimensional array of interconnected state machines (SMs) that are synchronized by a single clock. Inputs are given to the SMs at one edge of the array, and outputs are taken from the SMs at another edge. An SM has a finite number of states, its state at time $t$ depending on its own state and the states of its neighbors at time $t-1$: *11*

table lookup   The act of searching a table to find the value associated with a particular key (e.g., searching a page table to find the page-frame number associated with a page address): *129*

tag  *See* address tag

**tagged token**  In a dataflow model, a token that contains, in addition to the datum, a tag that provides information about the history of the computation that generated the token: *388*

**tag subsystem**  The subsystem in a cache memory that processes the addresses: *199*

TAN  An 8087 coprocessor instruction: *270*

Tandem/16  A fault-tolerant computer (circa 1976) by Tandem Computers: *19*

Tandy Corporation  *See* Radio Shack

tap  An connection point in an interconnection network: *194*

tape  *See* magnetic tape

tape cartridge  A compact container for holding a magnetic tape: *185*

tape drive  An I/O device that reads and writes to a magnetic tape. The device may use a reel-to-reel tape or a tape cartridge: *158, 165*

target address  *See* branch address

target instruction  *See* branch-target instruction

target register  *See* result register

task  *See* process

task initiation  *See* process initiation

task termination  *See* process termination

TCH  *See* TEST CHANNEL

TDM  *See* time-division multiplexed pin

telephone transmission  *See* serial data transmission

temporary address register  *See* DMA temporary address register

temporary count register  *See* DMA temporary count register

temporary floating-point number, of the 8087 coprocessor: *269, 270*

temporary register  *See* DMA temporary register

terminal  An I/O device consisting of a keyboard, a video display (or printer mechanism in some older models), and the appropriate interface for connecting it to a computer; when set up for input from a computer operator, called a console: *154*

**terminal count**  When a device, e.g., an 8237A DMA controller, transfers data, it maintain a count of the number of bytes that remain to be transfers. The DMA controller reaches terminal count when it transfers the final byte of data in the block, i.e., when the count of remaining bytes reaches 0: *255, 268*

termination  *See* process termination

TEST  An 8088 microprocessor instruction that tests the status of a TEST signal and suspends its own operation until the signal is *false;* used for synchronizing itself with an 8087 coprocessor: *240*

*See also* TEST signal

TEST AND SET  A synchronization instruction that reads the value of a designated bit in memory and places it in a register, and then sets the memory bit to $1_2$ in an atomic operation: *64–67*

TEST CHANNEL  An I/O instruction that gets the status of a channel; called TCH by IBM: *70, 159, 160*

TEST I/O  An I/O instruction that tests the status of an I/O operation; called TIO by IBM: *70, 159, 160, 163*

**test node**  In a dataflow graph, a node that produces *true* and *false* tokens in response to its input tokens; control nodes can then use the *true* and *false* tokens to regulate the flow of other data tokens through the graph: *385, 387*

TEST signal  A signal that an 8087 coprocessor sends to, e.g., an 8088 microprocessor for process synchronization. When the 8087 starts executing an ESCAPE instruction, it sets TEST to *true;* when finished, it sets TEST to *false: 271*

**test vector**  *See* vector mask

**test-vector operation**  *See* vector comparison

Texas Instruments Corporation: *290*

*See also* TI ASC

TF  *See* trap flag

Thinking Machines Corporation: *344*

*See also* CM-1; CM-2

**third-generation computer**  A computer that uses integrated-circuit technology and provides multiprogramming with good support services. Most third-generation computers were developed between about 1963 and 1975: *8*

**thread of control**  The sequence of statements in a program and its subprograms that the CPU has executed: *386, 388*

three-dimensional display processor  A special-purpose computer with special hardware for rapidly generating and manipulating three-dimensional displays: *20*

three-dimensional hypercube  *See* 3-cube

**threshold of firing**  A value — generally determined by the weighted sum of inputs to a neuron — that determines when the neuron will fire: *391*

TI ASC  Texas Instruments Advanced Scientific Computer; an early supercomputer (circa 1970) that was a memory-to-memory vector processor by Texas Instruments Corporation: *290, 293, 294, 304, 308*

**tightly coupled multiprocessor**  A multiprocessor in which the CPUs share a common main memory;

approximately equivalent to the group of multiprocessors with global memory: *18, 322, 364, 365, 367*

**tightly synchronized multiprocessors** Processors that operate in lock-step, often to provide a fault-tolerant computing environment: *380*

**time-division-multiplexed (TDM) pin** A connection on an integrated circuit chip that supports different purposes at different times (e.g., a pin that delivers an address during one part of a bus cycle and data during another part of the bus cycle): *245*

time multiplexed Any control paradigm in which the controller allocates a fixed amount of time per cycle to each device: *157*

time-of-day clock A computer circuit that keeps track of the correct time: *143*

   in the IBM PC: *268*

timer A special-purpose circuit for generating various types of signals at specifiable times: *234, 239, 256*

   IBM PC programming of, during system initialization: *274*

   use in the IBM PC for interrupt processing: *251*

timer interrupt An interrupt initiated by a timer: *143, 191*

time-sharing operating system An operating system that, by allocating to each user a small amount of time per second, gives them the appearance of each one having exclusive use of the computer: *8*

TIO *See* TEST I/O

TLB *See* translation-lookaside buffer

**token** A datum in a dataflow model of computation: *384–386*

token matching *See* token-processing system

token-processing system In a dynamic dataflow architecture, the system that processes the tokens: *388*

TOP An instruction for the top operation: *47*

top-down processing In the dataflow model of computation, the processing of nodes on a data-availability basis: *389*

   For contrast, *see also* bottom-up processing

top-of-stack register A register that points to the top of a stack in memory: *96*

topology The geometric structure of an interconnection network: *327–338*

**top operation** The operation on a stack that returns its top element without altering its contents: *47*

toroidal topology The topology of a doughnut; an interconnection topology formed from a two-dimensional grid by connecting the opposite ends of each row together and then connecting the top and bottom element of each column together: *332*

TPI *See* clock ticks per instruction

TPS *See* transactions per second

trace A signal conductor manufactured on the surface of a printed-circuit board (e.g., by photoengraving): *413*

track On the surface of one disk, the set of memory cells accessible to the read-write heads without moving; hence one circular ring of memory cells: *166, 165*

trackball An input device, sometimes called an upside-down mouse, in which a user moves a screen cursor by rotating a small ball with a finger. The ball is embedded in the keyboard or an external device, designed to replace a mouse: *154*

**training rule** A procedure for modifying the coupling weights in a neural network (e.g., a perceptron) so it responds in a desired way to a set of inputs: *391*

transaction processing The electronic processing of transactions, such as money transfers, often by using special-purpose terminals called instant-access machines: *29*

**transactions per second (TPS)** A measurement of the number of transactions a computer can execute in 1 second: *29*

TRANSFER IN CHANNEL In a channel program, the equivalent of a branch instruction: *160*

transfer modes *See* 8237A DMA controller, transfer modes in

transfer rate *See* bandwidth

transient event A momentary event (e.g., power surge, electrical spark, or cosmic ray), generally not repeatable, that may cause a component or system fault or failure: *150*

transistor A solid-state switching or amplifying device: *4, 7, 9*

   count of, in microprocessors: *9*

**transistor-transistor logic (TTL)** A common technology for switching circuits in which *true* is represented by a voltage level of 2.5 to 5 volts and *false* by a level of 0 to 0.7 volts: *413*

TRANSLATE An 8088 microprocessor instruction that does table lookup: *240*

**translation-lookaside buffer (TLB)** A cache in the CPU of many virtual-memory computers that holds the most recent associations between logical and physical addresses; part of the memory-mapping hardware: *207, 208, 212, 214*

   in segmentation: *212*

transmission error An error in transmission, caused, e.g, by noisy signal lines or differences between the sending and receiving devices: *265, 266*

*See also* framing error; overrun error; parity error

**transmission rate** *See* baud rate

**transmitter clock** The clock that regulates the speed of transmission of a serial I/O device: **266**

*See also* receiver clock

**transpose** *See* matrix transpose

**trap** An exception triggered by a program event, such as a memory-access violation or an arithmetic overflow; also called synchronous interrupt: *51, 71, 104,* **144**, *146, 149, 161, 196, 208*

*See also* trap flag

**trap door** In an insecure system, a way that an unauthorized user can gain access to the system: *196*

**trap flag (TF)** A processor status flag in the 8088 microprocessor (and others) that, if set, initiates an interrupt after each instruction; used for diagnostic tests and debugging: *250*

**trap handler** The operating-system procedure to which the CPU transfers control when a trap occurs and which processes the trap: *51, 144*

**tree-structured network** An interconnection network that has the topology of a tree; hence a loop-free network with a unique path connecting any pair of nodes: *330, 331, 333, 340*

**tristate buffer** A buffer that uses tristate-logic devices to generate its outputs and hence can be disabled: *428*

**tristate logic gate** A gate whose output impedance is controlled by an enable or disable input. When the output is disabled, the device enters a high-impedance state (floats its outputs) and appears to be disconnected from the circuit (as opposed to producing a 0 or 1 output): *413, 415*

**TRS-80** Tandy Radio Shack–80. The first personal computer from Radio Shack; released in 1977, it used a Zilog Z80 microprocessor: *233*

**TTL** *See* transistor-transistor logic

**two-dimensional array** An array having two subscript positions; a matrix: *342*

**two-dimensional grid** A uniformly spaced arrangement of horizontal and vertical lines: *331, 339*

**two-dimensional pattern** A two-dimensional array of values, such as a matrix or a digitized image: *390*

**two-phase clock** A clock that generates two independent sequences of timing pulses; used by some microprocessors for timing purposes: *427*

**two's-complement adder** An adder that operates on two's-complement integers and produces their sum, also as a two's-complement integer: *424*

**two's-complement integer** An integer representation in which negative numbers are obtained from positive numbers, and vice versa, by complementing all the bits of a number and adding 1 (discarding the carry); e.g., $+3$ in 4-bit two's complement is $0011_2$ and $-3$ in 4-bit two's complement is $1100_2 + 1 = 1101_2$: *38,* **39**

in the 8087 coprocessor: *270*

in the 8088 microprocessor: *239*

*See also* ones'-complement integer

**two-way set-associative cache** A set-associative cache having two sets: *201–203*

**typeless data** Data with an unspecified usage: *51*

**UART** *See* universal asynchronous receiver-transmitter

**unary-to-binary encoder** An encoder that has $n$ inputs, $I_0$ to $I_{n-1}$, of which only one is assumed to be on at a time, and $\log_2 n$ outputs. The output is the binary representation of $i$, where input $I_i$ is on; thus a device for converting unary values to binary values: *417, 419*

**unconditional branch** A branch that will take place unconditionally: *133*

**unconditional branch instruction** An instruction that causes the normal sequential flow of control to stop and the CPU to select the next instruction from a specified location, the branch target: **68**

**underflow** The condition that arises when a number is too small for the intended representation: **44**

**UNIBUS** A system bus for the PDP-11: *120*

**unifunction pipe** A pipelined functional unit that can perform only a single operation or a group of closely allied operations (e.g., addition and subtraction, or division and square root): *289*

For contrast, *see also* multifunction pipe

**unimplemented instruction** An instruction that is not implemented on a particular computer; e.g., some instructions implemented on high-performance family members may not be implemented on low-performance members of the same family: *104*

**unimplemented-instruction trap** The trap that occurs when the control unit decodes an unimplemented instruction, which has an op code for which there is no corresponding machine instruction; can occur, e.g., in computers with 8-bit op codes, which often have fewer than 256 instructions: *195*

**uninterruptable operation** *See* process synchronization instruction

**uniprocessor system** A computer system with only one processor (e.g., a von Neumann machine): *19, 63*
   in multitasking: *63*
Univac Universal Automatic Computer; the first commercially successful computer, introduced by Remington Rand in 1951: *6*
**universal asynchronous receiver-transmitter (UART)** An I/O device that sends and receives information in bit-serial fashion: *234,* **255**
   in the IBM PC: *260, 265–268*
   *See also* 8250; serial I/O
University of Illinois: *8, 27*
University of Pennsylvania: *5, 6*
UNIX An operating system that AT&T Bell Laboratories introduced in the early 1970s and is now a favorite operating system for a wide variety of systems: *107*
unlatched address, on the IBM PC AT Bus: *258*
**unnormal number** A number in the IEEE representation that the hardware can represent, but that is too small to be normalized: **44**
   *See also* normalized floating-point number
unpacked decimal A representation that uses a full byte to represent a single digit in a binary-coded decimal (BCD); the least-significant 4 bits hold the value of the BCD digit, while the 4 most-significant bits hold 0: *240*
unprivileged mode The state or mode of a computer in which the CPU disables privileged instructions; given different names in different systems (e.g., problem state in the IBM System/360 or user mode in the DEC VAX family) and also generally called unprivileged state: *53*
   *See also* executive mode; kernel mode; privileged mode; user mode
unprivileged state *See* unprivileged mode
unsigned binary integer *See* absolute-binary number
**unsigned-binary number** *See* absolute-binary number
**upward compatibility** The characteristic of the computers in a family that allows programs from one machine to run on later or larger machines in the same family: *5, 106, 310*
user-friendliness The ease with which a user can interact with a system: *30*
**user mode** The processor mode in which application programs normally execute with little privilege: *71*
   *See also* unprivileged mode
**user segment table** In a segmentation system, the segment table that the hardware uses when the machine is in user mode: *212*

user trap A trap that occurs when a user program is executing (i.e., the machine is operating in an unprivileged mode), as opposed to one that occurs when the operating system is executing (i.e., when the machine is executing in privileged mode): *194*
**utilization ratio** The ratio between the time a device spends doing productive computations and the time during which it is operational: **28**, *29*

V *See* overflow flag
V80 An NEC microprocessor that is pin-compatible with the 8088 and has the same instruction-set architecture; a replacement for the 8088: *236*
vacuum tube A switching or amplifying device that preceded the transistor: *4, 6*
   technology: *175*
**validity bit** 1. A cache tag bit that, when set, indicates the presence (validity) of an associated refill line: **201**, *206, 207*. 2. A bit used in some paging and segmentation systems that indicates the presence of a segment or page in memory: *211*
variable A value in memory that a program can access and alter: *85, 86*
variable-precision data Data that accommodate a variety of precisions, such as block floating-point: *51*
VAX Virtual Address Extension; refers to Digital Equipment Corporation's family of minicomputers: *5, 11, 19, 23–27, 42–44, 51, 57, 71, 102, 106, 108, 179, 219, 220, 304, 307, 309*
VAX-11: *5, 308, 309*
VAX 11/780: *219*
   LINPACK benchmark of: *307*
VAX 8600: *219*
VAX 8700: *219*
**VAX MIPS** The MIPS rating of a computer relative to the performance of a VAX: *26*
**VAX unit of performance (VUP)** Approximately the speed of the VAX 11/780. The CPU component is nominally 450-K VAX instructions per second or 1-M RISC instructions per second: *27, 28*
vector A one-dimensional array; a collection of variables, called vector elements: **26**, *47, 96*
vector addition The operation of adding corresponding elements of two vectors to give a third vector: *344*
   on bit-slice processor: *351*
vector code Code specifically intended for execution on a vector machine: *76*
   in pipelining: *294*

**vector comparison** The vector analog of COMPARE; the vector operation that checks each element of a vector to see if it satisfies a specified test condition and produces a vector mask of the results. Also called test-vector operation: *75, 76–78*

**vector compression** A vector operation that has two arguments, a data vector and a mask vector. The result vector consists of the elements from the data vector whose corresponding mask-vector elements are *true*; thus the result vector has only as many elements as there are true elements in the mask vector: *77*

For contrast, *see also* vector expansion

**vectored exception** An exception that uses a jump table to find the address of the exception handler. The hardware uses the vector number as an offset into the jump table, which holds the addresses (vectors) of the exception handlers: *92, 148, 149*

   interrupt: *238*

**vector element** A single variable within a vector: *47, 76, 77*

**vector expansion** A vector operation that has three arguments — a data vector, a mask vector, and a replacement vector. The data and mask vectors have the same length, and the replacement vector has as many elements as there are *true* mask elements. The operation produces the result vector by replacing elements of the data vector whose corresponding mask element is *true* by the next element of the replacement vector: *77*

For contrast, *see also* vector compression

**vector instruction** An instruction that specifies a vector operation: *58, 60, 72–81, 209, 304*

**vectorizable code** Code that lends itself to vectorization: *28*

**vectorization** The compilation of programs to run efficiently on computers with vector processors: *27*

**vectorized loop** A loop that has been modified to run on a vector processor: *78*

**vector length** The number of elements in a vector; same as vector size: *47, 339*

**vector machine** A computer whose hardware has been optimized for executing vector instructions, typically by pipelining; also called a vector processor: *26, 322, 361*

   memory-to-memory: *339*

   pipelined: *304–306*

**vector mask** A logical vector used as the control argument for various vector operations, such as vector compression, expansion, and merge; also called a test vector: *76*

**vector operation** An operation that processes one or more vectors to produce either a vector result or a scalar result (a vector-reduction operation): *72, 305*

vector processor *See* vector machine

vector product The result of multiplying corresponding elements of two vectors together: *74*

**vector-reduction operation** A vector operation that produces a scalar result, such as sum reduction (the sum of the elements of the argument), AND reduction, and OR reduction: *73*

**vector register** A register that holds a vector or part of a vector and consists of a number of simple registers (typically 32 to 512) that the hardware accesses sequentially; vector registers hold the operands and results of vector operations in machines that perform register-to-register vector operations: *72, 313*

vector-scalar addition The vector-scalar operation of adding a constant to all elements of a vector: *74*

**vector-scalar operation** A vector operation in which one of the operands is a scalar and the result is a vector (e.g., multiplication of all elements of a vector by a scalar): *72, 73*

vector-scalar test A test operation whose arguments are vectors and whose result is *true* or *false* (e.g., a test for whether two vectors are identical): *76*

vector-selection operations Operations that use a test vector or index array to restrict the number of elements they process (e.g., scatter, gather, compression, expansion, merge), or operations that create a test vector (comparison): *75*

vector size *See* vector length

**vector stride** The offset in memory between successive vector elements for a specified vector operation; also called increment or stride: *47, 81, 82*

   in matrix multiplication: *81*

**vector-vector operation** A vector operation in which both operands are vectors and the result is a vector: *73*

Veen, A. H.: *389*

**vertical control** Said of an implementation in which control signals are encoded into bit patterns and then decoded prior to use: *134–136*

For contrast, *see also* horizontal control

**very large scale integration (VLSI)** Characteristic of integrated circuits containing over 1 million transistors on a single chip: *8, 322, 392, 393, 411*

VGA *See* Video Graphics Array

video controller The I/O interface that controls a video display

   IBM PC test of, during system initialization: *275*

Glossary/Index **539**

video-display terminal   An output device that displays information on a cathode ray tube (CRT); a monitor: *233*
**Video Graphics Array (VGA)**   An IBM standard video display consisting of 480 × 650 pixels with 16 colors or 320 × 200 pixels with 256 colors: ***235***, *236*
  IBM PC address assignment: *278*
video-screen buffers   The random-access memory that holds the values necessary for creating a full-screen image
  in the IBM PC: *277*
video-screen refresh   The process of rereading the values in the video-display buffers and using them to repaint the screen display: *255*
virtual address   *See* logical address
**virtual-addressing range**   The range of logical addresses that a program can conceivably access: *98*
  For contrast, *see also* physical-addressing range
virtual-address space   *See* logical-address space
**virtual memory**   *See* virtual-memory system
virtual-memory hardware   Hardware that efficiently supports virtual-memory systems, such as page and segment maps, translation-lookaside buffers, and memory-protection hardware: *206*
**virtual-memory system**   A memory system that maps the user's logical addresses into physical addresses; hence parts of the program may reside at physical addresses that bear no relationship to the logical addresses. Examples are memory systems that use paging and segmentation: *8, 86, 100, 188, **191**, 204–221*
**virtual-page number**   The logical address of a page in a paged, virtual-memory system: ***206***, *207*
VLSI   *See* very large scale integration
**volatile memory**   Memory that requires continuous power to retain its contents; hence it loses its contents when the power is turned off: *184, **185***
von Neumann, J.: *6, 9, 10, 13*
von Neumann bottleneck   The pathway between the CPU and main memory, so called because of its limited bandwidth: *11, 312, 322*
**von Neumann machine**   A machine whose operation, at least conceptually, is based on the von Neumann machine cycle; a single-instruction-stream, single-data-stream processor that uses a program counter to control the instruction sequencing: *4, **11–16**, 55, 56, 69, 122, 127, 158, 322, 323, 368, 383*
**von Neumann machine cycle**   The cycle of fetching an instruction from memory, decoding it, incrementing the program counter to point to the next instruction, and then executing the instruction: ***13***, *126*
**voting logic**   Logic in a fault-tolerant computer that compares the outputs of a number of duplicate subsystems and generates for its output the majority opinion of its inputs: ***381***
VUP   *See* VAX unit of processing

WAIT   An 8088 instruction, used in conjunction with an 8087 coprocessor, that causes the CPU to test the status of the TEST signal (from the coprocessor) and suspend operation if TEST = *true*: *240, 270*
**wait state**   A dummy bus cycle that a CPU executes when an attached device (or memory) cannot deliver the requested datum within the required amount of time; e.g., a 1-wait-state machine inserts one wait state for each memory access if the processor's clock speed is too fast for the attached memory chips. This term generally applies to microprocessors: *183, 246, **247***
wait-state logic   In the IBM PC, the logic that controls the inclusion of wait states in bus cycles: *239, 241, 249, 256*
WAN   *See* wide-area network
watchdog timer   *See* heartbeat
**weighted arithmetic mean**   An arithmetic mean in which the individual measurements are weighted according to their importance; useful for factoring the workload distribution of a computing center into the performance evaluation: ***28***
  For contrast, *see also* geometric mean; harmonic mean
**Whets**   Units in which the results of the Whetstone benchmark are quoted: *27*
Whetstone Algol Compiler: *27*
**Whetstone benchmark**   A benchmark test of CPU floating-point scalar performance: *27*
Wichmann, B. A.: *27*
**wide-area network (WAN)**   A collection of computers whose interconnection network spans large distances, often by using telephone lines or microwave communications: ***371***
  For contrast, *see also* local-area network
Wilkes, M. V.: *6, 308*
**window**   A range of physical addresses through which a CPU can access banked or expanded memory: ***216***, *217*
**window register**   In the Cm* computer, a physical address that a processor can write to alter its system tables: ***376***
word   The basic unit of storage for integer data in a computer; generally the size of the computer's fixed-point operational registers: *83–85*

**word address** For a computer that uses word addressing (e.g., the CDC 6600), the same as the address; for a computer that uses byte addressing (e.g., the IBM System/370, the PDP-11 and VAX-11 families, and most microprocessors), any address evenly divisible by the number of bytes in a word: *83, 84*

**word boundary** A point in memory that falls between words, as opposed to one that is between bytes but not between words (e.g., on a 32-bit machine with byte addressing, addresses 0, 4, 8, 12, ... are word boundaries): *84*

word offset The address of a word relative to the beginning of a page or segment: *206, 213, 214*

word-parallel operation An operation where all of the bits of a word operand are processed concurrently: *342*

**word size** The size of the natural datum for a computer, a function unit, or component, and generally also the size of its operational registers: *36*
For contrast, *see also* bit-serial operation

**WORM memory** A type of disk that can be written only once but read many times (WORM = Write Once, Read Many), like some optical disks: *189*

WRITE A channel command for a magnetic-tape operation: *160*

**write-around cache** A cache that transfers data to memory without updating its own RAM when a miss occurs on a write operation: *198*
*See also* write-back cache; write-through cache

WRITE A TO DEVICE N An output instruction for transferring the content of the accumulator (A) to output-device N: *154*

**write-back cache** A cache that delays the transfer of data into memory until after it has updated its own RAM: *198*
*See also* write-around cache; write-through cache

write cycle  *See* I/O write cycle, memory write cycle

write request A request made to a memory-port controller when a device wants to write to memory: *156*

WRITE TAPE MARK A channel command for a magnetic-tape operation: *160*

**write-through cache** A cache that transfers writes from the CPU to memory while simultaneously updating its own RAM: *198, 368, 370*
*See also* write-around cache; write-back cache

Wyse Technologies: *236*


XBA  *See* XBA registers

**XBA registers** The operational registers of the CDC 6600, where X, B, and A refer to accumulator, index, and address registers, respectively: *298, 301*

**XBA result-register designator** A value used by the CDC 6600 to indicate which XBA register is to get the result produced by a functional unit: *298, 301*

XGA  *See* Extended Graphics Array

X*n* Designates an accumulator in the CDC 6600, where *n* ranges from 0 to 7: *298, 303*

XOR Exclusive OR; an instruction for performing a bitwise exclusive-OR operation on two binary operands: *240*

XOR circuit Exclusive-OR circuit; has two inputs and one output and outputs a 1 when either input is a 1, but not both of them: *414*


Z  *See* zero-result flag

Zenith Data Systems: *236*

Zero-address instruction  *See* 0-address instruction

zero-result flag (Z) The status flag that a CPU sets when the result of an operation is 0: *53, 125, 126*

zero-wait-state line A line on the PC AT Bus that allows high-speed memories to operate without wait states: *257*